Baltic Sea

• Stolp

olberg

Neustettin •

Königsberg

East

Prussia

Vistula River

POLAND

• Posen

WARSAW

◉ Lodz

Breslau ◉

Silesia

Cracow •

WEST EAST

BERLIN

CHOSLOVAKIA

GERMANY

VIENNA

AUSTRIA

THE GERMANS

THE

The German should learn all languages, so
that no stranger would feel uncomfortable
in his home, and so that he too can be at
home everywhere.

Johann Wolfgang von Goethe
MAXIMEN UND REFLEXIONEN

GERMANS

ADOLPH SCHALK

PRENTICE-HALL, INC.   Englewood Cliffs, N.J.

TO MY IMMIGRANT AUSTRIAN-BORN MOTHER, WHO TAUGHT ME THE GERMAN
LANGUAGE AND CULTURE IN THE HEART OF THE UNITED STATES.

CONTENTS

CONTENTS

PREFACE

THIS BOOK WAS written over a period of nearly five years. It is based on my accumulated experience in West Germany (with several visits to East Germany) over the past fifteen years. During that period I lived in Bonn for one year, in Munich for several months, and in Hamburg for nearly eight years. I have traveled extensively *bergauf, bergab* (up hill and down dale) throughout the country.

This study is not intended to be either scholarly or scientific. It does not try to prove or disprove a "thesis." I have purposely kept footnotes to a minimum. Although a great deal of research was required, and I have tried to develop the topic systematically, this is essentially a popularized, personal report. I have tried to describe the German people as I found them, as I know them and, with all my foibles and shortcomings, as I love them, with all their foibles and shortcomings.

Wherever I was able to discover something beautiful or noble or good, I said so—and such examples abound. By the same token, I have not hesitated to call Schmaltz, Schmaltz, whenever the situation required. To criticize is to care.

The idea for this book came to me during my Hamburg stay. Here, under the sponsorship of Atlantik-Brücke (Atlantic Bridge), a German organization devoted to furthering American-German friendship, I established a monthly newspaper called *The Bridge*. This paper was distributed primarily to American servicemen stationed in the Federal Republic and attempted to explain German life and culture to them. It soon found an enthusiastic following as well among Americans back home who were especially interested in German affairs.

My experience with *The Bridge* taught me two things: first, that most Americans know very little about the Germans, and second, that a great many Americans nevertheless have a keen interest in all things German and eagerly read about German life if presented in an attractive way.

ix

Although there are a great many books on the general market about Germany, there are relatively few dealing in detail with the daily life, culture, mentality, and problems of the German people as such. There is a lot of material in this vein available from the West German press office and from semiofficial as well as private organizations. But much of this material is presented in a scholarly framework and appeals to a limited audience. Moreover, many people are, rightly or wrongly, suspicious of information designed to put an organization's or a country's "best foot forward." There is nothing wrong with this, of course, "so long as it is a foot." But even organizations with impeccable credentials are reluctant to go very far in showing the seamy as well as the presentable side of the causes they represent.

I felt, therefore, that the time had come to write a book about the Germans as they really are—warts, underwear, and all.

Perhaps my biggest handicap during the writing period was the constant need to raise money to pay for the considerable necessary research and frequent travels. But all of my efforts to receive financial aid from established institutions failed. My study was either too critical or too popularized. Somehow a work is suspect if it is attempted with a light and humorous approach. Thus the venture took me at least three years longer than I originally intended.

In retrospect, I can only be grateful that the various organizations and foundations I approached for help turned me down. This gave me the tremendous advantage of being able to develop the book completely independent of outside influence whatsoever. For better or for worse, I have tried "to tell it like it is."

In the process of writing this book I interviewed literally hundreds of persons. Inevitably I encountered strong opposition and a great deal of criticism. Several questions were raised so often that it seems to me appropriate to comment on them here. I have reduced them to five main questions:

1) How can you write about "the" Germans? The topic is too broad, too general, and furthermore "the" Germans do not exist.

Strictly speaking, it is of course impossible to write about "the" Germans, anymore than one can write about "the" universe or "the" Supreme Being known as God. Theologians have observed that you cannot know what God is, only what He is not. It is obvious that a report on the seventy-eight million citizens of West and East Germany must be a report of seventy-eight million exceptions to anything that one might say about "the" German people as a whole.

Yet books about God and the universe are appearing all the time. And if I insist on the broad title, *The Germans,* it is because like the authors of those books I need a point of reference. It is only within the framework of "the" Germans that one can intelligently discuss the relationship of the Prussians, the Bundeswehr, the West or East Germans, and Jews in Germany to one another and to the ethnic group to which they belong. Even for the purpose of demonstrating that "the" Germans do not really exist and that there are countless areas of differentiation, one still needs the collective term as a point of departure. Moreover, there are some things that one can observe about a people as a whole—their ethnic development, their language, their culture, their mentality—no matter how great the differences within those categories may be.

Limited topics have their shortcomings too. It is possible to write a dissertation on "The Ecology of Snail-Eating Flies on the Left Bank of the Nile Between Idfu and Luxor." But I rather doubt that such a study would be of much direct help to scientists, educators, and politicians concerned with the burning question of world ecology and environmental pollution.

"The proper study of mankind," as the poet has said, is still "man." And the proper study of the German people is "the Germans." This is a legitimate field for study, no matter how much the efforts of an individual writer may fall short of the "big picture."

And fall short I did. First of all, I have focused this study primarily on the German people in the period since World War II, which is a considerable restriction to begin with. Inevitably I have had to ignore such interesting topics as sports, recreation, tourism. A great deal more could have been said under this collective title on political issues and personalities. I did not begin to enter into the problems of aggression, peace research, and psychological problems peculiar to the Germans. I was only able to devote a short section to education and the whole ramification of related problems.

I reluctantly dropped a chapter originally planned for this

book, which was entitled "How Was Hitler Possible?" This was partly because I restricted this study to the period since 1945, and partly because only a book-length treatment of this question could do justice to it. However, in a sense this entire book is an answer to that question.

It is my observation that too little has been said about the democratic traditions of the Germans, to which I did devote a chapter. I felt that the time has come to stop condemning this people for their Nazi past and to emphasize some of their positive contributions.

Bismarck and his profound influence on the Germans received rather short shrift—for reasons given above. Similarly the extremely important subject of French-German relations and the entire complex of problems and opportunities raised by West Germany's participation in the Common Market could only be alluded to briefly.

For space reasons too I had to drop plans for a comprehensive chapter on recent German developments, East and West, in the sciences and the arts.

I regret these omissions. In spite of them, however, I feel justified in retaining the generic title. Surely no one expects me to write about "Some Considerations of Ethnic and Cultural Characteristics of the Citizens of the Federal Republic Between Bingen and Cologne Since 1945." Whatever its obvious limitations, my book is about "the" German people as a whole.

2) How can you write about the Germans from Switzerland?

The answer is simple, I happen to live in Switzerland. Nevertheless, my first impulse upon signing the contract for this book was to rent a room somewhere in West Germany and write the book from there. But I decided against it.

First of all, I was already intimately acquainted with daily German life. Then, no matter where I settled in the Federal Republic, I still had to travel a great deal. And I frankly didn't see the sense in renting three places at once—my Swiss flat, a room, and on top of that, a hotel room as I traveled throughout West Germany.

Besides, it is only a forty-five-minute drive from my flat to the West German border. As a German colleague said to me, "Why throw away such a tremendous advantage? By constantly being forced to enter and leave Germany from another country you are repeatedly receiving fresh impressions that would be lost to you if you lived in Germany all the time."

Moreover, in Switzerland you can get the bulk of West German newspapers and magazines, including regional publications, at nearly every kiosk, hear most West German radio programs, see the telecasts of the major West German networks, while easily half of all German-language Swiss TV programs are of West German production anyway.

Most important of all, the very fact of living in Switzerland— with its famous position of neutrality and as the home of countless international organizations—gave me a perspective I wouldn't otherwise have had. I am deeply indebted to my Swiss colleagues for helping me toward a greater sense of detachment. Threatened throughout World War II by the possibility of a Nazi invasion, the Swiss have a special interest in keeping a close watch on German affairs. They are easily the world's best German-watchers, as their superb coverage of German events by their mass media shows. Some of the best books on Germany are written by Swiss authors (for example, *Bonn Ist Nicht Weimar* by Fritz René Allemann).

"Whenever I want to know what is going on in Germany, " Adenauer used to say, "I read the *Neue Züricher Zeitung*"—in reference to the internationally respected Zürich daily.

3) Have the Germans changed?

I personally dislike the wording of this hackneyed question. When you say, "Have the Germans changed?" which Germans do you mean? And, changed from what to what? Taken at face value, the question implies racist undertones, for it suggests that there might be something inherent in the German character which accounts for past evils. It also has the suggestion of arrogance, for it assumes that the questioner is in a morally superior position to be able to demand changes of the Germans.

To me it is more appropriate to ask: What changes have taken place in the two Germanies since World War II? How have they affected the mental habits, behavior patterns, living methods, and daily life of the German people? The answers to these and many related questions have been the preoccupation of this book.

But if this question must be asked, I can think of no better answer than that given by Dr. H. G. van Dam, secretary general of the Central Council of the Jews in Germany. In a press statement issued in April, 1970, he said, "I believe that the Germans change or fail to change just as much as any other people. There are certain characteristics which come to the fore under specific conditions and develop along certain lines not only in individuals but in humanity as a whole, not only in individual Germans but in the Germans as a whole. People influence each other reciprocally, they effect changes in one another. The form of government, the economic order and social systems as well as political systems all exercise their influence. The same is true of school and home.

"The Germans, like the citizens of other countries, behaved quite differently at the time of Goethe than they did at the turn of the century.... The Weimar Republic was unable to cope with the inferiority complex that swelled up in the wake of World War I. . . . The Third Reich demanded total dedication of conscience—it commanded teachers every bit as much as soldiers. Thus it succeeded in typifying the German people by regimenting them in half-military and para-political formation.... With the collapse of the Third Reich. . . excessive nationalism dissolved into an absence of patriotism.

"The civic consciousness of the Germans in the Federal Republic is weak.... The successful economic policy, which goes by the name of 'Economic Miracle,' has produced a strong dominance of economic interests. The Germans have become Americanized.

"Although the process of democratic maturation is still at the beginning stage, one can say that the Germans of 1970 have different ideals and concepts of success than earlier generations .... Whether the German of 1970 will prove to be better than his predecessor is hard to say. But he cannot afford to remain the same if he wishes to survive. He has really tried to change many things."

4) The worldwide wave of unrest and social upheaval has affected West Germany too. How can you write about the German people now in the midst of so much change?

To be quite honest, this question calls attention to my greatest problem in writing this book: how to discuss the rapidly changing scene in such a way that it will still be valid at the time of publication and afterwards.

But the necessity of having to spread the writing of this book over a long period proved to be a blessing in disguise, for this circumstance compelled me to assume a greater sense of detachment from topical events than I might otherwise have had.

Easily half of the book deals with background matter, historical references, and the like, which will, I hope, be valid for some time to come. This in turn, however, created new difficulties. In a book that purports to discuss the Germans as they are now, I have put an awful lot of history. I didn't plan it that way. In fact, I started out with the good intentions of keeping history to a minimum. I also wanted to keep Hitler out of the book to the utmost possible extent. But this proved to be impossible.

Just as you meet history on every other German street corner, with thousands upon thousands of relics from the past, so too the German people today are completely unintelligible without a considerable knowledge of their past. You can't explain the Germans without discussing the Prussians, the revolution of 1848, the years 1870-71, and the Weimar Republic, not to mention the Romans and Julius Caesar. They are all of a piece and must be considered *in toto*. Nothing is more topical than the current controversies over Federalism, but this cannot be understood without a knowledge of the historical developments that brought it into being. Nor can the political parties be understood without considering their historic origins.

I have the greatest sympathy for many of the demands and aims of the New Left and all those rebels who would like to wipe the slate of life clean and start from scratch. Wouldn't life be easy if from time to time we could chuck everything aside and start over? To me the radicals' very human wish to return to point zero and ignore history is as unrealistic as a mature person who has made a mess of his life and wishes to reenter his mother's womb. There is in the last analysis only one thing to do with history and that is to live with it. And there is only one way to overcome the past and that is by first of all trying to understand it, by building on it, and by making your fresh start from where you are.

Seen in the light of history the topical events no longer appear so fleeting and irrelevant. It is true that events in the Federal

Republic are changing so rapidly that the observer is hard put to find many constants in a sea of variables. Even within the period between 1965 and 1970, when this book was being written, there were more changes in the Federal Republic than in the two decades preceeding.

Nevertheless, it seems to me that it is possible to record basic trends. More than at any other period in postwar West Germany, 1969-70 were watershed years. They were the great years of penal reform, education renewal, women's lib, youth rebellion, liberation from disciplinary restraints, and the socialist break-through of President Gustav Heinemann and Chancellor Willy Brandt. The broad outlines of the new Ostpolitik began to take shape in this period. It was the time of revolution in the Christian churches and the ebullient outburst of grass roots democracy.

Perhaps as good an example of the new German spirit as any is the bouyant atmosphere already in evidence among the people involved in the 1972 Munich Olympics preparations. Mindful of the vivid memories of the pompous structures built by Hitler to overwhelm visitors to the 1936 Olympics in Berlin, the present Olympics committee is going out of its way to make the present structures functional, graceful, and technically excellent rather than showy. "Our buildings," explained Willi Daume, president of the 1972 Olympics committee, "will be considerably smaller than any erected at recent Olympics, especially those built in Mexico in 1968."

"We want," he said simply, during a news conference in January, 1971, "to show that Germany today is different from the Germany of the past."

"In West Germany, Dr. Theo Sommer, an editor of the respected weekly *Die Zeit,* has said, "democracy has passed the point of no return. Its sixty million citizens will not let go of it....They are no longer *cavalier seul,* but a member of the club. There is little danger of Germany going off again on a tangent of its own. It is now part and parcel of a much wider grouping than it has ever belonged to. And just as its problems are general problems, so the solution to these problems will have to be general solutions too."[1]

By 1971 it appeared that the young republic had steered onto a course that it might follow for years, perhaps for decades to come.

5) *What are your overall impressions and conclusions after writing this book?*

As I write these lines, I pause to look over my desk at a map of the world and let my eyes sweep across the continents. I suddenly realize that there really aren't too many truly democratic countries in the world. By most standards, West Germany is better than the worst of them and among the best of the best of them. It is less socialized than Sweden, but it has bigger problems and bigger burdens. It is not even remotely as divided as the United States and far more stable than the United Kingdom or Italy.

But there are dangers too. It is my conviction that even the holiest of men, with the exception of a Christ or Buddha, if pushed far enough can be provoked to the most heinous of crimes, and the same is true of nations. This is not because of anything inherent in this or that national character—for such a tenet is racism—but because the unfathomable mystery of evil in human nature has not been solved by all the scientists and all the philosophers and all the theologians put together.

"The Germans," writes the respected British historian Arnold Toynbee (*The Encounter,* April, 1964), "have the same nature as the rest of us; and there is comfort, as well as horror, in this fact. Human nature has a fiendish vein in it, and our fiendishness is never irredeemable. If America and Russia get together (as they now seem to be inclined to do) to save mankind from liquidating itself, the human race's expectations of life on this planet is said to be of the order of about 2,000 millions of years. How many years did it take for human nature in Germany to be conditioned to those bad fruits? This process of German mis-education took an infinitesmally short span of time compared to the length of time that we all have ahead of us; and habits can be unlearnt as quickly as they can be learnt. For all I know, a majority of the Germans may have already sloughed off those unfortunate habits that made Prussianism and Hitlerism possible."

Clearly then, an honest appraisal of the Germans must include an acknowledgment of the dangers lurking in the human nature under their peculiar social and mental behavior patterns, every bit as much as a similar appraisal must in dealing with other ethnic groups.

xvii

The biggest "if" regarding postwar West German democracy is the fact that thus far it has enjoyed rather smooth sailing. It is easy to be democratic when things are going your way. The unknown factor remains: How would the Germans react in a real financial or political crisis? Could West Germany survive a shakeup like that which spelled the downfall of the Weimar Republic? There is overwhelming evidence to suggest that the answer is an optimistic "Yes!" But this is mere speculation and no one can anticipate such an answer with certainty.

There is a popular parlor game among some Germanologists to the effect that: the Bundeswehr is the opposite of the Wehrmacht, ergo the Germans are the opposite of militaristic; the Germans are now internationalized, ergo they would never again be tempted to conquer the world; there is not a trace of nationalism in West Germany, ergo there is no danger of chauvinistic nationalism.

This popular argumentation appears always to proceed from the same old worn-out premises. I think this is a mistake. It is just as hackneyed as the question, "Could the Germans do it (meaning the Nazi thing) again?" What these phrases do not take into account is the possibility of conflicts and problems arising from an entirely new relationship than heretofore, which are nevertheless nourished by lingering mentality and behavior patterns.

I have gone to great pains in this book to try to show that there is no such thing as a national German character or "the" German mentality. Nevertheless, certain behavior patterns are so widespread and so persistent, and confirmed so often by observers, Germans and non-Germans alike, that I cannot dismiss them as optical illusions.

The great sin of us Americans is that we do not take democracy seriously enough. Oh, we can get worked up emotionally about it. But when it comes time to practice it, it is another matter. Whenever racism rears its ugly head somewhere in the States, our attitude seems to be, "Nothing to get excited about. Just a problem that has to be worked out. Everything is going to be all right."

The great sin of the Germans is that they take democracy (and themselves) too seriously. German extremism is capable of pushing democracy so far until it becomes the opposite. In the new situation the danger is not that the Germans might go off on a tangent of their own. Rather, they could be so carried away by international idealism that they could take others along with them.

The great weakness of us Americans is our excessive optimism. The great weakness of the Germans is their excessive idealism. Unlike the French, who are more logical and therefore more realistic in their dealings with other nations, the Germans too easily succumb to *Wunschträume* (pipe dreams) and are thus too easily disappointed. Then they go to the other extreme in cynicism, relativism, and vindictiveness. Historian Theodor Schieder once spoke of the ill-fated German Reich "as a giant wishing to reach for the stars and losing the ground under his feet."

Another phenomenon that is characteristically German is their abiding inner insecurity, which has led them to great heights, superiority complexes, and great depths of inferiority complexes. I once saw a skit in the Düsseldorf cabaret *Das Kom(m)ödchen* depicting a watchmaker, in which the whole recitation centered around the word *Unruhe*. This means both restlessness and the balance mechanism in a watch. Using the word as a pun, the actor quipped, "The Germans may not have invented the clock *movement,* but it was German 'movement-itis' [restlessness] which made it necessary to invent clocks!"

You will not find a shred of nationalism in most places of the Federal Republic these days, but you can find restlessness on every street corner.

German cafés and taverns are just as overflowing with relaxing Germans as similar establishments in other countries. And German *Gemütlichkeit* is legendary. But proportionately there appear to be conspicuously fewer idle persons in the Federal Republic and East Germany than in countries also enjoying full employment like Belgium, the Netherlands, or Denmark. There are nowhere near the number of nice old ladies looking out the windows all day in Germany as there are in the Netherlands. And there is nothing even remotely as relaxed about the German *Platz* as the Italian *piazza*. "No loitering" signs are an innovation in Germany, and they are being installed in places like train terminals for the benefit of the Italian, Greek and Spanish "guest workers" rather than Germans. Germans, of course, like to relax just as other people, but for many of them it is much harder to do so. Even when they play, many Germans tend to be much

xix

more intense about it. It is said that the Italians are the world's worst organizers but the world's best improvisers—the opposite can be said of the Germans. There is—proportionately—far less spontaneity. Switzerland is just as industrially booming as West Germany, but—again proportionately speaking—the Swiss people have an almost suffocating calmness about them in stark contrast to large segments of restless Germans. "I should be flattered, I suppose," an American student said to me in Marburg, "that German students imitate American casualness so much, but I do wish they wouldn't be so intense about it."

According to the Giessen psychosomatic institute, one out of every three West Germans suffering from heart ailments is organically well. Their illnesses stem entirely from the stress of daily life and from emotional causes.

I shall have to leave it to the psychologists and psychiatrists to diagnose these phenomena. My own theory is that, in addition to the international uneasiness arising from conflicts and upheavals affecting all of us, the Germans are hung up on their past. They have never known political, social, or national security for very long in history. Perhaps this explains why they have placed so much emphasis on order—precisely because they never had it.

Today the West Germans are still trying to work their way out of an identity crisis. Bogged down by psychic trauma, the guilt-shame syndrome, they don't know where they belong. At the end of nearly every interview with a German I made it a point to ask, "Do you feel yourself to be a German?" By far the majority replied in the negative, many were evasive, and only very few replied affirmatively. Many said they felt more European than anything else. There is no word for "citizen of the Federal Republic." And the word "German" only underlines the ambiguity of the West Germans' identity. The generation-long uncertainty of the German question (in the larger context, indeed, the uncertainty goes back centuries) has undoubtedly left its psychological mark on the German psyche. "The self-confidence of the Germans," writes the well-known publicist Johannes Gross, "is characterized by the fact that they have no self-confidence."[2]

In spite of this—or, more likely, because of this—there is a growing spirit of national self-assurance. But this appears to be based on the Germans' economic security rather than any sense of national pride. This is not necessarily chauvinistic nationalism but the emerging consciousness of being "somebodies" and members of a world community. Disliked by the world for so long, the Germans don't know quite what to make of the fact that all of a sudden they are loved. It has gone to their heads. It is too much at once. They are intoxicated.

This is on the whole a healthy development. But the Germans are not yet used to being so universally accepted. Inevitably, there are unpleasant side effects. Many observers find that the Germans are becoming increasingly overbearing, calculating, and downright cocky. And some of them are aggressively defensive of the Nazi past.

For a growing number of Germans, and especially—and surprisingly—the younger generation, Adolf Hitler is simply too bad to be true. I personally won't be a bit surprised if in the near future we witness Hitler's rehabilitation. I emphatically do not mean by this any new outburst of nationalism, militarism, or neo-Nazism. That is certainly out of the question. No, it will be rather an indirect rehabilitation in the subtle way that legends multiply around men of such staggering proportions, good or evil. The relentless anti-Hitler indoctrination has just about reached the breaking point. Sooner or later someone will emerge with a book, play, or film, showing Hitler "in another light." Then before you know it, he will assume the mystique and fascination of a German Napoleon.

"The German recovery from nothing," writes the respected West German television reporter Thilo Koch, in a nationally syndicated column (June 19, 1970), "has provided them with the *Lebenslüge* [lie of life] that the Nazi catastrophe is somehow reparable."

I have called attention to German dangers. But there are also German achievements and contributions. If many Germans are restless, much of this is a creative restlessness. The West German theologians may well be among the world's most nervous, but they are also among the world's most dedicated and most dynamic. The tension in education, institutions, economics, and politics is a highly productive tension. If there is widespread German psychological insecurity, there is to a far wider extent German leadership in social problems, in development aid, economics, technology, industry, science, legislation, and politics.

In an opinion poll conducted in June, 1970, the West Germans led all the other West European nations (except Luxembourg, with 75 percent) in affirming their preference (69 percent) for a politically integrated Europe.

In the past, the Germans have been accused of being followers, not leaders. Today the West Germans are among the foremost leaders of Western democracy. They can be proud.

Adolph Schalk

Thalwil, Switzerland

INTRODUCTION

SOME OBSERVATIONS ABOUT GERMANY

THE GERMAN STATE as a political or geographic entity does not exist. For this reason maps of "Germany" still provisionally include the boundaries of the German Reich as it existed in 1937, and area covering 182,471 square miles, or roughly the size of Montana.

Technically, the German Reich has not ceased to exist as a state, but is "temporarily" deprived of its competence to perform legal acts as a result of the nation's collapse and the destruction of its governing apparatus at the end of World War II. Today we know two *de facto* political entities whose "provisional" borders may remain unsettled for years to come: The Federal Republic of Germany (West Germany), which is allied to the West, and the German Democratic Republic or GDR (East Germany), which is under Soviet control.

Following its defeat in World War II, Germany, as provisionally established by the Potsdam Conference, was divided into four zones occupied by Allied forces and administered through an Allied Control Council. National unification, although theoretically endorsed by the Soviet Union and the Western powers, foundered in the animosities of the Cold War.

At the end of World War II, the Soviet Union consolidated its hold on its occupied zone, which became the Soviet Zone and later East Germany, while the Western powers—the United States, the United Kingdom, and France—in turn consolidated their three zones, which became the Federal Republic. Thus, the Federal Republic is not a state founded by Germans, but by the three Western powers. And the GDR too was created by an outside power, the Soviet Union.

The former German provinces of Pomerania, Posen, and Silesia, including the large city of Wroclaw (Breslau), were turned over to Polish administration in 1945, while East Prussia was partitioned for administration by Poland and the Soviet Union.

Altogether Germany lost an area of some 34,000 square miles, somewhat less than the size of Virginia, or about a fifth of its original size. The migration of some ten million German expellees from those regions followed.

What we know as the Federal Republic or West Germany is a provisional government, which will remain so until its borders are permanently established by a peace treaty. It operates under a provisional "Basic Law" rather than a Constitution, and its "temporary" seat of government is at the university town of Bonn, theoretically awaiting the time when Berlin—today divided into East and West and situated 110 miles inside Red territory—may again become the capital of a unified Germany.

For many years the Federal Republic regarded the Soviet Zone as an illegal usurper of twenty-three percent of the former German Reich, and for this reason claimed sole right (*Alleinvertretungsrecht*) as the only democratic, freely-elected government to negotiate or act in behalf of Germany as a whole. It regarded itself as the sole trustee of the remaining territory of the former German Reich, whose origins as a state go back to 1871.

Since September 1, 1969, the coalition government under Socialist Chancellor Willy Brandt, taking a more realistic view of the situation, no longer attempts to be the sole spokesman for all the German people, and has begun to shift toward a *de facto* acceptance of two separate Germanies for the indeterminate future. It is no longer a foregone conclusion that East Germans would necessarily wish reunion with West Germany or that they might not prefer a socialist state similar to the GDR even if they were allowed to choose their government in a free election.

Some Facts and Figures

The Federal Republic is just over half the size of the former German Reich and could fit snugly inside the state of Oregon with room to spare.

At the last census (1969), there were nearly 78 million persons living in the two Germanies, 60.6 million in the Federal Republic and 17.1 million in the GDR. This is a population density of 611 persons per square mile, as compared to 100 persons per square mile in California and 49 persons per square mile in the United States as a whole. Despite these figures, Germany is less crowded than the Netherlands with 906 inhabitants per square mile or Japan with 650.

Once the greatest European military and economic power, Germany lost two world wars in the space of one generation and in them 8.5 million people. Twice in twenty-five years her people have seen their money and their securities devalued by more than nine-tenths.

In 1945, at the end of World War II, the entire state apparatus was destroyed, together with all the machinery of government, and German territory was wholly occupied by foreign troops.

The people existed on a starvation diet amounting to only 40 percent of the minimum recommended by nutrition experts. When cold and hunger came, they brought with them epidemics causing the death of infants and the aged. Contagious diseases threatened to spread. Fuel and clothing were hardly to be found, and the level of production in 1946-1947 was such that, had it continued, it would have provided only one suit for each inhabitant every forty years and only one shirt every ten years.

At the end of the war, millions of men who were capable of working were still in captivity. More than two million dwellings were completely destroyed and another two million partially destroyed. Buildings and factories lay in ruins. Communications were cut, bridges were destroyed, and the entire merchant marine was lost.

With its territory divided into four Occupation zones and its Eastern regions cut off, the economic structure of the country disintegrated. In Berlin, 80 percent of industry was lost through dismantling. The nation as a whole had no economic security. In 1945, such expressions as "frustration," "hopelessness," "anguish" and "lack of aim in life" were commonplace among Germans in the midst of a hostile world, a world which had crushed the German forces with overwhelming might and was now calling the German people to account for the Nazi disregard for human life and dignity.

Today the Federal Republic's share in world trade has attained that of the Reich's in 1929. The present living standard surpasses what it was before the war. The Deutsche mark is one of the world's hardest currencies.

Basically the Federal Republic has been a prosperous country in the postwar years. Although the average worker earns less than in the United States, there are far fewer slums in either West or

East Germany. Full employment has been the norm throughout most of the fifties, sixties, and into the seventies.

Regarded as a nation of poets and thinkers and composers in previous centuries, Germany had by 1900 become noted for foremost advances in science and technology. The old pastoral scene has been radically replaced by its new role as an industrial giant. Urbanization has become a way of life, with only 8 percent of the population still working on farms, as against 40 percent at the turn of the century. Women employees, formerly a rarity, today number 5 million.

Germany is at once the key and the Gordian knot of the emerging integration of Europe. With her frontiers of 1937 she would have taken up one-tenth of Europe, the Soviet Union excluded. In population, the two Germanies are exceeded in Europe only by the Soviet Union.

The Federal Republic is a charter member of Western Europe's Common Market and the European Coal and Steel Community, its *Bundeswehr* (armed forces) are directly under NATO command. Because of its provisional status, it is not eligible for membership in the United Nations, but it is active in UNESCO and other sub-organizations of the U.N., in the International Red Cross, and numerous international movements and organizations. It has a peace corps program and contributes substantially to the developing countries.

Germany lies in the heart of Europe. The Federal Republic adjoins Denmark to the north, Holland, Belgium, Luxembourg, and France to the west, Switzerland and Austria to the south, Czechoslovakia and East Germany to the east, and adjoining the GDR in the east, Poland.

Germany is divided into five main geographical features from the North Sea to the Baltic in the north, to the Alps in the south, and from the Rhenish slate hills in the west to the East Prussian lakes and the Silesian mountains in the east. These include, from north to south: the north German lowlands; the escarpment of the *Mittelgebirge* (mountains of medium height); the west and south German terraces and mountains; the south German foothills and, further west, the Black Forest Hills and the Bavarian Alps, to the southeast.

The Federal Republic is divided into ten *Länder*, which are roughly equivalent to American states. Each state is subdivided into *Landkreise* (similar to counties) and *Gemeinden* (communes).

The ten states of the Federal Republic are, from north to south: Schleswig-Holstein, Hamburg, Bremen (the latter are city-states), Lower Saxony, North Rhine-Westphalia, Rhineland-Palatinate, Saarland, Hesse, Baden-Württemberg, and Bavaria.[1] The special status of West Berlin is taken up in Chapter 12.

The East German states are: Mecklenburg, Pomerania, Brandenburg, Saxon-Anhalt, Saxony, and Thuringia. East Prussia, Silesia, and the eastern part of Pomerania belong to the disputed Oder-Neisse territories now under Polish and Soviet administration. The former state of Prussia was abolished in 1945. (See Chapter 7.)

The German climate is far from ideal, having one of the world's heaviest rainfalls. Air conditioning is conspicuous by its redundance. The temperature rarely goes above 90 degrees Fahrenheit, and when it does, the newspapers carry front-page headlines screaming, "Heat Wave!" In my eight years' residence in Germany and extensive travels over an additional eight years, I can recall only a few times when I didn't require a blanket at night during the summer. Psychologists often attribute to the weather the brooding, introverted character of many German thinkers and writers and the melancholic streak that permeates much of German literature. It is just as hard to imagine Goethe, Beethoven, or Wagner coming from the Isle of Capri as it is to imagine Verdi spending *Walpurgisnacht* in the Harz mountains. There are infinitely more bookstores in Germany than in sunnier countries. One reason, perhaps, is that the Germans are forced by nature to live indoors more of the time.

Modern Germany can claim almost no primeval forest, but "Der Wald" (the forest) is part of the mystique of the German language (Chapter 4). Forestation is fostered to a large degree. The legacy of the deep-dark forest, and the frequent fog, showers, and regular incidence of violent thunderstorms remains. This setting has colored the Nordic folklore with its tales of dwarfs, fairies, goblins, and witches. It is a romantic country, rich in thousands of traditions and customs many of which are zealously preserved to this day. In spite of the destruction of two world wars, there are still some four hundred castles, hundreds of medieval towns and villages, and Roman ruins galore.

Germany is also an extremely modern country with atomic reactors, psychedelic cafés, skyscrapers, and one of the most extensive superhighway systems in the world.

Democracy

The Federal Republic is still only an infant democracy. Before World War II, there was the twelve-year dictatorship of Hitler. Today it has already outlived the Third Reich as well as the ill-fated fourteen-year democratic effort known as the Weimar Republic.

Politically the Federal Republic is a welfare state with mild overtones of socialism, including obligatory health insurance, family allowances, and social security.

As a nation, Germany is a relatively new country. It is only twice as old as the Soviet Union and almost a century younger than the United States of America.

Even the word "Germany" is extremely broad and, seen from the perspective of history, constantly changing designations, meaning different things over the centuries to different people.

It has been applied to the aggregate of princely territories that made up the Holy Roman Empire.

From 1815 to 1866, Germany meant the German Confederation. But it was Austria which was then considered to be the foremost German state.

The unification of a variety of duchies, kingdoms, and assorted republics into a single nation didn't take place until 1871. Before then it was rightly said that Germany was a geographical entity rather than a country. To a surprising degree, each section of the country has retained unique characteristics, although the petty chauvinism associated with them—notably the antagonism between the Prussians and the Bavarians—has all but disappeared.

The present usage of the word "Germany" dating from the German empire of 1871-1918 defines Germany as the principal German-speaking area of Europe, apart from Austria and Switzerland. From 1919 to 1933, Germany was constantly referred to as the Weimar Republic, and under the Nazi rule as the Third Reich.

One of the most significant influences on Germany since World War II is the dispersion of refugees and expellees. This has had profound repercussions on the previous cultural, linguistic, social, economic, and religious patterns of various regions. Indirectly this migration has undoubtedly been a decisive factor in the emerging pluralism in politics, culture, and religion.

Religion

More than 96 percent of the population belongs—nominally— to one or the other of the two big Christian denominations, Evangelical Lutheran or Roman Catholic. This figure is misleading because, unlike the United States, a vast number of church adherents do not take an active part in church life, though adamantly perferring to remain registered as church members, even though this means that under West German laws they must pay a compulsory church tax—about 10 percent of their income tax or 1 percent of their total income—administered by the Federal and state authorities.

In recent years numerous Protestant sects have made impressive gains in membership, thus upsetting the previous pattern of a predominantly Evangelical-Lutheran Protestantism and injecting new currents of pluralism.

Under the present distribution, the membership of Catholics and Protestants in the Federal Republic is almost equal: 45 percent of the population is registered as Roman Catholic, while 51.2 percent is Protestant. By contrast, East Germany including East Berlin has about 14.8 million registered Protestants (over 80 percent) and some two million Roman Catholics. About 75 percent of the refugees in the Federal Republic are Protestant.

Only an estimated number of some 30,000 Jews are now living in the Federal Republic, compared with 560,000 in pre-Nazi Germany. In recent years a number of Jews have started returning to West Germany hopeful that a genuine Jewish community may thrive in the new symbiosis. By contrast, only about 1,500 Jews live in East Germany and this number is steadily decreasing because the majority are over sixty years of age.

Meanwhile, at the start of the seventies, the Social Democratic administration in coalition with the Free Democrats led by Chancellor Willy Brandt and Foreign Minister Walter Scheel, has made bold overtures toward reconciliation, both toward the East (GDR, Poland, Soviet Union) and toward the West (the Netherlands). In West Germany, at least, a new, politically-alert, internationally-minded German has emerged.

PART ONE

The Legacy

◄ I ►

MAIN STREET, GERMANY

SHORTLY AFTER ARRIVING in Germany, I was enjoying my first Wiener schnitzel in a *Gasthaus*. In spite of my crewcut, American clothes, and the fact that I didn't hold my fork continental-style in my left hand to convey food to my mouth, I did not think I was unduly conspicuous.

But suddenly from clear across the room a German tot shouted to his parents loud enough for everybody to hear, "Mommy! Look at how that man with the funny haircut eats! Isn't he naughty?"

The incident painfully reminded me that it wasn't these people with their "strange German ways" who were the foreigners, but that the foreigner was none other than myself. It also jolted me to the realization that the clue to the German people, or any people for that matter, is, more than anything else, their mentality.

An American college girl said to me that her biggest surprise on arriving in Germany was, "Everything was so much the same as at home. I didn't expect men to wear lederhosen or women to be in costume. But I did expect to be abruptly confronted by another world."

It was only after living for some time in Germany that this girl began to realize that, for all its sameness, Germany *is* another world. "But more than any physical or geographical differences, it is the world of the mind that separates or unites people. This is the biggest lesson I got out of my stay in Germany."

As the little child reminded me, good manners in one country may be bad manners in another: the difference lies in the state of mind. "The frontier," wrote George Bernard Shaw, "is only the difference between two ways of looking at things. Any road will take you across if you really want to get there."[1]

The trouble with trying to explain the customs, living habits, and mentality of a people is that everything explains them. It is,

1

as Chesterton once pointed out, like trying to explain the advantage of civilization over barbarism. Where do you start?

At first there are the little things that catch your eye. Knifelike door handles instead of round ones. Windows that open inward like a door instead of up and down. The absence of screen doors and windows in summer because the relatively cool climate attracts few insects. The colorful frescoes, with a religious theme in Bavaria—good old St. Christopher is ubiquitous in spite of his removal from the calendar of saints by the Vatican—and modernistic themes elsewhere on the facades of apartment buildings. The hundreds of ancient churches vying with startling modern ones. The abundance of flower boxes, bubbling fountains, beautifully laid-out floral plantings and striking monuments. The wonderful variety of thick, genuinely nourishing bread that you have to slice yourself (Germans regard American factory-produced bread as "odorless, tasteless cotton"). The medieval towns with their half-timbered houses and narrow, winding streets that end abruptly in a modern square with skyscrapers. The confrontation with history on nearly every other street corner. The incredible number of opera houses, theaters, bookshops, even in small communities.

Americans traveling in Europe are often annoyed by the necessity of filling out intricate forms when registering in a hotel. However, most German states have drastically shortened the forms or even abolished them, and passports are no longer required in many places. A very useful instititution is the hotel accommodation agency, usually sponsored by the local branch of the tourist office or *Verkehrsverein*, located in nearly every German city, usually in or near the main train terminal (*Bahnhof*).[2]

Once in their rooms, Americans are often frustrated to find no soap. This lack originates from wartime shortages and continues to this day. On the other hand, many German hotels polish guests' shoes in the wee hours of the morning if they are left in front of the door.[3]

A surprise awaits the American in the morning: the continental breakfast. This intriguing name soon loses its luster when our American friend realizes that it consists merely of a couple of hard rolls, butter, jam, and coffee or tea, and sometimes, a soft-boiled egg.[4] However, no American is displeased by the welcome restraint regarding tipping. So far, the everlasting outstretched hand is the exception and not the rule in Germany.

What, no ice water? No, in Germany this "beverage" is not only not automatically served in restaurants, its existence as an item of consumption is unknown. Waiters have to be asked repeatedly, and even then may bring a bottle of mineral water unless tap water (*von der Leitung*) is specifically requested. More than likely the waiter, believing that you want to down a pill will bring you lukewarm water. Soft drinks are rarely served with ice. Waiters usually excuse the lack by insisting "ice is unhealthy anyway."

With the increase of industrial canteens, German workers have begun to abandon the habit of carrying briefcases (*Aktentaschen*) that are used as lunch boxes. School children "wear" their briefcases on their backs with the aid of two shoulder straps, call them *Ranzen*. German mothers believe these *Ranzen* keep their children's backs straight and leave both hands free.

In Germany "man's best friend" is a privileged being and is allowed to accompany his master unmuzzled nearly everywhere, is nearly always permitted in cafés, taverns, and restaurants, and sits in all his dog glory under the table. There are approximately 2.5 million dogs in the Federal Republic, the most popular being der *Pudel* (poodle), der *Dackel* (dachshund), and der *Schäferhund* (German Shepherd). It is wise to keep your eyes on the ground on German streets. A roadsweeper can't be reserved for every dog.

Americans soon notice that the bicycle population is much greater here than at home and people from six to ninety-six take to the bike. All over the country many cities construct special lanes. between the street and sidewalk, especially for bicycles. Cars must give cyclists right of way before making a right-hand turn. The increase in automobile ownership has not really put a dent in bicycle traffic. On the contrary, bicycle manufacturers are enjoying a bigger boom than ever selling collapsible bikes that health-conscious Germans take with them in their car trunks.

Like the rest of Europe, Germany has a generous distribution of outdoor lavatories, some of them with ornate facades and pompous titles, such as *Bedürfnisanstalt* (literally, convenience establishment), or the simple designation "OO".

A fascinating sight in spring, summer, and autumn is that of many Germans, noticeably pretty women, sitting on park benches, with eyes closed, faces lifted skywards, sometimes for

3

minutes on end, trying to catch every possible ray of sunshine. I picked up the habit myself, and when visiting relatives in blistering St. Louis, dismayed them as I tilted my face to the sun and closed my eyes meditatively to drink it all in.

Americans are often puzzled by the "shanty towns" frequently appearing on the outskirts of German cities. But the "shanties" are anything but ramshackle. Usually painted in bright colors, they are spaced apart with small vegetable gardens in between. These huts are actually glorified tool sheds and summer cabins for city dwellers who rent garden space outside of town. They are called *Schrebergärten* (Schreber gardens) after a Leipzig physician who decades ago developed this idea as a means of combating industrial air pollution.

In Germany never ask anybody in *Lederhosen* (leather trousers), Tyrolean hat, or *Dirndl* (Bavarian peasant dress) for directions. Chances are, he or she will answer in perfect Bostonese, "Sorry, Mack, I'm a stranger here myself." Also, the famous Hofbräuhaus in Munich is the last place to meet Germans.

Spazieren gehen (taking a stroll) is part of the German way of life. If there is anything the Germans like to do more than talk, and talk they do, it is taking a walk. All over Germany the forests have neatly laid out foot paths, so that many Germans think nothing of going for an outing in their Sunday best—suit, tie, and polished shoes. Even for picnics some women will show up with high heels and nylons! However this formalism is beginning to peter out, sometimes in strange ways. For example, I met a charming middle-aged couple in a plush restaurant one evening, they wearing casual sport clothes, I, a suit and tie. The next morning I took a cue from them and appeared at the informal breakfast room of our hotel in sport clothes, but they (and not on my account, as all around us our neighbors wore formal clothes) arrived in suit and gown.

You must always be careful to have small change in your pocket. Waitresses, newspaper vendors, and street car conductors do not look kindly on even a ten-mark ($2.50) note. Many cities have an honor system of conductorless trolleys (not because of brotherly trust in fellowmen but because of manpower shortage) and let you cancel your own transfers with special machines located at every stop. Regular spot checks are made, and violators fined.

4

As a rule a man walks to the left side of a woman—not necessarily on the outside. The place on the right is always the "place of honor"; a young girl walking with an older woman would also walk on her left. The custom is believed to originate from the Middle Ages when the gentleman, wearing his sword at his left side, would walk to the left of the lady in order to be able to draw it quickly for her protection. Upon entering a restaurant or public place the man goes first. This is because in former times it was necessary for the escort to see if the place was fit for a lady to enter.

Movies

Children under six are not allowed in German movie theaters, and all movies are screened and evaluated under a Federal Youth Protection Law, which classifies them according to admissible age groups: 6 to 12, 12 to 16, 16 to 18, and adult.

Adult movies, however, are exempt from government censorship, but are processed by a voluntary censorship board of the motion picture industry (Chapter 14). In recent years, the impact of the permissive age has hit West Germany too, and the norm for adult movies is "anything goes," or, well, almost anything.

In the Federal Republic it is advisable to order by telephone movie tickets for popular films in advance, because all seats are reserved. Even if the theater is nearly empty, the usherette will inevitably squeeze you into an already occupied row rather than let you choose your own seat.

Movies do not run continuously, so that it is necessary to see the picture from the beginning. "This is where we came in" is not known in Germany. Double features are rare.

Sidney Poitier and John Wayne do their thing *auf Deutsch* in Germany, since most foreign films are dubbed. This is done not only to help Germans understand the dialogue better but also because of their penchant for "germanizing" everything.

The Little Shop Around the Corner

That little "shop around the corner" is closing at the rate of some 10,000 a year. An estimated closing of some 100,000 small retailers by 1980 is expected.

Nevertheless, in spite of the inroads of American-style supermarkets, the numerous small specialized shops still abound. In

5

the smaller towns and rural areas they will probably see the year 2000. Very often they specialize in a very few products, such as milk and milk products, bread and pastry, wines, shoes, linen, draperies. Most conspicuous are the perennial, spotlessly-clean meat shops, lined with dozens of sausages, not to mention the numerous sausage stands everywhere. Even in supermarkets people must often bring their own shopping bags to carry the goods they buy. Many bring their own milk bottles or cans, to be filled from a large milk container, since this is cheaper.

Germans are notoriously thrifty. Even in supermarkets they often shop in small quantities. If you want just enough Brussel sprouts to feed two people, the clerk will measure and wrap them just as politely and painstakingly as if you had ordered two pounds. Cheeses and sausages can be ordered by the quarter or even eighth of a pound.

Frequently on German streets one finds little shops named *Reform Haus.* But persons are not reformed here, merely eating habits. These health food stores specialize in items not usually available elsewhere. Peanut butter, certain types of mushrooms, rattlesnake steak, ant soup, and the like can be found here.

The German *Apotheke* sells, believe it or not, mainly drugs. A second institution called *Drogerie* sells only medicines which can be had without prescriptions and mostly toilet articles, cosmetics, sometimes camera supplies, wall paper, paints, and seeds. A number of experimental *Drogeries al la Amerikanisch* have been established, but it remains to be seen if they revolutionize German drugstores. Meanwhile the *Apotheke* as a prescription drugstore is protected by law.

The *Milch Bar* has only a slight resemblance to the Malt Bar, and it is almost impossible to get a creamy, thick malt in Germany. For one thing, the ice cream comes mainly from Italy and is far too rich for the American-style malts. Hamburgers are a rarity even in Hamburg.

Drive-in movies are few and far between—there just aren't that many warm summer nights—and so are drive-in restaurants. Motels are a recent innovation.

No Billboards and Restricted Advertising

There are no billboards in Germany and advertising on highways and roads is conspicuous by its absence. But there is much lobbying for this bane of Western civilization, and who knows how much longer the Germans can enjoy unblemished scenery?

Meanwhile in the cities you will find trim, small twelve feet high, forty-two inches in diameter *Litfasssäulen* covered with advertising posters. Named after the Berlin printer, Ernst Litfass, they were first erected in Berlin in 1855, in a successful campaign against unsightly advertising on fences and building walls. The famous French advertising columns (*Morris Collonnes*) were copied from Litfass, differing from the German columns only by their more decorative cap.

Located at the rate of about one per 1,000 population, the columns (made of prefabricated cement rings mounted on a poured cement base) are very effective. Constructed at eye level and stationed near bus stops and on street corners, they are relatively unobtrusive, aesthetically acceptable, and allegedy reach 93 percent of the population.

The Truth About Sauerkraut

One common American nickname for Germans is "Krauts." No one knows for sure where this originated. One version goes back to World War II when American troops captured a German commissary depot somewhere in Africa, and found out that every single can contained sauerkraut. No meat, no poultry, no fruit, only sauerkraut! In their disappointment they invented the name Krauts and it stuck.

In a survey taken by the Emnid Opinion Pollsters of Frankfurt, only 3 percent of the Germans named sauerkraut as their favorite dish. The poll showed that meats of all kinds receive priority among the majority of Germans, followed by vegetables with or without meat or noodles, spaghetti, and "miscellany."

The stereotyped notion that Germans have a predilection for starchy foods, especially bread and potatoes, also has been subject to scrutiny. Dr. Irmgard Landgrebe-Wolff, director of the Nutrition Advisory Service of the German Nutrition Council, Stuttgart, recently said that the last half century has shown a steady drop in the consumption of bread per person from 287 pounds to 176 pounds annually. At the same time consumption of eggs has shot up 100 percent. There is also a growing preference among West Germans for more refined products and delicacies.

This change of West German diet is partly because of the

7

influence of fashion houses. But the main reason is surely that living standards have considerably improved.

While tastes in the types of food are gradually changing, eating habits remain generally the same. Between 60 and 80 percent of all West German families still eat their main hot meal at noon. Many regions, especially Bavaria, still observe long lunch periods from one to two hours. Twenty-five percent eat two hot meals a day.

Also, there is some truth to the widespread belief that Germans are heavy eaters. If they diet at home, many of them make up for it by their eating habits at work. The German *Zweites Frühstück* (second breakfast) is still commonplace and is much more substantial, with a sandwich or two, than the coffee break, which has become standard in the larger industries.

A newly arrived American accountant gasped in horror as his German assistant calmly unpacked a picnic lunch in a client's office and started eating. Many Germans find gastronomical satisfaction in slipping out to the nearest delicatessen and preparing themselves a tasty lunch on the office desk. Noon has become the busiest time of day for food stores in business districts. Even in firms that provide cafeterias, thousands still favor bringing their own food to work, for many Germans tend to eat intermittently throughout the working day.

Employers in tune with the times provide electric kettles to brew up coffee or tea, and one of the later additions to the office equipment is the wood-paneled refrigerator. How far the trend will go, nobody knows, but if bosses started putting stoves in their offices, the Germans would be the last to show surprise.

Recipes and All That

When it comes to recipes, things are not so easy. Germans were late in using measuring cups and spoons and are more used to rule of thumb estimates—literally. Their recipes are far from precise and leave much to the individual imagination, such as "brown the meat, add *some* onions, *some* tomatoe puree, and *some* water and flour . . . "

Americans are frequently frustrated by the German—or for that matter, European—measuring system. An American housewife, trying a German recipe is suddenly stopped by the notation "150 grams flour." A German friend complains that it was 40 degrees during his Italian vacation and you don't know whether he sweltered or froze. A filling station attendant leaves you puzzled as he asks, "How many liters, please?"

What most Americans don't realize is that the United States and Britain are two of the very few countries in the world that still use the archaic system of feet and inches, ounces and pounds. Actually, the European system makes so much more sense.

The foot originates from ancient attempts to measure with that part of the body. And if in the seventeenth century there were as many as 265 varieties of this measuring unit, it is probably because of the fact that it was based on the feet of 265 different people.

The logical-minded French rebelled against this chaos and in 1795 devised and adopted the simple metric system, which rapidly spread to other countries.

While U.S. schoolboys, and adults for that matter, still fumble over 5,280 feet in a mile, 16 ounces in a pound, the European schoolboy simply uses measurements based on 100. All he has to remember is the prefix "centi" which means hundred and, "kilo" which means thousand. Thus a meter (slightly more than a U.S. yard) has 100 centimeters; a kilometer (0.6 miles) has 1,000 meters. Similarly, a kilogram 1,000 grams, a liter 100 centiliters, and so on.

School Life in Germany

All German children attend school from the age of six to fifteen, and part time to age eighteen. Although education is under state, not federal or local, jurisdiction, school standards are about the same throughout the country. At present there is a severe kindergarten shortage, with only 20 percent of three- to four-year-olds finding a place.

On any given day German children usually spend fewer hours at school than American pupils, staying only until noon or 1 or 2 P.M. However, many German children go to school on Saturdays, but this may change. A hot lunch is therefore not served, but at recess the kids can eat a sandwich brought from home. Sometimes a glass of milk is served at school. At home, the pupil must sit down to a sizable stack of homework. Even first and second graders must do some homework.

Compared with American schools, there is relatively little social life at a German school, high school or college, though in

9

recent years intensive political activity has developed (see Chapter 16). Dances and social events are rare, but there is a trend toward more of the American-style activities. School associations, fraternities, sororities are not known in German secondary schools. There are student clubs and fraternities of various types at the universities, but they bear little resemblance to comparable American institutions.

On their first day of school, the tots are consoled by their mothers with huge cones filled with sweets and maybe a small toy. In some states, the school year begins around Easter, in others in the fall. The vacation schedule also varies from state to state. There is a summer vacation lasting approximately six weeks and shorter ones of only a few days around Easter, Whitsuntide, in the fall, and at Christmas.

All German pupils must attend four years of elementary school or *Grundschule*. Then, after taking an entrance examination, they may either go on to an "intermediate" school *(Mittelschule or Realschule)* or to a secondary school. As in other European countries, the Germans have a long tradition of apprenticeship in commerce and the skilled trades. Thus the Mittelschule is designed to prepare the pupil for a trade or business profession; students who wish to qualify for university training attend a secondary school, or *Gymnasium* (not to be confused with the American gym). This is the equivalent of the American high school plus junior college. There is a stiff entrance examination and a nine-year program ending with the final examination called *Abitur* (or graduation). Since annual examinations are not customary in German schools this carries much weight and entitles the graduate to be admitted, usually at the age of nineteen, to any university without further examination.

There are three types of Gymnasiums, emphasizing either classical languages, modern languages, or mathematics and science, though all three are correlated in their basic curricula and requirements. Students must take all the courses offered but some electives are permitted. Though largely non-coed, this pattern is beginning to change.

Only 40 out of 100 Gymnasium students continue all the way to Abitur. Most leave after six years at the age of sixteen and receive a certificate called *Mittelere Reife,* which is the same as the diploma earned by Realschule graduates and roughly equivalent to a U.S. high school diploma.

A major educational reform program, however, is under way.

This calls for a fourteen-year, three-stage plan, expanding kindergarten facilities, lowering obligatory schooling to age five, and replacing half-day with whole-day schools. The program especially calls for drastic improvements of university-level education and adult education (Chapter 16).

Holidays

Germany is plagued by a plethora of legal and religious holidays. The Germans do not merely observe *a* Christmas Day, but *two* Christmases, *two* Easters. And as if that were not enough, Whitsunday has the rank of Easter and also is observed over a two-day period, usually with the first spring outing. The "second" Christmas is December 26; Easter Monday is also a legal holiday. This system enables the Germans, who have a deeply ingrained sense of privacy, to observe the "first Christmas day" usually in the strict family circle, while opening their doors on the "second Christmas" to friends and more distant relatives. Although countless numbers of German families no longer adhere to such a rigid pattern, the practice is still so widespread that American students, for example, sometimes complain that they are left out in the cold on Christmas eve and day and only get invited to join in the festivities on December 26.

In Catholic regions the religious feasts of Ascension Thursday, Corpus Christi (observed by huge outdoor processions), Immaculate Conception, and Assumption are observed, usually as legal state holidays. In Catholic Bavaria firms annually have to pay 30 percent more holiday wages than Evangelical Lower Saxony.

Labor Day is observed, usually by parades and speeches, on the same day as Communists celebrate theirs, May 1.

There is a kind of German Thanksgiving (Erntedankfest), but it is mostly observed by religious services, Catholic or Protestant, during which crop samples are symbolically blessed. But there is no historic event commemorated, nor a wide consumption of turkey on Erntedankfest.

In addition there are countless festivals: Oktoberfest in Munich, Fasching, Karnival, Schützenfeste, which are duly explained elsewhere in this book.

Picturesque Market Places

The picturesque market places stemming from the Middle Ages

11

have changed little and are a common street scene all over Europe, and in virtually every German town, with colorful umbrellas, and overflowing stalls with eggs, salamis, cheeses, fruits, vegetables, household utensils, clothes, sometimes tended by women in ancient costumes. Flea markets are found in several cities, notably in Munich and the Fisch Market in Hamburg's harbor section. Hamburg has no less than 36 open air markets. An estimated two-thirds of all German housewives like to shop at outdoor markets whenever they can.

Shopping

Daily life in Germany is much more regulated than in the United States, and nothing reveals this more than West German shopping laws. Sales are not held at just any time, but only twice a year, two weeks each in winter and summer (starting on the last Monday in January and in July respectively). All West German shops have their big sales called *Winter* or *Sommer Schlussverkauf* or *Ausverkauf,* and these are fixed by law. A shop that closes down, however, may offer a clearance sale or *Räumungsverkauf.*

One of the most unpopular laws in the statute book is the fourteen-page West German one regulating shopping hours. All shops must close on weekdays at 6:30 P.M. On Saturdays, closing time is 2 P.M., except on the first Saturday of the month, when it is 6 P.M. Barbers may stay open Saturdays until 6 P.M. but are required by law to stay closed on Mondays until 1 P.M. Florists may stay open Saturdays until 5 P.M. if they are within three hundred yards of a cemetery. During the month of December these restrictions are relaxed slightly. On Sundays, newsstands may stay open only to 1 P.M., and bakeries from 11 A.M. to 3 P.M.

Refreshment stands and news kiosks in train terminals and airports are open late in the evening and on Sundays and theoretically may sell only to customers who can prove they have a train or plane ticket. Although this is rarely checked, the selection is poor, the food stale, and the prices exorbitant.

By contrast, retailers in Belgium can open and close their shops whenever they wish, Sundays included. In France shops may stay open until 10:30 P.M. And in the Netherlands and Switzerland shops stay open on Saturdays until 6 P.M.

As a result of these restrictions, millions of working men and

12

women rush into the stores at the same time at the end of the day or during the lunch hour. On their day off, they find their shopping hours severely limited.

The protests of public and press have been ignored by the government, the shop owners, and the trade unions. Unions oppose the law's repeal because they say sales clerks already have a 42½-hour week and will not work any longer.

An opinion poll conducted by the respected Allensbach Institute revealed that while the majority of farmers and white collar workers preferred longer shopping hours, the majority of unskilled and skilled workers preferred the present restrictions. As one spokesman for the Institute put it, "The results indicate that the Germans would rather suffer the inconveniences of shopping restrictions than depart from their accustomed order."

The mass-circulation Berlin newspaper *B.Z.* editorialized recently: "The shopping restrictions will last until shoppers stop acting like sheep."

Traffic

Nothing is more frustrating to German and non-German alike, than the maze of German traffic signs and regulations. Germans themselves like to quip about *Der Deutsche Schilderwald* (the German forest of signs). Countless thousands of intersections and congested roads have such a conglomeration of signs, many of them with detailed instructions in small print, that you would become a traffic hazard if you actually stopped long enough to read them.

The new *Strassenverkehrsordnung* (traffic regulations code) of 1970 has been soundly condemned by the press as worsening the situation.

The weekly news magazine *Der Spiegel* sarcastically calls the new regulations "The catechism of good conduct," while the national daily *Die Welt* dubbed them "the sovereign police edicts from the nineteenth century." Even the Mannheim chief of police, Dr. Alfred Stümper, predicted that the 1970 traffic regulations are "so lacking in imagination that they will only create the utmost confusion among motorists."

Journalist Ferdinand Ranft wrote in *Die Welt* that the West German driver is compelled to drive defensively.

The confusion arises mainly from the German penchant for perfectionism. The traffic laws spell out in infinite detail how

13

motorists and pedestrians must conduct themselves in case of accidents, when and where children may or may not play in the streets, where parking is legal, when lights may be used. There are even large sections regarding how dirty a car may get, especially its windshield. Much of the legal fine print is because of an understandable concern for safety with a view to cracking down on aggressive driving and traffic deaths, discussed elsewhere in this book. But critics think that the regulations, which took twelve years to draw up in their present state, will require another score of years before they are humanly workable.

The Corner Tavern

Let's face it, the American bar has become a worldwide institution and Germany is no exception. In spite of this, however, the traditional German *Gasthaus* (literally, guest house) or *Gaststätte* has held its own and very often still preserves its old-fashioned *Gemütlichkeit* (coziness) if not downright medievalism. Most of them are warm and friendly places full of knickknacks or exquisite wood paneling, sometimes with a seventeenth century porcelain stove, and very often containing outstanding examples of prints, paintings, carvings, and wrought-iron signs (such as "At the Golden Ox," or "Augegottes"—Eye of God).

On a cold winter night the Gasthäuser are a joy to behold and an even greater joy to relax in for hours. Many have their own *Metzgerei* (butcher shop) and inexpensive hotel rooms. Usually there are no stools at the bar, but booths with benches instead. Steady customers automatically seek out the proprietor and shake his hand. If the owner's wife is present one shakes her hand. It is not at all impolite for any stranger to join someone already seated, even though other tables are unoccupied.

Umpteen times in the course of a day or evening the proprietor makes the rounds of all the customers, and makes a point of nodding to each one, often shaking their hands.

The average German *Gasthaus* has far more social acceptance than the American tavern, and women are frequent visitors. On Sundays whole families will esconce themselves, children and all, and spend the greater part of the day, especially in bad weather.

Unfortunately *Gasthäuser* near garrisons often have a bad reputation. Alcoholic consumption for youth is strictly regu-

14

lated. At sixteen a young person may drink beer until 10 P.M. At eighteen he or she may drink beer, but only beer, until midnight, and play the slot machines. After nineteen, he or she may imbibe something stronger than beer. And from twenty-one onwards, he or she may stay until the bar closes, usually at 2 A.M.

A standard item in most German taverns is the *Stammtisch,* a special table reserved for regular customers, usually marked by a little flag. Here they play dice or traditional German card games like *Skat* or *Max.*

If Herr Maier orders a "large" beer, it is usually about half a liter, or about seventeen ounces, although in Bavaria it is served in a quart-sized mug. There are those who insist that they went to Munich's Oktoberfest and drank beer with 18 percent alcohol. They are mistaken. The highest alcohol content of any German beer is 5 percent. When breweries refer to 18 percent beer, they are speaking of the percentage of wort (barley extract), not alcohol.

Since in German beers the carbonic acid is produced naturally and never removed from the beer, they are not kept too cold, for with the carbonic acid "bound in," beer will not fizz if drunk directly from the refrigerator. In many German taverns there are small cigar-sized "beer warmers" which Germans put into their beer glasses. Lukewarm or slightly chilled is the way Germans prefer their beer and, for that matter, their soda. In the United States, the carbonic acid is removed and added artificially before bottling. German beer is not pasteurized, except for export. Beer connoisseurs say unpasteurized beer tastes better, while pasteurized beer keeps longer.

Legend credits the mythical king Gambrinus with the discovery of beer, but archaelogists claim to have found recipes for beer in ancient Egyptian hieroglyphics making beer one of the oldest alcoholic beverages known to man.

The famous dark brown beer, called Bock Beer, which was brought to the States in the nineteenth century by German brewers, is attributed to the brewers of a small north German village called Einbeck. In 1248 they decided to make a special beer to celebrate the arrival of spring. They chose cereals for the malt with special care, and only the best hops, and lagered (*i.e.,* aged) the product in underground caves. The beer tasted so good that the demand for "Einbeck beer" spread all over northern Germany. In German, of course, Bock means goat, and since the

15

goat was usually depicted as the companion of Gambrinus, it was inevitable that "Ein Beck" should become "Ein Bock." Hence, the name "Bock Beer."[5]

Statistically, every man, woman and child in the country imbibes no less than 34 gallons of beer every year.

Although German breweries deliver their beer by modern trucks, most of them keep a few dray horses and ponies for festivals and just for old time's sake. Probably the happiest ponies in the world are harnessed to delivery wagons of German breweries. Like the human brewery employees, they are provided with a daily beer ration which, in contrast to the regulations of most other jobs, must be drunk during working hours.

Weinstuben (wine parlors) and the original *Ratskeller* (*i.e.*, town-hall basement, after *Rathaus*, town hall) of course also abound. Most of these are elegant restaurants specializing in fine wines and brandies. Germans tend to drink many fine German brandies, such as Steinhager, Kirschwasser, and the like, much more than whiskey.

The Café

German cafés are what the name implies: coffee houses primarily, though a few alcoholic beverages and snacks are sometimes served.

When you enter the café the first thing that usually catches your eye is a large, highly-polished metal machine that looks like nothing so much as a miniature locomotive standing on its end. With about ten yards of piping and anywhere from four to ten spigots and handles, it sits there, steam pours out of it, it makes funny hissing noises, people keep running around and putting things in and taking things out. And to think all it does is just make coffee!

Because it is heavily taxed, coffee in Germany is four times as expensive as in the States. As a result German cafés and housewives have developed dozens of tricks and techniques, notably the paper or cloth filter, to squeeze the utmost aroma and flavor from that little brown bean. Thus, a cup of coffee costs only around twenty cents and the consumption is immense.

The German café is a godsend to the weary pedestrian. Here you can sit for hours on end, read newspapers and magazines—most cafés supply a dozen or more, free, on special racks usually individually clamped into the slots of long sticks for easy handling. You can write letters, read, gossip. No one will dare ask you to leave if you don't order more, even if you sit for half a day. In summer the café usually sprawls over the sidewalk. The tables are shaded by huge colorful umbrellas, and "people watching" is in full swing.

German cafés make up in comfort and *Gemütlichkeit* for what they lack in charm and camaraderie. They are a disappointment to the artistic-minded and bohemian set who prefer the austerity of the French café, or the old (and dying-out) Viennese-style establishments with their plain marble-top tables, straightback chairs, Kaiser Franz Josef clothes racks and prints, wallpaper and wood paneling, and wooden booths. For the young, the Italian "Milch Bar" or "Eis Café" has replaced the more sedate café.

German cafés, like German hit tunes, are schmaltzy. The word for them is "bourgeois." It is unthinkable to enter one in overalls. Frequently they are embellished with upholstered arm chairs, the tables are covered with impeccable white or pink cloths, the sparkling windows are lined with potted plants (daily dusted by the waitresses) and covered with elaborate and frilly lace curtains. The decor is like that of an upper-class living room. Although people of all ages and both sexes frequent them, their main customers are well-groomed women of a certain age hunching over huge cuts of *Kuchen* and *Torten* (layer cakes) topped with generous helpings of *Schlagsahne* (whipped cream).

At the Post Office

West Germany does not have an equivalent of the Greyhound bus lines because the *Bundespost* (Federal Post Office) runs an extensive bus system which distributes the mail to the country post offices and at the same time transports passengers. If you want to make a long distance phone call or send a telegram and do not have a telephone of your own, you go to the post office. In fact, to order a telephone, you also go to the post office. The West German Post Office is the biggest "firm" of the Federal Republic and employs some 465,000 people. And no wonder! What Americans think of as normal postal services are only a fraction of the transactions handled by the West German post offices.

In addition to the business of stamps and mailing, it offers banking services including savings and checking accounts; pays out social security money and certain Federal pensions; handles subscriptions to newspapers and magazines; owns and controls the equipment (but not editorial decisions) of West Germany's radio and television networks; licenses and collects fees for radios and TV sets; provides the country with its telephone and telegraph network.

Among the advanced countries of the world with the highest telephone density, West Germany is seventeenth. However, an estimated twenty-six billion DM's will have been invested by 1975 in research work, rationalization methods, and data processing techniques. By the year 2000 West Germany hopes to be part of the worldwide visual telephone network and STD press-button system, enabling vest pocket connections anywhere in the world, as well as "torpedo" mail delivery.

Meanwhile, the Federal Post Office is hopelessly behind in carrying out its normal services. Its telephones are overloaded. To get a new one installed takes months, sometimes two years or even more.

Paradoxically, West Germany has one of the longest and most comprehensive lists of telephone services in the world. In many cities, for example, there is a "suicide number," advertised in the streetcars and buses. Persons who no longer know where to turn are urged to dial 555536, where an Evangelical or Roman Catholic clergyman or welfare worker will answer and try to arrange institutional or individual help.

Not only do West German telephones provide time signals, wake-up service, and weather reports, but some twenty other services. By dialing 1150 in Frankfurt, you can get a physician, dentist, druggist, or ambulance at any hour of the day or night. By dialing 1168 you can hear a recorded stock-market report. There is a movie-guide service, theater service, menu service, weather-travel service, newscast, sports-news summary, and a *Fussball Toto* service that lists the winning combinations in a soccer lottery. Special temporary services are often installed during big sports events (162,000 calls in Frankfurt alone during the Mexico Olympic games). The recipe and menu service *(Kuchendienst),* 1167, might produce a wild burst of beat music, followed by a recipe *aus Amerika* (from America), which might :urn out to be an appetizer and Boston baked beans.

All over Germany there is a shortage of outdoor phone booths, so that a long wait is common. While waiting, though, you can console yourself with the thought that if you *could* dial 1155, you could get the *Wasserstandsmeldung* and immediately learn the hour of high tide in Bremerhaven.

◄2►

ONE MAN'S FAMILY

IN PREPARING THIS chapter I wrote to the editor of a weekly newspaper in the industrial Ruhr district. I wanted him to help me find a German family in his area willing to talk openly about their problems, hopes, fears, and daily life. Although personally acquainted with dozens of German families, workers and professionals, artists and intellectuals, farmers and engineers, I wanted to find a family to write about with the complete detachment of an outsider. "The story of this family," I wrote to the editor, "should be the keynote chapter for the whole book."

He was furious.

"How can you even suggest such a thing?" he wrote back in a temperamental, closely-typed, three-page letter. "There is no such thing as a typical German family. By focusing on one family you will only help perpetuate the clichés about the Germans."

The editor was right, of course, and he himself proved his own point, for he was not even a "typical" German editor, since he turned out to be Austrian. But in the end I did find a family in the Ruhr to write about, and I found it mainly through the kind, albeit reluctant, help of this editor.

In spite of his warning, or rather because of it, this chapter is the story of one German family and their town. No one German family of course is typical of all or even most German families. At the same time, nothing illustrates the profound changes that have taken place in West Germany since World War II, the trends, spirit, atmosphere, and daily life of today's Germany, as well as the example of a single family in a single place, whose provider works in a specific industry.

Accordingly I had to draw up some norms of my own in selecting the family. Although a "typical" family and its city was neither possible nor desirable for this purpose, the family portrayed, nevertheless, should include certain elements common to the largest possible segment of German families, and the city should have historical roots. The Federal Republic being pre-

20

eminently an industrial nation, I decided to seek a workers' family in the Ruhr industrial district. Narrowing my choice, I sought a family whose breadwinner worked for the controversial Krupp firm in Essen. Krupp, whose origins go all the way back to the Middle Ages, surely comes as close as any German firm can to mirroring the tragedy, the schizophrenia, and the profound upheavals of German history.

Even the name Essen is the German word for smokestacks, though by coincidence. Few persons, even Germans, realize that Essen, whose origins date back to the ninth century, is older than Berlin, Munich, Stuttgart, or Düsseldorf, and that it had an illustrious past long before the name Krupp made it notorious and famous throughout the world. Three of the famous abbesses of the convent that ruled Essen for a thousand years came from imperial families. As a small town of 4,000 inhabitants, it was annexed to Prussia in 1802, and it was not until 1851, more than half a century after the industrial revolution had swept over England, that the world's then largest cast-steel foundries overnight made the name of Krupp and Essen famous. One of its main streets, Hellweg, was laid out by Napoleon.

During World War II, Essen endured 1,162 air raid alarms, 272 bombings, which killed 6,800 persons and destroyed 60 percent of the city, leaving a pile of debris six times the volume of the giant pyramid of Cheops. On March 11, 1945, 1,100 bombers dropped over 8,000 demolition bombs of up to ten-ton caliber.

In spite of two world wars, occupation, bombings, and wholesale dismantlings, Essen, today with over 700,000 people, is the fourth largest city in the Federal Republic, the largest coal mining and electrical center on the continent, and "the desk" (*i.e.*, administration center) of the Ruhr area, the largest industrial concentration on earth next to Manchester. It has 5,000 persons per square mile (compared to 50,000 in Paris and 20,000 in New York).

I arrived in Essen on a crisp but unseasonably sunny afternoon at the end of October. A family had been found for me, and I was to meet them the next afternoon. I checked into my hotel and spent the rest of the day, evening, and following morning getting acquainted with Essen.

At first sight downtown Essen differs little from countless American cities with its traffic jams, imposing department stores, and hordes of pedestrians. However, *Gemütlichkeit* is still abundantly in evidence. It is only recently that downtown shops started remaining open through the lunch hour, and in outlying regions as in much of Germany the long midday break from twelve to two o'clock is still common.

Although it was October, the shops were already decorated for the Christmas rush, the downtown streets were illuminated with the celebrated Essen Christmas outdoor-lighting displays, this time on the theme, "A World Journey in Lights."

Essen is actually the heart of a megalopolis of several dozens of communities concentrated in the Ruhr valley. They are so interrelated that it is possible to travel by streetcar all the way from Düsseldorf, through Duisburg, Mühlheim, Oberhausen, Essen, Gelsenkirchen, Herne, Bochum, to Dortmund—a total distance of some 100 miles.

It did not take me long to rid myself of several extremely false impressions of Essen. As the heart of the Ruhr I had pictured it as an ugly city surrounded by belching smokestacks, shrouded in smog caused by the steel furnaces and coal pits that produced the weapons and materiel for two world wars and the postwar economic miracle of West Germany. The air pollution was so great that Esseners joked that every time you wanted to kiss a girl you had to wipe the soot off her face first.

To my great amazement the air is crisp and pure, and all year round. Although it lacks the romance of Heidelberg or the cosmopolitan aura of Berlin, Essen is a neat, modern city with a smart, tree-studded central plaza, called Kennedyplatz after the late American president, with bubbling fountains and reserved strictly for pedestrians. The city boasts of its own opera house, concert hall, convention and exhibition halls, parks, zoo, numerous forest preserves, the beautiful Baldeney Lake region, an amusement park, and a tiny subway only four blocks long.

Although the area is still the center of the country's industry, there has been a gradual, almost unnoticed shift of industry southward, which is rapidly transforming the former agricultural province of Baden-Württemberg, known for its Black Forest, cuckoo clocks, and medieval villages. Today Baden-Württemberg produces 17 percent of West Germany's total industrial output. Manufacturing already accounts for the 54 percent of the state's $18 million gross product, a higher percentage than in any of the other nine German states. Some 10,600 industrial firms produce more and export more per capita than those in any other area of the country. According to the *deutsches Industrieninstitut*, Stuttgart, the state capital (pop. 614,000) has overtaken the Ruhr's Duisburg as the German city with the highest percentage of industrial workers: 24, compared to Duisburg's 23, out of every 100 employed.

Meanwhile the Ruhr, is slowly dismantling its outmoded coal-and-steel-based industrial pattern, and the coal mines are closing one by one. Thousands of coal miners have been reemployed in other industries. With the use of cheaper oil and natural gas instead of coal, the air has cleared in the Ruhr. (The famous Krupp gardeners even export orchids.)

Thus, precisely by seeking out a family in what I thought was *the* industrial area of Germany I inadvertently rid myself of a stereotype impression. The cliché "industrial Ruhr" doesn't quite fit any more.

Essen is, more than anything else, a family city. It has precious few nightclubs and, except on Saturday nights, the city folds up at around 9:30 P.M. Everything about it is respectable, and the exception that supports this rule is the neat way an entire village of prostitutes is literally tucked away on the wrong side of the railroad tracks on the outskirts of the city.

This village, located in the dimly-lit spooky warehouse district, is hard to find at first, but then around 9:30 P.M. you can see a strange "motorcade" of sorts: the continuous traffic of cars that lasts until 3 or 4 A.M. going to a tiny dead-end street called Nordhoffstrasse. The motorists park their cars in a small parking lot at the end of the block and then disappear behind a high stone wall.

When you walk around the wall you are immediately confronted with an overpowering stench emanating from a pissoir. Once past that, you enter the village of some fifteen attractive, two-story farm houses with potted plants, cozy living rooms with oversized picture windows, flanked by romantic street lamps. About thirty or more women, most of them under thirty-five and attractive, stand in the doorways, or lean out of the windows, some of them provocatively clad in high-laced boots or revealing undies, whispering sweet come-ons to the all-male procession of dozens of leering men meandering from window to window (going rate: five dollars a trick). "Want to come inside, *Schatzie?*" Just outside the village there is a police station, from

23

which the proceedings are supervised and *Ordnung* is preserved. All the girls are registered and are regularly inspected by health authorities. I could not help but smile at the advertising poster at the street's exit, with the legend, *"Strom—Energie Unsere Welt* [Electricity—Energy of Our World]*."*

The next day I waited in a café until appointment time with my selected family and browsed through the newspaper rack. The headlines of the three local dailies were: "Berlin—150 Wounded in Street Battle Between Police and Students"; "Soviet Spaceship Circles Earth 34th Time"; "Hitler's War Minister To Testify Here in Concentration Camp Trial"; "Bonn—After January 1st Traffic Violators Can Be Fined On the Spot"; "Hildegard Knef Wows Them in Essen Stadium."

After lunch I bought a bouquet of flowers and was taken by my editor acquaintance to meet the family selected for me. Since it was Saturday, they were all at home. They lived in a residential district not far from downtown Essen, in a five-story apartment house on the third floor, and shall here be named Reichert. I was warmly received. Coffee and *Kuchen* were served, along with *Schnaps,* and gradually the family unfolded their story.

For all the Americanization of Germany, this business of "just call me Joe" just isn't done, so it was "Herr Reichert" and "Herr Schalk" all the way through. Even the Reichert's immediate neighbors, with whom they have been on friendly terms for many years, are still formally addressed each and every time they meet as "Herr" or "Frau Schmidt."

Before me sat Herr Wolfgang Reichert, forty-eight, Frau Ingrid Reichert, forty-five, and their two sons, Dieter, fourteen, and Kurt, twenty-three. There is also a daughter, Ingrid, twenty-two, who lives in southern Germany, but she is considered the black sheep of the family, and I'll tell more about her later.

Herr Reichert is a stocky man with severe, rugged features, a sonorous voice, and combs his hair, close-cropped at the sides, straight back. Frau Reichert, not at all the buxom blonde one might imagine a German *Hausfrau* to be, turned out to be a frail wisp of a woman, with a birdlike, drawn face, coal-black hair in a toy doll style. Kurt is a handsome, shy youth with Beatle-length hair and a fuzz of a beard, while Dieter, brash, adventurous, and inquisitive, restlessly ran around the house.

Herr Reichert, like his father, was born in Essen, his grandfather having come at the turn of the century from

Halberstadt, which today lies in East Germany, in the Harz mountains.

Reichert says he was neither for nor against Hitler during the Third Reich days, but that he almost joined the Nazi Party, not out of conviction but because "it was the thing to do," and served as an *Oberfeldwebel* (first sergeant) in the *Wehrmacht* on the Russian front.

During his service on the Russian front, Reichert got a taste of the legendary severe Russian winters and suffered frostbite in both legs. Today he is minus both big toes and several small toes, but is able to walk, not run, normally.

"Toward the end of the war we were fighting in the Harz mountains near my grandfather's home. On my birthday, April 10, I was taken prisoner by the Americans. I must say that on the whole they were rather decent. They even gave me a glass of milk, a rare item then, as a birthday present. We were taken to a prison camp near a small town on the Rhine, from which I was released at the end of the war."

A brother, Werner, was taken prisoner by the Russians and was released after ten years of confinement.

Conditions immediately after the war were terrible. There was mass unemployment, hunger, chaos, and much of Germany lay in a sea of rubble. As a young boy, Reichert had begun in 1936 as an apprentice at Krupp, but toward the end of the war, the department he had worked for had been transferred to Elsass, and with the advancement of the Allies, again to Bamberg and Nürnberg.

"I shall never forget," he said, perhaps for my benefit, "how much we appreciated all those American CARE parcels that came at the time."

After tramping the streets looking for work, Reichert finally found employment as a coal miner in Gelsenkirchen in 1948. By 1950 he found work as a streetcar conductor and later as a motorman in Essen. It wasn't until 1951 that the Krupp works were again in full operation in Essen, and he was finally hired by his old firm.

Frau Ingrid Reichert comes from East Prussia, which today is under Polish and Soviet administration. "We had a big farm, which the Soviet soldiers appropriated. Our house, situated on a hill, was a natural target and was ironically destroyed by German artillery in the valley below. Before the Russians came, our family was quickly evacuated. Many women fled to the forests and cemeteries, fearing rape by the soldiers."

The future Frau Reichert lost contact with her parents, found refuge with an old Polish farm couple. The farmer hid her under a wagonload of potatoes, hitched his horse to it, and took her to the Red Cross center in Danzig. When she finally found her mother, her father had died from bronchitis and undernourishment. The two were transported, with several hundreds of other refugees in cattle cars to Braunschweig.

"It was awful. Several old people died en route and their corpses were not removed. We had to relieve ourselves in front of everyone and the stench was overpowering. We received a daily ration of salted herring and water, and our only possessions were small bundles we were able to carry in our hands."

A seamstress by trade, Frau Reichert had been a Red Cross volunteer nurse during the war, and met her husband while he was recovering from frostbite in a field hospital in the Bavarian Alps. When they were finally reunited in Essen in 1945, they married immediately.

Although Frau Reichert has kept a youthful appearance, her husband looks easily ten years older than he is.

Reichert is a foreman in one of Krupp's factories. He started out as a welder. By dint of his seniority and sheer hard work—he was still going to night school at the age of forty—he now earns 1,500 DM's ($415) a month, which is beginning pay for a minor executive. A welder normally earns from 700 to 900 DM's ($185 to $250), slightly less than a policeman (800 to 1,050 DM's). There are sixty employees in his section and he is responsible for fifteen. He receives three weeks paid vacation annually, sick leave, and a Christmas bonus. All told, his fringe benefits amount to about half a month's additional salary. He believes that in the near future most German workers will have a full thirteen-month's pay. Reichert's work week lasts forty hours, with rare overtime and Saturdays free. There is talk of a four-day work week by the year 2000, or even sooner.

Reichert's day begins at 6:15 A.M. At 6:30 his wife has the typical spartan continental breakfast of two hard rolls, coffee, butter, jam or honey on the table, sometimes a soft-boiled egg. He usually buries his face behind the local newspaper. He subscribes to the independent *Westdeutsche Allgemeine Zeitung*, the Ruhr's largest daily, rather than the other two Essen-based dailies, *Neue Ruhr Zeitung,* which he regards as too closely identified with the Christian Democratic Union (CDU), or the *Ruhr Nachrichten,* which favors the Social Democratic Party (SPD), and he regards that as "too socialist."

At 7 A.M. Reichert hops into his five-year-old Volkswagen which is parked on the street, and heads for work. The drive takes him about ten to twenty minutes, depending on the traffic. At 7:30 his working day begins. Like millions of German workers, Reichert carries a battered briefcase with him, which the Germans prefer to a lunch box. With the spread of the company cafeterias, many workers no longer bring their lunch, but still carry a briefcase, which contains their personal effects, sports magazines, newspapers, a pack of cards, soap and towel (for that after-work shower).

The American-style ten-minute coffee break with sweet rolls is rapidly replacing the *Zweites Frühstück* (second breakfast) which formerly consisted of wurst and bread.

The lunch break lasts half an hour, and Herr Reichert gets a warm meal for twenty-five cents at the Krupp cafeteria, which is only half the normal cost. His work day ends at 4:30. Sometimes he stops to relax for an hour or so at his favorite tavern, then drives home for supper, which begins at 7 P.M., although in many German households, 7:30 or even later. Supper is called *Abendbrot* (evening bread) and is hardly more than that. It usually consists of open-faced sandwiches, with cold cuts, a boiled egg, sliced tomatoes, and radishes with tea. But here too the American influence is felt—the customarily long two-hour warm lunch break is being replaced by the warm supper.

The Reicherts eat relatively little meat, partly out of habit acquired during the lean postwar years, but partly because meat is very expensive in Germany, except for chicken which has become increasingly popular and is imported (mostly from the United States) in immense quantities. When I asked her if they ate much sauerkraut, Frau Reichert laughed. "We hardly touch it."

It is significant that throughout all my talks with the Reicherts, both parents kept using one phrase over and over, *"früher . . . und jetzt"* (then . . . and now), and almost as frequently the phrase "the American influence."

"Things have changed radically in Germany," Herr Reichert reminisced, "not only in my short lifetime, but especially in the past five to eight years. Why, I can remember as a child of four hearing my father say 'thou' to his father, using the *'Sie'* form that we reserve for strangers and acquaintances today. This was the custom well into the present century. The old notions of *Untertan* (subject) and *Obrigkeit* (the authorities) are nearly dead. And so is the patriarchal concept of father."

The "then and now" theme is one which runs zigzag throughout the Reicherts' lives, the past and present interchanged and intertwined in much the same way as ancient historical buildings in Essen and all over Germany are sprinkled among modern streamlined ones. His relationship with Krupp is a good example.

The "then and now" theme meandered in and out of our conversation and became evident again in the visible elements of the vast Krupp plant, through a small part of which Reichert escorted me. The same firm which has some of the world's ultramodern equipment has other buildings and equipment that go back more than a century, notably the soot-covered *Turm Haus* (Tower House) administrative complex, with its blunt, cannon-shell-like tower, its uselessly high ceilings, old-fashioned office rooms, cumbersome elevators and paternosters, and endless corridors. "The Kaiser used this elevator," Reichert said proudly.

I took time out from the Reichert interviews to make an "official" visit to the Krupp establishment, of course without their knowledge of my visits with the Reichert family. Here I was met warmly by Count Georg-Volkmar Zedtwitz-Arnim, an official of the information department, who led me into his office, furnished like the plush office of a 1925 mid-western American bank executive. Count Zedtwitz is a boyish-looking, dapper, white-haired man in his early fifties, who took notes on the white margin of a 100-mark note during the telephone conversations, has never been to the United States, but claims to be distantly related to Mark Twain.

Although I came prepared with a whole list of questions about the firm's present and future plans, the count spoke almost without interruption for one and a half hours "justifying" Krupp in the face of voluminous publicity as the notorious family-run German armaments firm. It was obvious that the burden of Germany's past hangs heavily over the house of Krupp, whose firm was founded in 1811, but whose origins go back to the late sixteenth century, when the Krupps were already selling a thousand gun barrels a year to the participants in the Thirty Years' War. The Krupp name (which sounds like nothing so much as the blast of a cannon) became especially notorious in the blood-and-steel relationship to the Kaisers, when Alfred Krupp (1812-1887) became the first *Kanonenkönig* (cannon king), and transformed Essen into the largest and most stable company town in history. Krupp also produced the munitions for the 1870 war with France.

Friedrich "Fritz" Krupp (1854-1902) tripled his personal income in his first seven years at the helm. His engineers perfected time fuses which so enchanted the English that they bought the patent and paid Krupp one shilling three pence for each shell fired. Thus Krupp was able in time to make a profit from the Reich casualty lists. He built the Kaiser's navy and artillery as well. His homosexual activities in that nonpermissive age eventually brought his downfall (he gave his boyfriends in Capri solid-gold pins shaped like artillery shells). When he died a mysterious death shortly after the scandal broke, Kaiser Wilhelm honored him with a state funeral.

It was the Kaiser who then selected a husband for Fritz's daughter Bertha, after whom the famous Krupp World War I cannon was called "Big Bertha." Adopting the Krupp name, Gustav von Bohlen und Halbach soon produced nine million shells annually, using conscripted Belgian slave labor for his factories. Although the French dismantled his factories in the 1920's, in the wake of World War I, Krupp was again in full production by the 1930's, just in time for Hitler, whom Gustav backed wholeheartedly.

Together with his son, Alfried (1907-1967), Krupp prospered with the help of slave laborers supplied by the Nazis. Alfried Krupp von Bohlen was sentenced as a war criminal to ten years by the Nuremberg war trials in 1947, while Gustav, crippled by a stroke in 1945, died a slow death until final release in 1950. With Alfried's death in 1967, the dynasty finally ended, as his playboy son, Arndt, preferred to live on $500,000 a year from the Krupp trust, and has abandoned all interest in the industrial empire, which is now a joint stock company.

As if obsessed with the subject of Krupp's wartime innocence, the count kept insisting, "You can't punish a man for a crime that has not yet been defined. *Nulla crimen sine lege.* No crime

29

without a law. *Nulla poena sine crimen.* No punishment without a crime. That seems to make the war crimes court unfair because it condemned men like Krupp on a *post facto* basis."

The count's attitude is shared by a vast number of Germans who become very emotional in their defense of the Krupps who, they insist, were forced by the Nazis to use slave labor. Gustav, Bertha, and Alfred are deeply loved by many older Germans and especially by the Esseners, and by no one more than Hans Reichert. Proudly he showed me a large, framed photo of the late Alfried Krupp shaking his hand on the occasion of his twenty-fifth anniversary with Krupp—a photo that shares the place of honor on the living room buffet, alongside photos of his family.

With great emotion, Reichert will become eloquent over the Krupps, tears misting in his eyes. On a tour of downtown Essen, he took me to the life-size statue of Alfred Krupp at one end of the long downtown pedestrian plaza, standing in front of the *Markt Kirche* (rebuilt from World War II ruins to half its former size, whose origins date back to 1054 and which figured in the Reformation); the inscription on the statue reads, *"Die Dankbare Stadt* [The Grateful City]*."* That same grateful city has named one of its main boulevards Frau Bertha Krupp Strasse.

But with equal emotion that same Wolfgang Reichert brought me just a few yards farther and showed me the city's main square, Kennedyplatz. In front of several massive department stores, big banners floated with the caption, "Italian Weeks," one of them displaying a genuine Venetian gondola for the occasion. "You see," said Reichert, "we are very international."

Just one block from Kennedyplatz is the Roman Catholic cathedral whose origins date back to the ninth century. On the square in front of it a Salvation Army quartet was praising the Lord and begging for (financial) ammunition. Opposite them two women and a man were selling lottery tickets, one for the Roman Catholic diocese (first prize, a General Motors' Opel), one for the Red Cross, and one for the veterans' association. Shyly crouched in a nearby doorway was a lone female Jehova's Witness selling *Wachtturm* (*Watchtower*), with the headline, "The Truth About the Catholic Church."

With the same pride Reichert drove me to the outskirts of Essen, to the beautiful Baldeney Lake, which is a widening of the Ruhr River, with sailboats and pavilions, parks and gardens, and the villas of the rich. Here on a hill with a view stands Villa Hügel, the three-hundred room "castle" which Alfred Krupp had built with hall-sized rooms, believing that his ailing lungs would benefit from such large doses of "rural" air. From a distance it looks like nothing so much as an oversized turn-of-the-century mausoleum, which in a sense it is. The atmosphere inside is eerie and visitors automatically lower their voices as if they were at a wake. Huge oil paintings of the Krupp dynasty and Kaiser Wilhelm look down with anachronistic disdain on the visitors. An adjoining building where once princes and kings were wined and dined now houses a museum of Kruppiana, while the "castle," now owned by the city of Essen, serves as an occasional art and cultural exhibition hall.

Before heading back to his flat, Reichert drove me around the vast housing areas and hospital and rest homes that the house of Krupp had built over the years for Kruppians. Krupp always combined the latest modern ideas of production with archaic paternalistic policies toward its workers. Long before social legislation became standard, Krupp had introduced a social housing program financed with bank credits. Of course this also proved profitable to Krupp, just counting the increase in property value alone. Moreover, in former times, the tenants of the "workers' villages" or colonies could more easily be controlled. Private police could check on tenants at all times, even inspecting newspapers read by them and printed matter in their wastebaskets. Alfred Krupp was a Big Brother long before George Orwell invented the term. Indeed, he boasted that the housing projects were a great aid in producing a "pure race of Kruppians."

The social program was considerably enlarged in the time of Fritz Krupp, and still further by Bertha Krupp who established a hospital for Krupp workers, a new housing settlement for retired Kruppians, and organized a visiting nurse service, often visiting homes of the old and sick Kruppians herself. Thus she created an "angel of charity" image for the Krupp firm, which is the one that so many Esseners and Germans prefer to remember.

The Reicherts obtained their four-room flat from Krupp for which they pay thirty-five-dollars-a-month rent, about half of the going rate on the open market. With housing very tight in Germany, the Reicherts regard themselves as very lucky to obtain one of the 52,000 flats made available by Krupp for its over 90,000 employees, half of whom live in Essen today, compared to 85 percent before World War I.

Reichert is one of the declining number of Kruppians who are

31

imbued with what is known as the "old Krupp spirit"—deep, almost religious sense of loyalty to the firm. He is currently serving a three-year term as chairman of his factory's *Betriebsrat* (workers' council), and he is a member of one of the leading trade unions, I. G. Metall. Although he represents the workers in the council, Reichert is not above making decisions "against the personnel when the greater good of the firm is concerned."

During my visit in Essen something unheard of was happening at Krupp—10,000 employees went on strike for higher Christmas bonuses. Reichert attributes this to a growing spirit of independence, although he said, "Until now strikes were rare in Germany. There is something in the German mentality that would rather endure a certain amount of hardship than disrupt the perfect functioning of law and order. That is, this *was* the German mentality. In the past few years, I have begun to wonder whether one can be sure of anything today.

"The plain fact is, the social benefits at Krupp don't mean much anymore, because every German worker and his family have government-guaranteed medical care, children's allowances, high old-age pensions. The new breed of workers no longer feel like a proletarian class. With their cars, television, comfortable living, they have become very independent. I had always hoped at least one of my two sons would become Kruppianers. But my oldest was drafted in the *Bundeswehr,* stayed three years instead of the required one and a half, in order to take advantage of the inexpensive training, which would have cost much more in civilian life. He wants nothing to do with Krupp, and is now working as assistant accountant at a publishing house. As for my youngest son, he doesn't have any interest in Krupp at all. Ever since Alfried Krupp died in 1967, an entirely new spirit has swept through the concern. It has become streamlined, Americanized, efficient, smooth."

In spite of his open declaration of the liberalization of German life, Herr Reichert gave the impression that his family life was still strongly influenced by tradition. The house was spic and span, the children obedient and unobtrusive, and Papa made no bones about who was boss. More than once the expression slipped out, "We do such and such this way because that is the way Papa wants it done."

One example of Reichert's strong emotional attachment to the past is his activity in the *Unterharzer Verein* (Lower Harz Association) of which he is chairman. This is a so-called

Landsmannschaft, (literally, an association of fellow country-men), one of the many migrant-refugee organizations throughout West Germany. Ostensibly these associations are social gatherings of persons from former East German or Oder-Neisse regions, and their offspring, who try to keep alive the cultural and social traditions of their former homeland. A great many of these associations have become controversial because of their nation-alistic coloring and aggressive political leanings. At some of the huge outdoor rallies of these organizations, speakers have been known to become quite emotional about what they regard as unjust usurpation of their former property, and their *Heimat* in the eastern regions.

It is interesting that although Reichert himself and his father were born in Essen, he should have such strong ties to the land of his grandfather. But he insists that his particular *Lands-mannschaft* differs from many others formed by recent migrants, since his was established more than seventy-five years ago, long before Hitler was even dreamed of. His children, by contrast, are just plain bored by all that *Landsmannschaft* business and Reichert is resigned to the inevitable destiny of the *Unterharz Verein*—its slow fading away. In this *Landsmannschaft* the activities are purely social, no more harmful than playing the German card game of Skat with fellow members and singing old Harz hymns.

Nor do the Reicherts belong to the popular *Schützen* (riflemen's) organizations, many of them with a rightist color-ation, which hold numerous target shooting contests, street parades with riflemen in green hunters' uniforms, accompanied by their wives in dirndl dresses, marching in step to oompah-pah brass bands, culminating in a *Schützenfest* (riflemen's fair), which is nothing more than a glorified kermis with shooting booths, sausage stands, and beer halls.

If the Reicherts' membership in the *Landsmannschaft* suggests a touch of nationalism and strong adherence to the past, nothing would be further from the truth than to conclude from this that they—and their fellow Germans—have not changed. Today's Germany is full of anomalies. And even the Reicherts, with the sentimental attachment to old times and ingrained habits and thought-patterns showing traces of the Kaiser era, have been carried along in the growing international fervor that is sweeping West Germany.

Although they are not an especially out-going type of family, they include among their closest friends a Dutch couple they met while on vacation several years ago in Bavaria. Since then they suddenly discovered to their own amazement "how close Holland is" to Essen and that Arnhem, their friends' home town, is "only sixty miles away," with the result that mutual visits have increased in frequency.

The Dutch husband is a NATO pilot, slightly younger than Reichert, recently grounded on account of health. "There is no resentment whatever," Herr Reichert said, anticipating my next question. "They accept us for ourselves and we accept them. They do not blame us personally for the brutal treatment of the Dutch during the Nazi occupation. However, some of their older relatives—understandably—will have nothing to do with us."

Although the Reicherts have learned a few Dutch words, they converse with their Dutch friends in German. "Why learn Dutch" the couple asked the Reicherts, "when German is so much more international?"

"You know," Reichert told me, "there is so much talk about the Common Market and the barriers to European integration. But if it were up to us, we would have already solved the European question, with our friends in Holland, Austria, and Switzerland."

Another anomaly is the tenacity with which many ancient customs, especially in southern Germany, are kept alive (not necessarily for the sake of tourism) in spite of the demands of modern life, while elsewhere, especially in the cities, the customs are dying. Relatively few customs are still observed in Essen. Next to Christmas and Easter—which become more commercial every year—the Reicherts observe Whitsunday, which has the rank of Easter in Germany. However, even this feast has lost its religious character completely and is hardly more than the first traditional outing of the year. For some reason, most Germans feel it a duty to go out into the country on Whitsunday, weather permitting.

When he was younger, Herr Reichert used to observe Father's Day, which takes place on the Roman Catholic feast of Ascension Thursday, and is a legal holiday in some regions. The German version of Father's Day is nothing more than a noisy stag party, all the men wearing straw sailor hats adorned with toilet paper, their car or preferably a run-down truck decorated with bawdy posters and bunting, ending up at a tavern in the woods where they sing and drink until dawn.

The famous Rhineland Carnival season is also observed in Essen, but in contrast to the public festival and outdoor parade in Cologne, Düsseldorf, and Mainz, and Munich's Fasching, it is more of a family affair.

When their children were small, the Reicherts helped them make paper lanterns and costumes for the still popular after-dark *Martin'stag* parade on November 11, commemorating St. Martin's famous deed of slicing his cloak in two in order to clothe a freezing beggar. The children go from door to door reciting verses and collecting candy and fruits in exchange, à la American "Trick or Treat." On December 6, St. Nicholas day is commemorated when a man, usually a student, dressed in a bishop's robes, with miter and staff distributes bags of candy, nuts, and fruits to children, usually while they are in school. The *Weihnachtsmann* (Santa Claus) also distributes goodies on Christmas Eve.

The reading of the Reicherts is confined to newspapers, magazines, and about a dozen, mostly American novels lining their single book shelf. But Herr Reichert is an avid soccer fan, spending many hours watching sports events on their television set. He often likes to kick a soccer ball around with his sons and on Sundays likes to go on long walks in the numerous wooded areas near Essen.

Herr Reichert belongs to no political party. In his words, "the ideal party doesn't exist." He is suspicious of the SPD's socialist origins and tendencies, but is also unhappy with the CDU because in his view it is too fragmentary, too much of a patchwork party. In spite of the fact that he is a practicing Roman Catholic, Reichert is uneasy about the Christian label of the CDU.

"The trouble with West German politics," he says, "is that there is no respectable folk party, a party truly representing the conservative middle. That is why the extremist NPD enjoyed some success, it gave an outlet to these people. That is the reason too why the so-called extra-parliamentary opposition, which is the term used to describe extremists of right and left, but largely the leftist student organizations, has grown to such sizable proportions.

The Reicherts vote for the CDU party at elections. They read avidly about political events, feel compelled to be informed and to vote. They have noticed a decided increase in political awareness and concern among Reichert's fellow workers in recent years. "The impact of world events mainly through the mass media has not been without results."

The Reicherts have mixed feelings about the growing unrest in Germany, the wave upon wave of student rebellion, the glut of sex information, and the worldwide crisis of authority that has left its impact on Germany too. As believing Roman Catholics they are uneasy about the birth control controversy that began in 1968 with Pope Paul VI's encyclical, *Humanae Vitae.* "It is getting so," says Frau Reichert, "one doesn't know what to believe anymore." Like most Roman Catholics in Germany they do not accept the birth control encyclical, "though we are past the age where it would make a difference in our lives."

But the Reicherts see positive seeds in all the unrest, both within society and within their church. "Before, we had the feeling that everything was too pat, and if I may say so, that the Church was asleep. Now everything is coming alive. We learned a lot from our Dutch friends. You know, in Holland the Catholic Church is far more progressive than in most other countries, and we witnessed people making a general confession together in Church instead of private confession, and receiving communion in their hands."

Herr Reichert is pessimistic about reunification. "This can only be settled within the framework of a greater Europe. Let us not be fooled. None of the great powers, or even more so the small European powers, really want to see Germany reunited and thus assume dominance in Europe, and the average German is more concerned about his job, his future, and his health than such far-off concepts as reunification."

They feel more strongly about the Oder-Neisse territories, understandably so, considering the loss that his wife's family endured there. "But it is unrealistic ever to hope for the recovery of these lands." In his view there is no other choice but to relinquish them to Poland, "where since the war a whole generation of Poles have grown up and have just as valid a claim to it as their *Heimat* as we did formerly."

The Reicherts have not associated with a single Jew in all their lives. Herr Reichert recalls that "as a boy I remember a Jewish tailor down the street, but we had no contact with him." Nor do they have any connections with the tiny Jewish community in Essen today. Neither do their children. Herr Reichert openly admitted to me that his children received only skimpy treatment of the Third Reich in their history classes. "It is hard," he said, "for any teacher of forty or older to willingly expose himself to inevitable humiliation by admitting the crimes of the Third Reich. And most of the men who determine the curricula and textbooks are over forty. Perhaps there will be a change when the younger generation advances. However, other regions are more advanced and treat the subject more forthrightly. Also, we Germans are continually reminded of our past by our press, radio, and television which sometimes gets on my nerves. Sometimes, you must understand how I mean this, sometimes I wonder if the world will ever stop handling us like ex-convicts."

I had to seek contact with the Jewish community on my own. I toyed with the idea of inviting the Reicherts along, but I didn't pursue the matter.

While first becoming acquainted with downtown Essen I had noticed an impressive large churchlike building standing conspicuously on a main thoroughfare. It looked like a synagogue. But I had noticed a sign over the entrance with the words *Gute Form* (good design) and I dismissed the idea. Present-day Germans, I told myself, wouldn't dare abuse a synagogue by turning it into a museum.

But now I took the trouble of going up to the building which did indeed turn out to be a former synagogue. A large stone sculpture of a sarcophagus with the Star of David contained the inscription, "More than 2,500 Jews of the city of Essen had to give up their lives in the years 1933-1945." Elsewhere on the facade an engraving of the tablets of the Ten Commandments could be seen along with an inscription in Hebrew and German, "Truly my house shall be called a house of prayer for all the people" and "Thou shalt love thy neighbor as thyself. I am the Lord," from the book of Moses.

But the "house of prayer" was now a house of good design, a museum. And just across the street from it stands the *Friedens-kirche* (Peace Church) of the Old Catholic confession with the incongruous inscription: "1914-1918. They died a hero's death for the Fatherland and Volk, faithful unto death," followed by a list of soldiers who had fallen in World War I. Even more incongruous was the shrill laughter and shrieks of delight pouring from the kermis immediately next to the synagogue, where hundreds of shouting, laughing Germans were enjoying the roller coaster, merry-go-round, and spook house.

I admit that I was shocked to see the Jewish synagogue turned into a museum of industrial design. Before jumping to any conclusions, however, I decided to ask the leaders of the Jewish community about the matter.

I soon learned that the Jews of Essen now have a beautiful, if small, synagogue of striking contemporary design just a few blocks away, also located on the main boulevard, and just behind it, an attractive, modern Jewish community center. Here I spoke with Herr Georg Jolles, a member of the community's board of directors, who explained to me that the original synagogue's interior was burned out during the infamous Crystal Night, the wave of terror all over Germany during the Nazi regime. However, it was not the Germans but rather the Jewish community which decided to turn the old synagogue into a museum.

"Look at it this way," Herr Jolles explained. "The city of Essen offered to restore the old synagogue and return it to us. But it is a huge building. With only 200 Jews left in Essen, out of more than 5,300 before 1933, and most of them elderly, it would be impossible for us to maintain it. We received many offers for the building, including from the Salvation Army. But the thought of turning it into a Christian Church, after all that happened, was abhorrent to us. Better it should be a museum."

The Essen Jewish community has no full-time rabbi, but it does employ a cantor, Herr Chaim Lipschitz. Its president has the very Teutonic name of Siegfried Neugarten, and told me that relations with the Germans are on the whole good. However, the future of the Jewish community in Essen looks bleak. "We have twenty-five youth under twenty and many of them want to go to Israel. They see no future here." I asked what the average age of Jews in Essen is, and he replied, "I hesitate to say. It must be close to sixty." Himself a born Essener, Herr Neugarten said that most of the Jews are from elsewhere. "It is a dying, not a living, community."

There is a small but active chapter of the national Society for Jewish-Christian Cooperation in Essen. During my stay, the Roman Catholic Bishop Franz Hengsbach sponsored a Chagall exhibit and "get acquainted" afternoon in one of the diocesan halls. Several hundred persons filled it to capacity, listened to a piano recital, a speech on Chagall, and a description of Jewish rites by Herr Lipschitz who also set up a display of Jewish scrolls, candlesticks, the Torah, and other religious objects.

Thus, while the average German, like the Reicherts, is untouched by Jewish events in Germany, the interest of a small elite is intense, genuine, and fruitful. There are frequent meetings with Protestant and Roman Catholic clergy, laity, and theologians, and tours of the local synagogue.

After leaving Essen I did not go straight home, but made a short stopover in southern Germany, in the university town of Freiburg-im-Breisgau. During my conversations with the Reicherts I had noticed that they were reluctant to speak much about their daughter. They seemed to be unhappy about her. I did learn that she was living in Freiburg, and it was easy to locate her address at the university. Ingrid Reichert did not seem to mind my unannounced appearance—she was in fact rather amused, and quite open. We went to a café where she told me her side of the Reichert story for over two hours.

Slight-framed like her mother, with a small boyish face and page-boy haircut, she wore chest-high bell-bottom pants, held up by oversized psychedelic suspenders, a striped men's shirt adorned by a daisy in her buttonhole.

Ingrid has ambitious plans. She is studying international law, plans to continue her education in London soon. Her studies will take about seven years. Meanwhile she has absolutely no intention of depriving herself of male companionship. "I don't want to buy a pig in a poke," she said, "and I'll be damned if I'll study seven years only to get married and not be able to use my knowledge."

She has a French boyfriend who visits her from nearby Strasbourg on weekends, and a tolerant *Hausmeister* (janitor-concierge) in the sky-rise student apartment house where she lives and enjoys a comfortable if frugal scholarship. "Neither he nor I wish any complications," she says. "He has his studies and I have mine. Thanks to the pill we don't have to worry. Is this immoral? I am honest. I have no illusions and as far as possible try to avoid destroying other people's, which is what I regard as immoral."

Ingrid frequently sprinkles her conversation with the word

Scheiss! (shit).[1] She sympathizes with leftist students but is too busy thinking of her career to "waste time jumping on the barricades."

Occasionally she drops a line to her mother and sends her a present, but finds it hard to accept the long preachy letters and tear-jerking scenes on the telephone. She has not been home for over a year, not even for Christmas. "I couldn't take the autocratic life with Papa any more. I am afraid I haven't lived up to their expectations of becoming a respectable girl, settling down, and raising a family.

"As for Papa, I am afraid he is old stuff. There is a new generation of Germans now. We are tired of the Nazis, the war, the self-pity of the older generation, the nostalgia, Hitler, and all that bosh. We want independence, opportunity, personal happiness, and reform.

"*Papa's Kino ist tot* [papa's cinema is dead], Papa's government is dead, Papa's way of life is dead, and for all practical purposes, Papa is dead. He means nothing to me. Nothing."

◄3►

WHAT IS A GERMAN?

WHO–OR WHAT —are "The Germans"?[1]

We can hardly apply this term solely to citizens of West and East Germany, for, as a single glance at history (Appendix A) will show, political affiliation of this people has been haphazard and continually changing. No one knows whether German reunification will ever take place, and if so, what the boundaries of "Germany" would then be.

The descendants of the colonists who were settled along the Volga by Empress Catherine II between 1763 and 1770 have long been recognized as "German" by the Soviet government. At the end of World War II millions of *Volksdeutsche* (ethnic Germans), in the biggest migration in history, were driven from Czechoslovakia, Poland, and other eastern territories. For more than seven centuries these large groups of peoples of German origin, sought after because of their skills, had settled in eastern and southern Europe at the invitation of rulers. Although they became citizens of their adopted countries, they retained their previous national characteristics and inherited speech. In Transylvania, for example, the Saxons are conspicuously different from their neighbors whether they are living in that region's Hungarian or Rumanian part.

In the Alsace-Lorraine area of contemporary France there are still many thousands of persons of the older generation whose preferred political allegiance is France, but whose language, culture, traditional dress, and cuisine remain predominantly and unmistakably German. "I have changed my national anthem four times in my life," one ninety-year-oldster put it. In a recent man-on-the-street television interview in Strasbourg, citizens of all ages unhesitatingly and unanimously mentioned as their most famous citizen, Dr. Albert Schweitzer, the great French humanitarian whose name and cultural formation were clearly German.

The enthusiasm with which the majority of Austrians welcomed the *Anschluss* (annexation) to the Third Reich reveals the

41

extent to which they felt themselves to be German, and this identity is not quite dead today. And there are many Swiss who regard themselves as linguistically and culturally German.

The national poet of Austria, Franz Grillparzer, for example, was devoted to the House of Hapsburg and despised the jingoism that developed in the north after the Napoleonic wars. He castigated the Germans, "a formerly quiet and modest folk," for turning into "fire-eating world-devourers [*Feuerfresser und Weltverschlinger*]." Yet, compared with the Czechs and Hungarians of the Austro-Hungarian empire, he preferred his German heritage, speaking of the former deprecatingly as mere "tribes." In his eloquent eulogy of Beethoven in 1827, he expresses the grief of "an entire nation, the whole German people."

Similarly the preeminent nineteenth century Swiss novelist, Gottfried Keller, cherished Germany as his spiritual home, and expressed his loyalty in favor of Germany during the Franco-Prussian War.

Literary experts classify the writings of the Austrians Grillparzer, Hugo von Hoffmansthal, the Swiss playwrights Friedrich Dürrenmatt and Max Frisch, and those of the Czech Jew, Franz Kafka, under German literature. Musicians tend to regard Austrian-born Mozart, Haydn, and Schubert as German composers. Scientists think of the great embryologist Karl Ernst von Baer as a German, even though he was born in Estonia when it was part of Czarist Russia.

The ebullient and chauvinistic publicist Ernst Moritz Arndt asked in his poem, *"Was ist das deutsche Vaterland?* [What Is the German Fatherland?]," which became the battle hymn of the new nationalism of the 1880's. Can it be Prussia, or Swabia, or any one of a dozen others? No, he replies, his Fatherland must be greater: *"So weit die deutsche Zunge klingt und Gott im Himmel Lieder singt* [The German Fatherland shall range as far as the German tongue is heard, singing in praise of God]."

But a closer examination precludes the German language as the decisive bond that identifies "The Germans." The prevalence of dialects—local languages with their own syntax and pronunciation—is still strongly characteristic of many German regions, notably in Swabia, Bavaria, and the Rhineland. *Schwytzerdeutsch,* the mother tongue of "German" Switzerland, is still the everyday language there and is unintelligible to most Germans, while most Swiss will tell you that high German, though used in pulpits, on solemn official occasions, newscasts, and in schools, is a foreign language to them.

And, in spite of cultural affinity with Germany, the national loyalty of the German-speaking citizens of Switzerland, Alsace-Lorraine, and Austria overshadows cultural and linguistic similarities.

Nor can there be, of course, any question of a German "race." No one demonstrated the ludicrousness of the Nazi "pure race" theory of dominant Nordic characteristics more than Hitler himself. Numerous jokes about Hitler and Goebbels, originating during the Third Reich, highlight the fact that the man championing the "pure race" idea, Hitler himself, was the least Nordic of them all, and if anything, more closely resembled the stereotyped version of certain alleged Jewish types, as so eloquently shown in Charlie Chaplin's poignant movie, *The Great Dictator.*

The general Germanic pattern reveals ethnographic and linguistic characteristics of great variety, with many differences of head shape, stature, customs, traditions, mentality, hair and eye colors, and bone structure. Some North German groups may well be as blond as some Scandinavians and markedly fairer than average continental Europeans, but the Fehmarners, whose stature is supposedly "Nordic" have a conspicuous number of brunettes. Taller stature is generally more common in the North, but Bavarian mountaineers are as often as not just as tall as Schleswigers.

The myth of a German race is further illustrated by famous German personalities. Immanuel Kant is probably the most illustrious of German philosophers. But he was partly of Scottish ancestry. Hermann Helmholtz was one of the glories of German science, but his mother was a lineal descendant of William Penn, the English Quaker. Ludwig van (not von!) Beethoven's grandfather, as his name implies, came from Flanders. And Hitler had to renounce his Austrian citizenship, remain *Staatenlos* (without a country) for years, and resort to an obscure German legal loophole in order to qualify for German citizenship and eligibility in his crucial race against Hindenburg for the German presidency.

Ethnically the Germans can be traced all the way back to the centuries before Christ. To Julius Caesar, they were known as

Germani and lived along the Rhine and, in the south, along the source of the Danube. The Romans referred to the vast area of moors and forests, swamps and sandy plains as *Germania Magna* (Great Germany), using the word Germany to refer to a region rather than a particular tribe. Thus one of the oldest geographical terms of European history is the word Germany.

It is the Roman historian Tacitus who attempts to trace the origin of the word *deutsch* in his monumental work *Germania* or *De Situ, Moribus et Populis Germanide* (Concerning the Location, Manners and Peoples of Germany) which appeared in A.D. 98. He states that the word *Deutsch* originates from the ancient high German word *diot* or *diet* meaning "people" or "popular." The adjective became *diotisc* and this became Latinized into *theodiscus* then to become *Teutonic*. But, unlike the Gauls and other European groups, the Germani for the most part resisted the Latinization of their language.

The people that the Romans found were warlike, evasive, primitive. The Germani were of Indo-Germanic stock, spoke an Aryan language, and were composed of aborigines and a mixture of outsiders, some of them coming perhaps from Sweden or southern Baltic regions. They lived in primitive huts made of reeds, mud on poles, usually on marshy ground or shallow lakes, easy to build and easier to abandon.[2] They were seminomads, settling in makeshift villages rather than stone houses or caves, and were hunters, fishers, and keepers of small herds of cattle. They cultivated small fields that could be left behind under sudden enemy attack. They had no written language.

According to available evidence the Germani were by no means literally blond, even in A.D. 50. They were as a group fairer than the Romans, which may account for the first distinctive trait of a Nordic people.

During the barbarian invasion—or *Völkerwanderung* (migration of people), depending on who is telling it—between the first and the fifth centuries, the Germanic peoples moved in tribal units from the Nordic concentration around the western Baltic (Denmark, Sweden) and the mainland between the Lower Elbe and Oder rivers. In the process of settling central Europe, they intermarried with the previous inhabitants, both Latin and Slav.

Throughout the Middle Ages a slow population expansion toward the east led to the assimilation of a large Slavic element. In the eastern part of Germany, the proper names, styles of villages, and physical types reveal the mixture of Slavic and Germanic elements.

"The Germans" underwent profound changes over the centuries, the differences over the different epochs being in fact more striking than the regional differences at any given period. To the refined and cultured Romans, the Germans were barbarians. It was only through contact with the high civilizations of their neighbors that they adopted urban settlements, learned to cast bronze and enamel, began to cultivate the grape vine, and learned to exploit the mines of the Eifel and Taunus.

The spread of Christianity and the formative influence of the Reformation were major civilizing factors. The industrial revolution and the lasting influence of two world wars have further conditioned the German people. Today the encroachments of technology, collectivization, economic and political interdependence, socialization, and infrastructure all take their toll and no one can predict the outcome.

But the roots go deep. No one knows to what extent the subconscious influence of the past still lurks in the German soul. Recently an aged Bavarian woman mentioned a house struck by lightning, using the expression, "Thor struck it." Although she lived in a district noted as the site of a famous monastery for a thousand years, the name and attributes of an old Norse god were still imbedded in her manner of speech. The neo-paganism of the Nazis and the glorification of ancient Teutonic legends and values in Wagnerian operas, and the lingering existence of a number of eccentric neo-pagan sects even today reveal how deep the ancient thought-patterns are rooted in the German mind.

At the same time, such current manifestations are so few and so sporadic that they must be dismissed as a reliable barometer of the general German character.

For one thing, the existence of an extraordinary degree of local and regional differentiation shows how precarious it is to make broad generalizations. Until 1945, when the moral as well as the physical order collapsed and new values descended upon a stunned Germany arising from the ashes, the Bavarian mountaineer had a very different set of values from those of a Mecklenburger or a Hamburger. In the north, an East Prussian and a Westphalian could not be put into one category except by contrast with foreign nationalities. High Germans despised the

Plattdeutsch as stupid and filthy, while the latter in turn denounced the former as charlatans. Westphalians look down upon Hessians. Saxons formerly regarded Prussians as slow-witted. The Swabians are even today repelled by the Bavarians' coarseness, and in Bavaria one still hears the expression *Saupreuss* (Prussian swine).

Especially in rural areas and within relatively restricted districts the variety is considerable. Villages separated by less than fifty miles may be decades apart in agricultural advancement, and even more so sociologically. In Paderborn, for example, matrimony has traditionally been a happy-go-lucky affair without thought for the morrow, while in Münster, less than sixty miles away, the emphasis on security dominates.

The difficulty of arriving at a common denominator of just what constitutes a "German" is aggravated if we limit the term to mean "a common German culture."

It may come as a surprise to be told that German culture is the product of a highly variegated, individualistic rather than nationalistic development. Berlin has never dominated the cultural life of Germany in the same way as cities like London, Paris, or New York have in their respective countries. Even today no country in the world boasts of so many towns as small as Springfield, Illinois, with their own opera houses, art galleries, theaters, concert halls, and museums, as does Germany.

Germany has never suffered the unhealthy concentration of culture in one center that is the bane of most other countries. The reasons are historical: Until 1871, Germany was split up into hundreds of duchies. It was the eighteenth century dukes, in competition with each other and highly jealous of one another, who founded theaters and opera houses and established universities, each trying to outdo the other in splendor and excellence, drawing to themselves the best poets, artists, musicians, and scholars that money could buy.

Nevertheless, in spite of linguistic, physical, cultural, historical, and geographical diversity, there *is* such a thing as a German nationality, a German ethnic group, German culture, and German traits and characteristics. Partly through natural diffusion, partly through the deliberate efforts of various prophets and dominating political leaders, partly through governmental action, certain similarities of attitude and social behavior have developed.

But it is only by being aware in the first place of the great variety and importance of the many differences within the German people that we can presume to discuss the similarities.

◄4►

"YOU GERMANS ARE TOO STIFF!"

ONE EVENING IN a Cologne bar, abetted by a couple of rounds of beer, I became involved in a conversation about the German character.

"You Germans," I told my friend, "are too stiff, too formal. You should be more casual. Like Americans."

My companion smiled tolerantly. "Yes," he admitted, "perhaps we should. In fact, I think we are learning from you. For example, there is *Bürgermeister* [mayor] Schmidt [whose real name we won't mention] of Oberunterdorf. He's a good deal less formal since his trip to the United States."

I requested, and got, a fuller explanation.

It seems that *Bürgermeister* Schmidt was asked to dedicate a new diving tower at a local swimming pool. He made a pleasant, if standard speech extolling the virtues of physical exercise in general, swimming and diving in particular. The crowd applauded politely.

Then the applause ceased abruptly. The *Bürgermeister,* clad in his dignified blue serge suit, was climbing up the ladder to the diving tower. "Now," he said, "I shall really dedicate the diving tower." And he jumped off.

"An admirable example of official informality," I admitted to my German friend.

"Yes," he said. "Before his trip to America, the *Bürgermeister* would have dived off the tower with top hat and tails."

There is of course no such thing as "the" German character. The coarse, fun-loving Bavarians are much more like the Austrians than their staid fellow Germans in the north (but there are thousands of staid Bavarians and fun-loving northern Germans). The German East Frisians, with their countless windmills, are ethnically related to the Dutch West Frisians, while the shrewd Swabians are strikingly similar in dialect, custom, and mentality to the German-speaking Swiss. And the Rhinelanders can't be compared with anybody.[1]

But everywhere one goes, one hears that the Germans are chauvinistic, arrogant, sentimental, stiff, humorless, extremist, methodical, blindly obedient, regimented, and at once overbearing and submissive. German men are said to be authoritarian, patriarchal, given to self-pity and martyr-complexes; while the women are accused of being excessively domestic, fanatical housecleaners, rug-beaters, and mattress-airers, inextricably bound to the three K's: *Kinder, Kirche, Küche* (children, church, kitchen).

The Germans are said to love to serve under a strong leader, to march in unison, and to eat more sauerkraut than anything else. Visitors to the Cologne Karneval or Munich Oktoberfest of Sylt's nudist colony will accuse them of being oversexed, flip, reckless, and boorish.

Others find the Germans warm, hospitable, generous, dependable, conscientious, honest, clean, orderly, practical, imaginative, romantic, cultured, refined, industrious, disciplined, and thorough.

At best one can speak of behavior patterns. The standard rebuke, "one should not generalize when speaking about any people," however, is in itself a generalization. Just as it is unobjective to dismiss the Germans with stereotype observations, it is equally unobjective to suppress mention of mental and social behavior patterns that have become ingrained in German life.

While there is no such thing as a reliable measuring stick for evaluating the German character, it is possible to illustrate some of the elements of the German mentality and social behavior, even while they defy definition and classification. But even here careful distinctions are called for.

On the whole, the new modes of life are sweeping away the old. Nevertheless, many traditions and customs have such deep roots that their complete disappearance is not at all a foregone conclusion. About the best one can do at this point is call attention to both the changes and the lingering patterns in a state of suspenseful coexistence.

The formal way of doing things, however, is definitely one German characteristic that is on the way out. Take the "stiff Germans" remark at the beginning of this chapter, for instance. Until fairly recently there was a decided difference between the posture and walking habits of large numbers of Germans and that of Americans. One constantly heard unflattering remarks about

49

the widespread American slouch. Germans were horrified by other "American" mannerisms such as chewing gum.

A standard joke tells of a deaf old lady in a train sitting across from a gum-chewing GI. After some time the lady leans over and says, "It is very kind of you, young man, to hold a conversation with me, but I am hard of hearing and I must ask you, please, to speak louder."

But the slouch and gum-chewing are only two of many "American" habits that Germans by the thousands have made their own.

Another German (and to a large extent, European) custom is the perennial handshake. It still happens that if you enter a room full of forty people you are expected to shake each and every person's hand and once again upon leaving. In many firms employees shake hands with each other in the morning, before meals, and again in the evening. In one large firm a survey revealed that employees spend twenty minutes daily shaking hands. But many Germans no longer take this so seriously.

Although many still cherish the hand kiss, 60 percent of women respondents in a survey and 80 percent of the men did not. The custom has assumed the character of an affectation.

Germans seem still to have a penchant for wearing especially nice clothes on Sunday. The respected Demoscopic Institute in Allensbach disclosed the results of a recent opinion poll: 93 percent of all rural respondents, 74 percent of urban interviewees, and over 90 percent of workers and craftsmen prefer to look their "Sunday best" by wearing clothes especially reserved for that day. An amazing number of German families, especially in rural areas, reserve their living rooms for use solely on special occasions, such as weddings, anniversaries, birthdays or to honor special guests, and spend most of their leisure hours in the kitchen.

Most German women take great pride in the appearance of their windows, which are usually covered with elaborate curtains and a profusion of potted plants. A recent survey showed that German families have an average of twelve potted plants in their houses, second in the world only to Denmark (fifteen plants).

Casual visits are the exception and not the rule. "Dropping by" just isn't done. It goes against the German *Hausfrau's* sense of order not to prepare meticulously for visitors. The house has to be spic and span, *Kuchen* has to be baked or bought, and the family has to be dressed up for the occasion. This is still fairly common practice, but here too American informality has made great inroads on German living habits.

The long cocktail hour before dinner is still rare, and if you are invited to dinner or coffee, Germans expect you to be on time. *"Pünktlichkeit ist die Tugend der Götter* [Punctuality is the virtue of the gods]!" The custom of bringing along flowers upon being invited to a German home remains. Only it is extremely important to remember that red roses can be poison ivy, as these are presented only by a lover to his sweetheart.

Shocking to many Americans is the Germans' earthiness about natural processes. Instead of the discreet "lavatory" or "powder room" the Germans use the straightforward *Toilette* or *W.C.* (literally, *Wasser Closet* and irreverently used in reference to Winston Churchill during World War II). Instead of showing pictures of their nude babies lying prostrate as Americans are wont to do, beaming German parents think it is hilariously funny to display snapshots of their toddlers sitting on the pot. One American writer has observed, "The Germans seem to have quite a preoccupation with the human behind."

On the beach the Germans quite often do without cabins, gingerly maneuvering in and out of their swimsuits under a bathrobe, while their neighbors presumably look at imaginary sailboats in the distance. Small children run around nude. (The joke is told about the three-year-old daughter of a refugee family from East Germany playing in the nude one day with the three-year-old West German boy next door. Taking a sharp look at her anatomy, he said, "How come you don't have one of these things like I do?" "Well," she said with a sigh, "you know we are refugees and have lost nearly everything.")

Fresh Air

The Germans have a thing about fresh air. In fact, one of the all-time popular German songs is *"Berliner Luft,"* which praises the qualities of Berlin's crisp, pure air. In many cities, if you walk down any residential street on a weekday morning, you will see bulging featherbeds, pillow cases, and blankets draped over countless window sills for their daily airing. Suits and dresses are often hung up for hours on balconies, and the daily resounding thumps of carpet beating sound like Verdi's "Anvil Chorus."

Germans who have been to the States consider American homes overheated and regard the sealed windows of air-conditioned buildings as a health hazard. Many Germans sleep with the windows wide open all night even in the coldest winter, in fact many persons keep their bedrooms unheated. Incredible as it may sound, Germans frequently have outdoor kermis in *winter,* and bundled up in overcoats swarm into them by the thousands, and take to the ferris wheel, shooting galleries, and roller coaster in the middle of January. On the other hand, landlords inevitably insist on heating flats according to the calendar not the actual weather conditions. Once the spring season (April 1) starts, no matter how cold your flat, there is no heat, whereas a sudden warm spell in March will not induce them to turn down the heat.

Above all, Germans prize their famous spas and health resorts noted not only for their mineral water springs but also pure air. In fact, some of them are called *Luftkurort* (air health spa). Which brings me to that unique German institution: *Die Kur* (the cure). A middle-aged German who wants to rejuvenate the juices of life will take off for one of the many *Kurorte, i.e.,* health resorts in cities and hamlets from the Baltic to the Black Forest. *Die Kur* is a Germanic way of life, the German search for the *Jungbrunnen* (fountain of youth). Most of these resorts have the word *Bad* (bath) as a proud prefix to their name. This means that the town, region, or village contains waters officially designated as having health-giving properties (and that prices are higher than elsewhere). Many *Kurorte* specialize. Bad Kohlgrub's mud is good for rheumatism, Bad Dürkheim's brine heals skin disease, Bad Münster is noted for the inhalation of vapors, Bad Ems' thermal springs assist heart and circulatory ailments. And the mecca of the *haut monde,* Baden-Baden at the fringe of the Black Forest, has a cure for everybody, especially for the affluent. Its waters are claimed to be beneficial for the sufferers of "rheumatism, neurotic ailments, gynocologic diseases, catarrhs of the respiratory tract."

The discovery of a new mineral spring or the unearthing of a particularly fine mud variety is the German equivalent to striking oil in Texas. If the water or the mud can be medically proved as having healing qualities, the prefix "Bad" is triumphantly adopted and the community is in business.

When the *Kurgäste* (cure guests) arrive they are warmly welcomed by the *Herr Kurdirektor* and his coterie of white-smocked attendants. The guests will be placed under the care of the *Kurarzt* (cure physician), who prescribes the *Kurdiät* (cure diet) and the special treatments with water, mud, or mineral water.

During the day the cure guests (they are never called patients) take their prescribed mineral water drinks, mud baths, submit to massages or therapeutic exercises, or take walks around the usually beautiful landscaped *Kurpark,* where every afternoon they can listen to an outdoor *Kurkonzert* performed by a *Kurorchester* in the *Kurpavillon.* In some resorts there is a gambling casino with roulette to while away the long evenings.

During free time the *Kurgäste* will relax on the benches provided by the *Kurverwaltung* (cure administration), watch the other *Kurgäste* promenading by and commiserate with each other's ailments in the hushed tones usually reserved for a funeral.

The whisper is characteristic of the *Kurort,* where quiet and serenity rule the day. Motorists entering a *Kurort* are always greeted by large signs, warning, "Attention, *Kurort*! Sounding of horns forbidden." Besides, guests and even the staff are discouraged from driving, so as to be compelled to walk as much as possible.

Many *Kurorte* qualify for health insurance rebates, so that a constant headache of German firms, and American firms employing Germans, is the frequent absence of employees, especially women, taking *Die Kur.*

Other Traits

One very gratifying German trait is their deep and genuine love of nature. Nothing irks them so much as the blithe "So-what-else-is-new?" attitude of many Americans to a breathtaking sunset or the stillness of a forest. *Wanderlust* is part of their way of life. Young people especially like to explore the country, and there are 730 youth hostels in West Germany alone.

Less attractive, however, is the penchant of many Germans toward maudlin sentimentality. I shall never forget stopping at a slick, modern restaurant on the Autobahn, with plush new fixtures and the latest decor. Yet there, conspicuously affixed to the wall was a Biedermeier pedestal with two Victorian-style vases filled with flowers and a big, sentimental, hand-painted plaque above it, reading: *Mutter ist doch die beste* [mother is the best after all]. I can't prove it of course—and the reader will forgive this lapse into subjective comment—but it is my considered impression that Germans are disproportionately inclined to bathos and self-pity. Many of them seem to be inordinately fond of kitsch.

Many Germans themselves deplore what they call the *Spiessbürger* (middle-class) mentality. Its symbols are the tuxedo and evening gown, the pretentious living room, frilly lace curtains, the potted palm, and candelabra. Its taste centers around the operetta, which still enjoys immense popularity, the *Kaffeeklatsch,* and an exaggerated sense of good manners. Its values are based on externals, on bowing and scraping, on the love of titles, and the preoccupation with business deals, profit and material comforts. Its code of morals is based, not on justice, but respectability.

Surely the worst example of German sentimentality is the *Schlager* (hit tune). German, Swiss and Austrian music and literary critics are unanimous in deploring that awful German pop music that nevertheless enjoys overwhelming popularity. The saccharine, drooling sob-sister stuff inundates you from countless thousands of juke boxes all over Europe. Germans call them *Schnulzen* (tear-jerkers). Some of the worst pop songs go all the way back to World War I, especially those dealing with St. Pauli and the Reeperbahn, Hamburg's notorious night club, red light, and striptease district. Freddy Quinn (taking over from the World War I matinee idol, the late Hans Albers) never fails to impress countless thousands of misty-eyed Germans with his heart-rending *Heimweh* (homesickness) for *Das Herz von St. Pauli* ("the heart of St. Pauli"). Just as bad is the profusion of *Heimat (i.e.,* "home sweet home") films and *Lieder.* Fortunately, there are also hundreds of stirring, uplifting and humorous German student songs, cabaret songs, chansons, beer songs and folk songs, not to mention classical *Lieder* that more than compensate for all this.

What Americans might regard as a busybody attitude, some older Germans regard as a tradition of public cooperation with the police. Whenever there is a street fight, some bystander might call the police within minutes. Their attitude is that their own safety is involved and that crime must not go unpunished. An extremely popular TV program—telecast at regular intervals simultaneously in West Germany, Austria, and Switzerland from Munich—*Akten Zeichen X, Y . . . Ungelöst* (Case Number X, Y . . . Unsolved), presents re-enactments of unsolved crimes, highlighting clues, followed by appeals for public cooperation. Two hours later on the same evening a follow-up program reveals the results of telephone tips submitted by the viewers in the three countries. In many cases suspects are arrested on the same evening. Although well over half of the crimes reported in these telecasts are solved, West German newspapers have strongly criticized the program because it sometimes allegedly encourages a vigilante mentality and police abuse.

I have been annoyed on numerous occasions when some self-appointed citizen went out of his way to call my attention to an expired parking meter. In some German cities retired persons are hired to roam the streets and report all traffic offenders. In some cases even children have been encouraged with occasional small rewards to become informers.

Er muss seine Unschuld beweisen (he must prove his in-nocence) is an expression frequently heard whenever a suspect is charged with a crime. Until recently this attitude prevailed in German courts. Extensive penal reforms (Chapters 14 and 22) are underway and German courts require proof of guilt before convicting. Nevertheless the guilty-until-proven-innocent attitude is still deeply rooted in the German mentality.

Another tendency, that is happily on the way out, is that of siding, not with the underdog in any uneven struggle, but rather with the top dog. I remember an incident just recently witnessed by a friend. A would-be suicide, a man on the roof of a high building, was hesitating about whether or not to jump. Instead of pleading for his life, several Germans in the crowd below shouted, "Jump, you coward!" and he did just that. An isolated case, perhaps, but a true one. One possible explanation is that the strains of insecurity run deep in the German soul and that, being hung up on their long, tormented history, Germans yearn to be, for a change, on the side of a winner.[2]

The Dirty Germans

According to the Allensbach Demoscopic Institute, 43 percent of the German people think they are the world's cleanest nation. But in recent months German mass media have raised cries of dismay over the alleged increase of German filth and have challenged the time-honored reputation of the German *Hausfrau* for cleanliness.

A series of ads appeared in newspapers across the land sponsored by the advertising agency "Special Team" promoting underwear and showing a German family wearing pig masks. The caption: "This year the average German father will wear the same underwear for an entire week without changing, the average German mother, 5 days, and the children, 4 days. This is German cleanliness. And you are one of them!"

According to the mass circulation weekly magazine *Der Stern,* Dr. Reinhard Bergler, a Bonn psychologist and hygiene specialist, has testified that most German men wash themselves during the week "only from the collar up," since they don't change shirts. The standard German lexicon, *Brockhaus,* doesn't even list the word "clean."[3]

Other statistics reveal that fewer than half of all German children brush their teeth daily. A frequent complaint of American GI's is that German girls do not bathe frequently or thoroughly. Americans, especially girls, staying with German families do not cease griping that their landladies, mostly for reasons of thrift (gas and electricity are expensive), refuse to let them bathe more than once a week.

A leading detergent manufacturer sponsored an exhibition called "The Clean Germans" in an effort to improve the washing habits of the German people (and sales, too, of course). Speaking at the exhibition, the Bavarian minister of the interior complained that many people prefer to look clean rather than to be clean. "When I tried to replace the green shirts of the Bavarian police with light gray shirts," he said, "I ran into great opposition. The men insisted that green shirts look clean longer than gray ones."

According to the mass circulation Sunday paper *Bild am Sonntag* "even the 'sloppy' French and the 'dirty' Italians do not sleep nearly so long in their bedclothes as we do—namely on an average of three to four weeks."[4]

It was not too long ago that Germans used to criticize Americans as prodigious wastrels. In the postwar years they were forced by shortages to develop thrift into an art. Littered roadsides and overflowing garbage pails were virtually nonexistent. But all this is changed. The filth, especially in the large cities, seems to increase in density day by day, in direct ratio with the increase of German prosperity and liberation from traditional restraints.

A Sense of Order

If there is one word which has traditionally been associated with the German mentality it is the word *Ordnung* (order). One of the highest compliments that can be paid to anyone is to say, *"Er ist in Ordnung* [he is in order]*."* When a German wants to settle a dispute, he says, *"Ich werde alles in Ordnung bringen* [literally, I will bring everything in order]*."*

From time immemorial a sense of order was drilled into the German from the time he began to walk until he was carried, *Ordnungsgemäss* (in an orderly way), to his grave. Cosmetics on tables, unpacked suitcases, clothes strewn around the living room, doors left ajar could soon lead to a cold war between the *Hausfrau* and her family or boarders.

It would be too much to say that the contemporary rebellious German spirit has abolished this deep-rooted German trait. The order is still everywhere to be seen, but in a new crazy-quilt pattern that makes the observer shake his head in disbelief.

The sense of order accompanies the German whenever he moves into a new community. Every person, foreigner and German alike, is required by law to register with the local police *(Polizeiliche Anmeldung)* and give notice again when he leaves the community or even moves within it. Police in this case are actually bureaucratic, plainclothes civil servants. I have often told Germans that such registration is unknown in the States, and invariably the first thing they say is, "How do you ever track down criminals if you do not keep a record on everybody?"

The systematic registration has its positive sides. A friend of mine knew only the city where I lived but not the street, and easily located me through the police registration, since I was not listed in the telephone directory.

In addition, foreigners are required to obtain an *Aufenthaltserlaubnis* (residence permit).

It should be pointed out that these procedures are common throughout Europe, and that we Americans keep a close track of foreigners too. Moreover, West Germany was the first European country to abolish the elaborate hotel police registration forms still required in other countries.

Although West Germans enjoy a thoroughly relaxed atmosphere, nevertheless, daily life does contain certain elements of what Americans would call regimentation, and which the Germans merely shrug off as a matter of *Ordnung* (order).

Related to this sense of order is the Germans' supposed highly developed sense of discipline. *Verboten* (forbidden) signs are so numerous that they are sometimes regarded as a symbol of Germany. The following sign, hopefully, is no longer so common as it once was, but it is nonetheless a type still found all over the country. It is conspicuously posted at the entrance of a playground in the downtown Horion Park in Düsseldorf:

> Children, get along with one another, do not destroy anything and behave yourselves. Respect all adults. Parents and guardians: Be mindful of your supervisory duties. The city is not liable for accidents or damages.
>
> IT IS FORBIDDEN FOR ANYONE: To climb walls or fences, to play soccer, to use this equipment after 6:30 P.M. between March 1 and October 31, or after 5 P.M. between January 11 and February 28, to ride or push bicycles, to take dogs along, to play music, to damage or pollute the premises. Directives of the park supervisor must be obeyed under penalty of the law.

Thornton Wilder is credited with this observation: "In England, everything which is not forbidden is permitted. In Germany, everything which is not permitted is forbidden. In France, even that which is forbidden is permitted. And in the Soviet Union, even that which is permitted is forbidden." To which the Germans themselves, no longer so obedient as they once were, like to quip: "Everything that is not forbidden is obligatory."

But German discipline is daily becoming more and more conspicuous by its rarity. People still line up at street crossings like so many grim soldiers waiting rigidly for the light to turn green, but they have to compete with a growing number of jaywalkers.[5] In parks strict regulations prohibit walking on the grass except in those areas clearly marked for this purpose and sometimes with a marked-off section called the *Liegewiese* (meadow for lying down). But many Germans refuse to take all this seriously. In Frankfurt, the Konrad Loews were taken to court by their apartment house owner for letting their children play on the grass. The case aroused considerable controversy, especially when the court decided in favor of the landlord, arguing that grass exists to delight the eye and that children playing on it disturb nearby residents. "But we won't give up the fight and are going to appeal," said the Loews, who have six children. Mr. Loew, an economist and business consultant believes that the time has come to do away with this kind of authoritarianism of the past. And the prevailing mood of West Germans, regardless how the courts decide, is decidedly on his side.

Meanwhile, jokes about German discipline abound.

A student returning to Germany from a hitchhiking tour of Sweden told me about a sign he saw posted on a youth hostel there:

Americans—come home before two A.M.

Germans—don't get up before six A.M.

Italians—no singing after ten P.M.

Swedes—no girls in dormitories

To the Germans, the *Verboten* pedantry is, like Charlie Brown's blanket, a symbol of security. Whenever critics tease them about being regimented, they counter with the observation that in England and the States there may be less police regulation, but on the other hand an infinitely more tyrannical public opinion that dictates conformity in dress, manners, morals, and thinking.

Teutonic characteristics, such as the reputed thoroughness, are not exactly loved by the outside world. This was illustrated when Lufthansa, the national airline, had to drop an advertising campaign in response to a barrage of foreign criticism. The ad featured a closeup of a glowing "Fasten Seat Belts" sign, with the caption, "At times you might be annoyed by the fanatical thoroughness of the Germans. But not at times like this."[6]

Any foreigner who has had to put up with the exasperating slowness of telephone installation or of many German businesses, notably service institutions, will wonder what ever happened to German thoroughness or efficiency. The ready smile, quick service, and "customer is always right" are a sheer matter of luck in German department stores, shoe repair, and dry cleaning shops. Especially with the growth of the economic boom and the accompanying help shortage, slovenly service has become commonplace. A good secretary is extremely hard to find. And I am told my experience is typical: I advertised for a secretary in Hamburg, received only ten replies, of which only two could be considered. One of these two applicants could not even spell German properly and unabashedly asked me—a foreigner—the meaning of a common German business term. Fortunately, I finally found a really first-rate secretary, but it took a lot of looking.

I shall never forget a visit to Assisi, birthplace of St. Francis, where my Franciscan guide, a German, complained to me about the "superficial" Americans who think they can "do" Assisi in three hours, while Germans stay for several days, poring over almost every stone, carry scholarly guidebooks around (not the five-dollar-a-day variety), and spend the entire evening in academic discussions about art, architecture, hagiography, while at adjoining tables Americans will unabashedly ask if St. Francis (1182) was a contemporary of St. Augustine (354).

"The Germans may be great ones for order," one American diplomat's wife told me, "but brother, they are even greater for a total lack of coordination. There is nothing more exasperating than dealing with German laundries, service people, cleaners, and fighting it out with the landlord . . . . Judas priest!"

Meanwhile the Germans go blithely on organizing and suborganizing. In 1969 the Interior Ministry announced that preparations were already underway for a system to give every West German a personal number. The system would be necessary, an official told parliament, for statistical purposes and to facilitate administration.

It is interesting that when applying for a job in Germany, one must not only fill in detailed questionnaires and supply photostats of one's diplomas or certificates, but write one's *curriculum vitae* entirely in longhand. This latter is usually analyzed for character traits by a graphologist. Even in private life Germans take handwriting very seriously and often make or reject friendships because of real or imagined traits detected in one's handwriting.

Titles on the Wane

A sense of order presupposes respect for authority, and this in turn has, in the past, led to a proliferation of titles. Until recently the greatest social prestige was attached to the title of professor. But the spate of student rebellions and spirit of unrest sweeping through West Germany in the late sixties has called this, like so many other sacred cows of German life, seriously into question. Some government department heads or ministers now make a point of asking to be called only by their last names, "Herr So-und-so," rather than the pompous "Herr Minister." In fact, it can be said that in West Germany there is far less to-do about titles these days than in the other German-speaking countries, Switzerland and, above all, Austria, where they still make such a fuss about them.

More and more Germans are dropping the formal address, *"Sehr geehrter Herr* [Very Esteemed Mr.]*"* and substituting the American "Dear Mr. "

Nevertheless, a professor is still a somebody in Germany and *Herr Professor* has not exactly lost its glow and respect. Not only medical doctors, but Ph.D.'s are still called *Herr Doktor.* The German chancellor is called *Herr Kanzler* or *Herr Bundeskanzler* (Mr. Federal Chancellor).

However, young people are much less title-conscious and north Germans use fewer titles than south Germans. To a Hamburg citizen a death announcement in a south German newspaper mentioning the status of a woman as *"Früchtegrosshändler's Witwe* [wholesale fruit dealer's widow] " appears just as quaint as to an American. Yet even in the north the picturesque chimney sweep, with his traditional if soot-covered top hat (which Germans touch for good luck) is respectively addressed as *Herr Schornsteinfegermeister* (Mr. Master Chimney Sweep).

The "Du" and "Sie"

A good clue to the German character is the use of *"Du"* and *"Sie."* Germans tend to make a very clear distinction between friends and acquaintances, and are apt to make only a few close friendships in a lifetime, even while being on the friendliest terms with a large number of acquaintances. The line is clearly drawn not only by the formality of titles, but also by the use of the two forms of "you", unknown in modern English: the intimate *"Du"* (comparable to the Biblical "Thou"), which is reserved for close friends, immediate relatives, animals, children, and God, and the formal *"Sie,"* which keeps all others at a distance and which says in effect, "You can penetrate into my private world just so far and no farther."[7]

The "Sie" is the invisible but unmistakable wall that the German carries with him wherever he goes, a mental and spiritual capsule of privacy in the midst of a hostile world, a refuge to withdraw into at a moment's notice, a handy instrument for saving face and preserving one's dignity.

While white collar workers generally use "Sie," teenagers, students, blue collar workers, and soldiers prefer to use the informal "Du" among themselves. With Americans many German girls rapidly adopt the "Just call me Joe" routine, but this is by no means a foregone conclusion. For the majority of Germans the formal distinction remains very much in force.

When two people decide to switch to "Du" from "Sie" there is usually a little wine or beer drinking ceremony. The two, glasses in hand, intertwine their right arms, then take a sip from their glasses. This is called Bruderschaft trinken (fellowship drink). If they are boy and girl, they may seal the ceremony with a kiss. But here too the younger set simply laughs at such formality.

Privacy

Another clue to the German mentality is their preference for privacy. Just as they do at home, Germans tend to close their office doors rather than leave them open. But the huge U.S.-style office rooms with countless rows of desks is rapidly replacing the luxury of individualism.

Germans build more fences around private homes than do Americans, though the trend toward high-rise apartment buildings is swiftly eliminating this custom.

But other privacy-assuring customs remain. For instance, whenever new neighbors move into a neighborhood, it is not the community which welcomes them, but rather it is expected that they introduce themselves to their new neighbors. Germans who have experienced the greater warmth and hospitality known in the States will point out that the American neighbors also expect greater conformity, such as joining the local church, signing up with different organizations, being active in the community. German aloofness, they claim, makes for greater privacy.

This highly developed sense of privacy may help account for

the slowness of some Germans to invite strangers into their homes. In recent years, however, much more widely traveled Germans have radically changed their thinking and many of them have become more casual and consequently more hospitable too.

German Humor

Perhaps one of the reasons why Germans have a reputation for being short on humor is that, strictly speaking, there is no such thing as German humor. Rather there is Berlin humor, Bavarian humor, Rhineland humor, Hamburg humor. One hears about Italian jokes, British jokes, Russian jokes, American jokes, but not German jokes. Aside from the inevitable sex jokes, which are international, German jokes are regional or political.

It is true, however, that certain German attitudes toward humor in general predominate in daily speech and life. Speeches are seldom sprinkled with humor and the opening joke or anecdote is rare. There are relatively few comic strips, although several German newspapers have recently modernized the traditional humor page, but more on the *New Yorker* level. Animal movies or television documentaries only recently have adopted the Walt Disney light touch. Thornton Wilder's moving epic of man's struggle for survival, *The Skin of Our Teeth,* bewilders many Germans who cannot understand how such a serious subject can be treated so lightly, and the same holds true for that British masterpeice, *Oh, What a Lovely War.*

The quick flash of an American smile is regarded as insincere, as is the American's penchant for immediate friendliness and "Just call me Joe" attitude. An advertisement for an American electric razor showing it shaving off the fuzz of peaches had to be dropped because the Germans didn't understand the humor of it. George Mikes, the Hungarian-born British humorist, accuses Germans of being able to laugh only according to the calendar (Fasching, Karneval, etc.), while the Italian film star, Victorio Gassmann, in a West German TV interview said the German language discourages humor "because it is a language with which one cannot play."

That having been said, there is German humor in abundance, but because much of it is in dialect or related to folklore, it is lost on the outside world.

63

Surely the most famous and sparkling folk humor in Germany is that of the Berliners. But it is more of a witty style than a fixed form of humor, such as jokes. It is so much dependent on the specific situation that the point is lost by the time it might reach print. There is a strong element of sarcasm and witty abrasiveness too, which the Berliners call *Herz und Schnauze* *(i.e.,* a lot of heart and a quick, biting tongue), or *Helle* (clever repartee), which other Germans call *Schlagfertigkeit.*

Berlin's Archbishop Alfred Bengsch, who lives in East Berlin, is as good an example as any. He says, for instance, of an inept East German official, "He is as apt for his post as a porcupine for a door handle." When he was harassed by East German border guards on one occasion, and one of them asked, "What is the difference between Catholics and Protestants anyway?" the Archbishop replied, "I don't have time to explain that to you now. But I suppose you might say it is like the difference between Lenin and Tito."

In northern Germany there are hundreds of jokes centering around the figure of a mythical German girl, *Kleine Erna* (Little Erna), usually of a risque nature.

In Aachen, during the Karneval season every February, an award is annually given to a prominent personality who showed the most humor during the previous year, *Gegen den Tierischen Ernst* (Against Animal-like Seriousness).

In the Rhineland two legendary figures, Tünis and Schäl (roughly comparable to Stan Laurel and Oliver Hardy or the comic strip figures Mutt and Jeff), noted for their unbelievable stupidity, are the subject of countless jokes, many of them of the shaggy dog variety.

Germans have a penchant for giving irreverent nicknames to public buildings. The West Berlin convention hall, with parabolic arches, is called The Pregnant Oyster. The ruins of the blown-off tower of the Kaiser Wilhelm Memorial Church on West Berlin's fashionable Kurfürstendamm, which have been preserved in that state as a reminder of the folly of war, have been affectionately dubbed The Decayed Molar. In Cologne, the tiered modern concert hall that resembles a sawed-off pyramid, is called Tomb of the Unknown Musician. Elsewhere a modernistic church whose main building includes several transcepts arranged in cloverleaf fashion, has been called Herd of Elephants Church, because from a distance it resembles the behinds of a group of elephants huddled in a circle.

Streets are also the subject of humor: "In Hamburg there is a street called Horse Market—but there are no more horses. Then there is a street called Goose Market—but no geese are sold there. And finally, there is a street called Jungernstieg (Virgin Promenade), but there are no more virgins."

Numerous political jokes abound, mainly dealing with East Germany: Two old men are sitting on a park bench. One of them keeps spitting, ostentatiously and often. Finally the other says, "Please, no political conversation, or I shall call the police."

A family is awakened in the middle of the night by a loud knocking at the door. They tremble with fear until they recognize a familiar voice. "Please," it said, "Don't worry. It's only me, the janitor, come to tell you that the house is on fire."

In Leipzig, East Germany, a man comes home only to find his wife in bed with another man. "Here you are wasting your time at home, Eva," he shouts reproachfully, "when you should be standing in line at the *Konsum,* where they just got a shipment of oranges!"

A form of humor that is highly developed in the Federal Republic (and to a restricted degree in East Germany) is that found in the political cabaret. All over the Federal Republic these cabarets, often basement cafés, mostly Bohemian in decor, produce an endless variety of satirical one-act plays, with pantomime, protest songs, poems, and humor often reaching a high literary quality. Their chief stock-in-trade is satire, and the objects of their venom range from American participation in Vietnam to German nationalism.

An example of the brutal and poignant force of these cabarets is the following narrative dealing with the failure of the church to stand up to Hitler during the Third Reich:

A Jew is arrested by the Gestapo but escapes them and is chased down the street. He dashes into a church for safety, which is filled with worshippers. He slips into a pew among the faithful and pretends to pray. But he is observed by the priest in the pulpit who has also just noticed the Gestapo entering the church. Perspiring with fear, the priest interrupts the sermon to announce, "All Jews please leave the church!" But the Jew bends his head and refuses to budge. Raising his voice the priest repeats his request, "I said, all Jews must please leave this church!" Again, no response from the Jew, while the Gestapo are going down the aisles scrutinizing every face. Finally the priest roars, "For the last time, I insist: All Jews must leave this church!"

At this, the crucifix over the high altar begins to stir, Christ descends from the cross, walks over to the Jew and says, "Come, Brother, we are not wanted here."

The Language Mystique

Perhaps the most revealing key to the German mentality, indeed to what has been called the German mystique, is the language. It inevitably comes away a poor second when compared to the melodic romance languages. Some of the sounds emitted in pronouncing certain words are so akin to clearing one's throat that certain variations of the language, such as Schwytzerdeutsch, the Swiss dialect, are humorously referred to as "not a language but a throat disease."

The Swiss poet Heinrich Federer has compared the German language as follows: "French is an elegant park. Italian is a large, bright, colorful forest. But German is more like a jungle, with so much undergrowth, so mysterious, with a thousand paths and yet without any large passage. One cannot get lost in a park, nor is there fear of danger in the bright and cheerful Italian forest. But in the German jungle one is swallowed up within minutes by the thickets."[8]

But anyone who has heard good German spoken in the great theaters of the German-language countries knows that it can be soul-searching in its beauty even as it is famous for its scientific precision. It may come as a surprise to be told that German is also picturesque, but it is true.

Take, for example, the word for thimble, *Fingerhut* (literally, a hat for the finger), or *Arbeitgeber* (work-giver), employer or *Arbeitnehmer* (work-taker), employee. *Stinktier* (stinking animal) is the word for skunk; *Weltraum,* for outer space (world space, literally); *Weltanschauung* (world view), for ideology; *Schreibtisch* (table for writing), for desk. And hundreds of expressions: *Mit dem ist nicht gut Kirschen zu essen* (literally, it is not pleasant to eat cherries with that fellow, *i.e.,* he is hard to get along with; possibly originating from the ill-mannered habit of spitting cherry stones in the direction of one's companion).

Vulgar pleasure is derived by some Americans from the frequent appearances of the word *Fahrt* (trip, journey, or, as a verb, *fahren,* to ride). Many service stations have a big sign at their exits, with the words, *Gute Fahrt!* (Have a good journey!), which mischievous-minded Americans prefer to interpret as

"Have a good fart!" Acute embarrassment to hearty laughter can be evoked by mispronouncing the word *schiessen* (to shoot) and saying *scheissen* (to eliminate) instead.

Words are symbols that express meanings, but there are some words so deep and pregnant with meaning as to defy definition: love, faith, charisma, hope. The same is true of words of evil: mental cruelty, hate, genocide. German words like *Weltschmerz,* (sorrow as the lot of the human condition), *Weltanschauung, Weltansicht* (world view, ideology), *Leitmotif, Wehmut* (melancholy longing), *Kindergarten* (literally, a children's garden) have become common in American usage. But so have, alas, other German words: *Nazi,* an abbreviation of the full name of the Nazi Party, *National Sozialistische Deutsche Arbeiter Partei* (NSDAP, National Socialist German Workers' Party); *Gestapo (Geheime Staatspolizei),* secret state police; *Führer Prinzip,* leadership principle upon which Hitler's New Order was based; *Konzentrationslager,* concentration camp; *Völkermord,* genocide, a new word that the Third Reich contributed to the world's dictionaries; and *Lebensraum,* living space. Obedience to authority has given rise to the expression *Kadaver Gehorsam* (blind obedience, *i.e.,* as compliant as a corpse). *Obrigkeit* (the powers-that-be, or the authorities) and *Untertan* (subject, underling) are words associated with Prussian authoritarianism. The latter word was formerly used in designating the status of a citizen. The American sociologist Gordon Zahn suggests that this note of rigid subordination had become something of a "principle" governing the German approach to political and social relationships and responsibilities: The so-called *Fahrrad* (bicycle) principle: *Nach oben bücken, nach unten treten* (bow to those above, tread upon those below).[9]

No English word adequately conveys the subtle shades of meaning implied in the German word *Volk,* though such words as "folk," "people," "nationality" are often used. The word has a certain mystique, especially when combined in words like *Volksstaat* (people's state), or *Volkssturm* (civilian mobilization) as used by Hitler. *Volkswagen* (people's car) though is surely devoid of such association.

The word *Heimat* is perhaps more difficult to explain and contains an even deeper mystique than *Volk.* The usual English translations are "homeland" or "native province," but they are inadequate. Like the word *Vaterland* (fatherland), there is also a mystical association suggesting a dominant note of a blood tie, a sacred identity linking past and future generations with the present. The same is true of *Blut und Boden* (blood and soil).

Similarly a kind of Teutonic other-worldly mystique has clouded certain words in the past, words like *Opferbereitschaft,* willingness to sacrifice personal well-being for the good of the whole community; *Treue,* dedicated sense of loyalty; *Pflicht,* binding duty (at opposite ends of the pole both Konrad Adenauer and Adolf Eichmann justified their deeds with the expression, *"Ich habe meine Pflicht getan"*—I have done my duty). Such words as *Ehre* (personal honor), *Ehrentod* (death with honor), and *Heldentod* (hero's death), and related concepts, are all part of the ponderous legacy of the German tongue.

No one can say how latent, widespread, or deep this mystique still lies rooted in the German character. A rash of new words seem to confirm the disdain of today's Germans for the Wagnerian mystique of the German past. The late American President John F. Kennedy's book, *Profiles in Courage,* enjoyed immense success in the Federal Republic. Its German version—and TV series based on it—is entitled *Zivilcourage* (civil courage), a popular word among the younger generation who have become intensely involved in political and social problems. This is an extremely interesting development inasmuch as the inability to relate theory and practice is said to have contributed considerably to the schizophrenic element of the German character. This fatal flaw is frequently cited by historians and psychologists as greatly responsible for the blurred thinking on war crimes, but also for the fact that such crimes took place at all on such an unprecedented scale, without the resistance of the mass population. In his zeal and reverence for the Law with a capital L, the average German was incapable of distinguishing between legal right and moral right. If the infallible *Obrigkeiten* (authorities) decide that it is necessary to act outside the accepted standards of morality, as in the annihilation of the Jews, then every good law-abiding German must obey them.

The famous counterpart to Alexis de Tocqueville's *Democracy in America* is Madame de Staël's book on the Germans. More than 150 years ago she observed, "The Germans . . . want everything in the line of conduct to be marked out for them beforehand. . . . They unite the greatest boldness in thought with the most submissive of characters. . . . With them obedience is not servility but regularity. They scrupulously execute all orders received as though every order were a duty. Enlightened Germans vigorously dispute in the speculative sphere, permitting no hinderance there. But they quite willingly yield all of real life to the powers that be. . . . The intellect and the character of the Germans seem to have no intercommunication; the one suffers no limitations, the other submits to every yoke. The former is most enterprising, the other very timid."[10]

"You Germans," an American colonel said to *Bundeswehr* officers at a Frankfurt social gathering, "would never win a war, because you can't improvise. You have to do everything from a plan." This alleged rigid adherence to activity planned in advance was brilliantly burlesqued by the German actor Gerd Fröbe in the comic film, *Those Magnificent Men in Their Flying Machines,* in which he played the part of a Kaiser-Wilhelm army officer who hopelessly foundered in a transchannel airplane race because he tried too hard to fly by following the minute rules of an instruction manual.

Today a new vocabulary dominates the German language, and dozens of words from American idiom and slang are a part of everyday speech: *die Babysitter; der Manager; der Boss; es ist okay; der Jazz; wir sind gehandikapped; der Astronaut.*

The legacy of the past remains, but to what extent and to what degree of intensity or how latently it is imbedded in the German character no survey or study can tell us. All of the phenomena and manifestations described in this chapter have to be measured against the countless other factors influencing modern German life: the ups and downs of personal fates; the economic condition of individuals and groups and the nation; the demands of modern life; the rising cost of living; the worldwide waves of student unrest; the rising tide of violence; the credibility gap; the generation gap; the conflicts with the Establishment and the numerous establishments within the Establishment; Americanization; urbanization; collectivization; pollution; escalating interdependence in business, politics, education, science, and culture; the booming tourist industry; the crushing weight of communications media; the European Common Market; automation, electronics, and cybernetics; infrastructure and permissiveness; and the price of coffee in Brazil.

◄5►

OF CASTLES, CUSTOMS, AND CULTS

NOTHING GIVES A better cross section of German life, not only in the present age, but also through more than twenty centuries of history, than the Rhine River.

Trickling in the heart of the Swiss Alps as a babbling infant, nurtured in the placid nursery of Lake of Constance, stumbling like an awkward teenager on the treacherous waterfalls (the most powerful in Europe) of Neuhausen, it then gently separates Switzerland from Germany, finally assuming the responsibilities of manhood at Basel. Here it abruptly turns northward, dividing Germany from France, only to swerve at Karlsruhe, penetrating deep into German territory. Much farther north, at Nijmegen, it rushes into the Netherlands, where at Rotterdam, it finally empties into the North Sea, some nine hundred miles from its source.

The river has been a major water artery since the dawn of history: Neanderthal Man was discovered near Düsseldorf, and all along its banks colonies were established by the Romans. Cologne was an important strategic, economic, and cultural center as early as A.D. 50, when the Roman Emperor Claudius granted city rights to the former military camp, called "Colonia Agrippina" after his wife, from which its present name derives.

Trier was conquered by Caesar's troops in 58 B.C., and was for some centuries the capital of the Western Roman Empire and residence of six Roman Emperors, and its name derives from "Augusta Treverorum." Its imperial baths were third in size after those of Caracalla and Diocletian. Coblenz, at the confluence of the Rhine and Mosel rivers, appropriately comes from "Confluentes" and dates to A.D. 9. The industrial city of Neuss was once "Novaesium," established A.D. 69.

Roman ruins, baths, amphitheaters, aqueducts, and fortresses exist in great abundance all through the Rhineland. Bonn's parliamentary building stands on Roman graves, and the chancellery covers the foundations of a Roman villa. Bonn's main street,

Koblenzerstrasse, was originally a Roman road. Boppard on the Rhine can boast of still possessing half of its original Roman town wall, while Mainz has a tower built in memory of Drusus, the Roman general who was the stepson of Emperor Augustus. Baden-Baden, the international spa at the edge of the Black Forest, still has relics of a Roman military bath house. Elsewhere the remains of blacksmith shops show that as early as the third century anthracite coal was being used as a fuel in Germany.

When the foundations of modern Europe were created in 887 with the division of Charlemagne's empire, Roman civilization deteriorated. Not being masters of engineering like the Romans, the Germans let the roads disintegrate and used the river as the great highway of the feudal age. This period is enshrined in the Romanesque and gothic cathedrals, monasteries, and walled towns serenely overlooking the Rhine. From Düsseldorf in the north to imperial Speyer in the south, the Rhine links a succession of picturesque towns and cities renowned as great repositories of medieval art—Cologne, Coblenz, Oberwesel, Mainz, Oppenheim, and Worms.

Kings and emperors of the Holy Roman Empire were crowned in the Rhineland. In the regions near the Rhine, in the cathedral of Aachen, the ancient Aix-la-Chapelle, thirty-two kings were enthroned, the first of them Charlemagne.

The banks of the Rhine became the main place of residence for the prince-elector bishops and the archbishops of Mainz, the Palatinate, and Coblenz. The great electoral palace built two centuries ago still stands today, an impressive relic of that era. The magnificent castles and princely residences in Düsseldorf, Bensberg, Brühl, Mannheim, Schwetzingen, and Karlsruhe recapture the baroque and rococo splendor of the seventeenth and eighteenth centuries.

Ministers and heads of state continue to meet on the Rhine at Bonn, and state visits are often held in palaces, while important guests stay at modernized castles. Today many castles have been converted into cafés, restaurants, elegant hotels as well as hippie youth hostels, outdoor theaters, artists' studios, chapels for weddings, picnic grounds, and pavilions. Many castles are up for sale at very low prices—but there is a string attached: the buyer of a *Schloss* must finance its restoration, often a matter of thousands of dollars, and preserve its historic character.

The capitals of three German *Länder* (states) are situated on the banks of the river. Historians like to point out that it was

71

part of Germany's destiny, and perhaps a fatal one, that no imperial capital was founded on the Rhine and that the functions of the capital were divided between three cities—the Holy Roman Emperor was chosen at Frankfurt, crowned at Aachen, and buried at Speyer. Today there is a similar dispersal of function, and the Federal Republic is essentially a Rhineland state: its political capital is Bonn, its financial capital is Frankfurt, its industrial capital is Düsseldorf, and its judicial capital is Karlsruhe.

It was in the Rhineland newspaper, the *Neue Rheinische Zeitung,* in the revolutionary year of 1848, that the young Karl Marx wrote his first appeal for violent overthrow of capitalistic institutions. And it was in the Rhineland that the ancestors of Freud were born. The Rhine evokes great memories: Gutenberg of Mainz, Beethoven of Bonn, Goethe of Frankfurt, Düsseldorf's Heinrich Heine.[1] Other famous Rhinelanders include Schiller, Schumann, and Adenauer.

For the wine-lover the Rhine evokes images of the Rheingau, that classic fifteen-mile stretch of slopes from Mainz to Bingen, the celebrated "Deutsche Weinstrasse" where the grape has been king for nearly two thousand years. Here grow the famous *Edelfaul* (nobly spoiled) grapes that give the Rhine wines their famous flavors. While there is less sun in Germany than in other famous wine countries like France, Italy, and Greece, the Rhine wines derive their unique qualities by lengthening the ripening time under a more gentle sun. The ancient process of gathering grapes when they are overripe actually has been mentioned in the Old Testament and by Homer, and the custom was brought into the Rhineland by the Romans. But the knowledge was lost and not recovered until the early part of the nineteenth century, when the Bishop of Fulda waited too long to begin harvesting the grapes in his Rheingau vineyards. To his amazement, the resulting vintage surpassed anything he had ever tasted.

The Rhine's hinterland is the Ruhr with the great industrial cities Essen, Mülheim, and Oberhausen in Germany's most densely populated region. Counterpointing this complex is Mannheim in the south, another giant inland port, and Ludwigshafen, important distribution and commercial center in the Rhineland-Palatinate. Still further south is the Saar.

In this age of cross-country tractor trucks and freight-speeding jets, most of us nostalgically think of river traffic as something that went out with Mark Twain, who, incidentally, once rode down a Rhine tributary, the Neckar, on a raft and wrote about his hilarious exploits in *A Tramp Abroad.*

The heavy barge traffic on the Rhine River proves otherwise. Thousands of black barges carry large cargoes of coal and timber, automobiles, and oil across the face of Europe, affirming the Rhine to be Europe's major freight and bulk goods shipping course. To the realists—the manufacturers and shippers—the Rhine is an industrial giant that annually shoulders seven million tons of shipping on 10,000 vessels of all shapes and sizes from many countries, carries 75 percent of Germany's 8,000 river barges, feeds the world's largest inland port of Duisburg-Ruhrort, and floats great fleets of "standard" barges, which have a capacity of 1,500 tons each, the equivalent of 80 railroad cars.

To the gourmet the Rhine used to mean a superb repast featuring Rhine salmon, which, alas, is no more, even though the dockside restaurants still feature the fish, now imported from Norway.

To the angler the Rhine means tales of creels full of eels, perch, and pike in the days before pollution. Today, Rhine angling is all but finished, what with the French factories of Alsace and Lorraine discoloring the waters with the wastes from potash factories, to the tune of ten thousand tons a day, in addition to the sewage from German cities and factories all the way down the line through the industrial Ruhr to the sea.

In spite of pollution, river traffic, and industry, the Rhine remains the visible monument of bygone romance as well as the region of modern-day escape. But fairy-tale enchantment is visibly a part of many regions of Germany. The famous Bergstrasse, from romantic Heidelberg northwards to Darmstadt, runs through lush wooded scenery, embodying a children's book image of Germany complete with cuckoos and castles, mushrooms and vineyards, fountains and half-timbered houses. The Bergstrasse's appeal—both historic and aesthetic—gains added glow from the atmosphere of legend that clings to the countryside like moss to its trees.

The Wagner Story

Dramatically perched on a steep crag near Füssen at the southern tip of Germany stands Neuschwanstein Castle, a nineteenth century imitation of a fairy-tale castle, built by the demented King Ludwig II of Bavaria. Ascending to the throne at the end of the American Civil War, Ludwig II was an eccentric dreamer who squandered the kingdom's coffers on the lavish construction of castles, notably Neuschwanstein, Linderhof Palace near Garmisch-Partenkirchen, Herrenchiemsee Palace on an island in the Chiem Lake, and the Berg Palace on the shores of Lake Starnberg. (Their tourist value today, however, has ironically proved Ludwig's mad splurge a most profitable investment.)

Nevertheless, it was he who rescued the middle-aged down-at-the-heels composer Richard Wagner and promoted him. Under his patronage, Wagner prospered and composed two of his most famous operas: *Tristan und Isolde* and *Die Meistersinger.*[2]

It was King Ludwig's idea to build a theater especially for the performance of Wagnerian operas. This dream was realized, but only after Wagner had begun to lose favor with the king. In 1871 Wagner went to Bayreuth, a small town in northern Bavaria, and a year later the foundation stone was laid for the Bayreuth festival house, which Wagner himself had designed. The theater was opened in 1876 with "The Ring of the Nibelungs."

Bayreuth was chosen by Wagner because its Frankish forests were so Germanic and "could not be penetrated by the Romans." Bayreuth preserved "and asserted the German tongue with victorious faith" and was subsequently able to survive the onslaughts of "French and other foreign cultures."

Wagner and Bayreuth have been fair game for much satire, buffoonery, and criticism, and by none more than the Germans themselves, since World War II, because of his excessive and morbid preoccupation with Teutonic lore, his intense nationalism (and anti-Semitism), and the preferred and exaggerated role his music played in Nazi Germany.

Today Bayreuth is known and loved by music lovers all over the world as the Wagner City, where annually thousands of Wagner fans attend the famous Bayreuth festivals. After Wagner's death the festival lived on in the hands of his nearest kin, most recently his grandson, Wolfgang Wagner. Today it is a foundation.

Stripped of its *Blut-und-Boden* mystique, Bayreuth's atmosphere has become cosmopolitan and the standard Wagnerian props—the horned helmets, the ladies in armor, and the Siegfried wigs—are gone. There is more being done to develop new talent and far-out free-form stage-designing—experimentation is the rule. The emphasis is on Wagner's "universality." Conductors from all over the world direct many of the festival performances.

A few years ago some of the old-guard Wagnerians started an Association for the Authentic Performance of Wagner's Dramas, but no one really believes that the old Teutonic winds will blow here again.

Goblins, Witches, and Dwarfs

Dwarfs, those small genii who live underground and have gray beards and pointed caps, are not only a beloved part of German folklore but a source of immense delight to countless thousands of Germans (and foreign tourists) who buy plaster statues of the famous figures for their window sills, gardens, and fish ponds.

The Pied Piper lives on in Hamelin where every year the famed legend is reenacted in the town square.

Tales of witches still abound in the region of the Harz Mountains, a great hilly area pushing out of the flatlands of Lower Saxony in Northern Germany. Though split in two by the East German border, the greater part is within West Germany, with its healing waters, pine-scented air, breathtaking gorges, and drowsy villages. Many of the ancient houses still have the original leaded glass windows, whose convex *Butzenscheiben* were blown long before the trick of making flat panes was mastered, and bulge with irridescent imperfections that wink gaily under sunlight or electric lighting.

The Harz is famous for a hardy breed of canaries and architectural wonders—notably Goslar, an imperial city that dates all the way back to the tenth century. Goslar's streets are a virtual museum. From Bad Harzburg directly at the Iron Curtain border tourists have two kinds of tales to chill their spines: the modern kind that are told about the visible Brocken East German border watch, with its watchtower, observatory and radar equipment, grim barbed-wire fence, and mine fields; the other kind, easier to take, is replete with stories of goblins and witches.

For Brocken was the setting for the *"Walpurgis Nacht"* scene in *Faust* in which Johann Wolfgang von Goethe revived an eighth century superstition concerning witches, and depicted them:

Jiggering and jabbering and boiling and roasting;
Quaffing and daffing and ogling and toasting. . . .

Today the Harz folk keep the old tale going. They stage annual witch-gatherings on April 30 called Walpurgisfests, and many of the villages, principally Bündheim and Bad Harzburg, thrive on the sale of handmade talismans to protect you from witches' spells. These are replicas of witches up to a foot high, with frizzled red hair and poised broomsticks. Bad Harzburg's *Sagenhaus* (house of legends) has devoted an entire museum to the evils brewing in them there hills.

Till Eulenspiegel

The Harz Mountains allegedly produced one of the most durable and beloved German personalities, a legendary medieval prankster by the name of Till Eulenspiegel (whose surname means "Owl Mirror"). He vies with the famous Baron Münchhausen, who actually lived from 1720 to 1797, noted for his tall tales and adventures into a world of fantasy, including a trip to the moon on a cannon ball.

Eulenspiegel was supposedly born in Kneitlingen, a Lower Saxony village, in 1300. His legends are very much alive today and he is a famous figure in folklore, music, and literature. Richard Strauss named a whimsical tone poem after Till in 1894. Jakob Grimm, the fairy-tale writer wrote about him, as did Hans Sachs, Fritz Reuter, and Wilhelm Raabe, and Charles de Coster of Flanders. And in Schöppenstadt near Kneitlingen there is an entire museum devoted to him.

Eulenspiegel refused to do a lick of work on the farm, was a dunce in school, and at the age of nine became a champion of social rebellion and reform. He protested against the social system, obsolete traditions, sanctimonious officials, and the feudal system.

A typical Eulenspiegel tale is the one in which he assumed the role of a visiting civic leader. He talked officials into permitting him to plant a pile of pebbles in the square to grow a new town hall. In another story he posed as an artist of renown and was commissioned to do a portrait of a ruling nobleman. When the canvas was unveiled before a large audience, Eulenspiegel pretended to be amazed that the onlookers saw only a blank canvas. "Oh," he said, "I forgot to mention that the portrait is visible only to legitimate children."

According to legend, when Eulenspiegel was buried, the ropes broke and the casket plunged Eulenspiegel into the grave feet first.

A statue of the year-round April Fool mischief-maker is to be found in a church wall in Mölln, near Hamburg, showing the clown with an owl and a mirror—his coat-of-arms. He is supposedly buried upright in the wall, and the epitaph reads, "This stone shall not be lifted by anyone. Here Eulenspiegel stands buried. A.D. 1350."

Picturesque Remnants

In spite of modern inroads, traditions live on in Germany. Regional costume has been dying out since the war, but *Lederhosen* (leather shorts) and *Dirndl* dresses are still frequent in Bavaria, and regional dress in many small towns, such as Marburg, and in the Black Forest region. In everyday life, two trades still cling to ancient dress, the picturesque chimney sweep with his top hat and ornamental jacket and the *Zimmermann* (journeyman carpenter), who wears a floppy wide-brimmed hat, occasionally an earring in one ear, bell-bottom trousers, and spends three gyspsylike years wandering on foot, bound by code not to ride, to lands near and far learning his trade.

Countless hotels and inns have colorful outdoor murals; in Catholic regions, depicting Biblical scenes, many of them with elaborate coats-of-arms and wrought-iron brackets. Dating back to the time when monasteries provided hospitality to travelers, many hotels have religious names, such as *Engel* (angel), *Drei Könige* (Three Kings), *Augegottes* (Eye of God), *Himmelreich* (Kingdom of Heaven). After 1450, with the establishment of Germany's postal system, many inns and restaurants sprang up near postal stations and received names like *Goldenes Posthorn*, *Alte Post*, and *Zur Post*.

The many names with "gold" attached to them originates from the preoccupation with alchemy in the Middle Ages and the search for gold by the futile effort to convert base materials, such as *Goldenes Lamm*.

The deep religious influence is especially evident in Bavaria with its numerous wayside crucifixes, shrines, religious frescoes (for example, Oberammergau), and religious street names. Even the word "Munich," in German *"München,"* means "of the monks," referring to the monastery that originally stood on the site. When I called at a Munich publishing house widely known as an atheistic center, I was greeted at the door by a secretary with the typical expression, *"Grüss Gott* [I greet you in the name of God]."

Customs and Festivals

Germany is the home of literally hundreds of festivals, including *Erntedankfest*, a kind of thanksgiving, and wine and beer festivals. The most famous are the Oktoberfest in Munich, and the Karneval season celebrated in hundreds of cities, but nowhere more than in Munich (where it is called Fasching), Mainz, Düsseldorf, Aachen, Cologne.

The Oktoberfest actually takes place in mid-September and goes back to 1810 when Crown Prince Ludwig I got married. This biggest beer festival in the world lasts sixteen days, is held on a big meadow named Theresienwiese, after the bride, where a million visitors annually consume 400,000 roast chickens, several oxen, tons of fish, 800,000 pairs of sausages, and wash it all down with a million gallons of beer.

In the pre-Lenten season, beginning in November and lasting through February, countless balls, masked and unmasked, often with many girls in topless costume, take place. The evenings are replete with "officials" wearing dunce caps and reciting satirical verse. The Munich Fasching culminates in a parade through the streets on the Sunday before Ash Wednesday. And on Shrove Tuesday, the day of the traditional *Kehr-aus* (last fling), the city drops all pretence of work. Thousands of people gather in the main square and dance to beat tunes blaring from loudspeakers in the Rathaus tower.

In Cologne and the Rhineland the last three days are called *drei tolle Tage* (three crazy days) and are climaxed in the famous Rose Monday parades, about five miles long, with huge floats of papier-mâché figures lampooning political figures, brass bands, and "regiments" of the "Fools Guilds" in traditional costumes. One of the highlights of the closing stages is *Weiberfastnacht* (women's carnival), the one-day supremacy of women. They hold boisterous hen parties, stop men on the streets and shower them with kisses, while stay-at-home husbands must cook their own meals. Adultery charges during this period are laughed out of court.

As the old monastic saying goes, "A wine barrel that goes untapped will surely burst."

Shepherds' Dances in Rothenburg-ob-der-Tauber; *Kinderzeche* (children's parade) recalling the repelling of Swedish invaders in Dinkelsbühl; Fishermen's Jousting in Ulm; Goat Auction in Deidesheim; Shepherds' Run in Urach—traditions live on.

Some of the most moving are the traditions observed at Christmas and Easter. There is the famous Advent Wreath, with four candles, which dangles from the ceiling or is placed on a table, to anticipate the coming of the Christ child, with the lighting of one candle on the first Sunday of Advent, and one additional one each week until Christmas; the candle-lighted Christmas tree, which still predominates over electric lights; and *Klöpfelnächte* in Bavaria when masked children sing carols and knock at every door for gifts of apples, nuts, and goodies, and the Epiphany singers go from door to door, carrying a large candle-lighted star commemorating the Magi.

In villages and towns of Swabia it is the custom every Palm Sunday to present a donkey ride portraying Christ's entry into Jerusalem. Elsewhere heavy oaken wheels six to eight feet in diameter, decorated with green branches and stuffed with straw are carted by six horses through the town and up the nearby "Easter Hill." After dusk many thousands of people from near and far watch from the surrounding hills and valleys. At the detonation of an old mortar, the first wheel—its straw set ablaze with torches lit from the "holy fire" (from Good Friday ceremonies)—is released and rolls down the hillside, accompanied by shouts and applause from the crowds. Colored Easter eggs—the custom originates from Germany—and "summerday sticks" (hazel rods decorated with flowers, pretzels, ribbons, and candy) are enjoyed by children.

Oberammergau

Repeatedly over the years there has been talk of filming the world-famous Oberammergau passion play, but so far nothing has ever come of it. Perhaps it is just as well, for literary critics appear to hold the prevailing view that the artistic merits of the play are far below that of its usefulness as a religious—or more bluntly—tourist attraction. A couple of years ago a maverick group of Oberammergauers went off on their own to perform a truncated version of the play in the United States, and it was a complete flop. I received an official letter from the passion play management disassociating themselves from the wildcat performance. The incident only illustrates how much the play's success depends on the picturesque environment of Oberammergau. Once stripped of its romantic setting, there is really very little artistic content to recommend it. The play begins at 8:15 in the morning and ends, broken by a two-hour lunch intermission, at 5:30. In the 1960 performance I was so bored that I left several times and only returned out of a sense of duty for my newspaper for which I was covering the event.

The custom of performing the passion play, a re-enactment of the passion, death, and resurrection of Christ on a huge, open-air stage, backdropped by alpine foothills, dates back to 1634. A terrible epidemic of the plague swept through the area and the Oberammergauers vowed that if spared they would present the Passion of Christ every ten years in gratitude. The town was "miraculously" spared and the vow has been kept for three centuries, interrupted only by World War II.

It has been argued that one should not apply standards of the secular theater or literary norms to Oberammergau, for these are simple peasant people expressing in their naive way the story of the passion. This argument would be more convincing if the town of Oberammergau really were one of naive simple farm folk. But a close inspection reveals that they are a sophisticated business community of the first caliber. This became clear to me when, during the intermission at the 1960 performance I attended, I left the passion play auditorium (the spectator part being under shelter) and saw directly opposite the building a smart little shop with a conspicuous sign reading, "Irmi Dengg—Souvenirs." On entering I was confronted with hundreds of salable pictures of the Oberammergau Virgin Mary, Miss Dengg, and was waited on by the "Blessed Mother" herself. A total of 518,052 spectators saw the play in 1960 at a minimum of five dollars a seat and up. Already in August, 1969, most of the 550,000 tickets for the 98 performances scheduled from May 18 to September 30, 1970, were sold, and officials said they had to turn down more than a million requests for tickets. Expected take: upwards of three million dollars, for a town of 4,800.

No one questions the Oberammergauers' right to earn a fair profit but numerous newspaper critics in Germany and elsewhere, notably Munich's *Süddeutsche Zeitung* have repeatedly charged the Oberammergauers with hypocrisy for holding up the passion play as a religious experience and excusing the shoddy performance on the grounds that it is a heartfelt effort of a simple peasant folk. "Let them make millions for all I care," one German reporter told me, "but if they are going to use the latest modern computing equipment and slick promotion methods, they owe it to the public to provide professional script writing and acting and directing too. There may have been a time when the Oberammergau play really was a deeply moving religious act without a trace of commercialism, but this is no longer the case."

An enterprising movie producer might do better to look behind the scenes at Oberammergau where the real passion play takes place and the villagers live out in real life the roles of Judas, Pilate, the apostles, and the mob.

Every time a "Jesus" or "Mary" changes marital status, buys or sells property, or becomes otherwise involved in the town's affairs, a new dispute breaks out, sides are formed, and woodcarver refuses to talk to woodcarver. Elections are decided on the basis of passion play issues, and at times some of the townspeople come to blows during heated quarrels.

Interest is especially intense some nine months before the beginning of a new passion play series, for of the 1,500 members of the cast only 17 are chosen—by a special committee including the mayor and town pastor—for the lead roles. Strict rules of personal conduct are also required, especially of the "Virgin Mary" who must actually be a virgin and is strictly forbidden to have a boyfriend. As one Mary-candidate put it to a reporter, "I was afraid to walk across the street with a boy for fear I would be disqualified."

The biggest controversy in recent years is the continuing hassle over text revision, not only for artistic reasons, but more importantly over allegedly anti-Semitic content.

During the 1960 performances, numerous critics, notably Robert A. Davis, professor of English at Columbia University, charged the play with anti-Semitic tendencies. Writing in the respected Jewish monthly *Commentary* at the time, Davis also alleged that the woodcarver Georg Johann Lang, who directed the play from 1920 to 1960, was one of the first Oberammergauers to join the Nazi Party, and that more than 60 percent of the town's farmers, woodcarvers, and innkeepers were members.

Erich Lüth, Hamburg's former press officer and a leader in the nationwide association for Jewish-Christian cooperation, has repeatedly spoken out against anti-Semitic lines in the play, which he attended in the company of Konrad Adenauer's son, Max.

The official 1970 English version of the text contains passages like these: "Nathaniel—'Tell the children of Israel . . . *the whole*

81

community shall stone him. . . . ' " Or the cry of the people: "The enemy of Moses is thrown down! Now he receives his reward!" Or, again, Caiphas' remarks: "Truly [through Jesus] *the honor of the nation* is attacked." (Pages 72, 106, and 116, respectively; italics added.)

Oberammergau passion play authorities have repeatedly announced that objectionable passages of the play have been removed or altered. The American Jewish Congress repeated the allegation in November, 1969, after changes were said to have been made, charging that it still contains anti-Semitic passages and asked the West German Government and Julius Cardinal Doepfner, Archbishop of Munich, to urge the Oberammergauers to change the text. Ironically, the 1970 season was opened with a sermon by Cardinal Doepfner, who insisted the play is not anti-Semitic.

Mr. Ernst Zwink, mayor of Oberammergau, insisted that the villagers despised anti-Semitism and that there are no longer anti-Semitic passages in the play.

In the foreword to the official 1970 Oberammergau Passion Play Text Book, Father Max Bertl, the parish priest, wrote:

> It was God's inscrutable decision as to when, where and how the redemption of mankind was to take place through Jesus Christ. This divine plan selected that area which today we call the Holy Land. The inhabitants of this land became participants in the trial of Jesus. "The Jewish authorities and those who followed their lead pressed for the death of Christ; still, what happened in His Passion cannot be charged against all the Jews, without distinction, then alive, nor against the Jews of today." (Vatican II: Declaration on the relation of the Church to non-Christian religions.) Jesus Christ took His Mother from among the Jewish people, had a small group of faithful followers from the Jewish people around the cross, gathered around Him men from the Jewish people, who later suffered pain and death for His sake. Others of the Jewish people met in front of Pilate's courtroom, demanding the death of Jesus with the cry, "Crucify Him!" Who could and should see in these the whole Jewish people? Must we not, rather, regard them as representatives of all mankind, who by their sins brought about the Lord's death?

The efforts to replace the colorless text, written in 1860 by a local priest, Alois Daisenberger, with a rediscovered play written in 1750 by a Benedictine monk, Ferdinand Rosner, have been unsuccessful. In fact, Hans Schwaighofer, a teacher of wood-carving who played Judas in 1960, resigned as director of the 1970 play in a hassle over the text change. The Rosner play would have satisfied artistic standards and was recommended by no less a person than the distinguished Munich composer Carl Orff, who was to have composed music especially for it. But it is hard to argue against success and the villagers voted over-whelmingly to keep the Daisenberger text. The new director, Anton Preisinger, a hotel owner who portrayed Jesus in 1950 and 1960, and a powerful village figure, said that "Rosner is too long-winded and not as dramatic. We don't attempt to create art that you can see in perfection elsewhere. For us this tradition is a duty. You know, the Bavarian is a very baroque person."

The villagers even rejected a new version written by the Reverend Stephan Schaller, a Benedictine monk and high school principal at the nearby monastery of Ettal, commissioned by Cardinal Doepfner, although a few passages of Father Schaller's version have been inserted into the Daisenberger text.

Veteran observers believe that the patchwork alterations have done little to prevent the impression that the play portrays the Jews as a fiendish, bloodthirsty group from whom the "kingdom of God will be taken away."

On the other hand, a number of Jewish spectators in 1960 and 1970 were quoted in German and American newspapers as finding nothing offensive in the play, and one couple invited "Judas" to visit them in Israel.

Just shortly before the 1970 play opened, the weekly news magazine *Der Spiegel* commented, in reference to the abundance of bearded extras all over Oberammergau, "This would be a nice place to produce the hippie musical, *Hair!*"

Dueling

Incredible as it sounds, the practice of *Mensur* or student dueling is not only still alive in Germany, but it is compulsory in some student organizations. Although banned by Allied occu-pation powers in Germany after World War II and still banned in East Germany today, the practice was revived officially in 1951 and in 1969 the Bundestag lifted penalties for dueling in the newly adopted legal code. Perhaps they did so in resignation since dueling is usually practiced in secret by the student fraternities and was hardly ever apprehended even when it was forbidden.

Until now, it has been standard practice at the 115 fraternities of the *Deutsche Burschenschaft,* Germany's oldest student fraternal association, that every student member be required at least once to fight a so-called "sharp match" with a rapier, which inevitably ends in some bloodletting, to be accepted as a full *Bursche* (regular guy) or senior member of a fraternity. Scars on the faces of older German men are fairly frequent and used to be regarded as a badge of honor, since the custom is supposed to show manliness, honor, and courage. Usually a duel is fought with a member of another fraternity. The contestants are dressed in padded aprons, arm protectors, leather collars, a nosepiece, and goggles, so that there really is no danger of serious injury. A match lasts from twenty-four to thirty rounds, and the whole point is not to flinch (move the feet), which is regarded as a dishonor.

Founded at Jena University during the Napoleonic wars in 1815, the *Burschenschaft* originally was a political movement devoted to the unification of German principalities. Over the years the *Burschenschaft* developed strong conservative characteristics, especially among the aristocracy, and was notorious for antiworker and anti-Semitic and anti-intellectual tendencies.

Some 5,500 active members belong to the *Burschenschaft* today, plus an additional 30,000 alumni. The fraternities hold many events, including duels, drinking sessions, with the participants wearing small-peaked caps, colorful sashes, uniforms, and leather boots, and singing old student songs.

Recently, however, there has been a liberal trend urging the substitution of parachute jumping, glider-flying, or some other modern form of courage in substitution for the old-fashioned dueling. To all appearances, the days of the sword and scar are numbered.

Nobility

Romance dies hard in Germany. Although royalty officially went out with the Kaiser, there is a deep and lingering hunger for everything connected with nobility. Whenever a "royal" wedding takes place anywhere in the world, German newspapers and television give it downright smotherage. During the state visit of the Shah of Iran and his young Empress in 1967, they received press and TV coverage far out of proportion to Persia's significance. A similar state visit by a nonroyal head would receive only a fraction of such coverage. Several big circulation newspapers, such as *Das Neue Blatt* thrive almost exclusively on gossip about celebrities, with at least half of their space devoted to royalty.[3]

In my more than fifteen-year association with Germany I have encountered this adulation of nobility again and again. I was appalled in one large West German city to see a Jesuit priest driving around in a big Mercedes, while his confreres in the very same religious institution had to share the use of a Volkswagen for transportation. The reason, I learned from his own lips, is that he happens to be a "count" and some wealthy matron donated the car to him. While the other priests were called simply "Father So-and-so," this priest was constantly addressed *"Graf* [Count]" and God help you if you forgot it! I once asked the Count-Jesuit if he didn't get tired of always explaining about the Mercedes, since the Jesuits take a vow of poverty, but apparently he took my remark amiss.

There is still importance attached in some circles to the "von" preceding some German names, which implies a former noble blood-tie. A leading Bonn politician, Baron Karl Theodor von und zu Guttenberg, former state secretary to the federal chancellor's office and an official of the Christian Social Union (CSU) insists on his title. As if the "von" weren't bad enough that "und zu" bugged me so much I even looked it up. And I found out that it means that the Baron is not only "von" (*i.e.,* "from") Guttenberg, but also "zu" (*i.e.,* "at"—still living at) the original noble Guttenberg palace. As the saying goes, it takes all kinds. . . .

It is of course common knowledge that the British royal family is of German descent and that German royalty has intermarried into numerous foreign courts. West Germany's unique system of a ceremonial president, with virtually no power, complementing the chancellor, who actually rules, is a modern substitute for a king. The Federal president functions much in the manner of the chairman-of-the-board kings of other countries, a kind of TV monarch who represents the country at state functions, dedications, and banquets.

The Queen Mother of Greece, Frederika, a German-born princess, was reportedly a power behind the throne of the mild-mannered King Constantine, now living in exile, and she has been criticized for her membership in the Nazi youth movement while in Germany. Otto von Hapsburg, son of the last Austrian Emperor, Karl I, has been a controversial problem for Austrian regimes for the past two decades, lives in Pöcking in Bavaria, and is greatly loved, celebrated, and admired by some older Germans.

It has been said that the Germans need a king as a reassuring parent who is always present, telling them that in spite of their mistakes they are good children after all. Shorn now of the military ambitions and the political self-seeking that made Germany the scourge of Europe, they appear to seek comfort in the continuity and magic of a nobility that has all but vanished but whose aura somehow hangs on with incredible tenacity.

◄6►

THE ROOTS OF GERMAN ANTI-SEMITISM

WHEN YOU STEP out of the main train terminal in Cologne, you need not inquire at the tourist information office nor look at a city map to find its famous and ancient cathedral. You have but to raise your head. There it looms in all its magnificence before you, truly a testimony of the great age of faith that was the Middle Ages.

But the splendid steeples towering into the sky high over the Rhine also point to a long history of persecution of the Jews under Christian auspices. Long before Hitler stood shivering on Munich street corners with the frenzied zeal of a holy roller, preaching his gospel of race hatred, the soil of anti-Semitism had been carefully tilled by the Christian churches.

The Cologne Cathedral itself provides an example. Imbedded in the inside wall of the southern steeple is a stone tablet, scarcely visible, on which certain rights are guaranteed to Cologne Jews. The tablet, the famous *Judenprivileg* of Archbishop Engelbert II, dated 1266, guaranteed Jewry of the Middle Ages, above all, the right to bury their dead without hinderance, and the right not to be charged any more customs duty or road taxes than the Christians. It also protected them against foreign money lenders who wished to settle in Cologne in order to ruin Jewish businesses. The "privilege" was an integral part of the legal structure of the Middle Ages and was continually renewed and continually disregarded.

If the "privilege" testifies to the efforts on the part of the church authorities to mitigate the un-Christian actions toward the Jews, it also testifies to the fact that anti-Semitism was a common practice of Christians. And it was the Jews of Cologne—easily the oldest Jewish congregation on German soil—who first suffered at the hands of Christians in the pogrom that accompanied the first Crusade.

As far back as the fourth century, through the conclusion of a peace treaty between the Roman state and the Church, the Jews were regarded as political opponents of the Christian state. Indeed, Emperor Constantine promulgated an edict on October 18, 315, which threatened that anyone who would throw stones at converts from Judaism to Christianity would be "tossed into flaming fire and together with his accomplices, burned to death. Moreover, whoever of the populace shall join this abominable religion or participate in their gatherings, shall receive deserved punishment."

The denial of civil rights to Jews became commonplace in the centuries that followed. In the Theodosian (439) and Justinian (534) codes the treatment of Jews was prescribed in detail and they were clearly marked as an inferior class of people, devoid of political rights.

Thus the Code of Emperor Theodosius of January 31, 439, proclaimed that "no Jew should be allowed to receive office or honors, he should not be allowed to take part in the administration of the city. . . . *It is an insult to our Faith* that [the Jews] . . . should because of the authority of a position have power to make judgments and decisions at will on matters pertaining to Christians, indeed even pertaining to the bishops of our holy religion. For the same reason we forbid any synagogue to erect any new buildings . . . ." (Italics added.)

Between the fourth and seventh centuries the ecclesiastical councils issued humane decrees regarding the Jews, which were not, however, very well observed. Pope Gregory the Great (590-604) established precedents for subsequent papal policy toward the Jews. He forbade every act of violence against them, prohibited enforced conversion, although he recommended the conversion of Jews by "gentle persuasion." Emperor Charlemagne (768-814) likewise permitted Jews to live in his kingdom and was kindly disposed toward them.

The flowering of German cities in the tenth and eleventh centuries induced many Jews to settle in these communities. To a certain extent they were actually invited by the city fathers and given special privileges. Numerous Jewish communities won recognition for their cultural and business contributions. Jews in Speyer were granted advantages, notably by Bishop Reudiger, that they could find in no other German city. And throughout this period a number of bishops were much loved by the Jews for their humane policies. There are existing records, dated 1015, showing that Bishop Adalbert II of Metz (984-1004) was daily mourned by the Jews of his region eleven years after his death.

With the coming of the Crusades, however, a wave of anti-Semitism broke out all over Germany. Synagogues were set on fire and thousands of Jews were massacred by Crusaders in Cologne, Neuss, Xanten, Kempen, and other cities on the lower Rhine, as well as throughout the German territories.

Scholars attribute this outburst of fanaticism to several factors. The immediate cause was the hysterical fear that Islam would engulf Christian civilization from Asia Minor to Spain, which led the panic-stricken Christians to strike out blindly at all non-Christians and especially at the—to them—"foreign" Jews in their midst.

Since the Jews were already regarded as enemies of Christianity and were theologically held accountable for the crucifixion of Jesus, an allegation commonplace during the Middle Ages, the Christian fanaticism took on all the aspects of a religious act of purification.

Not least, of course, there was the economic or scapegoat motive. In the course of the eleventh century the Jews had become economically prosperous, and this ironically as a result of the strict ecclesiastical regulations restricting the professional activities of Jews, compelling them to specialize in money-lending. Since the Christians were forbidden by injunctions to profit from usury the Jews became wealthy by default. Small wonder that the Christians' envy easily transformed into hatred, which was not helped by the fact that the spiritual warriors for the honor of God, the protection of the Church, and the terror of the unbelievers, as slogans of the day described them, owed vast sums of money and interest to the hated Jews.

When in 1096, the same year that the first Crusade burst like fire on the earth, a severe crop failure caused widespread famine, the masses vented their wrath by plundering the ghettos. The massacre of the Jews that followed in the wake of the Crusades caused a mass migration of the Jews toward the East—Bohemia and Poland—where centuries later the Nazis were to catch up with them and names like Auschwitz were to become bywords.

The following historical account, quoted by historian Dr. Ernst Ludwig Ehrlich, is typical of the countless incidents of enforced baptism on the part of fanatical Crusaders, even though such was forbidden by Pope Calistus II:

> As they [the Crusaders] neared Trier, some of the Jews who lived there plunged a knife into the bodies of their children, saying that

they had to send them to Abraham's bosom, so that they won't become a football for the fury of the Christians. Some of the women filled their brassieres with rocks and jumped from the bridge into the river. The rest, who still regarded life as worth living, hastily scraped together their personal belongings and fled to the palace, where Archbishop Eglibert lived, and with tears streaming down their faces pleaded for protection. He took advantage of the situation to admonish them to convert. . . . A rabbi by the name of Micha stepped forward and begged the archbishop . . . "Baptize us quickly so that we can escape from persecution!". . . . But a few years later they fell away [from the Church]. . . .[1]

During the second Crusade a monk by the name of Radulf, a pious but poorly educated man, went up and down the Rhine, preaching in behalf of the Crusades, urging that the Jews living in that region must be killed as enemies of the Christian religion. These teachings were heeded in many cities and towns throughout France and Germany. St. Bernard of Clairvaux, founder of the Cistercian Order, warned against the teachings of Radulf and sent messengers to various parts of France and Germany with letters in which he clearly "proved" that, according to the Scriptures, the dispersion—not the killing—of Jews was the proper punishment.

In July, 1236, Friedrich II used the expression *servi camerae nostrae* in reference to the Jews who were, it is true, under his special protection, but with this humiliating designation as chamber servants. Friedrich II thereafter extended the *Judenprivileg* that his predecessor, Friedrich I, had applied to the city of Worms, to all of Germany, and for the first time officially designated the Jews as an inferior class of the population.

When in 1348-49 the bubonic plague broke out all over Europe, the Jews were accused of having poisoned the wells. In spite of the pleas of Pope Clement VI that the pestilence was the curse of God and that the Jews themselves were victims of the plague, many thousands of Jews were massacred. In Silesia, where the plague had not even appeared at that time, 1,349 Jews were slaughtered in Breslau. More than 350 Jewish congregations from the Lake of Constance to Prussia, from Flanders to Silesia were destroyed. Tens of thousands of Jews were murdered. Even in regions containing no Jews but those who had already been converted to Christianity, the baptized Jews, were burned to death.

Throughout the Middle Ages and the centuries that followed, the *Judenordnungen* (Jewish regulations) of the cities became more and more numerous and the list of prohibitions even longer. From 1372 to 1427, except for a short interruption, no Jew was permitted to live in Cologne. Every Jewish merchant passing through the city was required to be outside the city walls before sundown. Even the famous guilds, so exemplary in other respects, discriminated against Jews, whose competition they feared. Between 1400 and 1410 the reigning dukes of the Palatinate and Bavaria issued decrees prohibiting "forever" the residence or even temporary presence of Jews.

It was otherwise in the territories of the prince-bishops, who continued to permit the Jews to settle, though under certain discriminatory restrictions. Jews were allowed to remain only on condition that they observe the rigorous *Judenordnungen,* which allowed the members of the suppressed minority to engage only in a few limited activities: moneylending, or trading in grain, livestock, wine, and jewelry.

Thus the daily activities of the Jews were considerably circumscribed. In order to make sure that the Jews would comply with these regulations, they were required to dress in such a way as to be recognizable as Jews. Thus Hitler's decree ordering all Jews in the Third Reich to display the Star of David on their external clothing was really not a very original idea. Pope Innocent III in 1215 had issued regulations requiring Jews to wear identifying garb. This custom spread widely so that in the middle of the thirteenth century, which some Catholic scholars unaccountably used to call "the greatest of centuries," the practice was enforced throughout France and had spread to Germany in the fifteenth century. According to a decree of the city of Cologne of July 8, 1404:

> All Jews, male and female, young and old, who live in Cologne or come to Cologne as strangers, must wear such clothing that one can recognize that they are Jews, in the following manner: Coat sleeves shall not be longer than half an ell. Shirt and dress collars may not be wider than a finger's thickness. And no fur linings may be worn externally....Coats must be fringed and reach at least to the calves. ... They may not wear gray shoes. ... They may not cut their hair past the lobes of the ears. ... Jewish women may not wear rings during the working day that weigh more than three guldens. ... They may not wear on work days gilded belts and may not wear any belts

91

more than two fingers thickness. . . . During Holy Week and on Easter
Sunday they must stay at home. . . . They may not at any time enter
the vestibule of the town hall. . . except when called by the councilers
to go there. . . .[2]

The rules and regulations governing the daily lives of the Jews
became so unbearable that Pope Martin V (1417-1431) found it
necessary again and again to raise his voice in protest against the
anti-Semitic utterances of Christian preachers, but to little avail.
It became commonplace for preachers to indulge in anti-Semitic
polemics.

When, with the establishment of a Christian moneylending
system, the Jewish monopoly in banking was broken, Jews were
hated more than ever. Instead of rejoicing that Christians could
now compete with the Jews in banking, Christian craftsmen and
merchants now feared Jewish entry into business and trade. And
the anti-Semitic sermons of the preachers gave them a convenient
moral crutch for venting their scorn against the Jews.

In a proclamation of July 5, 1498, Emperor Maximilian I
(1493-1519) banished the Jews from the city of Nuremberg.
Some Jews migrated to Frankfurt, others went to Prague. By the
end of the fifteenth century and the beginning of the sixteenth,
the Jews had disappeared from nearly all cities of the empire.
The greatest number went to Poland, others to Bohemia and
Hungary. Since Germany was not a nation in its own right but
was splintered into hundreds of duchies, a number of Jews were
able to remain in midget states in southern and western
Germany. The three archbishops of the Rhine banished them
from all the cities in their territories, but did permit them to live
in the surrounding countryside.

The irony of all this persecution is that throughout the history
of Germany the Jews were felt to be indispensable in many areas.
About 1,000 Jews lived in the Cologne region between 1500 and
1800, especially in Deutz and the electoral capital of Bonn,
where they served archbishops as court managers, court economists, and court physicians. The Jewish physicians of Deutz, who
had studied mostly in Holland at Leyden, or in the small Prussian
Brandenburg University of Duisburg, were noted for their great
ability, and were called in for advice again and again by Cologne
burghers, in spite of the admonition of the city council. The
Jewish tribunal of Cologne was regarded as the highest legal

authority in the Roman Empire; the saying "the wisemen of Cologne" was known all over Europe. Numerous cities and monasteries, bishops and archbishops, and even the kings of Denmark and Sweden were indebted to the Cologne Jews.

The French Revolution finally brought freedom to the Jews in the Rhineland and paved the way toward civil rights. In 1797 the prohibition to work and live in Cologne was abolished. In 1801 the first Jewish congregation was formed, which five years later included 124 persons. Even though the officials of the city, which in the meantime had become Prussian, only reluctantly admitted Jews, the number of Jewish citizens increased steadily.

In the revolution year of 1848 Jews were finally allowed to hold public office, after the Cologne banker Solomon Oppenheim as early as 1822 managed to become a member of the Cologne Chamber of Commerce. Oppenheim, whose firm by 1810 had an operating capital of a quarter of a million thalers, was the first Jew who was able to obtain a position of eminence in Cologne. His two sons, Abraham and Simon, were among the best known philanthropists of the city. Abraham Oppenheim was one of the leaders in the development of a railroad network in the Rhineland. As for the many other great German Jews, whose names and stories are already familiar—Heinrich Heine, Albert Einstein, Felix Mendelssohn—well, they belong to history.

To history belongs also, alas, certain anti-Semitic writings and outbursts of no less a person than the great Reformer Martin Luther (1483-1546). In the tradition of his time, he likewise held the theological position that the Jews rejected Christ and through their very existence as Jews they confirm this rejection. At first, the young Luther took a kindlier view of the Jews and regarded them as brothers in mankind under God, who like all other men are called by grace and salvation. "If one will help them," he wrote in his early years, "one must exercise . . . the law of Christian love on them."

But Luther's love for the Jews was with an eye toward conversion. When he realized that kind treatment of the Jews did not result in the hoped-for conversions, the chief reason—for him—for treating them in a friendly manner vanished. In deep disappointment, Luther altered his attitude. Convinced of the stubbornness of the Jews, he became imbued with what he thought was the impassioned anger of God against Israel and finally rejected them, even defending his position with theological arguments.

The following remarks, written by Luther in 1543, a few years before his death, were published in the official brochure which was distributed in connection with the Tenth Evangelical *Kirchentag* (national church rally), held in Berlin in July, 1961, as a sign of public confession of the Evangelical Church for sins against the Jews:

> What then should we Christians do about this rejected, damned folk, the Jews . . . . I will give my dependable advice. First, set their synagogues or schools on fire. . . . Then break up and destroy their homes. . . . Third, take all their prayer books and Talmudic writings in which such idolatry and lies and curses and defamatory things are taught. Fourth, let their rabbis be forbidden, as they value their lives, to teach henceforth. . . .Put them under a roof or stable, like the gypsies. . . .Let them wallow in misery and captivity as they incessantly lament and complain to God about us. . . .Do not dispute much with Jews about our Articles of Faith, for they are taught thus from their youth. . .so there is no hope there. . . .They must be forced through their misery. . .to profess that the Messias has come and He is our Jesus. . . .[3]

Four centuries later, Nazi leader Julius Streicher was able to justify the Nazi atrocities by declaring that he merely carried out the instructions of the great Reformer Martin Luther.

WHAT EVER HAPPENED TO PRUSSIA?

RIGHT IN THE middle of Berlin stands a monument that more than any other structure in Germany sums up the country's tormented history for more than 250 years. It is the Brandenburg Gate, and its meaning as a symbol is full of the contradictions that characterize the divided nation.

It faces East Berlin. But it leads to West Berlin.

It was the rallying point of the anti-Communist Soviet Zone uprising of 1953, in commemoration of which West Germany observes the 17th of June as a national holiday. And before the erection of the Wall, it was the literal as well as symbolic exit for thousands of refugees to West Germany.

It is the main link of the Wall, and it stands inside the Soviet sector of Berlin. But it is considered by West Germany to be one of its most cherished symbols, equivalent for West Germans to the American Statue of Liberty in emotional significance.

Built in imitation of the propylaeam, the vestibule of the Acropolis—a kind of squared-off Arch of Triumph—the ostentatious and somewhat pompous-looking monument witnessed Napoleon's triumphant entry into Berlin in 1806, the cossacks of the Czar, and the victorious Stalin Red Army in 1945.

Yet it is one of the few war-damaged historical structures of East Berlin that the GDR has restored.

It is ironical that this great symbol of a new, free Germany was originally constructed in 1791 in honor and memory of King Frederick the Great of Prussia and was for years the symbol of Prussia and subsequently of imperial Germany.

Today Prussia no longer exists. In 1947, the Allies, haunted by the image of "militaristic" Prussia, abolished the old Prussian province. Its former territories were distributed among all except four states in the four occupied zones of Germany, while East Prussia together with Silesia and Pomerania were placed under Polish and Soviet administration. And Königsberg, the city where Prussian kings were crowned, now bears the name of Kaliningrad.

Nevertheless, there is still widespread fascination with the word Prussia and all that it stood for. Indeed, the Germans cannot be understood without knowing something about the Prussian way of life. For while the Allies destroyed Prussia, they did not destroy many of the traces of the Prussian State and Prussian character and mentality, good and bad, that remain to this day.

The word "Prussia" is usually associated with purely negative concepts, such as autocracy, absolutism, and militarism. And the Prussian way of life is widely regarded by historians as one of the primary historical developments paving the way for Hitler. However, there are also reputable historians who attempt to account for Prussianism in a more favorable light.

It is true that until well into the last century, Prussia was an "absolute monarchy." It must be remembered that democracy as we know it is a new concept. It is not quite fair to measure a predemocratic state with the yardstick of twentieth century popular rule. The old Prussian doctrine, which seems paternalistic to us, was "all *for* the people, but nothing *through* the people." It was unthinkable to Prussian kings that the people themselves could be sovereign. Moreover, the office of ruler was deeply rooted in religious belief and held that governing was not just a means of enjoying power but was a duty and a gift of God. A deep sense of obedience inculcated by the Protestant reformers Calvin and Luther, who stressed subservience to the *Obrigkeiten* (secular authorities) prevailed.

Prussianism was characterized by a rigid caste system, with fixed rights and duties spelled out for every class.

The ruling and privileged class was the nobility. Strictly speaking, the nobility as such had no political rights, but it was an unwritten law that they alone were entitled to high military and political appointments. Their positions were not necessarily regarded as primarily a means of obtaining and exercising power or accumulating wealth, but were also endowed with an almost sacramental mystique or *Pflichtgefühl* (sense of high honor and duty) which has become deeply ingrained in the German character. (Adenauer once remarked, "When I die I want it to be said of me, *'Er hat seine Pflicht getan'*—He did his duty.")

This profound sense of duty may throw some light on the blind devotion to duty that led to the fanatical allegiance of some of the noblest and most refined officers to Hitler. The almost religious association of office and honor also helps explain why the Prussian nobility bitterly opposed reforms that would have lightened their duties.

The composite picture of the noble class with its egocentric concern for caste interests remains unattractive. This goes so far as even now and then to override the traditional loyalty to the king, an attitude satirized in an oft-quoted couplet:

> Unser König absolut
> Wenn er uns den Willen tut.
> (Let our king be absolute,
> So long as he does our will.)

Then there is the arrogance of a militaristic caste that recognized only martial values.

The lowest Prussian caste was the peasants, who were technically slaves, even though their lot under a paternalistic feudal system was probably a good deal better than that of the Negro slaves in pre-Civil-War United States. Until their emancipation in 1810 more than half of all Prussian citizens were practically the personal property of the land owners (*Junkers*) and even long after that were in *de facto* bondage to their masters. It was from this class that soldiers were drafted into the army.

Special privileges were granted to the middle class, the professions, and the merchants, who were excluded from higher government office but also exempted from military service.

Moreover, the Prussian middle class supplied the rank-and-file civil servants whose efficiency and loyalty became legendary all over the world. And they, together with the highly-disciplined standing army, formed the backbone of the Prussian state.

Paradoxically, this regimented and absolute monarchy also permitted considerable academic and religious freedom and gave birth to an unprecedented flowering of cultural and academic life.

Territorially the word "Prussia" meant different things in different periods of history. It should be remembered that Prussia was not Germany or a part of Germany but first a kingdom of its own, and only much later did it become a state within Germany. Its greatest personality, Frederick II, better known as Frederick the Great, was never a king of Germany, which didn't exist as such in his day, but king of Prussia.[1]

Prussian history may be said to begin in 1417, when Frederick von Hohenzollern, the *Burggraf* of Nuremberg, usurped the province of Mark Brandenburg from Emperor Sigismund I. This territory became the core of what was later to expand into the Kingdom of Prussia.

Just as you cannot separate German history from Prussian history, so you cannot separate Prussian history from the Hohenzollern family. By waging a series of successful wars of conquest—the normal method of diplomacy all over Europe at that time—by clever marriages, intrigues, and fortunate inheritances, astute management and political shrewdness, the Hohenzollerns gradually developed the poor and underdeveloped province into one of the mightiest states of Eurpoe. The family produced an illustrious array of eleven *Kurfürsten* (prince-electors, *i.e.*, princes who had the privilege of electing the emperor), six kings, and three emperors.

Some of the Prussian rulers who stand out are: The Great Elector, Frederick Wilhelm (1640-1688); Frederick Wilhelm I (1713-1740), whose father crowned himself king of Prussia in 1701; his son, Frederick the Great (1740-1786); and Wilhelm I, who became emperor of Germany at its founding as a modern state in 1871.

Frederick Wilhelm I had the nickname *Der Soldatenkönig* (the Soldier King). He was the actual founder of the famous-notorious Prussian Army, which was noted for its intensive drilling and rigid discipline. And he also reorganized the state along military lines. He was an extremely robust, tough, and often cruel leader and was notoriously stingy. One of his eccentricities, which is an example of his military obsession, was his "hobby" of finding unusually tall men to serve on the palatial guard, *Die Langen Kerls* (the tall fellows).

Frederick Wilhelm I represented one prototype of the Hohenzollern family. With his spartan, severe, and disciplined character, he represented Prussianism at its worst.

There was, however, another type that emerged from the Hohenzollerns, while not always innocent of such nasty habits as waging wars of conquest, nevertheless also noted for their intellectual, artistic, humane qualities and sometimes too for romantic and ostentatious predilections.

To this latter group belonged Prussianism's greatest personality, Frederick the Great.

He won his nickname "The Great" in early life by reason of

military conquests: in two wars with Austria (then ruled by Empress Maria Theresa), Frederick conquered Silesia. In the Seven Years' War, he fought with England against the Austrians, Saxons, French, Spanish, Swedes, and Russians—and won.

Although he devoted much of his time and budget to the military, he is credited with a great deal of social reform, some of whose benefits remain to this day.

Only three days after taking possession of his throne, at the age of twenty-eight, Frederick the Great abolished torture, and three years thereafter, public ecclesiastical penance. This was in 1740, thirty-two years before torture was abolished in Austria and at least a hundred years before it was abolished in Italy and France.

Frederick the Great also restricted the arbitrariness of monarchs. In his political testament of 1752 he wrote, "Before the tribunal the sovereign should remain silent and only the law shall speak." And in the Testament of 1768 he wrote, "The law alone shall rule. The duty of the ruler is limited to its protection."

His reforms, which later became the general legal code of the land, were characterized by the concepts of secularization, humanization, and demythologization in the sense of rational testing, *i.e.,* to test everything by reason.

If he was nationalistic, he was so only in terms of his own, individual state, Prussia, and not in regard to greater Germany. He promoted industrial and agricultural activity, encouraged innovations, and reformed elementary education. He waged his own version of a "War on Poverty" which included legal aid for the poor. His version of freedom of speech and religion would be restrictive in our view; nevertheless, his modified liberalization policies in those areas were sensational in his day. His motto was, *"Jeder soll nach seiner façon selig werden* [everyone should be happy in his own fashion]." However, much of his religious tolerance was actually just plain indifference.

However that may be, he promoted the arts, cultivated an atmosphere of free expression that produced an undreamed of flowering in literature and music. Among his friends were Voltaire, Rousseau, and Johann Sebastian Bach. He was a composer himself and no mean flute player, author, and poet.

It may surprise some readers to be told that this greatest Prussian of them all could not write or speak German properly. Like all the nobility and elite of his time throughout Europe and even Russia, he wrote and spoke in French. He lured French celebrities to his court, and poured the vials of his scorn upon the incipient classical literature of his native country.

In later life Frederick the Great became more and more isolated and bitter. His parsimony and fiery temper lost him most of his friends. He died surrounded only by his servants and a few pets. His last words were an expression of solicitude for one of his dogs.

The Hohenzollern dynasty came to an end with Germany's defeat in World War I and the abdication of Kaiser Wilhelm II in November, 1918. An intelligent, refined man, he lived in a dream world of royal romance and splendor, oblivious that the age of kings was gone. He died in exile in the Netherlands in 1941 and the great Prussian age died with him.

The evaluation of Prussia and Prussianism defies analysis. It was indeed an absolute monarchy, but it was not a totalitarian dictatorship either.

It produced philosophers like Immanuel Kant, Hegel, Schelling; scientists like Leibniz, von Humboldt; historians like Leopold von Ranke; democratic-minded political reformers like Freiherr von Stein, von Hardenberg, and Scharnhorst; poets like Heinrich von Kleist, Josef von Eichendorff, Theodor Fontane, E. T. A. Hoffmann, and Walter Rathenau. The great Evangelical theologian, Dietrich Bonhoeffer, who perished in a concentration camp, and the late Fritz Erler, one of postwar Germany's most brilliant and respected parliamentarians, were both of Prussian background.

It was a Prussian officer, Baron Friedrich Wilhelm von Steuben, who had fought in the Seven Years' War alongside Frederick the Great, who transformed George Washington's ragged and demoralized 9,000 troops at Valley Forge into a crack fighting unit. The idea of a "general staff" also came from Prussia.

But Prussia also produced, alas, philosophers like Johann Gottlieb Fichte, the acknowledged leader of intellectuals of his day, who frequently raised his powerful voice denouncing Jewry as a State within a State, and Jewish theology as incompatible with civil loyalty. In response to this ideology, a successful and respected lawyer in Trier, Hirschel Marx, going a step further than his rabbinical father who had dropped the original family name of Levi, changed his name to Heinrich. And, although Protestants were a small minority in Trier, he and his family were baptized in 1824 into the Lutheran Church. In joining the State

Church of Prussia, Marx wished to emphasize his devotion to Prussian institutions. His eldest son, Karl, the father of modern Communism, thus emerged from a decidedly Prussian climate.

Countess Marion Dönhoff, editor-in-chief of the respected West German weekly *Die Zeit,* herself of Prussian background, eloquently defends some elements of Prussianism. She has repeatedly pointed out that "Hitler was no Prussian," but rather the antithesis of everything Prussian, "a man without restraint, without tolerance, and without self-discipline," lacking those virtues which were also a part of the Prussian way of life.

How different, she wrote in one editorial, are the words of Frederick the Great who wrote, at the age of thirty-two, to the Duke Karl Eugen von Württemberg, "Do not think that the province of Württemberg was created for your benefit, but realize that Providence permitted you to enter the world in order to make people happy."[2]

Prussianism and socialism go hand in hand. In East Germany there is in this sense more Prussianism than in commercialized West Germany. Dönhoff thinks that there are some things to be learned from Prussianism: in an age characterized by pseudo-brilliance, television-image, status symbols, and public relations, a bit more independent thinking, a lot more of doing things for their own sake, not always asking about a thing's usefulness, less concern for self-interest, or one's "image" is called for.

But some Germans reject Dönhoff's concept of Prussianism as too romanticized. Hitler, says the Hamburg author Erich Kuby, would never have had a chance if Prussianized Germany did not pave the way for him. He argues that it is precisely the virtues rather than the vices of Prussianism which contributed to Hitler. Prussianism's paternalism never allowed the people to develop a political consciousness and responsibility. *"Ruhe ist der Bürger's erste Pflicht* [Peace and quiet, *i.e.*, order and obedience, are the citizen's first duty]" was a common Prussian slogan. Prussianism, Kuby pointed out, "had private virtues, but no binding ideals, which might have relevated the attainment and exercise of power. Moreover, the virtues had no other purpose than to serve the expansion of power."[3]

Clearly, Prussianism alone by no means accounts for either the good or bad elements that have shaped the German character. But for better or for worse it played a significant, perhaps decisive role in making the Germans what they are.

◄8►

"DEUTSCHLAND ÜBER ALLES"

Von der Maas bis an die Memel,
Von der Etsch bis an den Belt;
Deutschland, Deutschland über alles,
über alles in der Welt.

NO OTHER HYMN in history has stirred up so much controversy as the German national anthem of *Deutschlandlied*, particularly its first verse quoted above. "Maas," "Memel," and "Etsch" are rivers and "Belt" is part of the straits that connect the Baltic and the North Sea, north of Denmark. Today the Maas flows through France, Belgium, and Holland. The Memel forms the border between former East Prussia and the Soviet Union. And the Etsch (Adige) lies in the former Austrian territory of South Tyrol in northern Italy. Add the words, "Germany above all, above everything else in the world," and the hymn obviously sounds like the most intense possible rallying call for nationalistic aggression and expansionism.

Although this interpretation unquestionably was applicable during the Third Reich, the hymn originally had quite a different meaning. "Rule Britannia, Britannia rule the waves" taken literally could also have a very expansionist meaning. Yet there is seldom if ever any outcry about this British hymn.

The poem with the much misunderstood phrase *"Deutschland über alles"* was written in 1841 by the German poet August Heinrich Hoffmann von Fallersleben. He intended it as an appeal to his countrymen to put the love of Germany "above everything else"—that is, above their allegiance to the country's numerous principalities. At that time, most other big states had already been unified, while Germany was still split up into twenty-two individual states, including tiny principalities and free cities, only loosely united in the *Deutscher Bund* (German Federation) at the Vienna Congress of 1815. The biggest German states were then Austria and Prussia. The states forming this federation had once

102

all been parts of the former German empire, and together they covered a much larger area than what remains of the two Germanys today. Thus the rivers and the Belt mentioned in the hymn actually did flow through or border on territory that belonged to the former Holy Roman Empire of the German nation.

Such an all-German concept was considered subversive in large parts of the country, as the many kings and princes reigning over the many states knew that the increasing national spirit threatened their thrones. In fact, Hoffmann von Fallersleben penned the famous-notorious lines while in exile from Prussia, on the North Sea island of Helgoland, then owned by Britain.

A liberal publisher—who was also the first to print the works of Heinrich Heine—brought out the poem less than a week after it was written, in Hamburg, under the title "Song of the Germans." It was set to music that had been composed earlier by Franz Joseph Haydn, and had become the melody of the Austrian anthem, *"Gott erhalte Franz den Kaiser* [God Save the Emperor Francis]."

To transfer Haydn's composition from the anthem of the Austrian empire to a new song for the Germans was a daring political affront to the established order and a challenge to the post-1815 conditions in central Europe. Liberal ideas and the goal of national unity had suffered severe setbacks in the wake of the Vienna Congress.

Hoffmann belonged to the circle of liberals that was working against the so-called Restoration, that is, the attempt by the Austrian chancellor Metternich and some German princes to restore old, regional ruling houses. Many Germans and Austrians felt the ferment of revolution. Under these circumstances, the urge toward German nationhood came to be closely identified with demands for liberal reform.

The Hamburg publisher Campe had commissioned Hoffmann to write words for what would be called "unpolitical songs." But the real intent of course was highly political. Hoffmann wrote his *Deutschland* lines on August 26th. By October the "Song of the Germans" was being sung at public performances in Hamburg.

Hoffmann was discharged from his post as professor of German literature at Breslau for what authorities called "demogogic activity." His song, in fact, helped to nurture the spirit that led to the calling of the famous revolutionary parliament of 1848 in Frankfurt.

103

After the 1848 democratic movement toward German unity failed, national unity finally came about under Prussian leadership in 1871. But the "Song of the Germans" was not chosen to be the national anthem. Instead, during the Kaiser Reich the national anthem was *"Heil Dir im Siegerkranz, Herrscher des Vaterlands* [Hail to Thee, in a Wreath of Victory, Ruler of the Fatherland]," sung to the melody that Britons know as "God Save the Queen" and Americans as "My Country 'tis of Thee."

It was Friedrich Ebert, president of the Weimar Republic, a socialist, a democrat, and a statesman, who in 1922 declared the "Song of the Germans" the anthem of the German Republic.

Hitler took over the anthem when he came to power in 1933, but he ordered that the first verse be sung only if followed by the Nazi Party song, *"S A Marschiert* [The Storm Troopers on the March]."

After World War II, the national hymn sung under Hitler was felt to be so compromised that one could not sing it anymore. And even if it was not really a "Nazi song," there were hardly any Germans left who were still proud of their nation and who cared to praise *"Deutschland, Deutschland über alles."* For some time there were attempts to introduce a new anthem, written by the poet Rudolf Alexander Schroeder, but it never became popular.

From 1945 to 1952 there was no national anthem in Germany. On official occasions a few passages of Beethoven's Ninth Symphony were usually played. On February 2, 1952, the president of the Federal Republic, Theodor Heuss, agreed with Chancellor Konrad Adenauer, and restored the Hoffmann words and Haydn music to the status they had enjoyed in the pre-1933 republic.

Aware of the widespread misunderstanding about the words *"Deutschland über alles,"* which are usually interpreted as references to ambitions of world supremacy, this stanza has been dropped. Today the third stanza of the famous poem is sung, whose lines call for "unity and justice and freedom" urging the Germans to strive for those aims "with heart and hand as brothers."

East Germany introduced its own national anthem in 1949, the product of Johannes R. Becher and Hanne Eisler, both well known communists.

It is interesting that two out of every three Germans in the Federal Republic do not know with which words the text of their national anthem begins. A recent poll showed that only 32 percent know the correct beginning, while 20 percent said they did not know, and 46 percent thought the anthem still began with *"Deutschland über alles."*

The second verse of the *Deutschlandlied* praises "German women, German fidelity, German wine and German song," which "shall sustain their fine old magnificence in the world" and inspire the Germans "to noble deeds throughout our lives."

But this second verse is all but unknown and hardly ever sung at all. And as for the "noble deeds" it calls for, it is one of the strangest phenomena of postwar Germany that the country is almost completely lacking in accepted national heroes. There is no one who enjoys the popularity and esteem of an Eisenhower or John F. Kennedy (the latter, even today, enjoys more popularity than most famous Germans). In France, Napoleon remains a national hero in spite of all the havoc he wrought for the country and for Europe. In England, Churchill will remain a symbol for years to come. But in Germany, even the great heroes of the past do not evoke emotions or national pride.

Monuments

Nothing reveals the ambiguous greatness of the outstanding men and moments of Germany's past so much as its neglected although frequented monuments.

Since 1905 a granite statue of Otto von Bismarck, the founder of modern Germany, towers some 100 feet on a Hamburg street over—what? The street below it, the Reeperbahn, is Germany's most wicked, replete with striptease houses and officially accepted brothels. And the unintentional disrespect accurately characterizes the indifference of the average German to Bismarck today.

Although there are no opinion polls to back me up, I feel it safe to say that the average German has not a fraction of the respect and emotional attachment to Bismarck that the average American has for George Washington. As the German writer Robert Musil has said, "Nothing is so invisible as a monument."

If you drive down the autobahn from Hamburg, and having passed Hanover you head for Westphalia, you can see a giant pavilion perching on a hill high overhead. It is the Porta Westfalica, the gateway to Westphalia. If you take the trouble to drive up to it, you will see a twenty-one foot iron statue of

Wilhelm I, king of Prussia and German emperor, who has been surveying the countryside since 1896, when 1,300 trumpeters celebrated its unveiling in the presence of Wilhelm II.

Tourists today swarm over the pavilion and gaze curiously at the statue. Their photo albums will record their visit, but very few of them will bother about who Wilhelm was, when he lived, or what he means, good or evil, to the German people.

In the Teutoburger Forest another monument of the German past towers over the landscape, near Detmold. From head to toe a German hero, who became the symbol of German nationalism in the nineteenth century, the precursor of German unity and liberator from foreign oppressors, Arminius or Hermann, towers in monument form 150 feet high. The statue's sword of vengeance alone weighs more than the sabers of an entire battalion, 400 pounds. Engraved on it are the words: *"Deutschland's Einigkeit, meine Stärke, meine Stärke, Deutschlands macht.* [Germany's unity is my strength, my strength is Germany's power]"—written in the 1860's, before there even was a Germany.

For over forty years this statue was the dream of an eccentric and mediocre poet, Ernst von Bandel, whose idea it was to build a monument on this site to commemorate the defeat of the Romans by Germanic tribes in A.D. 9—and no one knows exactly when or where that battle was fought. Bandel squandered his entire savings on the realization of the statue, going blind in the process, but lived to witness its dedication on January 18, 1875, when, four years after the founding of modern Germany, Wilhelm I came to preside at the ceremonies and press the dreamer's hand.

Today the ambiguous hero Hermann is a curiosity. Donald Duck is better known among German children or, for that matter, among adults.

There is a sadness and pathos about the tragic atmosphere that surrounds nearly every German monument of distinction. The same is true at Coblenz, at the famous *Deutsches Eck* (German Corner), a sprawling monument on the river banks at the confluence of the Rhine and Mosel rivers. The heart of the monument, an equestrian statue of old Kaiser Wilhelm, is gone, having been destroyed by a shell in World War II and never replaced.

It is somehow a commentary on Germany itself—that empty pedestal, its tiered terrace and the coats-of-arms of all former

German states, including those of East Germany, and that poignant inscription that is so ironic today, *"Nimmer wird das Reich zerstört, wenn ihr einig seid und treu* [The Reich will never be destroyed, as long as you remain united and loyal]." A monument of glory—today a truncated memorial, a monument that warns more than it celebrates.

In Rüdesheim a goddess, presiding over the land, disdainfully looks westward towards Germany's former enemy, France. It is Germania, built to commemorate the victory over Napoleon III in the Franco-Prussian War and the establishment of Germany in 1871. Embedded in the monument are reliefs of Bismarck, Moltke, of Prussian artillerists, Hessian riflemen, Baden dragoons, Württemberg infantry—in short, the monument was intended to represent all Germany. The buxom dame weighs two and a half tons. But the monument is dead weight in the light of the Franco-German Friendship Treaty signed by Charles de Gaulle and Konrad Adenauer, and it stands today as a useless tourist attraction.

Wagnerian music should be played as the reader immerses[1] himself into the next dip of the German past, an imitation Doric temple called the Walhalla on the banks of the Danube near Regensburg, a Bavarian Acropolis, completed by Ludwig I of Bavaria in 1842 after thirty years of construction, and today crumbling from neglect. This "seat of the gods," a Madame Tussaud in marble, was intended as a giant hall of fame where Germany's great—118 in all—are enshrined in a vain search for tradition. Here Lessing and Mozart are arbitrarily placed next to Field Marshall General Diebitsch-Sabalkanskij, while Beethoven, Wagner, and Bach are off in a corner to themselves.

Saddest of all are the monuments of Berlin. The Victory Column, with rows of cannons embedded upright like candles in its sides instead of flutes, commemorates the conquests of 1864 and 1871. But, standing as it does at the Königsplatz, it is a monument of failure, for it is in line with the Brandenburg Gate, the entrance to East Berlin and Unter den Linden, once the German Champs Élysées, today only a memory. And at the foot of the Victory Column is another of the 166 statues of Bismarck found all over the country, typically almost hidden by surrounding bushes.

Germany has no monument of pride at all that inspires its onlookers as does an Arch of Triumph, a Lincoln Memorial, a Trafalgar Square, a Roman obelisk. No foreign dignitary ever lays a wreath at a German "tomb of the unknown soldier," for there is no such monument. Nor would the Germans dare to have one—the stigma of the Nazi past, World War I, and Prussian militarism hangs heavily like a black cloud even over its highly democratized Bundeswehr (Chapter 17). As one German writer has said, "Our monuments are the counterfeit currency of Germany."

And in the new Germany the search for a hero so far has only ended in frustration. Naturally it must be someone who is a great democrat or fighter for freedom, to fit the image of the new democracy itself.

Too often, though, the likeliest candidates—such as the leaders of the unsuccessful 1944 attempt to assassinate Hitler—have the disqualifying aspect of failure. This last mentioned event is commemorated, it is true, every year on July 20th, with speeches and wreath-laying ceremonies, but it is an event associated with the ignominy of defeat.

The first postwar chancellor, Konrad Adenauer, was respected more than loved, but he was too old-fashioned to appeal to the young, and even for the older generation he was too aloof and forbidding. Former Chancellor Ludwig Erhard, revered as the father of postwar economic recovery, was forced out of office for his ineptitude. The late President Theodor Heuss is still held in veneration and esteem but did not during his lifetime and does not now elicit anything even remotely resembling passion or idealism.[2]

Among the great leaders of the Social Democratic Party, from Kurt Schumacher to Fritz Erler to Erich Ollenhauer, there is always the stigma of failure. Even Willy Brandt, internationally popular as former mayor of Berlin and since then as foreign minister and chancellor, only helped bring his party into power through a coalition compromise. Moreover, for many years there was widespread distrust among the German population because he returned to postwar Germany from his Norwegian exile in a foreign army uniform, with a Norwegian wife, and was denounced as a deserter. Even if as chancellor he emerges as a new kind of political hero, he will never be more than a limited one, because large numbers of Germans will harbor reservations to the end. Marlene Dietrich still enjoys great popularity, but she is widely regarded as a traitor for leaving Nazi Germany.

The closest thing to passionate idealism is associated with

sports figures, and here it reaches a feverish, almost fanatical pitch. It is a shattering experience to sit among Germans at a soccer match when a German team is winning, and the chant of "Toooor [goal]!" thunders over the field like an earthquake. Whenever a German team reaches the finals of some international competition, German cities assume an eerie, other-worldly character. The streets are as empty as for a civil defense evacuation exercise, as millions stay indoors glued to their TV sets. Cries of "Uwe! Uwe! Uwe!" (after the soccer star, Uwe Seeler), reach the proportions of a national tidal wave. The former heavyweight boxing champion, Max Schmeling, now almost 70, is still the object of unqualified affection for millions and is remembered for his famous knockout of "The Brown Bomber" Joe Louis in 1936. But even this kind of longevity has begun to fade in the wake of new stars, such as Fritz Walter and Gerd Müller.

As for TV personalities and pop singers, strangely enough, by far—an estimated 60 percent—the most outstanding and most frequently appearing entertainers on German television are foreigners. When the German singer Peter Beil appeared on one national telecast, the Italian-born Caterina Valente remarked, in English, to the American pop singer Gus Backus, "What's this German doing on this program?" Some of the best known personalities on West German TV are: Bill Ramsey (U.S.), Chris Howland (England), Vico Torriani (Switzerland), Rita Pavone (Italy—whose rendition in German brings down the house even though she doesn't understand a word she sings), comedian Rudi Carrell (the Netherlands), Chris Andrews (England), Howard Carpendale (South Africa), Peggy March (U.S.), Gitte Haenning (Denmark), boy-wonder singer Heintje (the Netherlands), Wencke Myhre (Norway), Karl Gott (Czechoslovakia), Marika Rökk (Hungary), Udo Jürgens (Austria), Vicky (Greece), the Bentley Sisters (the Netherlands), Vivi Bach (Denmark), Dietmar Schönherr (Austria), and Mireille Mathieu (France).

The exiles form the biggest group of potential heroes, but the Germans are uneasy about them. Up to now there has been a sort of double standard about them. Perhaps it is because the Germans are ashamed to acknowledge as heroes those whom they have driven out. At the same time they bend over backwards to show honor to scores of eminent men who fled during or before the Third Reich: Albert Einstein, Thomas Mann, Paul Tillich,

109

Walter Gropius, Paul Hindemith. They are revered, but they are not heroes. The exiled Nelly Sachs was awarded the peace prize of the German book dealers, but she lived in Sweden, and the late Erich Maria Remarque *(All Quiet on the Western Front)*, who did not live in Germany for thirty years, received the Federal Service Cross, usually bestowed on men who elevate the name of the Federal Republic of Germany. Carl Zuckmayer *(The Devil's General, The Captain of Köpenick)* prefers to live in Switzerland.

Even the German flag is a symbol of failure. The three broad horizontal stripes colored black, red, and gold display the imperial colors of the Holy Roman Empire, an association which the Germans just can't seem to shed, as well as the colors of the unsuccessful 1848 Revolution and again of the Weimar Republic, a democratic effort that failed.

There is no such thing as a German equivalent of the Americans' July Fourth, commemorating the day of their founding. On the centennial day of the founding of the Second German Empire or Reich, January 18, 1971, Germans, East and West, observed the day with mixed, overwhelmingly negative, sentiments. President Gustav Heinemann in a nationally televised speech said, "What was achieved in 1871 was external unity without full internal liberties for the citizens."[3] But there is no official holiday commemorating the founding day of modern Germany.

A century after the founding of Bismarck's Reich the combined states of West and East Germany were only two-thirds of the former German Empire. At the end of World War I the Germans had to return the conquered French provinces. And, as a result of World War II, they lost Silesia, East Prussia, East Brandenburg, and a large section of Pomerania, now ceded to the Soviet Union and Poland. A few relics of the German Reich remain, such as the railroad system in the GDR, called the *Deutsche Reichsbahn* and the rebuilt *Reichstag* (parliament) building in West Berlin with its inscription, "To the German people." But it stands mostly as an empty and useless reminder of the past.

A handful of rightist politicians in Munich rallied around Herr Gerhard Frey, publisher of the extremist *Deutsche National Zeitung* (Chapter 14), to launch a new party, DVU (German People's Union), on January 18, 1971.

Every year on June 17th West Germans commemorate the East German uprising of 1953 as a legal holiday. It is observed with solemn speeches, patriotic gatherings, but mostly by picnicking and taking off for the beach or woods. And this too is a commemoration of a failure. The day has become so lackluster and, with the passage of time, meaningless that some politicians are beginning to urge its abolition.

And their Labor Day *(Tag der Arbeit)* coincides with the Communists' May Day, May 1, because of the socialist influence of the labor unions. This comes closer to a national day of pride, when parades are held and speeches are given. But here too it is mostly celebrated by not working.

"It is a simple matter to be a German," observes a typical West German student with whom I chatted in Bonn, "but this is a sober fact completely without value one way or another. But to *feel* as a German is something else again. I don't *feel* German, but neither do my friends and fellow students. I believe that hundreds of thousands of my generation also lack this feeling of being German."

Baldur von Schirach, the war criminal who had been leader of the Hitler Youth, said after his recent release from prison that it "would be impossible" to mobilize Germany's youth today in the way he had after World War I because the new generation was too smart and skeptical to be seduced by romantic nationalism.

"The German ideal," writes the well known German publicist Johannes Gross, "is total harmlessness. . . ."[4]

It would be wrong to leave the impression that undercurrents of nationalism are not existent. In West Berlin, for example, Adenauer Allee had a very short existence. Less than a year after Adenauer's death the street was again given its original name, Kaiser Allee, upon the demands of citizens. In spite of a fierce controversy and widespread protest, a West German destroyer was named after an officer of the Nazi *Wehrmacht,* Admiral Guenther Luetjens, an officer who went down with his ship and 1,976 men in 1941 after pledging loyalty to Adolf Hitler.

But such incidents as these are the result of efforts of the older generation, unable to accept the stigma of failure and longing for some kind of national identity and continuity. Another incident strikingly illustrates the schizophrenic element of the Germans' desperate attempt to hold on to some kind of national values. A couple of years ago a big controversy arose over the film *Cat and*

Mouse based on the novel by Günter Grass. In it the two sons of Willy Brandt (the then foreign minister), Lars, fifteen, and Peter, eighteen, played a student (at two different ages) who ridicules one of Nazi Germany's highest awards.

The story concerns a schoolboy, Joachim Mahlke, whose Adam's apple is bigger than normal. He tries to compensate for an inferiority complex by wearing a Knight's Cross that he stole from a German naval officer visiting his school. He is expelled from school for the theft and later joins the German army, where he is eventually decorated with the Knight's Cross.

The main criticism was directed at an ecstatic dance preformed by Lars, in which he wears swimming trunks and the cross. He wears the award not only around his neck but also—for a few seconds—at his waist. The sexual innuendos of this action caused German readers of *Der Spiegel* and *Der Stern* to flood the publications with letters of protest. Much of the criticism fell on Mr. Brandt for permitting his son Lars to perform the dance. Typical was a letter to *Der Stern* from a Berlin reader, who said that the film shows "how the Brandt family regards the military profession and military honor." Noting that Mr. Brandt was then foreign minister, the reader commented, "Poor Germany'"

In an interview with an American newsman, a Czechoslovakian journalist put the German enigma this way: "In Czechoslovakia history has a sort of continuity. Everyone agrees that the founding of the republic in 1918 was a good thing. It was something which had been worked up to. But in Germany, history goes in zigs and zags. There is no agreement on what was good and what was bad. Some people think the end of the kaisers was a good thing. Others don't. The same is true of the Weimar Republic. So there is a big conflict about history."

◄9►

THE ROCKY ROAD OF
GERMAN DEMOCRATIC TRADITION

THERE IS A very widespread notion abroad in the world that German democracy is something very new and that one of the reasons Hitler managed to come to power was that the Germans did not have a democratic tradition to build on. And this notion is nowhere more prevalent than in the Federal Republic itself.

West German pundits sometimes use the self-effacing expression *Verspätete Nation* (belated nation), mindful of the fact that Germany as a nation didn't even exist until 1871, when most Western countries boasted of established traditions and even the "young" U.S.A. approached its centennial. Many German writers limit German democracy solely to the Federal Republic, thus reducing German democratic experience to a mere generation.

"The German nation is nothing," Goethe wrote to his friend Friedrich von Müller on December 14, 1808. "But the individual German is something. Yet they imagine the reverse to be true. The Germans should be dispersed throughout the world, like the Jews, in order fully to develop all the good that is in them for the benefit of mankind."[1]

But German democracy is not something invented by Adenauer or Brandt. Actually, some rudimentary elements of democratic procedure can be traced all the way back to the Germanic tribes whose blue eyes and blond hair fascinated Caesar and Tacitus. Perhaps an important distinction should be made: Germans may indeed be short on practical democratic experience, but German history is studded with examples of outstanding democratic leaders and movements. If there is comparatively little awareness of them, it is because Germans have never before been able to enjoy the enduring experience of a viable, lasting democratic state. Whenever, throughout Germany's tortured and complicated history, the tender shoots of democratic thought or act began to appear, they were inevitably crushed by the relentless sweep of events.

113

German democratic origins might be compared to the source of the Danube: Nobody knows precisely where it really is, since it runs for miles and miles underground, appearing and disappearing in fits and starts, until finally it emerges as a bona fide river of life.

Among the many factors that figured in the evolution of German democracy, three main trends stand out: 1) the supranational imperial dream, 2) the tenacious and enduring particularism of the German nobility, 3) the struggle for national unity.

It is impossible to understand the present democratic Federal Republic and the evolution of German democracy without an awareness of these dominating historic factors. At the same time they are interwoven to such an extent that no one of them can be considered apart from the other two. Within the context of this three-way tug-of-war, German democracy was simultaneously fostered and stifled from the very beginnings of the German peoples all the way to modern times.

The Supranational Imperial Dream

The same flag that today flutters over the Bundestag, with its broad horizontal stripes of black, red, and gold, draped the coffin of Konrad Adenauer in 1967, the great architect of postwar German democracy. That flag was the standard of the anti-Establishment German students of Jena in 1817. Those colors were raised aloft during the Revolution of 1848. And it was the proud banner of the short-lived Weimar Republic (1919-1933).

But black, red, and gold were also the imperial colors of the German and Roman emperors. Ever since Charlemagne let himself be crowned Holy Roman Emperor by the pope on Christmas Day, 800, that grand imperial illusion—that the German emperors should be the legitimate successors to the Caesars—became a major German preoccupation and, at times, obsession.

"The Empire of the Middle Ages," writes British historian Sir John K. Dunlop, "was regarded as a Universal State, not as a national German institution. Though in practice the Emperor was by race a German, he tended to regard himself as the secular head of Western Christendom, and not as the leader of the German people. Thus, 'the Imperial Dream' delayed the formation of a

German state around a central kingly family, as happened in England and France."[2]

For centuries, during the late Middle Ages, even after the German Reich had lost all influence and cohesion, "The Holy Roman Empire of the German Nation" and its universalist myth doggedly persisted as an ideal. With the shift of power to the Hapsburg hegemony in the fifteenth and sixteenth centuries, the supranational character of the imperial idea developed, even while it lost its claim as the unifying principle of the Germans.

The pinnacle of imperial universalism was reached when the Hapsburg King Karl V became German Kaiser, as he was simultaneously ruler of Spain and as such exercised jurisdiction over its American possessions. The sun literally never set on his empire. But the Reformation, the Thirty Years' War, and the Peace of Westphalia radically reduced the Hapsburg empire, which subsequently focused its attention on its Slavish and Hungarian neighbors. In the end it ruled over more Hungarians and Slavs than Germans. Finally in 1806, Francis II willingly dropped the title "German Emperor" and substituted that of "Austrian Emperor."

Three factors awakened the German spirit of nationalism—and with it, democratic freedom: 1) the Napoleonic Wars, 2) the Congress of Vienna and the despotic influence of the Austrian Chancellor Prince Metternich, and 3) the awakening nationalism among the Czechs, Hungarians, and Croatians.

To a growing number of Germans the famous slogan of the French Revolution, "Liberty, Equality, Fraternity," was a welcome improvement over the anachronistic feudalism of their multiple regional autocratic princes. The "German spirit" really emerged between 1806 and 1812 when Napoleon was master of all Germany up to the Elbe and controlled Austria and Prussia. The Vienna Congress of 1815 created the German Bund, the loose confederation of German states that was dominated by Prince Metternich, under whose autocratic leadership the German princes consolidated their own possessions and thereby delayed German unity for years to come.

When German unity finally came into being in 1871 under the "Iron Chancellor" Bismarck, he resolutely sought to destroy once and for all the universality myth of the Holy Roman Empire. He created a "Reich" but it was a strictly German Reich. When on January 18, 1871, King William of Prussia was acclaimed German Emperor in the Hall of Mirrors in the Palace of Versailles, the imperial colors black, red, and gold were replaced by the black, red, and white flag of the North German Confederation, emphasizing the north German (*i.e.*, Prussian) influence in the new Empire.

The *Kulturkampf* must be understood not so much as an anti-Catholic measure per se, but as Bismarck's attempt to separate Prussian Catholics and the German Reich from Rome. But the backlash of Catholics, notably from Prussian-administered territories of the Rhineland, developed into a militant-front mentality that led to the establishment of the Center Party. Konrad Adenauer's strong pro-West and pro-France leanings, his and the CDU's hard-line policies toward East Germany and the Social Democratic Party cannot properly be understood apart from this development.

It remained for Adolf Hitler to restore, in the perverted form of pan-Germanism, the mystique of the Holy Roman Empire, with his "Third Reich" (after Bismarck and Charlemagne) and "Thousand Year Reich."

Particularism and Federalism

The hopelessly unwieldy and impractical German imperial idea was doomed from the start. Only a genius like Charlemagne was able to hold his empire together, whose division after his death led to the formation of Germany, France, and Lotharingia. It is a decisive fact of German political thought that throughout the centuries that followed, no German dynasty succeeded in securing the claim to the Carolingian heritage. The imperial-universalist idea was essentially an illusion. This supposed principle of German unity was actually a principle of German division. For it inevitably led to the enduring characteristic of the entire Reich development: the tenacious particularism of the German princes in continuous opposition to any kind of centralized power. Throughout German history until well into modern times, German feudalism jealously guarded its interests against all centralist and liberal movements.

Ironically, these same princes, in the wake of the Reformation, created an institution which, although it was designed to protect the interests of the elector princes, the clergy, the feudal lords, and the cities against imperial demands and encroachments, turned out to be a democratic forerunner of German parliament, the Reichstag: Notably, the permanent Reichstag of Regensburg, established in 1663, which handled religious questions in separate departments, a Corpus Catolicorum and a Corpus Evangelicorum. Although the subjects of the princes continued to remain serfs, their Reichstag idea was adopted by the Bismarckian Reich and subsequently by the Weimar Republic and by the Bundestag of toady.

It was the Emperor Napoleon who in 1806 dissolved the Holy Roman Empire of Germany forever and reduced the "Reich" conglomeration of states to the number that, in the main, comprise the contemporary West German (and East German) provinces.

Today federalism, or the relatively autonomous parliamentary states of the Federal Republic, despite its shortcomings, is a direct result of German particularism. It will undoubtedly be a part of West German political life for years to come.

The Struggle for National Unity

Along with the grand illusion of the Holy Roman Empire and the resulting particularism of German feudalism, the centuries-old struggle for German unity has been one of the biggest obstacles—even while it was a primary force of motivation—to German democracy.

In the fourteenth and fifteenth centuries the peasant uprisings failed to overthrow the oppressive rule of the German princes.

In contrast to the French revolutionary movement and that of other nations, the German struggle for freedom was far more complex. When in 1789 the French revolted against the despotic rule of monarchy, they already had a national state. All they had to do was overthrow the ruling powers and decree a new constitution. With the Germans it was otherwise. When they met in 1848 to establish a parliament and constitution, they succeeded only in creating a state on paper, powerless against the established might of the princes and, above all, Prussia. In the end the effort failed because the revolutionaries did not have the means to oppose the military might of the nobility.

Martin Luther's Reformation was not only a humanist rebellion against Church formalism and abuse, but also, to the very core, a German nationalist movement calling for a German church independent of Rome.

One of the greatest tragedies of German history is that Luther,

117

in order to oppose the imperial Roman idea and the Catholic hierarchy and popism, found it necessary to align himself with Protestant princes, and thereby with feudal absolutism, at the expense of political freedom for the *Untertanen* (subjects) and democratic development. Blind obedience to authority and the status quo was the tragic Lutheran teaching whose dire consequences were seen in the Third Reich.

Against the background of such formidable obstacles it is no wonder that German democracy failed for so long to find fruitful soil. Nevertheless, German history is replete with examples of democratic men and movements. Today greater attention than ever before is being paid to the sources of German democratic tradition, in a new focus on German history.

Examples of German Democracy

It would be farfetched to attribute to ancient Germanic tribes anything even remotely resembling democratic thought or procedure as we understand them today. Still, certain democratic elements should not be overlooked.

The early Germans, whom we discussed at length in Chapter 3, had a rudimentary form of assembly called "Thing." From time to time, representatives of various tribes, usually the tribe elders, met at these assemblies to decide over matters of war and peace, to hold court, and to observe manhood rites admitting the youth as full-fledged warriors.

It is interesting to note that, according to the Roman writer, Tacitus, these "Things" were haphazard affairs, sometimes dragging on lazily for days on end, interspersed with heavy drinking and brawling. At these "Things" decisions were made by vote, though only freeborn farmers exercised the "franchise." Even these primitive Germans had slaves, who of course had no voice in decision-making.

Out of these assemblies evolved the ancient German folk-moots and rural associations that were formed when communities wished to protect themselves from invaders, notably the Alemanni, the ancestors of the present-day Swiss. Today there are still five Swiss mountain communities which observe the custom of outdoor elections, with voting by a show of hands, a custom that scholars trace all the way back to the ancient German tribes.

The very germ cell of freedom-loving principles on the European continent was contained in the constitution of the three original Swiss cantons of Schwyz, Uri, and Unterwalden, which in 1291 "in view of the evil times," united to defend themselves against feudal encroachment.

Along with these cantons, the southeastern part of today's Federal Republic comprised the heart of the old German Empire at the time of the Hohenstaufen emperors. This area of Germany—Württemberg—belonged to the same movement that later led to the establishment of modern Switzerland, which is frequently described as "the world's oldest democracy."

During this same period too the phenomenal rise of the free cities played an important role in the struggle for civil liberties and independence from feudal lords and princes. Located throughout the territory of present-day Württemberg, these free cities were actually city-states exercising sovereignty beyond their fortified walls, and they maintained their independence for centuries.

Unfortunately the ambivalent role of the new class of society that emerged from these cities simultaneously fostered and hindered German democratic development. Unquestionably, the middle-class burghers were the ones who built the great cathedrals, sponsored the artists, artisans, scientists, inventors, and manufacturers and sparked the economic life-power that led to the industrial revolution.

In northern Germany the famous Hanseatic League, the maritime and commerical association, linked more than two hundred towns in common solidarity against feudal despotism. Even today the West German airline, Lufthansa, proudly associates itself with this medieval institution. In a search for democratic tradition, the Germans eagerly seize such links with the past. The license plates of Lübeck, Hamburg, and Bremen, the former leading Hanseatic cities, differ from those of all other German cities today by having the letter "H" for Hansa prefixed.

But the German middle class in the centuries following also became identified with hypocritical respectability, bourgeoise philistinism, and the decadent values that often appear in modern capitalism. Their symbols are kitschy plaster garden dwarfs; candelabra on dinner tables, pompous titles, and tuxedos.

"Partly as a result of the multiplication of small courts and the resultant formalism," writes historian Dunlop, "there grew up in

119

Germany a marked stratification of society and a strong class-consciousness. The landed gentry, the armed forces, the officials, and the professional classes had each their own pride of place and a rigid code of social behavior. The professional middle class, whether well-to-do or impoverished, jealously guarded its privileged status. Such a middle class was conservative, traditional, and, especially in Prussia, monarchist. It survived the shock of the French Revolution. It survived the liberal movement of 1848. It was hard hit by the defeat of 1918 and by the flight of Kaiser Wilhelm II; it was harder hit still, perhaps, by the inflation of 1922. Yet it still influences German political and social thought."[3]

However that may be, many of these free cities were also the birthplaces of state legislatures. In the late Middle Ages the peasants were finally admitted, along with the free burghers, clergy, and, at times, the nobility, in the *Landtag* (state legislature) which existed for centuries in Leonberg, Ludwigsburg, Ehingen, Freiburg, Sigmaringen, Bebenhausen, and especially in Karlsruhe and Stuttgart.

The first Landtag was established in Württemberg by Count Ulrich in 1457, who needed the citizens' support for his political ambitions.

The Württembergers laid down their constitutional rights for the first time in a treaty with Count Eberhard I. This Treaty of Münsingen was concluded on December 14, 1482—ten years before Columbus discovered America and 307 years before the Constitution of the United States was adopted.

Eberhard's son, Ulrich, chafing under the constitutional restrictions which the Treaty of Münsingen had imposed upon his father, attempted to disregard it by levying taxes without the consent of the representatives of the people. The Württembergers in defiance took up arms against their ruler and compelled him to sign the famous Treaty of Tübingen on July 8, 1514. In it constitutional government was formalized.

The Treaty of Tübingen set forth the most vital principles of natural and moral law upon which the American Constitution also rests:

1) The Duke cannot declare war without the express approval of the people's representatives

2) The Duke cannot levy taxes without the express approval of the representatives
3) No Württemberger may be punished without a fair trial
4) Every citizen accused of a crime must be furnished counsel for his defense
5) Every citizen has the right to emigrate
6) The national treasury is controlled by the representatives
7) The cities retain the right of home rule
8) No future duke can claim the allegiance of his subjects until he has sworn to fulfill the obligations imposed upon him by the treaty. Until he has taken his oath and sealed the Charter of Confirmation in the General Assembly of the people's representatives, his subjects owe him neither fidelity nor obedience. . . .

The old liberties of the Württembergers endured throughout the sixteenth, seventeenth, and eighteenth centuries, until King Frederick I of Württemberg, who had been appointed king by the victorious Napoleon Bonaparte, in December, 1805, deprived the people of their rights. In 1815 he attempted to dictate a new constitution to the representatives of Württemberg. But they stubbornly insisted on their old rights, and a new constitution— now a genuine agreement between the people and the king—was reached in 1819.

In the eighteenth century the British statesman James Fox declared that in his opinion there were only two constitutions in Europe worthy of the name: the English and the Württemberg.

Bavaria and Baden had also been granted new constitutions after Napoleon's fall, but the Württemberg constitution was the only one that was based on mutual agreement between the sovereign and his representatives.

The constitution of Baden, adopted in 1818, was regarded as the most liberal in Germany, even though the executive power was still vested in the sovereign, the Landtag had no right to introduce bills, and the right to vote or be elected was restricted to the wealthy.

When, after World War I, the German emperor abdicated and the old monarchy vanished, new republican institutions were adopted in Baden and also in Württemberg. They were in effect until abolished by the Hitler regime in 1934.

The present state of Baden-Württemberg was not formed until April 26, 1952, out of the former states of Württemberg-Baden, Baden, and Württemberg-Hohenzollern, following a plebiscite.

Today the tradition of the Landtag is continued in the capitals of the West German states.

Democratic Ambivalence in German Culture

The same anamoly and complexity that characterizes German democratic consciousness in other areas marked the development of German culture. The famous Westphalian Peace Treaty of 1648, which ended the Thirty Years' War, is regarded as one of the most fatal blows to German independence, and indirectly to German democracy. For, although it destroyed the might of the German emperors forever, it consolidated the power of numerous despotic princes and kings.

But, as so often happens in life, sometimes the worst of men unwittingly create conditions favorable to phenomena they never intended. The same ambitious greed that caused them to rule their subjects with an iron hand also involved them in feverish competition with one another. Each outdid the other in the construction of sumptuous palaces, opera houses and patronage of the arts.[4] Paradoxically, the French Enlightenment movement found fruitful soil in this cultural frenzy. And it was in this climate that, despite the authoritarian rulers who sponsored them, great democratic-minded playwrights, poets, composers and essayists emerged. There was the dramatist Gotthold Ephraim Lessing whose play *Nathan der Weise* was essentially a German *plädoyer* for human reason and religious tolerance. And, emerging out of the Enlightenment Movement in the late eighteenth century, came Johann Friedrich von Schiller, whose early dramas, notably *Die Räuber,* were passionate protests against feudal despotism and eloquent appeals for personal freedom.

Not only Schiller, but Goethe, Kant, von Fichte, and many other German greats also enthusiastically welcomed the new freedoms of the French Revolution. In the middle of the nineteenth century, Georg Büchner in his drama, *Danton's Tod*, depicted the French Revolution in an eloquent outcry against the oppressive *Obrigkeiten* (authorities).

The literary group, *Junges Deutschland,* whose prominent members included Heinrich Heine, was dedicated to German unity and social justice. But since the ordinary serf had neither the education nor the opportunity to read or see these works, the eloquent democratic pleas remained safely out of reach.

Most Sacred German Shrine

Surely the most sacred shrine on German soil today—and not because it happens to be a former church—is the secularized Pauls Kirche (originally the parish church of a wealthy Evangelical congregation) in downtown Frankfurt. For it is the cradle of German democracy. It was here that the first national German parliament was held in 1848.

The events leading up to this historic event were described in the previous chapter. Here it is interesting to note that in the aftermath of the Napoleonic wars the gradual awakening of independence and nationalism swept throughout Europe, including the German states. In 1848 there were uprisings in Paris, Vienna, Berlin, Munich, Budapest, and parts of Italy. And in eastern Europe the Czechs and the Hungarians were rankling under the yoke of imperial Austrian rule. In essence it was a universal rebellion against the anachronistic absolutism of monarchy.

On May 18, 1848, the first national assembly met in the Pauls Kirche with 585 deputies. There were freedom fighters from the Napoleonic wars among them, such as Ernst Moritz Arndt; there was the father of the gymnastic clubs, Friedrich Ludwig Jahn; there were writers like Ludwig Uhland and Jakob Grimm, the famous (along with his brother) fairy-tale collector.

The organizers defiantly chose Frankfurt, because this was the city where the German emperors were chosen by the elector-princes and where they were crowned.

The revolutionaries drew up a national constitution based on the American Declaration of Independence of 1776 and the French declaration of human rights of 1789. Among other things, they proclaimed: equality before the law; religious liberty and freedom of conscience; freedom of the press; the inalienable rights of the individual; the right to assembly; the right to a fair trial; and the right of private property.

The reformers, who were mostly scholars and theorists, had little practical experience in democratic politics. Thus their efforts were easily frustrated by the opposition of the Prussian King Frederick William IV and some other rulers of German principalities who resented giving up their royal prerogatives. The assembly was not truly representative of the German people, but rather a gathering of an intellectual elite: 49 professors, 213 judges and lawyers, 110 representatives of business, but only a few skilled tradesmen, one farmer, and no workers. The reformers had absolutely no power to implement their lofty aims. Their executive had no way to enforce the people's will, their minister of justice had no courts, their minister of the interior had no police, and their minister of war had no troops.

Even their most distinguished representative, Arndt, is today regarded as a dubious hero and patriot. Nothing underlines the ambivalence of this man more than a striking coincidence I experienced in Bonn in January, 1970. On the same day that I visited the Arndt home in Bonn, today a museum of Arndt archives and personal effects, I read a story in *Die Welt* that the entire body of students in Bonn's Ernst-Moritz-Arndt-Gymnasium (public secondary school) protested against the name of their school. "It must be renamed. Arndt cannot be our model." For Arndt's patriotism was anti-cosmopolitan, anti-French, often anti-Semitic, filled with mystical enthusiasm for the destiny of the Germanic race.

In preparation for this chapter I took time out to visit the Pauls Kirche. The eighteenth-century neoclassical redstone building, completed in 1833, was all but destroyed in a bombing raid in 1944. Today the exterior is reconstructed along the same lines as before, but the interior is more like a modern auditorium. The building is restricted for use to serious conferences, exhibits, and solemn public gatherings, notably the annual peace award ceremony of the German Book Trade Industry.

I was shocked to find the building in a seeming state of neglect. Cars were haphazardly parked right up against its walls, the building and entrance were downright filthy, its roof and tower a popular target for a large segment of Frankfurt's pigeon population. When I tried to enter, it was locked. A dirty sign, with sloppy, scrawled letters, read, "Closed for the winter." I immediately betook myself to the office of the lord mayor, right across the street, and protested against this treatment of Germany's democratic birthplace.

Officals there assured me that plans were underway for eventually improving the site. They explained that funds were simply not available to heat the church in winter. Then one of them escorted me on a guided tour of the building which was, on the inside, indeed a stunning, beautifully designed meeting hall.

But that is not the end of the story. Just about two blocks away from the Pauls Kirche is the Goethe Haus, the parental home of Germany's greatest poet. This of course is preserved perfectly. Hordes of tourists file through here daily, winter and summer, and there is no heating problem. During my visit I tagged after a group of some sixty American servicemen's wives who made the tour. Afterwards we had to pass the Pauls Kirche, and I asked several of them whether they knew what this building was. Not one of them had even heard of it before. Nor did any of them know that among the 1848 revolutionaries was a young man by the name of Carl Schurz, who emigrated to the United States to become a Union general under Abraham Lincoln and subsequently U.S. Secretary of the Interior.

In a letter to the lord mayor I described this incident and suggested that a godsent opportunity was being wasted in not explaining German democracy via a tour of the Pauls Kirche to the countless thousands of Americans, military and civilian, who pass through Frankfurt. I received a polite letter of acknowledgement and a handsome book about Frankfurt and its priceless treasures. It is interesting that this book dismissed the Pauls Kirche in one paragraph, while proudly boasting that the Hauptwache, the subway exit and plaza arrangement at the main downtown intersection, cost 70 million DM's (about $16 million) to construct. The Hauptwache building itself, a former police station dating back to 1730, is preserved intact. But unlike the nearby Pauls Kirche, it is illuminated every night, even in winter.

This is not to suggest that the Frankfurt authorities or the Germans have a callous disregard for their democratic birthplace. Rather the example shows, I think, that the Germans are not yet really conscious of their democratic tradition. They have not yet begun to realize that this is something that they should preserve and hold up in pride. Or, as the Federal Republic's first president, Theodor Heuss, put it, "The Germans are still in the stage of evolving their political life."[5]

The Weimar Republic

The Weimar Republic (1919-1933) has gone down in history as the monumental failure of the one democratic state that the

Germans ever had up to the time of Hitler. And the precise reason for this was that the Weimar Republic was, if anything, too democratic.

Named after the constitution of 1919 adopted in Weimar, the home of Goethe and Schiller, the Weimar Republic was a very democratic government. Its constitution included a bill of rights, universal male and female suffrage, proportional representation, and popular referendum. Ratified by the national assembly in July, 1919, the Weimar Constitution provided for a bicameral parliament, a chancellor, and an elected president. Moreover, the German people themselves compelled Kaiser Wilhelm II to abdicate his throne and flee into exile to Holland, thus ending the German Reich.

But the Weimar Republic had so many strikes against it that it would have been nothing short of miraculous if it had succeeded.

For one thing, it was born immediately after the end of World War I, when the people were completely demoralized. There was widespread unemployment and the ominous threat of economic collapse.

Although 75 percent of the seats in the national assembly were held by members of the parties supporting the republic (Social Democrats, Catholic Center Party, and Democrats), the republic stood on shaky ground. Radicals of the Right and Left were agitating throughout the land. During the winter of 1918-1919 the Communists even succeeded in temporarily establishing a Soviet regime in Bavaria. And on the Right the republic was opposed by the Nationalist Party and the right-wing members of the People's Party.

And internally, two inherent weaknesses inevitably led to its destruction:

PROPORTIONAL REPRESENTATION. This was intended as a democratic feature, but it allowed an unlimited number of political parties, none of which was able to obtain the required majority in the Reichstag, so that there was an overdependence on coalition governments.

Inevitably the coalitions collapsed whenever confronted by a crisis, because disagreement among so many coalition partners was just too great.

THE NOTORIOUS ARTICLE 48. Fighting for survival against the growing influence of the antidemocratic extremists of both Right and Left, the fathers of the Weimar Constitution felt it necessary to include an emergency clause which would give them the necessary instrument for dealing drastically with extreme situations. But to do so, it had to provide for a martial law, emergency measures, and temporary suspension of certain civil liberties. Although they provided as a safeguard the approval of the chancellor, and gave parliament authority to repeal such measures, there were too many loopholes. For example, the president could still invoke this article to dissolve the legislature before it could repeal any of his decrees. This is exactly what Hitler did.

Hitler did not need a *coup d'état,* or a civil war, or a revolution to come to power. He succeeded by defeating his opponents of the Weimar Republic with their own weapon—the ballot box. On July 31, 1932, the Nazis polled 37 percent of the votes cast, the strongest single party in the new Reichstag. The Communists emerged second. Thus the majority of the German people voted for one or the other form of dictatorship. And the Weimar system of democracy made it possible.

Today it is generally agreed that the vindictive spirit of the Versailles Treaty imposed unnecessarily harsh, indeed downright inhuman terms, on the defeated Germans.

It was contrary to President Woodrow Wilson's Fourteen Points and contrary to the spirit of the League of Nations, of which the new German republic was a member. The notorious "war guilt" clause of the Versailles Treaty, Article 231, put the entire blame for World War I on Germany alone. Germany had to forfeit all of her overseas colonies and adopt unilateral disarmament. The German army was not allowed to exceed 100,000 men and its navy was restricted to a few ships and no submarines. It had been excluded from the peace conference. Most humiliating of all, it was made to sign a carte blanche document that allowed the allies to dictate to the Germans at a future date how much reparations they had to pay. Further humiliation was suffered with the extension of French military occupation in the Ruhr industrial area in 1923 as a reprisal against a minor default in reparations payments.

Then, in the wake of the worldwide economic collapse of 1929, followed hunger, runaway inflation, continuous riots, streetfighting, uprisings, thuggery, and rampant unemployment.

There was extreme bitterness everywhere. The German generals never did admit Germany's defeat, but argued they had been betrayed, "sold down the river." They hadn't even surrendered, as the armistice of November 11, 1918, was signed by Matthias Erzberger, a civilian, who was assassinated by Rightists. Another civilian, Count Brockdorff-Rantzau, signed the Versailles Treaty.

Thus, when Hitler told the Germans that they were "stabbed in the back" by civilians, Socialists, Communists, and Jews, the myth gained widespread approval. It did not take much for the German people to repudiate the republic and its seemingly obsequious *Erfüllungspolitik* (fulfillment policy), which accepted the "war guilt" humiliation of the Versailles Treaty.

One of the few who dared to stand up to Hitler during his rise to power was Dr. Heinrich Brüning, chancellor during the last years of the Weimar Republic, from March 29, 1930, to May 30, 1932, when his forced resignation brought an end to German democracy. Hitler was named chancellor eight months later.

The Nazis labeled Brüning "the hunger chancellor" after he levied heavy taxes on the country. But it was his efforts to break up the estates of the Junkers of East Prussia, backbone of the officer corps, and distribute their land to the small farmers that brought his government to an end.

Probably nothing irritates the Germans today more than the tiresome and inadequate comparisons of the Federal Republic to the Weimar Republic. Yet the present government in Bonn cannot be understood apart from Weimar, to which the student of German affairs must necessarily turn, not for comparisons, but for lessons and for roots.

Even here, the ambivalent streak is clearly in evidence. Chancellor Willy Brandt is often compared to Gustav Stresemann, the Weimar foreign minister who tried to reconcile Germany with its former enemies despite considerable resistance from rightists at home. But Stresemann was the head of the German People's Party (DVP), whose right wing was sympathetic to Hitler, and which retained to the end an unrealistic goal of the restoration of the Hohenzollern monarchy.

Moreover, each of the major Bonn parties can trace its lineage back to the stormy Weimar period. The Social Democrats of course are their own heirs. The Weimar Center Party, established in 1919, sought to create a huge bourgeoise mass party to oppose the SPD, but failed, primarily over the issue of whether to support a monarchy or a republic; the Christian Democratic

Union (CDU) is its historic descendant. And the CDU's sister party, the Bavarian Christian Social Union (CSU) of Franz-Josef Strauss, is likewise the heir of the Bavarian People's Party of the Weimar period.

And Bonn's small Free Democratic Party plays an important role as a pivot between the two giants, currently as the coalition partner of the SPD. It is the product, established in 1948, of political refugees from the shattered German Liberal Movement, represented in the Weimar period by Stresemann's DVP and the socially progressive German Democratic Party (DDP).

In the light of all this, it should not be surprising that Bonn-watchers continuously make comparisons with Weimar and uneasy references to Germany's ambivalent democratic tradition.

Freedom Fighters

But there are changes in the wind. *Bonn Ist Nicht Weimar* (Bonn Is not Weimar) is the title of a popular book by the respected Swiss journalist Fritz René Allemann.

In West German schools today more attention is being paid to history's freedom fighters and other liberals, and less to wars, emperors, and dates of famous battles.[6] A new focus on social problems and a concern for human rights has encouraged Germans to take a new look at their own history and rediscover men and movements fighting for democratic values.

Thus the general strike of 1844, vividly portrayed in sketches by the late Käthe Kollwitz, is seen as a battle for industrial justice.

The Prussians, General Gerhard Johann Scharnhorst and Freiherr von Stein, are being belatedly lauded for democratic measures they introduced in the Prussian state.

The *Deutsche Burschenschaft* of 1817, the famous student fraternity association still in existence, was originally a movement against the Establishment of the time.

Political leaders like Friedrich Ebert (the first Weimar president), August Bebel, Walther Rathenau, Ernst Reuter (mayor of West Berlin during the airlift period), and Kurt Schumacher are emerging as heroes worth emulating.

Even Karl Marx and Friedrich Engels are enjoying a partial rehabilitation. In Wuppertal, a new stone plaque carries this engraved message: "Friedrich Engels, the great son of this city, was born on this site. He is one of the founders of scientific socialism." Not only did Chancellor Willy Brandt willingly accept an invitation to speak in Wuppertal on the occasion of Engels' 150th birthday (the town council allocated 200,000 DM's for Engels' celebrations), but he went to Trier as well to celebrate the 150th anniversary of Karl Marx. Engels' spiritual banishment from Wuppertal ended as early as 1945, when Adolf Hitler Allee was renamed Friedrich Engels Allee.

Recalling that intellectuals' scorn for the ill-fated Weimar Republic was also a factor in bringing about its downfall, today's West German literary groups have shown a pronounced increase in intense political activities, as we shall try to show in Chapter 14.

In a widely quoted speech in the Bremen Town Hall, February, 1970, Federal President Gustav Heinemann said he regretted that the German people have been made more conscious of the wars waged by their long-dead emperors and kings than the long succession of uprisings against oppressive ruling classes.

> It is a poor reflection on a democratic society, if even in this day and age it regards, for example, peasant uprisings of past centuries as nothing more than the quickly crushed schemes of "mutinous reds."
>
> This is the way German history has been written up to now. It is about time that a free and democratic Germany takes a new look at its past, to the extent even of rewriting the history books. . . . Nothing ought to prevent us in the Federal Republic from giving due credit to and tracing those forces in German history that lived and worked for a politically free and morally responsible German people able to lead their own lives as they see fit.

◄ 10 ►
VERGANGENHEITSBEWÄLTIGUNG
OR
THE NATIONAL GUILT COMPLEX

I SHALL NEVER forget one beautiful Sunday afternoon when I had the privilege of accompanying a Nigerian diplomat on a tour of Hamburg. He decided to wear his colorful native costume in bright yellows, reds, and oranges. Everywhere we went people stared curiously at us. Children boisterously ran up to my companion and playfully tugged at his robe.

I was somewhat concerned when people became too friendly and even familiar as we embarked on a tour of the harbor in a crowded tugboat. In fact, two rather bold women, giggling as they did so, reached out and rubbed their hands on his handsome shock of quite kinky hair. Fortunately the diplomat took it all good-naturedly and so all was well. Throughout the tour I noticed that a middle-aged man, standing at the other end of the boat, continued staring at us uninterruptedly.

When we left the boat about an hour later, this man came up to us, broke into a big smile and then, for no apparent reason at all, made a remark that speaks volumes.

"We Germans," he said, "aren't really so bad, are we?"

Since then I have often asked myself, "What deep psychic burdens in that man's soul made him feel it at all necessary to apologize to total strangers on behalf of himself and his countrymen?"

But this example is only one out of countless other experiences that I have observed and still observe in everyday German life. In plain English the generic term that applies to many of these manifestations of traumatic fallout is, simply, guilt. Some psychologists speak of a national guilt complex. The Germans themselves have invented a euphemism for it: *Vergangenheitsbewältigung* (coping with the past), and hardly a day passes that it doesn't pop up in conversation or the mass media.

Similarly, the Nazi past, Hitler, the incidents relating to World Wars I and II, have preoccupied and continue to preoccupy the press, radio, TV, the theater, and literature to a degree that is

downright suffocating even to a detached foreigner. To understand the extent of this grisly, almost morbid breast-beating and
infinite revelation of the bloody details of the Nazi nightmare,
imagine how Americans would feel if their entire mass media
would devote roughly about the same amount of space now
devoted to the comics or fashions, and even sometimes reaching
the fever pitch of sports, to our American genocide of the
Indians, the outrageous atrocities against the blacks, the brutality
associated with the conquest of the Philippines, and the World
War II herding of 110,000 Nisei in concentration camps.

As if this were not enough, imagine how the Germans must
feel to see the props knocked out from under many of their
postwar democratic leaders, whom they began to hold up in
esteem, only to be told in the end that they are besmirched with
an ignominious past.

Fallen Idols

During the Adenauer era there was a continuing controversy
over Dr. Hans Globke, secretary of state in the chancellory and
Adenauer's special assistant to the very end. A Catholic, Globke
was revealed by the German press as having served as a
high-ranking official in the Nazi ministerial bureaucracy and was
credited with drafting important sections of Hitler's anti-Semitic
legislation. His defenders, including Adenauer, maintained that
by remaining in office he was able to act as a kind of spy, that he
helped Jews escape, and used his influence to soften the
application of the race laws. Many witnesses, including Jews,
have since exonerated him. Nevertheless his critics are still
appalled by what they regard as a monstrous toleration of a man
compromised by his service to Hitler.

In 1966, State Secretary Albert Pfitzer, in charge of Chancellor
Ludwig Erhard's office, was disclosed by the press as having been
a member of the Nazi party and Hitler's SS Elite Guard.

That same year Countess Marion Dönhoff deplored, in an
editorial in *Die Zeit,* the moral bankruptcy of the CDU, that it
should find it necessary to nominate as a candidate for the
chancellorship, Kurt Georg Kiesinger, a man of unquestionably
high moral caliber since but who had been a member of the Nazi
party and served in the Reich Propaganda Ministry.

In 1968 no less a person than the Federal president himself,

Heinrich Lübke, had to appear on a nationwide television and radio program in order to defend himself against charges by *Der Stern* magazine that he had helped to build concentration camps during World War II. Although he vigorously denied the charges, he had to admit that during the war he was employed by the Schlempp architects' bureau, which designed barracks for laborers at construction sites in northern Germany, and that "after nearly a quarter of a century has gone by, I cannot remember every paper I signed." He completed his term of office prematurely and in the eyes of many Germans was discredited as a wishy-washy, lackluster president. "If he really was innocent," many observed, "he would have sued *Der Stern* for defamation of character."

Then in 1969 Dr. Eugen Gerstenmaier (who received his Ph.D. in theology), co-publisher of the distinguished Evangelical weekly, *Christ und Welt* (now called *Deutsche Zeitung*), prominent member of the Evangelical Church and president of the Bundestag—and candidate for the Federal presidency—was forced to resign for alleged misuse of funds. This was the man whom the British weekly *New Statesman* once called "headmaster of democracy," and was praised by prominent publicist Paul Sethe as "conscience of the nation." Although his salary was 130,000 DM's ($36,000) per annum, he received 281,107 DM's ($75,000) in reparations for alleged Nazi injustices toward him. These funds were granted in part for his supposed participation in the anti-Nazi activities of the *Bekennende Kirche* (Confessing Church) in the Third Reich. But the leader of the Bekennende Kirche movement, Dr. Martin Niemoeller, testified that he could not remember having even met Gerstenmaier at that time.

Although it has never been positively proved that Gerstenmaier acted improperly, the German press made no bones about the fact that he received many times more compensation monies than persons who suffered far more than he. Numerous concentration camp survivors have received only a pittance in compensation and then only after many years of legal proceedings. Professor Ernst Niekisch, for example, first received a modest pension shortly before his death after twelve long years of negotiations—and then only because the European Human Rights Commission intervened on his behalf. Of course Jewish claims generally have been processed more swiftly. It is only the borderline cases, where evidence was incomplete or lacking, that caused so much grief. And then Gerstenmaier comes along and receives preferred treatment, even though his claims are also insufficiently "proved"—that rankles.

On a lower level, Germans have been regularly confronted by embarrassing disclosures. Teachers have been abruptly suspended because of pro-Nazi indoctrination. Persons in government positions, as did German Ambassador to Portugal Herbert Roschach, have had to cut short a tour of duty when press reports suddenly leaked out that he had served in the notorious "Jewish Section" of the Nazi Foreign Office.

Dr. Theo Sommer, an editor of *Die Zeit,* has pointed out that among the 15,000 judges and prosecutors in the Federal Republic today, between 5,000 and 10,000 served in legal positions from 1933 to 1945. Some time ago, when Martin Sommer (no relation), one of the most brutal and sadistic torturers among SS concentration camp guards, was tried and convicted in southern Germany, it was learned that the judge's own record was highly dubious. Since it is impossible to read the hearts of men, who can say how many of them should be prosecuted today for collaboration with the Nazis? In most cases there is not enough evidence to press the matter.[1]

Even Israeli Foreign Minister Abba Eban made a *faux pas* in early 1970 by inviting Economics Minister Karl Schiller to Israel during the diplomat's official visit to Bonn, the first by an Israeli government member. When Eban was discreetly informed that Schiller was once a member of the Nazi party, Eban said, "Oh my God! I didn't know that!"

The Churches

Just as everything else in German life cannot be understood apart from the years 1933 to 1945, the same is true of the Christian churches. A vast number of Christians are disillusioned by the cowardly role of their churches during the Nazi era. The late Evangelical bishop of Berlin, Dr. Otto Dibelius, publicly repented his former Nazi allegiance and lamented the immense harm wrought by Luther's *Obrigkeit* teaching, which stressed blind obedience to authority. According to the well known American theologian-sociologist Harvey Cox, "The vast majority of [Protestant] pastors despised the Weimar Republic and prayed publicly every Sunday for the Kaiser."

And the Catholic Center Party, continues Cox, "voted with the Nazis to make Hermann Göring the first Nazi President of the Reichstag in 1932, and under Monsignor Kaas voted in 1933 for the notorious 'Enabling Act' which in effect throttled the republic and made Hitler dictator."[2]

One wonders too at the un-Romelike haste—thanks to the influence primarily of Papal Nuncio Eugenio Cardinal Pacelli—with which the Vatican signed a Concordat with Hitler, giving him ecclesiastical endorsement only months after his assumption of power. When Rolf Hochhuth came along in the early sixties with his provocative play *The Deputy* charging Pope Pius XII (the former Nuncio Pacelli) with criminal negligence for not acting forthrightly on behalf of the Jews, many Germans welcomed the shift of blame from the German Catholic Church to the Vatican—forgetting the close ties between Pacelli and German Catholicism.

In 1967 Prince Karl zu Löwenstein, president of the Central Committee of German Catholics, the coordinating association of all West German lay Catholic organizations, was accused in a radio broadcast by West German Rundfunk of pro-Nazi sentiments and support of the Third Reich and therefore of being ill-suited for a prominent Catholic leadership role. Although he was defended by the Catholic hierarchy, he was replaced shortly thereafter.

Then in 1969 the weekly newsmagazine *Der Spiegel* broke the Defregger Affair. According to the magazine disclosures, Matthias Defregger, auxiliary bishop of Munich, in his World War II capacity as Wehrmacht captain had passed on orders in the Italian village of Filetto di Camarda to shoot seventeen men between ages seventeen and sixty-five in retaliation for the killing of four Wehrmacht soldiers by partisans. The Defregger Affair at this writing is far from closed and will haunt the German Catholic church for years to come.[3]

The Manhunt

During the post-World War II occupation, allied military courts prosecuted 5,025 Nazi criminals, condemning 486 to death. The Soviet Union sentenced 10,000 German war criminals. And in 1962 Adolf Eichmann, who was responsible for Hitler's "final solution" of the Jewish "problem," was apprehended by Israeli

135

agents in South America and tried and convicted by an Israeli court and then executed (1962) for crimes against humanity. But while the Eichmann trial and the Nuremberg trials received worldwide publicity, relatively little attention has been given to the fact that *German* courts and *German* lawyers have been attempting to solve an unprecedented moral problem of unprecedented legal dimensions in trying the accused of National Socialist crimes of violence. These are not military crimes but civil trials for civil murder.

Between the time of West Germany's sovereignty in 1949 and 1970, nearly 85,000 persons, most of them former members of the notorious SS, have been investigated. Since 1958 some 170 major trials have taken place in the ten states of West Germany at a cost of $280 million, and in all of them the defendants were accused of specific acts of murder or of being accessory to murder. For more than a decade, 250 prosecutors and judges and 300 police officers have worked full time investigating Nazi crimes. Of those investigated, 12,882 have been prosecuted, 5,243 imprisoned, and 76 sentenced to the maximum penalty of life imprisonment (before the abolishment of the death penalty, 12 had been executed).

Reparations

Shilumin is a Hebrew word invented by Israel to describe West Germany's reparations to Israel. Through the Reparations Agreement of September 10, 1962, German goods and services to Israel in an aggregate value of over 2.5 billion DM's (about $600 million) were supplied by 1970. This is in accordance with the agreement made between leaders of international Jewish organizations and West Germany that Germany should pay for the crimes committed against the Jews by making some kind of collective reparation to the Jewish people as well as to individuals who suffered under National Socialism.

In addition, thanks to the Federal Republic's famous *Wiedergutmachungs Gesetz* (Compensation Law) nearly 15 billion DM's (over $3.6 billion) have been paid directly to individual Jewish victims or their heirs. And an additional 500 million DM's ($130 million) has so far been paid to the Conference on Jewish Material Claims Against Germany.

Money can never make good the horrendous atrocities of the Third Reich. But, as one Jewish leader has said, "This law proves that German leadership is prepared to make good to the extent that this is materially possible."

Observers have also pointed out that the Federal Republic through this law has set a precedent. No other nation in history has demonstrated its willingness to correct its past mistakes on such a gigantic scale. No moral outcry is heard about the alleged thirty million peasants slaughtered by Stalin, and relatively little publicity has been given to the first genocide of the twentieth century, the annihilation of one and a half million Armenians in the Turkish atrocities of 1915. The "open season" on Brazilian Indians by land-greedy whites in 1969-1970 long went largely unnoticed by the world press.

And the biggest group of all moral escapees is the Austrians.[4] Dr. Simon Wiesenthal, director of the Jewish Documentation Center in Vienna, vigorously negates the widely held Austrian view that the extermination of the Jews during the Third Reich was largely perpetrated by Germans and that therefore the Austrians are not morally bound to make reparations. According to a study published by him in 1966, based on many years of research, roughly half of all Jews murdered by Nazis are on Austrian consciences. Wiesenthal reminds us that Adolf Eichmann and Adolf Hitler were Austrians. When Eichmann began his mass deportation of Jews, he did so—according to Wiesenthal—via Austria and Czechoslovakia. Because of the historic relationship between the Austrians and those areas of Czechoslovakia and Poland where the concentration camps were located, mostly Austrian guards were appointed to these posts, since it was believed they knew best how to deal with the people there.

Wiesenthal charges in his study that the Austrian authorities have done very little to call Austrian Nazi criminals to account, nor have they exercised more than lip service regarding reparations. Since German authorities can only undertake action against German citizens, the Austrian Nazis have got away for the most part scot free.

Few tourists or visitors to Austria think of that country as a collaborator with Hitler, but rather as an innocent victim. Even Charlie Chaplin in his otherwise classic movie, *The Great Dictator,* inaccurately depicts the Austrians as the helpless victims of Hitler's *Anschluss* when in fact the vast majority of Austrians jubilantly welcomed Der Führer and went along in complete accord with his program. On March 11, 1938, as German troops marched into Austria (which is predominantly

137

Catholic), Vienna's Theodor Cardinal Innitzer sent Hitler a telegram: "The bells of Vienna will greet you as you enter." One day later, according to *Der Spiegel,* Hitler the Austrian was greeted as no other politician before him.

I shall never forget the chill that went down my spine during a visit to Austria in 1968 when a middle-aged Austrian farmer showed me with pride his scrapbook of World War II. He even boasted of pictures showing him in SS uniform hovering over an aged Jewish rabbi forced to clean an outhouse. On the front cover a famous picture was missing, but the inscription was still legible: *"Unser Führer."*

"Lest We Forget"

All over the Federal Republic monuments have been erected to commemorate the Nazi holocaust. Even World War I monuments have been renamed to include not only the fallen soldiers of World War II, but also all of the "victims of rule by terror." In downtown West Berlin the stump of the former tower of the bombed-out Kaiser Wilhelm Memorial Church has been left standing, pointing to the sky like a sore thumb, a grim reminder of the past. The former concentration camp sites of Dachau and Bergen-Belsen have been converted into memorial parks, and the Berlin execution site, Plötzensee, honors the martyrs who there shed their blood.

I shall never forget one Easter weekend I spent with a pious Catholic family in Hamburg. Instead of going to church on Good Friday, they decided it would be more meaningful to spend that day at the Bergen-Belsen site in prayer. Since this was some miles in the solitude of the Lüneburg heath, the family expected to be nearly alone. To our amazement it was *crowded* with repenting Germans of all ages. The parking lot was completely filled with automobiles from all over Germany. In spite of the crowds, it was deathly still. The quiet family groups reverently strolled from one mass grave to another where the victims of the camp were buried. Children scattered flower petals on the mounds, whose markers read, "Here lie 1,000 dead . . . 700 . . . 1,500. . . ." From mound to mound they walked like pilgrims following the way of the cross, men carrying their hats in their hands, women holding their rosary beads or reading quietly from a prayer book. At one mass grave I overheard a father, tears in his eyes, explaining it all to his teenage daughter. She was sixteen, about the same age as the Jewish girl, Anne Frank, who had been apprehended with her family by the Nazis in their attic hiding place in Amsterdam, and is buried anonymously in one of the graves. Anne Frank's diary, found accidentally by her father after the war, became a world best seller as a book, play, and movie. When the play appeared in Germany the audiences were so stunned that they left the theaters in silence, too moved and filled with remorse to applaud.

On the outskirts of the small town of Dachau, near Munich, where Himmler set up the first concentration camp in March, 1933, a memorial park has been developed. Housed in the former administrative buildings is a museum which contains relics and elaborate posters explaining the nightmarish events of the camp, where some 200,000 prisoners were detained and at least 30,000 were executed. Two of the original barracks have been reconstructed and the old cremation ovens may still be seen. Tombstones mark the places where ashes were buried. During my last visit a woman at the entrance sold booklets and postcards. Among the latter were some showing the cremation ovens. I cannot imagine any right-minded person sending these to anyone.

High in the Bavarian Alps at Berchtesgaden a few underground bunker rooms remain of what was formerly Hitler's famed "Eagle's Nest" hideaway. In December, 1968, the American Air Force, which controls part of the tunnel-rooms, was forced to abandon an exhibit on Adolf Hitler, which included redecorating the rooms as they were when Hitler lived there with his Eva Braun. The Germans protested against this commercialization of Hitler. "We have no interest in the business to be made from remembering Hitler," editorialized the Berchtesgaden newspaper, *Anzeiger.* Since then, the American armed forces and Germans both offer tours at opposite ends of the tunnel—but the rooms are bare.

The biggest and most notorious Nazi concentration camp on German soil was located at Buchenwald (which is in East Germany), where 56,000 persons were annihilated. Here on March 19, 1970, West German Chancellor Willy Brandt laid a wreath at the stark stone monument to the dead, during his historic visit in Erfurt with the East German Premier Willi Stoph.

However, none of the memorial sites in West or East Germany today even remotely evoke the horror and magnitude of the "crime beyond all human judgment" as does the far-away concentration-extermination camp site of Auschwitz (Oswiecim) near Cracow, Poland. While Bergen-Belsen had its thousands of victims, and Dachau, its tens of thousands, Auschwitz, the most monstrous camp of them all, was the scene of between two and four million persons killed between 1940 and 1945.

But few Germans ever get to see the Auschwitz site, which is even more remote psychologically and figuratively as it is physically. If they did, the impact would surely be many times what one might experience at Dachau or Bergen-Belsen. For the Polish government has made a point of preserving everything just as it was, as far as this is possible—the grim watchtowers, the barbed-wire fence, the prison blocks, and the rusty steel arch with the words *"Arbeit macht Frei* [Work Liberates]." School and tourist buses daily unload their live cargo of children and adults—mostly from eastern European countries—who make the grisly tour.

During my visit I recall my first gut-wrenching scene inside one of the barracks: a huge glass compartment, behind which I saw a mound, large enough to fill two boxcars, of what at first looked like steel wool. My guide then explained that this was human hair that had been shaved off the prisoners' heads.

"In the adjoining case," continued my guide, "is a roll of matting made from this hair. During wartime shortages, this was used to make mattresses for the Germans to sleep on."

After that first shock, everything else that followed was anti-climactic. In a second block a similar glass case contained a twelve-foot-high mound of children's shoes. In a third, the victim's clothes. In a fourth, toothbrushes, broken glasses, false teeth, and several mounds of old pots, pans, commodes, scrub brushes.

"To keep the death list," my guide continued, "seven typists clacked day and night . . . and toward the end the camp was setting new records. More than 6,000 gassings a day. The oven manufacturer was so proud of the achievements of his product that he had it patented."

During the Auschwitz war crimes trial in Frankfurt-Main in 1964, sixteen West German lawyers and a judge impressed Polish authorities by making a personal tour of the Auschwitz site in a conscientious journey into the past. One gray-haired lawyer, after inspecting the dungeons where men and women were hung up by their thumbs in nearly air-tight cells, and others so built that inmates could neither stand nor sit, fled from the spot, shouting, "Let me out! I can't stand this another minute!" Another started to vomit after he visited one of the gas chambers. There were still traces of human bones and ashes. One of the German delegation found a half-burned page from a Hebrew prayer book, part of the prayer for the dead.

The first high-ranking West German politician to visit Poland since World War II, West Berlin's governing mayor, Klaus Schuetz, wrote in the Auschwitz camp visitors' book in 1969, "These crimes must never be forgotten."

On December 7, 1970, thirty-one years after Nazi Germany's attack on Poland launched history's most devastating war, Polish Premier Jozef Cyrankiewicz and the West German Chancellor Willy Brandt signed a bilateral normalization treaty designed as a first step toward reconciling the two peoples. But the real significance of this event was poignantly symbolized some minutes before, when Willy Brandt, enroute to the historic signing ceremony, made a brief stop at the memorial commemorating the half-million Polish Jews who died at Nazi hands in the Warsaw ghetto. The chancellor, his face rigid, placed a simple wreath of white flowers in front of the monument. Then he dropped to his knees, bowed his head and folded his hands as if in prayer. He remained motionless for a few moments, then rose with trembling lips and continued on to the treaty-signing ceremony.

According to a public opinion poll sponsored by the weekly newsmagazine *Der Spiegel* 48 percent of West Germans thought that Mr. Brandt's gesture had been overdone, while 41 percent thought the act of atonement had been fitting. Behind these cold statistics feelings of West Germans toward Brandt's Ostpolitik run deep. Among the 48 percent there are many who believe Brandt is slowly selling Germany down the river, while among the others "he has restored my pride in being a German again." Inevitably some critics recalled a remark regarding the Germans attributed to Churchill: "They are either at your throat or on their knees."

."Nothing we Germans do is right," once sighed the respected TV personality Werner Höfer in front of millions of viewers, during an international press panel, "it's damned-if-we-do and damned-if-we-don't."

Repentance

Among those groups of Germans who have done most to show a genuine repentance for the Nazi abuses, it is my view, even though I am a Roman Catholic, that credit must go preeminently to various leaders and groups of the Evangelical Church.

"The depth of the guilt with which the Christian Church is burdened," stated the official brochure distributed in connection with the tenth German Evangelical *Kirchentag* held in Berlin in July, 1961, "is immeasurable. This guilt must be discussed with all candor. If Christianity does not repudiate unambiguously all those horrible declarations of her Fathers and teachers, she will never find a way to her Jewish brothers. A distinguished Jew once said, 'Whenever I hear the name Jesus, I think only of pogroms.'

"We owe the Jews a confession of a terrible wrong."

In numerous *Denkschriften* (memoranda) the Evangelical Church has forthrightly acknowledged the Church's co-responsibility for anti-Semitism and the Third Reich, and has approved recognition of the Oder-Neisse territories as part of the price the Germans must pay for the past.

One significant postwar Protestant institution is the Ecumenical Sisterhood of Mary at Darmstadt. You have read correctly: A Protestant convent of nuns named after Mary, which takes the traditional Roman Catholic vows of poverty, chastity, and obedience, and bases much of its life on the Rules of St. Francis of Assisi and St. Benedict. Atonement for the sins against the Jews is one of its main concerns. During the Eichmann trial in Jerusalem, unnoticed by the world press, which was pouring out reams of copy about the wicked Germans, these nuns quietly opened the Israeli branch of their congregation just a short distance from the court in which Eichmann was tried.

The congregation is the outgrowth of a Bible class of several women who had come together during World War II for the purpose of prayer and meditation. When the Allies on the night of September 11, 1944, nearly obliterated Darmstadt, these women vowed, in the event of survival, to establish a congregation of nuns. "It was the night of the air raid," wrote Mother Basilea Schlink, the woman who became the first superior of the congregation, "which was the turning point. Within twenty minutes Darmstadt was laid flat and thousands had to appear before the judgment seat of God. . . . We were moved to offer up prayers and supplications for our country, and we saw that repentance is not something done once for all, but that it must be constantly renewed, and our will constantly surrendered."[5]

A Lutheran pastor, Berlin's Dr. Lothar Kreyssig, in the sixties launched *Aktion Sühnezeichen* (Mission Atonement). Through his "penance corps" young men and women of all faiths have been volunteering their physical labor and talents (carpenters, painters, architects, laborers, designers) toward the reconstruction of buildings destroyed by the Nazis or the construction of buildings for the victims of the Nazis. Among many structures, they have rebuilt a part of England's famed, Luftwaffe-blasted Coventry Cathedral, a Jewish center in Lyon, France, a youth center in Rotterdam, and a number of Israeli *kibbutzim*.

In Chapter 15, I shall discuss the *Gesellschaft für Jüdisch-Christliche Zusammenarbeit* (Society for Jewish-Christian Cooperation) in which both Protestants and Catholics cooperate with Jews in various programs and projects.

To be sure, it is not as though the Roman Catholic Church has done nothing toward repentance and reconciliation for the past. In the mid-sixties the German bishops with their Polish colleagues wrote the famous letters of reconciliation. At the Dachau concentration site, a convent of Carmelite nuns has been constructed, whose main entrance is a former watchtower and one of whose walls was a prison block. It was consecrated by a former inmate (No. 26 680), Dr. Johannes Neuhausler, who, like Defregger, is also an auxiliary bishop of Munich. Near the convent, an expiatory chapel in the form of an open tower and named Christ in Agony was built in 1960.

Many outstanding interfaith leaders have emerged, notably the expert on Jewish affairs, Father Willihad Eckert, a Dominican friar in Cologne.

But one has the impression that the Evangelical Church has had the courage to meet the guilt syndrome head-on, while in the Roman Catholic Church only individuals here and there, but not the church as a whole, have met the challenge. For the long shadow of guilt hovers over German Catholicism to a far greater degree than any other German institution or group. Like it or not, the historic roots of anti-Semitism are mainly traceable to German Catholicism, as I have described at length in Chapter 6.

It is true that many priests, nuns, and laity suffered martyrdom during the Third Reich, and that men like Clement Cardinal August von Galen, The Lion of Münster, and Bishop von Preysing of Berlin, are rightly lauded for their heroic stand in the face of the totalitarian demands of the Third Reich, as are Alfred Delp, S.J., and the forgotten pioneer of interfaith "Una Sancta" movement, Father Max Josef Metzger, who both lost their lives for defying Hitler.

Throughout the entire postwar era, even up to the seventies, the leaders of German Catholicism have made a poor showing in coming to terms with the revelations of Rolf Hochhuth, or the American Guenter Lewy (*The Catholic Church and Nazi Germany*, McGraw-Hill, 1965), or Gordon C. Zahn, an American Roman Catholic (*German Catholics and Hitler's Wars*, Sheed & Ward, 1962). Still another indictment of German Catholicism's default in the Third Reich, *Die Kapitulation oder Deutscher Katholizismus Heute,* was written by a German Catholic, Carl Amery, and became a German best seller.

It is not, of course, for any of us to say how we would have acted if we were in the position of, say, a Bishop Defregger. Nor do we have the right to judge the souls of persons who were formerly compromised by Nazi abuses but might be genuinely reformed persons today. But the position of the Church toward the objective deeds of the Third Reich is another matter. And here I can only shake my head in disbelief at the monumental callousness or shrill self-righteousness with which the Roman Catholic leadership in Germany, clergy and lay, has in the main responded to the profound questions raised by Hochhuth, Lewy, Zahn, Amery, Defregger all the way to the present time.

An example of this kind of indifference is the bland tolerance of the *Festwoche* (Festival Week) in Deggendorf, where every September some 10,000 "pilgrims" commemorate a pogrom that occurred in 1337. Sixteen oil paintings in the town's main church recall the incident, vividly portraying Christians dragging Jews out of their homes and beating them to death. The Jews were killed for allegedly desecrating Eucharistic hosts and, according to a legend, the Christ Child appeared miraculously at that moment. Intensive research by scholars has revealed absolutely no evidence that the Jews actually did any such thing, but has uncovered abundant evidence showing that the Deggendorf Christians had acquired additional wealth from the massacre.

When asked about this, even Germans who should know better brush it off as an eccentric custom, a vestigial country practice that will inevitably die a natural death. Others see this as a shocking example of callous indifference in rural areas of today's Federal Republic toward the past. Even worse, it shows how much the responsible bishop, Dr. Rudolf Graber of Regensburg, really cares about repenting for the past. Ironically, Bishop Graber is an honorary chairman of the Munich branch of the Society for Jewish-Christian Cooperation. I was told by an informed insider that the reason Bavarian Jews have not made an issue out of this is to avoid an even greater outbreak of anti-Semitism that might result.

Statute of Limitations

In July, 1969, the West German parliament unanimously passed a law extending the statute of limitations on war crimes ten years. Had it expired on December 31, 1969, the estimated 16,000 undetected war criminals still at large in West Germany, would have become immune from further prosecution.

This statute of limitations may seem strange to Americans, especially lawyers, but it is rooted in the German penal code, which dates back to 1871.

In addition, the new law abolished the statute of limitations completely on outright genocide, thus creating the legal machinery by which the West German authorities can continue to hunt for such VIP Nazis as Martin Bormann, a top Hitler deputy, and Heinrich Müller, a Gestapo bigwig—both believed to be alive and hiding—as long as they live. As for the "small fish," those who have not been caught by 1980 under the new extension will either be dead by then or too old or infirm to stand trial in most cases.

The archives of the Soviet Union and East Germany have barely been exposed to western scrutiny. It is believed that the communists are deliberately withholding this source of incriminating evidence in order to embarrass West Germany if it should ever let up on the manhunt for Nazi criminals.

To many humanistic, morally concerned outsiders, the passing of this law may seem the most natural thing in the world. But in the light of postwar developments, this was not a foregone conclusion in West Germany.

145

In fact, back in 1965, the statute of limitations on Nazi murders was already due to expire. The dogged efforts of one man, Deputy Ernst Benda (CDU), who under great difficulty obtained fifty signatures on a petition, brought the extension bill to the Bundestag floor for a parliamentary debate. It was an open secret that most deputies of both the Social Democratic Party and the Christian Democratic Union (especially the sister party, Christian Social Union) were tired of the manhunt and wanted it to fade into oblivion. But Benda figured, rightly as it turned out, that once the issue got into public debate few deputies would have the courage to oppose the extension of the statute publicly. This is in fact what happened.

The statute of limitations was a major issue during a revolt that almost upset the CDU-SPD "Grand Coalition" in 1969. Finance Minister Franz-Josef Strauss, head of the CSU, argued that it was time to restrict the search for war criminals to major offenders. He demanded a "differentiated approach" which would be more lenient toward "small fry" Nazis. In effect, this is what the July, 1969, law achieved.

The statute-of-limitations issue has been hotly debated in the Federal Republic for years. Just as the U.S. Constitution prohibits *ex post facto* laws, so does the West German Basic Law, and the Ministry of Justice and leading lawyers have argued that the extension of the statute of limitations is that kind of law. Other German lawyers say that the extension is perfectly legal if it covers all murders, including homicide by civilians in peace-time.

It has been widely argued that the greatest danger of the statute's extension is psychological. The psychic fallout from continuous exposure to Nazi revelations is believed to have a special negative impact on the 50 percent of the German population that was under fifteen when World War II ended. Psychologist Erwin Scheuch, who is a graduate of Harvard, found in a study of German university students that 25 percent regarded their parents as Nazis and were themselves haunted by a sense of national guilt.

Many observers believe that the obsessive prosecution of Nazi criminals and an overdose of self-introspection about the past could create the opposite effect desired. Many young people either turn a deaf ear to the past or, worse still, start defending it.

"I Could Scream!"

I don't know how many times I have heard a remark like this from young Germans: "Sometimes I think if I hear that word 'Jew' just once more, I'll scream. If they—church, school, press, government, television—don't stop telling us to love the Jews, I think I'll end up hating them."

"No matter where we go," a twenty-year-old West Berlin student told me, "—and we young people travel a lot all over Europe—we are always asked about the Nazis and the Jews. Frankly, we are sick and tired of constantly being expected to account for the sins of our parents. When will we finally be let alone, to be ourselves?"

With the older generation the reactions are even worse. I visited a middle-aged couple whom I have known for years in Bonn. It is hard to find any German who is more genuinely sincere about the repudiation of the past and more intelligently committed to democratic life than this couple. Yet, when I casually mentioned, and then only because I was asked, that I was doing research on the Jews in Germany, the wife suddenly dispelled the extremely cheerful atmosphere of our little group and erupted in a highly emotional outburst: "The Jews! The Jews! When will the outside world ever, ever let us alone? Day in and day out you people keep coming here to dig up dirt about our horrible past, our terrible crimes against humanity! We are tired of being the world's whipping boy. When, oh, when will you ever, ever treat us like normal people!"

The momentary display of hysterics was not of course typical, but the woman's attitude and reaction are. Baron Karl Theodor von Guttenberg, former state secretary under Chancellor Kiesinger, and an official of the powerful CSU, has said repeatedly, "I really get bored hearing people talk about the German menace. It is something that I will not listen to."

The historic Auschwitz trial, began in the spring of 1964 and lasted for more than twenty months, the biggest trial in German history. Brought into this court were 359 witnesses to tell what they knew of mankind's most heinous crime—more than 20,000 spectators, most of them teenagers, many of them members of the Bundeswehr, watched the trial sessions, which were chronicled regularly and in detail by the mass media.

But the typical man-on-the-street reaction to the trial was, "We have had enough of this! Why must the name of Germany be continually dragged through the mud, because of a few bandits?"

The lawyers of the small prosecution staff said at the time that they estimated as many as 90 percent of the German people were opposed to such trials. They based their judgment on their own mail and the difficulties they frequently encountered (and still encounter) trying to get local authorities to ferret out and arrest suspected Nazi criminals.

Public opinion polls appear to bear them out, showing that more than two-thirds of the people are against continuing the manhunt more than a quarter of a century after the war. When in 1967 three middle-aged doctors were acquitted of charges of complicity in mass murder for their role in Hitler's euthanasia program in a Frankfurt court, the spectators broke out in a burst of thunderous applause. Although the verdict noted that it had been proved that the defendants had participated in the gassing of thousands of mental patients, they were excused on the grounds that they were acting under orders.

West German television produced a poignant film, *Murder in Frankfurt*. It told the story of a Polish survivor of the Auschwitz concentration camp who comes to Frankfurt to testify in the Auschwitz trial. The film unequivocally shows general German indifference to the trial, or frequent strongly voiced opinions against it. During the witness' visit, there is a noisy demonstration downtown by hundreds of taxi drivers who lean on their horns, block traffic, and display banners pleading for a return of capital punishment—in protest against the fatal robbery of a taxi driver.

The film drove its point home—Germans can get aroused over the murder of one taxi driver, but remain callously indifferent to the Auschwitz trial, which concerns the murder of millions, all in the name of Germany. I would like to emphasize that this is not my commentary, but that of German television making a judgment about Germans.

The notion of collective guilt of course must be categorically rejected as racism every bit as much as anti-Semitism with its collective hate. It is interesting to note, however, that while German leaders have gone out of their way to speak of "collective shame," and "shared responsibility," rank-and-file

Germans seldom use the first person plural in reference to Nazi crimes. While the Federal Republic, as we have shown earlier in this chapter, unhesitatingly has taken on "collective" responsibility in the matter of Nazi trials and reparations to Jews, the individual German, as likely as not, prefers to relegate the responsibility to some third party: "A *handful of bandits* besmirched the German name. . . . *those* Nazis. . . . Pope Pius XII, *he* didn't speak out. . . . *We* have to suffer for what *they* did. . . . "

I am not at all sure that it is necessarily callousness or even bad will that turns off the Germans whenever the past is mentioned. They have reached the saturation point. One family I have known intimately for over fifteen years has never in all that time really opened up on the Hitler era at any length. Whenever the subject did come up in passing, they made some strong anti-Nazi statement and immediately changed the subject. In fact, of all the thousands of Germans I have met, I can recall only one who had the courage to say to me, "Why, yes, I was a Nazi." Among the younger generation I frequently hear arguments like, "The Jews would not have been killed if it wasn't for the war." Or: "We suffered too. Look what the Allies did to Dresden." Or: "Hitler wasn't all bad. He solved the unemployment problem and after all, he built the Volkswagen and Autobahn." One hears these clichés over and over. Among older people I frequently hear, mostly in reference to the permissiveness of modern youth, "At least under Adolf we had law and order." Or even: "Who can believe such statistics. Six million Jews supposedly murdered by us Germans. How do you know this wasn't invented to discredit us?"

"The German people," says *Staatsanwalt* (District Attorney) Richard Dietz, "too easily and too conveniently interchange two different kinds of killing. They say the Russian civilians were killed because they were helping partisans, and the Jews were the casualties of the war. But it isn't true. They killed out of principle. The Jews, gypsies, mentally ill were regarded as *Untermenschen* [subhumans] to be eliminated. They were murderers, and it is our duty to prosecute murderers."

"One unpunished murderer among us," Mr. Benda has said, "is one too many. If we abandon the hunt, we might as well abandon the republic and head for the caves."

"We Didn't Know"

By far the most common remark that the visitor to Germany hears from the older generation in regard to the extermination of the Jews is, "We didn't know."

No less a person than the late Federal President Theodor Heuss said, at the dedication of the Bergen-Belsen memorial on November 30, 1952, "Those who are wont to say, 'We didn't know anything about all this,' should not use [this expression] as a crutch. We *knew* about those things."

The anti-Semitic laws, the public confiscation and destruction of Jewish property, the violent demonstrations, the visible arbitrary arrests and deportations, the fanatical radio diatribes, not to mention the odors drifting from Dachau toward Munich—all these were common knowledge.

I think this very standard excuse "we didn't know" must be interpreted psychologically. When older Germans use this expression, chances are they are telling the truth. For the Nazi criminals directly involved there can be no excuse. But for the average citizen in a crisis situation such as the Third Reich, his vision was blurred. It is possible to understand, while not necessarily endorse, his action as one of pushing the enormity of evil all around him out of his mind except where it touched his very survival. I think the mental process might be compared to the familiar one of many white American suburbanites who blithely commute past the Negro slums daily to the office without ever consciously admitting even the existence of a problem. They have conditioned their minds to a complete blackout. When an older German of today says, "I didn't know," what he really means is, "I couldn't let myself know. If I had, I wouldn't have been able to live with myself." Call it rationalization. Call it cowardice. Call it moral evasion. Call it anything that is human nature.

As Rabbi Hans Isaak Gruenewald of Hamburg said to me, referring of course to the ordinary German citizen and not to the Nazi criminals, "The German people in the Third Reich weren't bad. They were blind."

Today it is virtually impossible to arrive at any reliable barometer of the true German attitude toward the Nazi past and the Jews. This is illustrated by the following two examples.

I had gone to say goodbye to a young German architect one day and then helped him move his belongings to his car. While he was sorting out his things he showed me a book about the group of men, today regarded as heroes in the Federal Republic, that unsuccessfully attempted to assassinate Hitler. It was inscribed: "To my loving son, on his thirty-third birthday"—a present from his father.

A few moments later, however, I accidentally dropped a pile of papers I was carrying and, lo and behold, a picture of Adolf Hitler fell in full view to the floor. Red-faced, my German acquaintance stuffed the photo into a briefcase, but not before I had had a chance to look at its reverse side. Here was another inscription, in the same handwriting as that of the above-mentioned book, which read, "To my loving son on his eighth birthday."

It is easy of course in such a case to point one's finger accusingly and say, "Hypocrite!" Yet who of us can say he would have acted differently under the circumstances, and, more importantly, who can say that the change of heart is not genuine?

Then in 1968, according to a UPI report (October 24) from Rendsburg, West Germany, 1,000 former Nazi SS (storm troopers) met in a beer-drinking reunion under a huge poster showing three SS troopers, machine guns and Lugers hanging from their necks, carrying a wounded comrade from the battlefield, and the caption, "Have you forgotten?"

The SS veterans cheered as a speaker read aloud a telegram from Helmut Schmidt, then a leader of the opposition Social Democratic Party, today defense minister, who pledged to support their demands for government pensions.

"We were only soldiers," a speaker said. "We want only to be good democratic citizens today."

My first impulse was to condemn Schmidt's seemingly inexplicable endorsement of a former Nazi group. However, I decided to discuss the matter with a spokesman for the defense department. "Look," he said, "put yourself in Herr Schmidt's shoes. If he withholds the pensions, he will only embitter those men and then they will really become democratic dropouts. On the other hand, it is very likely that they are in fact quite sincere about being democratic citizens today. Why not give them the benefit of the doubt, namely that they regret their past mistakes, and give them a sense of belonging in the new Germany?"

Changing Relationship

Meanwhile it is not the past but the present and the future that are preoccupying Germans. University students are more interested in revolution than Nazis. And the overwhelming mood of the Germans is one of international participation.

As for the Israelis and other Jews, some of them are beginning to complain that the "special relationship" that has developed between West Germany and Israel is on the wane. What with Willy Brandt's preoccupation with "normalization," not only with Moscow, Warsaw, and Eastern Europe but also with Israel, there are decided signs of impatience with the bowing and scraping attitude of many West Germans toward the Jews. For his government, unlike that of Kiesinger and Adenauer, is not burdened by guilt.[6] Not only was Brandt himself a refugee of Nazism but his cabinet and entire government are predominantly men who either spent time in concentration camps or were untainted by Nazism. Ironically the Jews got along better with the earlier West German governments whose guilt feelings made them doubly eager to please them. Brandt has made no bones about promoting friendly ties with the Arabs and spent his very first vacation as chancellor in Tunisia.

During the immediate postwar years the Germans, ashamed of their own heritage, looked up to the United States as their moral ideal. Today, as a German friend wrote to me in a letter, "We don't even listen to AFN (Armed Forces Network) anymore." What with the alleged U.S. My Lai massacre in Vietnam, the moral compromises in the Nigerian-Biafran War, the Israeli blitzkrieg and dubious Palestinian policies, the Indian murders in Brazil, the racial turmoil in the United States, the weakening of the British pound, the French franc, and the U.S. dollar, and their own emerging economic power, the Germans are awakening to a new appreciation of their own strength and moral leadership.

Author Günter Grass, whose first successful novel *The Tin Drum* dealt with the guilt of yesterday, is now shifting his attention—as is the majority of the younger generation—to social involvement and political engagement.

"The German *Vergangenheit*," one colleague said to me, "is not something that can or should be 'solved.' Rather it is something we have to live with. And now suddenly it seems as though there is a turning point. The lessons of the past and our responsibility for it cannot and should not be forgotten. But we are beginning to see them now from a larger perspective. Instead of a preoccupation, the Nazi past has fallen into place as part of a transcendental whole."

◄ I I ►

GOD AND MAN IN EAST GERMANY

HORST BLOCK WAS a thirty-year-old construction laborer. With his brother waiting for him on the West Berlin side of the Wall, Horst decided to make his dash for freedom.

To get to West Berlin, he had to dodge several machine-gun toting *Vopos* (*Volkspolizei*—People's Police) guarding him and others working near the Wall, climb two barbed-wire fences, jump into a deep trench, run two hundred yards along the trench, crawl under another high barbed-wire fence, cross a ploughed strip, crawl under two more low fences.

·Horst managed to reach the second to the last fence, when he was spotted by a guard.

"Halt!" the guard shouted.

The guns chattered. Caught in the wire, Horst hung screaming as the other guards joined the firing. Then he was silent, his body spread-eagled in the wire, his coat in shreds, his head hanging. The guards cut him down.

In the decade since the Wall's erection by East German *Vopos* and People's Militiamen on August 13, 1961, Western observers have counted more than 200 known fugitives trying to cross it. And during that same period, some 30,000 persons have managed to escape from the German Democratic Republic (GDR) across that part of the Iron Curtain that separates the two Germanies, despite the tight controls established by the GDR. Among them were over 3,000 members of the East German police or armed forces, 600 from East Berlin alone.

The Berlin Wall, a twelve-foot-high barrier of reinforced concrete blocks, is nearly thirty miles long. The barbed-wire barricades, in parallel series up to six in number, are eighty miles long. They form the boundary around West Berlin and separate it from East Germany. In addition, there are 208 bunkers and fortified positions, as well as 193 watchtowers encircling West Berlin and manned by GDR border guards. About 14,000 GDR troops guard the barriers on foot, in towers, from bunkers, and in

154

armored cars. They are assisted by 200 highly trained police dogs.

Frequently the Wall on the West Berlin side is scrawled with the letters KZ, the abbreviation for *Konzentrationslager* (concentration camp), and many streets abruptly end at the Wall, where West Berlin authorities usually have a sign, reading, "Road blocked by Wall of Shame." In West Berlin, children play "fugitive and *Vopo*" instead of "cowboys and Indians" like West German children.

According to an investigation committee of lawyers in West Berlin, more than 10,000 arrests on political grounds have been made by East German authorities since the erection of the Wall, with 8,569 sentences passed, of which 5,851 were connected with attempts to flee to the West. For "crimes against the State" five of these persons received the death penalty, 59 were sentenced to life imprisonment, and 261 received sentences of 10 to 15 years.

In fairness, it must also be said that West German newspapers also report undisclosed numbers, estimated in thousands, of disillusioned former refugees who return to the East, and countless cases of bitterness and frustration on the part of refugees from East Germany who find it difficult to adjust to the West. Many West Germans deeply resent the social benefits and government aid extended to the refugees and often show their resentment by discrimination in housing, jobs, and social exclusion. The Berlin Wall has also become big business in an ugly way, by which some West Berliners, under the pretense of helping refugees escape, make a handsome profit out of human misery. East Germans pay upwards of $100 for forged West German identity cards and much more for access to tunnels and organized escape routes. In many cases, the refugees are caught, as the "refugee helpers" make a point of disappearing whenever risks are involved.

Like a Concentration Camp

Not only East Berlin but all of East Germany has many characteristics of a penitentiary or concentration camp, its western borders hemmed in by 860 miles of fortifications, with machine guns pointing inward at the East German people themselves.[1]

In my frequent tours of the eastern frontier of West Germany, I saw roads abruptly ending in blockades of barbed wire and ditches, rails ripped from the ground and replaced by ram-blocks, ghost towns and rotting farmhouses just past the border in East Germany. While West Germans stroll nonchalantly right up to the very border, East Germans can only be seen at a distance, past a "no man's land" filled with mines.

The zigzag demarcation line irrationally splits villages, forests, houses, yes, even trees, in two. In Berlin the Wall runs right in front of the Evangelical Church on the Bernauer Strasse, with the ironically appropriate name "Reconciliation Church," from which a gentle Christ beckons to West Berliners from the steeple. Elsewhere the Wall cuts off St. Michael's Catholic Church from half of its parishioners on the western side, who use the facilities of an Evangelical hospital for Sunday Mass. The Wall even divides a cemetery, separating the very dead of the two Berlins.

Zicherie, a village near Brunswick, is split down the middle by the East German border, which even divides a farmhouse (no longer occupied). Villagers on the western side can only visit their fellow villagers and relatives on the eastern side on rare occasions, and must make a detour of over 100 miles to reach the other side of the village. As one farmer on the western side told me, "It is easier for me to go to France to visit the grave of my fallen brother than to visit my live brother at the East German end of the village, just two blocks away."

A few miles further, only 300 yards from the border town of Hohegeiss in West Germany, lies the East German *Lungenheilstätte* (TB Sanitarium) whose electricity still comes from Hohegeiss. Every time the Hohegeiss inspector goes to the hospital to read the meter, he cannot take the direct road—a five-minute drive—but has to drive a 150-mile detour via official crossing points into East Germany.

The S-Bahn (suburban elevated railway) and U-Bahn (subway) still regularly cross both Berlins, while West Berlin's sewage system flows as it always has to East Berlin outlets. West Berlin's post office makes eight deliveries and pickups daily to East Berlin.

Since the erection of the Wall, foreigners and West Germans have been able to obtain entry permits to East Berlin with relative ease, and to East Germany proper only with difficulty, except for the annual Leipzig trade fair. Entry permits for West

156

Berliners, however, have been issued only at arbitrary intervals of several years. In individual cases, the permits are sometimes granted to them when a near relative is sick, dying, or getting married.

For me, it is always reassuring to be able to sign in before entering East Berlin at Checkpoint Charlie, the American military post (also for civilians) on the Friedrichstrasse, which will make inquiries in the event of no return.

Nevertheless, the somber prison atmosphere abruptly vanishes once you pass the Wall and *Vopo* guards. Just a short distance further, East Berlin's Alexander Platz bustles with activity. At 1,170 feet, the new television tower is the tallest structure in central Europe. The Centrum-Kaufhaus (department store), skyscraper hotel, and scores of swank nightclubs, restaurants, cinema, bars, and modernistic office buildings give East Berlin almost as swinging a look as you can find in West Berlin. The massive gingerbread apartment blocks along the Karl Marx Allee are as obsolete as that street's former name: Stalin Allee. Conspicuous by their absence are the estimated 200,000 Soviet troops discreetly ensconced in barracks far from population centers. They have strict orders not to mingle with East Germans, and appear quietly as tourists, mainly in civilian clothes, along with wives and children of officers and NCO's.

The political banners with their provocative slogans still hang from buildings, but they are played down. "Down With West German Militarism!" has been replaced by "The GDR Is a Reality!" "The Soviet Union, Our Eternal Friend!" "Freedom Is the Realization of Necessity," and "The GDR Brings Peace!"

For the Reds, the Wall Is a Success

From the Communist point of view, the Wall is a success. Before it was erected more than 3.7 million East Germans, mostly youth, voted with their feet and poured into West Germany, and with them the cream of GDR's scientists, skilled workers, technicians: No less than 20 percent of the total postwar population of East Germany.

The Wall has stabilized the East German state. It cut the flood of refugees to a trickle, and preserved much needed labor for the regime. And psychologically it compelled the East Germans to live with the GDR.

The result has been what has been called the "Economic Miracle" of the East: increased production, improved living standards, relative relaxation of restrictions.

Today, over twenty years after its founding, the GDR ranks as the second greatest industrial power in the East bloc, after the Soviet Union, and ninth in the entire world. According to U.N. Economic Commission statistics, East Germany now produces per capita more steel than Italy, more electricity than France, more cement than Britain, and more chemicals than any country except the United States. It is world famous for its optical products. It is constructing new industrial complexes all over the place, has developed a thriving shipbuilding industry, and its growth rate increases by 4 percent annually.

Moreover East Germans today enjoy the highest living standard of the Communist world, including the Soviet Union. Every second family owns a TV set. Forty out of 100 households have a refrigerator. The five-day workweek has been introduced. Although restricted on traveling to the West, East Germans flock to resorts in eastern Europe. The GDR is also the country most frequented by Czechoslovakians, who are unable to visit western countries since the Soviet invasion of 1968, and who prefer the large selection of meat and consumer goods not available in other eastern countries.

The number of automobile owners has nearly tripled over the past decade, now surpassing the one million mark. This gives East Germany a per capita automobile density one-third that of West Germany's, and the larger cities of the GDR, the proud and dubious status symbol of parking headaches.

Gone are the meat and potato lines. Stores are laden with merchandise. Fashions are hard to distinguish from most consumer-level haute couture of the West.

The monthly average wage has risen 15 percent in the past decade to over $175 monthly.

The low-income majority can get along far more easily than their counterparts in West Germany. Bread costs only twelve cents a loaf; potatoes, two cents a pound; a haircut, twenty cents. A four-room apartment goes for as little as eleven dollars a month, including kitchen and bath, but countless thousands are on the waiting list and the jerry-built structures deteriorate rapidly. Some 70,000 units are built annually, but the prospective tenants must "volunteer" to spend at least 600 hours shoveling dirt on the construction site before they can qualify.

Service costs, transportation, and entertainment are also cheap. Social services (family allowances, medical care for young and old alike, social security) are far more comprehensive than anything comparable in West Germany or the United States.

That bane of the prosperous western countries, the labor shortage, has also hit the GDR. Over half of all adult women and some 30,000 Hungarian "guest workers" are now employed in the GDR and officials put the number of open jobs at "over 100,000."

The "Farmers-and-Workers State," as the GDR likes to call itself, has really gone modern in its efforts to computerize itself. The same regime that ten years ago denounced cybernetics as "a pseudoscience" is now deeply immersed in data-processing and the production of computers. In 1969 the GDR had fifty Robotron 300's, a medium-sized computer-type, as compared with 600 electronic computers already operating in the Federal Republic, but the GDR is expected to close the gap by 1975.

Collectivized Agriculture Has Paid Off

Contrary to outside predictions, collectivization of three-fourths of East Berlin farms has paid off handsomely. At a time when the small individual farm so typical of Europe is doomed anyway, and the rationalization and mechanization of agriculture on a big scale has become an absolute necessity for survival even in the free world, collectivization proved a godsend to countless thousands of East German farmers foundering hopelessly, unable of themselves to adjust to the demands of technological necessity. Thus East Germany has ironically enjoyed more success with its farm production per capita than West Germany, which is still bogged down because democratic adjustments take infinitely more time. The value of GDR agricultural products has increased over 65 percent by 1970 from 1959, the year of final collectivization. Milk alone has increased 25 percent even though the number of cows has dwindled by one-fifth. Potatoes are up 18 percent; grain, 21 percent; sugar beets, 34 percent; while the number of farm employees has dropped by one-fifth, freeing 300,000 persons sorely needed by industry.

"While Bonn and the Common Market are still struggling with their labyrinthine farm chaos," said a proud East German farmer, "we have long ago solved ours."

159

There Is Humor, Too

There is even outspoken criticism—which always falls short of outright disapproval of the regime—which has spilled onto the editorial pages of the newspapers, TV documentaries, and café satire.

At the Pfeffermühle (Pepper Mill) in Leipzig, a performer tells his audience that new banana machines have been erected all over the city. "Really?" asks an amazed colleague. "Yes, you put a banana in at the top and a mark comes out at the bottom."

Of all places, even in East Berlin it is possible to poke fun at, of all people, that most German of all ideological Communist forefathers, Karl Marx. In a brilliant satire, *Der Herr Schmidt*, by East German playwright Günther Rücker, the first political trial of Communists, which took place in Cologne in 1852 on the orders of King Friedrich Wilhelm IV of Prussia, is humorously depicted. Prussian police spies come across like Keystone Cops, whose antics are enhanced by oompah-pah music, while Marx himself is satirically lampooned as a kind of Sun King. Of course, West German figures, notably CSU leader Franz-Josef Strauss, are drawn into the act. The play drew packed houses in a long run during 1969 at the Deutsches Theater in East Berlin.

"We Are the Better Germans"

"We know life is better in the West," one East Berlin hausfrau told me, "but what we have built we have built with our own hands and from scratch. After all, West Germany was getting Marshall Plan aid from the United States, while we were being milked dry by the Russians." (The Soviets have drained $16 billion in reparations so far and have not stopped.)

"Just what do you people want?" an East German worker asked the well known West German publicist Dr. Felix Rexhausen during a visit. "Are you perhaps going to come here again next spring and test us again and see how far things have gone with us, physically and morally, and then go on like this? Do you find that interesting?"

It is quite obvious that East Germans are tired of the everlasting words of pity, the hollow phrases from the West. An old teacher said to Rexhausen, after talking with him at length, "Now if you are going to use all this let me tell you one thing: I do not wish with this to contribute to the deepening of the West

160

Germans' malicious smirk about our Republic." One of the most bitter remarks the West German publicist heard was, "One day you will blame us for having lived here."

Unbelievable as it sounds, a growing sentiment of national pride is beginning to emerge in East Germany. "Make no mistake about it," a Dresden factory worker said, "this part of Germany was always more leftist than West Germany and the people here like the social benefits won under this regime, even if they don't accept the regime itself. Most of us have long resigned ourselves to the probability that there will *not* be a reunification ever. We still long for a day when a liberal form of socialism emerges with free elections. But if that day ever comes, East Germans would still vote overwhelmingly socialist."

It is an open secret in West Germany that Adenauer paid only lip service to reunification because in his heart he feared that the Catholic-oriented CDU could not survive in a reunited Germany. East Germany has long been the traditional stronghold of German socialism and is predominantly Protestant. Historically considered, socialism is a very natural German development. Marx and Engels are about as German as you can get. And Marxist thought owes much to nineteenth century German philosophy—notably the works of Hegel and Feuerbach.

What is so often overlooked by western observers is the profound fact that East Germany, hermetically sealed off from western and especially American influence, has vigorously restored the national consciousness. Far more than the Federal Republic which has become thoroughly westernized, East Germany has preserved the old German character with tenacious continuity. Once you leave East Berlin, much of the GDR outwardly still looks like the relics of the German past preserved in formaldehyde. The observations of Israeli author Amos Elon in 1967 (*Journey Through a Haunted Land*) are still valid: "When you are in East Germany, it appears as if the war were only yesterday."

Jean Edward Smith, a professor of political science at the University of Toronto, wrote in a study after touring East Germany:

> Orderliness, tidiness and the rigid observance of established forms remain a much more prominent feature of East Germany than of West Germany.

161

In addition there is a new . . . consciousness of being German, and the government exploits it. Newly coined medals depicting the likenesses of Bismarck and William II are prominently displayed in state-owned stores. The historic center of Berlin, located in the East, has been carefully restored to its former grandeur: it differs strikingly from the garish atmosphere of the Kurfürstendamm [in West Berlin]. . . . Isolated as the East Germans have been for the past twenty years, their last best hope seemed to dwell in the maintenance of a German heritage. For in spite of alleged socialist solidarity, the East Germans continue to share a traditional disdain for their Slavic neighbors. And in such a case, their "Germanness" seemed all the more precious.

The GDR fully exploits the deeply ingrained German sense of respectability and middle-class morality. East Germany is riddled through with a paternalistic Father-State-Knows-Best tone that permeates all of life. Hence the ever-present banners with Boy-Scout-like admonitions, often in rhyme, *"Jeder Mann an jedem Ort/mehrmals in der Woche Sport* [Every man in every place, takes part in sport several times a week]" or *"Du sollst sauber und anständig leben* [Thou shalt live decently and clean]."

But the puritanical restrictions are loosening and the mini skirts, the pill, and permissiveness rule the day among the youth. There is no longer any penalty attached to "concubinage." Universities are copying their West German counterparts with endless surveys of sexual habits of East German youth. According to Professor Helmut Rennert, director of the clinic for psychiatry and neurology at the Martin Luther University of Halle-Wittenberg (East Germany), "Our youth certainly cannot be called prudes, but their heterosexual relations are on the whole reserved."

The enforced absence of many Western stimuli and endless distractions gives East Germans more time to occupy themselves with basics, to enjoy a quiet evening sitting on a bench and looking at the sunset, or a long hike in the forest, or daydreaming alongside a bubbling brook. The vicarious thrills that sap the energy of the Western city dwellers with their daily exposure to the glut of material goods and entertainment are, for the present at least, a blessing in absentia for East Germans. Even personal

162

relationships are deeper, friendlier, less complicated or hectic. They still have time for you, time to listen and to learn, to look and to meditate. In West Germany the constant complaint is "I have no time."

East German cities and towns are full of great historic associations and memories. It was in Wittenberg that Luther tacked his famous Ninety-five Theses on a church door and launched the Protestant Reformation. At Weimar the graves of Schiller and Goethe, who lived and worked there, lie side by side. And only fifty miles further, high on the Wartburg fortress, Luther translated the New Testament, laying the foundations of the modern German language. At Dresden a theater whose traditions go back over three centuries is still packing them in to see classical plays. Nor can the citizens of East Germany forget for a moment that it was at Eisenach that Johann Sebastian Bach lived and worked.

East Germany's youth especially have a keen sense of pride in their country's material accomplishments. Not having experienced the war, they know only improvement since the days of postwar hardship.

The visitor from the West keeps hearing phrases like, "We are the better Germans!" They watch West German TV and gobble up American and West German books and magazines that pour in, despite restrictions. In a survey conducted with great precautions of anonymity by West German mass circulation magazine *Der Stern*, East German youth said West Germany is the western country they *least* wished to visit.

"West Germans are so bloated and arrogant, superficial, and greedy," was a typical comment by a twenty-eight-year-old female factory supervisor. Three-fourths of the youths questioned said they got their negative impressions from West German TV, West German relatives during visits, and their own frequent treks to West Berlin before the Wall went up in 1961.

The Walter Ulbricht regime shrewdly invested heavily in education, which received top priority next to industry. From six universities for only 8,000 students in 1946, the GDR now boasts forty-four universities with an enrollment of 220,000. Even West German observers admit that in many ways East German students have decided advantages over the students in crisis-ridden West German universities. Under Honecker 40 percent of the students are from workers' families, versus only 8 percent in West Germany. And the GDR requires no tuition. Of the students, 95 percent receive scholarships that include living expenses.

It is true that the students are required to be members of the Communist paramilitary Free German Youth Association and that too open criticism of the regime can lead to expulsion. Political science students must show evidence of "political aptitude." Communist propaganda permeates all studies, especially the humanities. But many scientific disciplines are regarded even by West German educators as superior to those in the Federal Republic.

Even in East Germany, which is regarded as the best disciplined Communist state in Europe, the clash between the conformist political doctrines of the FDJ (Free German Youth) and the restless spirit of rebel youths exists, though on a far more minor scale than in the west. During the finale of the GDR's twentieth anniversary celebrations in October, 1969, more than 1,000 youths staged a demonstration near the Wall. Most of them were turned on because of a rumor, which proved erroneous, that Britain's Rolling Stones were giving a performance in West Berlin, and a large number were merely out-of-towners who gravitated to the Wall out of sheer curiosity.

From time to time there are scuffles with the police.

During and after the Soviet and Warsaw Pact invasion of Czechoslovakia in August, 1968, in which GDR troops took active part, the Pankow (a district in East Berlin where the chief government buildings are located) regime showed uneasiness over the signs that the Prague spring fever had infected East Germans. Students in Leipzig brazenly protested against a government decision to raze the city's ancient University Church. In Rostock two undergraduates were sentenced to five years in jail for criticizing the regime.

But even the GDR's inner circle was divided over the Czech problem into hard-liners like Ulbricht and his right-hand man, Erich Honecker, member of the Politburo, and soft-liners like Prime Minister Willi Stoph.

Ulbricht's pro-Arab and anti-Israel policy is finding growing opposition among the GDR's intellectuals. Most embarrassing of all is their star member of the Jewish community, author Arnold Zweig, whom they used to display to the West as an ideological convert, and who has openly declined support of the anti-Israel policy.

The students and intellectuals link their emerging political involvement and resistance with the spread of the New Left in the West. But nothing would be further from the truth than to deduce from this the birth of an incipient uprising along the lines of the famous national revolt of June 17, 1953.

Paradoxically, the student rebels draw their inspiration from the Fathers of German Communism, Marx and Engels, along with Lenin, Mao Tse-tung, Ché Guevara, and New Left philosopher Herbert Marcuse.

"But make no mistake," the students tell Western visitors. "We are not anti-Communist and are loyal members of the GDR. We want to live in a socialist world. Our ideals are a democratic form of socialism."

The Christian Churches

Although nominally there are some 15 million (85 percent) Protestants and 1.6 million Roman Catholics in East Germany, the number of actually practicing Christians has dwindled by 75 percent in most towns. On the other hand, the fervor of the remaining Christians is unusually high. Few countries can boast of a greater spirit of cooperation and ecumenism than the GDR, where Catholics and Protestants are drawn together by the common bond of oppression by the regime. For years they have endured constant harassments (for example, funds have been withheld for repairs, with 2,000 churches still in their wartime state of ruin).

The arbitrary arrests of priests and laity have stopped and there is no outright persecution. The Constitution guarantees freedom of religion. Nevertheless, the regime has openly and systematically sought to discredit and ultimately replace formal religion. The regime even went so far as to create a macabre state religion, with its own Ten Commandments ("Thou shalt perform good deeds for socialism"), and sacraments, especially *Jugendweihe* (youth consecration), a substitute for confirmation. In addition, pagan rites for birth, burial, and marriage have been developed. Practicing Christians have been denied jobs, promotion, entrance to universities. Only 7,000 out of 104,500 teachers in the GDR are acknowledged Christians.

Financially the Christian churches in East Germany manage to keep afloat. For one thing, the GDR pays 15 percent toward the salaries of priests, an anomaly for an antireligious state. Also, generous donations continually flow from West Germany, which the GDR encourages because it sorely needs hard western currency.

Until 1969 the two Christian bodies were the last remaining institutions which transcended the two Germanies. Eventually Ulbricht persuaded certain Protestant ministers to plea for two separate church organizations and denounce the unity of an all-German Protestant administration. In 1967 he frustrated the joint meeting of the annual Evangelical Synod held simultaneously in both Berlins, by forcing East German clerics to meet twenty miles outside of East Berlin.

Ulbricht finally won out, and on June 10, 1969, the Federation of Evangelical Churches (BEK) in the GDR was created, thus formally severing ties with the Evangelical Church in Germany (EKD). Organized twenty-one years earlier, the EKD attempted to maintain an all-German church organization with eastern and western synods despite the political division.

Nevertheless, the new constitution of the BEK specifically refers to the first confessional synod held in Barmen in 1934, which repudiated National Socialism, and then goes on to require member churches to assist one another "toward a common defense against destructive false doctrines." In Article IV it emphasizes "common action" while drawing attention to "a special fellowship towards all of Evangelical Christianity in Germany" for which the BEK is to fulfill certain tasks in "co-responsibility" and "in fraternal freedom within its own organizational structure."

Four Roman Catholic dioceses in West Germany, those of Osnabrück, Paderborn, Fulda, and Würzburg reach far into East Germany, while a small region of the see of Breslau (Wroclaw), now Polish, extends into East Germany's southeastern corner. The Vatican is reported to be considering the establishment of new dioceses in East Germany to conform with the realistic postwar borders, but is loathe to appear to endorse prematurely either the Oder-Neisse border or the GDR regime.

Cardinal Alfred Bengsch, archbishop of Berlin, in contrast to his predecessor, Cardinal Julius Doepfner, presently the archbishop of Munich, deliberately moved to East Berlin, even though over half of his diocese (300,000) live in West Berlin. The regime lets him go as often as he wants (via Vienna) to Rome, but he may visit West Berlin only three times a month. And the West German bishops of the above-mentioned overlapping dioceses have not been permitted entry at all.

For all practical purposes the Roman Catholic Church in Germany is already divided into East and West, inasmuch as Bengsch is chairman of the East German Bishops' Conference and Doepfner is chairman of the West German Bishops.

No Illusions

Any observer who looks beyond the showcase cities of East Berlin and trade-fair conscious Leipzig will soon lose any illusions that the GDR is quite as glamorous as it first seems.

Many country areas still have horse-drawn carts and unmechanized farms, highways are potholed, and traffic is so slight that many cities look almost deserted. The cities are shrouded with soft-coal haze and omnipresent odors of disinfectants and cabbage. East Berlin's theater Thistle (*Distel*) timidly ventured one socialist solution for East Germany's ills: nose plugs.

The stores, it is true, are laden with goods, until you ask for the item you want and are told, "Everything is to be had—but not here." There is a thriving black market where coffee costs eight dollars a pound; a shirt, ten dollars; a TV set, nearly five hundred dollars; brandy, seventeen dollars a bottle. Baby food, nylons, blue jeans, luxury soaps, cosmetics, and most types of machinery are hard to get.

The GDR produces 120,000 automobiles annually (compared with 2.3 million in the Federal Republic), from the midget Trabant ($1,400) to the medium-sized Wartburg ($3,500). But there is a waiting period of four years and even the Trabant costs the average worker nearly a full year's salary. And gasoline costs $1.40 a gallon. Anyone placing an ad offering a used car for sale usually gets a phone call from the newspaper staff and the car is sold before the ad even reaches print.

High party functionaries never have to wait for goods, since they have exclusive access to the *Handels-Organisation Spezial* (HOS) which supplies them with every conceivable item from the East or West.

Because of a lack of natural resources, except lignite and potash, the GDR must make a large number of imports, which must be paid for with machinery, chemical products, food, mineral products, and consumer goods—and it is the consumer who has to do without.

Moreover, planned economy of the predominantly state-owned concerns, mostly organized in the *Vereinigung Volkseigener Betriebe* (VVB-Association of the People's Own Industry), makes competition virtually impossible. Preoccupied with quotas, priorities, and five-year plans, the East German firms still manufacture many inferior, outmoded, or downright useless products, while sorely needed goods are overlooked. This is carried to such extremes that a firm might leave its lights burning all night because at the beginning of the year it overestimated its kilowatt needs and would create widespread havoc if it wavered from the plan. In estimating payroll needs a year ahead, a firm must allow for sick leave. If it underestimates the latter, it could happen that the firm is unable to pay salaries toward the end of the year.

The GDR is still recovering from the massive pre-Wall exodus, mostly of young people, so that it has a disproportionately high percentage of senior citizens. Thus it is not surprising that its population has been decreasing at the rate of about 3,000 a year, whereas in the Federal Republic the population increased by 514,000 in 1968 (half of these being guest workers from the Mediterranean countries).

There are over three million pensioners in the GDR, which is 17.5 percent of the entire population (11.2 percent in the Federal Republic). While the GDR has a more comprehensive social security program than West Germany in other respects, it is far behind in caring for the aged, who receive less than 200 East marks monthly (about $40), compared to over $75 in West Germany.

The large number of female traffic cops in the GDR is a reminder that most East German women work, more per capita than in any other country in the world. Of the 17 million citizens in the GDR, 9.26 million are women, and 48 percent of them are employed full time. If one includes part-time work, the percentage is 71 percent. In order to accommodate working mothers, the number of kindergartens and nurseries has been increased from 110,000 (1949) to 554,000 (1968). "Woman," according to the East German constitution, "is a citizen with a firm socialist conviction, with many-sided interests, is well educated, enjoys the benefits of professional competence and training. . . . . In respect to her husband she is an equal partner, a loving mother to the children and an understanding friend."

East German men apparently regard their women differently, for after Romania and Hungary, East Germany has the highest divorce rate in Europe: 15.6 out of every 10,000 population (as compared with 10 per 1,000 in the Federal Republic). And the percentage of weddings has simultaneously gone down, 32.8 per 10,000 population. East German newspapers speak frequently of a growing envy of men who complain that their wives often earn more than they, or at any rate are becoming "bossier." East German psychologist Dr. W. König notes a growing "inferiority complex among GDR men."

While there are far more working women in the GDR than in the Federal Republic on the lower level, there are also proportionately more women in the higher professions in the GDR: 34 percent of judges, 70 percent of teachers, 31.5 percent of physicians, and nearly 13 percent of mayors.

However, the East German woman, for all the preaching about female equality, is still poorly represented at the top echelons of government. Only 21 women are included among the 181 members of the central committee of the SED (Socialist Unity Party), which runs the country. All members of the politburo and secretaries of the central committee are men. Only one woman, Margot Honecker, is represented among the 40 members of the cabinet, as minister for adult education, and she happens to be the wife of party secretary, Erich Honecker, Ulbricht's right-hand man and often mentioned as his successor. As for the regional SED secretariats, they are all run by men.

While goose-stepping has been abolished in West Germany because it evokes memories of Nazi times, the People's Army of East Germany, 126,000-strong, maintains the practice. For all its peace talk and banners with peace slogans, in practice the GDR keeps fanning the military spirit. Older observers who have experienced World War II shudder at the many similarities between the flag-studded, pompous Wagnerian-like parade demonstrations of the GDR, and the mass rallies Hitler used to stage at Nuremberg and Berlin.

There is no such thing as a free press or free elections in the GDR. The leading newspaper, *Neues Deutschland,* which is the official voice of the SED, sets the tone and the other publications follow.

All political power is concentrated in the politburo of the

169

SED, a twenty-one-man committee with party secretary Walter Ulbricht at the head, which dominates executive, legislative, and economic policy. Members of the SED central committee administer GDR districts (formerly *Länder, i.e.,* states). Politburo member Herbert Warnke controls the FDGB (Trade Union Association). Dependable functionaries of the SED manage and organize the various "daughter associations," from the Democratic Women's League to the Democratic Farmers' Party. The SED has 1.8 million card-carrying members.

Citizens are eligible to "vote" at the age of 18 and to hold office at 21. But there is no such thing as an election campaign. Every four years an "election" takes place, which is called "account-taking of the past four years" and "developing a perspective for the next four years." At the 1963 elections, 99.5 percent out of 11,621,158 eligible voters, voted for the government's National Front, while only 0.05 percent voted against.

In addition to 111 SED representatives in the *Volkskammer* (People's Chamber), there are also representatives of East German CDU, the Democratic Farmers' Party, the National Democratic Party (no connection with NPD in West Germany), the Free German Youth, and women's and cultural associations, but they cannot vote and are hardly ever consulted. Candidates are set up by the National Front voting commission, mostly SED members, and gradually eliminated in a whole series of regional elections, so that on election day in 1967, for example, the voters had a choice of only 500 out of 581 candidates.

On May 3, 1971, the East German news agency, ADN, in a sudden announcement, revealed that the seventy-seven-year-old Walter Ulbricht, for reasons of health, resigned as first secretary of East Germany's Communist party, SED. Although he retained the post of president of the Council of State, which he held since 1960, he thereby relinquished the actual seat of power to his successor, Erich Honecker, long regarded as Ulbricht's heir apparent. As secretary of the Central Committee, Mr. Honecker had been in charge of running the party's day-to-day affairs for several years.

An impeccable dresser and former head of the secret police, Honecker is regarded as a cool and efficient administrator who never shows his feelings. Western observers are virtually unanimous in the view that Honecker, long identified with a hard-line policy toward the West and a Stalinist brand of communism at home, is very much a man in Mr. Ulbricht's image. Neither they nor the Bonn government anticipate any significant change in relations between the two Germanies in the foreseeable future.

Whatever the outcome, there is hardly a politician left in Bonn who seriously questions the continued existence of the GDR. By 1970 it had won diplomatic recognition from twenty-one countries, where it now has envoys, and had established consulates in ten others, trade missions in fifteen more, and had sent representatives to the chamber of commerce of twenty nations.

To all appearances the boast of Ulbricht, made years ago, has come true: "One day the world will have to deal with us."

◄ 12 ►

THE GERMAN QUESTION AND BERLIN

THE FIRST THING that strikes the stranger on arrival at West Berlin's Tempelhof Airport is that nothing particularly strikes him, unless it is the airport's convenient location in the heart of the city. As he rides in his cab to his hotel, he passes several miles of broad, bustling boulevards and apartment houses not unlike those on Chicago's Sheridan Road, hundreds of shops, and hundreds of thousands of well-fed, well-groomed pedestrians. Not a sign of the Wall at all.

When, after checking into his hotel on the famed Kurfürstendamm (nicknamed "Kudamm"), West Berlin's Broadway and Times Square rolled into one, he inquires about the Wall, he learns that it is still a long way off. Advertising posters announce a poodle show, a soap exhibit, a forthcoming appearance of the Rolling Stones, and *I Am Curious (Yellow)*. Elsewhere thousands of Berliners are cramming the fun house and roller coaster at an amusement park. In spite of the 2.2 million persons crowded in the city's 185.7 square miles, West Berlin is very much a farming town. Some 163,000 chickens on 830 poultry farms, 22,000 pigs, and more than 2,000 registered cows and countless thousands of bees in 6,500 hives occupy more than 5,000 acres of farmland comprising about a fifth of the city. With the memories of the 1949-49 Berlin blockade still vivid—the Communists cut off all ground routes to this Western enclave 110 miles inside East German territory. West Berliners are holding on to all the farmland they can. At the vegetable institute at Berlin's Technical University, a $25,000 hothouse tower contains 2,000 potted lettuce plants which ride up and down an elevator all day long catching the sun while passing through spraying water.

Many of the farms can be reached by subway. A Dahlem farm, for instance, is separated by a wire fence, behind which twenty-two pigs grunt approvingly at the goings on of a fashionable business street lined with Mercedes-Benz sedans.

172

One-fourth of the city consists of parks—there are 50,000 boats on West Berlin lakes.

Physically at least, it is possible to live and die without ever seeing the Wall.

Life for West Berliners has aptly been compared to the eye of a hurricane—while all around tempests are swirling, life within is routine and normal. During one of many tense moments in Berlin over the past decade, I asked a middle-aged man at a bus stop about the crisis. "Crisis?" he asked. "Which crisis do you mean? You want to know something? I don't even remember what last year's crisis was all about." A few moments later he made a comment, seemingly unrelated. "What burns me up," this Berliner said, shivering in the cold, "is that they don't put enough buses on this line. I've been waiting here half an hour." I was reminded of a moving description by the late World War II correspondent Ernie Pyle who had asked a GI at the front what his greatest wish was, and the latter replied, "a hot shower and clean underwear."

More than two decades of the cold war, with its waves of crises—rape and looting by Russian soldiers, postwar destitution and starvation, the Communist blockade and the airlift, the periodic brinkmanship, and then the Wall—have hardened West Berliners. The same brusque, aggressive, outspoken Berlin manner—called *Schlagfertigkeit*—with its blunt sarcasm and sassy repartee and fierce local patriotism that infuriates and exasperates other Germans, has also proved to be a built-in safety valve. "We have calluses on our nerves," West Berliners will casually observe.

From his hotel the visitor rides over half an hour in two buses before he finally turns onto the Bernauer Strasse where, suddenly, like the subconscious reality of death, there it is—the Wall, the watchtowers, the death strip, the sulky East Berlin guards with their submachine guns and broken mirror fragments that they hold up to frustrate photographers. And just as suddenly it becomes clear to the visitor that the West Berliners' apparent blasé indifference doesn't ring true. One sympathetic word too many will bring a flood of tears from a housewife. "My mother is still over there," she sobs. "I haven't seen her since the Wall went up in 1961. At first, my husband, children, and I used to carry a ladder to the Wall, lean it against a lamp post and from that position take turns waving at mother and sisters on the other side. Since the death strip this is no longer possible." (Nearly one out of every three West Berliners has relatives in East Berlin.)

Isolated as they are, and repeatedly harassed by East German roadblocks of the three highway arteries from West Germany, the citizens of the "Island City" never tire of hearing pledges of support from the West. Newspapers play up American support for Berlin in a childish way, much like a jealous wife insisting on endless affirmations of love from her husband.

The Federal Republic's four chancellors so far—Adenauer, Erhard, Kiesinger, Brandt—inevitably made their official visits to the United States and just as inevitably the very first thing they would say on their return to hordes of West German reporters, "President Eisenhower . . . Kennedy . . . Johnson . . . Nixon [respectively] has given us assurance that the American people will remain firm on Berlin." President Kennedy's memorized one sentence of German, *"Ich bin ein Berliner* [I am a Berliner]*"* that he shouted to Berlin crowds still stirs emotions. When President Richard Nixon visited Berlin in February, 1969, 6,000 wildly cheering Siemens' factory workers sang—in parody of the New Left chant, "Ho, ho, Ho Chi Minh"—"Ha, ho, he—Nixon ist okay."

"The American president could issue a daily promise on Berlin," one West Berlin editor told me, "and every day it would be a banner headline."

Official West German concern for Berlin is overwhelming. Immediately after the erection of the Wall on August 13, 1961, West Berlin police drove panel trucks mounted with loudspeakers all along its twenty-five-mile snakelike length. "Remember Eichmann!" the loudspeakers blared at the *Vopos* behind the Wall. "One day you too will be called to account for collaborating with a dictatorial regime as he was. Murder remains murder," the speaker referred to the *Vopos'* shooting and killing of escaping refugees, sometimes even shooting escaping dogs, "even if exercised under command. Remember Eichmann!" Big posters were erected along the Wall, urging East German police purposely to miss when they shot at refugees. Showing a sympathetic-looking East German border guard, the posters were captioned, "I aim to one side."

Elsewhere West Berlin police appealed to East Berlin guards' consciences by displaying, across from observation slits on the East Berlin side, huge enlargements of photos showing human

174

misery caused by the partition. Sixty West Berlin police, equipped with miniature cameras, documented numerous inhumane acts by *Vopos,* sometimes even catching them in the very act of shooting refugees.

Looks Are Deceiving

Meanwhile, West Berlin has emerged as an internationally famous cultural and business center. The average visitor can be quite impressed by the galaxy of fashionable theaters, nightclubs, boulevards, bustling business complexes, international hotels, and an unending round of international conferences, seminars, and exhibitions.

The *Klinikum* of Berlin-Steglitz, with 3,000 employees is one of the world's most modern hospitals, handles up to 1,400 patients at a time (is nicknamed *die Heilfabrik,* the healing factory). The controversial West German publishing tycoon, Axel Springer, built a twenty-story glass and concrete structure right up against the Wall to demonstrate his belief in a reunited Germany with Berlin as its capital.

The number of industrial workers of West Berlin equals that of Norway. Its electrical industry, which comprises 27 percent of its entire industry, is greater than the combined electrical industries of Switzerland and Austria. Its growth rate, 6 percent to 7 percent, is about equal to that of West Germany, and in 1969 its GNP had already exceeded 22.5 billion DM's (20.8 billion DM's in 1968). Every second light bulb, every third cigarette, and every third dress bought in the Federal Republic is produced in West Berlin.

More than 30,000 students attend two universities and several academies. Eighteen theaters daily perform plays and the Berlin Philharmonic and the *Deutsche Oper* enjoy international acclaim.

In spite of all this, West German publications continually speak of West Berlin as a "dying city" and bemoan its predicted ultimate economic collapse. More than 20 percent of West Berliners are over sixty-five years old—as opposed to 8.9 percent of the senior citizens of pre-1939 Berlin and 11.8 percent in West Germany today. The World Health Organization has said that West Berlin has the highest suicide rate for any city in the world. 1967 figures showed that 49 percent of the 897 suicides (2,000 attempts) were persons thirty to fifty years old, 23 percent from twenty to thirty, and 7 percent over sixty. A psychiatrist explained that people in West Berlin, Hong Kong, and the depressed textile towns of northern England commit suicide at double their national averages because so many young people have left to get jobs elsewhere, creating a social isolation for the elderly.

Young people leave West Berlin constantly, and the Federal Republic has to virtually bribe them to keep them there. In 1968, for example, more than 8,000 or 1 percent of the young worker force left the city. Berlin newlyweds who promise to stay receive attractive bonuses at low interest rates, which are reduced with the birth of each child. Income taxes are nominal, corporation taxes are slashed to the bone, prices for consumer goods are appreciably lower than in West Germany. Airlines are partly subsidized for flights to Berlin. In 1969 more than 150,000 pupils from West Germany were sent to Berlin for study trips at government expense.

Two plush information centers in West Berlin supply vast quantities of printed matter to visiting journalists, and the Federal press office in Bonn spends millions of Deutsche marks annually entertaining hundreds of journalists and educators from all over the world, providing all-expenses-paid chauffeured tours of West Germany and especially Berlin. Tons of printed matter on East Germany and Berlin are distributed by the press office all over the world in many languages. Generous government grants are available to dozens of West German cultural and political organizations which directly or indirectly deal with the German problem. In 1969, a total of 596,000 visitors, half from West Germany, toured Berlin, many of them as a result of clever government-sponsored promotion. A whole fleet of promotion buses tour all over western Europe regularly loaded with slides and printed matter, staffed with pretty hostesses who try to convince potential tourists (travel agencies offer special reductions and discount shopping coupons) that *"Berlin ist eine Reise wert* [Berlin is worth a visit]*."* TV documentaries in West Germany week in and week out keep the consciousness of Berlin alive. Berlin-oriented radio programs remind millions in Germany and around the world. In 1969 alone the "blood transfusion" of Federal aid to Berlin amounted to a cool 1.1 billion Deutsche marks (over $300 million).

The reason for all this feverish activity is clear: Berlin is in trouble and its economic future looks bleak. Many observers believe that the tough, we-can-take-it West Berlin stance is beginning to crack and that its saturation point as an island city may soon be reached. In the second half of the sixties, it was West Berlin where the New Left began its stirrings, where the student rebellions rocked the educational Establishment to its foundations, where "Red Rudi Dutschke," student leftist leader, was shot and crippled for life, where anti-American demonstrations have been the most rampant, violent, and vociferous.

The mood of hopelessness has infected just about every Berliner. More than two decades ago Mayor Ernst Reuter told them, "If we want to win our fight, we will win it." Now they are no longer sure what the fight is all about. The clear-cut fronts, the lines of battle are gone, and no one is more confused than the leaders of West Germany and West Berlin.

West Berliners Are Worried

De jure, West Berlin is a *Land* (state) of the Federal Republic, and is so recognized by the Basic Law. But *de facto* the application of the Basic Law to Berlin is still subject to certain restrictions. Thus the West Berlin representatives at the Bundestag and Bundesrat plenary meetings have only a consultative status. They may not vote.

Because of the Four-Power agreements of 1945, West Berlin cannot be governed by the Federal Government, since all Federal laws must be approved by the West Berlin House of Representatives (140 members). The City Government (the Senate) consists of a Governing Lord Mayor (or *Bürgermeister*), a deputy Burgermeister, and eleven Senators.

On February 6, 1957, the Bundestag confirmed Berlin's status as capital of West Germany. But the seat of government and *de facto* capital is Bonn.

The Western troops in West Berlin number only about 11,000 and are completely encircled by twenty-two Soviet divisions, plus the armed forces of the GDR itself. Since West Berlin is under the protection of the Western Powers, it has no troops of its own, nor are troops of the Federal Republic stationed there, nor may West Berlin recruit for the West German Bundeswehr. For this reason, West Berlin is a haven for draft dodgers.

Although West Berlin obviously has never constituted a

military threat to the GDR or the Soviet Union, it has been frequently exploited as a lever for political pressure by the Soviet Union and the GDR in the hope of gradually wearing down the inhabitants' resistance, securing recognition through Berlin for the GDR, and ultimately absorbing the city in a separate communist state.

West Berliners are tired of the nonentity status of their non-city and the feeble ambiguous relationship with the Federal Republic. They are uneasy about the growing talk about concessions, the recognition of the "reality" of the GDR, and the frightening prospect, no longer farfetched, of actual recognition of the GDR by western countries, including, eventually, West Germany itself.

In such an eventuality West Berlin would be either a freak enclave, isolated more than ever from West Germany, or it would be hopelessly compromised by its exposed position and completely vulnerable for rapid absorption by the GDR. They know full well that the United States is not prepared to defend Berlin "down to the last American" and that as time goes on the allies will be less and less interested in identifying Berlin with the West German—and Western world's—cause. The allies have never recognized West Berlin as an integral territorial part of the Federal Republic of West Germany. And the East German constitution specifically claims the entire city, not merely East Berlin, as the GDR capital.

While conservative West Berliners feel betrayed, the proliferating New Left groups have become increasingly sharp in their criticism of *Rathaus* (Town Hall) policies, which they say are tainted with Cold-War sentiments. The most vociferous and influential of these groups is the Republican Club, a loose collection of individuals and organizations, including journalists, writers, professional persons, militant student organizations, such as the Socialist German Student Federation (SDS). The Republican Club demands a policy toward the GDR independent of Bonn, recognition of the GDR, without endorsing the regime, rejection of German reunification as a goal, and an independent economic policy designed to turn the city into an international East-West trade and cultural center.

The moderates urge an accommodation with the Communist system for trade purposes, but as part of a West German idcological disengagement that would bring about the removal of the Wall and all physical and psychological barriers.

And by 1971 there were indications that the Bonn government, in exchange for human concessions to West Berlin, might modify previous insistence that Berlin be regarded *de facto* and *de jure* as being necessarily a part of the Federal Republic.

Rudolf Augstein, the influential and provocative Socialist publisher of the weekly newsmagazine *Der Spiegel,* thinks any link of West Berlin with West Germany is unrealistic. He has been urging the city for years to make its own arrangement with Eastern Europe or face economic collapse. He does not rule out the possibility that the United States might some day sell out Berlin to the Soviet Union in return for concessions in Cuba, Red China, or the Middle East.

For a while, there was much mention of solving the German problem within the framework of a wider settlement involving a nuclear-free and neutral zone in Central Europe. This plan calls for the complete withdrawal of Russian and Western troops from East and West Germany, Poland, Czechoslovakia, and possibly Hungary. And these states would withdraw from NATO and the Warsaw Pact respectively and accept strict arms limitation enforced by East-West or UN inspection. Under such conditions Berlin would be the capital of a completely neutralized but reunited Germany.

This proposal, however, is rejected by most experts as not only utopian but, in the event of unlikely realization, even dangerous, as a neutralized reunited German state could too easily become a pivot between East and West and unpredictably shift allegiance at will. Moreover, the success of Western European economic development is greatly dependent on a close alliance of West Germany with western Europe—not to speak of its military security.

Large numbers of West Germans, in spite of comprehensive mass-media coverage of Berlin and East Germany, are poorly informed on life in "the other Germany." Paradoxically, growing numbers of West Germans are also willing to make large concessions to the Pankow regime, and their attitude toward reunification and the whole German problem has changed profoundly.

According to psychologist Peter R. Hofstätter, West Germans

still associate their fellow countrymen in East Germany with concepts like "slavery, destitution, exhaustion, death." The respected Allensbach Demoscopic Institute reported the results of an opinion poll prepared for their second German television program. They revealed that in 1966 nearly half of all West Germans had not heard of the construction of the Berlin Wall in 1961, that two-thirds did not know that there was a city in the GDR named Karl Marx Stadt (formerly Chemnitz). Half of the respondents erroneously believed that East Germans still need ration tickets to purchase bicycles or buggies, and the same number did not know that East Germany produces its own brands of automobiles.

West Germans' Views on Reunification

In another opinion poll, however, conducted by the Institute for Applied Social Science at Bad Godesberg, it was shown that the great majority of West Germans have shifted from an ideological attitude toward the GDR to a very pragmatic one. Only one-tenth of the respondents stated that recognition of the GDR was avoidable as a step toward reunification. The number of those believing a hard-line policy must be maintained toward the GDR declined within the space of one year from 27 percent at the beginning of 1966 to 19 percent at the end of that year. Nearly three-fifths were in favor of a policy of "small steps" toward reunification; 48 percent in the spring of 1966, but 59 percent by the end of the year. There were 11 percent willing to talk about the possibility of the presence of Soviet troops in the West. And 20 percent said they would consider the nationalization of basic industry.

Opinions on the standards of living in East and West Germany were quite differentiated. Nearly all agreed that West Germany provides more consumer goods and takes better care of the aged. Yet opinion was sharply divided on educational possibilities: 40 percent believed the Western educational system to be better; 39 percent, the Eastern. It is interesting that those who had personal contacts with citizens of East Germany tended to regard the Eastern system as superior (62 percent).

The number of those who are concerned about reunification has been steadily declining from year to year. At the end of the year 1966 only 26 percent still found the partition "unbearable" (in 1965 it was 38 percent). Only 18 percent said they would "get anything out of it personally" if Germany were reunited. Many of the respondents stated bluntly that reunification was quite secondary to their greater concern that the Federal Republic maintain economic stability. Only 18 percent insisted that the East Germans who will take part in the Olympic Games in Munich in 1972 be denied the right to use GDR flags and sing their national anthem, which the Kiesinger government permitted in 1969. (Both flags use the same broad horizontal red, gold, black stripes. The GDR, in addition, has superimposed a hammer and compass in the center.)

New Flexibility

The basis for a more flexible West German eastern policy had already been created by the grand coalition under CDU Chancellor Kurt Georg Kiesinger, although even here credit must go in large part to the junior partner in that coalition, SPD Foreign Minister Willy Brandt. The Social Democrats' thrust for "human, economic, and spiritual ties" between the two German halves, including contact on the official level proved to be a fiasco. However, ambassadors were exchanged with Romania, diplomatic relations resumed with Yugoslavia, an offer of mutual abjuration of the use of force was extended to all East European states, including the GDR, and a willingness to hold "preparatory talks" with the then Polish head of state, Wladyslaw Gomulka. The West German post office even issued a commemorative postage stamp honoring Karl Marx.

But it remained for Willy Brandt, upon assuming office as chancellor in October, 1969, to say the hitherto unmentionable: In his famous policy statement of October 28, he officially conceded the existence of two German states, the one capitalist, the other communist, ruffling feathers from Munich to Kiel. In the same statement he insisted that the SPD/FDP coalition government would never grant sovereign recognition of East Germany. But numerous sweeping changes were implemented that were unthinkable a few years earlier. The Federal Ministry of All-German Affairs—a name which presupposed reunification—was changed to the Ministry of Inter-German Relations. The new government also did away with the disparaging expressions previously used in reference to the GDR (for example, "*so-called* German Democratic Republic," "the Soviet-Occupied Zone," "the other part of Germany," "Middle Germany"), and references to the Soviet Union as "the enemy" (Adenauer frequently said *Tod-Feind*—deadly enemy). Brandt even foresaw the possibility of a legal settlement that would acknowledge the *de facto* existence of the two Germanies within a German nation until a final settlement of the German problem. Under postwar allied agreements, this settlement can only be reached through a still pending peace treaty, a development that seems farther away today than it did more than twenty years ago when the two states were formed.

West German pundits frequently say that a unified Germany will be achieved only within the framework of a much broader European structure, a pluralistic structure that permits national ideological diversity, and the existence of competing social systems. Many of them urge a greater cooperation with the Common Market and the Council of Europe.

At any rate, the SPD/FDP coalition introduced informality, flexibility, and a new openness in West Germany's approach to the East. They foresaw a treaty which would establish a kind of confederation granting "regulated coexistence." But there would not be an exchange of ambassadors, as the heart of the SPD/FDP policy is that East Germany is not a foreign country, and that Germans in both East and West are a common people living in a common nation. C. L. Sulzberger, writing in the *International Herald Tribune,* suggested a loose confederation of two Germanies like that created by Metternich for the hodgepodge of German states after the Napoleonic Wars. "The Metternich system allowed participating members," he wrote, "to retain their own rulers, armies and foreign policies but established a customs union and a talkative but largely powerless assembly, thus feeding the concept of German unity without either achieving it or worrying the neighbors."[1]

Situation Modified

When the SPD/FDP coalition assumed responsibility after the September, 1969, elections Leonid Brezhnev described it as "an indisputable victory for the forces of democracy." Observers attributed the sudden friendly attitude of the Soviet Union toward West Germany as an effort to cover up the clumsy handling of the ill-advised Soviet invasion of Czechoslovakia in August, 1968, and as a bid for greater stability in central and eastern Europe. Lengthy notes were exchanged between the two countries suggesting a nonaggression agreement.

But formidable obstacles to a genuine *detente* between the Federal Republic and Eastern Europe remained. Until then, the Soviet Union, East Germany, and Poland refused to budge from five basic conditions that they laid down as a prerequisite for the solution of the German problem:

1) That West Germany give legal recognition to East Germany

2) That West Germany recognize all existing frontiers, including the Oder-Neisse border between Poland and East Germany

3) That West Germany abandon Berlin as part of the Federal Republic

4) That the 1938 Munich pact be declared invalid

5) That West Germany forfeit all claims to nuclear weapons

While Kiesinger refused to budge on any of the demands, the situation since Brandt assumed leadership has changed drastically.

Thanks to Brandt's Ostpolitik a transition has already taken place in eastern Europe, notably Poland. It remains to be seen whether his dramatic eastward thrusts—his meeting with East German Premier Willi Stoph in March, 1970, his signing of the nonaggression treaty in Moscow in August of that same year, and on December 7, 1970 his signing of the normalization pact in Warsaw, acknowledging the Oder-Neisse line as Poland's western frontier—will bring lasting results. The two treaties must still be ratified by the Bundestag, and this in turn will depend a great deal on whether or not there is a satisfactory solution of the Berlin question. The Ostpolitik has been severely criticized by the opposition CDU/CSU, as well as by such leading American elder statesmen as John J. McCloy, the first postwar high commissioner in Germany, and General Lucius Clay, who was military governor of Berlin at the peak of the cold war. It is widely feared that Brandt's policy might lead to the weakening or conceivably even the severance of West Germany's ties with the West. German critics fear that the SPD/FDP coalition government under Brandt is selling German interests down the river with nothing to show in return.

However, the prevailing view is more optimistic. If the present developments continue, a general *detente* will eventually bring western and eastern Europe closer than they have been since World War II.

The SPD/FDP coalition has declared outdated the *Alleinvertretungsrecht* (the Federal Republic's claim to be the sole representative of the people of the two Germanies, on the assumption that the GDR is an illegal usurpation of territory against the will of the inhabitants). Also tossed into the scrap heap is the Hallstein Doctrine (severance of diplomatic relations with any country that recognizes the GDR). Almost since its inception in 1949, the Bonn government had spent literally billions of marks, mostly in underdeveloped countries of Asia, Africa, and Latin America, to purchase the favor of governments in those areas with the specific aim of encouraging them not to have any dealings with—and above all not to recognize—East Germany. The Bonn policy was "our friends are our friends only if they are enemies of our enemies." The Brandt government has announced that it will no longer pay hush money to foreign governments interested in relations with the East German state. (West German newspapers made a laughingstock out of United States Ambassador Kenneth Rush, who speaks hardly any German, but when asked about the Hallstein Doctrine, reportedly replied, "I'm not very well acquainted with that, but I think it is a good thing.")

With the signing of the nuclear nonproliferation pact on November 28, 1969, the Federal Republic reaffirmed its earlier (1954) renunciation of nuclear weapons.

With regard to Czechoslovakia and the Munich pact, the situation is much more complicated. Although Bonn had already under Kiesinger declared that the Munich pact no longer gives West Germany any territorial claim, it still is reluctant to renounce the pact outright.

The Communist regime in Prague has repeatedly accused Bonn of striving to recover the Sudetenland (which was returned to Czechoslovakia at the end of the war) by not renouncing the 1938 agreement of England, France, and Hitler's Germany.

Four international lawyers, Professor Humbert Ambruster of Mainz University, Professor Friedrich Klein of Münster, Professor Fritz Muench of Bonn, and Professor Theodor Veiter of Liechtenstein (who is also a senior official of the International Research Society for World Refugee Questions), in a statement on January 12, 1966, said the Munich agreement was still valid. They warned that annulment of the Munich pact might have an opposite effect from that intended, in that it could revive old problems by restoring the situation existing before it was concluded.

"This," they said, "would particularly apply to nationality and property rights and to the claim of the former Sudeten German population [expelled from Czechoslovakia in 1945] to the right to live again in the home of their origin."[2]

Although Brandt has firmly stated that a *de facto* acceptance of the GDR can never mean *de jure* recognition, the fact remains that reunification can no longer be regarded as the only acceptable solution of the German question. From a historical perspective, the case for reunification loses much of its force. The borders of Germany or, rather, numerous German states have changed so frequently, why must the more recent one of 1937 Germany be regarded as the sole criterion? Why not the borders of the Vienna Congress of 1815? Or the borders of the Kaiser Reich, including Alsace-Lorraine, of 1871? If the recovery of Alsace-Lorraine is unthinkable, is the recovery of the Oder-Neisse area any less unthinkable, or for that matter the GDR? "If we look at history," says Swiss historian Professor Walter Hofer, "we see that not unity but division was the norm of political existence in Germany. To be sure, German unity existed from 1870 to 1940, but three-quarters of a century is a very short period in the history of a people. The decisive question is: How can such a unity be integrated and reconciled with a European order in which all the other states, especially Germany's immediate neighbors, can, together with Germany, develop in freedom and security?"

Prevailing democratic opinion of course overwhelmingly supports the legitimate aspirations of the German people in both Germanies for reunification, and their sovereign right to choose in free elections the government of their choice. Undoubtedly the vast majority of the citizens of the GDR would in free elections decisively repudiate Ulbricht's kind of regime and radically uproot the police state machinery that has held them in bondage for so long. But would they necessarily and automatically opt for reunification? As has been indicated in the preceding chapter, there is overwhelming evidence to suggest that East Germans might very well prefer a democratic version of their socialist state to reunification. At any rate, reunification can no longer be regarded as a foregone conclusion.

Moreover, it is an open secret that large numbers of Europeans of both East and West prefer to keep Germany divided. BERLIN IS NOT THE NAVEL OF THE WORLD headlined the leading Swiss weekly *Weltwoche* during the 1969 Soviet threat to Berlin. The number of Europeans is legion who believe that the loss of the Oder-Neisse territories and the division of Germany is a small enough price to pay for the havoc that the Hitler regime wrought in the world. Reunification, they argue, cannot be based on any supposed "right" of the Germans to create a Reich like it once was. "We share their justified indignation over the humiliations and restrictions suffered under the Soviets," a Czech journalist said to me, "but what about the neo-Stalinism in Czechoslovakia? Or, for that matter, what about the Poles, Hungarians? They have no Berlin to wave like a red flag at the world. Why are the over-fed, bourgeois Germans so excited? Even in East Germany they do not even remotely have the problems, say, of Biafra, Hong Kong, or the blacks in Rhodesia and South Africa. Just what do they expect?"

Sir Geoffrey Defretas, former president of the advisory committee of the Council of Europe, has said, "For many the German division is a reassurance. Many Europeans sleep better at night because Germany is divided."

In an opinion poll conducted in 1968 by the Allensbach Institute, 60 percent of the French still fear German might, but only 44 percent of the British and 28 percent of the Americans. But in the same survey, paradoxically enough, 70 percent of the French said that the Germans have a right to be reunited, while 62 percent of the British endorsed this right "but not on the same basis," while 62 percent of Americans favored reunification without qualifications.

The famous French novelist François Mauriac once said, "I love Germany so much, I am glad that there are two of them."

Sebastian Hafner, the well known West German publicist, regards reunification as a hopeless goal, urges speedy recognition of the GDR. He argues that the estrangement of the two Germanies, including even the evolution of separate languages (West German is highly Americanized, while East German is riddled with ideological expressions), is because of nonrecognition. "Only recognition can bring us together again and remove the barriers, physical and psychological, which now separate us."

No longer feared militarily except in a few countries, the two Germanies of today have emerged as powerful economic forces which even in their divided state cause great concern, as I shall attempt to show in Chapter 21. Countries like the United Kingdom, France, Italy, Poland, and the Soviet Union are not about to encourage the muscle-flexing economic giant that is West Germany to almost double its production capacity by a merger with that eastern giant known as the German Democratic Republic.

East German Dilemma

For East Germany the new breezes of accommodation and flexibility flowing out of Bonn have been a frightening rather than a pleasing development. This should not be surprising. The secret of Ulbricht's success has been precisely because his "socialist model" of the farmers' and workers' state could only be accomplished in virtually total isolation. In addition, East Germans have risen to be the Soviet Union's biggest trade partner and to undisputed leadership in Eastern Europe next to the Soviet Union. Closer ties with the West would inevitably weaken this privileged status of the GDR.

But the same "realistic acceptance" that has shaken West Germany out of its stalemate position, has also penetrated the GDR.

Few West Germans are aware that hundreds of products that they buy for daily use come from East Germany (especially the big mail order houses, like Quelle and Neckermann, buy up the cheaper East German radios, tape recorders, sun lamps, etc., under license and sell them under their own names). In 1969, trade between East and West Germany increased by 25 percent over the previous year, breaking the previous record of 1966, when $750 million worth of goods were delivered in both directions. West Germany already ranks third, after the Soviet Union and Czechoslovakia as East Germany's trade partner. At the East German trade fair in Leipzig in 1969, West Germany was represented by 765 firms, who were received with open arms and continuous rounds of cocktail parties by the East German hosts.

Der Spiegel reported in November, 1969, that West German television crews suddenly received red-carpet treatment while covering East German activities. The GDR has had an "Office for Inner-German Trade" in Frankfurt since 1950 and another in Düsseldorf since 1956.

West Berlin's exports to communist countries, including Red China, rose 30 percent in 1969 compared to only 2.9 percent rise in the Federal Republic's exports.

On January 25, 1971, the postal authorities of the two Germanies signed an agreement that reopened ten direct telephone lines between East and West Berlin. Since 1952, when 5,000 lines were disconnected, there have been no public telephone connections at all. Even now the ten new lines will hardly meet the demand, so that most callers will have to reckon with a long wait. But at least West Berliners, who have been unable to visit their relatives in the eastern sector since 1966, will now be able to talk with them on the phone.

Plans are under way for the extension of inner-German trade, the liquidation of the Allied Travel Board in West Berlin and the allied visa-control station for GDR citizens traveling to West Berlin or West Germany, for the admittance of the East Berlin Schönefeld airport to the international air network, and the establishment of general consulates of the GDR in West Germany that will issue transit passes to West Berlin and East Germany.

Normalization is still far away, but small improvements like these go a long way toward a more hopeful, human relationship for the people of the two Berlins and the two Germanies.

PART TWO

The New Germans

PART TWO

The New Germans

◄ 13 ►

THAT LITTLE TOWN ON THE RHINE

"BONN," THE SAYING goes, "is half the size of the cemetery of New York City—and twice as dead."

When I stepped out of the whistle-stop-sized *Bahnhof,* I thought of the American GI who asked a policeman, "Say, where are all the girls in this town?" "Well, I'm sorry," replied the *Wachmeister,* "but she went to Cologne today to visit her grandmother."

Until 1971, you could whisk through Bonn in a matter of minutes and, if you weren't careful, not see a single building or setting to suggest that the sleepy university town and the preferred retirement town of senior citizens was the capital of Western Europe's industrial and military giant. Bonn's citizens have a nickname for it: *Bundesdorf* (Federal Hick Town).

Nothing is funnier to the visitor than the comic-opera setting—which older Germans take with deadly seriousness—of an official state visit, with the backdrop of the sedate eighteenth century university with its restful *Hofgarten,* or the Poppens-büttler Castle, or the colorful open-air marketplace, or the operetta-like gingerbread town hall, or the humble birthplace of Ludwig van Beethoven, or the miniature Romanesque cathedral, or the railroad tracks which literally divide the town in two and drive its citizens up the wall when its dozens of barriers block the streets countless times daily, or the romantic Rhine promenade with its Drachenfels ruins, Siebengebirge hills, and ponderous river barges.

Indeed, in 1971, so help me, some of its streets were still lighted every night by gas lanterns tended by a frustrated lamplighter tediously driving from lamp to lamp in a battered city Volkswagen. And just a few yards from the *Bundeshaus* (parliament building) sheep graze peacefully along the Rhine.

The "provisional capital" is the more polite phrase used to identify Bonn, meaning a town that serves as an emergency makeshift capital pending reunification of divided Germany and

191

a presumed restoration of Berlin as capital of the German nation.

A persistent myth has it that Bonn was chosen as capital because Konrad Adenauer, the first West German chancellor, wanted the capital to be within easy commuting distance from his home in Rhöndorf, a village on the other side of the Rhine. Others said Adenauer insisted on Bonn because the "old fox" knew that the Rhine valley climate (muggy like Washington, D.C.) made everyone tired except him.

Actually, the explanation is much simpler. The Parliamentary Council, which in 1948, under the auspices of the Western Allies, began to prepare the new constitution, had difficulty finding a place to meet. The Rhineland was chosen because it lay somewhere in the middle of the three western occupation zones which were going to be joined in the new political community. Cologne and Düsseldorf were simply much too destroyed by wartime bombs to house the Council. But the teachers' college of Bonn was relatively undamaged and therefore was chosen for the assembly.

The sixty-five "Founding Fathers" of the proposed new Federal Republic, who were chosen by the legislatures of eleven states, worked for eight months in the modest rooms of the college to lay down the basis for the new, democratic government in the western provinces of Germany. When the temporary seat of the government had to be chosen, Frankfurt received twenty-nine votes, and Bonn, thirty-three. It was precisely to emphasize the provisional nature of the "temporary" capital that tiny Bonn was preferred over Frankfurt, a large city. On May 8, 1948, Konrad Adenauer, Dean Acheson (U.S.), Robert Schumann (France), and Clement H. Atlee (Britain) signed the Basic Law.

Paul La Roche, chef of the Bonn parliament's restaurant, vividly recalls how popular in those early days his rich "pea soup with bacon" was with the emaciated, skinny members of the first Bonn parliament. Cookstoves from old English ships served as kitchen ranges, there were no refrigerators, and meals had to be carried across the open terrace. Today, nearly a quarter of a century afterwards, the old teachers' college, much enlarged and improved, is still the parliament building of West Germany and deputies discreetly ask La Roche for low-calorie menus.

But as time goes on, and reunification with the reinstatement of Berlin as the capital becomes a hopeless illusion, "provisional" Bonn has begun to assume more and more the atmosphere of a permanent establishment. Realistic measures have been taken to convert Bonn gradually into a full-fledged modern capital city with all the trimmings. The first step was the merger in 1969 of Bonn with several surrounding suburbs (notably Beuel and Bad Godesberg) into a "greater Bonn" with 300,000 inhabitants, not counting sheep that continue to graze contentedly along the Rhine. Although still a village by American standards, ambitious city planners already call it the "Manhattan on the Rhine," and there are even a handful of skyrise structures that dominate the otherwise picturesque landscape.

Basic Law

A "provisional" capital of a "provisional" country, of course, cannot have a constitution, but rather a *Grundgesetz* (Basic Law), which was also intended originally to be only a temporary settlement pending reunification. In fact, one of its main provisions aims at reunification of the constituent parts of the former German Reich, a section which has become controversial in view of the more realistic attitude toward East Germany and its probable recognition in the foreseeable future.

Meanwhile, the Basic Law guarantees the sacred and inalienable rights of the individual with a recourse to legal protection. It is superior to the power of the state, and it is subject to the Federal Constitutional Court (Supreme Court) in Karlsruhe. A famous passage in the preamble states that the Federal Republic is "animated by the resolve . . . to serve the peace of the world as an equal partner in a united Europe," and emphatically disassociates the Federal Republic from narrow nationalism.

The Federal President

While in the United States Americans have one man to govern as well as to represent, in the Federal Republic these two functions, representing and governing, are executed by two men, the Federal President and the Federal Chancellor respectively. Although the greater power resides in the office of chancellorship, the Federal President is the actual head of state. His role is very similar to that of the Queen in the United Kingdom, and some German observers hold that it is a psychological father-figure Ersatz for a Kaiser. At official functions, the president enjoys higher rank than the chancellor.

The Federal President is elected every five years by an assembly called the Federal Convention, which consists of the members of the Bundestag and an equal number of members elected by the state legislatures. The Basic Law does not allow for the election of the head of state by popular vote as was the custom in the Weimar Republic. Because the presidency has a dignified representative status like that of royalty, Germans do not regard it as fitting that their head of state should be exposed to the "degrading" turmoil of an election campaign. Haunted by the fear of abuse of autocratic power, such as was granted to the Reich president in the Weimar era and which provided the legal apparatus for Hitler, the Parliamentary Council in drafting the Basic Law restricted the president's power and limited his tenure of office to two consecutive terms.

The president's duties consist of representing the country at official functions and on state visits abroad, and of formally appointing both the Federal Chancellor (elected by the Bundestag) and the ministers (cabinet members) chosen by the Federal Chancellor. The president's proposal of chancellor could assume importance if the parliamentary majority should waver in the choice of several candidates, in which case his initiative could tip the scales in favor of one or the other.

The president exercises the power of pardon in individual cases and grants the Federal Order of Merit and other awards, chiefly in connection with cultural events. He also appoints Federal judges and public servants and promulgates laws. The first president of the Federal Republic was Professor Theodor Heuss (FDP), who was elected on September 12, 1949, and served two terms. Dr. Heinrich Luebke (CDU) succeeded Professor Heuss in 1959 and served two terms. In 1969 Gustav W. Heinemann (SPD) succeeded Dr. Luebke.

The Federal Chancellor

The most important man in the West German government is the Federal Chancellor, who determines and assumes responsibility for general policy. Although he is not directly elected by the people but by the majority of the Bundestag, it is the people who elect the Bundestag for a four-year term in free, direct, secret elections. The Federal ministers have relative autonomy within the scope of the chancellor's general policy.

The Bundestag may express its lack of confidence in the

Federal Chancellor only by a majority vote of its members and by requesting the Federal President to dismiss the chancellor. Thus, a chancellor's position is more secure than that of a prime minister in most other European countries, where a simple lack-of-confidence vote or defeat of a major piece of legislation can topple a government.

Federal legislation may be introduced by the Federal Government, by the Bundesrat, and by the Bundestag.

The Federal Courts

The Basic Law also provides for four High Federal Courts in the spheres of labor and social, administrative, civil and criminal, as well as finance jurisdiction. The Federal Constitutional Court in Karlsruhe has been functioning since October, 1951. For the first time in German history, a judicial body—unique in Europe—has been created that is capable of outlawing both legislation enacted by the parliament and actions of the government if such laws and actions violate the Basic Law.

Like the U.S. Supreme Court, this court also has the power to decide whether political parties and organizations are constitutional. In the fall of 1952 it denied the legality of a new-Nazi party. In the summer of 1956 it outlawed the Communist Party. In 1969 the court studied the rightist National Democratic Party (NPD), but permitted it to continue in existence. And, while it did not repeal its previous ban of the Communist Party, it permitted a new version of the Communist Party to organize and solicit members.

Twelve of the twenty-four judges of the court are elected by the Bundesrat and twelve by the Bundestag. Eight of the judges have a life tenure, the remainder are elected for terms of eight years.

While 3,000 out of 13,000 present judges in the Federal Republic are under thirty-four years of age, the entire judiciary system is urgently in need of reform. "The judges," according to Gerhard Jahn, Minister of Justice, "are in a difficult position. They must apply outdated laws."

Voting in West Germany

Electoral law in the Federal Republic combines features of both the American and the British systems. Every citizen, male

195

or female, who has reached the age of eighteen (reduced in 1969 from twenty-one) is entitled to vote. The West German election system knows no primaries and no electoral delegates, nor do West German voters register with (though many join) specific political parties.

Each voter has two ballots. The purpose of this dual system is to combine the advantages of plurality vote (*i.e.,* simple majority or largest number of votes, even if under 50 percent) and proportional representation. Proportional representation is designed to give a minority party a share in the legislature. This is how the Free Democratic Party, for example, won 49 Bundestag seats in 1965, even though it could not carry a single district in the country.

The voter casts his first ballot for a candidate of his choice; the winner of the largest vote represents his election district in the Bundestag. The second ballot is cast for a party which is entitled to send representatives to Bonn in proportion to its share of second-ballot votes.

The country is divided into 248 constituencies, each sending one deputy to the Bundestag. One half of the Bundestag membership is elected through the first ballot, the other half through the second.

The lists of candidates for the second ballot are made up by the parties in each state. Each party nominates a full slate of candidates for each of the second-ballot seats. In effect, the system benefits smaller parties and prevents the kind of landslides that occur under majority representation.

Although the lists of second-ballot candidates are publicized, their names do not necessarily appear on all the ballot sheets. Consequently, they need not campaign on their own behalf. The positive result of this is that political parties can sometimes nominate on the second-ballot extremely capable men who may not, however, have voter appeal.

An unexpected "by-product" of this dual system is the increase in the number of legislators with specialized backgrounds, such as finance, administration, health, education, and the like.

Haunted by the vivid memories of political fragmentation of the Weimar Republic, the Federal Republic has introduced the famous "five-percent clause" into the electoral law, which seeks to avoid the weakening of political life by the emergence of many splinter parties without sufficient authority to constitute either a stable government or responsible opposition. Any party which does not obtain a majority of "first votes" for its candidates in at least three constituencies, or a minimum of 5 percent of all valid votes cast in the entire Federal area, cannot be represented in the Bundestag. This clause prevented extremists of both right and left from entering the Bundestag in the 1969 national elections, notably the new-Nazi NPD and the Communist Party.

West Germans are conscientious voters. In all national elections from the beginning of the Republic to 1970, more than 80 percent of all eligible voters went to the polls. Special arrangements allow for absentee voting.

The Bundestag

The most important Federal organ is the *Bundestag* (parliament) which is elected for a period of four years by the people in general, equal, direct, and secret polls. It passes laws and supervises the executive. Both the government and Federal administration are under its control. It is roughly comparable to the British House of Commons and to a lesser degree, the U.S. House of Representatives.

In addition to the presiding officers and secretaries, the Bundestag has the so-called Council of Elders, a permanent committee of fifteen deputies proportionately representing the party groups (*Fraktionen*) in the Bundestag. The Council of Elders elects the Bundestag President and advises him in the conduct of business.

West Berlin is represented in the Bundestag by twenty-two "observers" who are not elected by the West Berlin population but by the West Berlin city parliament, and they cannot vote. This exceptional procedure is necessitated by the peculiar position of the former capital city in international law.

Any member of the Bundestag may introduce a "bill" or "motion." Preliminary work is performed by the special committees. After being read before the assembly three times, debated, and voted upon, bills become law by approval of a simple majority at plenary sessions. Amendments to the Basic Law, however, require a two-thirds majority of the Bundestag and Bundesrat. But the basic rights laid down in the Basic Law,

197

the distribution of powers, and the federative nature of the Bund cannot be altered by law under any circumstances.

A bill that has passed the Bundestag then goes on to the Bundesrat. If the Bundesrat does not approve the bill, it can appeal to the Mediation Committee that stands between the Bundestag and Bundesrat. This committee consists of eleven members from each of the parliamentary organs and they are not bound by instructions from either house. Should the committee propose amendments to the law, both the Bundestag and the Bundesrat have to debate the matter further.

Once a bill has been passed by both houses, the Federal President signs it, and it is countersigned by the chancellor or the competent departmental minister. It is then promulgated as law in the "Official Gazette" (*Bundesgesetzblatt*) and usually becomes operative fourteen days afterwards.

Parliamentary Reform

In practice, the Bundestag is bogged down by hopelessly outmoded parliamentary machinery and bureaucracy much of which dates back to Bismarck. On the other hand, Bundestag Deputy Günther Müller complains that in many ways the present parliamentary system is inferior to that of the relatively uninfluential Reichstag of the Kaiser. Then at least, he points out, a deputy meant something. He enjoyed authority. When he spoke, the press and people listened. Today the deputy is an anonymous cog in a gigantic bureaucratic machine. Bundestag Deputy Olaf von Wrangel speaks of his mandate as an "amputated function."

Much of the work of the Bundestag Deputy is dissipated in endless committee activity. During the parliamentary year 1961-62 the Bundestag spent only 166 hours in plenary session, compared with 1,428 plenary hours in the House of Commons.

The frustrated deputy learns too soon that even in committee he exercises an inferior position to established civil servants in the administrative apparatus. As for the district he represents, he frequently obtains precious little cooperation from his own local and regional authorities, who resent what they consider Bonn interference in their domain. Many regional and local government functions and agencies overlap, and the harried deputy has to waste countless hours merely to wade through jurisdictional regulations. Even then, the tedious wrangling has only just begun.

Worst of all, the Bundestag Deputy is all too often poorly informed on the very matters he is expected to debate and vote upon. He has not had access to a parliamentary information service, nor was there any kind of provision for consultation with experts and scientists on technical matters.

Reform measures foresee the eventual elimination of regional matters from plenary sessions, the reduction of German long-winded speeches to forty-five minutes, the creation of research institutes, and a data-processing system. The committees which have had to operate in the shadow of pompous plenary debates, will be granted new functions and powers: for example, if 25 percent of a committee deems it necessary, any matter relevant to an important problem can be aired in public hearings. A petitions committee will investigate Bundestag failings and spot possible loopholes in the law—in an effort at maximum parliamentary control. A change of standing orders is designed to let experts and consultants debate among themselves in parliament and to permit deputies to contradict and question the experts' opinions.

After twenty years in crowded offices, sometimes three to a room, the deputies can now enjoy their own air-conditioned office in their new skyrise building on the Rhine.

The Bundesrat

The *Bundesrat* (Federal Council) is the federative organ through which the *Länder* (states) cooperate with the *Bund* (Federation) in legislation and administration. It consists of forty-one members appointed by the Länder governments from their own ranks, as well as four representatives from West Berlin, who have merely an observer status. Thus the Bundesrat has only slight resemblance to the U.S. Senate.

Many federal laws—such as those affecting certain rights and interests or financial matters of the Länder—can be enacted only if the Bundesrat has expressly approved of them. In considering federal legislative proposals they are more apt to focus more attention on enforcement aspects of legislation than the Bundestag.

Theoretically the Bundesrat has no legislative term and is independent of national elections.

The Bundesrat possesses a veto power on certain types of

legislation passed by the Bundestag. It has absolute veto power only in those areas expressly so stated in the Basic Law.

Federalism

The Federal Republic is not only a parliamentary, democratic state, but a federative, constitutional state. Article 28 of the Basic Law guarantees the greatest possible autonomy for the member states in their relation with the Bund. The Länder possess primary, not secondary, sovereignty, thus differing from the United States or provinces of many other countries. Länder maintain their own policies in educational, cultural, social matters and their own separate police forces. The composition of most Länder differs considerably from that of the Bund. This was one reason why, after the collapse of Germany in 1945, such quick recovery could be made—the individual Länder, and the communities within them, as self-contained entities could rely on their own inner structure.

In many matters both Bund and Länder have the right to pass laws—a situation known as "concurrent legislation."

Federalism, however, is not only a product of German tradition, but also a product of fear of a strong central authority. The Western Allies in postwar Germany in fact exercised their utmost influence, which was considerable at the time, to emphasize the federal character of the new republic, far more so than the majority of German parties had intended.

But Federalism has proved to be a curse as well as a blessing. According to Dr. Theo Sommer, an editor of the influential weekly *Die Zeit*, "Federalism is this country's sacred cow: It consumes unnecessary resources, produces few results and hampers progress." According to Sommer, outdated administrative techniques in the Federal states make it extremely difficult to implement even the best reforms emanating from Bonn. "The Bundestag and the Federal government want to provide modern foundations for the state and society; and yet the states seem to want to strengthen the institutionalized bureaucracy of their financial and cultural sovereignty.... The prime ministers [governors] scornfully reject Bonn's 'proferred dictatorship' while generously accepting federal aid. But they deny the central government responsibility for educational planning, for a centralized security for hospitals, water supplies, and efforts to reduce air pollution and noise."[1]

The Parties

Political parties in Europe have a structure quite different from those in the United States. They are much more centrally organized, have contributing members, a kind of functionary hierarchy, and elaborate party programs. Until quite recently the German parties especially were identified with specific ideologies.

Nothing demonstrates West Germany's break with past political tradition so much as the development of the Federal Republic's political parties since 1945. Two trends predominate: the decline of the former multi-party system toward fewer viable parties, and even more significant, the clear ideological distinctions have given way more and more to pragmatic considerations, that is, to issues and personalities. Nevertheless, a certain relationship with the ideological past remains an important element of the leading West German parties, as we shall see.

It is interesting that in the Federal Republic there is no such thing as a "fund-raising dinner" to help defray campaign expenses of political parties, and there is no need for the candidate for a high office to dip into his own private fortune, if any, to pay for the high cost of public service.

It is the parties that finance the election campaigns in the Federal Republic, partly through their own funds and partly through tax monies allotted to them by law. In 1968 the Federal Constitutional Court ordered the Federal Government to extend financial support to splinter political parties, and reaffirmed the constitutionality of federal aid (2.50 DM's or 70 cents for every vote) to defray election campaign costs of any party polling more than half of 1 percent of the total vote. In so doing, it rebuffed the new-Nazi National Democratic Party (NPD), which opposed such aid. Ironically the NPD by receiving 4.3 percent of the national vote in 1969 became eligible for federal aid and received about $375,000 for its campaign costs. The Christian Democratic Union and Social Democrats each received nearly $9 million for the 1969 campaign, the Christian Social Union (CSU) received just over $3 million, and the Free Democrats (FDP), $3 million.

While no less than nine political parties were represented in the first Bundestag in 1949, there were only five political parties in the second Bundestag in 1953, and four in the third Bundestag in 1957. Since 1961 there have been only three represented in the Bundestag: the two "sister" Union parties, the Christian Democratic Union (CDU) and its Bavarian affiliate, the Christian Social

Union (CSU), counting as one; the Social Democratic Party (SPD), and the Free Democratic Party (FDP).

By 1970 the Federal Republic appeared to be heading for the two-party system. As early as 1949 the "big two," the CDU/CSU and the SPD, together received 60 percent of all valid votes. Four years later their share had risen to 74 percent, and by 1957 four out of five voters (82 percent) opted for these two parties, which received 81.6 percent of all votes in the national elections of 1961, and which jumped to 86.9 percent in 1965 and to 88.8 percent in 1969.

Of the several small parties in the last national election of 1969, only the democratic-oriented FDP was able to squeeze into the Bundestag with 5.8 percent of the votes. And the extremist parties didn't get in at all. The new-Nazi NPD received only 4.3 percent of the votes. The extreme left in the shape of the ADF, standing for Democratic Progress Campaign, polled fewer votes— 0.6 percent—than ever before.

An important feature of West German, and to a large extent, European, politics is the coalition system of government. Under this system an absolute majority is required to form a government. Consequently, even if one of the big parties "wins" an election by pulling the most votes, it may still be unable to form a government if it does not have the required 51-percent majority. As a result, a small party can play an extremely important role if it is able to form a coalition with one of the two large parties and thus create an absolute majority.

Thus in the 1969 national election the actual "winner" was the CDU/CSU with 46.1 percent of the votes, as against only 42.7 percent polled by the Social Democrats. But by forming a coalition with the FDP, the SPD gained 5.8 percent or a total of 51.9 percent of the votes, a very slim majority, but a majority. Thus the "winner" lost and the "loser" won. Many conservative Germans felt betrayed by the outcome of the 1969 elections. They argued that the coalition government of Willy Brandt and Walter Scheel does not really represent the will of the people.

Meanwhile the coalition system has been under heavy fire and many German political leaders have been arguing for the adoption of the simple majority system which would result in a standardization of the two party system. The arguments against this are that a simple majority system would virtually eliminate the FDP. Others point out that by permitting the victorious party of a simple majority to rule, such a government could too easily succumb to crises and all too soon be squeezed out of office by a strong opposition. As a buffer party between the two giants, the FDP has often prevented such a stalemate.

But the FDP, which is described in greater detail below, has lost a great deal of its credibility. In the *Landtag* (state parliament) elections of June 14, 1970, held in three states and involving nearly half of the West German electorate, the FDP was ousted in two states from representation, and lost many of its votes to the CDU. Many Germans have been disappointed by the FDP's shift to the left, from a previous partnership with the CDU/CSU to the coalition partner with Willy Brandt's SPD in 1969, while left-wingers in its own ranks threatened to bolt the party on account of its rightist leanings.

The coalition system also leaves the door open to the possibility that some day a partnership could be made with an extremist party. Had the NPD polled more than the FDP in the 1969 national elections, it would have been theoretically possible for the CDU/CSU to form a coalition with the neo-Nazis. This would have been highly improbable at the time, but political observers are uneasy about the fact that such a liaison is at all possible, even theoretically.

The Ideological Ties

The "big two" parties of West Germany, the CDU/CSU and SPD can more readily be compared to the Conservative and Labor parties respectively of the United Kingdom than to the Republican and Democratic parties in the United States. The CDU, for example, though regarded as conservative in West Germany has social welfare features along Democratic rather than Republican lines.

In a sense these two parties, which were established in 1945, are the heirs of much older parties, with the SPD being the oldest German party of all. The SPD revivers felt pledged to Socialism and regarded Karl Marx and August Bebel as their intellectual forefathers, while the CDU was influenced by and created by former leaders of the Catholic Center Party.

The common persecution by the National Socialist Antichrist and the danger of Communism were the aegis under which politicians of both Roman Catholic and Evangelical confessions founded the Christian Democratic Union in 1945. The material and moral defeat had smoothed over the differences between classes and conceptions of government. Aside from democratic socialism, Christianity was the only thing to have survived the catastrophe. The political merger of Protestants and Catholics thus became a unifying principle for non-Socialist workers and industrialists, farmers, craftsmen, and other citizens of varied professions.

Some of the CDU's first meetings were held in a monastery, the Dominican House of Studies at Walberberg, near Bonn, and its first draft was co-authored by Father Eberhard Welty, O.P.

With such a heterogeneous allegiance, both ideologically and sociologically, the CDU was hard put to create a party program. To put it bluntly, it could only engage in pragmatic politics. And the party was lucky to find in Konrad Adenauer, the retired mayor of Cologne, puttering around in his rose garden, and then past seventy, their master pragmatist and chancellor candidate. ("Don't commit suicide," the Occupation guard had told Adenauer during his detention. "Your life is over anyway.")

Wisely the CDU's leaders abandoned the idea of reviving the Center Party, which was more of a religious pressure group protecting the interests of the Catholic Establishment. In the new party the aim was to get Christians to work together and apply Christian values and ideals to politics. But the pragmatic fox, Adenauer, did not let go unnoticed the fact that the majority of German Protestants were concentrated in East Germany, while West Germany was almost evenly divided between Catholics and Protestants. It is widely believed that Adenauer gave only lip service to the cause of German reunification because the people of the German Democratic Republic have a long socialist tradition and presumably might vote socialist even in a democratic state. But as long as Germany remained divided, the CDU/CSU had a good chance of dominating West German politics.

At first that controversial "C" in the party's name proved to be an asset. In 1957 more than 60 percent of the Catholics voted CDU, 24 percent for the SPD, while 40 percent of the Protestants voted CDU and 37 percent, SPD. The CDU/CSU's following was especially strong in purely Catholic rural areas. It was the preferred party by far of women, who were numerically preponderant as a result of two wars and an otherwise longer life span. Until very recently, and to a large degree even now, German women have voted more conservatively. In the early postwar years women were also attracted by the patriarchal image of Adenauer and were noted for their loyalty to the church and their accustomed obedience to the clergy.

During the 1957 national elections, the late Bishop Michael Keller of Münster publicly declared that as long as the Social Democratic Party was a Marxist party no Catholic could vote for it. A typical remark in preelection sermons in Catholic churches was, "All Catholics of good conscience will vote for that party that regards the word Christian as important." Even in the state elections of 1970, Catholics were told by their bishops to vote for candidates "with Christian principles."

Unlike the United States, separation of church and state in West Germany is not a foregone conclusion. Although growing voices of dissent both within and without the churches are pleading for greater separation, the fact is that religious issues are intricately woven into the fabric of West German politics. *Proporz* or proportional representation according to religious affiliation continues to play a significant if declining role today. It has long been an unwritten law that countless thousands of positions, not only in politics but also in education, administration, and welfare, be distributed proportionately among Catholics and Protestants, sometimes to the point of absurdity. For a long time it was taken for granted that important posts in Bavaria be held solely by Roman Catholics, while in Hamburg and Bremen the preference was given to Protestants. On the national level, Adenauer was severely criticized for his partiality to Catholics, while Protestant Ludwig Erhard was accused of making too many Protestant appointments.

The tie between the churches and the CDU/CSU remained especially strong in the field of educational policy. For years German politics was riddled with controversy over confessional schools, divorce, and family questions. To this very day, concordats between the Vatican and the Federal Republic, and between the Vatican and individual West German states, regulate delicate questions of education and other church-state matters. One of the hottest issues was and still is the confessional school question. In the German tradition religious instruction has been guaranteed for generations in public schools. Indeed, until recently the majority of public schools (parochial schools are virtually nonexistent) were confessionally oriented with curricula and teaching staff designated according to the predominant religious confession of a given neighborhood.

The confessional pattern, however, lost all meaning in the wake of World War II when countless thousands of refugees and displaced persons scattered all over the country and completely upset previous patterns. Gradually the various Länder introduced a new community school system, abolishing the old confessional structures, but permitting religious instruction for the two big confessions and provisions for minorities within the school system. For many years church leaders, mostly Catholics, opposed this inevitable trend, and several die-hard bishops are still holding out against it today. But thanks to the influence of the second Vatican Council and leaders like Julius Cardinal Doepfner, archbishop of Munich, the ecumenical—and economical—wisdom of confessionally mixed schools is now being accepted.

The CDU/CSU, while winning the largest number of votes in most national and state elections, has never enjoyed a large membership, since only about 2 percent of its voters are enrolled in the party, or about 300,000.

The SPD, by contrast, with nearly one million members is the largest party organization and enjoys a far greater *esprit de corps* than the CDU/CSU.

Like the CDU/CSU, the SPD is also plagued by one of the letters in its name—the "S." In contrast to the CDU/CSU, the SPD is not really a postwar product but a revival of a party that for many Germans carries the stigma of socialism and communism. Adenauer made no bones about hammering home a single theme in most of his election campaigns: "The great issue before the German people is whether Germany will remain Christian [*i.e.*, vote CDU] or become communist [if SPD wins]."

Deep Roots

As a matter of fact the SPD's roots penetrate deep into the nineteenth century, into the beginnings of the German workers' movement. Karl Marx and Friedrich Engels, the great theorists who laid the groundwork for communism, also contributed to the social philosophy of Germany.

The beginnings of German social democracy are definitely traceable to Karl Marx, but the SPD's history as a party actually began with the establishment of the *Allgemeine Deutsche Arbeiterverein* and the *Sozialdemokratische Arbeiterpartei* (Social Democratic Workers' Party). It completely repudiated the Bismarck Reich and opposed the Kaiser Reich throughout its existence, and energetically promoted social legislation.

However that may be, Karl Marx is not even mentioned in the party's founding literature, nor did he write its program. In fact, he severely criticized the social democratic program of 1875. But Marx's thinking was an integral part of the party's early program, through the influence of one of its founders, Ferdinand Lasalle, a student of Marx and Engels.

By the end of the nineteenth century, however, the Social Democrats had already parted ways with their Marxist leanings. They have been the staunchest of German advocates for human rights and were one of the strongest groups opposing Hitler. Nor is their concept of socialism alien to the notion of personal freedom. Often attacked by church leaders as enemies of religion, they tended to regard religion as a private matter and were indifferent rather than hostile to it.

It is important to point out too that Europe has long had a more kindly attitude toward socialism than the United States, especially the advanced, democratic forms existing in Scandinavia. In a country where obligatory health insurance, family allowances, generous subsidies for cultural activities, compulsory state-administered church taxes, state ownership of railroads, telephone, television, and radio are taken for granted, even the CDU/CSU is a party somewhat left of the American Democratic Party and "socialist" by American standards.

Nevertheless, for a long time after its reestablishment in 1945, the SPD suffered from the Marxist label. Its first postwar leader, Kurt Schumacher, was deeply respected, but he died in 1952. He was succeeded by Erich Ollenhauer, who ran twice against Adenauer, but he was a colorless, uninspiring figure, and he too has died since.

It was Herbert Wehner, the mastermind of the party and its party whip in the 1969 Bundestag, who engineered the brilliant breakthrough that brought the SPD into the government. For years his previous role as a leading official of German and international communism was held against him. But since his complete break with Moscow in 1942 he has become a driving force behind his party's move to the center, bringing it further than ever from the old socialist line.

The break away from the Marxist past became complete in 1959 on the occasion of the party convention in Bad Godesberg, with the adoption of its famous "Godesberg Program." It dropped its time-honored socialist principles such as unconditional nationalization of key industries, planned economy, and the definition of the party as an "ideological entity." Nowhere in sight were the red banners of international socialism which previously dominated Social Democratic assemblages in Germany. And Herbert Wehner, then deputy chairman, dropped the customary "comrades" and instead addressed delegates with "ladies and gentlemen."

For many years the SPD's foreign policy opposed membership in Western European defense organizations, emphasizing the provisional nature of the Federal Republic, so as not to jeopardize chances of German reunification. By the time it met for its Hanover convention in 1960, the SPD instituted still further reforms and finally came out for NATO and strong Federal armed forces.

Like the SPD's ideological "S," the CDU/CSU's "C" has come under heavy fire. Thanks to the liberalizing influence of the second Vatican Council, changed attitudes towards socialism and the secularization trend within the churches, large segments of Catholics (as the Protestants before them) switched to the SPD. And the SPD in turn has gone out of its way to woo Catholic voters by showing an affinity between their social concern and the papal encyclicals on labor, poverty, and development.

Similarly the Christian label is beginning to prove more of an embarrassment as more and more voters realize that no political party can claim a monopoly on Christian virtue or, for that matter, Christian mischief.

By 1970 the ideological character of both the CDU/CSU and the SPD had disappeared so completely that personalities, issues, and policy became the distinguishing features. Nevertheless, formidable obstacles remained. While the SPD, for example, stands for long-term social planning, the CDU talks in terms of restricting social planning by the state to indirect help only. While the SPD seeks penal income, wealth tax, and death duties, CSU favors "classless taxation law."

The Free Democrats

The diminutive Free Democratic Party is extremely hard to

describe, let alone define. Its leaders themselves like to use the word "liberal" to identify the nature of the party, in an unconvincing effort to link it with the men who fomented the democratic revolution of 1848 (see Chapter 9). German liberals, in the sense they mean it, may perhaps be roughly compared to progressives in the American Republican Party, or "enlightened conservatives." One telltale nickname tags it "the commuter party," because many of its members are suburbanites who commute to white collar jobs in large cities.

The FDP finds most of its members among the urban middle class, as well as the professions, the trades, small- and medium-sized industrialists. They wield little influence among workers or in rural areas, and have more Protestant than Catholic adherents.

Because of the conglomerate of members ranging from free-wheeling reformers to industrial lobbyists, the FDP is also called "the party of individualists." In the past it has placed particular emphasis on economic safeguards for private property and small businesses and was influential in increasing military conscription from twelve to eighteen months.

Within the context of the coalition system of government, this tiny party has played an extremely important role in the postwar Federal Republic. One of its most important contributions has been to prevent any one political party from obtaining an absolute majority in the Bundestag, and thus significantly restricting the power of the big two.

In 1956, when the FDP still had many refugees among its members and had a more nationalistic bent than it has now, it left the coalition of Adenauer's CDU because he wanted the Saar region to have some kind of European status. The Saar subsequently was returned to Germany in a plebiscite.

The since-prominent investment broker, Dr. Erich Mende, also of a nationalist-conservative bent, then assumed chairmanship of the party in a new coalition with Adenauer—although reluctantly, as it tried unsuccessfully to send him to retirement. The FDP played a decisive role in toppling Defense Minister Franz-Joseph Strauss for his notorious police raid of the weekly newsmagazine *Der Spiegel* for alleged treasonable publication of defense secrets.

In 1966 the FDP broke the coalition with the CDU/CSU under Chancellor Ludwig Erhard and thereby brought about the downfall of his government.

In 1968 Walter Scheel took over the chairmanship of the party when its fortunes were very low and tried to give it a more progressive policy. In 1969 in Berlin the Free Democratic delegation cast the decisive votes that guaranteed the election to the presidency of reform-minded SPD politician Dr. Gustav Heinemann rather than the conservative CDU candidate, Dr. Gerhard Schroeder.

(And of course the first president of the Federal Republic, Professor Theodor Heuss, was a member of the FDP.)

In the coalition government formed with the SPD under Chancellor Willy Brandt, Walter Scheel has been one of the persons most responsible for the coalition's open approach to East Germany, the Soviet Union, and Eastern Europe.

In addition, the Free Democrats are pushing for greater separation of church and state, and the complete removal of church influence from schools. They favor the election of the president by the people and greater freedoms for the individual. They appeal for more plebiscites on issues that are stalemated in the Bundestag, and advocate legal reform of the courts.

The Free Democrats have also been called the "Schizophrenic party." It is a truism that the average citizen prefers parties with a clear-cut line and policy. The Free Democratic Party, inconsistently jockeying from right to left, and internally dominated by factions of the right and the left, is frustrating to many Germans, and mystifying to many more.

In the spring, 1970, state elections in Lower Saxony, the Saarland, and North Rhine-Westphalia, involving nearly half of the entire Federal electorate, the FDP was ousted from the parliaments of the first two above-mentioned states and barely managed to jump the 5-percent hurdle in the third. Indirectly, this was a severe blow to the SPD-FDP Bonn coalition and their open policy toward the East.

Many observers predict the inevitable demise of the FDP. In any case, there is a decided polarization between the SPD and CDU/CSU with the nation split right down the middle.

Postwar Developments

Observers of the West German political scene like to divide the postwar developments until now into three periods: the Period of

Occupation, from 1945 to 1950; the Period of Recovery, from 1949 to roughly 1961; and the Period of Change, since 1965.

During the first period, the Germans had to concentrate on mere survival, clearing the rubble of the obliterated cities, recovering from the trauma of a humiliating defeat, and "de-nazification." Two separate Germanies emerged, with a democratic structure slowly taking shape in the western half.

The indisputable symbol of the second period was that Grand Old Man, Konrad Adenauer. Whatever its shortcomings, the CDU/CSU government under his stern, autocratic hand unquestionably led the young republic along pro-Western paths and implanted the seeds of democratic government. It launched an economic boom unparalleled in German history. It strongly supported and subsequently joined NATO and established a democratic-oriented Bundeswehr, in spite of the great reluctance of the German population ever to rearm. It fostered the European Common Market and has vigorously promoted the European movement. Its slogans, "assistance for the family" and "prosperity for everyone," were in fact backed by effective legislation that included everything from family allowances to savings and bonuses and subsidies for family housing. Its refugee act and restitution law are models of great humanitarian legislation.

In three successive national election campaigns, Adenauer hammered home order and stability as his great trump card, under the slogan, "No Experiments!"

But profound changes were in the offing and Adenauer's version of stability and order soon threatened to degenerate into something more like stagnation. By 1961 Adenauer lost his parliamentary majority, and in 1963 the stubborn champion was retired to his rose garden on the Rhine. At his death in 1967 at the age of ninety-one, the mortal remains of the Grand Old Man were carried by boat down his beloved Rhine after a solemn Requiem Mass in Cologne Cathedral, and laid to rest in the shaded village graveyard of Rhoendorf.

In spite of excellent credentials as the architect of the "Economic Miracle, " Ludwig Erhard, Adenauer's successor, was unable to cope with the recession that hit the Federal Republic in 1966 or with his faction-ridden party. With the help of his popular image he managed to win the 1965 elections but his

211

naive notions of politics and his Pollyanna attitude toward problems soon plunged him into the midst of a leadership crisis which led to his inevitable removal from power.

Then, under the dynamic leadership of the "boy wonder," Willy Brandt, the personable former mayor of West Berlin, the SPD for the first time emerged from its opposition role to assume a partnership in the government. Previously relegated to running state governments (although they did this extremely well), they were now admitted to the power center in the "Grand Coalition" regime, with CDU's Kurt Georg Kiesinger as chancellor and Willy Brandt as vice-chancellor and foreign minister.

The Grand Coalition proved to be neither a success nor a failure. There was a significant shift away from the Cold War attitude toward the East and improved relations with the Soviet-bloc countries, including East Germany. There were sensible pump-priming measures. The budget was balanced by stringent cuts. And a start was finally made, after a decade of bickering, on penal, educational, and judicial reforms.

But it proved to be an unsatisfactory arrangement. For one thing, the very existence of a Grand Coalition left an unhealthy vacuum. When it was created in 1967, it marshalled the biggest majority bloc that any freely-elected German parliament has ever had—with a total of 447 out of 496 Bundestag votes. This left only the tiny Free Democratic Party with 49 Bundestag votes in opposition. This unhealthy situation fostered the *Ausser-parlamentarische Opposition* (APO), or extra-parliamentary opposition, the conglomeration of disgruntled political groups, mostly of the left. It launched a period of unrest, sit-ins, demonstrations, and protest movements throughout the nation.

In the view of most critics, the Grand Coalition marked the first radical break in West Germany's postwar history. But it was only a phase of a much bigger break to come, the Socialist surge to power, a new coalition in 1969, with the leftist-reoriented FDP and—for the first time—the ruling SPD under Willy Brandt. For the first time too in the Federal Republic's history, the CDU/CSU was in the opposition.

Within the space of a few weeks, the new regime signed the nuclear nonproliferation treaty, revalued the Deutsche mark, and launched preparatory talks with Poland and the Soviet Union toward a proposed nonaggression pact. And within a few short months Willy Brandt made history by meeting with East German

Premier Willi Stoph in Erfurt, East Germany and again in Kassel, West Germany—the first time the heads of the two Germanies met since the existence of the two states.

But Brandt's initiative searching for improved relations with the German Democratic Republic and Eastern Europe soon bogged down. The talks produced few tangible results, except the symbolic one that they came about at all. The vociferous CDU/CSU opposition, notably the CSU leader Franz-Josef Strauss, warned against a unilateral sellout to the Soviet Union. And the GDR itself insisted on full diplomatic recognition as the basis for "normalization"—a step that would be as premature as it is inevitable and which would surely plunge the Federal Republic into the deepest crisis imaginable. Time alone will tell whether Willy Brandt's program, "venturing more democracy," will ultimately produce fruitful results.

◄ 14 ►

HOW STABLE A DEMOCRACY?

NOTHING IN GERMANY'S authoritarian history prepared the citizens of the Federal Republic for the rip-roaring election campaign preceding the national Bundestag elections of September 28, 1969.

Bonn politicians swarmed all over the country to meet the people in Waldshut, Neckargmünd, and Marburg an der Lahn. Kurt Georg Kiesinger, then chancellor, found himself drinking Pils beer with the boys, shaking hands to the tune of John Philip Sousa, and delivering folksy speeches in his singsong Swabian dialect.

Herr Rosenthal, the owner of a big porcelain firm, clad in knickerbockers, red stockings, and a knapsack on his back ventured onto the dusty country roads to plug for the CDU in the hinterland. While elsewhere, the noted author Günter Grass traveled up and down the country in a minibus with a camping bed, distributed campaign literature on street corners, telling the people about the SPD. Pelted with farm produce in one town, he moved on to another, where he was handed a rooster and a basket of fresh eggs.

On the streets across the land, trucks with loudspeakers bellowed at potential voters, and everywhere there were handouts, slogans, leaflets, brochures, lectures, and heated discussions.

In Cologne, citizens by the hundreds called Number 235931 to ask political questions and had them answered by prominent politicians over television. In Clausthal-Zellerfeld housewives stood in driving rain to get a peek at Bonn bigwigs making a campaign appearance.

Newspaper and magazine reports around the world spread the news of "the new Germans" whose grass roots democracy was bursting out all over. Grass called it "voter initiative."

The former silent majority of the West German Parent-Teachers Associations were becoming articulate partners demanding a voice in the policy-making decisions of education. The

214

youth were examining the institutions of the Establishment and finding them lacking. The church members were demanding more say in the allocation of church funds and the right to elect their own bishops. Journalists were insisting on the right of participating in the shaping of editorial policy. And in factories, universities, institutions everywhere, employees, students, and collaborators were pounding the doors of rectors and managers with one word more than any other on their lips: *"Mitbestimmung* [co-determination]."

The question that remains to be answered is: How viable is this emerging German democracy? Do hidden dangers lurk beneath democratic appearances? Is this a mere passing phenomenon, or is it the confident self-assertion of West Germans suddenly aware of their political maturity?

"Democracy," stated the *Stuttgarter Zeitung* in an editorial (June 27, 1967), "has never come easy to the Germans. An unfathomable mysticism, a propensity to extremism and the eternal search for perfection have always dimmed their vision of what is possible and what is impossible."

There are many critics who are concerned that the very zeal with which the Germans pursue their new-found freedom could bear in itself the seeds of some new form of extremism quite different from nationalism or fascism but every bit as devastating.

The 1969 elections themselves are widely regarded as the symbolic watershed of a new phase of West German history. In the person of the socialist Chancellor Willy Brandt and the men around him, many Germans see a new breed of dynamic German leaders breaking away more completely with the past than ever before, and dedicated to fundamental reform. "We are creating the modern Germany," their campaign posters had read. "We have the right men."

With a national sigh of relief, the West Germans went to bed on election night with the assuring knowledge that more than 90 percent of the electorate voted for democratic parties and that neither the rightist National Democratic Party (NPD), with only 4.3 percent of the votes, nor the various leftist parties, with a mere 0.6 percent, garnered enough votes to enter the Bundestag.

For a time the NPD had caused great concern, not only in the Federal Republic itself, but especially on the international scene. Newspaper editorials around the world speculated whether the

215

Nazi beast was again rearing its ugly head, as the NPD successfuly won its way into one state parliament after another, under the leadership of party leader von Thadden, whose first name is Adolf.

In spite of the booming prosperity from which most West Germans profited, there were inevitably a number of persons who were bypassed. The NPD, which was ousted from three state parliaments in 1970, is a motley grab-bag party for disgruntled nationalists: small farmers, who disapprove of the stiff competition from Common Market imports; small business men who feel overrun by the aggressive chain stores; and old Nazis unable to adjust to the ignominy of Hitler's defeat. Actually they are more of a patriotic petit-bourgeois party than neo-Nazi, but nonetheless bear close watching.

There have been right-wing parties throughout the history of the Federal Republic, but like the NPD, none of them enjoyed much success for very long. The *Deutsche Reichspartei* polled only 0.8 percent in 1961. The *Sozialistische Reichspartei* was outlawed by the Supreme Court in 1952. The Refugee Party DG/BHE was completely wiped out by the wave of affluence.

The NPD's supporters include rifle club enthusiasts and the regulars in taverns of small towns. Only 17 percent of its members are under thirty. Its program is at once grotesque and illusory: It is against foreign workers, development aid, urges the withdrawal from NATO and the EEC, is opposed to the Franco-German peace treaty and the recognition of the German Democratic Republic. It glorifies paternal authority, urges strong disciplinary action against youth, and is against intellectuals and modern art. It is imbued with romantic and mystical notions of womanhood and modesty.

The Kiesinger cabinet wisely resisted the temptation to give in to worldwide demands to ban the party, which would have given it a beneficial martyr-status, driven it underground, and made it potentially attractive for many who otherwise find it boring. Rather, it decided to tackle right-wing radicalism in the open. It was a calculated risk and it paid off. Even at the height of its "success," the NPD made a poor showing as a backlash party. In comparison, the U.S. rightist George Wallace has wielded considerably more influence; nor did any of the West German rightists even remotely reach the heights of hysteria of the American McCarthyism of the fifties.

The Fascist Left

Many observers are deeply concerned about the pronounced fascistlike characteristics that are all too often emerging from many sectors of the New Left.

During Chancellor Kiesinger's 1969 election campaign in the nine-hundred-year-old town of Biberach, he was continuously interrupted by noisy youth waving banners and red wooden crosses, shouting: "Beat us dead, we are the new youth!" The enraged townspeople finally snatched the crosses and banners, broke them up, and used the sticks as clubs to drive the protestors from the scene. The peaceful election campaign ended up in a bloody melee that hardly deserves the name "democratic electioneering." The chancellor shouted angrily, "This is an abuse of our democracy!"

The frenzy and downright fanaticism with which many leftist demonstrators poured their wrath upon the NPD campaign assemblies compelled von Thadden to speak from behind a bulletproof glass booth. NPD meeting halls had to be encircled by barbed wire and guarded by burly NPD orderlies that reminded Germans of Hitler's SA troopers. Still, it was usually the leftist demonstrators who provoked them to action. At a rally in Essen, von Thadden was dragged from the rostrum by a youth who then shouted into a microphone, "Get out of here, Nazi swine!" Elsewhere youths shouted "Sieg, Heil!" and threw tear-gas grenades into assemblies.

Such bullying methods remind the observer of a ditty composed to describe conversion tactics in the Middle Ages: *"Willst du nicht mein Bruder sein, so schlag ich dir den Schädel ein* [If you won't be a brother mine, I'll beat your head to powder fine]."

Similarly during the historic visit of East German Premier Willi Stoph, in his summit meeting with Chancellor Willy Brandt in Kassel, in May, 1970, it was hard to tell which of the demonstrators were the greater fanatics, the fascist right, who opposed Stoph's presence, or the fascist left, who urged recognition of the German Democratic Republic.

"Brutality at the NPD meeting in Frankfurt," wrote journalist Roderich Reifenrath, "and bloodshed at the extra-parliamentary opposition's Berlin demonstration, show that violence is no longer a chance product but an essential part of political

217

disagreement. These events cannot be played down. On the right-wing, a 'fight-to-the-death' mentality, very reminiscent of the Nazi era, is coming to the surface.

"Nor is the left-wing free from criticism. The originally justified protests against the abuse of both written and unwritten democratic principles have now degenerated into unprincipled riot."[1]

These comments are all the more significant inasmuch as they appeared in a leftist-oriented newspaper.

The Communists

The "new" Communist Party in the Federal Republic was founded in Essen in 1968 to the tune of beat and partisan songs. Young left-wing rebels and veteran revolutionaries from the previous underground movement debated the party's statutes and action program, elected their executive committee and pre-sidium. They deliberately avoided such designations as "central committee" and "politburo."

The present party's name differs simply in a transposition of letters, DKP (Deutsche Kommunistische Partei) instead of KPD. The previous Communist Party was declared illegal by the Federal Constitutional Court in 1956. The present party has departed from its predecessor's aim at revolutionary overthrow of society, a condition for its rehabilitation. But it has attracted little interest. It reportedly has some 22,000 registered members and virtually no influence on the political scene. Its platform urges recognition of East Germany, the adoption of East German socialism, the withdrawal of NATO, and demands for 15 percent wage increases for industrial workers, which most trade unions reject as illusory.

In addition to the German Communist Party, there are a number of other left-wing groups such as the Deutsche Friedens Union (DFU); the Humanistische Union; the Women's Peace Movement (WFFP); the Socialist Worker Movement; the Democratic Farmers Action Party (DBA); and the Democratic Progress Party (ADF). But their political influence has been virtually nil.

The New Left

The West German New Left was originally concentrated among a group of new-Marxist students and was born in West Germany just about the same time as von Thadden's NPD. At first fighting for university reform, many of the rebel students (though not all, and at best only 14 percent of the entire student body) sought a socialization of society as a whole. They tossed around words like "neo-capitalism," "revolution," and *"Umfunktionieren* [restructuring]," "Basis Groups," "infiltration," and frequently provoked bloody clashes with the police.

They call for a "destruction of the state apparatus." Much of their talk and activity is the blind unleashing of emotions without any effort to spell out clear aims or to work painstakingly toward realistic goals. At one 1968 demonstration, posters read, "We need a Lee Harvey Oswald." At a more recent demonstration cries of "Let all over forty be gassed," could be heard, or, "Concentration camps for the deadwood over forty!"

They reject Bonn's representative democracy, organize infiltration groups who attempt to convert workers and apprentices to Marxist ideologies, and systematically if artificially seek to foster class struggle, or at least a class consciousness in a bourgeois Germany where there are hardly any distinctions left between blue and white collar workers.

Efforts along this line have been a miserable flop, nor do they have any connection with the Communist Party, which wouldn't dare risk its shaky status by admitting them to its ranks even if they wanted to. Ironically, words like "revolution," which the New Left glibly bandies about, are taboo for the German Communists who are not about to risk a second ban by the Supreme Court.

The strange thing now is that the New Left is no longer confined to a handful of rebel students. It has become a fashionable nationwide movement, or, more accurately, parlor game—something like the milquetoast solidarity of long sideburns. The leftist fad has become *"Salon-fähig"*—fit for the living room.

You can find the new leftists especially in the communications fields, in the trade unions, in education, and among the younger theologians and pastors of both confessions. It has become quite respectable for a bourgeois journalist, trimly dressed in suit and tie, who drags his family to church every Sunday and dutifully pays his taxes, to speak knowledgeably about guerrillas in South America, exploitation of the masses, abolishment of private property, stiff taxation of the rich, redistribution of capitalist

219

profits among the workers, while he of course comfortably enjoys the benefits of the very system he deplores.

A "typical" example of the new middle-aged leftist is the lord mayor of Frankfurt-Main, Walter Möller. Noted as a leader of the leftist-radical wing of the SPD, Möller is an unabashed adherent of Karl Marx, seeks to create an ethical synthesis of Marx and Kant, and promotes a modified form of class struggle. He favors the ultimate elimination or at least drastic reduction of most private property, and promotes new structures that would provide a fairer democratic control of the means of production by the workers.

However, when you try to pin him down, he will admit that even in a completely socialized society new power structures and a kind of hierarchy would emerge. Although he favors the recognition of the German Democratic Republic, he calls East German society "the most retarded and repugnant form of Communist domination imaginable." Möller even regards the progressive version of Yugoslav communism as falling far short of the democratic socialism he envisages.

But in the evening when he is tired, this formidable leftist *Bürgerschreck* (citizens' fright), as the German press calls him, likes to relax by playing on his electric organ.

"Red" Jochen Steffen, the undisputed boss of the SPD in Schleswig-Holstein, "the Franz-Josef Strauss of the North," inevitably creates newspaper headlines with his picturesque and flamboyant criticism of the capitalist Establishment of West Germany. Surprisingly he has won widespread respect even from conservative farmers. They like a person who says what he thinks. At the same time, the forty-two-year-old revolutionary is the very model of an "English" gentleman, wears a waistcoat, and keeps his pencil-thin moustache carefully trimmed. In the 1971 state elections, he won 41.2 percent of the votes, a considerable gain over the SPD's 39.4 percent in 1967, but lost the election to the CDU, which won the absolute majority with 51.7 percent of the votes cast.

However, it is from quite another quarter that the leftist trend in West Germany is causing growing concern at the beginning of the seventies. All over the country numerous "red cells" have been sprouting at the universities. The membership of these independent groups of the New Left has been recruited mainly from the Socialist Students' Union, which was dissolved on the national level. Recognizing that street clashes only provoke rightist reactions and opposition from the silent majority, and that their militant provocations have not had much success in winning over the workers, New Left students have now gone over to a more subtle, quiet revolution in the universities. They demand appointment of Marxist teachers, the organization of lectures under a "Socialist Study Program," and oppose the "bourgeois indoctrination" of the present curricula. There are no reliable statistics available on their numerical strength, but they have groups in Munich, Berlin, Bremen, Heidelberg, Frankfurt, Münster, Bochum, Hanover, Göttingen, and Regensburg. According to ASTA, the national student-government association, about one thousand students are currently taking part in a Marxist-Leninist study program organized by the red cells, which frequently create their own elaborate courses parallel to existing university curricula.

Some observers prefer to see this development positively. The New Left at least keeps the universities alert and provokes discussion of political and social problems to a degree never before known in Germany.

A similar phenomenon is taking place in the political parties. Although leftists and rightists alike have made a poor showing in national and regional elections—so far—they have been creating considerable unrest within the established political parties in recent years. The year 1971, for the Social Democrats, was the year of confrontation with the rebellious *Jusos* (young socialists) within their own ranks. In Munich these Jusos' frenzied demands for a greater radicalization of party aims caused the popular mayor, Hans-Jochen Vogel, to withdraw his candidacy for reelection, and thus jeopardized the party's chances for staying in office. For the Jusos the SPD has betrayed its name by becoming a bourgeois party hardly distinguishable from the CDU. They want to turn it into an ideological Marxist party once again, with a decidedly communist and anti-capitalist program. It was only with the greatest adroitness that Chancellor Willy Brandt was able to prevent a party split that could have toppled his government. "Social democracy and Communism," he told the Jusos, "are incompatible."

In the eyes of the Old Guard the utopian demands of the Jusos completely ignore the hard realities of political survival. If the Jusos would indeed succeed in turning back the clock and revoking the Godesberg Program, making the SPD once more a left-wing socialist cadre party fighting class distinctions, the party would soon land back on the opposition benches. It was only when the SPD broke out of the ghetto of 30 percent of the votes through the Godesberg Program (Chapter 13) that it finally achieved the breakthrough of becoming a popular mass party.

Franz-Josef Strauss & Co.

On the Right, there are decided indications of far more subtle nationalistic and rightist tendencies that have penetrated far into the thinking and activity of existing democratic parties and institutions, notably the right-wing factions of the CDU and CSU.

It is widely believed that the real reason why the NPD failed to gain admittance to the Bundestag in the 1969 national elections is that the CDU/CSU already were so far right that it wasn't necessary to vote NPD.

Symbol of the conservative front in the Federal Republic is the indomitable leader of the Christian Social Union (CSU), Franz-Josef Strauss. "Strauss" is the German word for ostrich, but the controversial politician has been more often compared to a bulldozer with a computer for a brain. He is far and away the most colorful politician on the West German scene and seems to be always in the thick of several battles at once. More than any other West German politician, he has intensely dedicated followers and equally intense opponents.

Hefty, bull-necked, Roman Catholic, Strauss has the figure of a beer barrel, the charm of a Bavarian, and a brilliant mind. His witty repartee in slightly accented English makes him a sought-after guest at British and American gatherings. A cartoonist suggested gifts for his fiftieth birthday: cushions for his elbows, a magnifying glass to help him choose his friends, and a muzzle.

A butcher's son of Munich's bohemian Schwabing district, Strauss was one of the brightest classics and philology students ever to attend the University of Munich. Avoiding Nazi involvement, he spent World War II as an artillery lieutenant on the Eastern front. A former mayor of a small Bavarian town, he co-founded the CSU, entered the Bundestag, and soon became one of Adenauer's protégés.

In 1962 the coalition Free Democrats forced him out of the cabinet as defense minister after a scandal involving Gestapo-like police raids (ordered by Strauss) on the anti-Strauss weekly newsmagazine *Der Spiegel*. The magazine allegedly used classified material as evidence charging Strauss' Bundeswehr with inefficiency. Police arrested the publisher, Rudolf Augstein, and top editors on suspicion of treason and disclosure of state secrets. The legal charges against Strauss have since been quashed, and he has emerged stronger than ever. Meanwhile, a former *Spiegel* editor, Konrad Ahlers, is head of the government press and information department and official spokesman.

Critics charge that Strauss' CSU is the Bavarian wing of the CDU only in theory. *De facto* it is regarded as a party in its own right. Strauss' critics are wary of his pugnacity, vindictiveness, ambition for power, and suspect him of trying to forge his fifty parliamentary deputies into a political lever capable of tipping the narrow parliamentary margins in his favor.

Thus in 1965 he nearly toppled Chancellor Ludwig Erhard from office by threatening to withdraw CSU support. Under Strauss' pressure Erhard had to appoint as minister of justice, the reactionary and nationalist-oriented Richard Jaeger, a proponent of the death penalty and a supporter of Portugal's Salazar and Spain's Franco.

During the Adenauer-de Gaulle era, he headed the group known as the "Gaullists" who favored some form of nuclear independence from the United States, and opposed the Common Market approach toward a politically united Europe, promoted a rigid defiance of the East, and urged closer ties with France. Strauss almost succeeded in ridding the Bonn cabinet of Foreign Minister Gerhard Schroeder, who favored closer ties with the U.S., negotiations with the Eastern European nations, and inclusion of Britain in the Common Market.

Strauss warned the Western allies in 1965 against barring his country from a share in nuclear defense. "They should be able to figure out from history," he said, "that if they do that a new kind of Adolf Hitler would arise to find nuclear weapons for Germany—and something worse," by which he meant "a radicalization of German politics." He has opposed the nuclear nonproliferation treaty and consistently urged a stronger Bundeswehr and German arms industry.

Although 62 percent of Germans in a recent opinion poll place the full blame for World War II on Germany (as against only 32 percent in 1950), Strauss has branded as false those accusations which put the chief blame for the war on Germany and urged

Germans "energetically to take up arms against the continuous defamation of Germany as the sole starter of two world wars."

The NPD's von Thadden was never able to dare use expressions that Strauss bandies about at will, and indeed his CSU is often described as "right of the NPD." Strauss was widely criticized for a fiery outburst he made in the heat of the 1969 election campaign. Referring to noisy youth demonstrators of the extra-parliamentary opposition (APO), he shouted, "The APO people behave like animals, for whom the application of laws made for men is no longer possible." To which the demonstrators replied with a barrage of animal noises ("oink, oink") and "Jawohl, Herr Zoo Direktor!"

This same Strauss, who still clings to the illusion of reunification, has been one of the staunchest opponents of Chancellor Willy Brandt's open policy to the East and has accused him of stupidity and weakness in his dealings with East Germany and the Soviet bloc.

Through his powerful weekly *Bayern Kurier* (circulation 110,000—up 10,000 since last year), Strauss lashes out against his enemies like a trigger-happy cowboy. Typical headlines read: "A Versailles of Cosmic Proportions" (referring to the nuclear nonproliferation pact signed by the SPD-FDP coalition); "Sellout Chancellor" (referring to Willy Brandt). It even takes up its editorial cudgels to defend American comic strips such as "Mickey Maus" (Mickey Mouse) and "Onkel Dagobert" (Little Orphan Annie's Daddy Warbucks), who were savagely attacked in leftist publications, which tagged the former as "ideological infiltration" and Warbucks as the "prototype of mono-capitalism."

A rightist group with which Strauss is closely identified and at whose rallies he is frequently a major speaker is the League of Expellees, and represents several million Germans driven out of former German territories in Eastern Europe.

Although these groups sometimes make a lot of demagogic noise, their language has been increasingly restrained in recent years. Most of their adherents are over forty-five years of age. The circulation of their numerous small newspapers is steadily going down and most of the ads are death notices. Many of these expellees once owned big properties and are now hopelessly embittered over what they regard as callous disregard for their human rights. But much of their activity is of a social nature. The groups keep alive old customs and songs and sponsor numerous festivals and outings.

Indirectly they wield some influence, as their leaders continually urge them to resist the current government's political dialogues with Poland and the Soviet Union, recognition of the GDR, and above all, recognition of the former Oder-Neisse territories now on Polish soil—where most of their homes were located. It is believed that the NPD gathered many of its votes from this group. But most of them are adherents of the CDU/CSU.

Observers are also uneasy about Rainer Barzel, opposition leader of the CDU/CSU, whose views on Brandt's Ostpolitik and nationalist leanings differ little from those of Strauss. Along with Gerhard Schröder, he is most often mentioned as a possible CDU chancellor candidate. Gerhard Schröder's chances are actually better from many viewpoints. He is much more international-minded and progressive; he is respected for his well-balanced approach to problems. But he is pushing sixty and is disliked for his seeming standoffish personality.

Barzel is relatively young, in his mid-forties, and is regarded as a hard-working, efficient, manager-type politician. However he often appears to assume aggressive airs and inevitably leaves the impression that he too easily adjusts his views to suit the whims of popular taste.

Many look hopefully to the dynamic, youthful, articulate Helmut Kohl, minister president (governor) of the Rhineland-Palatinate, as the most qualified chancellor candidate for the CDU. He gives convincing indications that conservative and progressive ideas can be harmoniously combined. Gerhard Stoltenberg, the former minister for scientific research under Chancellor Georg Kiesinger and newly-elected minister president of Schleswig-Holstein, is also regarded as having chancellor qualifications, but is discredited in the eyes of many because of his recent position as a manager for the Krupp concern. Ex-chancellor Kiesinger's chances for reelection are virtually nil.

In the meantime, while the NPD's fortunes are declining, other rightist organizations and political parties have emerged, notably the *Deutsche Volks-Union* (DVU), and *Deutsche Union* (DU), both founded in 1971. A nationwide, rightist resistance movement to Brandt's Ostpolitik, called *Aktion Widerstand* (Resistance Campaign) has assumed worrying proportions. Even the supposedly dying League of Expellees *(Landsmannschaften)*, mentioned above, could again assume importance if rightist and leftist polarization should intensify. At its annual rally in Nuremberg in May, 1971, attendance swelled to over 30,000 mainly with Akton Widerstand people demonstrating out of solidarity against the Ostpolitik.

In addition the Free Democratic Party (FDP), has been further weakened by the establishment of the *National-Liberalen Aktion* (NLA), a rightist party, composed of disgruntled former members of the FDP. According to official figures of the department of the interior, in 1971 there were 316 radical groups or organizations in West Germany with nearly 100,000 members.

And within the CDU/CSU the young turks are likewise restless, demanding a greater share in policy-making decisions and a shift from its rightist course to a progressive center position.

Thus the success of the democratic parties in national and regional elections is at best a highly vulnerable one. So far, the Federal Republic has successfully steered away from extremist adventures of the Right or Left. But the old saw about "eternal vigilance" being the "price of liberty" was never more true than now.

Emergency Laws

The hottest single domestic issue throughout the sixties and well into the seventies, in the Federal Republic, was the controversial *Notstandgesetzgebung* (Emergency Legislation). The laws give emergency powers to the West German government to limit certain civil rights in the event of national danger. They provide for a rule by a truncated, temporary parliament of twenty-two deputies and eleven representatives of the West German states who would run the country in the event of natural disaster, armed rebellion, or nuclear war, until such time as the regular government could reassemble.

Some of the emergency powers the new laws give to the Federal Republic are: the right to draft women; the right to draft adult males from their jobs for defense functions; the right to use the army for civilian purposes; the right to employ the Federal border guard as police; and the right to limit states' rights. Some of the main clauses provide for the right to tap telephone calls, open mail, restrict travel, impose strict censorship, abolish the right to strike.

An important aspect of the legislation is that it cancels the

226

residual rights of the victorious World War II Allies—Britain, France, and the United States—to intervene in the governing of West Germany in the event of a threat to the country's security.

One controversial ruling is the provision for the creation of an air-raid warden force on a block-by-block level. This latter particularly frightens many Germans because of vivid memories of the *Gauleiter* (district leaders) who arrogantly terrorized everyone during the Third Reich.

The laws have been strongly opposed by labor unions, the New Left and student rebels, as well as much of the nation's mass media. For the laws are reminiscent of the notorious emergency laws, the famous Article 48 of the Weimar Constitution, which abolished all freedom in Germany in the event of circumstances that made it necessary to "protect the nation and state." It was Adolf Hitler who invoked this article on March 1, 1933, to consolidate his dictatorship.

Dr. J. C. G. Roehl, a British legal expert of the University of Sussex, has stated that the current West German emergency legislation is among the most democratic and progressive in the world.

But many Germans are almost pathologically opposed to the laws. Dr. Eugen Kogon, professor of political science, a former concentration camp prisoner and author of the book, *The Theory and Practice of Hell,* has called the laws the "first step toward paramilitarization of our society."

Perhaps the most depressing aspect of this emergency legislation for its opponents is that the laws were passed very quietly by the Bundestag, and that the overwhelming majority of the West German population was not the least aroused by its passage.

Power Centers

The Swiss sociologist Dr. Urs Jaeggi, who is attached to the University of Bochum, West Germany, wrote a widely quoted book, *Macht und Herrschaft in der Bundesrepublik* (Fischer Bücherei, 1969, Frankfurt) in which he claims that democratic pluralism is more of a West German pipe dream than a realizable fact of life.

According to Jaeggi, the Federal Republic is dominated by big business and industry. Over 35 percent of the nation's private property is owned by a mere 1.7 percent of the country's households.

Contrary to the widely held view that in West Germany there

are no class differences, Jaeggi argues that the consumer and the average employee is becoming more and more the helpless victim of class manipulation by the all-pervasive cartels that exercise increasing control over German life.

Jaeggi points out that the number of West German employees increased from 20,376,000 to 26,979,000 between 1950 and 1964. In that same period, however, the tendency toward concentration has increased by leaps and bounds. Where 35 percent of workers in 1933 were employed by enterprises with fewer than fifty employees, the number of firms with fifty employees or less decreased to 11.6 percent by 1957, while the number of businesses with more than two hundred employees climbed to 68.9 percent in that same period.

According to the Godesberg Program of the SPD, "The leading men of big industry by means of cartels and associations are able to exercise influence on the state and politics to such a degree that it is no longer reconcilable with democratic principles. They usurp the power of the state. Economic power has become political power."

Dr. Friedrich-Wilhelm Doergo of the Academy for Economics and Politics, Hamburg, categorically calls the *Bundesbank* (Federal Bank) a *Nebenregierung* (Parallel Government).

In fairness, it must be pointed out that no mean share of power and influence are exercised by the trade unions, the churches, and the political parties in their own right. Nevertheless, the trend toward monopolies and cartels is causing great concern.

The merger of Thyssen and Mannesmann in the pipe and tubing industry, for example, which was approved by the European Economic Community authorities, has meant virtually the complete eradication of competition in the pipes and tubing business. More recent examples of mergers are those of Hapag and Lloyd, and the great electrical concerns, Siemens and AEG, not to mention the automobile merger between NSU and Volkswagen.

On the other hand, the formation of large, efficiently operating industrial units is in many cases indispensable, if an exporting country, such as the Federal Republic, is to hold its own on the extremely competitive international market, notably against the rising industrial giant, Japan.

The process of concentration, however, if continued, could

eventually destroy rivalry altogether, that great motivator, accelerator, and brake of the economy.

In 1971 the Bonn cabinet approved reforms of laws governing major corporate mergers. Merging companies with a volume of 1 billion Deutsche marks (about $280 million) or more must first seek the permission of the Cartel Office, which will have the power to order the merger dissolved if this leads to or strengthens what it believes is a monopoly. Companies with a market share of over 40 percent will become subject to tighter control over possible abuses of their "monopoly" position and over possible merger plans.

Conscious of the unequal distribution of wealth in the Federal Republic—90 percent of the citizens must share a mere one-fifth of the entire national income—the Bundestag is preparing legislation for the so-called *Vermögengsbildung der Arbeit-nehmer* (Wealth-Sharing Program for Workers).

Various plans have been proposed. One version foresees the deposit of one Deutsche mark (28 cents) each working day, or 312 Deutsche marks a year, for each worker, tax free and with high-interest premiums, to be applied to the purchase of stocks and bonds. Another plan calls for the deposit of 20 Deutsche marks a month (about $4.50), or an annual deposit of 240 Deutsche marks, with 30 percent interest, provided there are no withdrawals over a given period. Provisions are also being considered whereby persons in the free-lance professions, small tradesmen, young married couples, and part-time employed pensioners can benefit from such arrangements.

Critics of the plan argue that this is mere tokenism, a cheap way of integrating the workers even more totally in the Establishment, so they will be less prone than ever to call it into question. In the last analysis, the workers will receive only an infinitely small share of the profits of industry, while the bulk of the wealth remains in the hands of the few. The Leftists especially argue that the only fair solution is an across-the-board distribution of profits among all the workers in industry.

Press Monopoly

The man whom the rebel students and the Leftists have singled out most often as the symbol of all that is bad in West Germany is a tall, handsome, silver-haired publisher by the name of Axel

Springer, who commutes among his six homes in Europe in a private jet, directs his $200-million press empire with 12,000 employees from atop a glass skyscraper directly alongside the Wall in West Berlin. Now pushing sixty, Springer is staunchly anti-Communist, unabashedly German, and touts a Cold-War line. He is a strong supporter of U.S. intervention in Vietnam and Cambodia. He owns fifteen magazines and newspapers, including the popular, nationally distributed, mass-circulation tabloid *Bild Zeitung* (4.4 million copies daily) which accounts for 40 percent of West Germany's weekday publications and 88 percent on Sundays. In West Berlin alone, Springer's 2,000 employees produce four dailies and two Sunday newspapers with a total of 1,017,000 copies daily for 65 percent of the West Berlin press, and in Hamburg (next to Berlin, the second largest city in West Germany), Springer produces 70 percent of the daily press.

Springer's newspapers echo their readers' contempt for the young radicals by calling them "political beatniks," "crazy half-toughs," and "the matriculated mob."

The students in turn charge Springer with managed and slanted news, with a dangerous monopoly and manipulation of public opinion to create a Fascist-style society in West Germany. A common slogan on lapel buttons and posters is *"Enteignet Springer* [Dispossess Springer]," to which *Bild Am Sonntag,* Springer's mass circulation Sunday paper, replies, "No terror shall bend us."

Springer seems to know what his readers want. During one particularly stormy week, when radical students mobbed Springer trucks and tried to destroy bundles of one of his newspapers, they enjoyed the best sales in their history.

The transfer of the Springer concern in 1970 into a joint stock company has further consolidated Springer's practically unlimited power over the firm as the sole shareholder and chairman. Springer reportedly owns 45 percent of the stock of the Hamburg television studio production company, 70 percent of whose vast production is destined for the biggest of West German national television stations.

However, the concentration trend, especially in the publishing field is causing grave concern in the Federal Republic. This is also true of the book trade. Erwin von Wehrenalp, the owner of the Econ Verlag, has said that the trend toward large enterprises in the book trade will continue. "Every week almost I could add another company to my gigantic undertaking. So many owners of small publishing firms come to me and ask me to help them out of financial difficulties."

The West German Press

Every day a total of 18.7 million copies of 1,328 daily newspapers with some 630 main editions hit the West German streets. They, together with some 6,482 periodicals (with 16.1 million readers of religious publications), make up the bulk of that new German forest, the *Blätterwald* (Forest of Printed Matter).

A significant factor of the West German press since 1945 has been the trend toward nonpartisan, independent newspapers. Over 80 percent are independent, with only 7.5 percent directly sponsored by political parties and 12.5 percent with close political ties. Nearly all are privately owned. (However, in a national telecast of ZDF, the second West German channel, pundit Gerhard Löwenthal alleged [June 24, 1970] that the SPD has secretly been buying up newspapers and already owns 10 percent of the nation's dailies.)

The deeply rooted sense of Federalism is nowhere more clearly shown than in the press, which has a long tradition of decentralization. Berlin has never been a press mecca like London with its Fleet Street. At least a dozen major West German cities have outstanding dailies. And newspapers in the Länder capitals play an important role in asserting provincial independence.

However, the number of local and regional newspapers has declined since World War II from 80 percent to 60 percent, and the trend is continuing.

Although Axel Springer's publishing empire is cause for serious concern, it is no real threat to West German newspaper freedom as long as it is offset by other powerful communications media. And that, indeed, it is. In addition to the progressive-to-leftist-radical newspapers and magazines, most of West German television studios are progressive and liberal rather than conservative.

Far and away the most controversial, hard-hitting, headline-making West German publication is that postwar phenomenon, the *Time*-like newsweekly, *Der Spiegel.* A single issue (circulation, one million) is about as thick as *Newsweek, Time,* and *US News and World Report* put together, and its smotherage

231

treatment of certain subjects is encyclopedic in scope. Because of its frequent bombastic, sensational, muckraking approach, it must be read with more than a grain of salt. However, it is indispensable reading for anyone who really wants to know what is going on in the two Germanies and, quite often, its reporting on other parts of the world is superior to the English-language coverage.

Der Spiegel was instrumental in toppling Strauss from the cabinet, hurried along the downfall of Chancellor Ludwig Erhard, helped push President Heinrich Luebke prematurely out of office, and broke the scandalous Bishop Matthias Defregger affair. Its in-depth and seemingly endless series on the Third Reich has no equal anywhere. At times the publication rises to greatness, especially in its superb interviews and original analyses of social phenomena.

Another anti-Springer publication, the mass-circulation (1.8 million) illustrated weekly, *Der Stern,* dispenses breathtaking exposés of German and international politics and social problems between layers of masculine and feminine flesh.

From its lofty editorial throne, the widely quoted weekly newspaper *Die Zeit* (circulation, 320,000) pontificates on national and international problems in long scholarly articles with excruciating fairness and timid progressiveness. It is an important status symbol for intellectuals and rookie politicians. It is widely regarded as the most balanced, best written German newspaper in existence.

Bild der Zeit is an important new pictorial magazine with outstanding photos and high-caliber writing, a combination of *National Geographic, Life,* and *Scientific American.*

An outstanding equivalent of the *Wall Street Journal* is the *Industrie Kurier* along with other important economic papers, *Handelsblatt, Die Welt der Arbeit,* and *Deutsche Zeitung und Wirtschaftszeitung.*

The two most important conservative dailies, both nationally and internationally respected, are the staid and old-fashioned *Frankfurter Allgemeine* and, I hate to admit it, a Springer publication, *Die Welt,* which is the intellectual counterpart of *Bild.*

The *Rheinische Merkur* is the influential conservative weekly in the Rhineland with close ties to the CDU. Since the party has gone into opposition, however, it has assumed a disconcerting nationalist tone. It is also considered to be a spokesman for the conservative wing of the Roman Catholic Church.

Two excellent progressive local dailies are the *Frankfurter Rundschau* in Frankfurt/Main and the *Stadt Anzeiger,* Cologne. A daily that enjoys international respect as one of the best in the German language and with international distribution, is the liberal *Süddeutsche* of Munich.

The Protestant weeklies, *Allgemeines Sonntagsblatt* (moderately liberal) and *Deutsche Zeitung* (conservative) enjoy a wide readership, as do such Roman Catholic publications as the scholarly *Herder Korrespondenz,* the avant-garde arty monthly *Kontraste* and the liberal weekly newspaper, *Publik.* Outstanding religious reporting and documentation are produced by the two church news agencies, the *Evangelische Pressedienst* (EPD) and the *Katholische Nachrichten Agentur* (KNA).

German cafés are flooded with a whole gamut of sexurated slicks, the notorious *Illustrierten* whose stock-in-trade is blood, guts, sex, and gossip. Thus they more than make up for the absence of society pages in the regular press. Among the most gaudy and revealing are *Quick, Neue Revue, Bunte Illustrierte,* and *Das Neue Blatt.* Typical headlines are: "Why Onassis Stood Up Jackie" and "Sensational Photos of Queen Elizabeth's Bedroom."

If there is one word to summarize much of the contents of the serious German press, it is verbosity. This is not strange considering that most mastheads list almost as many Ph.D.'s as a U.S. college catalogue. And, alas, the copy all too often shows it. Many of the pages and pages of *Feuilleton* (culture) articles read like doctoral dissertations. Ironically, Springer's *Die Welt* is by far the most attractive serious German daily in typography, layout, readability, snappy feature style, and simplicity. The famous five W's (Who, What, Why, When, Where) are very much buried in the long, long, often tendentious stories in the more serious German newspapers.

Although the German press devotes an enormous amount of space to exposés, the German attitude toward such washing of dirty linen in public is quite different from that of other countries. Countess Marion Dönhoff, editor-in-chief of *Die Zeit,* pointed out in an international TV press panel discussion (*Frühschoppen,* February 22, 1970), that "in England, when the press criticizes, there is a feeling that something is being settled.

In West Germany the people react differently—by telling so much about problems, they think, they only get worse."

Professor Tobias Brocher, the noted Frankfurt psychoanalyst, once observed, "In Germany one condemns those who uncover dirt, not those who make it."

The American publicist Melvin Lasky has complained, "The German press seldom has columnists with opposite points of view. There are few debates."

Comics are virtually absent from most serious newspapers, but appear sparingly in a number of tabloids. The "Blondie" strip is called "Dagwart," and "Dennis the Menace," "Fritzchen." The one bright spot in the otherwise stuffy *Die Zeit* and *Süddeutsche* publications are their humor page, which is a mixture of *Playboy*-type jokes and *New Yorker*-style cartoons and satire. The famous satirical magazine, *Simplicissimus,* which reached its heyday prior to World War I with barbed cartoons attacking the Prussian officer system, petered out in 1967. In its place is an irreverent modern satirical magazine called *Pardon* and a nudist-studded muckraking publication, *Konkret.*

But there is no such thing as a German Art Buchwald, and sprightly American-style columnists are conspicuous by their absence.

There is heavy coverage of sports, and frequent scholarly articles on jazz, soul, beat, and pop, all of which, like the banal comments of every pop and jazz artist who changes planes in Frankfurt, Munich, or Hamburg, are studied and analyzed with religious intensity. Leave it to the Germans to make a *Weltanschauung* out of every conceivable trend from Carnaby Street to neo-voyeurism. A frequent word that appears in many newspaper dissertation headlines is *"Spannungsfeld* [area of tension]"—*"Spannungsfeld zwischen Sexuellebefreiung und Moral* [Area of Tension Between Sexual Liberation and Morality]."

Extremist publications have an estimated combined circulation hovering at around 250,000—compared with over 22 million for democratic-oriented publications. The only extremist paper worth mentioning is the *Deutsche National Zeitung* with an estimated circulation of over 100,000. It is a strictly private venture of one Gerhard Frey published for over twenty years out of Munich. Its sensationalism is revealed by its headlines: *"Brandt's Grosser Verrat: Er Liefert Deutschland An Moskau Aus* [Brandt's Great Betrayal: He is Selling Out Germany to Moscow];" or "The Mass Murder of the Arabs."

German observers tend to regard this kind of publication as part of the price you have to pay for press freedom. In a true democracy you have to let extremists blow off steam.

An amusing oddity of the German press is the weekly *St. Pauli Nachrichten* published in the honky-tonk striptease section of Hamburg. Filled with titillating sex stories, it enjoys a high circulation all over the country. It is the voice of a new Sex Party, which seeks to enter the Bundestag on a platform of sexual freedom and "Reunification With East Germany Through Sexual Encounters."

West Germany surely enjoys about as absolute a press freedom as you can find anywhere—some say even more than in the U.S. or Britain, where libel laws are severe.

The Basic Law states simply, "There shall be no censorship." But it also stipulates that "these rights are limited by the provisions of general laws." In other words, it is only possible to prosecute journalists, authors, or editors for published matter if the plaintiff can prove that they have otherwise violated the law.

The German Press Council, organized in 1957, is an organ for the self-control and protection of the press. The Federal Government's Press and Information Office in Bonn spends millions of DM's in PR promotion of the German image, and sponsors visits of hundreds of journalists annually from all over the world. But it has no control over the German press whatsoever, although it serves as spokesman for the government. In 1970, however, the Press and Information Office was vociferously criticized and denounced by much of the press because it spent large sums of money promoting its image during the election campaigns preceding the Bavarian and Hesse state elections.

In 1969 the editorial staff of *Der Stern* successfully staged a revolt when one of the weekly's owners, Richard Gruner, wanted to sell 25 percent of the partnership. The prospective buyer, Heinrich Bauer, a publisher of sex magazines, found stiff resistance from the editors who felt they would be mere puppets in the new arrangement. The deal fell through when they threatened a walkout. In addition, the editors pressed their advantage, and forced the new management to sign an agreement declaring that no employee had to write against his convictions and gave the staff "participatory say" in ownership or top management decisions and personnel changes.

The revolt then inspired the socialist-oriented *Der Spiegel* in

January, 1970, to similar steps. The publisher, Rudolf Augstein, persuaded the employees to form a corporate organization, gave it half the annual net profits to be applied in a comprehensive pension fund, and, for good measure, threw in 50 percent of company ownership over a ten-year period. In so doing, Augstein headed off a potential drive for editorial participation in day-to-day decisions and management. In a compromise solution, he is allowing the staff to vote in the selection of business managers and editors.

This participatory trend shows signs of becoming a movement and has already spread to other publications. Meanwhile the free-lance writers established the Association of Federal Republic Writers, including the membership of the noted author Heinrich Böll, which seeks to improve royalty- and fee-agreements for writers and will lobby for their social rights in Bonn "if they do not want to meet a paleontological end as the dinosaurs of the cybernetic era."

Radio and Television

Radio and television in the Federal Republic differs profoundly from the United States. For many observers they are outstanding examples of institutions completely independent of commercial interests. Programs are never, but never interrupted by advertising, which is restricted to solid five-minute blocks of spot commercials one after the other, and then only between six and eight P.M. (and even then may not exceed twenty minutes in a two-hour period). And on Sundays there is no advertising at all. Sponsored programs are prohibited by law. There are no local stations, and no commercially-operated broadcasting corporations. Regional broadcasting stations serve not only individual cities but also the individual Länder.

On the whole, the Germans of any given region have a choice of three West German channels and one or more from adjoining countries, including the German Democratic Republic. West German radio and TV are beamed into East Germany and have a wide following. The choice of radio is broader, since most sets are able to pick up a large number of local German stations, American and British forces' broadcasts, a large number of regional German broadcasts, and many European stations.

While radio broadcasting is mostly on a twenty- to twenty-four-hour basis, television is limited, for economic reasons, to the hours of 5 P.M. to midnight, and all day on Saturdays and Sundays. There is also elementary- and secondary-school television during the day, and *Telekolleg,* adult-education TV, which is combined with correspondence college courses.

In the Federal Republic the main TV channels are subdepartments of radio broadcasting stations, which are nonprofit corporations under civil law and are owned by the Länder in which they are located.

There are three channels:

The First Program (German TV-ARD) consists of joint productions nationally transmitted according to a fixed quota for each of the nine state broadcasting stations. Thus this program telecasts productions originating from all parts of the country. On weekdays these studios also broadcast programs dealing with regional problems, lasting on an average of twenty minutes daily.

The Second Program *(Zweites Deutsches Fernsehen-ZDF,* Mainz), is produced since 1962 by a central studio for national transmission as an alternative to and in competition with the First Program with its various state studios.

The Third Program is produced by the state studios but independently of the other programs and channels. This channel is deliberately highbrow and is roughly comparable to the BBC's Second Program or educational TV in the United States. Numerous foreign telecasts are beamed to viewers, often in their original languages, highly technical scientific programs aimed at particularly bright viewers, and such American imports as *CBS Reports, White Paper, Meet the Press.*

If West German radio and TV are so independent of commercial interests, who pays for them? One big source of revenue is advertising, but it is not enough. Most of the money comes from compulsory subscriptions. If you buy a radio or TV set in West Germany you are automatically required by law to apply for a viewing license, which costs 2 DM's (60 cents) a month for every radio set, and 5 DM's ($1.45) for every TV set. This money is collected by the post office, which is responsible for the technical operations and transmitting equipment of radio and television (and also runs the telephone system, telegraph, and telex). It is possible to cheat, of course, but stiff penalties are meted out to "black market" viewers, when detected.

The reason West German broadcasting differs so much from that in the United States and many other countries is primarily because of its historical development. Like most European countries, radio in Germany evolved as a state institution and not as a private enterprise. This of course was abused under the National Socialists, who exploited radio as the state's most important vehicle of propaganda. Radio and TV are still controlled and manipulated by the East German regime today.

However, the West German system has built-in guarantees that have made it probably the most effective German democratic institution of all. The basis for the present structure was laid in 1945 when the American, British, and French military governments of their respective occupation zones stipulated that radio devote ample attention to all representative philosophical, social, religious, political, scientific, and artistic problems and trends.

Although the Federal Post Office retains jurisdiction over the allotment of frequencies and transmission techniques (625 line system), and retains 20 percent of radio receipts and 27 percent of TV fees for this purpose, the individual broadcasting stations enjoy full editorial freedom.

All broadcasting stations in the Federal Republic and West Berlin enjoy self-government under three important civilian structures: 1) the Broadcasting Council, a body including representatives of important public organizations and associations, such as industry, the trade unions, consumer associations, the churches, youth, women, and minority groups; 2) the Administrative Council, the body supervising the general operation of the station, which also must be representative of the entire citizenry; and 3) the *Intendant* (manager), who supervises programming and production.

The various broadcasting stations of course are bound by laws and agreements which are not made with the Federal Government at all, but with the various Länder they are located in. This is to assure that the stations preserve their independent character and do not become themselves manipulators of power and information. For example, the stations do not have the same freedom to propagate their own views as newspapers do, but are required to permit independent journalists, writers, and public figures of all political and religious tendencies to unequivocally state their views.

Since these broadcasting stations are Länder-oriented, two additional, but likewise independent radio stations have been created in Cologne, the *Deutschlandfunk,* which produces radio broadcasts with a more comprehensive view of Germany and is beamed all over Europe, and the *Deutsche Welle* (German Wave), which emits short-wave broadcasts via directional beams in twenty-eight languages all over the world.

Obviously, even with all these safeguards, the system is not 100 percent foolproof. Inevitably this or that *Intendant* will lean too far right or left, or will evoke violent differences from his staff or listeners and viewers. West German newspapers frequently publish exposés of radio and TV scandals involving alleged suppression of programs, or highhanded ousting of editors, power struggles, and the like. A recent allegation (by *Der Stern*) claimed that Axel Springer caused the last-minute suppression of a TV documentary, by the respected reporter Thilo Koch, critically dealing with the Springer concern. However, other TV programs have not failed to bring exposés of Springer and others like him; somehow the truth gets across.

Journalists and educators of many countries, and with the highest possible critical standards, are inevitably impressed by the overall high caliber of West German broadcasting and telecasting. Its in-depth documentary reporting and analyses of complicated political events are surely among the best in the world. And it has far and away more programs of artistic and literary merit than the United States. The chief reason for this may be attributed to the independence of West German TV from ratings and public opinion polls. Above all, the men and women who do the programing have no obligations whatsoever to test any program in terms of its sales-stimulating effect. The commercial aspect does not even enter their minds. Close attention of course is paid to the viewing public's television preferences as revealed through polls, it is true, but the programing is still designed to meet people's entertainment and artistic and educational needs in terms of standards and competence, not sales.

It is doubtful whether any other television country anywhere has nearly the number of outstanding plays, avant-garde theater, dancing and music, brilliant features, imaginative humor and satire, and cultural programs as does West German TV. Some American observers even regard its coverage of American events superior to that in the States itself. And no German medium has shown more courage and honesty in critical reportage of the domestic scene, from neo-Nazi trends to student revolts. There are at least two first-rate discussion programs a week. It is an interesting commentary on West German democracy that the

Internationaler Frühschoppen (International Cocktail), a lively Sunday-noon press panel dealing with controversial political topics and chaired by the personable and brilliant Werner Höfer, has consistently enjoyed immense popularity for more than a decade.

A common complaint against West German TV is that it is "weak on entertainment." But there has been considerable improvement. Germans are enjoying *Smokey Bear* talking in their own language, not to mention *Julia, Flipper, Flintstones, Petticoat Junction, I Dream of Jeannie,* and such personalities as Doris Day, Sammy Davis, Jr., Mahalia Jackson, Barbra Streisand, Frank Sinatra. They like *Bonanza* so much they gave it the top West German TV aware one year, the Bambi.

A large number of Germans, especially adherents of the conservative CDU/CSU, have become increasingly unhappy over what they regard as a leftist-dominated and manipulated TV apparatus. For some critics, Gerhard Löwenthal, the commentator on the Second German TV (ZDF) is the only conservative counterpart to a whole series of leftist-orientated commentators—notably Hans Merseburger. Some of these disgruntled viewers have joined a new organization called *Funk und Fernsehmitgestaltung* (FFM) which demands a greater co-determination on the part of the viewing public. West German TV, it seems, shares the dilemma of most television countries—the great problem of allowing for opposite points of view.

There has been considerable agitation in West Germany in recent years in favor of the establishment of commercial radio and TV à la the United States, notably by influential businessmen and, you guessed it, Axel Springer. But even if they succeed, it is more than likely that the present system will continue on a parallel basis, just as does the BBC in the United Kingdom.

Film Censorship

There is no such thing as West German censorship of movies as far as adults are concerned, but its "youth protection law" stipulates that all films must be examined first to determine whether they can be harmful to children. Children under six years are forbidden to see any motion picture, while movies, in typical German thoroughness, are classified according to three groups: children from six to twelve years, from twelve to sixteen, and from sixteen to eighteen. In other words, adults can see any movie, while children are restricted.

And as for the procedure by which movies are classified, this "censorship," if the word must be used, is carried out by the film industry's *Freiwillige Selbstkontrolle der Filmwirtschaft* (FSK), the voluntary censorship board, which was created by the film industry itself through its head organization, *Spitzenorganization der Filmwirtschaft* (SPIO), which has its headquarters in an old castle near Wiesbaden.

According to FSK guidelines, German voluntary film censorship has two main characteristics: the government has no control, and it is designed to tell the truth rather than hide it.

Every year the FSK, which is composed of leaders of youth, workers, religion, and government appointees (but not officials), examines around 3,000 films. The government appointees, however, only have a voice in films considered for youth and even then their decision can be overruled.

FSK guidelines oppose movies that are militaristic, imperialistic, or nationalistic, or that discriminate against races or minorities, violate the Basic Law, or falsify history. This last rule is aimed at the Nazi era. FSK board members if anything encourage films about the Nazi period but believe that films must stand the test of fact not fiction. That they have approved such brutally honest films as *Mein Kampf* and *Wir Wunderkinder* show that there is no attempt to hide the ugly facts. The former, a Swedish-produced documentary based on secret Nazi films and old newsreels, shows graphically, in all their horror, the Hitler atrocities. The reviewing board permitted even children from twelve onwards to see it, because, as one board member put it, "we thought it that important."

Outright pornography so far has not appeared in West German films, but there are heated debates as to just what pornography is, and the complete freedom on this score in Denmark is being considered by German lawmakers too. Even now, West German films are more permissive than those of most Western countries.

Meanwhile, voices are growing louder and louder for "total democracy," and West Germany is bursting at the seams with experiments in all directions, from protest songs to anti-art, to anti-authoritarian kindergartens, to Living Theater.

241

Total Democracy

In the Federal Republic there are numerous civil rights associations, such as the *Bund für Bürgerrechte* (Civil Rights Guild) in Frankfurt, and the *Humanistische Union* in Munich, the equivalent of the American Civil Liberties Union, and the *Vereinigung für Staatsbürgerlich Freiheiten* (Civic Freedoms Association) in Bonn, which aims to inform the population of its rights under the Basic Law and the laws of the land. The *Bundeszentrale für Heimatdienst* (Federal Center for Patriotic Service), which is supervised by a committee of members from the Bundestag, acts as coordinating agency and information center for these bodies.

The latest rage in the Federal Republic is the anti-authoritarian kindergarten. In many places throughout the country experiments are being conducted to discover new ways to educate children with a maximum of freedom.

In West Berlin's John F. Kennedy *Vorschulklasse* (preschool class—the word "kindergarten" is avoided), children are encouraged to follow every whim and to decide for themselves how they will occupy their time. Teachers build on spontaneity and experience and try to help the children lead themselves to knowledge by nourishing their own widening horizons. Completely absent are drills, commands to "sit still," regimentation, and rows of seats. Uncombed, shrieking, running, jumping, they receive crayons if they want them, toys if they want them, and guidance only to the degree it is desired.

It is too early to say whether or not such methods will have satisfactory results and to what extent this approach will help children become better, more responsible adults. But the issue has become highly controversial.

For instance, in West Berlin, a youth center operated by scientists of the city's Free University was closed down in April, 1970, by City Senator Horst Korber of the city's youth department, after he learned that school children were encouraged by the scientists to undress and attempt sexual intercourse.

The center was run by graduate students of the Institute of Psychology under Professor Klaus Holzkamp, the director, and his assistant, Professor Rudiger Kock. The scientists explained that the purpose of their activity was "to emancipate working-

class children from the repressive influence of their home
education by exposing social exploitation and sexual com-
pulsions."

But this center was only one of many such experimental
groups. There have been some fifty *Kinderladen* (literally,
children's stores), private day-care centers in West Berlin run by
young parents, mostly intellectuals, artists, and liberals, who wish
to bring up their children "free of inhibitions" and according to
"progressive psychology."

In many of these centers the "anti-authoritarian" methods
include drilling the children in Marxist and Maoist slogans and
ideology. Many people are especially shocked by the fact that in
some of these experiments, children are used whose parents are
not even consulted.

But for the parents there is very little choice. In the country
that gave "kindergarten" to the world, there is a kindergarten
capacity for only one child out of every three applicants.

The Word Is "Anti"

Nothing indicates the universal confusion about democracy in
the Federal Republic so much as the turmoil that has characterized the cultural scene over the past few years. There is
anti-theater, anti-opera, anti-art, and anti-directors. Gangs of
leftists will interrupt a play or satirical performance to force the
actors to stop and "discuss" with them what they are trying to
perform. "True theater," the gang spokesman shouts, "requires
audience participation."

All over the country outstanding *Intendants* (directors) are
leaving for greener pastures in Austria and Switzerland because
they cannot cope with the constant demands for co-determination and democratization of the theater to such a degree that
stage hands, actors, and in some cases even cleaning women are
supposed to have a voice in how a play must be directed, written,
acted, and performed.

On the positive side, though, the West German theater has
contributed so very much to the awakening of a social
consciousness and an enrichment of new dramatic forms to a
degree hitherto unknown that the above-named aberrations are
little enough price to pay.

Whatever one may think of Rolf Hochhuth's playwriting qualifications (or lack of them), the fact remains that the 1963 production of his controversial play *The Deputy*—which blames Pope Pius XII for failing to intervene in behalf of the Jews in Nazi Germany—not only shook up the national German conscience but launched a whole new era on the West German stage. Produced in the theaters of over twenty countries, the play brought political documentation to the stage and social involvement to countless theater audiences.

Hochhuth's *Soldiers,* in which Winston Churchill is posthumously cross-examined, was likewise condemned as poor drama, but it enlivened recent contemporary history. His more recent *Guerrillas*—an exposé of American politics and the CIA—is described as "a masterpiece of mediocrity," but it is an enacted lecture on American demoralization.

In 1964 Heinar Kipphardt's dramatization of the protocol of J. Robert Oppenheimer portrayed the dilemma of physicists in the atomic age.

The Investigation by Peter Weiss in 1965 was the protocol of the Auschwitz trials set to music in a dialectically constructed "oratorio."

The man who directed these first efforts at documentary theater, the late Erwin Piscator, was known for his political theater both in Germany and in the United States (where he sat out the Nazi era).

In another production, *Gesang vom Lusitanischen Popanz(The Song of the Lusitanian Bugaboo),* Peter Weiss attempted to portray conditions in Portuguese Angola.

The experimental theater of the German Academy of Acting discovered the Austrian Peter Handke, who introduced *Publikums Beschimpfung (Abusing the Audience),* a one-hour harangue at the audience, spoken by four actors, repeating deliberate clichés in rhythmic cadences. This technique has been copied and used since all over the world.

The Nazi themes have meanwhile given way to world themes: Vietnam, colonialism, racial discrimination, exploitation of the masses, guerrillas, rebellion. In 1968 three plays, by Peter Weiss, Armand Gatti, and Megan Terry, all dealing with Vietnam were enjoying successful runs on German stages.

Günter Grass, with his *The Plebians Rehearse the Uprising* in 1966 for the first time brought to the stage an incident of

244

German postwar history: the workers' revolt in East Berlin on June 17, 1953. His 1968 play *Davor* dealt with student demonstrations.

However, the West German theater is in a state of prolonged crisis. Just as in most bourgeois countries, the theater world in West Germany is leftist-oriented. In the German system the "star" is not the leading actor but the *Intendant* (stage director). He enjoys about the same social status as the football coach in America. If his "team" wins (this is not necessarily box-office success but also talked-about critical recognition), he is lionized by the prestige-conscious community. But if his "team" loses, he may have to start packing his bags. As a result successful *Intendants* are lured from one community to another like prize football coaches.

But because theater and the arts in Germany are heavily subsidized—a tradition that goes all the way back to the time of the German duchies before the country's unification in 1871—the contemporary *Intendant* finds himself in a very schizophrenic situation. If he caters to the bourgeois public, which prefers traditional classics, he will become rapidly stigmatized as the director of a museum. If he creates a workshop for experimentation, he will enjoy the raves of critics and the New Left against the background of rows of empty seats.

There is a lot of hot debating going on about who the theater public should be. Many *Intendants* and avant-garde playwrights, actors, and critics go so far as to say the middle-aged bourgeois should be kept out of the theater altogether and leave their seats for a "better public," the progressive-minded young generation. Trouble is, the new generation avoids the theaters in droves.

The very subsidization which should relieve *Intendants* of financial woes has proved ironically the cause of deep inner frustration. In Germany the theater has never been an institution of mere entertainment but the very heart of *Bildung, i.e.,* the education of humanist values. Its themes of revolution are not something that began with Hochhuth but date back to Schiller, were revived again in the 1920's with Bertolt Brecht and continued in the wave of protest plays of the sixties. For *Intendants* the stage is an instrument of social commitment, not a setting for amusement. The more subsidized they are, the more they insist on demonstrating their independence, with far-out plays.

245

One attempt to solve the dilemma has been relatively successful, that of adapting classical plays, from Aeschylus to Shaw, in such a way as to reveal their "hidden" revolutionary message relevantly for our times.

Nevertheless, the dilemma of the German theater is very real. Sometimes an *Intendant* and his repertory company become innocent political footballs. In West Berlin in 1970 the *Schaubühne*, an experimental theater, was playing Maxim Gorki's *The Mother* in Bertolt Brecht's adaptation to full houses. But as municipal elections neared, the Christian Democratic opposition, in an effort to unseat the Social Democratic administration, made a public issue out of the production, charging the *Intendant* with "subversive indoctrination." In spite of the defense of the Socialist city senator for cultural affairs, the Socialist city council, in obvious reaction to the CDU campaign, summarily suspended part of the subsidy allotted to the *Schaubühne*.

In Hamburg, on December 19, 1970, Gerard Hirsch, aged 47, *Intendant* of the world-famous *Schauspielhaus*, committed suicide. In a note he left behind he had written, "I could not stand the general lack of courage any more."

Meanwhile, "the show must go on," and, in spite of everything, theater, opera, and music in West Germany are far from dead, and the arts are still subsidized to a degree unknown in most other countries.

How stable is West German democracy? Perhaps the following remark by a young theologian is as good an answer as any. "For a long time," he said to me, "I toyed with the idea of emigrating. But I asked myself: Where? Britain, with its immigration quota, economic malaise, and race problem? The United States with its Vietnam, My Lai, Cambodia, Black Panthers, and George Wallace? Italy, with its unending waves of strikes and government chaos? France, with its anti-Semitism and economic doldrums? South Africa or Rhodesia, with their apartheid? Australia, with its whites-only immigration policy and splendid isolation?

"And then all of a sudden I realized that, as nations go, the Federal Republic really isn't such a bad place to live."

246

◀ 15 ▶

THE JEWISH COMMUNITY

DURING THE VERY beginnings of the Middle East conflict in 1967, before the actual Six-Day War began, Israel purchased 20,000 gas masks from West Germany as a precaution against possible use of gas by the Arab forces. There is profound irony in the thought that the survivors of the gas chambers of Auschwitz, Buchenwald, Bergen-Belsen, Dachau, Theresienstadt, and their children should appeal, of all people, to the survivors of the Nazis and their children for protection against gas.

On the very first day of the shooting, June 5th, an estimated six hundred West German youths volunteered at the Israeli Embassy in Bonn to fight or work for Israel. Within hours the embassy was deluged by phone calls, express letters, telegrams from thousands of German citizens offering sympathy, solidarity, money, service, and support.

These examples are only two out of many that underline the change of 180 degrees among the leaders and citizens of the "new" Germany and the improved relations between the Gentiles and Jews in the Federal Republic's short existence.

Outwardly at least there are signs of hope everywhere. New and reconstructed synagogues, some of them gleaming in white marble and built in striking contemporary design, have been constructed in Hamburg, Frankfurt-Main, Bremen, Hagen, Bonn, Düsseldorf, Duisburg, Dortmund, Cologne, Paderborn, Worms, Münster, Mülheim, Saarbrücken, and West Berlin—all financed by the Federal Republic or the individual Länder.

But as soon as one delves deeper, the picture becomes much more blurred and uncertain. The symbiosis that characterized pre-Hitler Germany included more than 550,000 Jews (the six million murdered Jews in the Third Reich were from all over Europe). Today the number of Jews in the Federal Republic is estimated at around 30,000. There is of course no racial or ethnical classification by West German authorities, but the Jewish Central Council keeps track of those registered in the various local Jewish communities—26,143 at last count. How, then, can these few Jews living in the Federal Republic today be compared with those who once were an important cultural and economic factor of German life?

The absence of a Jewish elite is keenly felt because today there are no longer such giants of the caliber of an Albert Einstein, Felix Mendelssohn, Heinrich Heine, Otto Brahm, Max Reinhardt, Ernst Lubitsch, Alfred Kerr, Kurt Tucholsky—to name only a few. Twenty-five percent of the German Jews are over sixty years old and live on pensions or social welfare. Those who have been helped by restitution aid to a "quiet" evening of life are not very numerous. The intellectual elite has either gone to the dogs or vanished. The number of those in free-lance professions—which in 1933 was astoundingly high—has declined considerably. There is a dearth of Jewish lawyers and physicians.

About 65 percent of the Jews living in West Germany today come from eastern and southeastern Europe. These form the actual living and above all youthful element in the congregations. They are predominantly small businessmen. Although most of them lack a regular trade or profession—for the younger Jews spent their youth in concentration camps, DP camps, and wandering—they have been able nevertheless to carry on a profession or trade.

However, Jews today hold high government posts and are represented in every walk of life. Two are members of the Bundestag. The late Dr. Rudolf Katz was vice-president of the Federal Constitutional Court. Dr. Herbert Weichmann is prime minister of Hamburg. Ludwig Rosenberg is the retired president of the Federation of Trade Unions. The late Ernst Deutsch was one of the country's best known actors. Dr. Jeanette Wolf is a member of the Berlin city council. Artur Brauner is a prominent producer.

Until a few years ago many Jews in the Federal Republic made a point of buying only extremely old furniture and investing their money in jewelry or other valuables small enough to put in a small valise. They literally carried a second passport (usually from Israel) at all times, ready to make a quick getaway if the ghost of Hitler should suddenly rear its ugly head.

"Today this is no longer so," says Heinz Galinski, chairman of the directors of the Central Council of Jews in Germany and chairman of the Jewish Community in West Berlin.

248

"We are not a liquidation community," the dapper, bald chairman explains. "Otherwise we would not have gone to all the trouble of building up the complex of Berlin Jewish institutions."

As the largest, most conspicuous, and most active Jewish community in Germany, the Berlin community is a natural barometer of Jewish life in the Federal Republic. Statistically this is revealed by an increase of 5,890 members in October, 1964, to well over 6,500 in 1970. Just a few years ago, the membership was declining, because of the high death incidence of the predominantly aged members. As in the Federal Republic, every second Jew was nearly sixty and the average age was over fifty. Today the average age, thanks to a slight increase in marriages and a trickling return of former German Jews, has dropped to around forty-five, especially in Berlin. It isn't a very impressive statistic, but in the light of all that has happened, it is encouraging enough to be ground for "cautious optimism."

Jewish activity in West Berlin is spread out over four synagogues, a kindergarten, a home for the aged, several schools for religious instruction, several youth organizations, two women's organizations, and especially the imposing, relatively new Jewish Community Center on the Fasanen Strasse, just off the glamorous Kurfürstendamm, West Berlin's swank theater and nightclub boulevard.

In this latter institution, religious services are held, an adult education program is in full swing, a kosher restaurant serves the ritual-minded. Here plays and poetry readings are held, concerts are performed, lectures are given, as well as courses in Hebrew, the Bible, Jewish religion, Jewish history, instructions in Israeli folk singing and dancing. So much has it become an important cultural center of Berlin that well over half of its visitors are Gentiles.

Throughout West Germany proper, entire high school classes, as well as Catholic and Protestant seminarians, regularly make tours of Jewish institutions or visit the various synagogues. Rabbis and Jewish scholars are flooded with requests for lectures. There is a constant stream of visitors from Israel and vice versa.

The *Gesellschaft für Jüdische Christliche Zusammenarbeit* (Society for Jewish-Christian Cooperation), with chapters in most of the larger cities, has sponsored numerous seminars, meetings with Jews, and symposiums on all aspects of Jewish-

249

Christian relations. Workshops on anti-Semitism and problems of Jewish-Christian relations are a regular part of the curricula of Catholic, Protestant, and secular adult education programs, institutes, and discussion groups. Numerous youth groups from the two big Christian confessions make regular pilgrimages, sometimes on bicycles, to former concentration camp sites.

Anti-Semitism Without Jews

Generally speaking, outright public anti-Semitism has been extremely rare in the Federal Republic. No doubt it exists among the older generation, but it is mostly latent. Elsewhere in this book, rightist extremism, with anti-Semitic manifestations, and the German attitude toward the statute of limitations on Nazi manhunts, and the like, are discussed at some length. From time to time there are incidents, mostly teenage vandals looking for thrills rather than anti-Semitic outbursts, such as overturning headstones in Jewish cemeteries or making swastika smearings on synagogues. But while these incidents echo in newspaper headlines around the world, much less coverage is accorded the genuine and massive public demonstrations against such incidents.

"If someone in London draws a swastika on a Jewish building," Rabbi Hans Isak Gruenewald of Hamburg told me, "the police will only shrug their shoulders as if to say, 'so what?' If the same thing happens in Germany, people want to tell the chancellor right away."

It was a high-ranking Jewish official who pointed out to me that West Germany is the only country in the world—including Israel—where anti-Semitism as such is punishable by law.

As for the vast bulk of Germans there is no way of knowing what they really think or how they would act in a crisis, for it is extremely "in" to be pro-Jewish and "out" to say anything disparaging of the Jews or even Israel (though, as we shall see, the latter has become the target for attack from the New Left).

While there is virtually no discrimination against Jews in respect to housing, employment, recreation, and hotels, there are constant court cases all over the country involving insults to Jews. The Jewish community of Berlin alone recorded more than 1,000 anti-Semitic incidents between 1959 and 1970. I have personally witnessed a number of anti-Semitic scenes or remarks on any number of occasions. Once I was with several German friends, including one Jew, in a Hamburg bar. We had been to a heated confrontation of Arab and Israeli students at the university, and we were continuing the animated discussion. After a while, a middle-aged man at the next table who apparently had been eavesdropping on our conversation, staggered to his feet, and walked directly to the Jewish member of our group and said, "What! They forgot to gas you too!"

It is significant that it was the Germans in our group who made the loudest protest, immediately sent for the police, while the Jew merely shrugged off the matter and was relieved when the man slipped out the back door. "Let the man alone," he said. "He is drunk. He doesn't realize what he is saying. If he has something of the past on his conscience it will nag him until death. After all that has happened, why make a big issue out of every little incident like this?"

But our Jewish friend in this case was very young. Some of his relatives had been in concentration camps, but he himself had not experienced the Hitler nightmare. An older Jewish survivor more likely would have pressed the issue—and who would dare oppose him?

The Research Center for Psycho-Therapy and Psycho-Pathology of the Max Planck Society in December, 1969, published the results of a ten-year study in the United States, Israel, and Europe made with 219 concentration camp survivors. According to Professor Paul Matussek, director of the center, 43.4 percent of this group were suffering from psychic disturbances, 14.7 percent were affected by paranoid tendencies, and 52.5 percent suffered from a regular incidence of nightmares and subsequent fits of shock. Only 12 percent of these persons were even relatively free from psychic disturbances, while the remaining 88 percent were victims of recurrent periods of depression, resignation, and despair, characterized by apathy, inhibitions, with a tendency toward fiery outbursts of temper at the slightest provocation. As a result, most of the former Nazi victims enjoy precious little professional success, lead unharmonious family lives, and have extremely little social contact. Most of these unhappy persons will remain psychological outcasts of society for the rest of their days.

According to Dr. Gerd Biermann, a Munich pediatrician, there are per capita more abnormal Jewish children of school age than Gentile, suffering from neuroses as a result of the ambivalent values absorbed in homes torn by spiritual schizophrenia of living in a land which they cannot love.

"My little girl came up to me the other day," one Jewish mother said to me, "and she said, 'Mommy, why do you have that number on your arm?'—referring to the concentration camp identification tattoo. A pang went through and through me. How could I tell her without teaching her at the same time to hate her German playmates? So I said, 'Never mind, that is an important telephone number I didn't want to forget.' But I know that I can't fool her for much longer and some day I will have to tell her."

In summer some Jewish women cover their ID tattoos with adhesive bandages whenever they wear short-sleeved dresses or go to the swimming pool, so as to avoid stares from Germans.

I remember attending a Jewish-Christian theological conference at a Benedictine monastery. One of the speakers was a Jewish scholar. But he was a survivor of Auschwitz, and never, never for a moment let his German hosts and partners forget this. All during the four-day meeting, on an average of about once every hour, he compulsively brought up his Auschwitz experience over and over again. "When I was in Auschwitz . . . "; "you Germans . . . "; "then the time the guard kicked me in the teeth . . . "; "'You Jewish swine,' the guard shouted at me"; "then the time I lay all night and screamed in pain . . . "

At the end of the conference I offered to drive him to Munich, a journey of about two hours. Although I made a point of reminding him that I was an American and we spoke only in English, only one subject was on his mind during the entire ride: "Auschwitz . . . Auschwitz . . . Auschwitz . . . "

Multiply his case by the thousands and you can understand why, for the older generation of both Jews and non-Jews the barrier is so great. Small wonder that very few Jews take an active part in German life or Jewish-Christian activities. They are reluctant to identify themselves with Germany, but unwilling to divorce themselves from it either.

Although the Jewish community in the Federal Republic is so tiny, never has there been such a tremendous interest in all things Jewish. There is something almost unhealthy and downright eerie about the preoccupation of many Germans with Jewish culture. It is a phantom interest, perhaps for many a therapeutic interest, through which some Germans hope to atone for the deep-rooted sense of guilt described in Chapter 10. Even anti-Semitism, when it does appear, has a likewise other-worldly quality, for it is an anti-Semitism without Jews.

But this intense preoccupation is at best the activity of a relatively small minority—in spite of occasional outbursts of favorable sentiment whenever some incident awakens the German majority to a need to publicly shake their fists against swastika smearings or the burning in 1970 of the Munich Jewish home for the aged (attributed to Arab extremists). By and large, however, the vast majority of Germans show little interest in meeting or working together with the Jewish community. Even though the clergy of both confessions are among the foremost leaders of Jewish-Christian activity, the Christian churches as a whole have done precious little to bring the two groups together.

Add to this the fact that until very recently world Jewry showed considerable apathy toward the German Jews. In fact, for a long time many Jews around the world, notably the Israelis, looked down on the German Jewish community with contempt because they were living in Germany. As a result the Jewish community has been isolated both within and without the Federal Republic.

On the Gentile side, Jewish-Christian cooperation inevitably tends to bog down after a time. Many persons, though unwilling to admit it, find it all a big bore. Year after year the Gentile Germans perfunctorily feel they must go through with the elaborate Brotherhood Week celebrations and regular concentration camp commemoration days. They feel it is their duty to do something "nice" for the Jews. Some critics even observe sarcastically that many of the activities are hard to distinguish from those of "Be Kind to Animals Week."

I remember on one occasion when I visited a Jewish-Christian program in a large German city, which shall here go unnamed. The hall was half empty, and (I might as well be honest) I sat near the rear door so that I could make a quick getaway if the meeting proved too boring. One of the officers noticed me, however, and immediately got up from his seat in the front row and walked all the way to my row and sat down right beside me, even though the seats all around were empty. After a moment, he

253

said, "Why don't you join us down in front?" I declined. Then, after a pause, he said, "But you *are* Jewish, aren't you?" When I replied in the negative, he said, "Well, in that case I don't have to worry about you then." And he got up and left.

This phenomenon of *preferred* treatment for Jews in today's Germany is known as Philo-Semitism.

Special Status—A Dilemma

The lack of visible presence of a sufficient number of Jews dooms many Jewish-Christian efforts at the outset by clumsy over-politeness, preferred treatment, and excessive adulation. It has become fashionable for Gentile Germans to attend Jewish social events or to send their children to Israel. "*My* daughter," Frau Schmidt will triumphantly boast to Frau Meier over the telephone, "is going to *Israel* this summer." Having a Jewish friend is a real catch for a social climber and all too often such a friend is displayed, talked about, and fussed over like a new-rich's first Mercedes. I recall how a neighbor in Hamburg was telling me about a newly acquired acquaintance, and at least four times in the course of the one-hour conversation he said, "Did I tell you that he is from Israel?"

Rudolf Augstein, publisher of the news weekly *Der Spiegel,* once wrote in an editorial, "Oh, how I wish I were Jewish, so that I could really open up and attack the Jewish publicist William S. Schlamm [noted for his conservative leanings]!" And Augstein is about as anti-Nazi a German as you can find.

Jewish leaders are concerned about this development, which they fear may only be a kind of inverted anti-Semitism. They deplore the special status that is accorded the Jews in today's Federal Republic. "During the Hitler era," complained one Rabbi, "we were *Vogelfrei* [*i.e.,* persecuted]. Today we are under *Denkmalschutz* [*i.e.,* under special protection, like a forest preserve or monument]. This present situation isn't healthy either, though of course far preferable."

"When a Jewish speaker appears at a Gentile school to give a talk," one Jewish leader told me, "he is stared at like a man from Mars."

At the same time the Jewish leaders face the dilemma of finding themselves contributing to this special status, even if their reasons for so doing are eminently understandable. It is, for instance, very easy for the son of Jewish parents to be exempted from military service because it cannot be expected that a Jew in today's Germany serve in the Bundeswehr under officers who were a part of Hitler's war machine.

Moreover, this separate status is conspicuously promoted by Jewish leaders themselves, notably Heinz Galinski. Born in West Prussia and bearing the physical and spiritual scars of three concentration camps, Galinski objects to Jewish "assimilation," opposes sending Jewish children to public schools, and comes out squarely for a "separate but equal" status.

A shrewd politician with little formal education, Galinski inevitably reminds American visitors of the local party "boss," a type he physically resembles. Some Jews in Berlin criticize him for alleged autocratic tendencies, but admit that his strong hand has been a major factor in developing the Berlin community to its present state of vitality and prestige. Galinski insists that it is precisely as Jews, by keeping their identity rather than by assimilation, that they must be accepted in the "new" Germany.

But this is easier said than done. For the Jewish community has also been strongly affected by that bane of the Christian churches—secularism. Only very few Jews regard the Sabbath as so holy that they will let it interfere with a weekend in the country. Of the 100 or so Jewish children in Hamburg only about twenty appear regularly for religious instruction. Many of the synagogues are so poorly visited that they are more of a successful symbol of German restitution than they are of Jewish piety. In only a third of marriages involving Jews are both partners Jewish, and the divorce rate is rising just as it is among Christian confessions. While Christian spouses occasionally convert to Judaism, Jewish youth, restless and sometimes neurotic from the ambivalence of a torn allegiance, prefer either to emigrate (mostly to Israel or the USA) or to assimilate altogether.

Within the Jewish community itself, I am told by some of its most prominent members, there is frequent rivalry and internal tension among the leadership: between the large and dominating Berlin community, on the one hand, and the national Jewish organization in Düsseldorf (near Bonn), *Zentralrat der Juden in Deutschland* (Central Council of the Jews in Germany), on the other hand—the latter representing the common interests of the autonomous Jewish communities, and promoting religious and social activity. Squeezed between the two and often playing a buffer role, is the Jewish weekly, *Allgemeine Wochenzeitung der Juden in Deutschland.* (Note: the wording of the above two titles—the Central Council of the Jews *in* Germany, or the General Weekly of the Jews *in* Germany—rather than "Jewish Germans" or "German Jews" in itself speaks volumes about the relationship of the Jews with the Gentiles in the Federal Republic.)

Hermann Lewy, the mild-mannered editor of the *Wochenzeitung,* reportedly finds it difficult at times to deviate from *Zentralrat* policies. Its secretary general, Dr. Hendrik G. van Dam, is irreverently referred to by fellow Jews as "the last Prussian" on account of his aristocratic bearing and uncanny resemblance to a film type-caster's Prussian officer.

One of the biggest internal Jewish problems in the Federal Republic is the constant tension between the sophisticated West German Jews and the disproportionately large number of Eastern European Jews. The latter are mostly former displaced persons who form the majority in some communities. In Munich the eastern Jews and their offspring comprise 90 percent of all Jews. To the much more educated German Jews, they are sometimes regarded as lower-class foreigners and resented for their alleged clannishness, their sheer numbers, for their poor German, lower standards of dress, lack of social amenities, and culture.

Pro-Arab Radicals

In the late sixties and early seventies the monolithic Pollyanna "a-Jew-can-do-no-wrong" attitude of German society came to an end, and a new phenomenon arose: the anti-Zionist, pro-Arab movement of radical students and intellectuals. In June, 1969, Israeli Ambassador Asher Ben-Natan was insulted with anti-Zionist slogans as he entered the auditorium of Frankfurt's Goethe University and kept from speaking to the Organization of Jewish Students in Germany for two hours by Arab and leftist German students. They held up posters reading, "Fascists Out!" "Nazi Kiesinger and Ben-Natan—A Clique with Dayan." Similar demonstrations and heckling have taken place frequently in recent years.

Opinion is divided over the emergence of these groups. While some critics see a striking similarity between these demonstrators and the Nazis and deplore the leftist unwillingness to discuss the issues, others see the development as a healthy sign. Many observers have long deplored the tendency in West Germany to identify everything Jewish with Israel and welcome the anti-Zionist movement—so long as it remains small—as a dramatic means to differentiate the Jews and attitudes towards them. Even former Ambassador Ben-Natan, while deploring the unwillingness of these leftists to discuss matters rationally, said that he was convinced that they are "not anti-Semites." However, the danger that less sophisticated individuals and groups would be drawn into outright anti-Semitism always remains. During one wave of anti-Zionist demonstrations the Bonn government was tempted to use this as an excuse to drop all pretense of leniency toward leftist student groups.

The well known publicist and writer Hans Habe calls the anti-Zionist development a "tragic phenomenon of Moscow-proselytism." He finds it strange that Rightists in Germany tend to be pro-Israel while Leftists are pro-Arab, and ironic that the Rightists are, according to him, "on the side of humanity."

Meanwhile, the Federal Republic is trying to keep alive its good relations without at the same time jeopardizing its bridge-building to the Arabs. When Foreign Minister Walter Scheel said to Israeli Foreign Minister Abba Eban, that the time is perhaps ripe for "normalization," the latter replied, "The relationship between Germany and Israel cannot be normalized!" And the schizophrenic Jewish-German problem appears to remain for the indefinite future.

Why They Came Back

The situation shortly after World War II did not encourage the slightest hope that a Jewish congregation could ever again be established in Germany. The 180,000 Jewish survivors, mostly DP's, who were still around at war's end, had only one wish: to get out—as soon as possible—of the country in which they narrowly escaped death itself. Very few of the survivors were German Jews, but they, of all people, wanted to stay, much more than the preponderate Eastern European Jews, who desperately wanted to leave.

The exodus of Jews who were still or again in Germany in 1945 was effectively taken care of. Numerous Jewish organizations helped in this respect and the overwhelming mood of Jewish leaders was a decisive rejection of any thought of reconstruction of Jewish congregations in Germany.

Yet, in spite of all this, it proved necessary to establish such Jewish organizations, if only on a provisional basis. Many German Jews and DP Jews were too old to start a new life elsewhere. And, to the surprise and even indignation of Jewish organizations, German Jews actually *wanted* to return to the land of their birth, their culture, and their memories. In the last analysis they were Germans. So to help them, some kind of help had to be extended. And it was with this tiny core that the new community was born.

Talks with a great many Jews in West Germany today, of all ages, gives me the impression that most of them do not fear a resurrection of Nazism. Although hesitant on a second point, a majority appear ready now to give German as their nationality, though with reservations.

Editor Lewy, mentioned earlier, is a Berliner. When he moved to Düsseldorf, which is located in Westphalia, to assume work on the newspaper, his teenage daughter was interviewed on television. Among other questions, the reporter asked, "Do you find it difficult to live here?" She began to reply, "Yes, I do—" and the reporter became visibly nervous, obviously bracing himself to hear still another indictment against the "wicked Germans." Great was his relief when the girl finished her comment, adding truthfully, "it is usually rather difficult for a Berliner to adjust to Westphalia."

In the course of my many visits to Jewish communities in West Germany I made a point of asking over and over again, "Why do you live here?" and the answers, of course, vary. Younger Jews will unabashedly admit that they like the privileged status and see no reason why they shouldn't enjoy it. Some Jewish boys make a point of letting their identity be known so as to have the edge over Gentile boys in attracting the prettiest girls. It is only human that older Jews should want, after so much suffering and privation, to enjoy the financial and other benefits that a guilt-ridden Germany holds out to them. One Jew even admitted to me, "I squeeze every damn penny out of these Germans that I can." (It should be pointed out that many anti-Semitic outbursts refer immediately to the restitution benefits enjoyed by such

Jews, and expressions like *Die Brüder*—a somewhat disparaging reference to the Jews meaning literally "the brothers"—provoke frequent comments among Germans.)

"You ask me why I as a Jew live in Germany," a sixty-year-old attorney told me. "My wife and I tried to live in Israel for five years. We love it and hope to visit it often. But the climate is very hot, life is hard, especially at our age. And, as an attorney trained in German law, it was hard to make a living.

"But to be completely honest—and this may be hard for an outsider to understand—we were homesick. You know, memories of our youth in Berlin are so strong that we find it impossible to live anywhere else."

Others put it more simply: "Where else can you taste Mosel wine at its source?"

If the truth be told—and this is what makes the Nazi persecution of the Jews so incomprehensible—there really is no one so German as a German Jew.[1]

The significance of this became especially clear to me when I had the privilege of escorting the well known American Jewish humorist Harry Golden to various Jewish institutions in a large German city. On this particular occasion, we were accompanied by the chairman of that city's Jewish community, and were walking toward the synagogue. All of a sudden, Harry Golden, hatless and unencumbered by German protocol, bounded across the street, leaving me and the very proper German-Jewish leader speechless.

Golden had spotted two teenage German boys in front of the synagogue and without further ado simply dashed across the street to stop and ask them what they thought about Jews. "Have you ever met a Jew?" he asked. "No," the astonished boys replied, "we haven't." "Well," said Golden unabashed, vigorously shaking both their right hands, "meet one now." Then he went on for several minutes and asked the boys what they learned about Jews. "Well," said one, "we are confused. At home the subject is taboo, and we get the feeling that there is something bad about them. But in school we are taught that they are good people."

The Jewish chairman was aghast. Wearing a black suit, Homburg, sensible oxfords, and a dark tie, and walking with a somewhat rigid, almost military gait, he was downright shocked

259

by this American casualness and openness. Right then and there I realized that from the tip of his Homburg to his precision-moving feet, this Jewish leader was *German*, while the other Jew in our group, Harry Golden, with his lack of inhibitions and chewing on an unlit cigar was every inch *American*. Both were Jews, but they were worlds apart. I knew then that I was closer, though a Gentile, to Harry Golden, than to the Jewish leader or to any German Gentile for that matter.

When Golden rejoined us, the chairman gulped and ventured a mild comment. "You Americans," he said, "you aren't very inhibited, are you?"

Jews in East Germany

Over in East Germany the future of the Jewish community looks bleak. Only 1,500 Jews still live there, about two-thirds of them in East Berlin. And 75 percent of them are over sixty years of age. In all of the German Democratic Republic, including East Berlin, there are only about twenty Jewish children under fifteen and only one rabbi—and even he had to be brought from Hungary (in contrast to more than twelve rabbis and fifty religion teachers in West Germany).

East German Jews, in contrast to those in West Germany, have no compensation for Nazi atrocities, except for small pensions and free medical care "as victims of political or racial persecution." In the GDR there are no Jewish publications, no religious school for rabbis.

Although the West German government has been trying more and more to stay neutral in the Middle East conflict, the overwhelming sympathy, in spite of the anti-Zionist Left, is for Israel. In East Germany the Arab nations are officially supported and Zionism is prohibited by law.

Although there are no Jews in the GDR government, Gerhart Eisler is president of the state-run radio and television network, where he has to take orders from the Politburo, but is well paid. His late brother, Hanns Eisler, composed the melody that has been adopted as the GDR's national anthem. Friedrich-Karl Kaul is East Germany's most prominent attorney.

During Stalinist days two prominent Jews were imprisoned because they demanded that East German Jews should be compensated for the atrocities suffered under Nazi tyranny. If there have been any anti-Semitic actions since then, the Communist press has not reported them.

Dr. van Dam has repeatedly pointed out to American Jews that the GDR and, for that matter, Austria, whose share of Third Reich crimes (it is after all the birthplace of Eichmann and Hitler himself), is far from negligible, have done nothing remotely comparable to the efforts of West Germany toward restitution (Chapter 10).

Future Uncertain

Meanwhile, opinion is divided over the fate of the Jews in West Germany. Many observers believe that Jewry is ultimately doomed because, in the words of Dr. Geis, retired rabbi in Düsseldorf, "no one cares enough to keep it alive." It is characterized by assimilation, gradual decimation through the deaths of the predominantly older members of the Jewish congregations, and apathy. There is much pressure from outside Jews that "those who wish to be Jews ought to emigrate to Israel."

The American rabbi Balfour Brickner, of the Union of American Hebrew Congregations, emphasized, after a visit to West Germany in 1966, that it is extremely important to keep Judaism alive in West Germany "to show that Israel and Judaism are not necessarily the same thing."

He is concerned that the Jewish community in the Federal Republic is officially neo-orthodox, with only one liberal rabbi practicing there today. "Unless this pattern is changed, Judaism will die among the young, who are now growing to maturity, groping for an expression of the Jewish faith in a more modern key."

Rabbi Brickner tells of an experience in Bonn, which more than anything underlines the ambiguous future of Jewry in Germany today. After attending services by the small Jewish congregation in Bonn, he asked the president of the congregation about the future of Jewry there. He replied to Rabbi Brickner that he thought it was dead.

In the very next breath, however, he indicated to Rabbi Brickner that he would like to buy the lot next door to the synagogue. Asked why, he said, "There should always be something here for those who come."

The dominating impression that Rabbi Brickner had from his visit—and his view is representative of many—is that "we must not abandon the Jews in Germany. From a practical point of view, it may not make much difference whether or not there are Jews in Germany. But from a philosophical and spiritual dimension, it would be a cruel and ironic offense to the memory of the six million were we to permit those few Jews who still remain to be lost. There may be an end to German Jewry—most think it will not survive—but so long as it does exist, it deserves our continuing concern."[2]

As for the Germans themselves, the loss of the Jewish community would be a great tragedy. They *need* the Jewish community not only in order to have a visible presence in order to exercise their repentance, but also and especially to preserve their own self-respect. Otherwise, there can be no genuine catharsis, German democracy will be unable to demonstrate its sincerity, and Hitler will posthumously triumph in his goal to eliminate Germany of the Jews.

◄ 16 ►

THE GENERATION GAP—GERMAN STYLE

AS RECENTLY AS 1962, at an elegant reception in Hamburg, I was suddenly confronted by a stunning young blonde woman who appeared to be about twenty years of age. I introduced myself and then almost dropped my cocktail glass as this full-grown, provocatively developed girl shook my hand—and *curtsied.* Only then did I notice that she was drinking orange juice. From her parents, who had now joined us, I learned that she was only sixteen, that is to say, a child, and was only doing what all good German children do when they are introduced to adults.

In 1966 Mrs. Alice Shabecoff, wife of a Bonn correspondent for *The New York Times,* wrote an article in that newspaper describing how German children differ from American children. Her explanation was simple: German children are obedient, in fact, compliant, helpful, disciplined, and quiet. They adapt to their parents and seldom the other way around. Above all, "They speak when they are spoken to." American children are loud, undisciplined, boisterous, and lazy. But they are also more natural, more sincere, and freer than their German counterparts.

Mrs. Shabecoff compared a single sentence from a book on child-rearing by the German psychologist, Dr. Johanna Haarer, "One gives the child spinach," to the same advice by the famous American pediatrician, Dr. Benjamin Spock, "One *offers* the child spinach."

In a survey conducted at that time by two German psychologists, Dr. W. Kemmler and Dr. B. Heckhausen, obedience topped the list of answers to the question put to German mothers: "What do you regard as most important in educating a six-year-old?"

If you visit the Federal Republic today you will find that curtsying *(Einen Diener machen)* and obedience are still "norms"—American women, especially servicemen's wives, are usually shocked to see a conspicuous number of German mothers, though a minority, blithely leading their toddlers around on leashes. In the course of my research for this book I visited many dozens of German families and was surprised that many parents, even the younger generation, still place considerable emphasis on discipline and obedience.

But they are on the defensive. A walk through any West German village or city will soon rid an observer of any preconceived image of blind obedience to parental authority. Especially once they pass the age of sixteen, and even before that, today's German children have had it. They are more apt to be defiant, cocky, hypercritical, completely undisciplined, and belligerently independent. Hands balled in their pockets, long-haired teenage boys slouch through the streets or test their jalopies for screech volume as they tear around street corners.

The days of the proper dark suit and tie, the correct gait, and deference to adults are gone. The German Fritz of today is more apt to wear a bright yellow pop jacket, blue jeans, and polo shirt, while his female counterpart prefers to go psychedelic. Born after the collapse of Nazi Germany, too young to remember the first phase of the Cold War, today's German youth are critical of the Federal Republic and the United States. They ally themselves with American blacks, South American guerrillas, the Vietcong. They engage in sit-ins, teach-ins, demonstrations. They call their professors *Fachidioten* (specialized idiots) and their teachers *autoritäre Dickschädel* (authoritarian knuckleheads). Like their fellow students all over the world, they are against the Establishment. And even more than elsewhere the German students have reason to reject the leadership of the older generation. From the alleged failure of their elders the young see the necessity for establishing their own norms for their role in society and the means to achieve it.

Until the student rebellions of the middle sixties, the West Germans never had it so good. Full employment, rising living standards, and the good life turned the country into a nation of calorie-counters. Slogans like "Security for All" and "*Seid nett zu einander* [Be Nice to One Another]" were the identification tags of a security-oriented society suffocating in material comfort and spiritual complacency.

The first rumblings began, appropriately enough, in West Berlin, in 1966. Exposed to almost hysterical anti-Communist indoctrination for a generation, the Berliners developed an exaggerated Front-mentality and oversensitivity to everything

264

connected with East Germany or the Wall. But the young generation born after World War II, and sickened by all this nauseous self-defeating ideology, wanted no part of the Cold War propaganda and the bogeyman of Communism. They were fed up with the stagnation that characterized the Federal Republic's relationship with the German Democratic Republic.

In January, 1966, Berlin students, indignant over American involvement in Vietnam, lowered the flag at Amerika Haus (the USIA cultural center) to half-mast and pelted the building with eggs. With that, the German-American postwar honeymoon was over.

In the summer of 1967 the Shah of Iran was received as an enlightened leader and honored guest of the West German government. Persian students studying in West Berlin easily persuaded several thousand German students to join them in demonstrating against the Shah, shouting slogans from behind barriers several hundred feet away from the city hall, where the Shah made a public appearance. Suddenly about eighty pro-Shah Persian demonstrators appeared, waving signs of welcome for the Shah and then turned violently on the student demonstrators behind the barriers. After watching indifferently for about ten minutes, the police intervened and arrested two of the students. Later it was learned that some of the pro-Shah Persians were members of the SAVAC, the Iranian secret police, and the others were hired for 80 marks (about $22) a day to follow the Shah and cheer him wherever he went.

That same evening in front of the West Berlin Opera House, the police brutally, without warning, beat and kicked defenseless demonstrators. About twenty students were hospitalized, and one of them, Benno Ohnesorg (whose last name ironically is the German word for "without a care"), was killed. Outraged, the students organized the greatest student mobilization in the history of the Federal Republic. A week-long strike was declared at the Free University, followed by strikes in numerous West German universities. Two decades of West German complacency were shaken to the core.

In Berlin a twenty-four-year-old student, Fritz Teufel, who enjoys the fact that his last name means "devil," became a symbol of rebellious German youth. Acquitted of charges of rock-throwing at policemen during a demonstration, he eagerly pleaded guilty to nonviolent rebellion against German society.

265

"It is far easier," he said at his trial, "to make a horned cow pass through a keyhole than to make one German civil servant doubt a statement by another German civil servant."

Baldur von Schirach, the war criminal who had headed the Hitler Youth, observed upon his release in 1967 that it "would be impossible to mobilize Germany's youth today" in the way he had after World War I, because "the new generation is too smart and skeptical to be seduced by romantic nationalism."

Within a few weeks Mayor Heinrich Albertz lost all control of the police, the courts, and the city assembly. He was ignominiously dismissed from his post by the ruling Social Democratic Party and replaced with the youthful, scholarly, and liberal Klaus Schuetz, himself a product of Berlin's Free University. Scheutz was then serving as State Secretary under Willy Brandt, then foreign minister, who in turn is nationally respected for his courageous term as former mayor of Berlin.

In spite of Schuetz's subsequent impressive leadership and agility in dealing with student uprisings, student riots continued to flare up in Berlin and soon spread all over the Federal Republic. Germans could remember nothing like it since the time their country was torn apart by roaring street brawls on the eve of Hitler's takeover. Inevitably the violent forays of the students reminded the Germans—and foreign observers as well—of the chaotic years before World War II when groups of left-wingers engaged in bloody clashes with Hitler's Storm Troopers. If continued unchecked, observers feared it could similarly arouse a rightist reaction among the general population as in the past. Observers were struck by many of the students' lack of humor, lack of fair play, and almost fanatical obsession in combating "The Establishment." Even the popular, liberal author Günter Grass soon dubbed them "left-wing fascists."

However that may be, the issues that the students have been rebelling against are real. For example, there is the Free University of Berlin. It was established in 1948 by a handful of professors and students of the East Berlin Humboldt University. Fed up with the communist indoctrination that permeated every branch of learning, and where even mathematics classes began with fifteen-minute lectures on Marxism, they literally carried their books in their arms and marched out of the school. In those pre-Wall days, they were able to walk straight through the Brandenburg Gate to the war ruins that still comprised the Kaiser

Wilhelm Institute in West Berlin. Thus, the Free University was born.

The new university received generous U.S. State Department aid, from $3 million between 1948 and 1954, to $18 million thereafter. The Ford Foundation donated another $3.8 million. The *Studentendorf*, the first U.S.-style college dormitory constructed in Germany was also an American contribution.

Anxious to eliminate the medieval structure of German higher education from the start, U.S. Occupation officials wrote the so-called "Berlin model" into the Free University's constitution. In contrast to other German universities, where students elect their own separate government, the *Allgemeine Studentenausschüsse* (ASTA), the Berlin model permits student representatives to sit on almost all university committees, including the academic senate, and to participate in decision-making in nearly all matters, from discipline to curricula.

But in practice this highly democratic tradition-breaking procedure was regularly sabotaged by the faculty. The conservative law faculty, for example, quite easily got around the matter of student participation on the constitution committee by changing its name to the legal committee, and then making admission requirements so difficult that the students were not qualified to sit on it.

Thus the very model of progressive university reform eventually became itself the bastion of conservatism.

The Exalted Professor

Then there is the German university system itself. Nowhere else in the world has the position of professor been so exalted and almost deified. He is applauded (by knocking on desks) before and after every lecture. The rector of a university until recently was addressed in the third person and called "His Magnificence." German professors are state officials with salaries starting at 60,000 DM's ($16,000). According to standard practice, institutes, clinics, hospitals, and the like, are headed by professors. The German professor, who enjoys life tenure, has been king in his own domain, is often given to patriarchal airs, and has unlimited authority over his assistants and graduate students.

In the main there have been three social classes, with the

professor at the top and the mass of students at the bottom. In the middle is the so-called *Akademische Mittelbau* (academic middle structure). These are the *Assistenten,* similar in rank to the American assistant professor. They often have to wait many years in time-consuming servility to the professors, even mowing their lawns, carrying their books, and doing onerous administrative work.

It is this caste system which is under attack. However, the student rebels unfortunately often fail to make distinctions and completely overlook the many dedicated new-breed professors. Many of them work sixty hours a week or more, often on Sundays and Saturdays during the school term. But they feel unappreciated in spite of their efforts at reforms in the students' interest and often to their own disadvantage.

"Egghead" Surplus

Although the universities are subsidized by the individual German states, countless thousands of candidates are annually turned away from the overcrowded institutions. A typical anatomy course turns into a morbid joke as forty to fifty scalpel-wielding medical students helplessly hover over one cadaver. The ratio of students to teacher is nearly three times as high as in the United States and four times as high as in Britain.

In the 1966-67 academic year there were 262,000 students attending universities and other institutions of higher learning in West Germany, a country of sixty million people. This was less than 8 percent of the eligible school population.

In 1970 only 45 out of every 10,000 West Germans attended universities, contrasted with 200 out of 10,000 in the United States and 117 out of 10,000 in the Soviet Union.

This is what is called "the scandal of *numerus clausus,*" or the quota system. Theoretically all German *Gymnasium* graduates have a right to study at a German university and in a department of their choosing.

In practice, however, restrictive admission policies have been more the rule than the exception since the end of World War II. Of course, there have been no restrictions on the basis of race or creed, and the German universities are, if anything, multiracial and totally international. Contrary to quotas in other countries, such as the Ivy League in the States, which sifts candidates scientifically to winnow out the cream of the crop, German universities in the past accepted applicants on a first-come, first-served basis or on the questionable evaluation of secondary school grades.

In 1968 the German Chamber of Commerce and Industry, the country's top business association, warned against an "egghead" surplus and urged a limitation of 10 percent of the school-age population to university enrollment. They argue that the West German economy and social structure are threatened by "one-sided" education policies that do not provide for a sufficient number of workers and technicians. Moreover, they predict a growing intellectual proletariat, university graduates unable to put their training to use, since there are simply not enough jobs for them.

In spite of scholarships, and tax exemptions for poor families with a university student, a working-class father often finds it impossible to send any of his children through college. Only 8 percent of West German university students come from workers' families.

In the Federal Republic most students do not leave high school until they are twenty, and the average age for completion of studies is twenty-seven, an age at which their counterparts in many other countries have a family and an established position. It is with considerable justification that German students complain of "protracted childhood."

Moreover, some 30 percent of university students end up with no degree at all, while those who do get a degree, especially in the humanities, or even in political science, end up with professional uncertainty.

This prolonged study period is partly because of the fact that in most universities students do not have to take any examinations at all for two years, a situation that differs little from that discovered by Mark Twain a century ago when he visited the University of Heidelberg. "One sees so many students abroad at all hours," he writes, "that he presently begins to wonder if they ever have any working hours. Some of them have, some of them haven't. Each can choose for himself whether he will work or play; for German university life is a very free life; it seems to have no restraints. . . . He goes to bed when it suits him, and does not get up at all unless he wants to. He is not entered at the

269

university for any length of time; so he is likely to change about. He passes no examinations upon entering college. He merely pays a trifling fee of five or ten dollars, receives a card entitling him to the privileges of the university, and that is the end of it. He is now ready for business—or play, as he shall prefer. If he elects to work, he finds a large list of lectures to choose from. He selects the subjects which he will study, and enters his name for these studies; but he can skip attendance."[1]

Meanwhile, there is mounting criticism that the "eternal student," with his fourteen semesters of studies, must go, that the structure must be streamlined to make room for the countless thousands who are turned away for lack of space. There is talk of reform, electronics and computerized education, and structure changes. But satisfying solutions are nowhere in sight.

Other Shortages

On the high school and grammar school level the situation is at least as bad. Between 1960 and 1970 the teacher shortage more than doubled. Already in 1961 there was a shortage of nearly 12,000 teachers for the 852,575 junior high school pupils of the Federal Republic. By 1970 the pupil volume had risen to 1,271,300, while the number of teachers increased to less than 25,000. To meet the demand, the required annual increase should be 8,000 teachers, but so far only 3,000 new teachers per annum have been added, with a yearly deficit of 5,000.

At the Immanuel Kant high school in Neumünster, in the 1969-70 school year, 156 hours of instruction had to be dropped because of the shortage. In the 1968-69 school year the state of Schleswig-Holstein had to drop a total of 3,601 hours of instruction in math, Latin, gymnastics, and German.

The biggest shortages are in the natural sciences. Already in 1965, according to a survey conducted by the Volkswagen Foundation, 14,400 instruction hours in chemistry, physics, and mathematics were given by teachers who had no training in these fields. It is estimated that by the year 1980 the shortage of teachers in these subjects alone will rise to 22,000.

Behind the shortages is a widespread disillusionment with the teaching profession, riddled as it is with problems of low pay, overcrowded schools, poor working conditions, and, last but not least, the growing reluctance, especially among the preponderant number of women teachers, to expose themselves to the daily, nerve-shattering struggle for respect and discipline.

The same bleak picture characterizes the technical institutions. Only eight students from the Federal Republic took up the study of metallurgy at the Technical University of Berlin in the winter semester of 1968-69. In the past ten years the number of metallurgy students in the universities of Aachen, Berlin, and Clausthal dropped from 1,508 to 639. And this at a time when the need for metallurgists grows year by year. According to the Federal Ministry of Scientific Research, the number of students in the engineering disciplines dropped 8 percent, from 34,647 to 31,983, while in all other fields the number of students has sharply increased.

The reasons for this decline are attributed to the nineteenth century humanist ideal of education that still places little value on science and technology in our highly industrialized society and in the widespread belief that so much has been accomplished already in these areas that no new horizons are open in these fields at present. According to the business daily, *Handelsblatt,* "If a fifth-former [junior college student] is asked how iron and steel are obtained from iron ore he comes out—if we are lucky—with the description from his chemistry book which perhaps gives the latest technological state of 1890 and the production figures for 1952. In general he does not know and is also not interested. He cannot explain how semi-conductors work, nor a fully-automated textile machine."[2]

From 1961 to 1968 the Federal Republic's private and public expenditure on research and development rose from 1.11 to 1.94 of the gross national product. But as early as 1967 the Soviet Union was allocating 3.1 percent, the United States, 3 percent, France and Britain, 2.3 percent each of their respective GNP, for research and development.

Clearly, the education syndrome in the Federal Republic presents many challenges in the years ahead.

Political Issues

But the education malaise in the Federal Republic is only one out of many factors responsible for the restlessness of German youth. Political issues also played an important and, at times, decisive role.

With the formation of the Grand Coalition government in

271

1967, the two leading parties, the CDU/CSU and the SPD closed ranks and the Socialists came to power for the first time in the young republic's history. But this left only the tiny, ineffectual Free Democratic Party (FDP) in opposition and created the kind of political vacuum that was very favorable to radical groups, students or otherwise.

With the student demonstrations against the Shah in 1967, a movement was ushered into existence that soon became known as the *Ausserparlamentarische Opposition* (Extra-parliamentary Opposition), APO. Not only students, but also progressives, intellectuals with socialist leanings felt betrayed by the SPD. Even before the coalition there was a growing disgust with the increasingly respectable character of the socialist party which became harder and harder to distinguish from the conservative CDU. In the eyes of the young and leftist radicals, the SPD through the coalition sold its soul for a few ministerial posts and the chance at least to be a part of the ruling government. The coalition, while effective in routine affairs, failed to carry out the radical rethinking of policy that was to have been its main justification.

In Chapter 14, the main political issues absorbing the interest of the APO are described in greater detail. There also have been never-ending demonstrations by the APO against the Springer publishing empire, for recognition of the GDR and acceptance of the Oder-Neisse border, for greater co-determination in industry, education, and government. The students conducted sit-ins against the increase in streetcar fares in various cities. In May, 1968, leftist student strikes against the emergency laws (Chapter 14) forced most West German universities to shut down and caused the resignation of the rector of West Berlin's Technical University.

A number of militant student organizations sprang up overnight, notably the most leftist of them all, the Socialist Student Federation (SDS). Its ideological leader, "Red" Rudi Dutschke, will probably never fully recover from an assassination attempt by a young house painter by the name of Josef Bachmann, an avowed admirer of Adolf Hitler; Bachmann has since committed suicide. At its heyday the SDS numbered some 2,500 students. The Socialist University Union, SHB, with about 1,500 members and the rightist Association of Christian Democratic students numbered about 1,000 members in 1969. Of the more than

272

300,000 West German university students, there has never been at this writing more than 3 percent belonging to a political university group.[3]

The radicals found that the majority of the students, who had joined them in countless nonviolent protests, backed out when physical violence to others and themselves became the rule. In fact, in Munich, when two riots caused deaths, some students made banners reading, "Stones Are No Arguments." In one demonstration inside the main train terminal, protesting students dutifully lined up to buy platform tickets first, thus literally fulfilling a Lenin prophecy: "You can never make a revolution with the Germans. If they were ordered to storm a train station they would first stand in line to buy tickets."

"The greater danger," one Munich professor has put it, "is not the headline-making radicals, but the rank-and-file, disinterested, apolitical students, who still comprise the majority. Let us not be fooled. An awful lot of this demonstrating is sheer youthful letting-off-steam." But this explanation is too simple. Although the vast majority of West German student rebels are probably motivated by many reasons other than political issues, there is no question that precisely the tiny minority of politically-dedicated students has contagiously affected the entire student body so profoundly that it will never be the same.

Of course, for the vast majority of them at first the Axel Springer issue, or emergency laws and the like were only symbols or even scapegoat reasons for expressing a deeply rooted, often indefinable sense of frustration, not only with the German Establishment, but with modern life itself. Many students were motivated by sheer boredom, by the contagious influence of Berkeley and other American student uprisings, and by mob psychology. Student protests, after all, have become fashionable. For a great many participants they indicate as much conformity as "law and order" does for bourgeois citizens. It would take greater courage and non-conformity for a student or group of students, say, within the SDS, to oppose the rebels, than it does for students to go along with what all the students are doing.

"Even though there are different immediate goals in East and West," writes the famous Yugoslav rebel author, Milovan Djilas (*International Herald Tribune*, October 20, 1969), "the protest of young intellectuals the world over stems from a common denominator: new and broader knowledge and advances in education which must eventually involve them in the modern economy and technology. Ironically, they have failed to apply their new knowledge in the way that society requires. The technological revolution has been so sudden, the growth in the number of educated people so vast that neither the intellectuals nor the society to which they contribute have been able to become accustomed to the change or to understand each other."

To a certain extent the long overdue and hurried introduction of political education in West Germany had a boomerang effect. On the one hand, its sketchiness and superficiality only provided cannon fodder for borderline and emotionally unstable students. How could politically uneducated teachers be expected to instill an adequate political consciousness?

On the other hand, the increasing popularity of sociology and political science over recent years has produced an intellectual proletariat at the universities, with extremely limited opportunities for employment. At the same time, by the very nature of their studies, these students acquired the mental equipment to create a social neurosis out of their own neuroses caused by their (especially in Berlin) artificial environment and the inevitable effects of the universal-guilt neurosis that was subconsiously transferred to the young. Small wonder that they became the intellectual storm troopers of student revolts.

It should not be overlooked that the older generation in Germany has left the younger generation no illusions whatsoever. If there is a single word to express the dominant impression that the older generation has left upon the young, it is disgust. At the same time, this younger generation knows nothing of the deprivation and misery of their parents. They accept material comforts unquestionably. One would have to be blind to overlook the ambivalence of the young people's extremely emotional reactions. They despise affluence and yet automatically claim the right to enjoy its benefits.

Twenty out of every hundred West German school children are overnourished. In Bavaria there are special sanitariums for overweight ten- to fourteen-year-olds. And more than 200,000 school children under fourteen are without adult supervision during most of the day. Seventy percent of all babies brought to German hospitals suffer from dietary ills, mostly from over-nourishment. The number of school-age children with neuro-vegetative disorders is increasing year by year.

"Never," says the director of the Hamburg association, *Kinderschutz* (For the Protection of Children), "have there been so many parents so intensely concerned about the rearing and education of their children. But at the same time never have there been so many who have let their children grow up wild. The plain simple fact is, parents are overburdened. Modern life just makes too many demands."

Recently the state supreme court of Frankfurt upheld the claim of a twenty-year-old student for a monthly allowance of 1,050 DM's ($290) from his wealthy parents. The court defended the "right" of the student to live in a manner commensurate with his family's status, "nor can the ownership of an automobile by a student with rich parents be regarded as a luxury."

Senior Citizens Unwanted

According to the sociologist Dr. Helmut Schelsky, the chief casualties of modern German family life are the aged. Day by day the eight million West Germans over sixty-five are relegated to greater isolation, greater uselessness, and greater superfluity. Although 21 out of 100,000 West Germans annually commit suicide, among those over sixty the number increases to 55, and among the over-seventy-year-olds, to 70. Twice as many women between fifty and fifty-five commit suicide as do women between thirty and thirty-five. Sometimes it takes weeks before the death of a senior citizen is discovered by a neighbor or an acquaintance.

There is still a strong family sense in German life, and in my personal experience I have been touched by the care with which many young couples look after their parents. But in a society where sexual prowess and professional achievement are steadily replacing the old values, there is little room for persons once they have reached a certain age. Moreover, the tremendous housing shortage forces even children of good will to try to tuck the old folks away, if possible, in a home for the aged. But most of these homes are already overcrowded and have a waiting period of five years. Once admitted, the strain of adjustment is so great that the senior citizen prematurely succumbs. One-fourth of all persons admitted to homes for the aged die within six months, while the number of aged requiring psychiatric treatment has greatly increased.

The process of becoming an outcast begins relatively early. Once past forty, the average German employee has to struggle for acceptance, by his own children, by society, and, often enough, by his co-workers and his employer. In the rapid technological convulsions that have become a standard part of daily life, firms rise and fall overnight. In such a situation the fate of the middle-aged worker or executive is highly precarious. Once dismissed from his post he is lost. In spite of the fact that at this writing there are three vacant posts for every unemployed, the middle-aged have only a slim chance of employment at one of the 723,000 positions open, no matter how qualified. A highly trained technician earning $1,000 a month may find himself grateful at forty-five to obtain a new position for $175 monthly.

According to the DAG trade union expert Siegfried Eike, "Of all the groups of society, it is the older generation that bears the brunt of the inhumanity of our society." A high school paper in Bad Lauterberg even went so far as to suggest that persons over sixty be slowly narcoticized out of their misery, a solution that under the Hitler regime went by the name of euthanasia.

In this context, it is ironic that the youths and older intellectuals of the APO have joined the youth rebels of the western world in placing their highly emotional allegiance with the late "Ho, ho, Ho Chi Minh," and Mao Tse-tung, a man already in his eighties—a most senior citizen. Along with very mature heroes like Marx and Lenin, Ché Guevara alone just barely can be mentioned as a true representative of their generation.

Most ironic of all is the fact that the unofficial but extremely popular intellectual spokesman for German student rebels in the late sixties and beginning of the seventies was the over-seventy-year-old Professor Herbert Marcuse of the University of California's San Diego campus. His books, *Eros and Civilization*, a Freudian interpretation of social change, *One Dimensional Man,* and *Negations* have been runaway best sellers among students seeking an intellectual basis for their hippie culture.

What made the Berlin-born Marcuse a guru of the student-rebels was his chilling and penetrating critique of modern industrial civilization, which he sees as an impersonal, all-pervasive, and crushing force overriding the individual. Instead of freeing and aiding man, modern technology, so argues Marcuse, has only worsened the collusion of military, corporate, and political interests.

A charming, mild-mannered man with a lifetime membership in the San Diego Zoo, Marcuse resembles anything but a revolutionary. His abstruse, Teutonic style defies readability, and his attack on industrial civilization is so unrestrained, lofty, and ambiguous that it breaks down on application.

A similar fate awaited the APO, or at least its most important organized groups. In the end, the SDS, in March, 1970, hopelessly split by Maoist, anarchist, Stalinist, and rightist-leaning factions within its ranks, dissolved for good. It had made little visible permanent impact on society as a whole, nor did it influence the 1969 national elections, either by winning votes for leftist parties (see Chapter 14) or by provoking a backlash victory for the extremist-rightist NPD.

Hans O. Staub, the well known Swiss editor and TV commentator, suggested that the APO "dissolved in its own aimlessness. This extra-parliamentary opposition, which thought that it had monopolized the theory and practice of the permanent revolt, forgot and continues to forget to study its own theoreticians and mentors thoroughly. If they had done so, they would have been able to read that in the long run there is no such thing as an 'uprising for the sake of uprising.' Every revolt and every revolution must, if it wants to survive, have clear goals."[4]

Impressive Changes

Taken as a whole, however, the West German youth rebellion must be put down as an impressive change in the daily scene. And its influence, albeit indirectly, on German structures has been considerable.

In response to student demands one university after another has initiated far-reaching changes. Heidelberg University, just to give one example, adopted a more liberal constitution providing for a greater voice by students in the choice of officials, curricula, and exam requirements. The Great Senate no longer is the sanctum of the "Herr Professor Doktor" and there are representatives of all groups, with the professors having only 38 percent of the vote. A student has been chosen for the first time in the institution's history as senate chairman and in February, 1970, a forty-four-year-old theology professor was elected as rector, "against the preferences of the professors." The university has only 190 full professors for 11,500 students. The rest of the 1,000-member faculty is composed of associates, assistants, and instructors.

The voting age in German states has been lowered from twenty-one to eighteen years, and the age at which candidates can run for public office has also been reduced—from twenty-five to twenty-one years. This is significant considering that in 1965 more than half of the country's population had been born after the Nazi era. Each quadrennial Federal election will bring approximately three million new voters to the polls. By 1973 there will be thirteen million people—nearly a third of the electorate—who will barely remember the German defeat of 1945. It doesn't take much imagination to foresee profound changes in German structures, thinking, and way of life in the near future, once these voters exercise their franchise.

If nothing else, the youth rebellion revealed that a large segment of the German population is not prepared to accept blind obedience as a norm of life; it provoked thought; it awakened political consciousness among a great many youths and older persons; it produced leaders and intellectuals as well as chaos and disruption; it stimulated reform measures that might have been delayed for many years; it provided new thinking on authority and freedom. And that is something.

A new generation has come of age in Germany since World War II—a generation whose style of life had changed strikingly from that of its elders. They reject the old ideas of authority in the home and on the drill field. They share a dream of union and a passion for freedom with their European kin across the Rhine and in the world beyond. They play an ever larger role in the country's political and intellectual life.

Many of the APO's have become IPO's, *Innerparteiliche Opposition* (Internal Opposition, *i.e.,* as party members). There is still a general shift toward the left, and many youth, along with the older intellectuals, talk a great deal about class struggle, reject Bonn's representative democracy, and constantly seek to provoke the constitutional institutions. Large segments of West German youth and older leftists have created their own neo-revolutionary parlance. A neo-Marxist ideology has emerged, a conglomerate of anarchist, socialist, and Marcusean ideas.

278

Thus far, the New Left has been unsuccessful in winning over the workers. It is significant that the Prague students in the famous uprising leading to the Soviet invasion of 1968, disapproved of Rudi Dutschke and that the French-German student leader Daniel Cohn-Bendit in his book, *Obsolet Communism*, ignored the events in Czechoslovakia.

At the same time, the riots and demonstrations of the APO and its successors have created a largely inaccurate picture of the thinking and aims of the vast majority of young Germans. This is no doubt because of the extensive coverage by the mass media of the articulate minority. In a survey conducted under the auspices of the Volkswagen Foundation, of 1,800 young people in 450 towns and villages chosen as a scientifically representative sample, there was little trace of the extreme left.

In Hanover a similar survey, conducted by another research center of 1,800 young people between fifteen and nineteen years of age, showed a decided rightist trend. Thirty-eight percent said they were mistrustful of the way modern publicity treated the Nazis and were of the opinion that National Socialism wasn't really so bad. However, over 50 percent favored the existence of the Communist Party in the Federal Republic, and nearly half favored U.S. withdrawal from Vietnam.

Officially at least there is greater tolerance for the young. Willy Brandt, often criticized for the leftist activities and hippie life-styles of his two young sons, simply says, "They have to struggle with their problems in their own way, the same as I have to struggle with mine."

The Federal President, seventy-year-old Gustav Heinemann, has won a wide following among the youth, partly on the strength of his impressive reform measures as minister of justice before assuming the presidency and partly for his brutal frankness in regular give-and-take sessions with young people. "If you make revolutions," he has said, "see to it that you have adequate garbage disposal. Otherwise the whole mess will come down on your heads."

Meanwhile the youth are reassessing values, evolving their own attitudes and forms of self-expression.

Countless dozens of new literary and artistic forms are emerging in the Federal Republic. Young, vigorous, critical, they are making their presence felt all over the world.

The genesis of this movement is Group '47, a literary

symposium founded, as its name suggests, in 1947, by survivors of the humanist tradition that survived Hitlerism. Today most of its members are hoary middle-aged men. Heinrich Böll is pushing sixty, and even the man who was described on a cover of *Time* (April 13, 1970) as "A Man Who Can Speak to the Young," Günter Grass, is hitting the mid-forties.

The author of *The Tin Drum* and *Local Anaesthetic*, with his drooping mustache and gypsy style of life, is a refreshing departure from the Olympian Thomas Mann-ish type of German writer. He consistently pokes fun at the Establishment, shares with the young his disdain of materialism and U.S. support of Greece and involvement in Indochina. But he also lashes out against the excesses of the young and the repressive power of the Soviet Union. Eschewing the aloofness of many older German authors from politics, Grass has become a symbol for West Germans' emerging grass roots politics (Chapter 14).

Other Group '47 writers have become pacemakers in other ways. Author Uwe Johnson won the six-nation International Publishers' Prize. Peter Weiss is noted for outstanding documentary plays on political and social problems, notably *Die Ermittlung,* dealing with the Frankfurt trial of the Auschwitz war criminals. Günther Eich is regarded as the father of the New Poetry in Germany; he likes to say of himself, "I was never avant-garde. I always moved sideways."

Rebellious, uncompromising, creative, their attitude is reflected in a ballad of protest by poet-critic Hanz M. Enzensberger, called "Foam."[5] These are its opening lines:

> at the hour of birth i was blinded with foam in my eyes
> crying with grief on a black friday thirty years in the past.

◄17►

"CITIZENS IN UNIFORM"

FOR TWO AND a half centuries German armies were associated with blind obedience, ruthless precision, and iron discipline. Among Germany's neighbors they evoked constant fear and terror. This spirit of militarism which the Prussians imposed on Germany since its unification by Bismarck in 1871 permeated all of German society, demanding loyalty and respect from every German citizen. The German army, which reached the epitome of efficiency, quite literally was a state within a state. Its officers swore an oath of loyalty to the Kaiser. Even civil offenses of soldiers were tried by military courts. As recently as 1918 an officer could be penalized if he neglected to punish civilians known to show disrespect to anything military. The Prussian atmosphere was so stifling that the personal emissary of President Woodrow Wilson reported to him just prior to World War I that in Germany "militarism has run stark mad."

Even in the short-lived democratic Weimar Republic, the 100,000 man *Reichswehr,* which later was absorbed by Hitler's armies, exacted the rigors and perfectionism of the Prussian tradition. It took the crushing defeat of the Germans in World War II to affect radical changes in their thinking about the military.

The Germans' attitude after 1945 was a radical change from 1919, when they had refused to accept the defeat of their armies and easily fell prey to the hypnotic spell of Hitler's "stab-in-the-back" syndrome. This time destruction and demoralization were so complete that the national mood was one of genuine revulsion against militarism in any form. The starvation diet of millions, the wholesale destruction of cities, the disappearance of hundreds of thousands of German POW's into the midnight of Siberia had left their mark. *"Ohne mich* [count me out]" and *"Nie wieder Soldat* [never again a soldier]"* were the outcries across the land. Veterans' meetings were continually disrupted by youths. Even Herr Theodor Blank, the commissioner appointed by Chancellor Konrad Adenauer in 1952 to prepare the groundwork for the new German armed forces, was hit in the face by a beer mug thrown by an antimilitarist youth at an Augsburg political meeting.

The opposition to the *Kommissgeist* (barracks-room spirit) was universal. Two antimilitary novels, *Fragebogen* (Questionnaire) and *0815* (the Nazi equivalent of GI), a humorous satire of heel-clicking authoritarianism, were runaway best sellers immediately after the war and a movie *Hauptmann von Köpenick*, blasting Prussian militarism, was a box-office success in the late fifties. EMNID, a West German opinion poll organization, found among 2,000 respondents questioned in 1952, only 21 percent in favor of rearmament, 63 percent opposed, and 16 percent with no opinion. Dr. Gustav Heinemann, who became Federal President in 1969, resigned from Adenauer's cabinet in 1950 in protest against the rearmament policy.

External developments finally persuaded the Federal Republic, despite overwhelming and articulate opposition by the majority of the population, in favor of remilitarization.

The decisive factor was East German rearmament under Soviet direction. By 1948, the German Democratic Republic began organizing the paramilitary *Bereitschaften* (preparedness forces), which numbered 50,000 by 1950 and included artillery and light tanks. In the space of one year it had grown to five fully mechanized divisions along Red Army lines. And in 1956 it was unabashedly named the People's Army. Conscription followed in 1962. The East German forces subsequently expanded to six fully trained divisions with more than 200,000 men. In addition, nearly a million civilians had organized in paramilitary organizations and were trained in the use of rifles and machine guns, including 320,000 so-called factory guards and 460,000 *Freie Deutsche Jugend* (Free German Youth).

Besides the frightening total of 750 million men at the Communists' disposal, compelling economic reasons figured in the reasons for West German rearmament. Mr. Anthony Eden, then British Foreign Secretary, urgently pleaded to the House of Commons on July 7, 1952, "If the Germans take no part in rearmament, it could mean that they alone of the free nations would be able to continue to devote their full industrial capacity to civil needs and export trade."[1] Putting it more bluntly, Sir Ivone Kirkpatrick, British High Comissioner, said, "If we do not support a German arms contribution, we shall be encouraging competition in the field of foreign trade which may eventually ruin us. . . . I fear German tractors more than German tanks."[2]

Thus, initial development of the new German armed forces came about primarily as the result of the political and military decisions by the western powers.

Prodded by the western powers and the eastern threat on the one hand and opposed by the majority of Germans on the other, West Germany, under the direction of the military commissioner, Theodor Blank, and his successor, the first West German minister of defense, Franz-Josef Strauss, began erecting the machinery for a substantial military force.

The problems were immense. The West German economy had been completely demilitarized and it would require monumental efforts to find the funds to support the new armed forces. Herr Blank not only had to build an army from scratch, but he had to create one which would eliminate every trace of all the ugly characteristics of previous German forces. Even the former names, *Wehrmacht* and *Reichswehr,* had to be discarded.

Built-in Safeguards

With typical German thoroughness, the new German military was redesigned in infinite detail, with built-in safeguards that should assure that the whole apparatus remain true to democratic principles. Basically three structures have been created within the *Bundeswehr* to assure this:

1) The position of Armed Forces Commissioner (*Wehrbeauftragter*), having authority to inspect the *Bundeswehr*, has been created, modeled after a similar Swedish institution which has enjoyed much success. This commissioner is elected by parliament and is responsible to its president. Although he is not a part of the executive branch of the government, it is his duty to supervise the protection of the basic human rights of individual soldiers within the armed forces and to make frequent on-the-spot inspections to see that these rights are respected.

2) As a further safeguard against possible militarism, all military administration is under the control of a civilian

apparatus almost one-third the size of the *Bundeswehr* itself. This office is not answerable to any general even though its daily decisions go all the way to the barracks level and affect the lives of every soldier.

3) To assure the proper implementation of these aims, a concept has been invented, one defying translation, which is called *Inneres Gefüge* (inner structure) or, more recently, *Innere Führung* (inner leadership, *i.e.*, leadership arising from the individual soldier's own inner convictions—as opposed to blind external obedience).

This collective term implies that the individual soldier is primarily a free citizen and that his dignity as such must be protected during his military service. The main task of *Innere Führung* is educational, teaching soldiers on the one hand to be technicians rather than combatants, and on the other, emphasizing personal responsibility and creating an awareness of traditional democratic values.

A whole staff has been appointed to work out the proper methods of applying this *Innere Führung*. The chief mastermind of this concept is General Count von Baudissin, a high-minded youthful idealist, who developed the details of this approach and coined the expression, "Citizen in Uniform," a concept which has become the symbol of the new spirit within the *Bundeswehr*.

The practical consequences of *Innere Führung* have led to the abolishment of parade-ground drill; soldiers are encouraged to take an active part in politics; military superiors may give subordinates orders only in matters pertaining to the military service. The regimental banners used when the Germans invaded Holland and Poland are gone, and regiments carry numbers instead of names. Gone too are the old Prussian and Nazi soldier songs.

By far the biggest headache for the *Innere Führung* personnel was the selection of officers. Most of the best military leaders were ruled out because of pro-Hitler leanings, illness, or age. A special committee was appointed to screen every officer from colonel on up before appointment.

Saluting is required only for a soldier's immediate superior officers and top brass ("Why don't they salute?" complained an American officer visiting the *Bundeswehr*.) The use of the obsequious third person singular when addressing a superior has been dropped. The notorious NCO bully—the *Schleifer*—has been abolished—no longer can noncommissioned officers command soldiers in their free time to beat carpets for their wives. The new German soldier may wear civilian clothes outside the barracks and is entitled to weekend leaves. Severe penalties are meted out to officers who abuse their position. Each unit may elect a *Vertrauensmann* (soldiers' confidant) who has a right to bring any serious matter to the attention of the authorities.

Already in 1950 the Western powers decided on the inclusion of the Federal Republic in their active defense organization, spurred on greatly by the war in Korea, whose division between communist and anti-communist territories was similar to the situation of the two Germanies. However, it took five years before the Federal Republic received the green light to join NATO. In less than seven years, with the appointment of Kai-Uwe von Hassel as new Commander-in-Chief of the German forces in January, 1963, the *Bundeswehr* had an over-all strength of 415,000 men. Its third armored division was assigned to NATO in 1965, thus reaching the goal of twelve army divisions set by NATO. These include seven mechanized-motorized divisions, three armored divisions, a mountain division, an airborne division. In addition, the German air force has transferred sixteen squadrons and six rocket antiaircraft battalions and the navy has placed fifteen squadrons with destroyers, speedboats, minesweepers, assault boats and naval planes totaling some 182 warships, 30 auxiliary vessels, and 35 naval planes under the High Command of NATO. It should be emphasized that the Federal Republic is the only NATO member to place all her combat-ready units under the NATO High Command and not retain an independent "national" military force under exclusive German jurisdiction. There is nothing comparable in Germany to a general staff organization or the American Chiefs-of-Staff. The Commander-in-Chief of the *Bundeswehr* in peace time is the civilian defense minister. The Prussian tradition of a general at the head of the armed forces has been abolished. The Basic Law in numerous articles provides for political control of the armed forces to prevent the possibility of a military "state within a state."

Only three categories of units remain under "national" German control: 1) various staff organizations and educational institutions of the *Bundeswehr;* 2) units still in training; and 3) the so-called territorial defense, *Bundesgrenzschutz,* with some 20,000 men assigned to defense, security, and guard duties, mostly along the East German border.

The Federal Government has scrupulously respected the four-power status of Berlin. None of the laws pertaining to the military apply to West Berlin. There are no German soldiers in West Berlin, nor is any advertising for the *Bundeswehr* allowed there. In contrast, the controlling authorities in the Soviet Zone have allowed the National People's Army to march into East Berlin, in contempt of the four-power status of the city.

Riddled with Crises

Today the total German armed forces (army, navy, and air force) comprise 455,000 men. It is interesting that the largest single contribution of conventional forces in the NATO defense alliance is supplied by the *Bundeswehr.* Together with some 400,000 United States troops in Europe, of whom some 200,000 are stationed in Germany, it is the mainstay of NATO.

In the event of a showdown, how much could NATO rely on the German forces? Not much, judging by developments so far. Since its inception, in fact, the *Bundeswehr* has been riddled with crises. Its accumulation of shortcomings is so great that *Der Spiegel* published a title story in December, 1968, entitled *"Armee Ohne Rückgrat"* ("Army Without a Backbone").

It was the *"Spiegel* affair" which toppled the CSU head, Franz-Josef Strauss, from his cabinet post as minister of defense in 1962. Strauss had become more and more angry over anti-Strauss articles in *Der Spiegel* and finally toward the end of 1962 ordered a raid on the editorial offices of the magazine in Hamburg. Charging the editors with treason for alleged revelations of secret military information, he had them arrested and investigated. Strauss was ultimately acquitted in 1968, and even before then made a comeback as finance minister in the coalition cabinet of Chancellor Kurt Georg Kiesinger. But many German critics still regard his action as undisciplined and autocratic and look with uneasiness on his aggressive mannerisms and the nationalist overtones of his speeches, even though he was never a Nazi and enjoys a wide following among democratic leaders both at home and abroad.

Then there is the Starfighter crisis. Lockheed's needle-nosed F-104, which the U.S. Air Force rates as its finest interceptor, has received the nickname "The Flying Coffin" in the *Luftwaffe* (air force). More than 127 Starfighters have crashed, 26 alone in 1965, and have taken nearly as many lives. The trouble apparently started when former Defense Minister Strauss, back in 1958, chose the Starfighter, the free world's most noted plane, presumably in the hope of bolstering the *Bundeswehr*'s position in NATO. However, in order to add bomber capabilities to the Starfighter, the Germans installed considerable additional electronic equipment. It has proved to be too complicated for West Germany's fledgling 100,000-man air force. The *Luftwaffe* pilots have been either inexperienced youngsters or fading World War II veterans with little or no jet experience. Even more difficult has been the maintenance situation. Over a third of the maintenance personnel are draftees who finish their eighteen months' tour of duty before they have really learned their jobs. Pilots have not had sufficient practice to master the plane, while an average of two-thirds of the Starfighters are grounded at a time. The average *Luftwaffe* flying hours for F-104 planes has been less than thirteen hours a month, as against NATO's recommended twenty.

The low-level flying required to stay under the Soviet radar net is extremely dangerous for the swift jets. And Germany's poor weather conditions aggravate the problem.

"Every time the telephone rings," Inspektor Lieutenant General Johannes Steinhoff told a reporter, "I fear it's another crash." Three high-ranking *Bundeswehr* generals resigned in August, 1966, because they could no longer cope with its incompetence. The number of volunteers for *Luftwaffe* pilot training nosedived from 471 in 1957 to only 134 in 1968.

Meanwhile pilot training has been transferred to Luke Air Force Base in Arizona, where the skies are clear and the German cadets can learn from seasoned U.S. instructors. Pilots' pay has almost doubled to $137.50 a month.

In 1967 the scandalous case known as the "HS-30 affair" broke out into the open. It involved the *Bundeswehr*'s 1957 order for 10,000 HS-30 tanks, even though no one in authority had seen anything but a small-scale wooden model.

In the end, Germany took delivery of only 2,176 of the tanks, paying millions in penalties for reducing the order, and so spent $65 million for tanks that proved unfit for combat. The tank was designed by the Swiss-owned Hispano-Suiza firm and was to be manufactured by its British subsidiary, British Marc, or by

German firms under license. The comptroller's report charges only incompetence. But several mass media, including the TV program *Panorama* and *Der Spiegel,* have alleged that the deal with Hispano-Suiza was signed so quickly because kickbacks were paid to individuals and parties. *Panorama* particularly pointed its accusing finger at the late Otto Lenz, State Secretary in the office of Chancellor Adenauer at the time the HS-30 contract was signed. Lenz allegedly was paid a large sum of money, which he shared with the Christian Democratic Union.

As NATO's largest land force and as such the backbone of Western Europe's land defenses, the *Bundeswehr* at the beginning of the seventies was notoriously under-equipped, inept, lacking in officers, training, morale, discipline, money, and, of all things, order. "From Prussian militarism to an army without a backbone, this is too much," one high-ranking officer told me.

In 1968 a man by the name of Hans-Georg von Studnitz, a journalist and military expert known for his nationalist leanings, wrote a book, *Rettet die Bundeswehr (Save the Bundeswehr),* which became a barracks best seller and created a national stir, even causing the defense ministry to issue a twenty-two-page rebuttal. Much of the book had a neo-nationalist tinge, but even the most democratic-minded German GI's and civilians realized that there was more truth than fiction in his savage attack on the "marzipan soldiers" and "liverwurst officers."

Studnitz's main point is that the armed services are "sick," riddled with an "anti-tradition complex," soft, an easy prey for ambitious politicians, lacking in discipline, and most likely would be unprepared in any real emergency.

His point is reluctantly admitted by some of the more outspoken *Bundeswehr* officers. During maneuvers, German soldiers are notorious for time-consuming blunders that would be disastrous in a real conflict: tank commanders leading their columns on hill tops as conspicuous targets for the "enemy"; armored units helplessly stranded by the smallest streams; tanks whose camouflage is useless because their tracks are still clearly visible to "enemy" reconnaissance planes.

Morale among enlisted men as well as officers is at an all-time low. Draftees begin their eighteen months of service with the greatest reluctance. Officers and noncommissioned officers, as well as experienced career soldiers, have been leaving at a steady pace. The number of volunteer soldiers dropped from 100,000 in

1966 to only 64,000 in 1968, while draftees comprise over 50 percent of the standing army instead of the hoped-for limit of 38 percent. In January, 1969, Military Affairs Specialist Matthias Hoogen told the *Bundestag* that so many young men were evading the draft that West Germany had the highest rate of conscientious objectors in the world, with one out of every 20 draftees as compared with one out of 750 in the United States and one out of 50 in Denmark. One reason is that West German CO status (*Kriegsdienstverweiger*), in the light of its past, is fairly easy to get, one does not have to prove religious or ideological pacifism. Some seventy chapters of the German War Resisters' League encourage draft dodging, while leftist student militants vigorously support their stand. The churches and the trade unions also support conscientious objection. In order to cope with this problem the Labor Ministry has made jobs available for CO's in hospitals, technical services, and charities, where they serve their equivalent 18-month term and receive the same pay as a private.

An obstructionist movement within the *Bundeswehr* created widespread havoc during 1969 when sabotage and disruption tactics were employed as a demonstration against the draft and the military establishment. Parts were removed from vehicles, bolts loosened, causing the malfunctioning and breakdown of equipment.

Officers and noncoms complain about the low pay and lack of prestige. The officers are frustrated. In former times, being a soldier meant something and being an officer was a passport to top society. The baggy, drab *Bundeswehr* uniforms, purposely designed to play down military chic, are not very helpful to troop morale. "Did you ever try to dance in one of these uniforms?" a *Bundeswehr* soldier asked me.

At social events in Bonn, high-ranking generals are by protocol on a par with state legislators. Officers have been known to carry their uniforms in a suitcase to their barracks and then change out of mufti.

They are underpaid. A full colonel has to get along on less than $600 a month, which is about the same salary as that of a head-waiter or master chimney sweep. In civilian life he could probably earn nearly $1,000 a month in a position of similar responsibility. A hotel doorman or secretary earns more than the $175-a-month pay of a master sergeant. It is not uncommon for officers' wives to work as salesclerks in department stores to bolster the family budget. A retired general was recently criticized by a Bonn newspaper for "degrading" his status by selling investment securities.

They are also understaffed. The 455,000-man armed forces lack 4,500 commissioned and 31,000 noncommissioned officers. At present, noncoms and officers must work many hours overtime and have so many men under their care that they have precious little time for personal attention to enlisted men. There is too much theoretical training and not enough field practice.

The biggest frustration of all is the bureaucratic military administrative apparatus. The civilian clerks constantly interfere with commanders' decisions. As a result, the officers and noncoms ("the backbone of the Kaiser's armies") have become more and more unwilling to assume responsibility.

"Nobody wants to go back to Prussianism," one exasperated noncom told me, "but sometimes I wish for just a touch of that old *Wehrmacht* discipline. It wasn't all bad."

Part of the reason for this state of affairs is the almost fanatical penny-pinching policy of the Bonn government toward the military. The *Bundeswehr* and rearmament have been so unpopular—and the staggering financial burdens of a welfare state bogged down by wartime restitution and one of the world's highest income taxes—that the Bonn government has been reluctant to invest too much money in it. This was carried to such an extreme that commanders even discouraged the use of electric razors to save current, that paratroopers lacked training because aircraft were grounded to save gasoline, and the infantry was inadequately trained because the German GI's don't get enough exercise with their automatic rifles because ammunition cost too much.

The *Bundeswehr* is so patterned after the civilian's nine-to-five routine that recently the trade unions have made considerable inroads. Nearly 20,000 officers and noncoms and even four generals have joined the Union for Public Service, Transportation, and Traffic. The union has already begun demanding better pay, promotion and retirement benefits, and the possibility of strikes within the armed forces is not at all farfetched.

Another factor that is said to lie at the root of the *Bundeswehr*'s sea of troubles is a lack of military tradition. British, American, French soldiers and officers can all look back on their military past with pride. The Germans cannot. Another trauma is the frightening prospect, in the event of a showdown, of *Bundeswehr* soldiers having to shoot down fellow Germans and fire shells on German soil.

Studnitz in his book emphasizes his point that the best weapons cannot replace tradition. But as the defense ministry has rebutted, this concept does not account for the notably successful forces of the Vietcong and the Red Army, while "on the other hand, tradition-rich armies, such as the Prussian forces at Jena and Auerstadt or the French army in 1940, have failed."

The popularity of Studnitz's book is decidedly not a barometer of nationalism in the *Bundeswehr,* regardless of its nationalist overtones. As the sobering realities mentioned above indicate, the prevailing mood of the overwhelming majority of the *Bundeswehr* comes closer to political apathy. Recent surveys indicate a trend away from a predominantly CDU/CSU army (allegiance to the Christian Democrats was strongest when Franz-Josef Strauss was minister of defense) to voters balanced among all of the three major parties. In spite of the rightist NPD's noisy publicity about being the party "for the man who has to fight for his Fatherland," there is no evidence at all of a large following within the *Bundeswehr.* The NPD does talk more about military matters than any other party and repeatedly demands withdrawal from NATO or participation in an all-European defense system. It demands a German national army with a German general staff and the restoration of the principle of absolute obedience and command. No precise *Bundeswehr* membership figures are available, but informed observers estimate less than 1,000.

However, about a tenth of *Bundeswehr* NPD members serve the party as active functionaries. The best known of these is *Luftwaffe* Captain Wolfgang Ross, who is the only active *Bundeswehr* member to be elected to state parliament. When he campaigned with big posters showing himself in uniform, Bonn defense officials protested and the posters vanished.

There are occasional public flare-ups over the naming of barracks, ships, and the like after former Nazi generals or admirals. Although there was a controversy over the naming of West Germany's largest missile-carrying destroyer, "the pride of the German fleet," it is called *Lütjens* after Admiral Günter Lütjens. Lütjens is the World War II admiral who went down with the notorious *Bismarck* on May 27, 1941, shortly after it sank the then largest battleship in the world, the British *Hood.*

Lütjens, however, was noted for his loyalty to Hitler, to whom he sent this last message, "We are fighting to the end with faith in you, my Führer, and with unshakable confidence in German victory."

During the uproar, the ship was supposed to be named instead after Field Marshall Erwin Rommel, who was driven to suicide for his part in the unsuccessful attempt to assassinate Hitler on July 20, 1944. But the "Lütjens" name was retained, while a secondary destroyer is named after Rommel.

The Hitler assassination attempt and the "generals' revolt" have been widely publicized in troop indoctrination pamphlets as an illustration of justified disobedience, but they have also sown widespread confusion among recruits regarding military obedience. "The problem today," one officer has commented, "is not blind obedience, but how to get any kind of obedience at all."

Changes in the Wind

But there are changes in the wind. West Germany hopes to increase its peacetime troop strength to 460,000 by 1973. Reforms are underway that may eventually restore prestige, self-respect, and morale to the *Bundeswehr.* There are moves for higher pay, more attractive uniforms. The Bundestag in January, 1969, voted by a large majority to require alternate service of every conscientious objector, such as male nurses, Red Cross medical aides, gatekeepers, and maintenance men, and called for swifter mustering-out processes for disturbing persons who might damage their fellow soldiers' morale.

In November, 1969, the new SPD Defense Minister Helmut Schmidt launched a whole series of far-reaching changes. The first prominent Social Democrat to take part in reserve maneuvers of the *Bundeswehr* just after its formation, Schmidt is acquainted with the armed forces from the lowest rung, and has emerged as one of West Germany's foremost military theoreticians. One of his first acts was to create a new post of State Secretary for Technology and Armaments and appoint to it a McNamara-like executive, Ernst-Wolf Mommsen, head of the

Thyssen works and a great-grandson of the famous historian Theodor Mommsen. He is expected to bring modern management methods to the *Bundeswehr*.

Schmidt, long a sharp critic of the *Bundeswehr,* drastically streamlined the cumbersome civilian administrative apparatus, which in his view has no business dominating the uniformed part of the *Bundeswehr* based on command and obedience. The commanders of the three armed forces have been given greater powers and responsibility and enjoy the same status as their civilian counterparts. The Inspector-General has the same status as a civil state secretary.

Critics have voiced concern that precisely such steps may lead back toward a renewed militaristic orientation. However, the Defense Ministry under Schmidt lost no time in removing Major General Helmut Grashey, vice-inspector and Number Two man in the army, a controversial officer who had sharply attacked the whole democratized concept of the new German Army, with its built-in parliamentary ana juridical safeguards against a military corruption of power.

Although the West German government signed the nuclear nonproliferation treaty on November 28, 1969, opposition leaders of the CDU/CSU—which had opposed the treaty for nearly three years during the Kiesinger administration—had strong reservations. They feared that the control provisions of the treaty would open the way for an outside power to obstruct West Germany's research and development work with nuclear energy for peaceful purposes. Worries are expressed about industrial espionage, and about the possible openings an unfriendly power might seize to interfere in West Germany's purely internal affairs.

Even before the treaty West Germans were prohibited from manufacturing or using any nuclear weapons by themselves. These restrictions were placed upon Germany by the victorious allies after World War II. All nuclear warheads, whether designated for the West German army, navy, or air force units, remain under United States control. The West German *Bundeswehr* has the rockets, airplanes, and other weapons to deliver a nuclear blow to an enemy in war, but these are stored under American control, with a "double key" system that gives the President of the United States the final authority to use them.

Since the entire West German armed forces is committed to NATO, there are widespread anxieties in Bonn that West Germany in the event of the deterioration or collapse of NATO would be left defenseless in a nuclear war.

West German leaders are also uneasy about the constant talk of substantial troop withdrawals from Europe and the Federal Republic.

Another factor that contributed to the strengthening and expansion of the *Bundeswehr* is its changed role in the light of NATO's changed strategy. Originally based on the assumption that U.S. nuclear superiority would prevent Soviet invasion, NATO was not too much concerned about a *Bundeswehr* which lacked nuclear weapons, in the push-button mentality of that time. It was at best a political instrument under the domination of the Western powers.

With the increase of Soviet missile strength, and the corresponding change of strategy under U.S. President John F. Kennedy and Defense Secretary Robert S. McNamara, the emphasis shifted to "flexible response." Under the new plan, NATO ground forces, in which the *Bundeswehr* suddenly became the decisive element, were to be prepared for conventional confrontation.

Allowed to decline during the Cold War thaw of the sixties, this deterrent system became important again after the invasion of Czechoslovakia by Warsaw Pact countries in August, 1968. Since then NATO under American leadership has sought to relax tension in Europe.

What all this means is that the *Bundeswehr* has been shifting more and more toward independence, at least in part. There has been a growing awareness of national consciousness that inevitably will affect the *Bundeswehr*. There has been a trend toward greater authority for officers and noncoms and more discipline.

Creeping Rearmament

Critics are concerned too about the significant changes in the German armaments industry. Until recently the German government assiduously avoided building up new German armaments. Large orders for heavy equipment, tanks, guns, and the like were placed mostly abroad, where production facilities already existed.

But this policy was short-lived, and quickly replaced by creeping rearmament. Small arms, up to a caliber of 40 mm, have been produced by the Federal Republic from the beginning. With some exceptions, so too have warships. The German aircraft industry, a "late returnee" to industry, has received an initial credit of 35 million DM's (about $9 million) from Federal funds. It builds primarily foreign aircraft types under license (transporters, training and liaison machines) and also the DC-27 aircraft of German construction developed abroad. It is also constructing tactical aircraft procured from abroad. In addition, the responsible parliamentary committees have decided to let the German aircraft industry build under license the U.S. F-104 Starfighter, and the Italian Fiat 691, a light machine for ground fighting.

Eighty-eight U.S. Phantom jets are to be bought from the U.S. but under the condition that some or all of the jets be manufactured in Germany. McDonnell Aircraft Co., which manufactures the plane, has this arrangement with Britain and is believed to be amenable to repeating it in Germany.

In this context it is not surprising that the notorious Krupp concern should join the race. After his conviction at the Nuremberg war trials, the late Alfred Krupp swore never again to produce weapons. For a while the firm was exclusively devoted to the production of peaceful products and services. Some examples are: the construction of a hydroelectric plant in Greece, an iron-ore smelting plant at Larynma, an industrial plant in Afghanistan, freight quays in Holland, a huge ore-dredging installation in Australia, and a $20 million harbor in Bangkok.

But in 1968, less than a year after the death of the last Krupp owner (it has since become a public corporation), the firm was in production for the *Bundeswehr.* It has since been revealed that as far back as 1961, Krupp had been assembling the Starfighter, and since 1964 had built small U-boats for the *Bundeswehr.* In addition, the firm produces tanks, warships, torpedo shafts, radar equipment, mobile bridges, blow-up tents, mobile hospitals, armored trucks, civil engineering barracks.

During a visit to the Krupp works in Essen, I asked Count Georg-Volkmar Zedtwitz-Arnim, the firm's information director, if he could explain the reasons for the policy change regarding weapons production. He insisted that they were still producing mainly peaceful products and virtually no weapons. "The question nowadays," he said, "as to just what is a weapon and what is not is hard to define. Look, you manufacture a truck. Paint it red and it is a vehicle for the fire department. Paint it gray and it can be sent to developing countries. But paint it olive drab and it immediately becomes a weapon! If we voluntarily renounce weapons, please, let us define what weapons are."

With similar hairsplitting the firm has coined its own house definition by which neither Starfighters nor submarines can be classified as "weapons" but rather as "weapons-carriers."

. The Krupp general director, Günther Vogelsang, who was a lieutenant in World War II, reportedly said, "A weapon is something that goes: 'boom, boom!' "

Meanwhile thousands of *Bundeswehr* GI's across the land daily go marching along, and pigtailed girls and apple-cheeked boys run behind them in admiration. The goose step has been replaced by the American quick step and the notorious jackboots of Nazi days are replaced by smart hiking boots. And, believe it or not, many of the songs they sing literally contain words like these:

> *Oh Susanna! Oh weine nicht um mich!*
> *Denn ich komm von Alabama,*
> *Bring mein Banjo nur für Dich!*

According to record industry statistics, German military band LP's are persistent best sellers, not only in Germany, Austria, and Switzerland, but also in France, Belgium, and Holland.

For, if there is one thing those *Bundeswehr* GI's *can* do, they can sing.

◄ 18 ►

THE GERMAN MALE—A NONPERSON?

THE POPULAR IMAGE of the German male has generally tended to be one of several stereotypes: a robust Wagnerian opera singer (more often than not represented by a middle-aged rotund Scandinavian); a ruggedly handsome, ruthless blond adventurer; a humorless, stubborn, autocratic family patriarch; a heavy-set middle-aged army officer; a strong-armed bully; a fanatic, full-bearded scientist; or the tall, haughty aristocrat with a monocle.

To most Germans, however, the symbolic German male is quite different. In fact, Germans have for several centuries identified themselves with a popular cartoon figure, whom they call the "German Michel," a short, nondescript, roly-poly male of indeterminate age, with spindly legs, always wearing a stocking cap and a blank, quizzical-to-harassed expression on his moonlike face. This is the German's idea of himself: a decent, law-abiding, patient, obedient, well-meaning fellow always being pushed around.

The cartoon figure has been compared to England's John Bull, France's Marianne, and good old Uncle Sam, but a more fitting American comparison is actually that other popular if pathetic U.S. cartoon figure, the mustached, middle-aged, bespectacled milquetoast, John Q. Public. If the stereotype of the arrogant German bully exists, then only as a counterpart to the "little guy" represented by the German Michel. It was the German Michel rather than the stereotyped bully who was the real villain in the Nazi era. More than anyone else, the millions of "Michels" who carried out orders created the backbone of Nazi strength. The German Michel fought Hitler's wars, built the concentration camps, and turned on the gas jets; the German Michel was the pushed-around, obedient, respectable "little guy" who didn't want trouble, who believed in law and order, and who would carry out unbelievable atrocities precisely because his basic

297

passion was order, decency, and middle-class respectability. This concept lies at the heart of the traditional German family.

Today the Michel is a more apt figure for the German male than ever before. Not only is he the pushed-around "little guy" of German society, but his identity and self-assurance have nowhere been so seriously threatened as in the family circle. Over the past several years I have observed countless newspaper and magazine articles with headlines such as, *"Ist der Deutsche Mann eine Null* [Is the German Male a Zero] ?" or "The Crisis of the German Male," "The Father Descends from His Throne," "The Age of Emasculation." Americans have a counterpart in the emasculated, henpecked pathetic comic-strip figure of Dagwood Bumstead.

The well known social critic Karl Bednarik called his book *Die Krise des Mannes—The Male Crisis* rather than *The Human Crisis—* because in his view the male has been affected by the changes and revolution in modern life far more than has the female.

Men, he argues, have throughout history been the leaders, protectors, inventors, philosophers, discoverers, explorers. For better or worse they have made history and in the main created the world we live in. Now we see a society emerging in which women play an ever increasing role, creating an entirely different world, perhaps even a better one than the one dominated by men.

But at what a price!

Until recently, argues Bednarik, men could find release for their natural aggressions as soldiers serving the state, or they could find outlets in their work where they were master and could witness the emergence and completion of a finished product, or at least as the central and authoritative person in the family. "We find today," he writes, "that by far the majority of men lose themselves in passive resignation and frustration to the mass media." In their professions, it is even worse. Man's activity is daily more circumscribed by the straitjacket of the Organization. Then when he seeks relaxation and release from his tensions at home he is again frustrated, for here he is no longer master. The advent of the pill, female emancipation, and increasing demands of a planned society on his children, not to mention his wife, complete his emasculation.

Forty percent of German men reject the pill because the awakened sexual desires of their wives have completely upset their time-honored notion of a well-regulated and peaceful family life.

A standard joke in West Germany is that the German male regards sex as a physical accomplishment like a track star at an Olympic game—one shouldn't put it past him to take a stopwatch to bed. As a result of growing sexual demands of his wife, he is stripped of his masculinity because he is no longer even master in bed. Professor H. H. Knaus, co-discoverer of the Knaus-Ogino birth control method, confesses that "the pill endangers the ethos of the civilized world and may ultimately lead to the collapse of order that has developed over centuries."

Professor Dr. Hofstätter of the University of Hamburg has said, "The German man is used up very early, so that all spontaneity is absent at home, and he develops his temperament only in eating and drinking." Psychotherapist Dr. H. Hahne, Stuttgart, says, "The male of today is no longer capable of genuine love. He is primarily concerned that his sex life functions satisfactorily."

"Sex and love," according to Rev. Alfred Ziegler, director of the marriage school of the Evangelical Academy of Bochum, "have become hopelessly separated."

According to one survey conducted among 5,000 families, the average German family spends only forty-six minutes daily, aside from meals, in common activity. At the same time, women are playing an ever increasing role in deciding family affairs. In another survey, conducted among teenagers, the majority of respondents stated that their fathers spend far too little time in family affairs. "My father," one teenage girl said, "ever since I can remember is simply someone who comes home from work every evening and in the morning goes to work again, someone who doesn't see us very much and is not interested in us. He is only a Thing who has to earn money." In a Stuttgart school, children of the sixth grade were asked to write an essay about their fathers, but many handed in nearly blank pages. The entire essay of one pupil was as follows: "I don't know anything about my father. Can't I write about my mother?"

According to the Federal family report, "The previous concept of the autocratic father, with his high collar and strict orders is rapidly disappearing. Today's father has descended from his symbolic throne and either he is a full participant in a democratically-oriented family or an outsider."

Rightly or wrongly, the world's concept of the German male

still persists: his inability to laugh at himself, his lack of gallantry toward women, his reckless use of high-powered cars to compensate for his sense of inferiority, his awkwardness, and his widespread habit of talking too loudly at social functions.

It is interesting that while Mother's Day is a family affair as in the states, Father's Day, which falls on the religious holiday of Ascension Thursday but is also a national holiday, is strictly an exuberant, boisterous, male outing. The "boys" traditionally wear old-fashioned straw sailor hats, carry ribboned canes, decorate a bus or car with silly bunting, toilet paper, etc., and take a trip out into the country to some nice tavern and stagger home, completely stoned, about four or five A.M. the next day.

In short, the modern German father is on the defensive. He is ostracized, frustrated, overtaxed by the demands of society and family, isolated, has fewer and fewer outlets for his energy, imagination, and talents. He finds his dignity and self-respect diminishing or nonexistent, and he is scared.

Divorce

There is a divorce in the Federal Republic once every nine minutes, one per thousand of the population, or nearly 60,000 a year. This is proportionately four times that of the British, but less than half the American rate, and much the same as France, the Low Countries, and Scandinavia.

The routine procedure for divorce in Germany is much the same as in most European countries.

The usual waiting time for a divorce is about two weeks, and the actual proceedings last about ten minutes.

Ironically, the most common form of divorce, the "conventional" divorce (by mutual consent) is explicitly prohibited. Officially there is no recognition of a divorce in which some kind of *Schuld* (guilt) cannot be established. German courts must attribute guilt to one or both parties, sometimes dividing the guilt into ¼, ⅓, or ½ "guilty" between the two parties. Even though German marriage is a contract between two persons by mutual consent, those same persons are not permitted to break the contract by mutual consent.

Thus a couple who agree to separate because they are convinced that they are not suited for each other must invent a marital offense—with one of them assuming the greater part or all

300

of the blame—in order to qualify for a divorce. They must further agree on alimony, rearing of children, and division of property.

If, however, the alleged innocent party refuses to divorce, he or she can block the legal action indefinitely. Thus a small businessman has been living with a *Fräulein* and their four children for years because his legal wife, whom he has not seen in ten years, refuses to grant him a divorce. And without a divorce he cannot marry the *Fräulein,* even though she eagerly desires to be his legal wife and mother of their children. If the courts had declared his legal wife "guilty" in their shattered marriage, then he could obtain a divorce, but since in the eyes of the law *he* is "guilty" he cannot obtain a divorce as long as his legal wife refuses.

In Germany the double bed and the indissolubility of marriage is still regarded by the marriage senate of the Federal Constitutional Court (Supreme Court) in Karlsruhe as sacred. The chief reason why divorce remains so difficult to obtain in West Germany is the dominating influence of the Roman Catholic Church and the CDU.

Nationwide controversy has centered for years around Clause 48 of the German marital code. This made it possible to dissolve a marriage, even against the will of the innocent party, if separation had lasted more than three years and if the court decided that the relationship was past saving. The Christian Democrats successfully abolished this clause in 1961, largely through the lobbying of Dr. Elizabeth Schwarzhaupt, a spinster who later became minister of family affairs.

The clause undoubtedly is an exception to the general basis for German divorce laws. Under this system a marriage can be dissolved only if one party is guilty of adultery, desertion, or other substantial marital offenses. The only other exception to this "guilt" principle is prolonged, incurable insanity. But even when the latter condition can be demonstrated, it is still extremely difficult to obtain a divorce from a partner afflicted with extreme insanity.

Clause 48 was inserted into the marriage code only in 1938—in the Nazi period—and those Christian Democrats, especially Catholics, who pushed for its abolition, denounced it as a "Nazi law." However, the preparatory work for the marriage code of 1938 had started far back in the Weimar Republic days. It had been the most liberal and left-wing lawyers and politicians in Germany who had long advocated some clauses making it possible to dissolve a "dead" marriage even if no party could be charged with the "guilt" for the marital failure.

It is true enough that the Nazis were less interested in the humanitarian reasons for this law than in fostering their population policy with easier divorce, since the law did help pension off aging wives by setting sprightly middle-aged men free to contract second and third marriages and hence produce more offspring. In practice, the conservatism of middle-aged German husbands and the quiet sabotage of German courts prevented the law from having its desired effect.

Although reform of the marital code is slow a-coming, drastic changes are being proposed. Among them: abolishment of the "guilt" principle; adoption of the wife's name if the couple so chooses; alimony to be paid to the weaker party regardless of sex; children of divorced couples to be left with the more suitable parent; strengthening of married women's position; and financial measures to provide divorcees with security in old age. A confusing aspect will be the expected proliferation of double-names, such as Schultz-Müller, already a German commonplace.

In spite of the encroachment of sexual freedom, divorce, and modern demands, the German family has remained on the whole remarkably stable. "Although divorce has increased fourfold since the turn of the century," says Dr. Max Wingen of the Federal Ministry for Family and Youth, "this factor by itself is by no means an adequate argument against the general stability of the German family."

Domesticity Still Reigns

The general mood of West Germany today is one of cosy domesticity. Although material prosperity, the growing consciousness of individual freedom, female emancipation, and teenage permissiveness have affected legal and social institutions including marriage, they have not shaken its fundamental stability.

In spite of gloomy predictions, notably by social critic Sebastian Haffner and apostle-of-doom Pater Leppich, S.J., that the family is on the way out in Germany, the fact remains there is no real evidence that this is actually the case and instead there is overwhelming evidence that marriage is more popular than ever.

In the under-twenty-five bracket alone, more than 250,000 marriages took place in 1969. Ninety-six out of 100 persons of all ages marry at some time.

An American sociologist, Professor Lee Rainwater, of the University of Washington, commenting on a study made under his direction of German and American married men, said, "Germans are better husbands." He attributed the strong marriage bond to a search for identity and community in a world increasingly hostile to the individual. The foundering male stripped of his masculinity in society, at work, and among his own sex, still seeks fulfillment in the family that has already begun to reject him.

In another survey, 87 percent of West German men said they felt happiest in the family circle.

"The Frenchman," says the German author Hans-Georg von Studnitz, "seeks in his wife a mistress, the Englishman, a nurse, the Swiss, a waitress, the American, a sugar-darling. But in Germany half of all married men call their wives, 'Mutti [mother]'."

In an opinion poll conducted by the Allensbach Institute more than 68 percent of German men said their ideal wife must be "thrifty," a smaller number (62 percent) said they must be faithful, and 60 percent opted for cleanliness as the most desired trait in an ideal mate. "Warmth" was fourth on the list, although "tenderness' wasn't even mentioned. Other qualities were "industriousness," "naturalness," "a sense of order," and "punctuality."

Seventy-eight percent of German men prefer their wives to spend most of their time at home.

Dr. Karl Bednarik, mentioned earlier in this chapter, points out that there need not be a crisis of manhood if the German male, learns to adjust to new challenges. He suggests that the solution may well lie in shared authority, and in the male's greater articulateness and participation in social and political problems. Here, he points out, is an endless sea of opportunity for men of imagination and courage, where they can rediscover their authority.[1]

In spite of all the attacks on the German family, it is today, according to Frau Anne Braucksiepe, former minister for family affairs, *"wunderbar in Ordnung."* And whenever a German says *"in Ordnung,"* he or she means that it is the greatest.

East Germany

In East Germany family life is at least as intact as it is in West Germany, if not more so. Paradoxically the pressures from the regime to sign up the children with paramilitary organizations, such as the FDJ (Free German Youth or Young Pioneers), or the exposure to professional reprisals if the parents are active churchgoers—all this has brought the family closer together. Moreover, the regime has found it to be in its own interests to vigorously promote family life.

For whatever motives, the fact remains that family legislation in the German Democratic Republic has some elements that are more humanitarian and progressive than in West Germany or, for that matter, many western countries.

The status of married partners in East Germany is considerably different from that of West Germany. Just to give one example, both partners in a marriage in the GDR can decide which of their family names they shall use in marriage. According to East German law the "expenditure and enjoyment of material and cultural needs and desires of marriage partners and children must be obtained together." Housework and education of children are a mutual obligation—which West German marriage courts are only slowly acknowledging. In regard to property, each marriage partner may keep for himself or herself whatever he or she earned or inherited before marriage—or receives as a gift after marriage—while anything earned together must be shared and, in the event of a divorce, equally divided.

In East German divorce laws there is no such thing as "guilty party," and "alimony" only to a limited degree. If the court decides that one or the other partner of either sex is economically handicapped by the divorce, the other partner must pay a temporary alimony that may not last more than two years. In rare cases, unemployable persons may receive alimony for an indefinite period. Thus if a sickly husband is divorced from a healthy, working wife, it is likely that *she* will have to pay *him* alimony. The children are allotted to that marriage partner, regardless of sex, who, in the eyes of the court, is best suited for their education and welfare.

East Germany law frowns on "free love" and makes divorce difficult, partly by imposing exorbitant fees. As in West Germany "conventional divorce" (by mutual consent) is not recognized, but on the other hand a hopeless marriage is not preserved if the court decides that a marriage has "lost its meaning for the partners, the children, and society."

The word "illegitimate child" does not exist in GDR lawbooks, and children of unwed parents have equal claim with legitimate children on the inheritance of their parents.

In spite of recent reforms, West German marriage and divorce laws are still considerably behind those of East Germany.

◄ 19 ►

THE VANISHING GRETCHEN

UNTIL FAIRLY RECENTLY the German woman's domain was restricted to the legendary "three K's"—*Kinder, Kirche, Küche* (children, church, kitchen)—and her fame as a *Hausfrau* had become an international byword.

But "the" German woman—who of course has never existed—is undergoing a profound transformation. The Gretchen of story-book fame has all but disappeared and in her place a modern woman has emerged, with all of the elegance—and neuroses—of her counterpart in other parts of the world.

Recently an American magazine coined the word *"Fräulein-wunder"* to indicate a welcome new look among German women. It reproduced color photographs of tall, slender beauties to prove its point. Among the glamorous new girls are such international film stars as Christine Kaufmann, Romy Schneider, Elke Sommer, Karin Baal.

The magazine *Germany International,* published in Bonn, observed that some German models (Ina Balke "with her apartments in Paris, Rome and New York"; Alexandra Kaack, who serves a world-famous Parisian fashion house; Dagmar Draegert and Wilhelmine Behmenburg in Manhattan) "are earning far more than a Bonn cabinet minister."

So, for that matter, are many women executives. Women in business for themselves have formed the Federal Republic's Association for Professional Women, with 800 members. Its president, Dr. Lily Jones, herself runs a plant employing 850 people that manufactures thermoelectric measuring instruments. Hildegard Roth, the treasurer of the Women Entrepreneur's Association, operates a cement works, with 100 employees. Another woman, Marianne Busch, is top "man" in a cigarette factory employing 500 workers. Käthe Kruse has developed a flourishing doll industry.

The world-famous Steiff toy animal firm, which is the home of the original Teddy Bear (named after U.S. President Theodore Roosevelt) is headed by Margarete Steiff.

The weekly newspaper, *Die Zeit,* which is widely regarded as the world's best German-language news publication even compared with dailies, has as editor-in-chief Countess Marion Dönhoff.

Of the nearly 10 million working women in the Federal Republic, some 726,000 are self-employed. Every eighth entrepreneur in West Germany is a woman.

Drastic Structural Changes

As far back as 1882, one-fourth of German women were working. If one includes the active participation of women in family enterprises or farms, the percentage was much higher. Since then, the percentage of employed women in Germany has more or less stood constant at around 33 percent, rising to 36.2 percent during World War II. Although this figure still holds today, female employment has undergone drastic structural changes in recent years.

Of the 7.23 million female employees in 1939, some 3 million (41 percent) were engaged in family-run enterprises. Today only 1.87 million women (19 percent) are active in family businesses.

While the percentage of female unskilled workers has remained constant from 1939 to 1969 at 37 percent of all employed women, the number of female white collar workers has risen from 14 percent to 35 percent. As a result, female employment has become more and more a characteristic of the middle and even upper classes of society, and is no longer regarded as something odious. Women employees in industry are still on the whole dissatisfied with their lot, while women in professions are happy in their work. In 1950 only 13 percent of employed women decided in favor of administrative, bookkeeping, or typing work. But the demand—and prestige—associated with such white collar employment has pushed this figure to 20 percent in 1965. Similarly employment in menial work dropped from 19 percent to 15 percent. In 1950 over one-fifth of all high school graduates wanted to become seamstresses, cooks, or seek domestic employment, today only 6 percent.

Compared to West Germany's 34.3 percent employed women, the Netherlands has only 24.7 percent, Italy 26.0 percent, and France about 34 percent.

During World War II and in postwar years many women had to take up work outside their homes, often being the sole breadwinners of their families. There were more than 400,000 war widows. And even after the return of POW's, many of their wives continued to work in order to replace the household goods which had been destroyed.

Far more girls have an education today than in 1900. The number of women in universities rose from 306 in the summer term of 1907 to 60,000 in 1969. More girls marry today than in 1900 and they marry much sooner. As a result ever more wives and mothers go to work. Between 1950 and 1962 the number of employed mothers with children under fourteen, rose by 74 percent.

More and more young wives continue working after marriage in order to provide a better economic foundation for their new households.

And, with full employment, there is a great demand for women in industry.

Not only in the professions but in the home as well, the German *Frau* has taken on entirely new dimensions. Nineteen million *Hausfraus* are emancipated as never before.

The mechanization of the household together with modern hygienic standards have prolonged the life expectation of the German woman and provide her with an undreamed of freedom to pursue a career, engage in sports or cultural pursuits.

Paradoxically, these same women, for whom the work-saving devices have won so much free time, have fewer children.

At the turn of the century nearly half of all German women in twenty years of marriage had four or more children. By 1960 only one-sixth have that many children. Two-thirds of German wives today have only two children or less. This is a big change since the seventeenth century when German women often bore as many as seventeen children. Johann Sebastian Bach was father of twenty, Maria Theresa, mother of sixteen, Franz Schubert was the twelfth of fourteen children. Dürer, Kant, Gellert, Bismarck, Robert Koch, Werner von Siemens, and Richard Wagner had five or more brothers or sisters.

Until the middle of the last century, childbearing was a dangerous adventure for most women—some 15 to 20 percent of pregnant German women died in childbirth.

At the turn of the century, the average German woman reached sexual maturity at the age of fifteen, married at twenty-five, gave birth to her last child at thirty-five, and had to provide for her children until she was fifty. Today she is sexually mature at twelve, marries before twenty-four, gives birth to her last child at twenty-seven, and is freed from maternal duties at forty-one. Whereas at the turn of the century women already outlived men on an average of 3.51 years, today this figure has increased to 5.81 years. A girl born between 1871 and 1880 had a life expectancy of only 38.4 years, while a girl born today can count on an average of 73.13 years. By the year 2000 the life expectancy of German women may well pass ninety. An interesting phenomenon is that the gap between women's life expectancy and that of men is continually widening.

History of Emancipation

The Federal Republic is one of the few countries in the world whose constitution specifically guarantees equal rights to women.

Article 3, paragraph 2 of the Basic Law reads, "Women have the same rights as men." But it took years of hard work and bitter struggle to have the laws of the country brought into line with this constitutional principle.

The German woman's emancipation followed in the wake of the suffragette movements in England and France and not primarily as a result of her own initiative. The first German suffragette, Luise Otto-Peters, made a slight public ripple during the revolutionary year of 1848, and later founded in Leipzig the *Allgemeine Deutsche Frauen Verein.* But her activity was received with surprise and ridicule in the German press. However, a breakthrough of sorts was won in 1908 when German women were granted the right to organize and/or join political organizations. Whereas in England suffragettes chained themselves (modern demonstrators please note) to the iron fence outside the House of Parliament or even threw themselves in front of the royal carriage, German women were quietly given the franchise after World War I. Article 109, paragraph 2, of the 1919 Weimar constitution guaranteed equal civil rights for men and women. In addition, female suffrage for the provincial parliaments and the Reichstag was laid down.

309

Only a few German women, however, have emerged as outstanding personalities in the country's history. In the early 1800's, Rachel Vernhagen was lauded by Heinrich Heine as the wittiest woman in the world, and noted for her literary salon in Berlin. Nelly Sachs, Marlene Dietrich, Pola Negri, and Käthe Kollwitz, "painter of the poor," are others. But what a short list.

Although motherhood has been lavishly praised in German literature as the true heroism, it has not really been too kind to the German woman. Modern observers cite the derogatory treatment accorded her in the classics. Gerhard Hauptmann's *Mutter Wolffen,* and Bertolt Brecht's *Mutter Courage* depict rather sex-starved, neurotic, perverse, or at best, pathetic creatures. Friedrich Dürrenmatt's *Besuch der Alten Dame (The Visit of the Old Lady)* is a brutal portrayal of materialism and vengeance. Birga Kristlein in Martin Walser's *Das Einhorn* receives her husband like a meal, and Thomas Mann's Rosalie von Thümmlar in *Die Betrogene (The Betrayed One)* is the victim of a cruel irony. In the novels and stories of the contemporaries Heinrich Böll, Uwe Johnson, and Wolfgang Koeppen, women, if mentioned at all, are unflattering secondary characters.

Come a Long Way

German women had clearly come a long way when on July 20, 1959, the Federal Constitutional Court heard a woman deliver a judgment which finally gave them equal rights in all questions relating to the rearing of children and signing documents in their behalf. The woman, clad in red judge's robes, was Dr. Erna Scheffler, member of the First Senate of the Federal Constitutional Court.

Numerous women hold executive positions in the Federal, state, and community governments. Frau Käte Strobel served as minister of public health in the Kiesinger cabinet, preceded by Dr. Elisabeth Schwarzhaupt, and Frau Anne Braucksiepe as minister for family and youth affairs. The rector of Heidelberg University was Professor Margot Becke. The mayor of Oberhausen in the industrial Ruhr, Luise Albertz, is known for her forthright fight for bettering the lot of the coal miners dispossessed in the wake of numerous shutdowns of Ruhr coal mines because of the increased use of oil. In the Grand Coalition administration three dozen members of the Bundestag were women, the youngest of whom, Ursula Krips, an attractive woman in her early thirties, won the unofficial title of "Miss Bundestag."

Dr. Maria Probst served as vice president of the Bundestag while simultaneously carrying out her role as grandmother until her death in 1968.

In the national elections of September 28, 1969, thirty-two female deputies (out of 518) were elected to the Bundestag, or four fewer than in 1965. On the other hand, four women were appointed to key positions in Chancellor Willy Brandt's cabinet: Frau Käte Strobel remained as minister of public health, whose office now included youth and family affairs; Dr. Katharina Focke, parliamentary state secretary in the Federal Chancellor's office; Frau Brigitte Freyh, parliamentary state secretary to the ministry of economic cooperation; and Dr. Hildegard Hamm-Brücher, parliamentary state secretary in the ministry for education and science.

Frau Elisabeth Weichmann, who is also the wife of the mayor of Hamburg, is a Bundestag deputy and president of the European Bureau of Consumers' Associations, which for the past fifteen years has been trying to help the bewildered consumer with specialists' advice about the quality and prices of consumer goods.

More than seventy women's organizations of various political leanings, the so-called "Working Communities" (workshops), are devoted to community affairs and democratic education. There is a unique information center, in Bad Godesberg, which is devoted exclusively to disseminating information on all subjects pertaining to women. Its membership of eighteen central organizations (representing eighty women's associations and mixed groups from the trade unions) includes six million women.

More Demanding, More Frustrated

The German woman, as a result of all these gains, has become more independent—and demanding. Some 7,000 beauty experts help her look and stay young, but in spite of all her emancipation and comforts, the modern German woman is frustrated. Less childbearing, modern hygiene, and labor-saving devices have increased her life expectancy. But the struggle to obtain all these

311

conveniences makes it necessary for the modern woman, who is not only freed from the drudgery of grandmother's day but full-time live-in servants as well, to go to work.

Medical experts, sociologists, and educators are divided as to the effect of all these trends. In the pessimistic camp a gynecologist, Professor Hugo Otto of Ludwigshafen, claims to have observed an increasing frequency of "premature invalidization" among many working mothers. Dr. Heinz Kirchoff in Göttingen categorically decrees that "no mother with children under fifteen should hold a job." The sociologist Dr. Alexander Rüstow, unsuccessfully attempted to make it illegal for mothers with small children to work.

A Munich pediatrician, Dr. Theodor Heilbrügge, speaks of "technological orphans," the *Schlüssel Kinder* (key children, *i.e.,* children with both parents working, carrying the house key on a chain or cord around their necks). An estimated 1.5 million such children are reported in the Federal Republic.

The optimistic experts favor working mothers. They point out that working mothers usually have a greater interest in the outside world, politics, and social problems, and communicate this to their families. They insist that the increased life expectancy of working mothers contradicts the "premature invalid" theory. In the same period (1952-1964) in which the number of working mothers increased, their mortality rate decreased by 100 percent.

Local investigations revealed further that employed mothers, who have the benefit of well-paid plant physicians and facilities, have a much smaller percentage of premature births than non-working mothers. In Krefeld pregnant employees of a large concern only experienced 2.3 percent premature births out of 100 women, as against 6 out of 100, the average for the area. A Hamburg physician explained this phenomenon: "Working women are not so cramped at birth and leave their confinement earlier because they are restless with nothing to do."

For some time plant physicians have observed another phenomenon: Until 1958 the number of cases of working women being declared incompetent for their jobs was consistently higher than the number of men. Since 1960, however, it is the other way around.

Professor Rüstow's appeal for the prohibition of working mothers couldn't be enforced even if it were law. For the plain facts of life are that nearly one-third of German brides already are pregnant or mothers, that 50 percent of all German brides no longer bring a dowry into their marriage, and that the complete outfitting of a normal middle-class household averages 12,000 Deutsche marks ($4,000). Thus working wives are a must.

This necessity in the first years of marriage all too often imposes severe penalties on the wives. About 50 percent of all female university students are dropouts, mostly for the purpose of marriage. If the wife wants to work later on, she is excluded from most higher professional work or even trades because she did not complete her studies. In Germany much emphasis is still placed on having all one's papers in order, regardless of that person's competence or qualifications.

Dr. Else König, adviser on women's affairs for the Federal Employment Agency, recommends the creation of sub-professions and sub-trades, so that women—and men for that matter—who are compelled to drop out, may in later life obtain employment on a sub-professional level and still be able to make use of their knowledge and training.

Women of a Certain Age

Especially problematical is the "over forty" group. It is humiliating for a woman, trained in a profession but without having that all-important diploma, to be rebuffed. Along with most other industrialized countries, particularly the United States, the Federal Republic is attempting to reassimilate the forty-to-sixty age group of women in gainful employment. Forty-two percent of all women seeking employment in 1966 were past thirty-nine.

"Desolation," "emptiness," "life deficit" is part of the standard jargon employed by psychologists and sociologists in regard to the psychological condition of the over forty-year-olds without professions. Such women can be seen by the thousands in dance halls like *Ball der Einsamen Herzen* (Ballroom of the Lonely Hearts). Every weekend most large newspapers carry a full- (or even two-) page spread of marriage ads, which include many from younger men and women, but by far the majority are from the middle-aged men and women.

"Attractive woman, 1 meter 70 centimeters tall, own apartment, automobile, loves travel, theater and sport, seeks acquaintance with a well-situated man between 45 and 60 for possible later marriage. . . . "

313

Enterprising gigolos advertise in the women's magazines. "Young man, 24 years of age, 1 meter 80 centimeters tall, seeks extravagant, well-situated lady under 45, with car, for the purpose of recreation. Full-length photo requested."

Actually, men and women of all ages, because of the dislocations of modern society and impersonal city life, advertise in matchmaking sections of daily newspapers that sometimes cover two entire pages in a weekend edition. Because of World War II casualties, however, there is a surplus of three million women, mainly between forty-six and sixty.

In addition marriage-broker institutions worth an estimated annual $15 million worth of business are located all over Germany. But many of these are outright rackets. The Central Office Against Corrupt Business Practices in Hamburg has a blacklist of 142 out of 250 marriage agencies for alleged swindle. However, a great many couples reportedly have been happily matched through newspaper contacts or some of the legitimate marriage institutes.

An unmarried woman has the right upon reaching the age of forty to be called *"Frau,"* and it is customary to address all older women with this title, whether married or not. In a survey, 58 percent of unmarried women over thirty preferred to be called *"Frau,"* 19 percent *"Fräulein,"* and 23 percent not caring one way or another.

It already has become quite correct for women past thirty-five (or younger for that matter) to travel alone, to go on vacation alone, and "pickups" are not necessarily regarded as improper. It is not at all unusual for an older woman to invite men close in age or older to a Fasching ball or to the theater. Unescorted women in the German *Gasthaus* or bars are still frowned upon, unless they are in pairs or groups.

More and more, however, the fading fortyish matron seeks refuge in some form of neurosis.

A woman gynecologist said: "The *Hausfrau*-only type tends to let herself go. The husband begins to seek escape, eventually takes on a mistress. The wife seeks refuge in real or imagined illnesses and appeals for pity or sympathy, hoping thereby to win back her husband. But he does not react, and then the mutual cruelties begin to set in."

Church-sponsored marriage advisory centers report that "especially in marriage where the wife is only a *Hausfrau* and does not work are conflicts particularly strong."

314

The unemployed middle-aged woman is a special problem for physicians, police, alcohol clinics, and tired social workers.

The comforts of modern life especially threaten to transform the *Villen Viertel* (mansion areas) into psychic slums. In former times a fading woman could find partial fulfillment in assuming the sewing, mending, and cleaning chores of a married daughter or relatives. Today labor-saving devices and the dread of in-law interference rob her of even this.

Dr. Klaus Thomas, founder of the Ecumenical St. Luke Order for the medical care of potential suicides and drifters, points out that "lonely women are our most frequent visitors." His most frequent therapy: work. He has found that employment, charitable activity, or even part-time work can do wonders in rehabilitating the frustrated, lonely middle-aged woman. The biggest dangers are addiction, especially alcoholism, which is counteracted by responsibility, contact with others, and preoccupation in some field of interest.

In a survey among several leading concerns, it is revealed that absenteeism is less among older women than among younger. The maturer woman showed a greater sense of responsibility, organizational ability and dependability, and was more adept in dealing with people. On the other hand, plant physicians note that older women tire more easily, sometimes suffer from memory loss. A compromise solution—the employment of older women on a part-time basis—has been widely adapted with considerable success.

More and More Complicated

With her emancipation the German woman has become much more complicated. The recent government report on *The Situation of Women in Professions, Family and Society* comprises 639 pages, in contrast to a similar report by the U.S. government on *The American Woman,* 50 pages. The German press is full of reports and studies on the German woman: "Woman and Culture," "Woman as Breadwinner," "The Eternal Woman," "Woman as Lover," but only a smattering of articles on "man" in German society. This is perhaps an indication of how much the patriarchal concept of the father and husband has vanished from the German scene. It is still there of course, in a subdued way, but the father role has not only diminished—it has become to a large extent subordinated to the woman.

315

Along with this, the phenomenon of *"Mutti-ismus"* (momism) is especially widespread in Germany. More than in the United States, German youth are dependent on their parents long after marriage. It often happens that even young husbands spend more time with their parents than at home. *"Mutti"* is also sentimentalized by women, and often plays a dominating role in German family life. There is even a hit tune with the line, *"Mutti ist immer dabei* [Mother is always around] ."

Whereas the transformation of the Fräulein from a portly, dowdy woman into one of Europe's most sophisticated beauties has been one of the most gratifying aspects of West Germany's postwar miracles, the transition from the patriarchal system to one of partnership between the sexes is still a long way from being realized. Although guaranteed equality in principle, the German woman is still discriminated against in industry, where there is a discrepancy of 31 percent between the earnings of men and women doing identical work, and in daily life, where men are still dominant in business, politics, and social prestige. In recent years I have noticed an increasing restiveness and aggressiveness among many ambitious German women. Television discussion panels often reveal the bitterness and downright belligerence of attitude and vocabulary of many German women who have become complex-ridden over the emancipation issue.

They regard as tokenism the special regulations for the protection of women in employment, such as maternity provisions (six weeks' leave with full wages before and after childbirth) and exemption from night work.

Although the number of female theology students in recent years has increased by 15 percent, the role of women pastors in the Evangelical Church is restricted and they are confronted on all sides by prejudice.

Only 4 percent of the 11,000 instructors at the Federal Republic's universities are women.

The Eternal Hausfrau

In spite of all the changes in the life of the German woman, something of the basic character of the eternal *Hausfrau* appears to be deeply ingrained in her after all.

Emancipated as she is, the German woman reveals on the whole a decidedly low quota of professional ambition.

In one survey in a south German concern only one-fifth of the women employees showed interest in professional advancement (compared with two-thirds of the men queried in the same concern).

According to the Hamburg sociologist Professor Elisabeth Pfeil, nearly two-thirds of all employed mothers work primarily for economic reasons, and only one-tenth out of "psychological" motives: "more contacts," "active in life," and love of a profession for its own sake.

A Wicker opinion poll survey disclosed that 66 percent of all German women prefer intellectually superior husbands.

To this day the German woman has remained preponderately passive in regard to politics, community action, or social reform. Only 6 out of every 1,000 German women are members of a political party (as compared with 40 men out of every 1,000).

In 1957 only 8 percent (45 out of 509 deputies) of the Bundestag were women (out of 18 million female votes). However this small percentage was still more than that of women in the parliaments of France, Norway, or even the U.S. (where the female population was represented by only 2 percent in the House of Representatives).

However, German women have consistently voted conservatively in national and regional elections and have been the mainstay of the CDU/CSU from 1953 to 1969: in 1953 the CDU/CSU received 20 percent more women's votes than the SPD did, contrasted with only 6 percent more male votes for the CDU/CSU; in 1957 women gave the CDU/CSU 25 percent more votes than they did the SPD; in 1961, although more men than before (39.7 percent voted SPD, 49.6 percent of women voters helped secure the CDU/CSU majority; 1965 might have been a victory year for the SPD, if it depended solely on male votes (44 percent voted SPD and only 42 percent CDU/CSU), but the women voted in the CDU/CSU with 51.7 percent—three-fifths of all votes for the CDU/CSU came from women.

By the same token, German women avoid voting for extremist parties. In April, 1968, the rightist NPD party received 13.4 percent of the male vote during the Baden-Württemberg state elections, but only 6.8 percent of female votes. Contrary to popular belief, even Hitler's NSDAP (Nazi Party) was at first primarily a man's party. It was only when it had "arrived" that the women endorsed it en masse.

Dr. Klaus Liepelt, director of the Bad Godesberg Institute for Applied Social Science (Infas Report) attributes the strong conservative preference of female voters to three chief factors: 1) women go to church more than men (two-thirds of all Catholic church-goers are older women); 2) only about a third of all female voters are employed as against 84 percent of male voters; and 3) there are far more women with inferior education than men. These factors are all the more decisive in German elections inasmuch as there are far more eligible women voters than men: 21 million women were qualified to vote in the September, 1969, national parliamentary elections, as against 17.5 million men—3.5 million more women. This is because of the five-year greater life expectancy of women and still noticeable male deficit caused by wartime casualties. "Wherever the CDU/CSU is elected in Germany," says Liepelt, "is decided by the number of church steeples, and wherever the SPD is elected, by the number of smokestacks."

According to the Infas Report, German parents, especially German husbands and fathers still consciously or unconsciously completely overlook the political education of women. Every second female respondent in the Infas survey, in response to the question, "When were you least interested in politics?" replied "at home with my parents."

CDU former Chancellor Kurt Georg Kiesinger, writing in the periodical *Politik und Geist,* has said, "I recall a saying of Immanuel Kant's: 'Women should be reserved in regard to politics, so that they will be able to reduce the enormous importance that men attach to it in daily life,' " and CSU head Franz-Josef Strauss was quoted in the mass-circulation daily *Bild:* "I am unable to decide that more women should be active in politics."

The fact that Willy Brandt and the Social Democrats barely squeezed into office in 1969 (and even then did so in spite of the actual majority of votes held by the CDU/CSU) is because of a leftist trend among young women voters. Among female voters between twenty-one and twenty-nine allegiance to the Social Democrats increased by 10 percent to 48.2 percent. To all appearances, this looked like the beginning of the end of the hitherto "safe" women's vote for the CDU/CSU.

Restrained Use of Makeup

No matter where you go in Germany, cosmetics are still

318

conspicuous by their absence, or at least restraint. American women are invariably regarded as overdressed, overdecorated, and above all, overly made-up. The majority of German women still prefer (or think their men prefer) the completely natural look. There are still strong prejudices against the use of makeup, especially in rural areas. "My mother," a typical young woman will reply upon being questioned on the subject, "is constantly reprimanding me on account of my makeup." Another girl replied, "My father refused to speak to me for days merely because I wore lipstick."

It is interesting that the product Angel Face, which enjoyed huge success in England and the States, has been a miserable flop in Germany because of the tremendous psychological difference. Whereas in England many wish to preserve the fair "angelic" look of their youth, German women, precisely because of their strong domestic backgrounds, are more inclined to a robust, temperamental, and self-confident appearance.

Paris, Rome, and London may lead the world in fashion, but it is Berlin that holds its own as one of the leading fashion producers. While Paris creates most of the new ideas in fashion, Berlin styles are worn by more women from Sicily to Stockholm. Even many French women are clad in Berlin imports, because Paris *haute couture* is far out of the average *mademoiselle*'s reach. "Berlin makes Paris Wearable" is the slogan of the more than 400 ladies' fashion manufacturers and 55,000 employees in the island of elegance.

"Not everyone can wear the Paris fashions as they are created," says Ruth Kerle, an editor of *Elegante Welt*. "The Berlin couturiers will make them wearable. Most German women are very busy and want practical clothes. The average woman thinks to herself, 'Can I wear it?' and on that basis, she buys or she doesn't."

The German female shopper looks for three things when buying clothes. First, she feels the material for softness and quality. It must be good material. Second, she looks at the cut of the garment to see that its lines will not be quickly outmoded. It must be of good cut. And third, she looks at the workmanship—the fine-sewn seam and the finishing details. It must be well-made. She is not likely to buy something just because it is cute or cheap.

"German women don't like fancy stuff and they don't like to

look overdressed." That's the way a German fashion photographer sums up the German woman's feeling toward clothes.

"They like plainer dresses and are more serious than frivolous about their clothes. Parisians wear more makeup and may have more charm, but the German women know how to wear color combinations better. Here you can't tell whether a girl is a waitress or an executive by her clothes."

American fashion, however, has found its way to Germany, especially in two styles: sports clothes and teenage apparel. California sportswear has an increasing appeal but is rivaled by Italian sweaters, shoes, and summer frocks. Blue jeans are still the rage among the teenage set and even older. However, 46 percent of West German women, according to an Allensbach survey, find miniskirts repugnant. It is interesting that miniskirts ordered from London's Carnaby Street are required to be two inches longer for German consumption.

The Bavarian dirndl dress, formerly worn only by peasant women, has if anything increased in popularity, so much so that an entire dirndl fashion industry has sprung up, with several firms specializing exclusively in dirndl dresses.

A surprising number of German women, even young girls, wear long woolen stockings in winter and long underwear, which, as one German Fräulein, who had been to the States, told me, "American women wouldn't be caught dead in."

According to a 1969 BBC TV documentary, the bulk of British government paper waste is converted into toilet tissue mainly exported to West Germany. British women, it explained, prefer colored tissues to match their walls, while German women are less particular in regard to this item.

For most German women it is still a "categorical imperative" to be wed in a full-length white wedding dress like their mothers and grandmothers before them. Statistics indicate that 80 percent of all German girls want to get married in the traditional white. Pastel shades, which have become fashionable in America, find little favor in West Germany. Even miniskirt addicts prefer the traditional length on their wedding day.

Gertrude Horn, a marriage adviser in Frankfurt, says that the time is long past when the bridegroom is not allowed to see the wedding dress before the wedding. Nowadays the groom is brought into discussions and tryouts of the dress and is consulted about the cost.

In Germany most women do not receive a diamond ring either for engagement or marriage. Both men and women wear a simple gold band, on their left hand during engagement and on their right after the wedding. Widows sometimes add their husband's ring to their own, and unlike the custom in some other countries, keep their husband's names, unless they remarry.

Even though Germany is the home of the Mendelssohn and Wagner wedding marches, neither these nor other marches are usually played at German weddings. Also, the big wedding cake, throwing rice or confetti at the church door, tying tin cans or ribbons or "just married" signs to cars, or continuously honking automobile horns on the wedding day—all this is unknown. And so is the pre-wedding stag party.

On the other hand, the custom of *Polterabend (Poltern* means "to make a loud noise") is very popular. On the eve of the wedding, friends of the couple go to the bride's house and smash old pottery and dishes at her door or under her window. It's an old superstition that the loud noise drives away bad luck. To assure future married bliss the bride is expected to sweep up the broken pieces all by herself.

Pre-wedding showers or baby showers are not known in Germany. Presents for the couple are either sent shortly before the wedding day, or delivered in person at the reception, or on *Polterabend.*

All couples are required by law, church wedding or not, to marry at the local *Standesamt* (registrar's office) in a simple but dignified civil ceremony. Those wishing a church wedding then have their second wedding ceremony a few days later.

Some 20,000 German women annually marry non-Germans, mostly because of increased contact with foreign guest workers from Mediterranean countries, the most marriage-minded for-eigners (with German girls) being men from Spain, Italy, Greece, and Yugoslavia.

Women in East Germany

In the German Democratic Republic, the SED, the Com-munist-run Socialist Unity Party, boasts of "creative partici-pation of women in the socialist reconstruction" and "the promotion of women to their professional qualifications."

As discussed more fully in Chapter 11, nearly 75 percent of all women are employed in East Germany—more than anywhere else in the world.

But even there middle-class respectability tenaciously survives all the onslaughts of the female emancipation movement. This is indicated by the results of a survey conducted in East Germany by the sociological department of the Martin Luther University in Halle. Only one out of four single male workers sympathized with the idea of their future wives working. And the women also seem less concerned about the "socialist construction of the state" than the needs of home and hearth. In an East Berlin survey over 70 percent of employed married women said they worked primarily "to modernize the household with new furniture and TV."

In 1969, some 2,000 East German women members of the DFU (Democratic Women's Union) convened in East Berlin to discuss the rights and needs of GDR women after twenty years of socialism. After lengthy speeches extolling the emancipated women of the socialist republic, the meeting ended with a long series of demands along the following lines: more kindergartens, better and more modern community laundries, better school lunches for their children.

Thus it appears that, in spite of East German socialism and West German sophistication, the German *Hausfrau* is here to stay.

◄ 20 ►

DAS DEUTSCHE VITA

FROM SCHLESWIG TO Füssen and from Aachen to Hof, West Germany is tingling with a sexplosion whose end is not in sight.

Nude women—and men—adorn the covers and insides of just about every mass-circulation magazine, and even the ads are completely sexurated.

Early in 1970, in a program called *"Das Deutsche Vita,"* a north German radio station broadcasted eye-witness reports of a sex orgy that allegedly took place in a prominent Hamburg businessman's basement. Hardly a day passes that teenage sex parties, group sex games, prostitution, rape, abortion, permissiveness are not shrilly proclaimed from newspaper headlines. "Underground" pornographic films are widely shown, including an animated color film in which the leading character is a talking penis.

Although outright pornography is still illegal, the stuff pours in by the ton from Denmark, where it is legal. Along Danish highways near the German border, slot machines dispense photos, films, and every kind of sexual paraphernalia.

While topless dress, mostly because of the climate, has not met with much public acceptance, except occasionally at the beaches, it has become common at numerous Carnival and Fasching balls, although most of the girls are covered with painted decorations. In a Düsseldorf nightclub, at one dollar a minute, a nude girl inside a booth can be fondled through a pair of holes admitting only arms.

All over Germany, notably on the island Sylt in the North Sea, there are nudist clubs (*Frei Körper Kultur*—FKK), and in Hamburg the city park has a nudist sunbathing enclave. Every year the nudists present their annual exhibit (photos) in the city's downtown fairgrounds. Several swimming pools permit mixed nude bathing at certain times.

Every weekend countless German newspapers display full or half-page classified marriage and friendship ads. While most of

323

these are regarded as innocent, the wording of many friendship ads gives rise to widespread editorial speculation that they are actually a contact vehicle for group sex games. Such an ad reads: "Young, attractive couple, middle thirties, unconventional, seeks acquaintance with other couples of same age interested in unusual forms of entertainment and indoor games. Box No.——."

Eyewitnesses of such "unusual indoor entertainment" in countless newspaper "confessions" say that a typical game is for all the men to toss their car keys in a bowl, the lights are turned out, and the women fish for the keys, each one spending the night with the man whose key she finds. Others tell of orgies and weird black magic rites.

Gross Familien (hippie communes) à la Sweden are much discussed, but it is doubtful if this practice is widespread in the Federal Republic, where the appearance of respectability still dominates.

Beate Uhse's *Fachgeschäfte für Ehehygene* (Specialty Shops for Marriage Hygiene), located in eleven cities, dispense pep pills, sex paraphernalia, chocolate-covered anti-impotence pills, and love-making devices and literature in a multimillion-dollar industry. She receives hundreds of thousands of letters from sex-hungry persons from ages twelve to ninety, which are automatically classified and answered by computer.

In another city an enterprising gadget manufacturer has clandestinely put on the market an erect plastic penis, which is filled and squirted like a water pistol by squeezing the lifelike testicles ("for best laughs, use milk"). Elsewhere toilet attendants sell condoms with cogged spirals or hard rubber ticklers shaped like miniature hands on the tips.

Hamburg's St. Pauli district, near the harbor, ranks among the world's wickedest, with its congestion of striptease bars, nightclubs, homosexual hangouts, and brothels. Its main street, Reeperbahn, is heralded in numerous sentimental sailor songs and evergreen hit tunes of the Marlene Dietrich and Hans Albers era. Here Lady Godiva nightly rides a horse down the aisles of a restaurant, nude girls wrestle in a ring of mud (nearest spectators are protected with plastic capes, while guests at the rear can watch proceedings via a huge tilted mirror over the ring). Café Keese, called "ball paradox," lets women choose their partners for nearly every dance. On a side street, Grosse Freiheit (the Great Freedom), ogling male customers disrobe girls with fishing poles, and elsewhere girls bathe in transparent bathtubs while directly across the street, from the top of a Volkswagen bus in front of St. Joseph's Catholic Church, the Jesuit "Pater Leppich" thunders against vice and abomination. Just a short distance away, homosexuals have their own nightly floor show in a basement dive.

Prostitution

Like most everything else in Germany, prostitution is controlled by strict regulations and efficient organization. Hamburg's Herbert Strasse, a small block-long side street, is blocked off at each end by tall steel gates marked "No minors allowed under police order." Nicknamed the "meat market," the street is reserved for prostitutes who occupy the double row of two-story brick houses and negotiate with customers through tiny glass slots built into the shop windows where the scantily-dressed women sit two abreast.

Since October, 1967, the famous street has to compete with Eros Center (named after the Greek god of love) an officially-approved apartment house especially designed for prostitutes' specific needs. Costing 4.7 million marks ($1.5 million), the concrete and glass four-story building contains 130 rooms, each with the same standard furniture, fittings, wallpaper, emergency bell. The building has nine units, each leased for 10,000 marks ($3,000), plus 2,000 ($600) for furnishings, for five years. The nine leaseholders are a hotelier, a jeweler, a car dealer, a pensioner, an insurance salesman, a club owner, two restaurant owners, and a retired tax official, and they are solely interested in making a good profit. In addition, they pay a monthly rent of 450 marks ($150). The girls in turn pay their particular renter 50 marks a day ($15) in advance for their room, and they in turn charge 30 marks ($9) a "trick." No customer stays longer than ten minutes.

Ingrid, thirty-two, has had a room in the Eros Center since it opened, but plans to leave it soon and go back to the streets. "At the Eros Center I had to stand around in the courtyard like a sausage on display in a store window. On the street, it happens more naturally, a man can size you up and it gives the illusion of romance. This is too clean, too clinical. The men miss the mystery of the dark alleys and the sense of doing something sinister."

Nevertheless, the nine leaseholders reportedly are doing well on their investment. At last report they were enjoying a profit of between 15 and 17 percent.

Periodically there are public outcries against the "scandalous goings on" of the Reeperbahn and St. Pauli, but nothing comes of them. Eros centers exist in several other large cities, Stuttgart, Düsseldorf, and even in small-town Bonn, and brothel districts are accepted fixtures in most cities, all with the blessing of the city and state authorities, even though strictly speaking, they are illegal. The German sense of *Ordnung* and keeping everything under control has overruled paragraph 180, section 2 of the West German penal code, which prohibits the maintenance of a brothel. Authorities feel that by controlling the women and requiring a regular health inspection, they can cut down on venereal disease. Not only that, but the fact that 45,000 registered prostitutes in the Federal Republic earn an estimated billion DM's annually has been realized by the federal tax authorities—and it is believed that there are at least three times that many prostitutes who remain unregistered.

Overlooking the stipulation of the Reichsfinanzhof of 1931 that "the bodily surrender of a woman is no profession," tax collectors have found the practitioners of the world's oldest profession fair game since 1964.

Since then, the tax officials of the nine West German states have reaped ridicule and headaches along with revenue in struggling to collect taxes from prostitutes. For there is no certain way to ascertain how much prostitutes earn. One tax collector admitted that, in order to make an estimate, one evening he personally observed a delinquent tax payer "at work" for hours from a dark alley. In Düsseldorf, after a four-hour negotiation with leading brothel owners, prostitutes were levied 8 marks ($2.00) a day income tax, payable, according to the time-honored German custom, in advance.

But in a tax-evasion trial in a Bremen court, the judge observed that "a nation of laws may not tax *future* punishable activity," and found this procedure invalid, arguing that while prostitution is not a crime in West Germany, soliciting is, and advance taxation "tends to encourage soliciting."

In Cologne, tax officials estimate the income of the girls according to the appearance, size, and year of their cars. A "star" prostitute was taxed 32,000 DM's for one year ($9,750). In Nuremberg and Hamburg the girls are required to make their own declarations. If they decline they are arbitrarily taxed for an estimated 12,000 DM's a year or $360 a month.

The 270 registered prostitutes of Düsseldorf, mainly concentrated near the Bahnhof, serve an estimated 8,000 customers daily, bring upwards of 800,000 marks ($250,000) tax revenues annually. Earnings range from 20 marks ($6.00) to over $1,000 a "trick"—and a girl of class can get even more.

Many of the girls now have a piggy bank in their rooms, with a sign attached, *"Für den Vater Staat* [For Father State] ."

Since in Germany the churches derive most of their income from the church tax, roughly 1 percent of members' incomes or 10 percent of their income tax, which is administered by the state tax authorities, such revenue poses a delicate problem; most Germans, churchgoing or not, are registered with a church. The Evangelical Church of Hanover as well as the Lutheran State Church of Hamburg want no part in the wages of sin. The Evangelical Church Association of Cologne, however, justifies its acceptance of the monies with the argument, "The Church is a community of believing sinners. There are no members of inferior quality."

Catholic authorities are also divided, but most districts quietly pocket the tax money.

Homosexuality

Homosexuality appears to be a growing phenomenon in West Germany; in most large cities, bars and dance halls "for men only" are in strong evidence. There are no reliable statistics available, but estimates range between one and two million homosexuals, allowing for the occasional and borderline instances. The notorious paragraph 175 of the German penal code, dating back to 1871, which made homosexuality a crime, has been repealed, along with penalties for sodomy and adultery. Nevertheless, according to the Erlangen theologian (Evangelical) Hans Joachim Schoeps, "The Third Reich, where homosexuals are concerned, has not yet ended."

Public opinion is still strongly opposed to homosexuality. In a 1969 public opinion survey carried out by the Allensbach Institute, 46 percent of respondents favored continuation of penalties for homosexuality, while 36 percent were opposed and 18 percent expressed "no opinion."

During the Nazi era, some 8,000 homosexuals were annually placed in concentration camps, compared to 800 annually arrested and sentenced to short prison terms before this period. Today, police have thorough "homo-lists" and automatically make systematic inquiries among known homosexuals whenever a sex crime occurs. In Kassel a teacher was dismissed from his post merely because he befriended a known homosexual, even though the latter was a highly cultivated and learned person. Homosexual couples who attempt to share an apartment together are exposed to constant humiliations and insults, even if their outward appearance is identical with that of other men.

In the GDR penalties for consenting adult homosexuality have been abolished, although severe penalties do remain for the seduction of minors.

Abortion

In the Federal Republic there are annually about 1 million births and an estimated 500,000 to 1.5 million abortions, or roughly one abortion for every birth. According to conservative estimates, about 250 women die annually as a result of attempted abortions.

Under present laws, only one form of abortion, the so-called "medical indication" *i.e.,* when the mother's life is endangered, is recognized as legal. They do not take into account economic or other factors in already large families ("social indication"), or indications that the embryo could be mentally or physically retarded ("eugenic indication"), or pregnancy as a result of rape ("ethical indication"). However, this issue is a subject of continuous debate. The proposed new abortion law would permit termination of early pregnancy on request, while consent of a medical jury would be required in advanced cases.

In spite of permissiveness and the gradual liberalization of sex legislation, which some interpret as immorality run rampant in Germany, sober observers are quick to point out that, from the long historic point of view, present manners and morals are tame compared with orgiastic periods of the past.

Around 1500 Hieronymus Bosch created his famous painting *Garden of Delights,* which portrays sexual depravity compared to which the "sweet, mild *Mädchen*" of today's Germany are as innocent as the marzipan candy creations of Nuremberg.

The wickedest dives of Hamburg are tame compared with the dance crazes in the sixteenth century—a chronicler describes one in which male dancers were lasciviously licking the exposed behinds of their partners. The sex parties of Bamberg or Heilbronn that make the headlines of West Germany's scandal sheets, pale in comparison to the Renaissance "naked games" of Nuremberg recorded in 1468, or to the bathhouses of the late middle ages where underwater orgies were a part of the daily scene. "What glorious swine our great, great grandfathers were," observed the historian Joachim Fernau recently.

With the Reformation and Counter-Reformation and the Lutheran concept of guilt came the new emphasis on sexual morality and related sense of shame, guilt, and abhorrence of the "lower" impulses of the human body. The epitome of Victorian prudery was reached in 1890 when leading physicians of Europe issued a decree stating that it is villainous slander to claim that women have sexual feelings.

It took the cataclysm of World War I to release the sexual repression of women. By 1922, during the Weimar Republic, a *Deutscher Bund für Mutterschutz und Sexualreform* (German League for the Protection of Motherhood and Sexual Reform) was established which tried to abolish traditional notions of guilt and sin in connection with sex and establish new norms for sex education. But in *Mein Kampf* Adolf Hitler wrote, "Public life must be freed from the stifling perfume of our modern eroticism," introducing a new puritanical era.

Once more, it was an upheaval—World War II—which fully unleashed the emancipation process.

A team of sociologists under the guidance of Professor T. Hitpass learned in a survey undertaken in 1965 that out of 100 respondents—unmarried twenty-year-olds—58 girls and 68 boys had engaged in intimate relations with the opposite sex.

Further investigations revealed a pronounced class difference in the sexual experience among young girls. Girls in trade schools and in rural areas showed a marked higher percentage of sexual experience than university students or city dwellers.

Considerable dust was raised when in the fall of 1969 eighth and ninth-graders in West Germany received a "Sex Atlas" which frankly describes the technique of sexual intercourse and provides information on methods of contraception. The book makes no moral judgment on premarital sex, includes color photographs of the reproductive process, the effects of venereal disease, and was prepared by the government. It was described by the Federal Health Ministry officials as one of the most comprehensive and advanced sex-education programs for school-children anywhere.

Only recently has the question of sex education in the schools been treated on a massive scale. And the Christian churches, long regarded as old-fashioned and intolerant on this question, have belatedly moved toward more liberal policies. Monsignor Paul Adenauer, son of the late chancellor, and previously regarded as highly conservative like his father, demanded in an article that church, school, and state work more closely in developing a "completely clear sexual pedagogy." He also insisted that German families take more responsibility in educating their children on sexual matters from an early age.

In a survey by sex researchers in West Germany, it was revealed that only a quarter of thirteen- and fourteen-year-olds in the country discuss sexual matters with their parents.

Something has begun to develop in Germany that until recently was regarded as a purely American phenomenon—the emergence of petting (*i.e.*, sexual play short of intercourse). The same young Germans who regard the morality of their parents and their churches as ridiculous and old-fashioned are imposing restrictions of their own. In an extensive study of "sexual knowledge of youth," the Evangelical theologian Heinz Hunger concludes that early and objective sex education among the young tends, contrary to popular belief, to promote rather than destroy sexual restraint.

In the same study Hunger discovered that rural youth, where promiscuity is found to be much much higher, is astoundingly ignorant of sexual matters. According to psychologist Dr. Esther Harding, "Young girls of today succumb just as easily to the new conventions that require sexual participation as their grand-mothers succumbed to conventions that forbade it." It is only because permissiveness has become respectable that it is so widely accepted. At least where Germany is concerned, respect-ability is the decisive factor in sexual morality.

The late Professor Hans Giese, director of the Institute for Sexual Research at Hamburg University, discovered to his astonishment that half of the coeds who answered his question-naires about sexual experiences were still virgins. "The mere fact that the old morality is no longer accepted as valid," he said, "does not mean that all morality has ceased. Somewhere within the traditional concept of immorality are the seeds of a new moral order."

As for the male students, sociologists, researchers, and church leaders tend to concur in the view that the permissiveness of the new society basically frightens them more than it tyrannizes them. There is a decided trend toward "steady partnerships" which psychologists explain as a kind of refuge from the impersonal collectivized loneliness in large universities.

Much of the sexual intensity and sex-cult activity is attributed to the ennui of married couples who enter their wedding night in boring repetition of a fixed habit. The glut of sex literature, films, and advertising has given rise to a national inferiority complex of individuals whose sex life seldom if ever is the ecstatic, immeasurable, seventh-heaven experience that the illusory world has made it out to be. As a result there is an almost frenzied preoccupation with love-making techniques, and more married couples than ever before seek relief from their boredom by endless experimentation.

Conspicuously often, physicians, psychotherapists, and religious marriage counselors report of masculine psychically-rooted impotence. They receive constant complaints from women whose husbands around the age of thirty "only go to bed with me about once a month or even every three months," according to marriage counselor, Reverend Adolf Sommerauer. He places the blame squarely on the continual exposure to superwomen, "so that they are no longer enticed by women who do not look like the oversexed dolls in the films and mass-circulation magazines."

"It is," says psychologist Ernst von Xylander, "an age of the over-evaluation of the orgasm which causes many women to accuse their husbands of being incapable of satisfying them."

Helga

Once they realize their deficiencies, leave it to the Germans to go about rectifying the situation with a super grim determination and thoroughness. While the French often regard sex as a game, the Danes, as a reality, and the Swedes, as poetry, the Germans seem to regard it as something to be analyzed—and explained and explained and explained.

It all started with *Helga* a seventy-five-minute *Aufklaerungs-film* (Enlightenment Film), a government-subsidized sex-education documentary, filmed at a university clinic, which depicts the story of a young married girl from pregnancy to birth. The opening scene shows a pollster going from tough dock workers to elderly women in shopping centers, asking if they received sex instructions as children. In nearly every case the answer was an embarrassed "no." Then it went on to explain the "facts of life." The highlight of the film was an actual birth scene, which caused hundreds of persons to faint at the sight and an estimated 90 percent to turn their heads.

The astonishing success of the film, which distributor Hanns Echelcamp slapped together on a skimpy budget of $200,000, most of it from the government grant, yielded over $3,500,000 in Germany alone. It was a runaway box-office hit around the world. According to *Variety* it easily rivaled *The Boston Strangler* and *Paper Lion* in Baltimore, while compiling big grosses all over the U.S.

Inevitably a whole rash of sex "documentaries" followed, notably by sexpert Oswalt Kolle, whose books and films dominate the sexology market in Germany: *Your Wife, the Unknown Creature,* in which actors demonstrate a variety of positions for sexual intercourse, while a narrator in a white smock, who of course is a *Herr Professor,* dryly explains the proceedings in clinical detail; *Miracle of Love; The Perfect Marriage; Helga and Michael,* the story of a courtship from first kiss to consummation, and *Helga and the Sexual Revolution,* in which the heroine discovers the orgy.

I have seen a number of these films and found them to be sentimental, preachy, responsible, and incredibly dull. My views are shared by dozens of experts and film critics with whom I have discussed these films. Non-Germans especially regard these films, as much of the German approach to sex, as too plodding, analytical, and above all characterized by *Tierischerernst* (animal-like seriousness).

Birth Control

In spite of the birth control pill there are proportionately more childbirths today than a decade ago. In 1959, 812,000 children saw the light of day compared with 1,052,000 in 1966. At the same time, thanks to the pill, the number of illegitimate births declined. Whereas 120 out of 1,000 newborn babies were illegitimate in 1860, in 1962 there were only 56 and in 1965 only 47. In this connection it is interesting that 12 percent of all German women of childbearing age, or only 2 million, take the pill, while 14 million adamantly decline, not only the 20 percent who want children, but the many German women who fear possible side effects.

Until recently such subjects as conception, birth control, contraception had surprisingly little official attention in German society. In 1969 there were only six major birth control information clinics run by the local branch of the international Planned Parenthood League (Pro Familia) in West Germany, compared with 650 in England.

Although birth control devices are widely available, the country's 1871 law, which held that prescribing them is immoral, was only recently liberalized, leaving physicians in uncertainty and inhibiting the expansion of public clinic programs until now.

The controversial papal encyclical *Humanae Vitae* issued in 1968 created a stir in Germany as it did everywhere else. According to a survey sponsored by *Der Spiegel* half a year before the appearance of the encyclical, 81 percent of Catholics in the Federal Republic were of the opinion that the birth control pill was none of the pope's business. Only one Catholic in six spoke in favor of a prohibition of the pill. Well over half of the married Catholic respondents admitted to using birth control pills and other devices.

The stock of the firm Berliner Schering AG, the largest West German contraceptive manufacturer (60 percent), rose in the aftermath of the papal encyclical. Five thousand participants in the Eighty-second German Catholic Conference *(Katholikentag)* at Essen in 1968 staged an open rebellion against Pope Paul VI's encyclical. Numerous demonstrators strutted around the meeting grounds with big signs captioned, "We don't talk about the pill, we take it." And the meeting ended with a resolution demanding a revision of the papal position.

The West German Roman Catholic episcopate endorsed the encyclical in a cautious statement, with the reservation that the pope's word on contraception "is not infallible" and left the door open for the individual conscience as the ultimate criterion.

Illegitimate Children

Until 1969 illegitimate children in the Federal Republic were still social and legal outcasts and widely discriminated against. In 1966 a Bonn court stipulated that illegitimate children were not entitled to a share in the inheritance of their parents as were the legitimate children of either parent.

Although illegitimate children have been the underprivileged of German society for generations, ironically Germany—and Europe—has produced a whole series of illustrious "bastards." Just as the Renaissance Pope Alexander VI unabashedly favored his bastard offspring, and William the Conqueror of England dubbed himself with a straightforward "Bastard" nickname, so Kätchen of Heilbronn was promoted to princess once the Kaiser recognized her as his "natural daughter." The victor in the famous Battle of Lepanto, Don Juan of Austria, is the progeny of a liaison of the Emperor Karl V and the daughter of a Regensburg burgher. Other historic illegitimate progeny were: the Prussian hero, Count Yorck of Wartenburg; Cosima Wagner, daughter of Franz Liszt; Hitler's father Alois Schickelgruber; and the assassinated (in 1934) Austrian Chancellor Engelbert Dollfuss.

Chancellor Willy Brandt makes no attempt to hide his illegitimate birth, which the late Konrad Adenauer snidely referred to at the height of election campaigns.

Traditional Roman Catholic theology still brands illegitimate children as embodied sin, technically labeled *irregulares ex defectu* (materialized defect). "Thus it occurs that they [illegitimate children]," according to moral theologian Professor Waldemar Molinski, "frequently develop psychic complexes, and soon are relegated to the role of outsiders."

The Evangelical Church permits the individual member churches to decide whether they will bless the illegitimate children or not.

However, the new breed of theologians in both confessions have rejected such forms of legalistic discrimination outright and the ultimate elimination of such discrimination from ecclesiastical jurisprudence is only a matter of time.

In this as in other matters related to sex, it is hoped that the new legal reforms will eliminate the crazy-quilt pattern of justice that has characterized German communities. The cases are legion of persons being imprisoned for what is a crime in one community but perfectly legal just a few miles away. Severe penalties were frequently meted out to individuals who were often helpless victims of a technicality, while blatant prostitution went on unpunished. Thus in the predominantly Catholic city of Passau a sixty-eight-year-old bricklayer and his sixty-three-year-old wife were sentenced to four weeks in prison for "pandering" because they "tolerated" the common-law relationship of their son (age forty-two) with a forty-one-year-old woman and their four illegitimate children.

The new reforms, initiated in 1969, are designed to remove the last remaining obstacles to complete rehabilitation. No illegitimate children in the future will be deprived of inheritance rights, and the age until which a father of an illegitimate child must pay for the child's upbringing and education has been lowered to eighteen.

Although the Germans will hardly retreat from their hard-won freedom from sexual repression, there is growing evidence of boredom with all that exposed flesh. The Danish porno slot machines near the German border are begging for customers. The slick, mass-circulation youth magazine, *Twen,* ceased publication, in spite of increased pornographic illustrations. Beate Uhse's international mail order house for sexual devices reportedly suffered a decline in sales in 1971. Just as in the United States, nostalgic romanticism is sweeping across the land. But, "Das Deutsche Vita" nonetheless is here to stay.

◄21►

"WE ARE SOMEBODIES AGAIN!"

"THE ITALIANS WORK to live, the Germans live to work."

This saying, of course, is a generalization and like all generalizations must be taken with more than a grain of salt. At the same time, the German attitude toward work is undoubtedly the secret weapon without which the now famous German "Economic Miracle" would not have happened. Other war-torn European nations received aid under the Marshall Plan, but none of them knew how to put it to such good use as the Germans.

The West German economic boom began on June 20, 1948, with the enactment of the currency reform in the three Western occupation zones. From 1945 to 1948 the Germans lived in dire poverty, many of them in a state of utter destitution. After Hitler had assumed power, he had pursued a reckless financial policy which steadily reduced the value of the Reichsmark. Owing to the immense expenditure of armaments and the war, the Reichsmark was only worth a fraction of its former value after the collapse. Consumer goods were virtually nonexistent and food was scarce. In Cologne Archbishop Josef Frings even preached in his sermons that "taking coal and other necessities under these circumstances cannot be regarded as stealing." The Rhinelanders coined a word for it—"fringsen." The black market with its runaway inflation, exorbitant prices, and illegal goods thrived.

Thanks to the currency reform, the populace soon possessed a stable currency once more—but at what a price! The reform wiped out the life savings of millions of Germans. But it did prevent the dreaded repetition of the Weimar period, when a wheelbarrow full of bank notes would hardly buy a loaf of bread.

Compared with the Swiss franc, one of the world's most consistently stable currencies, the German mark at first enjoyed little confidence abroad. Shortly after the currency reform only 18 Swiss francs were needed to purchase 100 Deutsche marks. By 1952, however, 100 DM's could buy 94 Swiss francs, and a year

336

and a half later the mark had already exceeded the Swiss franc in hardness, with the exchange rate rising to 100 DM's for 105 Swiss francs. In 1969 the DM was revaluated, increasing its exchange rate to 116 Swiss francs for 100 DM's, or 3.68 DM's to a dollar (up from 4 to a dollar).

The real proof of the economic strength and hardness of the DM came in February, 1953, when the Federal Republic confidently signed the London Debt Agreement, acknowledging her pre- and post-war debts, a total of $3.6 billion, to be paid over a period of years. For the first time foreign investors gained confidence in German credit.

Between the time of the currency reform in 1948 and mid-1954, West Germany increased her overall industrial production by 230 percent. By the end of 1953 the West German shipbuilding industry attained second place in world construction—an astounding feat, considering that her wartime merchant fleet boasting over 4 million gross tons, was reduced to less than 144,000 tons of battered and obsolete shipping. In the chemical industry, traditionally one of Germany's strongest concerns, she won one-sixth of the world trade by 1952.

German Fairy Tale

Nothing symbolizes this economic recovery more than the Volkswagen story, which reads like a German fairy tale. It originated as a massive Nazi swindle which milked $225 each from some 336,000 gullible Germans who foolishly believed their small investment in the construction of a plant producing the "people's car" would materialize in their proud ownership of an otherwise unattainable automobile. Instead, the regime used the money for armaments production and not one civilian received a Volks until after the Allied Occupation.

Ironically, the British, who are now suffering greatly from German competition, especially in the automobile market, went out of their way to restore the Volkswagen plant (65 percent destroyed by bombs) to a production of twenty vehicles a day.

In Hamburg they found a penniless former director of the Opel (General Motors) works, Dr. Heinz Nordhoff, with only one suit and two neckties to his name, and persuaded him to take over the Volkswagen management. Helped by Marshall aid, Nordhoff transformed the ugly beetle project into one of the world's most successful industries. He liked to tell his workers the old Prussian motto, "Work hard, don't brag, and be bigger than you appear." But his methods were American. Hard sell American-style played a big role in Volkswagen's success, as well as the "German Miracle" itself. From Wolfsburg, headquarters of the Volkswagen plant, dozens of smart, well-groomed "customer consultants" fly regularly to all corners of the world equipped with the latest psychological know-how. They carry half a suitcase full of multilingual booklets that break the human race down into forty-one basic types for the salesmen to convince: "The Hesitator," "The Smart Alec," "The Tightwad," and "The Bully." With endless illustrations and pedantic German explanations the salesmen are told how to manage every situation.

I shall never forget my first visit to the VW plant in 1960. Another American journalist, who was an official guest of the German government, and I were picked up at the plush Atlantic Hotel in Hamburg, the famous haunt of people like William Holden, Marlene Dietrich, and the royal couple of Thailand. The VW firm was building only the small beetle at that time, and I couldn't help but break into a belly laugh while waiting for a Rolls Royce to get out of the way, as we squeezed into a tiny Volks, driven, so help me, by a burly six-foot, smartly uniformed chauffeur with white gloves, which he kept on the entire ninety miles to Wolfsburg. He disapproved of my poking fun at his uniform but relaxed on the way back by sharing a beer with us—without hat, coat, gloves, and insignia.

Today the gigantic Volkswagen plant looms like a latter-day fortress in the Lower Saxony wheat fields and pine woods, where the Mittelland Canal surrounds the plant like a moat. Here a swinging, modern town of over 100,000 inhabitants has emerged with even the churches and schools decorated with the famous beetle design in mosaics and murals, and the main street is called Porsche Strasse after the designer of the Volks.

All employees have modern housing and every worker automatically receives a 100 DM ($28) bonus on his wedding day and 50 DM's on the birth of each child, even if illegitimate. Some 30,000 workers receive the highest wages in Germany, turning out some 1,800,000 vehicles a year, out of a total production of 3,500,000 annually produced by the West German automobile industry (Opel, Ford, Daimler-Benz, Auto-Union, NSU, VW, and BMW).

At the beginning of 1970 there were 720,000 jobs vacant in the Federal Republic, less than 200,000 unemployed (under 1 percent). In addition, there were 1,230,000 employed foreigners from Italy (25 percent), Turkey (14.9 percent), Yugoslavia (14.3 percent), Greece (13.3 percent), Spain (10.3 percent), and Portugal (2 percent).

From a material point of view, German families never had it so good. According to the Federal Economics Ministry, the average male German saves nearly 2,000 DM's (about $550) annually, smokes 2,214 cigarettes and drinks 163 quarts of beer. A family of four, according to an Allensbach Institute survey, requires 650 DM's ($180) minimum monthly to live. A German worker must work five minutes for a quart of milk, compared to fifteen minutes by a Soviet worker, eight minutes by a French worker, six minutes by a British worker, or three minutes by an American worker.

More than two-thirds of all German households have a refrigerator, more than 50 percent, a TV set, and German families own some fourteen million motor vehicles, or about 200 automobiles for every 1,000 inhabitants, just behind the USA, Sweden, France, and Britain, but ahead of Switzerland, whose wage level and standard of living is actually higher.

In 1969 alone more than 700,000 automatic washing machines and 170,000 automatic dishwashers were sold in West Germany. In 14 percent of all households and in over half of all apartments constructed in 1969, thermostated oil, electric, and remote-control heating units have taken over the traditional use of briquets for home heating. According to a DIVO Institute (Frankfurt) survey, 75 percent of all households purchase packaged soups, 79 percent own vacuum cleaners, 23 percent regularly have their clothes laundered, and six million eat lunch daily at the plant cafeteria.

Income has increased to 6,067 DM's per inhabitant, or 13,369 DM's (nearly $4,000) per adult employee annually. The weekly salary of an industrial worker has topped $50 and thus increased 241 percent in sixteen years. Although inflation has taken its toll, an estimated salary increase of 139 percent within this period still remains after taking its effects into account. Thus, while many products costing 100 marks in 1950 today cost 143.10 marks, the buying power of the German mark remains formidable. An average industrial worker needs to put in 932 hours and 36 minutes to buy a Volkswagen, which is 54 hours less than a year previously.

The prevailing social status in the Federal Republic is middle-class respectability. Skid row, slums, the Bowery—such concepts are foreign to the German scene. But there are pockets of misery in the midst of prosperity. The differences of income between individual cities and country regions is often extreme, though never as bad as parts of Italy, Greece, Spain, or even the United Kingdom. And there is nothing even remotely like Harlem, West Virginia, or Chicago's Sixty-third Street.

Nearly half of the population of rural Selfkant-Geilenkirchen (49 percent) earns less than 6,000 DM's ($1,700) a year, while the number of persons earning such a small salary in Düsseldorf is under 39 percent. More than four million pensioners have a monthly income of only 200 DM's ($60). Even if planned reforms raise this to $80, the senior citizens still have to compensate their meager pensions with part-time work merely to survive. Many old-age pensioners are said to receive "too much to die on, not enough to live on."

In the Volkswagen town of Wolfsburg the average wage earner pays over $200 in annual income tax, while in rural Zweibrücken, 200 miles away, only 41 DM's ($8.50) annual income tax is paid.

However, the dominant note on which West Germany entered the seventies was one of exuberant prosperity.

How It Was Possible

Credit for West Germany's prosperity of course is due to many persons and many factors. But there is one man more than any other with whom the "economic miracle" is most closely associated: Ludwig Erhard, the corpulent, cigar-smoking minister of economics in the Adenauer cabinet, himself no mean symbol of West German prosperity. A member of the resistance movement, he became economic advisor to the Allied military authorities as early as 1945. He had a decisive influence in the administration of the "Bi-Zone" organized by the American and British military governments in the establishment of currency reform. Against the advice of most experts, he immediately abolished rationing and price control. It is true that his image as father of the economic miracle was tarnished by his short stint as chancellor, being ousted for ineptitude. Nevertheless, his brilliant stroke formed the basis for a free-market economy and the recovery leading to economic boom and stability.

However, the success of Erhard's policies would have been impossible without many other important elements. We can briefly mention five chief factors here:

1) The fundamental factor that made the German economic miracle possible was of course the Marshall Plan. In pre-Marshall aid days, Germany received G.A.R.I.O.A. funds (Government and Relief in Occupied Areas), which reached its peak between 1947-49, with an annual expenditure of some $580 million. After the currency reform, the European Recovery Program, more popularly named after U.S. Secretary of State George C. Marshall who proposed it, became effective, which poured over $3.5 billion into Germany up until 1953.

Although West German leaders and publicists have not ceased repeatedly to acknowledge the importance of Marshall Plan aid, American friends of Germany are constantly disappointed in everyday conversation by the prevailing attitude that all their successes are of course a result of their own ability and Erhard's stroke of genius. No other nation in history has shown this kind of generosity to its vanquished foes, yet few if any Germans ever stop to think what Americans might have expected had Hitler destroyed American cities and marched triumphantly to the White House.

2) Another important development was the influx of more than ten million refugees from the German eastern territories and East Germany. Although at first this migration evoked the specter of mass unemployment, this proved a blessing in disguise, for it created at once a gigantic consumer market, aggravated the housing need (while stimulating the housing boom), and provided an almost unlimited reservoir of—mostly skilled—manpower from all branches of industry.

3) British colleagues I meet in Germany never fail to point out that economically the real victor of World War II was Germany. Grotesque as it may sound, the dismantling and destruction of German factories gave them the unique opportunity of starting from scratch with a complete reorganization of their entire industry from the gound up and with completely new machinery

341

and equipment, while Britain and other European countries were for the most part saddled with outmoded methods and machinery.

4) The Equalization of Burdens Law, enacted in 1952, was a gigantic scheme applying internally some of the same principles and procedures as the Marshall Plan externally. The State was simply unable to provide compensation to the vast number of refugees, and to those millions who had lost their homes, property, savings, businesses, and old-age pensions during the war and subsequent period of inflation. The Government saw only one possible way to provide blanket aid for massive recovery, and that was the equalization of burdens idea. Under a long-term plan spread over several decades, levies were imposed on farmers, businessmen, and property owners with undamaged assets, in order to raise the billions of marks needed to aid those who suffered damage or loss of property, especially those who were bombed out, and to give them the initiative and means for a new livelihood. Through this plan some 40 billion marks (over $9 billion) were allocated for all categories of assistance, from old-age pensions to the revival of businesses formerly located in the east.

This revolutionary Equalization of Burdens Law (*Lastenausgleichgesetz*) made it possible to put into operation an entirely new, dynamic social policy that automatically increased old-age pensions on a blanket basis according to cost-of-living indexes, introduced children's allowances, and launched a massive housing construction program.

5) The German "secret weapon" is their *Fleiss* (industriousness). Without the invisible asset of the German attitude—and capacity—for work, the "German miracle" would be unthinkable. This assertion of course is a touchy matter and requires qualification, which will be given later in this chapter. Moreover, as we shall see, this German dedication and thoroughness, has been on the wane in recent years. Nevertheless, it cannot be dismissed as a vital factor in West Germany's postwar recovery.

When a German returns from a vacation his friends and neighbors do not ask, "Did you have a nice time?" but rather, *"Haben Sie sich gut* erholt [Have you *recovered* well]?"— vacation is not regarded as a pleasure in itself but an opportunity to "recover" from two periods of work.

342

Or take as another example, the exceptionally few strikes in West Germany—at least until the seventies—as compared with other countries. In 1965 only 6,300 German workers went on strike compared with 880,000 in the United Kingdom, 1.2 million in France, and 2.4 million in Italy. The Germans in that year lost only 49,500 working days compared to England's 2,900,000, France's 980,000, and Italy's 7,600,000. Also, 46.5 percent of the German population is employed compared with 51 percent in Eastern European countries and only 39.5 percent in the other Common Market countries.

In 1966 some 27,000 West German employees struck, with 196,000 lost working days. In 1967, some 60,000 persons on payrolls took part in strikes with about 390,000 working days lost. In 1968 the Federal Office of Statistics reported that a total of 25,167 employees of 36 firms went on strikes, accounting for a total of 25,249 lost days.

The average duration of a strike, measured per worker, is only about one day. In many strikes, the time lost from work is measured in hours.

The reasons for this can be found not only in the German mentality, but also must be attributed to a comprehensive social legislation that is older and far more advanced than most other countries. It was Bismarck after all who in 1881, when most other European countries were caught in industrial turmoil, assured himself of the German workers' loyalty by giving them the first social insurance system in the world.

The Trade Unions

West Germany's trade unions never fail to puzzle visitors and infuriate native extremists who cannot understand this labor movement's complete indifference to *Klassenkampf* (class warfare). Rugged individualism and laissez-faire have been completely foreign concepts to the German mentality with its deeply ingrained sense of order and discipline.

In the period prior to World War I Germany's trade unions turned their backs on the leftist revolt led by Rosa Luxemburg and Karl Liebknecht. In 1918, in the face of the Bolshevist threat, they made a pact with management in return for substantial benefits. And since World War II, trade union leaders have dismissed the militants with a disdainful, "Why kill the cow you are milking?"

When the democratic trade unions, which were prohibited by the Nazi regime, were reestablished, they had a unique opportunity to restructure the labor system from scratch. Abandoning the idea of organizing workers in the traditional small crafts unions covering many industries simultaneously, the unions now cover whole industries. Contrary to the American system of company contracts, collective bargaining in West Germany is carried out exclusively by the industrial unions for whole industries. There are no closed shops in Germany. Hiring rackets cannot develop because the state's employment agency *(Arbeitsamt)* has a monopoly. Corruption and racketeering have not so far besmirched the image of German trade unions, not because they are above human temptation but because the German structure enables them to achieve most of their aims through hard bargaining. Until the fall of 1969, wildcat strikes were virtually unknown in West Germany because three-fourths of the members of a given union must approve a strike before it is legal. A wave of strikes throughout the country coinciding with the 1969 national elections gave rise to much speculation as to whether the relatively strike-free period was over and a new trend was in the offing. The prevailing view of experts appears to be that the stability of West German labor will remain a constant even if here and there occasional strike waves cause momentary unrest.[1]

The heart of the German system is *Mitbestimmung* (codetermination) or worker-management participation. Many outsiders shudder when they first learn about the extensive amount of labor participation in German industry and immediately cry, "Socialism!" And, for that matter, codetermination is still a controversial issue in Germany too, but it is a question of degree and not of kind. At any rate, limited codetermination has successfully been a part of labor-management relations for many years.

The Industrial Constitution Law *(Betriebsverfassungsgesetz)* of 1952 provides that all businesses with five or more employees must create a plant council *(Betriebsrat)* to represent employees' interests. In stock companies, employees' delegates comprise one-third of the supervisory board *(Aufsichtsrat)*, which appoints and supervises the board of directors *(Vorstand)*. In family-owned companies that have no supervisory board or less than 500 employees, codetermination is limited to the plant council. In enterprises with more than 100 employees, industrial committees are established. These must regularly be kept informed of manufacturing and operational methods, production programs, the financial status of the enterprise, production and sales figures, and any development substantially affecting the employees.

Workers in the Federal Republic are among the highest paid for almost the shortest working weeks in Europe. The acute manpower shortages of Germany's booming industries in the fifties and sixties compelled them to outbid one another in offering benefits to workers already accustomed to the protection of national social legislation, family allowances, old-age pensions, sick leave, and health insurance.

Although the right to strike is guaranteed by law, West German labor leaders for the most part find this self-defeating because the interests of the labor unions are so intricately woven into the fabric of German society, and because West German unions have become cooperative and responsible partners in industry and government to a degree unknown elsewhere. Union representatives sit on the boards of all major German industries, in the bodies governing radio and television, in the Bundestag (there are no less than 242 unionists among the 521 deputies), and in many supranational European organizations.

Of the nearly twenty-five million employed persons in the Federal Republic, about one-third are organized in unions (in comparison, about 25 percent of the U.S. labor force are members of trade unions). In individual occupations, however, the proportion of union members is even higher. For example, four-fifths of miners, two-thirds of railway workers, one-half of metal workers are members of a trade union.

The German metal workers union, with two million members, is the largest individual trade union in the free world. It is one of the sixteen autonomous trade unions belonging to the German Trade Union Federation (Deutsche Gewerkschaftsbund—DGB), the central organization of German labor and the largest employees' organization in Europe, with its headquarters on Kennedydamm (after John F. Kennedy) in Düsseldorf. This federation contains more than 6.5 million members, including the largest percentage of all the manual and clerical workers organized in German trade unions. More than 80 percent of the members are skilled and unskilled laborers, 11 percent white collar workers, and 8 percent civil servants. One million are women.

In addition to the DGB, several other important trade union umbrella organizations should be mentioned: the German White-Collar Trade Union *(Deutsche Angestellten Gewerkschaft—DAG)* with nearly 500,000 members; the Christian Trade Union Federation, with 200,000 members; the German Federation of Civil Service employees *(Deutscher Beamtenbund)*, with 680,000 members.

Officials at the Düsseldorf DGB headquarters share the concensus that what is good for the economy is good for labor. Management to them is not a class enemy but a somewhat phlegmatic "partner." Nationalization or union shops have long been dropped as union's goals. Walkouts do sometimes occur, but because of the years of relative peace, strike funds (provided by the well-heeled union banks) have become an "overkill" deterrent which has wheedled many a compromise from management.

And the unions themselves believe in being reasonable. As one DGB official put it, "Our research staff keeps us informed what a given industry can afford, and how far we can go." The German dread of inflation, which has twice in less than two generations wiped out their savings, is a powerful deterrent to abuse.

For the unions, the "partnership" concept has paid off. Germany's trade unions employ 24,000 persons, own banks, insurance companies, construction firms, a total of 143 enterprises at home and abroad. They produce furniture, jam, detergents, matches, razor blades, cigarettes, *Schnaps,* and hair spray.

The Bank für Gemeinwirtschaft in Frankfurt, the fourth largest in the Federal Republic, is the hub of labor's expanding economic empire. Built from a pittance in war reparations funds paid to unions victimized by the Nazi regime, it has sprawled out to 190 branches whose clientele includes some of the giants of German industry itself. From its penthouse executive suite you can look out the window to the distant, high-rise towers of Nord-West Stadt, a self-contained city developed primarily by union-controlled building and real estate investment companies for $50 million.

To avoid conflicts of interest, the bank strictly follows a policy against owning industrial stock. Yet it has helped bail out any

346

number of firms, and it has also extended credit to a plastics firm, hit by a strike, that needed it to survive.

As a result of all this prosperity West Germany's trade unions have become, in the eyes of its growing number of critics, fat, complacent, and stagnant. While in 1952 some 6 million out of 15 million employed were members of trade unions, in 1969 with 25 million employed the membership increased by only half a million to 6.5 million. Because of overemployment, firms have been compelled to cater to workers' demands to such a degree that unions are often superfluous.

Thousands of union members and functionaries of the individual trade unions belonging to the DGB are disenchanted by the DGB's failure to reduce West German taxes, among the highest in the world, to improve social legislation, and to implement more comprehensive codetermination in the factories. There is still widespread dissatisfaction about the manner of handling hardship cases of employees dismissed as a result of rationalization or automation, with demands ranging from more severance pay to fully-paid-for retraining programs, to "study vacations," a plan by which an employee at full salary could go on a "sabbatical" year in order to take courses improving his professional standing.

The effectiveness of the DGB is curtailed because many of its individual member unions, resenting curtailment of their power, have denied the DGB amendments in its statutes, and otherwise restricted its power in order to preserve their own independence.

The greatest body of disgruntled unionists are the 600,000 leftist-oriented under-thirty *Jugend des DGB* (DGB Youth), which has no voting power in the DGB. Among their demands: recognition of the GDR and the Oder-Neisse territories; contracts with the *Freie Deutsche Gewerkschaftsbund* (FDGB) of the GDR and with communist trade unions in Western Europe; ideological and financial support of the DGB for disarmament and pacifist organizations; and the establishment of a permanent watchdog committee with the machinery to launch a nationwide general strike instantly in the event of undemocratic government abuse, especially in respect to the controversial emergency laws, which restrict democratic procedure in the event of a national or international emergency.

The DGB has also been severely criticized for alleged dishonesty in the disclosure of its funds. Thus in 1968 the Deutsche Industrie Institute in Cologne, a management-oriented organization, estimated the total holdings of the DGB at 1.5 billion DM's (nearly $400 million), while the DGB itself places its assets at only one-tenth of this or 164,349,000 DM's.

Even though *Mitbestimmung* already is a part of West German worker-management structure, the trade unions are now pushing for *paritätische Mitbestimmung, i.e., equal* mandated codetermination, which would compel large companies to give workers up to half the votes on boards of governors.

Under the previous system, codetermination and consultation of the workers' council were confined to personnel and social matters, working conditions, working hours, vacation schedules, wages. It did not extend to decision-making of management investments. The workers' council, for example, has had the right of codetermination in the administration of the company's welfare facilities, but has had no say about determining how the funds should be spent.

What the unions are now aiming at is not a change in the distribution of capital, but greater control in the employees' interests, more right of decision in the expenditure of capital, *i.e.,* a share in decision-making by partial control of management.

In the eyes of the unionists *Mitbestimmung* represents nothing more than the final merger of the workers' movement with the system it once attacked. Labor unions have invented such phrases as "industrial democracy," and refer to codetermination as simply a "comprehensive plan to achieve the integration of the working people in industry . . . for active partnership and the right of codetermination in all those industrial enterprises which by their importance for the entire population affect the entire economic life of the country," as one official put it.

The DGB wants to introduce this new version of *Mitbestimmung* to all enterprises that have 2,000 employees or more, with an annual turnover of more than 150 million DM's, or profits exceeding 75 million DM's. This would apply to 393 companies and approximately 70 percent of West German industrial manpower.

This highly revolutionary issue is of course hotly debated in the Federal Republic and will probably remain a controversial issue for some time. Opposition is strong, as is the growing fear that the unions are becoming too powerful already. There are cries of "socialization!" and "a threat to the social and economic system!"

Even Chancellor Willy Brandt's Social Democratic Party has cautiously proposed a milder form of codetermination (partly out of deference to the somewhat more conservative Free Democratic Party of coalition partner, Foreign Minister Walter Scheel). They would give the unions less say in determining delegates to the supervisory board and prefer a two-thirds majority for the managing board. Critics point out that full codetermination would create opposing blocs and eventually cripple management effectiveness. They argue that basic rights of private property are threatened, and that the unions selfishly want to share the benefits of free enterprise without assuming the commensurate risks.

The Common Market

European unification is still a distant goal, if not a Utopian dream. The fluctuations of NATO; the immense difficulties afflicting the common agricultural market; the complications of West Germany's opening to the east; the problem complex accompanying the United Kingdom's possible membership; tensions in the wake of the devaluation of the French franc and the revaluation of the Deutsche mark in 1969—all these are typical obstacles standing in the way of Europe-wide harmony, not to mention such far-ranging goals as eventual political union or a confederation of states à la Switzerland.

The integration of West Germany's 1,400,000 farms, over a third of them full-time enterprises, into the modern overall national economy is headache enough. But it is a major factor in the failure of the Common Market nations to work out a unified farm policy. The ultimate goal of making the Common Market countries one great trade area like the United States as the basis for continuing prosperity and eventual European integration depends in large measure on the success of the EEC's farm policy, which in turn hinges on the West German farm problem.

In spite of city migration and dwindling farms (see Chapter 22), the ratio is still such that there are far too many farmers on far too little land, making for high prices.

This in turn has required large-scale protectionism in the form of subsidies and high duties on foreign products. Since all farmers belong to the West German Farm Federation, which is vehemently opposed to any reduction in subsidies, they are a powerful

349

political factor. Composing 13 percent of the population, they overwhelmingly support the Christian Democratic Union and its affiliate Christian Social Union, and it is from their ranks that the extremist NPD has been drawing much of its strength. As a result the government has been reluctant to alienate them.

Consequently, grain prices are 20 percent higher in West Germany than the average for the other member nations of the EEC. Wheat sells about $115 a metric ton (36.7 bushels). That is $3.13 a bushel. Barley brings about $100 a metric ton. These West German prices would have to be reduced drastically to be in a single price level in the EEC. But the West German Farm Federation vigorously opposes this.

West Germany's high duties and import quota are based on an obsolete structure dating back to Prussian Junkers (great land owners) who in the 1880's received protection against the inflow of cheap grains from abroad.

It is the West German hausfrau who has to pay for all this special treatment to the farmers. Food costs on an average of 35 percent of consumer income as against 19 percent in the United States. West German taxpayers feel the bite again as they shell out for a subsidy program that costs upwards of 2.4 billion marks ($650 million) annually.

However that may be, important advances have been made through the European Economic Community on the economic level, which has had profound and most favorable effects on the Federal Republic. The affluence of the Federal Republic with an increase of exports of 233 percent and imports of 262 percent between 1958 and 1967 owes a great deal to the EEC.

Since 1958 the EEC has expanded to become the third largest steel and electricity producer in the world. With a population of 186 million persons, it is the second largest consumer market, and it is far and away the most powerful trade association. West German industrial profits within the EEC have risen nearly fourfold over the past decade. "No one," according to Sicco Mansholt, vice-president of the European Commission, "has profited more from the EEC than West Germany."

Barring unpredictable catastrophes, leading economists foresee for the seventies an even greater golden boom period than before. According to a study published by the Basel (Switzerland) Prognos-Institut, the annual comsumption per capita in the Federal Republic will rise from 4,751 Deutsche marks by 1985. The Prognos experts say further that surplus income in private

West German households will rise by 7 percent. The monthly income of retired persons will double over the next few years. Social benefits will increase by 100 percent in the next decade, and the country's GNP will increase by 1980 from 591 billion Deutsche marks (1969) to 1,260 billion Deutsche marks.

The Giant Flexes Its Muscles

Before European integration can ever become a realistic goal, however, the problem of Germany's future must be solved. Yet reunification appears ever more unrealistic as time goes on. In the Preamble to the Basic Law of the Federal Republic, Germans are called upon to strive for reunification in peace and freedom, and in that same constitution they are urged to work for European security, European-wide creation of law and order and peace in the world. Many astute political observers, including some of Germany's most loyal friends, see a contradiction in these two goals. There is widespread apprehension, especially among the Common Market countries and aspiring members, that a reunited Germany would be the greatest obstacle to a peacefully integrated and politically united Europe.

This fear is no longer one of Germany's potential military might, but its dominating influence as the world's fourth largest economic power. In November, 1969, the distinguished French daily *Le Monde* asked whether "German economic machinery will accomplish what its weapons cannot?" Around that same time *Paris Match* observed that "German ministers move confidently among their friends and arrogantly among their enemies. . . . The economic might of West and East Germany if put together would be three times greater than that of France."

"Economic success," the former West German minister of finance (and of defense), Franz-Josef Strauss, told American columnist Joseph Alsop in 1969, "has almost the role nowadays of the infantry divisions in the time of the Kaiser."

This was seen in the international monetary crisis of 1969 when the Germans defiantly postponed the revaluation of the mark for months and compelled the whole world to acquiesce to their demands. Again in 1971 the West Germans revalued the mark, and forced the U.S. to postpone plans for its withdrawal of half the American troops in Europe; not least was the fear that the Federal Republic might demand immediate payment in gold for its vast dollar reserves.

"Wir sind wieder wer! [We are somebodies again!] ," a phrase coined by Ludwig Erhard, frequently falls from German lips. Veteran friends and visitors to Germany notice an increased aggressiveness, arrogance, and cockiness all over West Germany. "I find the Germans," a responsible American professor, an expert on German affairs, told me, "decidedly more calculating than a few years ago."

Second only to the United States, the Soviet Union, and Japan, the Federal Republic has evoked the envy of such hard-hit, strike-ridden countries as Britain, France, and Italy. "One would almost believe that the real victors of World War II were the Germans and that it has paid them handsomely to lose the war," observed a veteran British newspaperman.

If the notion of a "big Europe" ever comes near realization, it will be Germany that will carry more weight than any of the other constituent powers. Many of them see something very Bismarckian in the German trend.

It only takes a little arithmetic to see why these fears loom so largely and realistically in the consciousness of Germany's European neighbors. If the Federal Republic by itself is already the strongest industrial power in Europe outside the Soviet Union, how much stronger would a reunited Germany be?

This question was answered in brutal frankness by a courageous television program shown on a nationwide hookup by Westdeutscher Rundfunk on April 10, 1969, entitled "The German Colossus." The documentary pointed out that even in Eastern Europe the GDR is the strongest industrial power outside of the Soviet Union and the tenth largest industrial power in the world. According to Soviet figures the GDR in 1964 led Eastern European production (without the Soviet Union) by 29 percent. And on a per capita basis the GDR produces 52 percent more than the Soviet Union. In 1970 the GDR will have increased its national income by 30 percent, a greater growth rate than in the west.

In the event of a reunification, the combined annual production of refrigerators in both Germanies would be 2.5 million, which is only 40 percent less than the remaining EEC countries and 30 percent more than Eastern Europe. In the two Germanies the population would swell to 76.5 million, compared with 122 million in the remaining EEC countries and with 82 million—or only 5.5 million more than in a united Germany—in all of Eastern Europe (minus the Soviet Union).

With a supply of 1.2 million tractors the two Germanies possess one-fourth fewer tractors than the remaining EEC countries but far more than double as many as Eastern Europe.

In the production of synthetics, television and radio sets, automobiles and rubber products, the two Germanies produce far more than all the other EEC countries together. Synthetics: 2,190,000 tons in both Germanies while the EEC countries combined produce 130,000 tons less, and Eastern Europe only a little more than a fifth of the German production. Automobiles: 2,840,000 in the united Germanies, or 300,000 more than in the other EEC countries, with Eastern Europe producing only 104,000, about the same amount as the GDR alone. With the production of 27.9 million automobile tires in the two Germanies, they exceeded by 4.5 million the other EEC countries and by 22.5 million the Eastern European countries.

For all practical purposes, the GDR already enjoys many of the benefits it would have if it were a member of the EEC. Strangely enough, a significant fact has been widely ignored, namely that the GDR benefits from special trade agreements with Bonn which dispense with customs obligations. Bonn justifies these regulations on the basis that as "the other part of Germany" the GDR cannot be regarded as a foreign country, and also as a means of easing tension. It is widely believed that the real reason the other East bloc countries are pushing so hard for GDR recognition is that as a separate country it would no longer be eligible for "inner German" trade exemptions and thereby be less competition for them. Since the GDR now enjoys almost the same customs exemptions as West Germany, it is able to sell its products all over the EEC market far cheaper than any other Eastern European country.

Meanwhile, more than half a century since Germany relinquished her African and Asian colonies, and a quarter of a century since World War II, industrial giants from the Rhine and Ruhr are comfortably ensconced in more than 100 countries. Just to give one example, the Siemens Electrical Firm produces generators in Spain, assembles transformers in Bogotá, has a telephone plant in Pretoria and a huge electrical plant in Australia. In 1968 its proceeds were 1.9 billion Deutsche marks ($500 million) or 18 percent of Siemens' gross income. "We are at home everywhere," says Siemens general director Dr. Gerd Tacke.

West German foreign investments have been rising since 1960, roughly, about 21 percent per annum, a growth rate exceeded only by the Japanese. During the same period American and British entrepreneurs increased their annual investments by only 8 to 9 percent. It is true that compared to British and American foreign investments, West German investments abroad are proportionately small. But from year to year West German investments abroad have galloped to staggering sums. In 1969 West German European investments totaled 8.9 billion Deutsche marks and in other foreign countries, notably well-calculated investments in developing countries with an eye to future markets, 6.7 billion Deutsche marks.

The giant IG Farben chemical concern, whose foreign holdings were liquidated by the victorious allies in the wake of World War II because of its imperial structure, today owns foreign properties worth more than 3.3 billion Deutsche marks.

"No one," editorialized the *Deutsches Allgemeines Sonntags-blatt* in December, 1969, "knows how German the world is today. But it is certain that in the past fifteen years it has become more German than ever before."

The Affluent Society

There is an old, rather corny saying, "The Germans work as the French sin." But anyone who has been to Germany these days knows that the Germans are not letting anyone have a monopoly as far as sinning goes. American visitors shake their heads in dismay and wonder what ever happened to all that *Fleiss* (industriousness), for it has ceased to be a principal aspect of the affluent German "economic wonderland." Service in restaurants and shops is excruciatingly slow, attendants and salespersons are surly, filling station attendants often have to be asked twice to wipe your windshield, and all over the country secretaries and receptionists in business and government offices are noted for their downright frivolity.

"The saying once made the rounds in Europe," quipped a Hamburg businessman, "that there would be fewer wars if Germans would work less hard. If that is right, we are likely to face a long period of peace."

There is no German word for "efficiency," and a more apt word to describe the success of past German dedication to work is "methodical." It has also been said that the Italians are the world's worst organizers and best improvisers, while with the Germans it is the other way around. But today this is highly questionable as a German characteristic, if it ever was one.

Germans now enjoy the forty-hour workweek, which will probably be reduced to thirty-five hours in a few years and even less by the year 2000. A typical year gives them 128 days off, including national and religious holidays, and paid vacations of three weeks will soon become standard. Thousands of Germans now enjoy working hours which enable them to adjust their work schedules to their own preferences and needs.

The German passion for work is further called into question by a recent survey conducted in ten countries of Eastern and Western Europe among adults between eighteen and sixty-four years old living in cities with between 30,000 and 300,000 inhabitants.

It was learned that the French work more than the Russians, Americans, or Germans, devote more time to household chores and the family than the inhabitants of the other countries studied. The French work, on an average, 46½ hours a week compared to 40 in the Federal Republic, 42½ in the Soviet Union, and 40 in the United States. The record is held by Hungary with 50 working hours a week.

The French sleep longest, 8¼ hours, compared with 7½ for Americans, 7½ for Germans, and 7¼ for Russians. In spite of the French reputation for eating, the survey showed that the average Frenchman spends only 1¾ hours daily eating, compared to nearly 3 hours by Germans. The fastest eaters are the Russians with only an average of 50 minutes daily.

The Germans—at least the West Germans—are the biggest drinkers of alcohol in the world. They drink more *Schnaps* (brandy) than the Russians, Swedes, Americans, and Poles, all noted heavy drinkers, or 500 million quarts of alcoholic beverages annually. And they hold the world's record as well for the consumption of the German national food, BEER. In 1969 West Germans drank 11 billion Deutsche marks (about $400 million) worth of beer, or over 130 quarts per capita.

The West Germans' consumer ebullience since World War II is characterized by a whole series of what they call "waves." Undernourished, underhoused, deprived, during and after the war, they became obsessed with an almost fanatical frenzy of

355

gratification as soon as prosperity began to rear its lovely head. First it was food, for which they invented the somewhat distasteful word *Fresswelle* (glutton wave). Then it was the housing wave. Then came the *Kaufwelle* (buying wave, *i.e.,* the purchase of such consumer goods as cars, TV sets, refrigerators). Then the *Reisewelle* (travel wave), when Germans began to inundate surrounding European countries by the hundreds of thousands (and today every second office clerk benefits from low-cost group tours to Tunisia, Cameroon, or Thailand). Recent waves were *Studenten Welle* (student wave) and *Sex Welle.*

Every week some 18 million West Germans invest an average of $8 million in the official state lottery. For as little as 23 cents a player can win $125,000 if the results are right when electronically drawn on color television every Saturday evening. All one has to do is pick six correct numbers out of a total of forty-nine. One can buy lotto tickets in thousands of tobacco shops all over Germany. Of course similar games are played in Italy, France, and Switzerland in a tradition that goes back to the fifteenth century. In Germany lotto was introduced in 1760 by the Prussian King Frederick the Great, who needed to replenish the exhausted Prussian treasury. Proceeds go to charitable institutions.

As a result of all this prosperity the Germans have become hopeless status-seekers. "Keeping-up-with-the-Müllers" has become an integral part of their way of life.

"Sind Wir Ein Volk Von Angebern [Are We a Folk of Braggarts]?" asked the leading mass-circulation weekly, *Der Stern,* in 1969.

The status value of a car is so great that it is an open secret that thousands of owners of Mercedes 200 will remove the "200" sign from their cars in the hope that it will be mistaken for a Mercedes 300, a class higher. Others will buy a Volkswagen and then change its chassis with that of a Porsche. Still others play the snob in reverse. The former Krupp manager Berthold Beitz was known to drive a Porsche with a Volkswagen chassis.

The number of factory workers is growing who go to work in their business suits, so that they might be mistaken for white collar workers. A hostess in a Hamburg bar told me, "I always look at the shoes if I want to know what the financial capacity of a male customer is. It is no longer possible to tell just from his suit."

The men's wives have their own status symbols: expensive hairdos, fur coats, clothes, maids from Trinidad, "snob" sports like golf, sailing, safaris, and travel to exotic places.

Even in an industry with more than a thousand workers, it is unthinkable for skilled workers to associate with unskilled workers, and a *Kegelklub* (bowling club) of foremen seldom includes their underlings in their group. It is almost impossible for a worker, even if he is just a slight grade below, to associate privately with someone a grade higher in employment.

A strange quirk is the "snob" appeal associated with membership in political organizations. Many men join not out of idealistic considerations but because it is "in" to do so. "Showy" furniture is also a common status symbol. Even if a worker's family does not have too many visitors, they want to be able to say "We just bought a new living-room set," or stove or refrigerator.

A fifty-one-year-old factory worker once told me, "We started out insuring our furniture for 500 marks. Now it is insured for over 25,000 marks."

According to the Wickert Opinion Poll Institute in Tübingen, "Two-thirds of all West Germans (exactly 65 percent) are very satisfied with the life they are leading."

◄22►

A MATTER OF LIFE AND DEATH

THE DIFFERENCE BETWEEN American and European cities, as columnist Russell Baker has pointed out, is that while New York makes people want to take a bath or curse the mayor, European cities, with their splashing fountains, promenades, and, joy of joys, trees, make men want to kiss women and sometimes even make women want to kiss men. American visitors to Europe invariably are delighted to find themselves for once in countries where one can walk the streets safely at night.

But I am afraid there is more to this "Europe's cities are safer and cleaner" cliché, at least where Germany is concerned, than meets the eye.

According to a survey conducted by the Allensbach Demoscopic Institute, the respected West German opinion pollsters, West Berliners are among the most timorous citizens in the Federal Republic. Every second citizen questioned was of the view that it was a risky thing to be out after dark. And in the Federal Republic as a whole two out of every five people are afraid to go out at night. Although only 15 percent of male respondents admitted having fears being on the street alone after nightfall, two out of three women questioned said that they had fears after dark.

According to the institute, which has conducted numerous surveys on the question of public safety, the consistent increase in the crime rate has become a more serious cause of fear than any other social or political problem in the Federal Republic. In an Allensbach survey 72 percent said they feared crime most, 5.8 percent gave the possibility of unemployment as their greatest fear, and only 2.9 percent said they most feared the rightist NPD party.

The number of known crimes—excepting traffic and security violations—has increased three times as fast as the population growth within one decade. In 1967 some 12,000 police and plainclothes officers, not counting traffic police, had to cope with an all-time record of 2.07 million crimes.

Every day in the Federal Republic, with a population of 60.6 million and covering an area roughly equivalent to Oregon, there are an average of five murders, three bank robberies, 158 stolen vehicles. Annually some 163,000 objects are stolen from cars, 142,000 burglaries are reported from businesses, warehouses, and factories, 61,000 instances of plundering coin vending machines (by police officers themselves in 1969 in Bonn) occur, 58,000 automobiles are stolen, 46,000 house burglaries and over 11,000 armed robberies of banks take place.

In April, 1969, more than 35,000 known criminals were at large. From year to year the percentage of solved crimes decreases. While in 1954 the police were able to solve three-fourths (73.4 percent) of all crimes and apprehend the law-breakers, by 1967 only 52.2 percent of all reported transgressions could be cleared up. (On the other hand, the percentage of solved murder crimes has increased, from 86.2 percent in 1953 to 95.4 percent in 1967.)

NPD chief Adolf von Thadden uses these statistics to great advantage in his "law and order" pitch for votes. "Our people," he has said, "are exposed to a wave of crime that can only be compared to the Wild West of the USA." The NPD newspaper *Deutsche Nachrichten* complains that the Federal Republic's lax laws and inadequate law enforcement make Germany "a paradise for criminals."

The biggest headache for West German police are the growing number of "white collar" crimes. Hardly a day passes without nonexistent houses being sold, watered-down wine being passed off by the barrelful, and thousands of marks being paid for nonexistent eggs. Even banks extend credit for millions whose collateral is nonexistent.

In an affluent society whose slogan is, *"Hast du was, bist du was* [You are what you have,]*"* public opinion readily condemns a shoplifter who pinches a transistor radio from a department store, while regarding as "cool" anyone who can get away with income tax evasion involving thousands or even millions. "Stealing," one observer has put it, "has become the German national sport."

The Police Force—Understaffed and Overworked

The police force is unable to keep up with this crime escalation because it is drastically in need of reform and expansion. In most cities and provinces the police are chronically underpaid and forced to bungle along with outdated or inadequate equipment. Morale is low. Few police officers earn more than $250 a month. In Cologne, for example, in 1969, there were the same number of policemen as in 1950, even though the population has increased since then by 17 percent. There is a dire shortage of experts and modern crime detection equipment.

It is not at all unusual for someone whose home has just been burglarized to be told on calling the police, "Leave everything just as it is, we'll send someone around in the morning."

The prisons are overcrowded and reeking of physical and technical neglect. The province of North Rhine-Westphalia has detention facilities for only 16,500, with the result that the provincial minister of justice has to periodically exempt minor offenders with less than three months' sentences from serving their terms. Sometimes these petty offenders are even told, "Come around later when we have room."

In regard to jurisdictional matters the situation is as grotesque as two labor unions quibbling over whether the installation of water spouts is a plumbing or roofing job.

For example, the tri-city area of Heidelberg, Mannheim, and Ludwigshafen, with a total of around one million population, divides its *Kripo (Kriminalpolizei)* jurisdictionally into twelve units overlapping three *Länder*. It frequently happens that someone will call the police on being assaulted, only to be told, "Sorry, but I only handle narcotics cases."

Retired Chief of Police Wilhelm Dahmen of Worms told a German reporter in an interview, "If a corpse appeared on the Hesse side of the Rhine, it was not unusual for the Hesse police to give it a shove so that it would land on the Rhine-Palatinate side."

Incredible as it may sound, manhunts in most places in the Federal Republic take place only during office hours or at best during a once-a-week night patrol. Only the large cities have twenty-four-hour shifts for the police.

On the Federal level the situation is even worse. The Federal Crime Office in Wiesbaden has no authorization to coordinate crime detection activities among the various states and even on a statewide level there are endless jurisdictional disputes between communities and within communities among the various branches of the police force.

In Bavaria it is very difficult for the crime investigation department to cooperate on crime cases with the municipal police force because no legal basis for this has been created.

Telephoto equipment is conspicuous by its absence in most police stations, so that police must still resort to special delivery to transmit photos and fingerprints of crime suspects. Budgets for crime detection are often so miserly that officers are forbidden to make long distance phone calls of more than thirty miles and underworld tips can only be rewarded if the informers are willing to sign a receipt with their real names.

In Frankfurt the apprehension of a gang of fur thieves was delayed for months because police authorities refused to provide expenses for one of its officers to go to Amsterdam to look at some of the stolen furs that had been found.

In 1969 a notorious gang of check forgers was almost caught, but the project failed because the state crime detection headquarters of Baden-Württemberg could not come to a jurisdictional agreement with other West German states.

On an individual level modernization and improvement of West German police forces and crime detection methods have been made—in Hamburg the latest equipment and methods have become a model for the rest of the country. But it will be a long time before this becomes standard throughout the country.

Police Brutality

The German press has vigorously condemned police brutality during numerous student uprisings, but in everyday life the long arm of the law tends to be more restrained. Most foreign visitors appear to find the German police cooperative and courteous. Some traffic police are downright funny in their efforts to put acrobatic humor into the drab routine of directing traffic.

In my more than fifteen years close association with Germany (eight as a resident) I have had numerous encounters with the police, and I can recall only one instance where this was truly unpleasant, but it was because of clumsiness and bureaucracy rather than bullying or abuse. I was living in Munich at the time and was aroused from sleep at 5 A.M. one Sunday morning. My landlady was hysterical. *"Herr Schalk!"* she cried, *"die Polizei ist da!"* waking up several neighbors in the process, who, or course, had to watch the whole embarrassing proceeding as a uniformed officer escorted me to the nearest police station. When I got there I learned to my indignation that my car insurance firm had neglected to send the required insurance registration duplicate to the police.

However, on another occasion when I was on the autobahn, I was suddenly waved down by a squad car and had to pull over to the side. It turned out that I had forgotten my wallet at the last restaurant and the police were returning it to me.

Penal Reform

While it may take years to modernize the Federal Republic's police force, considerably more progress has been made in the matter of penal reform.

The death penalty has been abolished in the Federal Republic, as it has in Austria, Denmark, Italy, Norway, the Netherlands, Sweden, Switzerland, Greenland, Iceland, Finland, and the Republic of San Marino. The Soviet Union and the Soviet bloc countries have retained it for murder and economic crime, even though Empress Catherine of Russia was the first to abolish it in 1769, followed by Joseph II of Austria in 1787. The Germans had written the abolition of capital punishment into their constitution of 1849, but it did not become effective until a century later, after the Hitler bloodbath, with the establishment of the Federal Republic in 1949.

Opinion polls show that a large majority of Germans actually favor the death penalty, particularly in view of the rising crime rate. To its credit, the government, backed by most of the younger generation of educated Germans, the intellectuals, and most of the press, radio, and television, have stood firm against the popular outcry for the return of capital punishment.

In 1969, after years of preparatory work, the Federal Republic introduced the first of a series of fundamental changes in its antiquated penal code dating from 1871. The old Prussian laws had been modified over the years, but it was only in 1953 that a parliamentary committee began to comprehensively review the outdated statutes. The reform measures, which are called "the work of a century," will be completed in 1973.

The emphasis of the reform laws are that the state will cease to regard itself as the "custodian of virtue" and that punishment should be directed toward rehabilitation rather than reprisal. For example, the new version of the laws dealing with sexual offenses, a key part of the bill, proceeds on the premise that "not everything that is distasteful by religious, ethical, or moral standards can be punishable."

However, penalties for sexual relations with a minor or coercion of an adult remain strict—up to ten years' imprisonment or more. Under the new code, chronic sexual offenders can, but only with their consent, be castrated, and a number have done so.

The man who more than any other is to be credited with the implementation of these reforms is, oddly enough, a member of the Council of the Evangelical Church in Germany, the Federal President Gustav Heinemann, who exercised his influence to the full in his prior capacity as minister of justice. His reasoning: God requires no protection, while atheists, freemasons, and pacifists should have the same rights as members of religious communities.

"Blasphemy," long a matter punishable by law in Germany, has been replaced by the term "religious defamation." Thus, in the new form the prohibition applies only to hindrance of religious services and especially the disturbance of a funeral service.

Procuring will now only be regarded as a misdemeanor, not a crime, although prostitution can still be punished as a legal offense, even though in many places prostitutes escape punishment as long as they are registered and under the control of health authorities.

One of the biggest innovations is the abolishment of penitentiaries and all sentences of hard labor. A uniform prison system has been adopted without classification of hard labor, confinement, and detention for investigation purposes. Most short sentences of six months or less have been abolished in favor of fines assessed according to the offender's income. Since previously some 130,000 persons annually have served such short-term sentences, which represented 85 percent of all prison sentences passed, this measure will greatly relieve prison congestion.

These reform measures include provisions for the establishment of sociotherapeutic institutions for habitual criminals with serious personality disruptions, as well as for compulsive criminals.

Other important changes include the right to make public demonstrations. Although this right was already guaranteed by the Basic Law, under previous legislation any person remaining on the scene of a demonstration after being told three times by the police to leave could be punished even though he had not participated. Under the new reforms much more freedom is permitted, although there are still stiff penalties for the exercise of violence.

A convicts' union was established in 1968 by a lawyer, Wolfgang Schwelte, which has grown to more than 2,000 members. The union seeks regular working wages, better living conditions for its members, and looks after convicts' families. Convicts in West German prisons earn from 0.50 Deutsche marks (12.5 cents) to 1.10 Deutsche marks (28 cents) a day plus 30 Deutsche marks ($9.50) as an annual bonus for regular work attendance.

Progress in judicial reform, by contrast, is much slower. As of July 1, 1970, the law assuring equal legal status for illegitimate children entered into force. Thus the child is considered related to its father with the mother exercising parental authority and exacts greater maintenance responsibilities. Illegitimate children will also be entitled to maintenance until the age of eighteen, and be assured a claim in lieu of an inheritance on the death of its father. Even before the father's death, the illegitimate child will be entitled to demand an advance settlement instead of inheritance.

Press critics have been loud in denouncing outdated courtroom procedure, such as the use of robes dating back to the French Revolution, the heavy use of ceremony, and the requirement that the defendant stand up when taking the oath and when a sentence is passed. Measures are underway for secularizing the oath.

Senseless Brutality

Murder and homicide have almost doubled in the Federal Republic since 1963 and the so-called "senseless" crimes of violence have likewise increased. One hundred children annually are beaten to death by their parents. Brutal assaults in parks, taverns, and on the street are rapidly becoming commonplace. According to Hamburg police commissioner Johannes Schmidt, crimes of "senseless" brutality with no apparent motive of robbery, revenge, or material gain, have risen to more than 100,000 annually in the Federal Republic.

According to criminologist Dr. Hans von Hentig, these "sense-less brutalities" are one of the symptoms of sick, modern society. "The over-stimulated 'needs' of people in a consumer society have all but obliterated the sense of balance of many persons." His colleague, Dr. Gustav Nass, attributes increased tendencies of aggression among fifteen- to twenty-year-olds to sexual frustration. "The control areas for sex and aggression in the brain lie directly next to each other. Thus the stimulation of the one can easily flow over to the other."

When on October 12, 1969, the psychoanalyst and social psychologist, Dr. Alexander Mitscherlich, received the Peace Prize of the Federal Republic's Book Trade Association for his studies on aggression, it aroused worldwide attention. "I can well understand that," said Dr. Mitscherlich in his speech at the award-ceremony. "In the history of the last two or three generations there are very few credible examples where the word 'German' has been linked with the word 'peace.' Our Peace Prize has been understood in connection with our attempt to divest ourselves of a trait of character that has become so dear to us, belligerency."

The German and His Car

Observers and psychologists alike continue to be mystified about the strange forms of aggression that a frightening if small number of German motorists exhibit regularly on German autobahns, streets, and roads.

On January 20, 1971, two women and a man were drowned when their sports car plunged into the Main River in Frankfurt after being chased through the city by a pack of angry taxi drivers. It seemed that the driver of the car, who managed to swim to safety, had cut sharply in front of a taxi. The infuriated taxi driver chased after the car, radioed his colleagues for help, and they then chased the car until it was forced into the river.

This is by no means a farfetched, isolated case. At regular intervals, German newspapers carry stories of brutal knifings, beatings, and forced accidents, sometimes ending in death. In Bonn a middle-aged engineer got out of his car at a red light, walked to the car in front of him, which was driven by a pretty coed, and punched her foursquare in the face. Reason: She had braked too suddenly for his taste at the preceding crossing. In

365

Nuremberg a gas station attendant shot and killed the driver of another car. Reason: He didn't like the way that driver had hogged the road. In Cologne a butcher jumped out of his car and smashed a pedestrian to the ground, who then died of skull fracture. Reason: The pedestrian had the gall to call attention to his defective lighting. On the Frankfurt-Cologne autobahn the driver of a Mercedes 220 SE pulled alongside a Volkswagen, while his companion sprayed the occupants with the contents of a fire extinguisher. Reason: The Volkswagen had committed the unpardonable "crime" of passing a Mercedes.

On a milder scale a rather frequent scene in German traffic is the notorious *Deutscher Gruss* (German greeting), roughly equivalent to nose-thumbing, or the Bronx cheer, *i.e.,* if a motorist wishes to express his disapproval of another motorist's driving manners, he sometimes taps his right temple with his right forefinger, which conveys the meaning of "Idiot!" Although Germans themselves deplore this habit, it seems destined for longevity.

Germans, like Europeans generally, have a much different attitude toward their automobiles than the average American toward his vehicle. Americans tend to take their cars for granted. True, they may well be a status symbol, but primarily they are a means of getting from one place to another. In the summer at least, every second German washes his car once weekly, according to one survey, and every sixteenth German more than once. Only a fifth of German cars are washed less than once a month. The slightest scratch or dent will drive Germans up the wall. They get extremely upset if you even tap their bumpers when parking and sometimes excitedly threaten to call the police. This is partly due to the unusually high West German insurance premiums, but psychological factors also play a significant role. For Germans, a car is not merely a status symbol but an emotional experience, a companion, an object of pride, a hard-won possession, with seemingly built-in therapeutic value. Germans as a rule keep their cars far longer than Americans and nurse them with tender care until they reluctantly part with them. Psychologists can only speculate about all this, but one educated guess is that many older Germans work off their wartime neuroses with their automobiles, while the younger generation compensates for its aggressive tendencies and anti-Establishment neuroses in the same way.

Traffic

In 1968 for the first time since the end of World War II, the number of road deaths in Germany dropped. In 1968 the total of traffic deaths dropped to 16,698 from 17,084 in 1967. Although the number of cars on German roads continues to rise, this downward trend may persist as a result of new traffic regulations. With stiff penalties for violators, it is now made a major offense not to stop and render assistance in emergencies.[1] Getting a driving license has never been a simple matter in postwar West Germany. The candidate is required to go to an authorized commercial driving school, which may cost from $60 to $200 and may take up to six months or longer. Then he must pass a stiff oral and written theoretical examination and a driving test. He must show a certificate of good health and pass an eye examination. The license costs fifteen dollars, but it is good for life. There have been proposals for requiring driving license renewals every ten years, but nothing has come of them.

As if that were not enough, candidates for class two driving licenses (trucks and tractors) must earn a Red Cross first-aid certificate, while candidates for class three (normal vehicles) must know the rudiments of first aid, such as how to stop bleeding and how to apply artificial respiration.

New laws require several safety features to be built into all motor vehicles. First-aid boxes, safety belts, and fire extinguishers are obligatory. Orange emergency telephones are conspicuously located all along German autobahns at regular intervals. In addition numerous agencies provide emergency medical services. The Cologne city council, to give one example, has introduced a new system providing rescue cars on call in seven major urban districts.

Compared with expressways that crisscross the United States, those in Europe are still meager. All six Common Market countries combined have fewer than 6,000 miles of superhighways, and a quarter of these are in Italy and about half in West Germany. Stretching from the Baltic Sea to the Alps the West German autobahn is the densest freeway system in the world. However, her reputation as the "classic" dual-highway nation is being threatened by Italy which is expanding its *autostrada* network at a fast clip, so that based on automobiles-per-road-mile ratio, it has already surpassed Germany.

The West German autobahn is a mixed blessing. There is no speed limit and, unlike Italy, France, and the United States, no toll (so far). It is possible to drive from Basel, Switzerland, to the Danish border, or from Salzburg, Austria, to Aachen, without passing through any large city, except Munich (pending completion of the bypass). But one goof, one flat tire, or momentary lapse of awareness by one driver at some of the bottleneck areas, such as the stretch from Cologne to Düsseldorf or between Heidelberg and Frankfurt, and the whole thing comes to a screeching halt. Pileups, bumper-to-bumper standstills for as long as an hour or even two, are the rule and not the exception. And the secondary German roads are even worse.

As for the numerous autobahn restaurants and filling stations, in spite of their modern decor and attractive landscapes, even fountains, they are more often an ordeal than a pleasure. In my more than fifteen years' of regular use of the autobahns, I have yet to experience any worthwhile major improvement on the poor service and poor maintenance of these establishments.

But there are compensations: the numerous fine parking places with picnic tables and rest rooms; the complete absence of billboards; and the comforting presence of dozens of "yellow angels"—yellow service cars of the ADAC, German Automobile Club—which continuously cruise the autobahns day and night helping countless stranded motorists (including nonmembers), usually free of charge or for a nominal fee to cover costs.

A mixed blessing too is the new regulation permitting police to fine traffic offenders on the spot for minor offenses. This eliminates time-consuming money transfers and court appearances, but often enough overly zealous police make the best use of the overly regulated German traffic legislation (see Chapter 1).

An estimated additional twenty million automobiles will be on German roads—the most crowded in Europe—by 1980, twice as many as now, and already plans are under way to double the present number of autobahns. At present trucks are banned from German roads on Sundays, except those with special permits. So far nothing has come of Transport Minister Georg Leber's plan to ban long-distance trucks (about a million) from the autobahns altogether, thereby diverting more freight to the government-owned railways now operating at an annual three-billion-mark deficit.

Whatever the shortcomings, the German autobahn system is the heart of the European superhighway network. With luck, you can speed from Vienna to Antwerp on the same day. One more link toward an integrated Europe—that's the German autobahn.

Housing and Cities

A new dwelling (*i.e.*, an apartment or equivalent) is completed in the Federal Republic every minute. At the end of World War II, more than eight million Germans in what is now West Germany were homeless, and accommodations in the years following had to be constructed also for seven million displaced persons and thirteen million refugees. As a result, half of the 20.5 million dwellings in the Federal Republic are new, *i.e.*, constructed since the war, at a cost of 260 billion DM's ($80 billion).

To facilitate this vast construction program, which was one of the chief factors contributing to the postwar economic boom, the Federal Government granted generous tax concessions, favorable loans, and savings bonuses. In addition, it financed dwellings for lower income groups, the aged, and provided substantial annual bonuses for low-income families who made savings contracts with various building societies enabling them to buy homes and apartments at agreeable terms. In 1968, 39 percent of all completed dwellings were purchased by low-income families through these societies. Nearly three million Germans own their own homes.

But this *Wiederaufbau* (reconstruction) did not come about without a price. Psychologically, many Germans who have long roots in the part now known as West Germany, resent the apparent preferred treatment given to refugees. Very often, the latter received so much government aid that they were able to improve their social status and even build up prosperous businesses in West Germany with far greater success than native West Germans. The Equalization of Burdens Law (explained in Chapter 21) by which property-owners are, in addition, made to pay for refugee aid, adds to the resentment. Moreover, German taxes are among the highest in the world, mainly of course as a result of their material and moral debt for losing the war and serving Hitler.

The removal of rent control at the end of 1968, after a ten-year phasing-out period, brought about an increase in rents which were already exorbitant. Although many three-room flats cost $60 or even less, most Germans must pay anywhere from $500 to $5,000 so-called *Baukostenzuschuss* (contribution to construction costs) in advance. Usually, but not always, this down payment, euphemistically called "key money" entitles the tenant to a ten- or twenty-year lease; the tenant in turn can exact the same down payment from his successor. But in countless thousands of cases, the house or apartment owner reserves this right to himself, so that the key money is, to be called by its right name, just plain extortion. In some cases the down payment is applied to the rent.

Although there are relatively few slums in Germany, there are numerous slumlike pockets. In West Germany an estimated three million persons or 5 percent of the population live in over-crowded conditions (more than one person to a room).

But for additional millions even living in a new apartment is a Kafkaesque nightmare. *Der Spiegel* reports (February 3, 1969) "the collapse of social standards, the abandonment of traditional city structures, the deprivation of acceptable aesthetic environment—all these are the result of the German reconstruction since the second world war."

"Like the Middle Ages," says architect Hellmut Maurer, "the authorities build primitive dwelling units for the broad masses." And social psychologist Dr. Alexander Mitscherlich has been saying for years that "nowhere else is so much wretchedness produced in the name of 'social' as in 'social housing.' " A Berlin physician reports that complaints from young apartment-block dwellers, such as sleeplessness, dizziness, heart trouble, restlessness, and extreme chronic irritability are his daily fare.

Megalopolitan Chaos by 2000

A corpse was first discovered in a Berlin housing project three weeks after death, even though the odors penetrated through the air vents of the building for days—the occupants as far as the fourteenth floor simply closed the vents.

City planner Otl Aicher, who is in charge of the construction and planning of the Munich Olympic Games site of 1972, predicts a nationwide megalopolitan chaos by the end of the century if measures are not taken soon to change from classical city planning to regional concepts. He points out that by 1980 the area between Krefeld and Bonn, which includes the industrial Ruhr region, will have 7.5 million population, or something approaching the population of Paris or London. But nothing is being planned to accommodate the administrative, cultural, and social needs of this population on an overall scale. He is frightened by the chaos that will inevitably result, since the area increases by 500,000—that is, by the population of a large city—annually.

Every year an additional 160 square miles of land are covered with more high-rise, jerry-built, monotone, cramped apartment houses, so that in two years an area as large as the Lake of Constance, Germany's largest lake, is built up, and in twenty years, the entire Black Forest region. By the end of the century, most of the Federal Republic will begin to emerge as one vast megalopolis with a dwindling few green patches and forest preserves in between.

The whole concept of community life centering around a single metropolitan area is rapidly being destroyed by the hard realities of urban collectivization. City planner Dr. Isbary points out that the German apartment dweller no longer thinks in terms of the city or community but of operational bases. His apartment is one base. The school (or very often schools) where he sends his children is a second base (or bases). The place or places of work of himself, wife, and possibly older children are further bases, often quite distant from home, and the church is still another, while recreation and other activities are scattered over a still wider area of bases. "The new development," says Dr. Isbary, "is no longer the city, town or village but operative bases." The trend is further hastened by the construction of peripheral shopping centers and hundreds of peripheral suburban housing settlements sprawling far into the countryside. City planners foresee the construction of administrative centers for whole regions, far removed from the downtown areas of cities, perhaps even located in the countryside, since the autobahns and highways provide easy connections.

Down on the Farm

German hens are laying more eggs than ever before and the fields are producing 50 percent more grain than fifteen years ago. But the number of farmers is decreasing steadily year by year. In Bavaria alone, 90,000 farms—or 7,000 a year—were abandoned between 1949 and 1967, leaving only 390,000. Since 1949 two million people have voluntarily migrated from the farms to the

371

cities. In the country as a whole the number of farmers has fallen 40 percent in twelve years, with the number of farms decreasing by 364,000 during that same period, and more than a million acres of land have dropped out of production altogether.

Meanwhile Germany's 2,800,000 farmers have already progressed a long way in the process of modernization. Their farms are fully motorized and to a large extent mechanized. Horses and cows pulling ploughs and farm carts, a familiar sight just a few years ago, are now a rare exception. The amount invested in new agricultural machinery in the past ten years must be in the neighborhood of 25 billion Deutsche marks (over $7 billion). Modern methods of cultivation, high-quality seed, and better fertilization have made it possible to raise the yield of each acre by 50 percent since 1955. Cooperatives and farm-machinery rental agencies make it possible for farmers with only small acreage to work their land at a profit.

Environment and Pollution

Tests taken in the Federal Republic reveal that 7 million tons of carbon dioxide, 3 million tons of hydrocarbon, 2.5 million tons of nitrous oxide, and 2.5 million tons of soot and dust escape into the air annually. Along with Japan, Britain, and the United States, West Germany's air is one of the world's most polluted thus prompting the Bonn government to commission a comprehensive environmental protection program.

Health and Welfare

Germans pay one of the world's highest taxes, but this is mainly because of West Germany's extensive social security program, which is especially designed to assist families and the aged; and some 30 percent of the average income is spent on compulsory and voluntary insurance or social security of some kind.

There are, for example, provisions for generous tax deductions from 20 percent to 50 percent for families. In addition, all parents with three or more children receive a monthly allowance of 40 DM's ($10) for each child except the first two. This is considered less generous than the children's allowances of many other European countries, such as Sweden, Finland, Denmark, Greece, Yugoslavia, Austria, Belgium, Holland, and Italy.

Nevertheless, the German social security system, whose foundations were laid by Bismarck in 1881, in the wake of mass internal industrial migration from 1850 to 1880, is noted as one of the first and most progressive of its kind.

The compulsory old-age and liability insurance of 1957 applies to all wage earners whose income is below 1,250 DM's ($352.50) monthly. The funds are built up by equal contributions of employee and employer, the former's share amounting to 7 percent of his income. Roughly four-fifths of the West German population is covered by compulsory health insurance, which provides for medical care, drugs, and hospitalization.

Other social legislation provides for maternity pay, and the maternity protection law of 1952 bans the dismissal of expectant mothers and grants them privileges during the weeks preceding and following confinement. There is also a provision that allows mothers one day a month for household chores on company time, and the law on disabled persons, which ensures them employment, especially war veterans, via compulsory quotas for all larger companies.

All employed persons in West Germany are insured against unemployment. Employers and employees alike are taxed 1 percent of wages, the ceiling of this type of insurance being 7.50 DM's ($2.00) a month per capita. Out of this fund, unemployed persons receive a certain percentage of their previous pay for a time, depending on their previous working time. Government unemployment relief provides for those not eligible for unemployment insurance.

Old-age pensions start for men when they have reached their sixty-fifth year, for women when they have reached their sixtieth. The amount they receive is based on individually paid contributions, but also on the national salary level during the last working years of the pensioners. Adjustments are made to allow for increased living costs. Pensions as a rule reach up to 75 percent of previous earnings. A widow receives 60 percent of her husband's pension, and special allowances are paid for children up to eighteen years of age.

One reason for the high income tax rate in Germany is that this is one way German families help pay for the damages resulting from World War II. Through the Equalization of Burdens legislation, all wage earners and home owners are taxed for the staggering costs of rehabilitating refugees and expellees from former Eastern German territories. The burden is designed to be paid off by 1979.

In recent years the medical and hospital situation in West Germany has been under heavy fire from press and TV. Yet there is hardly a reputable physician or hospital head who does not openly admit that the medical schools and hospitals are hopelessly overcrowded and urgently in need of reform. At a Munich conference in 1969 the German Association for Surgery admitted a sober fact: the heart centers are hopelessly overtaxed, the waiting lists keep growing longer and longer. At the Düsseldorf hospital, for example, there is a waiting list of five years.

In an interview with *Der Stern* in April, 1969, Dr. Werner Klinner, director of heart surgery at the University of Munich medical center, and the first German surgeon (together with Dr. Fritz Sebening) to make a heart transplant, conceded that "many patients on the waiting list die before the operation can be performed. This is saddening for us. There are children whose hearts are so weak that they have to ride in a wheelchair. Even if a patient has only three months to live, we can't operate."

In 1968 ninety persons on the Munich waiting list died before operating day. "Sometimes," said Dr. Klinner, "the next of kin sends me a death notice."

In the United States there are 120 heart centers for over 200 million inhabitants, or one for every 1.66 million persons. In West Germany five heart centers, with a maximum capacity of 3,000 patients each, must serve 60.6 million persons.

As for birth deliveries, the Federal Republic has been described as an underdeveloped country. More than 10,000 prenatal deaths occur annually and in 1967 nearly 25,000 infants died in their first year. Thirty-three thousand German children die before, during, or soon after birth annually, which is thirteen times more than the number of traffic deaths.

The infant mortality rate of West Germany is 100 percent higher than that of Sweden. It has 6 more out of every 1,000 infant deaths than Japan, 7 more out of every 1,000 than the Netherlands, and 3 more out of every 1,000 than East Germany. Over 6,000 spastic, mentally retarded, or crippled children are born in German clinics annually.

This state of affairs is attributed to overcrowded, poorly equipped hospitals and maternity wards. Nearly 70 percent of all

German children are born in clinics that have fewer than 1,000 births annually. Hospitals that are zealous in requiring the painstaking filling out of questionnaires about personal data, including the infant's religion, are all too often lax in observing basic requirements of natal care, such as pregnant women's blood pressure measurements, blood and urine specimen examination.

Germany's former fame as a country of great medical achievements was further besmirched with the notorious thalidomide affair (the drug was known in Germany as Countergan). Between 1957 and 1962 an estimated 8,000 deformed babies were born in Germany after their mothers took a tranquilizer produced by the firm of Chemie Gruenenthal, one of the oldest and most respected pharmaceutical firms. An additional 4,000 cases were reported in dozens of other countries where thalidomide was sold.

More than half of the deformed babies have since died, while an estimated 3,000 or more have survived, most of whom are now of school age. A controversy has arisen as to whether to integrate these deformed (limbless or flipperlike appendages) children in public schools or send them to special institutions. Although most parents favor integration, with physicians preferring special treatment, less than half of the children have been admitted to public schools. Since there is no standard system for medical care in the Federal Republic, much is left up to the initiative of the individual state or the parents. In the state of North Rhine-Westphalia, for example, of 294 registered thalidomide victims, 124 attend regular schools, while the others go to special classes. The advantage of the private rehabilitation centers, which take other malformed children too, is the availability of technical devices and care.

On December 18, 1970 the "thalidomide trial"—the longest criminal proceeding in German history—ended inconclusively. Lasting two and a half years, through 283 court sessions involving 120 witnesses, 60 experts, and 72,000 pages of testimony, the trial was closed by the court because it was felt that the charges were too difficult to charge specific persons. The Chemie Gruenenthal Firm set up a fund of $27.3 million for the children and $1.1 million for the involved adults. The government set up another fund for deformed children, with $14 million being reserved for thalidomide cases.

375

A German Mayo Clinic

In 1969 construction began in Wiesbaden on the first European "Mayo Clinic" or *Deutsche Klinik für Diagnostik*. The father of the idea, Dr. Leo Krutoff, admits that his brainchild stems from a visit to the famed clinic in Rochester, Minnesota, in 1963, whose 400 doctors see 200,000 patients in a year from all over the world. The German version has begun on a modest scale, with a staff of 40 doctors assisted by several dozen nurses and laboratory technicians. "Everything will be under one roof," says Dr. Krusoff, "and it will eventually cover the entire field of medicine. Not only will the patient have the advice of medical teams, but a computer will also aid in the diagnosis. The first building, of a planned complex of four connected structures, will be an eight-story, air-conditioned one costing 9 million DM's (more than $2.4 million) and a high-rise 100-bed hotel for persons accompanying patients to the clinic.

The German Way of Death

Death in Germany is conspicuous by its absence. Even if you live in Germany for twenty years, chances are that you will never see a funeral cortege for the simple reason that there aren't any. (The elaborate state funeral and funeral procession of Konrad Adenauer was an exception.) Mortuaries, hearses, and above all, the stately mansionlike funeral homes so common in the States, are virtually nonexistent. The Forest Lawn-type of cemetery as satirized so brilliantly by Evelyn Waugh in his novel *The Loved One* is unknown.

The German attitude toward death and funerals is to get the matter over with as quickly and inconspicuously as possible and the less said about it the better. There is none of this business of making a corpse look lifelike and asleep. And for all practical purposes, no embalming. And there are no wakes in the usual American sense of the word, though the family of the deceased may provide refreshments.

Practices differ from place to place and there are surely exceptions to the above observations as well. But generally whenever someone dies, one contacts a *Beerdigungs Institut* (literally, Burial Institute) which has little resemblance to American-type funeral homes. The deceased is placed in a station

376

wagon, panel truck, or limousine, usually painted black, sometimes decorated with a simple cross, but hardly the elaborate hearses known in the States and some other countries.

"The Germans don't like to talk about death or be reminded of death," a Roman Catholic priest told me. A mortician who wishes to open an institute has extreme difficulty finding anyone who will rent him a shop or building. *Beerdigungs Instituten* are usually located inconspicuously in back side streets, even in alleys, in industrial areas or far out of town. They are most often drab, little shops that display caskets, and nothing else. The *Institut* provides the caskets, death notices, transportation of the deceased to the cemetery. It also sells or rents *Sterbewäsche* (burial clothes), which usually consist merely of a kind of nightshirt with laced fringes, since only the head and shoulders are exposed. Rarely is the departed one attired in a suit or street dress.

The *Beerdigungs Institut* does not have a funeral parlor, but immediately takes the body straight to the cemetery. In most German cities the cemetery contains a large building, traditionally designed like a pagan Roman temple, with a dome, and grimly called *Leichenhalle* (literally, corpse chamber). Inside, the body is placed in one of a dozen or more cells, similar to those of a monastery and just as austere. Here the body remains until the day of the funeral. The relatively cool climate makes it possible to leave the casket open. The head of the deceased rests on a white pillow and is surrounded by flowers.

There is usually a refrigerated cell available if required, and in extreme cases the casket is kept closed.

The funeral itself is held in the interdenominational chapel of the *Leichenhalle,* but is usually restricted to a short service. The actual funeral Mass for Roman Catholics or funeral service for Protestants is held in the parish church, but without a catafalque.

After the simple funeral service, the body is lowered to the *Leichenhalle* basement where it is either cremated or taken out for immediate burial. The ashes of the cremated deceased are placed in an urn and then buried in smaller plots prepared for this. The urns are never allowed to be taken home.

Most German cemeteries and the *Leichenhallen* are public property, and the actual fees for burial are minimal. The average cemetery fee is around $50, but this does not include the costs of

377

the *Beerdigungs Institut.* Every citizen of Hamburg, rich or poor, for example, has a free grave plot at Ohlsdorf, which is regarded as one of the most beautiful cemeteries in the world, with only a nominal one-time fee of $12 for "perpetual care." Elsewhere in Germany grave plots may cost from 25 cents to several dollars. Some 700,000 West Germans die annually or about 1.2 percent of the entire population, and the average burial, including the *Institut,* costs about $375.

Although the mourners wear black clothes at the funeral itself, afterwards they wear small black ribbons on their coats or collars or armbands for several weeks.

In West Germany there are no regulations for licensed morticians. Anyone who owns a black tuxedo and has five marks ($1.50) for a license can go into the mortuary business. Among the 3,000 undertaking establishments in the Federal Republic some are operated on a supermarket basis, with a systematic daily screening of death notices, routine checks at homes for the aged, and hospitals. Many hire spotters, especially at homes for the aged.

Although Germans do not like to be reminded of death or talk about it, strangely enough they spend far more time and effort than many other nationalities in caring for the graves, visiting the cemetery, and in recent years are spending more money than ever on luxury funerals. Once the body is out of sight, it seems, the sting of death is easier to endure.

Pallbearers are usually professional mourners, decked out in long gowns, three-cornered plumed hats, ruffles, and white gloves. There is a growing trend toward more flowers, elaborate rites, fancier and more expensive caskets, organ and choral accompaniment. An entire industry has developed devoted exclusively to the sale or rental of burial accessories. Morticians can claim up to 20 percent profit from a funeral. "One can live decently," one of them put it, "on seven burials a month." According to one newspaper headline, "The German motto is, 'Live and let live—die and let die.' "

The growing sums of money spent on the dead provides evidence for the theory that the Germans not only live beyond their means but also die beyond them, justifying Sigmund Freud's observation at the turn of the century that the real reason one spends so much money on one's departed is thereby to pay for the riddance of guilt feelings toward the deceased.

378

Recently German newspapers have exposed racketeering in connection with burial practices. Many burial "institutes" have been accused of removing expensive casket fittings prior to burial and then reselling them. If questioned, the morticians' standard reply is, "We can easily prove that. Let's exhume the body and see."

Paradoxically, the same Germans who push death out of their minds as much as possible, set aside the entire month of November as officially devoted to it. On November 2, All Souls' Day, Catholics attend Requiem Masses and go out to the cemeteries by the hundreds of thousands to light candles and lay wreaths, while on the last Sunday of the month *Totensonntag* (Death Sunday), it is the Protestants' turn.

Then, as if that were not enough, there is a national memorial day, *Volkstrauertag* (People's Memorial Day). Originally this was to commemorate the fallen of the two world wars. In postwar West Germany, however, the meaning of this day has officially been extended to include *Die Opfer der Gewaltherrschaft* (Victims of Despotism).

During the month of November the Germans are inundated by radio, press, and TV with lengthy meditations, poems, documentaries on death, plays dealing with war, the Nazi past, and much funereal symphonic music.

But during that same month another spirit begins slowly to emerge. In Bavaria, the season gets its traditional start: "On the 11th, 11th, 11, 11 [*i.e.,* November 11, at 11:11 A.M.]"—and how that sentence ends nobody knows, because the slogan means simply that the Carnival season has begun. By the end of the month the rest of Germany too has forgotten about death and every German worth his name is trying to think of what costume he will wear at the round of Fasching, Carnival, Fastnacht balls that will preoccupy him until Ash Wednesday.

◄ 23 ►

THE CHRISTIAN REVOLUTION

"WEST GERMANY TODAY," the American humorist Harry Golden once said during a visit, "can be defined as 'Prosperity in search of a soul.' "

If buildings alone were a criterion of spirituality, one would not have far to look: from Münster to Munich there is a super-rosary in brick and mortar, from magnificent ancient cathedrals to a dazzling array of provocative modern churches. More churches have been constructed in the postwar Federal Republic—an estimated 10,000—than in the four centuries between the Reformation and World War II.

However, most of the modern churches after a few years show the telltale ravages of time. A century from now chances are people will still visit the Cologne cathedral, whose origins go back to the Middle Ages, but very few modern German churches, if they are around at all, will be worth looking at.

Perhaps it is just as well. The indignation of German Christians is mounting over the *Kirchenbauwut* (church-building obsession). Demands are growing for all-purpose churches that can be used as community centers and meeting halls, for social events as well as services.

In 1970 many hundreds of these churches stood nearly empty Sunday after Sunday, while an unprecedented mass exodus from church membership was in full swing. A survey conducted by *Der Stern* in January, 1970, revealed that Catholics and Protestants have been serving notice to their churches at the rate of thirty to forty daily in towns as small as Kiel (300,000). In Munich (population: 1,250,000) 1,800 Catholics left the Church in 1969, compared with an average of 900 over the preceding nine years. In West Berlin more than 13,000 Protestants left the Church by November, 1969, which was 70 percent more than in the previous year. Although there were no national figures available, the trend continued throughout the year and ultimately spread from the cities to the countryside.

It is important to point out that in the Federal Republic all citizens are required to register with the police authorities and also give their religious affiliation. Adults are then automatically required to pay an annual church tax (which amounts roughly to 10 percent of one's income tax), which is administered by state tax officials. In reimbursement for the state's tax collection service, the churches turn back about 4 percent of the total collected. In 1970 the vast majority of West Germans were church-registered: 51 percent in the Evangelical Lutheran Church and 43.8 percent in the Roman Catholic Church, with just a few hundred thousand in the so-called free churches (which are outside the church-tax system and depend on voluntary contributions).

This system evolved in the aftermath of the Napoleonic confiscation of church properties in 1803. In compensation the subsequent German state agreed to collect taxes in support of the church.

Today church authorities are loath to relinquish the church-tax system, even though there is growing pressure to drop the state-administered system in favor of voluntary support, as in the United States. The Roman Catholic bishops in 1970 issued a joint statement upholding the system, arguing that it spreads the burden of church support, protects them from special-interest groups, and assures a dependable income for church employees.

The German churches are enormously wealthy. In 1968 alone the Roman Catholic Church received about $310 million from church taxes. Many dioceses and church institutions own industrial properties. A whole chain of exquisite brandy distilleries is owned by the Benedictine Monastery of Ettal. Vast sums are collected from real estate and stock market investments.

It does not come as a surprise that church officials are alarmed by the church dropouts, which they see as a threat to their very existence. For the majority appear to be leaving in order to get out of paying the church tax. Deeper probes, however, reveal that many are leaving out of disillusionment with a church that no longer has relevance in daily life. According to one survey, 52 percent of all Christians in West Germany do not believe in life after death. The Institute of Applied Social Science in Bonn revealed in 1970 that only 37 percent of the population (in cities as few as 20 percent) regularly attend religious services compared to 43 percent a year previously, and that the greatest decline is in the Catholic Church.

Some observers see the dropout trend positively. *Oberkirchen-rat* (High Councillor) Hermann Kalinna, of the Evangelical Church's Diplomatic Office in Bonn, told me in an interview, "The present situation is far healthier, because we prefer that people stay in the Church out of conviction rather than habit or respectability as in the past. Especially in the immediate postwar years people joined the churches in droves because it made them look good professionally and socially. Why, only a few years ago it would have been unthinkable for a teacher to leave his church. He would have been instantly dismissed. Today, the waves of crises that have inundated the Christian churches have discredited them. There is no longer a social stigma attached to leaving. On the contrary, it is becoming fashionable to quit.

"But, to me the significant thing is that people now are at least stopping to think why they are in the church. If they leave, then they do so because *they made a decision.* While those who stay also were compelled to ask themselves: 'Why am I a member of this church and what am I going to do about it?' In the long run, this may actually save the Church because those who stay, really care."

Paradoxical as it may sound, the mass exodus is actually the result of dynamic social awakening that is shaking the Christian churches in Germany to their very foundations. Thus, large numbers of conservative Christians are leaving in protest to the increasing social involvement of the churches, while progressives are leaving because in their view the churches should be even more socially involved. Still others are leaving in protest to the state church-tax system. In many areas the free churches, such as the Seventh Day Adventists, Mormons, and Jehovah's Witnesses are gaining members who are leaving the Evangelical Church, which they think is straying from fundamental religion.

At the same time, never has interest in religious questions been greater in West Germany, especially among the younger generation, than now. The manager of Herder's (Roman Catholic) book store in downtown Cologne told me, "There is no such thing as a book sales crisis, but rather a shift of interest. Pious books, meditations, are 'out,' but controversial books on theology and the social aspects of religion are very much 'in.' In fact, more lay people are reading theology than ever before. Moreover, one can hardly speak any longer of 'Catholic' and 'Protestant' book shops. Most of them have long been interconfessional."

German mass media are constantly giving full treatment to religious subjects. An editor of the religious affairs department of Bavarian Broadcasting told me that his colleagues in the other departments envy his inevitably larger mail response. The Catholic Academy, an adult education center in Munich, often has standing room only, even for seemingly abstruse subjects as Zen Buddhist meditation.

The Authority Crisis

As for reform in the Catholic Church, it is pretty much a matter of the tail wagging the dog. In spite of their reputation as the foremost liberals at the Vatican Council, the German Catholic bishops are notorious for foot-dragging at home. (One close adviser to Cardinal Julius Doepfner, chairman of the German Bishops' Conference and archbishop of Munich, told me, "The bishops are poor theologians and had to rely at the Council on their *periti*. These happened to be people like Karl Rahner, S.J., for the best theologians were liberal. Had there been any articulate conservative theologians around at the time, the German presence at the Council might just as well have gone conservative." Of Josef Cardinal Frings, retired archbishop of Cologne, it has often been said that his position was usually that of the last person who left his presence.)

Cardinal Doepfner told me in an interview that he opposes a change in celibacy regulations "at this emotionally charged period," and was decidedly cool toward suggestions like female rights or priesthood in the Church, intercommunion, interfaith news services, or electing bishops for limited terms of office.

"Not only does the German Catholic hierarchy offer precious few solutions to the burning problems of our time," sociologist Dr. Paul Eckert, O.P., told me, "they are not even asking the right questions."

Some of the German bishops still have, if unconsciously, prince-bishop mannerisms. Most of them live in sumptuous villas. Julius Cardinal Doepfner resides in a palace that was renovated twice in a decade and rides in a slick Mercedes with a shining brass-framed coat of arms with the insignia "I preach Christ crucified." The German Protestant bishops attending the World Council of Churches' Fourth Assembly—devoted to world poverty—in Uppsala, Sweden, in 1968, were severely criticized for being the only delegates to come in chauffeur-driven limousines.

The articulate laity and impatient clergy accuse the Catholic bishops of still fighting the Bismarckian Kulturkampf of 1872. They are worried about mixed marriages, at a time when marriage itself is questioned. They balk endlessly about intercommunion when all around them people have stopped going to communion altogether, and they fight for the purity of doctrine when theologians are asking whether even the most elementary of doctrines still has value.

To my astonishment, the official representative of the German Catholic bishops in Bonn, Monsignor Wilhelm Wöste, a kindly fiftyish man who looks like a country doctor and still wears the clerical garb that was vogue in 1920, spent the greater part of an hour emotionally telling me that German Catholic parents have a "right" to state-sponsored confessional schools. This, at a time when the Wickert Institute of Tübingen revealed in a survey that 77 percent of all Christian parents prefer nondenominational schools.

The die-hard Catholic bishops base their case on a concordat signed between Hitler and the Vatican in 1933, which was upheld as still valid by the Federal Constitutional Court in 1957, as well as regional concordats signed by the Vatican and individual provinces.

However, progressive Catholics and Protestants argue that the "days of concordats are over" and that in a time when the churches are fighting for the survival of religion at all, it is silly to argue over confessional schools. Even so, the biconfessional system, with neutral religious instruction, swiftly becoming standard in most areas, is after all in the interest of ecumenical understanding. Germans, they say, should be glad to have religious instruction in public elementary schools at all, considering that other countries, like the United States, prohibit such instruction.

In spite of the communications gap between the bishops and the clergy, between the clergy and the people, and, within the various groups, between progressives and conservatives, the West German churches in 1970 had not fostered an "underground church" or free church movement, such as that which swept the United States or the undisciplined movements in the Netherlands. "But," one cautious observer said, "we cannot rule it out as a possibility either."

At the beginning of the decade the greatest impetus came from the rank-and-file clergy and faithful, who were prodding their leaders into action.

A few examples can be cited here:

BIRTH CONTROL. The turning point for Roman Catholics came in September, 1968, during the Eighty-second German Catholic Conference at Essen, when 5,000 participants staged an open rebellion against Pope Paul VI's encyclical *Humanae Vitae* on birth control.

Even monks and nuns joined the ranks of the rebels. Benedictine Abbot Alcuin Heising pleaded for freedom of speech. (Several months afterwards he became laicized in protest against Roman Catholic authoritarianism and then married.) Sister Johanna Eichmann demanded the abolition of "maternalism in convents" and called for the emancipation of nuns.

While the West German episcopate timidly issued a carefully-worded statement admitting that the Pope's word on contraception "is not infallible," some 60 percent of German Catholic women of childbearing age unabashedly took the pill.

CELIBACY. Well over 76 percent of West German Catholic clergy opposes compulsory celibacy as a requirement for the priesthood. But in February, 1970, the German episcopacy, led by Cardinal Doepfner, adamantly upheld traditional celibacy, thereby taking an opposite stand from that of their Dutch colleagues who had urged modification of the celibacy regulations earlier that year.

However, the number of West German laicized priests is relatively small. Between 1964 and 1968 1 percent (195) of the diocesan Catholic clergy left the priesthood and 1.7 percent (85) of order priests. Celibacy is regarded as only one problem among many in the current crisis, and not even the most important. One can speak rather of an "identity crisis," which is riddling the Protestant clergy as well.

Many German priests share the sentiments so eloquently expressed by a group of French priests in an open letter to their bishops in November, 1968, in which they raised fundamental questions about the nature of the priesthood itself. "Whose priests? Priests for what? These are the questions we are asking ourselves and they are continually being asked of us. Clearly they reveal numerous contradictions: between on the one hand what we say in faith, in the name of the Gospel, and on the other hand what we are forced to do and live as members of the clergy;

between the manner in which we live and the manner in which most men live."

DISSENTING GROUPS. An estimated 2,000 out of 20,000 West German Catholic clergy (not counting religious orders) are members of twenty-one priest groups (Pipeline, SOG—Solidarity Group, etc.) which are struggling for a democratization of the Church. Since 1965 they have been holding continuous meetings aiming toward more autonomy for local and national churches; for the election of bishops by priests and laity and for limited terms; for the abolishment of compulsory celibacy; for the reform of marriage laws (more rights for non-Catholic partners in mixed marriages, divorce); greater freedom of theological differences; the abolition of the college of cardinals, nuncios, and Vatican diplomacy; the subordination of the Vatican curia under the synod of bishops; and, above all, the election of the pope by all 2,108 bishops instead of by the college of cardinals—and for a limited term.

Inevitably the activity of these "rebel" priests aroused and mobilized the conservatives, and a polarization has set in. On the far left, *Kritische Katholiken* (Critical Catholics) wish to overthrow the Establishment altogether and replace it by an amorphous, unrestrained church movement, and on the far right, the *Una Voce* group (no relation to an international movement by the same name) upholds veneration of the Virgin Mary, loyalty to the Pope, *Humanae Vitae,* celibacy, and traditional doctrines. In 1969 they demonstrated in front of Cardinal Doepfner's residence, denouncing him as a heretic—while progressive Catholics never cease to insist that the cardinal is an archreactionary.

DEMOCRATIZATION. There is a saying in Germany, "Wherever two or three Germans are gathered together, there you have four organizations." Since "democratization" is very much "in" in the Federal Republic these days, and nowhere more than in the Christian churches, the Germans immediately set about democratizing with a fury, which means of course a frenzy of organization. There are parish councils, regional councils, diocesan councils, priest councils, and an endless array of conferences, conferences, and still more conferences. In 1972 the first West German Roman Catholic Synod will take place, which aims to establish guidelines and reforms for the future of German Catholicism, but already there is widespread dissension about what some regard as heavy-handed manipulation by the hierarchy.

The bishops, it seems, are not about to relinquish an authority which they haven't even noticed has already begun a process of rapid deterioration. Over the heads of the officials of the Central Committee of German Catholics, which represents all lay Catholic organizations in the country, the hierarchy in January, 1970, published statutes for the proposed synod parliament, with the controversial paragraph, "The right for the enactment of legislation in church matters is exclusively reserved to the bishops." Moreover, the bishops insist that over half of the proposed parliament consist of persons of their choice.

One-fourth of all officers of the Central Committee are hierarchy-designated. Although the 1,500 priests of the Freiburg diocese may elect thirteen members of their priests' council, four of them are appointed by the archbishop.

On the parish level, councils are elected by parish members. But here the picture is even more confusing. Nowadays people no longer take parish boundaries seriously but shop around for churches with liturgy and sermons to suit their taste. With increased ownership of automobiles, more German families than ever spend many weekends away from home, for many it is only a matter of hours or even minutes to hop over to Austria, Switzerland, France, Belgium, the Netherlands, or Denmark. Then there is a growing parish turnover, so that elections are often meaningless in a parish where hardly anyone knows personally more than a handful of parishioners. Even then, a parish is lucky if 40 percent vote at all. To play it safe, many parishioners simply vote for the candidate with a Ph.D. As a result parish councils are often poorly or unevenly representative.

There is much talk about letting clergy and laity elect their bishops. In Münster in 1969 some 400 lay leaders supposedly had a voice in the selection of the new ordinary. But, according to Bernd Feldhaus, a schoolteacher and chairman of the Catholic Society for Church and Democracy, "It was a farce." He reportedly intimated that after the votes of the 400 were submitted, the results were hushed up, so that there is no way of knowing whether or not the actual choice, which was made by the cathedral chapter behind closed doors, was guided by the votes.

It is my considered conviction that the German bishops, like their colleagues around the world, are frightened by the convulsions within the Church and cling to the last vestiges of their authority out of sheer desperation and helplessness. "Democratization? What's that?" Cardinal Doepfner asked me when I brought up the subject in an interview. "Who," he asked, "would elect the bishops?" "Why, the faithful," I replied sheepishly, "the ordinary parishioners." To my amazement the Cardinal actually lost his cool and literally began pounding on the table. He enunciated every word slowly. "That," he said, "is just the point. *Who-are-the-faithful?* Can you tell me? I'd like to know!"

I realized that I was sitting in the presence of a very lonely man, who feels betrayed on all sides and sees all the things he loves and believes in vitally threatened by a whole avalanche of forces that he cannot even identify, let alone understand.

"Can you imagine what would happen in such an election campaign?" he continued. "Factions, strife, demonstrations, insults, bitterness, perhaps violence. Progressives and conservatives unleashing their passions to the full! If the progressives won, would the conservatives follow? And if the conservatives won, I most seriously doubt that the progressives would democratically accept the results of a democratic process they so emotionally promote now.... The big thing missing in the present upheaval all over the world is: *There is precious little concern about the essential matters of the Faith itself.*" The *Herr Kardinal* slumped into his chair and breathed heavily. He looked much older than his fifty-six years.

To be sure, democratization of the Church has its limits. Time and again I was told by church leaders, journalists, and lay intellectuals, you cannot vote on whether Jesus Christ was an historic person or on the existence of God any more than you can on whether the grass is green or the ingredients of water are anything other than H_2O. As Dr. Friedrich Carl Schilling, assistant editor-in-chief of the Evangelical Press Agency in Frankfurt-Main told me, "If it were put to a vote, the death penalty would most likely be legal in the Federal Republic. Our Bundestag abolished the death penalty—but against the wishes of the majority."

Meanwhile the rank-and-file clergy and laity are increasingly restive. The bishops are beginning to come around to meet their priests and people and to listen more. Most dioceses now publish their financial statements. The church tax has been lowered and representatives of clergy and laity have more authority in the distribution of funds. More money than ever is being allotted to development aid, community centers, adult education, the training of lay theologians and specialists, modern parish planning, and social problems.

WOMEN IN THE CHURCH. West German women are for the most part second-class citizens as far as the Christian churches are concerned. In the Evangelical Church some 250 female clergy compete with 10,000 male colleagues, and of these less than half—only 100—have pastor status. The others are restricted to subordinate positions. Moreover, female pastors must abandon their positions in the event of marriage. Dr. Hans Timme, vice-president of the Westphalian Regional Church, belongs to a growing minority of church leaders who are striving for a more equitable treatment of female pastors.

In the Roman Catholic Church the situation is even worse. Cardinal Doepfner has been extremely reserved about even discussing the possibility of the female ministry, which the Vatican in 1970 definitely ruled out. That same year, in January, the official Vatican newspaper, *L'Osservatore Romano,* even went so far as to state that it would lead to the death of the Roman Catholic Church if it gave in to the demands for women priests. In January, 1970, the Vatican refused to grant accreditation to a West German diplomat, Mrs. Elisabeth Müller, because she was a woman. However, the majority of West German Catholic or Protestant women have themselves shown more lethargy than interest in promoting their own cause. West German Broadcasting turned down my suggestion for a script on women in the church on the grounds that "there would be very little interest in it."

In January, 1970, some 90,000 German nuns were still active in hundreds of hospitals, schools, homes for the aged, and convents. As everywhere else in the world, they are undergoing the agony of the crisis syndrome. Nuns and priests are continually giving talks on such subjects as "Does Religious Life Have a Future?" "Do Nuns Still Have a Meaning?"

Mother Maria Theresita, chairwoman of the Association of Religious Superiors in Germany, admitted that in her own congregation alone, which numbers 1,100, the number of candidates has been dwindling. In 1968 only 41 new candidates applied, compared with 79 in 1957.

However, she sees the future optimistically. Radical changes

389

are already underway in most congregations. There has been streamlining in dress, increase in recreational activity, contact with the outside world. Nuns may now read newspapers, the most permissive modern literature, and attend far-out plays. They have more vacation time, more independence, and a greater professionalism is required in their work. Many are trained as psychologists, physicians, technicians, and journalists. There is a trend away from big, sprawling convents to small teams working in apartment houses.

THEOLOGICAL PLURALISM. Without a doubt the proliferation and polarization of theological thought in West Germany has unleashed widespread confusion, disillusionment, and deep inner insecurity. *Oberkirchenrat* Kalinna goes so far as to attribute much of the frenzy of young Protestant clergy over social problems to their inner distress, as an escape from the hard problems of fundamental theology. Many young theologians are eager to plunge wholeheartedly into sociological ventures but assiduously avoid parish assignments, where they have to pretend a faith they no longer can defend or even explain. "Historical and biblical studies," Kalinna said, "are suffering. Indeed, they are not even taken seriously. The young clergy regard themselves as primarily socially committed. It is not an accident that church groups, pastors, theologians are right there among the student demonstrators, protestors, New Left.

"Strangely enough, others are attracted by the radical new theology, in fact many join the church in order to have an opportunity to improve the world. But the emphasis is social. Theology is for this very reason a central problem in the Church today, but unfortunately very few recognize this fact."

On the Roman Catholic side, Professor Hubertus Halbfas, theologian on the faculty of Bonn University, was removed in 1969 from his teaching position with the Academy for Youth Affairs and from the Institute for Catechetics and Homiletics and generally restricted by the Catholic authorities from teaching and publishing. According to Roman Catholic biblical scholars and renowned theologians, as well as the German hierarchy, his demythologization of events in the New Testament went far beyond the bounds of acceptable Catholic teaching. For example, Halbfas sees only symbolism, not fact, in such traditionally accepted miracles as the multiplication of loaves and fishes or Christ's walking on the water.

Halbfas is not alone. The Munich theologian, Dr. Thomas Sartory, a former Benedictine monk (now married), published a much-discussed book, *In der Hölle Brennt Kein Feuer* (*No Fire Burns in Hell*), in which he questions traditional Catholic concepts of heaven, hell, sin, eternal punishment. The number of theologians, Catholic and Protestant, is growing who question the literal interpretations of the Virgin Birth, original sin, transubstantiation of bread and wine into the body and blood of Christ, the existence of angels.

This trend is causing so much concern that even former avant-garde theologians like the internationally renowned Karl Rahner, S.J., and Swiss-born Hans Küng, who were under heavy fire during the Vatican Council and both of whose writings have repeatedly been suspect by the Vatican curia, have become downright conservative in the eyes of the New Left theologians. In February, 1970, Rahner published a lead article in the Catholic weekly, *Publik,* entitled, "Am I Right or Left?" The former black sheep of the Establishment now finds himself defending the German bishops in their restrictive stand against Halbfas and speaking forthrightly in support of traditional Catholic teachings. The radical theologians have coined a term for him: "Adaptive Theologian." Another Roman Catholic theologian, Johannes Metz, has gained considerable attention, especially in the United States, for his explorations in "political theology." He emphasizes a transcendental God and the "we" of salvation, which is a departure from the previous "I" dominating Roman Catholic God-relationships. He himself calls it "the theology of the world."

"The secularity of the world," he writes, "as we see it today in a globally heightened form, has fundamentally arisen not against Christianity, but through it." However, the young radicals dismiss his thought as merely "the liberation as dogmatic projection."

As for the Protestants

In West Germany one sometimes wonders if it is not the Protestants who were mostly shaken up by Vatican II, since they have been in a state of continuous turmoil every bit as great as the Catholics. Their watershed year in the present upheaval was 1966 when more than 20,000 Evangelicals assembled in the

Dortmund sports stadium, thundering their battle cry, "No Other Gospel," in protest against "dangerous modernism" which they believe is shaking the very foundations of their traditional faith.

It is from this group that a large percentage of the dropouts, mentioned in the beginning of this chapter, come. They have become very insecure by the new political orientation of the progressive pastors. Nothing symbolizes this more than the public withdrawal from Evangelical Lutheran Church membership of the Federal Republic's most prominent publisher, the controversial newspaper tycoon, Axel Springer, who switched membership to a small splinter sect, the Old-Lutheran Church of Berlin, which only has 40,000 adherents. In an open letter to the Berlin press officer of the Evangelical Church, Springer wrote, "I am disturbed to a high degree that the Church continually presumes to give me unsolicited advice on political, economic, and industrial matters, while at the same time abandoning more and more precisely those things which I need from the Church, namely peace with God, consolation, and encouragement, and, for matters of conscience, the absolute criterion of the Gospel." Springer speaks for many (*Die Welt, Hamburger Abendblatt, Hör Zu, Berliner Abendblatt, BZ,* and the national mass-circulation daily, *Bild,* with over 4 million readers), and no doubt his influence played a big role in the Church exodus of 1970. However, it is not exactly irrelevant to point out that politically-conscious Evangelical clergy have been among the foremost opponents of the Springer press monopoly (see Chapter 14).

Evangelical theologians and pastors have been deeply involved collaborators with the New Left, with student rebels and demonstrators. The Evangelical Church has issued a whole series of *Denkschriften* (Memoranda) on political and social issues, such as recognition of the Oder-Neisse border, a realistic attitude toward the GDR, opposition to U.S. Vietnam policy, support for codetermination in industry, opposition to the Federal Republic's emergency laws which would limit democratic procedure in the event of sudden danger—all issues on which the Springer press usually takes a conservative point of view.

Even the Roman Catholic bishops have made joint statements on Polish reconciliation, and have encouraged Christian involvement in social and political questions. Only a few years ago priests were still urging from the pulpit that the faithful vote for the CDU or CSU. Today the CDU/CSU can no longer count on the Catholic vote. On the contrary, it has become fashionable in many Catholic circles to vote socialist.

Numerous Evangelical pastors have been suspended, transferred, or otherwise penalized for their political activities. But nobody any longer seriously doubts that the Evangelical and Roman Catholic churches have cast their lot squarely with the political and social issues of the day. Evangelical Bishop Kurt Scharf of Berlin, who has been expelled from his East Berlin headquarters and home by the GDR, and who vividly recalls the Christian default in the Third Reich, has unremittingly and eloquently insisted that a Church divorced from politics is unrealistic and contrary to the teachings of the Bible. "The Church," he has said, "belongs in the center of the controversies of our times. Without interest in the outside world, the Church would be no more than an introverted sect."

On the theological level the principal target of the fundamentalists has been the Reverend Dr. Rudolf Bultmann, professor emeritus of Marburg University, and his existentialist "demythologization school" of theology, which has been dominating German Protestant theology since World War II. The traditionalists are frightened by the radical Bultmann skepticism concerning the historic character of Christian revelation and the thesis that the miracles performed by Christ and basic tenets of Christian faith such as the Virgin Birth, Christ's divine nature, and the Resurrection must be interpreted symbolically.

The late Dr. Karl Barth, the internationally renowned Swiss theologian, had dismissed Bultmannism as "of no consequence," but even such giants as he and Paul Tillich are also belittled by the New Left theologians for having no concrete answers to today's problems.

Meanwhile, even Bultmann is rapidly becoming old hat. The young radicals dismiss him as basically conservative, personalist, *bürgerlich*, with little awareness of social ethics, a concern for only a handful of experts at the universities. Bultmann, they argue, merely improved on the writings of men like David Friedrich Strauss and Friedrich Nietzsche (who coined the famous "God is dead" phrase in the nineteenth century).

The son of a Nazi customs official, fortyish Wolfgang Pannenberg of Mainz University, and a new school of young theologians known as the "Pannenberg Circle" argue that Bultmannism is merely a kind of "Biblical authoritarianism" of God's word. Pannenberg dramatically asserts that the Resurrection is, properly understood, a decided historical event. The fact of the Resurrection, he argues, was one of the primitive elements of Christian teaching, and is God's proof to man that biological death is not the end of existence.

But Pannenberg inevitably comes in for attack from progressives who say his theology is only an updated version of traditionalism and, on the other hand, traditionalists are offended by his contention that the Virgin Birth is probably a legend. American theologian William Hamilton accuses Pannenberg of being a "medievalist" because he revives God as the supreme supervisor of the forces of the universe—an idea repugnant to our secular age.

A young Reformed Church theologian, Jürgen Moltmann, pleads for a "theology of hope," arguing that the churches have neglected the central fact of Christianity—the forward-looking paradise of the future. Instead the church has been morbidly preoccupied with the past, it is a Church "that lives on memories." Even atheist philosopher Ernst Bloch, on whom Moltmann bases much of this theology, says that man's hope for the future is the basis for transcendence in the universe.

An Evangelical woman theologian, Dr. Dorothee Sölle, married to a former Catholic priest, has created a stir for her "political theology," political church services, and "atheistic faith in God."

All in all, West German theology today is pretty much of a merry-go-round affair. Small wonder, then, that so many German Catholics and Protestants seek refuge in "that old-time religion," arguing that "it is better to believe in the tried and true than in the confusing hodgepodge of modern Christianity." Even *Oberkirchenrat* Kalinna admitted to me, with a sigh, "Most of the current theologians are completely unrelated to one another. There are precious few bridges."

In spite of all this, the mood of the West German churches these days is one of boundless optimism. The decade-old book, *Die Bibel Hat Doch Recht* (*The Bible Is Right After All*), by Werner Keller is a continuing best seller. Religious controversy draws capacity crowds everywhere, and Ernst Bloch finds himself saying, "Where there is hope, there is religion."

The New Christianity

As the polarization *within* the two big church bodies grows greater and greater, paradoxically unifying trends *between* the two are also rapidly increasing. As time goes on, it is getting harder and harder to distinguish the Roman Catholic Church from the Evangelical Church in the Federal Republic. On the official level, of course, differences remain. But in the challenging reality of daily life, they are rapidly disappearing out of pragmatic considerations. While the hierarchy and officials of the Catholic and Protestant establishments pedantically and timidly measure out the future with teaspoons, a growing, articulate minority of restless clergy and people are bursting out all over.

In Frankfurt/Main, at the main downtown subway exit, where an estimated 300,000 persons pass daily, a small "shop" located alongside a fashion store, gently invites passersby, hardly mentioning religion at all, to take advantage of the *Beratungs-stelle* (counseling service). Anyone seeking advice on any problem whatsoever may drop in on any weekday until 10 P.M. Inside, religion is played down. A Catholic and an Evangelical clergyman are on hand, but there is no way of telling them apart. And there are two lay specialists. No forms are filled out, no registration takes place. No one even asks the caller's name. The center merely keeps track statistically of the number of callers, topics discussed, and approximate age and sex, but without asking for any of this information. It is interesting that very few persons seek financial help, but most ask advice on marriage, family, and vocational problems. The center has been a godsend for countless foreigners, especially the many thousands of guest workers in the city, who find adjustment in the strange country hard for them.

Like most West German cities, Frankfurt also has a *Telefon-seelsorge* (Telephone Ministry). By means of a widely advertised telephone number, persons may anonymously seek help over the phone seven days a week. Protestant and Catholic clergy and laity are "on call" around the clock. For those who wish it, specialized agency help is also available. The greatest success of this venture has been in dealing with potential suicides. Both the *Beratungsstelle* and the *Telefonseelsorge* appear to be made to order for the impersonal cruelty of modern urban life. For many persons they are a last place to turn when life no longer has meaning.

But while new forms are being invented for the ministry, some of the time-honored forms are stirring with new life. Roman Catholic monasticism is of course riddled with crises. There is very little these days to distinguish a Benedictine monk wearing a tie and suit from a Franciscan friar in a turtleneck sweater. More and more monks and religious are required to specialize in technical fields, to become sociologists, city planners, psychologists, editors, or to learn the intricacies of data processing. The encroachments of TV, mass media, expanding urbanization, the increasing work load commensurate with declining vocations—and it seems that all that is left are the buildings, occasionally worn habits, the medieval nomenclature, vestigial rules perfunctorily observed by only that third of monks or religious who are not dashing hither and thither giving lectures or running projects.

Strangely enough, however, monasticism is discovering new possibilities precisely in the hectic age of distraction. People are beginning to ask, "What is so irrelevant about a heaven-sent retreat with good men, prayer, meditation, and quiet?" The point is, until now this was a possibility open only to a select few who were willing to devote their entire lives to monasticism—if they met the requirements.

Many West German religious institutions are rediscovering their own identity, and at the same time making enriching new contacts with people "in the outside world," under an experiment called *Kloster auf Zeit* (Temporary Monasticism). Under the new plan, lay persons, sometimes married couples, may live as monks and religious at these institutions for short periods, sharing the routine of prayer, meditation, good food, wholesome walks on the monastic grounds, with no obligation to join permanently—and at low cost. It is interesting that precisely at a time when the death toll has sounded for Roman Catholic monasticism, these ancient religious forms have been adopted by the Protestants, notably the Marian Sisters at Darmstadt and the famous Brothers of Taizé, France.

It is also important to point out that many West German monasteries have long been deeply involved in social projects. The Dominicans at Walberberg coauthored the original draft of the CDU, but they also initiated talks between the Roman Catholic hierarchy and the SPD, paving the way for Catholic acceptance of German socialism. They were the first to send German priest-workers to the coal mines of the Ruhr, and they developed an entire new concept of industrial ministry that has become standard in many dioceses.

It was the Benedictine monastery of Maria Laach that protected Konrad Adenauer all during the Hitler years as a secret guest living inconspicuously in a basement cell. That same monastery, along with that of Beuron, launched the Liturgical Movement that swept throughout the Roman Catholic world a generation before Vatican II. Maria Laach today is irreverently compared to the extinct prehistoric volcano on its premises, as it sticks stubbornly to an old-fashioned interpretation of the Benedictine Rule as well as Latin rendition of the Mass and sung office. Nevertheless two of its monks regularly don blue jeans, go to a Cologne tenement, and live there for long periods, ministering to workers' families and offering Mass in their living rooms.

Most West German theology students, Catholic as well as Protestant, now live in small groups in student homes and apartments, rather than in large buildings, mingle with other students, and get their degrees from the secular universities. Catholic seminarians have a *Freies Jahr* (free year), in which they can take time out to travel, visit another university, savoring the beer in Munich or the mountains in Switzerland. They are exposed to all the rigors and adventure of *Studentenleben,* and although only a third of all theology students go on to ordination, those who persevere are usually far better adjusted than their older colleagues who studied under the old not-so-splendid isolation of pre-conciliar seminaries.

"The Priesthood of All Believers"

In Cologne, too, I visited St. Alban's Roman Catholic parish in the heart of the working class neighborhood. Here I was received by a mild-mannered man in his fifties, wearing a turtleneck sweater and smoking jacket, who turned out to be the pastor, Dr. W. Poth. He has realized for some time that the old patriarchal concept of a pastor was inadequate for modern urban life. And he has accepted the consequences.

For one thing, his parish is called *Angebots Pfarrei, i.e.,* it has no boundaries and people come here from all over the city and environs. Here too is located the city's Montessori school, open to children of all faiths, who come from all over the area.

Because of the critical priest shortage attributed to declining vocations, Dr. Poth is the only priest at St. Alban's. As a result, he was compelled to initiate a step that has already become part of the revolutionary new pattern of modern parishes. Realizing that he could not do all the work by himself, Dr. Poth was one of the very first Roman Catholic pastors to hire a lay administrator (a married man and a father of seven children), who is paid a good salary. It turned out that this administrator had a knack for dealing with people, so that he gradually took over many ministerial duties, including the establishment of a rehabilitation center for ex-convicts. He makes most of the house calls, and is a big hit with the aged. "He is warmly received," says Dr. Poth, "and people are not at all disturbed because he is not a priest. On the contrary, because he is married they confide all the more readily in him."

"The ministry," he added, "is no longer the exclusive task of ordained priests. Luther's 'priesthood of all believers' has become a reality. So you see, necessity is also the mother of spiritual invention."

Although some 4,300 Roman Catholics are registered at St. Alban's, only about 1,200 regularly attend Mass, and less than half of these—or 10 percent—really take an active part in the parish's life.

"I have no illusions," Dr. Poth admits. "A large percentage of our 'families' have highly irregular marriages—by previous moral standards, that is. We have ever so many common-law marriages, mixed marriages, divorcees, unmarried mothers, some of them with children by more than one father—but they have crucifixes in their bedrooms, holy water fonts on their doorposts, and send their children to first communion. We even have Corpus Christi processions every year. But I am not fooled. Most of this is little more than folklore, something like Karnival."

In Dr. Poth's view the days of laying down rules and keeping track of sins are over. He has cut down his time in the traditional confessional box to only an hour a week and then only "because there are some who still want it." He actually discourages private confession, and urges people to use one of twenty-six new prayer forms he composed for general confession recited in common before Mass.

"The Church is no longer a lofty institution that, from above, tells people what to do. It must rather help them find their own guidelines for deciding themselves what is right." In regard to birth control, for example, Dr. Poth says each situation has to be handled for itself. "And I merely try to help them realize all the moral considerations. Morality cannot be imposed by a priest but arises from free inner choice. The first virtue is not chastity but love. I always emphasize this in every problem: In this situation, what does love dictate? If a couple needs birth control for their love, then that is the answer."

The authority crisis is very real to Dr. Poth. "The decline of authority is immense. What the pope says means nothing anymore. And as for the bishops, people are fed up with their know-it-all condescension."

Dr. Poth sees institutionalization as the biggest obstacle to general religious reform. "Everything is so thoroughly organized that it stifles genuine dynamic religious involvement. Renewal has become too much of a super-plan prepared by experts wearing white smocks in a clean office, far removed from the grease of a truck driver or the grime of a factory worker. This plan is pompously imposed from above, instead of letting people jump into action, letting them make mistakes, and seeing the natural organization grow out of the situation."

The other big difficulty is the tremendous communications gap between bishops and clergy on the one hand, and between clergy and people. "They are simply not on the same wave length."

Perhaps the biggest headache of all is the overwhelming atmosphere that is too complex and subtle to be defined or even identified: the overriding, crushing, omnipresent, all-encompassing influence of the "Affluent Society." It is not sexual permissiveness that concerns Dr. Poth so much as the materialistic exploitation that accompanies it—the luxury cults, hypersexuality, the frantic search for thrills, and the frustration that can only come from endless pursuit of sheer material and physical pleasure.

In spite of all this, Dr. Poth exudes an astounding spirit of optimism. "You see, those few who remain in the Church are more active, more articulate, more involved than ever before." Dr. Poth is enthusiastic about the action group in St. Alban's which has demonstrated against U.S. participation in Vietnam, protested against the murder of Indians in Brazil, and stirred up interest in former Biafra. Special collections at Christmas, 1969, jumped from 9,000 DM's in 1968 to 19,200 DM's—113 percent more—because they were designated for Third World causes instead of previous German charities. "You see, the people are awakening to social responsibility."

Church of the Future

On the outskirts of Frankfurt/Main is a sprawling modern satellite settlement called Nordwest Stadt, built largely with trade union funds in 1961. Here I spent an evening talking with Dekan Hermann Raiss, dean of nine Evangelical parishes in the area.

A soft-spoken, medium-sized man in his mid-forties, just beginning to gray at the temples, Dr. Raiss immediately admitted that his Church is in the throes of an authority crisis. The main support of the Evangelical Church in Germany, he said, comes from the conservative majority, who are extremely uneasy about the growing sense of political and social involvement. The young people, however, are leaving the Church in droves because they regard it as so much historical baggage. "We are seeking a middle group, who can help us build for the future, not by rejecting the past, but by building on it. But they do not yet exist."

Then Dr. Raiss used the same expression of Luther's that Dr. Poth had quoted to me: "the priesthood of all the faithful."

"I see the present crisis positively," he said. "For the first time since primitive Christianity we have a chance to realize that priesthood of all the faithful that Luther called for. Luther, however, died in bitter desperation because he failed to win the people. What he didn't realize was that it was impossible for him to implement the priesthood of all the faithful under the authoritarian system of the Church."

For Dean Raiss the future has already begun. "Thirty-three percent of our youths here in Nordwest Stadt are under fifteen years of age, the biggest percentage of youth in any West German community. More than any other Evangelical community we have to cope with youth. Our efforts here could be decisive."

Like Dr. Poth, Dean Raiss has done away with the patriarchial parish structure. He has united with two other parishes in the area in order to create a team of pastors with differentiated functions. The word is *"Gruppenamt"* or team ministry. In addition, the three pastors have added a lay educator to their team, and foresee adding specialists in group dynamics, psychology, etc.

Although these parishes still use traditional church buildings, they also forsee all-purpose parish structures of the future, serving simultaneously as community centers, meeting halls, theaters, and youth centers. The present church already has adapted to such differentiation.

Religious worship has also been differentiated to fit the needs of different segments of the community. While there are sermons and organ music for the older generation, worship includes such forms as teach-ins, film services, soul meetings, pop, and beat. "However," warns Raiss, "it is a grave mistake to impose pop or beat on youth. What you must do is always let them discover their own forms of expression, and then help them coordinate and cooperate.

"The big problem with young people," Raiss continued, "is that they get bored so easily. It was Mao Tse-tung who once pointed out that the trouble with a revolution is to keep it going for forty years. You know, the opponents of youth rebels use the wrong strategy. What they should do is encourage them to rebel for forty years. And then you'd see how soon they would peter out.

"That is why I am so optimistic about the future. When youth gets bored, resignation usually takes two forms, pot and violence. But there is still a vacuum. And if we work it right, the new Christianity can fill that vacuum."

The *Sex Welle* (sex wave) that has inundated West Germany as it has all over the West, must be considered, according to Raiss, in the entire context of the social crisis. "It has many healthy aspects. It is a genuine liberation for the frustrated. But young people are easily saturated. If you leave them alone, they will soon create a new morality. It is actually very easy to convince them that sex is not everything, that love is necessary."

Raiss favors legalizing pornography and adopting the total permissiveness of Denmark. "Children with a healthy upbringing," he said, while his own five-year-old daughter was avidly perusing an illustrated "Sex Atlas" in the corner, "are not endangered by exposure to pornography. And those who do not

401

have such an upbringing are just as much in danger from other influences. I think that people who need pornography should have it."

In Raiss' view nothing is timelier than the Bible. "It just needs a new vocabulary. Instead of Christ, the word 'Future Man' can be used. Instead of 'Kingdom of Heaven,' 'Future Society.' And nothing is timelier than the prophets. If they were not anti-Establishment people, who were? For that matter, so were Christ and the apostles. They were all politically involved. The opportunities are immense."

Nor is religious instruction, which is compulsory in West German public schools, a problem for Raiss. At the age of fourteen, pupils can drop out of religion classes, "but we have found that if you divide the class into seminars, and teach religion as comparative ethics, including individual psychology, oriental religions, Marxism, Mao, Ché, and the rest—why the interest is tremendous. Students flock to such classes."

People often ask Raiss why do we need a church at all for political commitment. "Couldn't we do this without belonging to a church?" He likes to answer that a true revolution is a change in society *and* the individual. "If you change only the society, you rape the individual. The whole man must be educated and affected. Somebody has to raise the question of the meaning of life, the universe. And right now the Churches are asking these questions more than anyone. Transcendental notions are returning. God-for-me is 'out.' But God-for-us is 'in.' The transcendental desire is very widespread. People are not yet conscious of it, but once awakened, you will see a flowering of new religious expression."

Thus, renewal, it seems, is arising not from the leaders of the Churches but from the pastors and the people themselves. "Something significant is happening," Kalinna told me, "to the German churches. What we have here could be the beginning of a new kind of grass-roots Christianity."

◄ 24 ►

THE GREAT AMERICAN INUNDATION

BACK IN 1955 on a warm day in May, I was straining against the railing of the top deck of the SS *New York,* as it slowly pulled into Bremerhaven, to get my first glimpse of Germany. The man next to me had turned on his transistor radio. "How appropriate," I thought. "Perhaps we shall hear some German music, or something suitable as we enter, for me, a new country."

But the first sound that I heard was an ear-splitting rendition of "Davy! Daaaaavvvyyyy Crockett!" at the end of which the announcer in unmistakable Americanese said, "This is the Armed Forces Network bringing you . . . . "

After that, everything else in those first moments in Germany was anticlimactic: the first people I saw on the dock were American GI's waiting for their arriving wives and sweethearts, the first automobiles were Chevys and Fords and Buicks, the first drink was a Coke, and the first food, a *Heisse Wurst* (hot dog).

Just a few days later, on my very first Sunday in Germany, I entered a café where a small band was playing, you guessed it, American jazz and hit tunes. Then, as a switch, the musicians donned ten-gallon hats and one of them grabbed the microphone and in a deep sonorous voice warbled across the room, *"Oh, ich bin von Texas, der Cowboy von der Plains. . . . "* The room was hushed in reverent silence, but the thick-accented Germanization of cowboy lingo was too much for me. I burst into an uncontrollable fit of laughter. Immediately about a hundred pairs of furious eyes fixed on me. I gulped, blushed to the roots of my crew cut, and headed swiftly for the john.

The Germans take their Wild West lore seriously. If in other countries children by the thousands play cowboys and Indians, in Germany countless thousands of adults are enthusiastically preoccupied with the great American morality play, the-Winning-of-the-West.

This interest was first awakened on a large scale by a German by the name of Karl May (pronounced "my"), who wrote more

403

than seventy novels around the turn of the century, mostly westerns, which have sold nearly twenty million copies and are still going strong. A ne'er-do-well in early life, May wrote the novels mostly while serving prison sentences for petty thievery (shades of O. Henry!), and didn't set foot in the United States until his novels brought him enough wampum to afford the trip.

May is still the main source of information for thousands of Germans who have gone just plain Wild-West loco. In spite of May's numerous inaccuracies (for example, Kit Carson— 1809-1868—reminiscing about his boyhood in Dodge City, which wasn't founded until 1872), Germans today probably know more about the folklore, history, customs, and ethnology of the early North American West than most Americans do.

In Bad Segeberg, Schleswig-Holstein, there is a permanent outdoor amphitheater built solely to dramatize May's works every summer. It is interesting that May idolizes the Indians, notably the exploits of one of his heroes, the Apache Chief Winnetou, and promotes red-white friendship. Julius Cardinal Doepfner, archbishop of Munich, willingly accepted the honorary title, "Big Chief Power and Courage" and an Indian headdress from an Indian tribe in Minnesota in 1966.

There are hundreds of Wild West clubs in Germany where one can see cowpokes, who have never been west of the Rhine, chewing on a knackwurst, and using such expressions as: *"Was ist los, Geronimo?" "Wie geh'ts, Davy Crockett?" "Guten Morgen, Sittung Bull!"* You may have interrupted the monthly meeting of the Lower Rhine *Cowherren* or the Upper Westphalian Branch No. 25 of the *Indianer Bund,* presided over by Herr *Rote Volke Schmidt ("Rote Volke"* being German for "Red Cloud"). The minutes are recorded by Hans Fitzlmeier, who prefers the nickname *"Schnellfuss,"* a free translation of "Swift Moccasin." And then they will go on to tell you things about Custer's Last Stand that old Custer himself never knew happened.

Perhaps more than most other non-English-speaking people, the Germans really have gone *à la Américan,* or rather *sehr amerikanisch.* They *gehen shoppen im Flower-Center, trinken Coca-Cola, lesen* [read] *im Digest-stil* [style] *eine Anzahl* [a number of] *Facts, bestellen* [order] *ein Babysitter. Am Abend* [in the evening] *sie mixen Drinks, geniessen* [enjoy] *Entertainment mit den Girls, und nehmen teil* [take part in] *Teach-ins, Sit-ins, und die Happenings.*

But the Germans are the first to admit that the Americanization is not all that bad and that they are inspired by the American penchant for simplification. Mark Twain used to complain that the German language is "so slipshod and systemless and so slippery and elusive to grasp" that he would "rather decline two drinks than one German adjective. . . . German books," he added, "are easy enough to read when you hold them before a looking glass or stand on your head. . . . My philological studies have satisfied me that a gifted person ought to learn English (barring spelling and pronouncing) in 30 hours, French in 30 days and German in 30 years. It seems manifest then that the latter tongue ought to be trimmed down and repaired. If it is to remain as it is, it ought to be gently and reverently set aside among the dead languages, for only the dead have time to learn it."[1]

Inspired by the American example, the Bonn government, with a grant from the Volkswagen Foundation, has undertaken, through its German language institute in Mannheim a monumental restructuring of the language into basic German for beginners. But the institute's director, Dr. Hugo Moser, warned that "we can't really simplify German but rather attempt to make its learning more logical to foreigners." Their "efforts at simplification" still goes by the name of *"Vereinfachungsbestrebungen,"* though they are a step in the right direction. But the fifteen scholars, trying to computerize the prose of 300 contemporary German writers and publications, sigh, *"wir sind gehandikapped."*

Leave it to the American GI, of course, not to wait around for any such scientific simplification. Unable to pronounce many German tongue twisters properly, he has invented his own parlance, now as standard as KP or CQ. *"Es macht nichts"* (it doesn't make any difference) has become *"moxnix"* (the directional flippers on older Volkswagen models are called "Moxnix sticks"). The European unit of land measure, kilometer (or 0.6 miles) is simply called "K" or "click." Kaiserslautern becomes simply "K-Town" and Aschaffenburg "A-Burg." The GI inevitably pronounces *"Ich liebe Dich"* as *"Ish liebe Dish"* and hence refers to himself as "Old Ish." The perennial German worker's briefcase is dubbed "Schnitzel Bag," and the German beer bottle with the porcelain cap on a wire is called "flip-top" and "snap-daddy." There are many more, which you can easily pick up at the nearest German *Gasthaus* (tavern), or "Gassed House," only ten "clicks" from "K-Town."

The Golden Ghetto

The United States has been maintaining six divisions under NATO command in West Germany, with some 200,000 troops, USAREUR (United States Army Europe) headquarters in Heidelberg and USAFE (United States Air Force Europe) headquarters in Wiesbaden. There are several dozen U.S. army and air force bases scattered all over Bavaria, Baden-Württemberg, and the Rhineland-Palatinate. Inevitably their continual presence since postwar occupation days has not left the regions and the country unscathed. Add countless thousands of American tourists, plus many thousands of other nationalities, and you can imagine what romantic old Heidelberg looks like in the height of the tourist season. The overwhelming congestion, the din of all-night rowdyism, drunkenness, and the suffocating presence of camera-laden sightseers has destroyed every vestige of the serene loveliness that once was Heidelberg. From a distance the castle looks as splendid as ever, but try to worm your way into a restaurant for a quiet meal at reasonable prices or to find a hotel room, and you are lost.

As for the day-to-day relations between the American "protectors" and their German hosts, the problems go far deeper than can be adequately analyzed here. Over the years I have talked with hundreds of GI's and their families, partly in my previous capacity as founding editor of *The Bridge,* an English-language monthly paper sponsored by the German organization, *Atlantik-Brücke* (Atlantic Bridge), which is specifically devoted to furthering German-American friendship. The paper, which ceased publication in 1970, attempted to explain the language, customs, and culture to Americans in Germany. Although sponsored by leading West German industrialists and including some of the country's most distinguished citizens in its exlusive membership, *Atlantik-Brücke* is primarily a prestige organization.[2] It has arranged an impressive number of conferences with intellectuals on both sides of the Atlantic discussing problems of NATO, Europe, and Germany, and it has published much useful documentation on Germany. But as a vehicle for grass roots understanding between Germans and those Americans actually living on German soil, its achievements are meager indeed. Even *The Bridge* whose overall budget was less than $15,000 annually was severly restricted in fulfilling its purpose, as the *Atlantik-*

Brücke had a parsimonious attitude toward the venture. It was dependent on the thousands of Deutsche marks received annually from the Federal Press Office, which was the actual subsidizer of the publication. As a result of such shortsighted budgeting, *The Bridge* was arbitrarily distributed to only a portion of American troops.

Both the American forces and German communities regularly organize official community relations activities and sponsor a community relations program. There are German-American weeks, sports events, barbecues, hoedowns, square dances, hootenannies, and festivals. Dozens of German-American clubs have been established in many cities. But they are not a genuine aid to a GI's adjustment in Germany.

For space reasons I can only illustrate the problem through the examples of two families, one American, one German, but their short case histories sketched here speak for many.

Captain Thomas H. Nelson and his wife, Marianne, and their two small children, Annemarie and Joan Catherine, were based at Ramstein, headquarters for the 17th Air Force, USAF, and also headquarters for NATO's 4th Allied Tactical Air Force, one of Europe's bigger air bases. During repeated visits to their military housing settlement—and I had to be cleared by guards every time—I spoke at length with the Nelsons about military life in Germany.

They confirmed what I had heard so often before: the American serviceman assigned to Germany receives precious little preparation from the military, such as a course in German customs, language, mentality, manners. Chances are he has already been stationed in another foreign country previously (especially Vietnam or elsewhere in Asia) and this probably colors his attitude toward non-Americans of any nation.

The Nelsons arrived in Germany in American civilian aircraft hired by the military, they landed at a military base and were processed by the military. "At Frankfurt," Marianne told me, "the only way we really knew we were in a strange land was the knife-handled doorknobs!"

If he goes over alone, the serviceman will live in barracks on base, work with Americans, eat with Americans, and shop American. Even if he seeks recreation outside of the numerous facilities provided by the military, he will most likely be surrounded by fellow Americans. If he has a family and is not a high-ranking officer, he usually has to find living quarters for the family off base "on the economy," at least at first. This may be his first real contact with the German people. And it is not always a happy one.

As a civilian living for the most part in regions far from an American base, I, personally, have enjoyed the friendship of a great many Germans. But Germans who live in a city or village near an American military installation often tend to have a different attitude toward Americans than Germans living far from such bases. There are many wonderful German families there too, but unfortunately the unwary GI is more apt to make his first contacts with those who know the value of the American dollar and do their best to get it. Often an apartment for rent will have two prices, one for a German family, one for an American. Even then many flats lack many things Americans take for granted: hot running water, built-in closets and cabinets, central heating.

During one trip to the Nelsons, the following happened to me: I stopped for lunch in a restaurant near Kaiserslautern and ordered a Wiener Schnitzel, which on the German menu was listed at 5 Deutsche marks. When I went to pay, another waitress showed up, speaking in English this time, and asked for 9.50 Deutsche marks. "But," I protested, "I distinctly remember the menu said only 5 marks." The proprietor happened to overhear the conversation, and obviously thinking I didn't know German, scolded the girl for not giving me the American menu. "What!" I said angrily, and now speaking in German, "you have two sets of prices for Germans and Americans?" "Ah," replied the proprietor, completely unruffled, "but the meat for the American menu is fresher."

"The only Germans most GI's encounter," said Captain Nelson, "are those who work on the base, such as secretaries, managing personnel, laborers. These Germans are often 'fat cats,' knowing just how much work to do for the Americans to get their money. Hence many Americans become extremely sensitive about these Germans."

"And as for domestic help, not to mention salesmen, and the like," added Marianne, "maids are quite visibly after the dollar."

In the Nelsons' view, what American military personnel lack is the opportunity for a "cultural shock," or the confrontation with another world. Marianne tells this story: "Although I had

had German in college, on my very first shopping trip in the little town of Bitburg (where we were first stationed) I kept walking up and down the streets window-shopping, never getting up enough nerve to actually go in. I ended up coming home without having bought a thing, and then went to the PX and bought what I needed. We always had 'Little America' to fall back on! Little did I realize that the shopkeepers in Bitburg were on to the ways of Americans and most of them spoke English.

"Even those brave Americans who do learn some German and try it out shopping are often answered in better English than their German, so they lose courage. The Germans feel they know what the Americans want, so they give it to them, frequently never giving the sincere American the real chance for an encounter with genuine German life.

"I know of one Air Force Colonel's wife," added Marianne, "who would not shop in a German store that would not serve her in English. If any German were 'uppity' to her she would in no uncertain terms tell them that she didn't like being here any more than they liked her being here, that if they had 'behaved' themselves in the forties, she and her husband wouldn't have to be here, and that they were here solely for the good of Germany, and the Germans had better appreciate it!" An extreme case, but one which illustrates the mentality which is, somewhat less crassly expressed, characteristic.

I asked Marianne about the German-American women's clubs. "Trouble is," she said, "many of these are big, fund-raising affairs but few German women have had experience as have American women with parent-teacher associations, Girl Scouts, Red Cross, church and school organizations. They tended to *Kaffeeklatsch* with other rather than with the Americans on their one day a week away from home. Most of the German women were older and were the same women year in, year out, while the Americans have a big turnover and were mostly much younger. As a result the German women often dominated the clubs, even though the younger American women were actually more experienced because of their club work at home."

One of the biggest problems is the highly developed sense of class consciousness among German women, who frequently snub a mere lieutenant's wife, while buttering up "Frau" Colonel. "One American woman invited her German landlady from the village where she lived to one of these club meetings. She was mortified all afternoon by the ruthless way the more proper *Fraus,* whose husbands were town merchants, snubbed the poor woman."

The Nelsons also spoke glowingly of numerous acts of kindness they experienced from Germans too. Once when they had a flat tire on the autobahn near Frankfurt, it was American cars which kept passing by them, in spite of their military license, but it was a German who proved to be the "good Samaritan."

"How do we feel about our stay?" the Nelsons asked themselves. "Well, we definitely did live in a 'Golden Ghetto.' Perhaps we should have tried harder to escape it, but you really can't. The problem is, the military housing is necessary because Americans are already imposing on a crowded German housing situation, and in the event of an emergency, concentrated housing facilitates rapid mobilization. But even if you try to go beyond this, the Germans won't let you leave the ghetto mentality either, because they are so damned sure they know how to act with Americans and always put that facade forward.

"Do we really feel we got to know Germany and the Germans? Yes and no. We finally became acquainted with Germans we liked but through a non-military friend. Here a real exchange took place. Clinking steins of beer together is fine, but to get deeper. . . . In our whole time in Germany we only got to know two or three persons with whom we could talk about the Jews or the war. Sometimes it burns you inside, when a German woman comes up to you and says she just can't understand the race situation in the U.S. You'd like to say that at least we didn't build outright concentration camps and furnaces. But you try to explain things as best you can, politely . . . . "

The Steiner Family

The Heinrich Steiner family lives in Augsburg, which is also a host city to an American military installation, and the Americans, including dependents, comprise about 8 percent or 20,000 out of 250,000 population. The couple is in their late seventies, with seven grown, mostly married children, including an engineer, a teacher, a sociologist, an historian, a language expert, living in scattered parts of West Germany, one of them in Rome.

Since the family is not really typical they are immune to the widespread cliché-notions about Americans; indeed, several of their relatives (cousins, etc.) are happily married to former American servicemen and there are regular visits to the States. And the family has been generous hosts to not only Americans but Africans, West Indians and Turks as well. Thousands of German families have done the same.

"But imagine," says Christoph, thirty-five, father of two children, and a junior executive at the world-famous Siemens electrical firm, "how the average German worker feels who reads week in, week out, in his newspaper about taxi drivers murdered by GI's, prostitution, rape, narcotics—all involving GI's. True, much of this is also the fault of the cooperating German parties, but the ordinary citizen doesn't think that far. But perhaps even worse is the conspicuous and ubiquitous presence of all the things that suggest the *privileged* American—the PX, special license tags, quartermaster gas stations, numerous clubs, and recreation centers. The exclusiveness, the preponderance of huge American automobiles, the GI self-assurance and downright vulgarity, rowdyism, and tawdry atmosphere of night life in Kaiserslautern and Frankfurt—that rankles."

The senior Herr Steiner recalls with sadness, but without a trace of bitterness, the confiscation of thousands of German homes immediately after the war. "I would say that the overwhelming majority of Germans were genuinely looking forward to liberation by American troops at war's end, with an aching longing. But this hope was soon dampened by the senseless denazification efforts, and the agony of looking on helplessly as thousands of Germans faced starvation while the GI's lolled in heavenly abundance, buying a girl for a chocolate bar."

"For a great many Germans," added Richard, twenty-eight, also married, one child, high-school teacher, "the American military is a reality they daily confront in terms of incredible noise, screaming jets, rifle practice, the constant frustrating presence of army convoys on the autobahn and country roads, maneuvers, and uncontrolled boisterousness which irritates many Germans. If the German citizen feels imposed upon by the Bundeswehr he can sometimes be heard and even accommodated, but this is impossible with the American military."

"I would say," continued Christoph, "that if the average German were asked how he feels about the presence of American troops, he would reply as follows: 1) 'We need them, otherwise we would be hopelessly exposed to the Soviets; 2) the Americans can get to know us—*respect* us—and our products in this manner.' " To which Christoph added, with emphasis, "Note, I said, 'get to know *us*' and not vice versa."

Christoph's judgment is somewhat harsh, for I have encountered many Germans genuinely eager to become acquainted with Americans. But somewhere along the line the fact that the American military is always the first to jump into action in any catastrophe with men, equipment, facilities, and its legendary generosity in bailing out ailing communities in the construction of soccer fields, community projects, and the like—all this seems to be lost on the Germans. In fact, recent West German opinion polls show signs of growing disenchantment with Americans and American policy.

"We used to admire the examplary way the Americans drove, in spite of their *Strassenfreuzer* [street cruisers]. With their increased use of European cars, they seem to have adopted European bad traffic manners as well. Americans neglect their cars far more than Europeans—you can tell their cars by the dirt—and are therefore a greater safety menace.

"In my student days in the fifties I used to devour American literature—Hemingway, Faulkner, Steinbeck—which dominated German reading. Toady Germans don't even listen to AFN [Armed Forces Network]. The picture that is now emerging of Americans is that only super-specialists can have success, half the nation is involved in a race riot, and that addicted hippies comprise 20 to 30 percent of the American youth. Much of this of course is the fault of German journalists who play up sensational stories. But the fact remains, the American image, which used to be our ideal, is tarnished."

According to a poll conducted by the Allensbach Demoscopic Institute in 1967, 52 percent of a representative sample of 1,000 West Germans said they wanted their country to cooperate most with the United States. This was the lowest percentage since the institute started making such surveys in the early fifties. In 1963, 90 percent opted for the United States, and in previous surveys the figure hovered at around 80 percent. A surprising 41 percent of respondents in the 1967 survey showed preference for the Soviet Union as the country they wanted West Germany to cooperate with most, the highest figure ever in the surveys. In

1963 the percentage for the Soviet Union was 27 percent and in 1962 it was only 22 percent.

On a personal level, 47 percent of the sample replied affirmatively when asked whether they like Americans. In 1964 the percentage was 58 percent. The percentage of those who said they do not especially like Americans rose from 19 percent in 1965 to 24 percent in 1967. Anti-American rallies and demonstrations were frequent throughout the late sixties, mostly in condemnation of American presence in Vietnam.

There is widespread resentment of the payments offsetting American troop costs in Europe, which have totaled over $1 billion annually, of which the largest percentage is shouldered by Germany. Franz-Josef Strauss, head of the CSU and former finance minister and defense minister, has repeatedly said that Bonn's contribution to offset the costs of stationing American troops in West Germany should not be considered "occupation costs. The Americans are not here because we are providing offset payments. They are here because they are defending their own interests."

One barometer of German feeling for Americans is that of German workers at U.S. military bases, where discontent, as indicated by the high rate of employee turnover, is consistently high. "We feel we're treated as second-class citizens," is a common complaint. Analyses of state election returns indicate that the rightist National Democratic Party (NPD) has consistently gained votes in election districts with a heavy concentration of Germans working for the U.S. Army or Air Force. The discontent seems to be shared, according to one survey, by many of the nearly 100,000 West Germans employed by the U.S. Armed Forces.

Interviews with these employees suggest that their chief complaints are that their wages and benefits are below those of their countrymen holding similar jobs with the Bundeswehr. A German nurse at the United States Army general hospital in Frankfurt is paid a maximum of $1,700 for her first year, while an American civilian nurse makes $5,331. German nurses, no matter how qualified, according to Kurt Kelly, chairman of the Employees' Council at the hospital, are given the most menial tasks. "They are treated like charwomen. Consequently, the hospital cannot attract German nurses." Non-American nursing positions must be filled by nurses from third countries. The Frankfurt hospital has Turkish, Pakistani, British, and Canadian nurses, but few Germans. The average wage of German civilians working for the Allied forces is about 82 cents an hour while those working for the Bundeswehr make slightly more than $1 an hour.

Black Illegitimate Children

After World War II some 10,000 illegitimate children were born to German women, who were fathered by U.S. Negro servicemen (of course the number of illegitimate white children was proportionately much greater). At first, the West German government clumsily segregated them. I recall visiting one children's home for illegitimate blacks some fourteen years ago. It was located far from any town and they were treated with hyper-paternalistic solicitude. I was asked by the housemother if I, as an American acquainted with the American race problem, could give her advice as to the children's supposed racial traits, "like primitive dancing," which would help her place the children eventually in some black country. I was appalled and immediately reported this to the authorities.

In fairness, I should mention that I also visited at that time a private German family that had adopted twelve Negro children whom they raised completely without distinction along with their own four children, with excellent results. (One neighbor, though, reportedly complained, "Every time I look out the window, I see black.")

In recent years, however, all of these children have been completely integrated, for the most part reared by their own mothers in a completely white milieu. Studies are being made to see how these young people, now mostly in their twenties, adjust in a culture that has no visible racial minority. I have heard of isolated instances of these children being victimized by insulting remarks, but in several communities where I spoke with their teachers and mothers, they are completely accepted, experience no discrimination in obtaining employment or in daily life, and are on the whole well-adjusted.

Black Panthers and Racist Housing

In recent years there have been growing complaints by black servicemen of over-priced apartments and racial discrimination in rental of off-post housing. In December, 1970, the U.S. Army's European headquarters in Heidelberg initiated a plan to blacklist off-post housing units whose landlords practice racial discrimination.

Ironically, West Germany on December 17, 1970, granted asylum to an American Negro, Sgt. James Henry Grant, officially listed as an Army deserter, on grounds of racial persecution. This judgment by the administrative court in Ansbach, if not overruled by a higher court, could open up West Germany as a sanctuary not only for American blacks but soldiers from other NATO countries as well, making West Germany a potential deserter haven like Sweden. The big question that is posed by this decision is whether more of the estimated 40,000 black American GI's serving in Europe will follow Grant's example.

Around this same time, according to an interview in *Der Spiegel* (December 14, 1970), the Black Panthers "information minister," Eldridge Cleaver, asserted that his party is growing and looks to the U.S. Army in Germany as a fertile field for the recruitment of followers. There have been numerous racial clashes, including a riot among infantrymen in West Berlin, throughout West Germany all during 1970.

Radio Free Europe and Radio Liberty

A perennial thorn in the side of many Germans, especially the Socialist-led coalition government of Chancellor Willy Brandt, is the continuing presence in Munich of the two controversial American relics of the Cold War, Radio Free Europe and Radio Liberty. The former beams nineteen hours of thinly-disguised anti-communistic propaganda daily to the Iron Curtain countries, while the latter broadcasts exclusively to the Soviet Union. Brandt, who sees the existence of these stations as a serious obstacle to his Ostpolitik, told a *Stern* reporter in March, 1971, that "it is incredible that twenty-five years after the war, foreign stations on German soil still send propaganda to third countries."

It is an open secret, confirmed by public disclosures made by Sen. Clifford P. Case (R., N.J.), in hearings made January 23, 1971, that these two stations have been clandestinely funded by the CIA at a cost to American taxpayers of $30 million annually. In Washington, plans have been discussed to replace the semi-secret CIA control with an "American Council for Private International Communications, Inc.," which will have a **board** of fifteen distinguished Americans appointed by the President with congressional approval.

Theoretically the Bonn government can stop the broadcasts by simply not renewing the stations' licenses, which expire every year. But politically this is a very touchy matter. Such an action might conceivably awaken suspicions in Washington that the "ghost of Rapallo" was being awakened from its historic sleep, and that Bonn was making secret deals with the Russians without Washington's knowledge. At the same time the situation is extremely embarrassing to Bonn, inasmuch as General Lucius D. Clay, and former U.S. President Harry S Truman, belong to Radio Free Europe's board of directors. Several Eastern European countries have informed Bonn that they would boycott the 1972 Olympic games in Munich if the two stations were still operating then. Meanwhile, the licenses have been renewed.

Germany—A Dollar Colony?

One of the first things I did when I settled down in my new flat in Hamburg was to order a case of German beer and a case of good old American Coke, both from the nearest *Lebensmittel Geschaeft*. Lo and behold, whose name showed up on the Coca-Cola bottle caps but that of Max Schmeling, the first German to win the world's heavyweight boxing championship. I located the champ in a downtown café one afternoon and, over steaming cups of coffee, not Coke, sounded him out not only about German sport but also about the American business invasion of Germany.

"Der Max" is still a handsome, heavy-set man in his sixties, has a sprinkling of gray now and enjoys a vast following. He is idolized all over Germany, continually appears on TV shows, at sports events and rallies. He is the boss of one of the 120 Coca-Cola plants in Germany, having a total of 12,500 employees.

But nobody regards *him* as a threat to German business.

Yet German newspaper headlines and *Gasthaus* gossip perennially raise the bogeyman of the second American invasion, the alleged dollar colonization of Germany and Europe.

More than 2,000 West German business enterprises belong to American firms—compared with only 350 in 1957—and the number is growing. West German newspaper headlines frequently

416

ask: *"Wird Deutschland Eine Dollar Kolonie* [Is Germany Becoming a Dollar Colony] ?"

How widespread these fears are, and not only in Germany, was shown in 1968 by the phenomenal success of the book, *The American Challenge* (Atheneum) by the Frenchman J. J. Servan-Schreiber, a best seller in several countries.

His main point: In a decade of the Common Market, this "European market is basically American." Unless there is an all-European coordinated counterprogram, within a federal framework, the only alternative, according to Servan-Schreiber, is "domination by IBM." In answer to Servan-Schreiber, IBM published a full-page ad that same year in *Der Spiegel* as well as in Servan-Schreiber's own *L'Express*. "For us," the ad boasted, "Europe is a country like any other."

Nevertheless, Servan-Schreiber's arguments are hard to contradict:

Currently more than one-third of the total United States investments abroad—some $14 billion—is in Europe. In one year, 1965-66, American investment rose by 17 percent in the U.S., 21 percent in the rest of the world, and 40 percent in Europe.

"The Common Market," writes Servan-Schreiber, "has become a new Far West for American businessmen. . . . Their investments do not so much involve a transfer of capital, as an actual *seizure of power* within the European economy" (italics his). For Esso, Europe now represents a market larger than the U.S. and growing three times faster. It is not surprising that an American executive in Frankfurt called the Common Market's Treaty of Rome, "the sweetest deal ever to come out of Europe."

Historic Background

It should be pointed out that some of these American enterprises have operated in Europe for generations, notably the International Telephone and Telegraph Company, which has been entrenched in Europe for nearly fifty years, and whose biggest European company is Standard Elektrik Lorenz Aktiengesellschaft of Stuttgart, founded in 1879, only three years after Alexander Graham Bell invented the telephone.

Although the firm of Adam Opel in 1924 was Germany's largest automobile manufacturer, it sold out to General Motors four years later.

One of the oldest American financial institutions in Germany

417

is the Bankhaus Bache & Co. in Frankfurt. Through its electronic instruments it is capable of placing its clients in direct contact with the New York Stock Exchange. Within a matter of seconds, it is able to obtain the latest returns of New York securities. As a pure stockbroker undertaking, it represents for Germany a new kind of bank primarily devoted to stocks and bonds rather than savings.

The McCann advertising agency in Frankfurt is the largest and oldest of its kind in Germany, established here in 1928. In 1966 it had a turnover of 160 million DM's ($50 million). Although it is under German management, its executives regularly visit the United States to keep abreast of the newest American advertising methods.

In Schönaicher Forst near Böblingen, International Business Machines Corporation (IBM) maintains a research laboratory. Here some 800 scientists, engineers, and technicians are tinkering with electronic computers, through which they are in continual contact with all the factories in the world that manufacture the computer model which they have designed. A sizable portion of the production of IBM factories in Mainz, Milan, Tokyo, Toronto, San José, and Boca Raton in Florida is controlled from Böblingen via the *Daten-Fernverarbeitungsnetz*.

The German "daughter-branch" of IBM, founded in 1910, is actually older than its "mother," which was founded by a German immigrant by the name of Hermann Hollerith. The German branch was renamed IBM-Germany in 1949, and this laboratory was established in 1959.

IBM, with some justification, declines the American label, and insists on the term, "multinational." The IBM concern has distributed its capital all over the world, among its individual national research laboratories and factories in India, Japan, France, and Germany, as well as in the United States. All of these firms work independently and control their own products in all the markets that they reach. As a result it is inaccurate to speak of a dollar invasion; rather it is a global business empire, and in the Federal Republic, IBM has virtually cornered the computer market.[3]

Even before the turn of the century American firms had established their first outposts in Germany. In 1882 the Berlin industrialist and engineer Emil Rathenau brought the French Compagnie Continentale Edison to Berlin, which was controlled by the largest electrical concern in the world, the General

Electric Company. Today General Electric controls about 12 percent of the *Allgemeine Elektrizitäts-Gesellschaft* (AEG), which Rathenau founded.

In 1890 Rockefeller established the Standard Oil Company, later to be renamed ESSO, in Germany, and Singer sewing machines were already a byword in Germany during the Kaiser Reich.

After World War I, Corn Products Refining Company set foot in Germany *(Maizena, Mondamin)*. This was followed in the twenties by Libby General Milk *(Glücksklee)* and Woolworth.

The real business invasion actually began after World War II in the fifties, when new life began to stir among the ruins. At first big American companies seeking European outlets set up shop in Britain. But after 1962, when de Gaulle blocked England's entry into the Common Market, more and more U.S. firms hopped across the channel to Germany. In 1966 the investments of American firms at home rose only 17 percent over the previous year as compared to 40 percent in Common Market countries. The Federal Republic emerged as the most important base of operations for U.S. expansion in European economy.

As internal tariffs were dismantled with the six Common Market member states—France, West Germany, Italy, Belgium, the Netherlands, and Luxembourg—American industry feared it would lose markets if it did not quickly establish plants inside one of the six, which represents a market of 165 million people.

Backed by the resources of the richest country in the world, the invasion has taken on huge proportions and ruffled the feelings of many Europeans. Americans dominate the computer industry, control a sizable portion of the automobile industry, run some of Europe's biggest hotels, manage many of the advertising agencies, and drain away thousands of the best brains.

As for Germany, all you have to do is pick up the telephone directory of any large city and you will find a staggering number of familiar listings.

American world concerns dominate the fuel and lubricating market. The Deutsche Erdöl A.G., one of the last independent gasoline firms in the Federal Republic, was bought out in 1966 by Texas Oil, together with a large share of Castrol GmbH, and Mobil Oil has purchased 28 percent of the shares of Aral, so that American oil concerns dominate a sizable portion of West German energy production.

In the village of Uentrop in Westphalia, the world's largest chemical concern, Du Pont de Nemours of Wilmington, has just built a 25-million DM ($7 million) nylon and Dacron factory at the edge of the Ruhr area. Some 350 workers at each shift will service the automatic machinery of this gigantic plant. This isn't the only Du Pont holding on German soil. In 1962 the U.S. concern bought the Adox Photo works in Wiesbaden, and it owns 26 percent of the shares of the Pigment-Chemie works in Homberg.

American firms like IBM, Burroughs, and Honeywell dominate nearly 90 percent of all data-processing electronic manufacturing equipment. Forty percent of the automobile industry, in spite of Mercedes and Volkswagen, is in the hands of Opel (General Motors) and Ford. Forty percent of the mineral oil industry is dominated by Esso, Mobil Oil, Texaco, Chevron, Marathon Oil, Philips Petroleum, and Veedol. Sixty-five percent of all razor blades manufactured in the Federal Republic are the product of the American-dominated Gillette Roth-Büchner GmbH.

Subsidy and Experience

The superiority of American industry in competition with European enterprises is primarily due to these two factors:

1) American managers, with their wide experience on the gigantic internal market of the United States, understand the problems and opportunities of big operations better than their European competitors. Their wider experience and know-how thus is effective in employing and interpreting opinion research for the most favorable sales possibilities in the Common Market area.[4]

As the New York Institute for Economic Research put it in one of its reports: "The creators of the Common Market can be proud of removing the barriers that divide and choke Europe. But it is the American enterprises that have understood how to exploit this market by using methods that built up their own huge American market."

2) The American government subsidizes enterprises with billion-dollar orders for research and development in key industries for technological development: space travel, aviation, and electronics. Although European countries have recognized the importance of underwriting ventures in these areas, their contribution thus far has been meager.

The Federal Republic spends 750 million Deutsche marks (about $215 million) annually for imported technical knowledge, more than three times as much as it receives for license exports.

The notorious brain drain affected large numbers of German scientists and technicians who were easily lured to the States, not only because of the higher salaries, but also because the American businesses were far more generous about providing research facilities and opportunities. Recently, however, this trend has declined—in fact, it has actually reversed—with many Americans seeking employment in Europe.

Prevailing opinion in Europe gloomily predicts that the technology gap between the old and the new world will widen rather than narrow in the coming years. According to the Hudson Institute in New York (which is subsidized by Washington), the countries leading in per capita income are: U.S.A., Sweden, Canada, West Germany, United Kingdom, France, U.S.S.R., Japan. The average: U.S.A., $3,500; West Germany, $1,800; U.S.S.R., $1,000.

In thirty years, according to the Hudson Institute, four countries will stand at the top of the list, with between $4,000 and $20,000 per capita income annually: U.S.A., Japan, Canada, and Sweden. All other countries will have under $4,000.

Servan-Schreiber predicts that by 1985 the third industrial power after the U.S.A. and U.S.S.R. might well be, not Europe, but American industry in Europe.

The Europeans face a dilemma. Restrictive measures might only boomerang. On the one hand, as Britain's former Prime Minister Harold Wilson expressed it, they fear becoming an industrial harlot. On the other hand, they need the investments of American companies, their know-how, research, drive, and experimentation, and have actually come to depend on them for employment, foreign exchange, and technological help.

Most American companies use only a skeleton staff of Americans. Nationals hold practically all the key jobs in the affiliates. In the entire European organization of ITT there are only sixty-one Americans, thirty-seven of them based in Brussels.

If there is a gap between the productive capacity of Europe and America, as many people on both sides of the Atlantic feel, then American investments can help to narrow it. Though Europeans may resent the new breed of conquerors, there is really very little they can do until their defenses are stonger. What the United States provides, Europe still needs.

The Organization of Economic Cooperation and Development (OECD) stated in a report in March, 1968, on the technical lag of Europe, that "as long as Europe remains splintered among petty national interests, and divided between the Common Market and EFTA, it will remain a second-class power and be dependent on the United States."

Why They Sell to Americans

The case of radio and television manufacturer Gerhard Kubetschek illustrates why German firms so readily sell out to American buyers.

A DP from Breslau, Kubetschek established his firm in an old army barracks building in Wolfenbüttel in 1948. His initial capital of 8,000 American cigarettes bought his first supply of radio parts on the black market. By 1966 he sold his firm, now called Kuba Imperial, with 4,000 employees, to General Electric for 80 million Deutsche marks ($25 million). "It wasn't as if we were losing money," Kubetschek explained later to reporters. "On the contrary, in 1965 our proceeds exceeded 220 million DM's, and we were the third largest concern in the field.

"But as an individual enterprise I did not see how in the long run we could continue to hold our own against the growing intensity of competitive firms. It was better to get out while we were still healthy.

"Before selling out, I accepted an invitation by General Electric to visit their plants in the United States. There I had the opportunity to see their research laboratories, especially in the field of television. And I began to realize that the staggering expense of such research and experimentation can only be made by a concern whose production spans the entire electronic field from space travel to computers down to the smallest transistor radio."

Self-made men like Gerhard Kubetschek were undoubtedly the backbone of German economic recovery immediately after the war. But this Horatio Alger atmosphere was artificial and short-lived. Inevitably more and more of these one-man enterprises sell out to American firms.

Why American firms? Why not German, or French, or other European firms? Dr. A. Zimmerer, head of a West German agency specializing in selling German businesses to American firms, says the reasons are usually subjective. "German business-men do not as a rule like to negotiate with their German competitors, but rather with a foreigner. If the negotiations fail, the competitor knows nothing about it, for if they did they could use this knowledge to their advantage.

"Moreover there just aren't many inland buyers. In recent years we have sold almost exclusively to Americans."

Asked why this is so, whether the Germans have too little money to buy out their own firms, Zimmerer replied, "No, it is not a question of money, but a question of drive that the Americans bring. For the Americans don't pay with cash anymore. They only finance a small percentage, and even then through German banks.

"We Germans," continued Zimmerer, "lack this spirit of enterprise, this energetic, dynamic management, self-confidence, the willingness to take calculated risks—and this we must learn from Americans."

A growing number of well-informed German economists see the American invasion positively. "Americans have good ideas, continually apply new methods and developments and new products to the German market, which they have manufactured here and to a large extent adapted to German needs and conditions. This American initiative has been responsible more than any other factor for a rationalization, for price reduction and stabilization, and surely for the economic upswing of recent years," according to a Frankfurt businessman.

It is significant that those branches that are most Ameri-canized, such as oil and drugs, best hold the price line, while in other areas of the German economy that Americans have not entered—banks, agriculture, breweries, mining—prices have risen.

More than anywhere else American production and business methods have been beneficial to the German aviation industry. The technicians who are advising the new air defense system of the seventies belong to the German firm *Entwicklungsring Süd* (Southern Development Ring) and the American Republic Aviation Division. The two enterprises have merged to become EWR-Fairchild International. Their task: The development and production of a vertical starting supersonic pursuit plane for the German and American Air Force, the successor of the ill-fated Starfighter.

The operations of two concepts, that of the German horizontal starter VJ-101D and that of an American pivot-drive aircraft, are to be united in a single new model for a joint assignment of Bonn and Washington.

One of the most striking examples of how American know-how vitally affected a German industry is that of the SABA radio and television firm in Villingen. Established as a clock factory in 1835, the firm was proud of its time-honored tradition of craftsmanship. Baden tinkerers, woodcarvers, and carpenters carefully constructed handmade but old-fashioned, ponderous radios and loudspeakers employing conventional construction methods.

But it soon became clear that these revered production methods would soon bankrupt the firm. SABA took the consequences and signed a contract with the Radio Corporation of America (RCA), which permitted it to study modern production methods in the States and apply them to their German plant. They have been paying $25,000 annually for these rights, but the investment paid off. Since then the firm has more than doubled its sales and production at less than 50 percent the cost of the old methods.

In Munich the firm Junkers manufactures Heos weather satellites. They learned all the basic techniques and knowledge with American technological and financial assistance. Today they are independent. "We learned so much from the project 'Heos,' " a spokesman for the firm said, "that we would now be in a position to design and manufacture a space sonde without outside help. The point is, we would not have been able to reach this stage without American help, and even with it, we shall continue to require their financial help for this kind of project."

Up to 1970 Americans have invested nearly 12 billion DM's ($3.7 billion) in German industry for the purchase of established firms or for the construction of their own plants. But German economy has enjoyed immense benefits from this through the introduction of new methods of technique and management.

A man who is not afraid of American dollar infiltration is Alfons Müller-Wipperfürth. Instead of complaining about the business invasion, he decided to beat the Americans at their own game. A tailor by trade, Alfons Müller-Wipperfürth today controls a sprawling textile empire by "commuting" from one country to another in his private de Havilland jet. One day he will land in Lugano, the next day in Vienna, Brussels, or

Hamburg. They call him the Henry Ford of the German textile industry, noted for lightning fast decisions as well as for his economic production methods. His office is literally inside his aircraft, where he holds regular press conferences. He owns fourteen factories in five countries, which manufacture suits, shirts, underwear, and overcoats. He produces his own yarn, silks, and synthetics with which he supplies his 200 clothing stores throughout West Germany. Although he has received many offers from American firms he has so far declined any mergers or even partial collaboration "because we want to remain independent."

The small town of Burghausen, one of the most beautiful places in Bavaria, is an example of where American investment proved to be a much-needed form of development aid. "We were virtually bankrupt," the *Bürgermeister* confessed, "before the Americans came. But instead of imposing 'the American way of life' on us, they rapidly became Bavarianized." The chemical plant of Burghausen was about to be torn down because it was too far from a refinery. With the construction of an oil refinery by Marathon Oil and a pipeline to Triest, Burghausen was saved.

Challenging J. J. Servan-Schreiber's *The American Challenge*, Mr. John B. Rhodes, vice-president, International Affairs for Booz, Allen & Hamilton, Inc., who was stationed in Europe for many years, thinks that the Common Market is actually a very vigorous competitor for the United States. Writing in the *Harvard Business Review*, September-October, 1969, he asserts that the reports of Europe's death are premature. "Americans," he writes, "find themselves competing vigorously, and not always success-fully, at home and abroad with a growing stream of European products."

One should not minimize the dangers, however. The fact remains, the Americans are overwhelming competitors for the Germans. Even the largest German enterprises are dwarfed in comparison with the industrial giants from overseas and their immense financial reserves. The situation is aggravated by the fact that the German lawmakers in the twenties encouraged foreign investments by granting considerable tax deductions. These laws are still in force and only encourage foreign expansionism in Germany, while they are a real handicap especially for the smaller German industries. Nor is it likely that the laws will be drastically changed because West Germany needs the American firms.

These reservations having been made, however, it is fair to say that American capital has stimulated Germany economy. It brought about the badly needed modernization of obsolete industry, it revolutionized daily life and made a substantial contribution to German prosperity.

GERMANS IN THE UNITED STATES

"From every corner of the ship one could hear the creaking of the masts. . . . the howling of the wind, and the constant thump of the sailors' heavy shoes. Meanwhile the passengers were moaning, screaming, cursing, complaining day and night. In one corner near my cabin thirteen hunting dogs barked constantly. And in a room nearby hundreds of empty wine bottles rolled with the waves continuously. Boxes, trunks, suitcases, furniture, flew from one end of the room to another. . . Tomorrow we will have been twenty days at sea. . . . "

Those lines are excerpts from a letter written on board ship by the German immigrant Julius Niese to his parents on November 23, 1860. Some years later he became a successful St. Louis merchant.

"I asked the hostess of a restaurant in the usual discreet tone for the whereabouts of the toilet. 'The ladies lounge is downstairs,' she answered. Now a lounge, as far as I remembered, was the lobby of a hotel or theater, certainly not the place I was looking for. Puzzled, I went downstairs only to find a door marked 'Powder Room.' I asked a woman coming out if she could tell me where the toilet was. Somewhat irritated, she pointed and said, 'Can't you see, the rest room is right there?' I opened the door, and thus found that powder room, ladies lounge, rest room and bathroom all mean the same thing in America. What a rich language!"

And those lines are taken from a letter by Frieda Meierberger to her girl friend in Mainz that she wrote shortly after her arrival in New York in February, 1970. Today she is a bilingual secretary for a New York import firm specializing in German products.

Between these two letters several million Germans have settled in the United States. Since 1683, when the ship *Concord* bearing thirteen German families from Krefeld anchored at Philadelphia, the number has totaled more than 6.5 million. Between 1850 and 1860 every second immigrant was a German. According to the census of 1900, some 2,700,000 Americans were German-born. Since then an estimated 35 million—about one out of every six Americans—can trace their ancestry to German immigrants.

Although the emergence of the United States is usually associated with Anglo-Saxon names—Washington, Lincoln, Adams, Wilson—German influence on the American way of life is greater than many people realize. To be sure, no German names are included among the great discoverers and explorers, for Germany, unlike Holland, England, Spain, or Sweden, did not boast of a seafaring tradition. Nevertheless, the penetration of German culture is considerable.

In fact the very name "America" is the result of a *faux pas* made by a German cartographer, Martin Waldseemüller, on his famous "Cosmographia Introducio," a map of the world that he designed in 1507. Subsequent cartographers continued to name the new continent after the Italian navigator Amerigo Vespucci, and the error stuck.

It is believed that the Hessians fighting on the British side in the Revolutionary War introduced the Christmas tree, which was known even before the time of Martin Luther. The first professor of German language and literature in the United States—at Harvard University—Charles Follen had immigrated from Germany for political reasons in 1819; he continued to decorate a tree each year for his son, "according to the custom of my former land." Other instances of the custom in America are recorded in Fort Dearborn in 1804 and by the German colony at Belleville, Illinois, in 1833.

Like the Christmas tree, "Silent Night" (though this is Austrian in origin), the Easter bunny and the colored Easter egg, kindergarten, the county fair, wieners, frankfurters, hamburgers, sauerkraut, liverwurst, noodles, pretzels, dumplings, singing societies (from which glee clubs originated), gymnastic societies *(Turnvereinen)*, and above all, beer—all have become a part of the American way of life.

Hundreds of cities and towns were named by their original settlers after the places of their birth in the "Old Country": Heidelberg, Pennsylvania; Germantown, Wisconsin; Anaheim, California; New Braunfels, Texas; Hamburg, New York; New

Bremen, Ohio; Bismarck, the capital of North Dakota—just to give a few examples.

A cursory glance at any U.S. telephone directory can only illustrate the impossibility of reporting the contribution of countless Schmidts, Meyers, Schulzes toward the building of a great nation. The names of famous immigrants, or their descendants, speak for millions of unsung citizens of German origin or background.

In the artistic fields, there are painters like immigrant George Grosz, or the first generation descendant Lionel Feininger. Leopold Damrosch, and his sons, Frank and Walter, became dominant musical figures. George Henschel and Wilhelm Gericke were the first conductors of the Boston Symphony Orchestra. Bruno Walter, Erich Leinsdorf, Paul Hindemith, Lukas Foss, Ernestine Schumann-Heinck, and Elisabeth Rethberg are just a few of the outstanding music personalities of German background.

Of German stock are writers like Nobel-prizewinner John Steinbeck, Theodore Dreiser, H. L. Mencken, Joseph Hergesheimer, the commentator H. V. Kaltenborn. And the forefathers of Adolph Ochs and Arthur Hays Sulzberger of *The New York Times* were German.

Countless thousands of refugees of the Nazi regime brought manpower, talent, and distinction to the United States, from a bricklayer whose name might be Hans Schmidt to a Thomas Mann. One hesitates to include on this list Albert Einstein, who was rejected by his native country as a Jew, but whose formation and development as a scientist and as a man was nevertheless unmistakably German.

On the occasion of the death of Ludwig Miës van der Rohe, an immigrant from Aachen, in 1969, *The New York Times* wrote, "The glassy skyscrapers and sleek-walled buildings that are the pride of modern cities and the symbol of modern life owe more to Ludwig Miës van der Rohe than to any other architect of our time." Then there is that other architectural giant, Walter Gropius, and one of the world's greatest photographers, Alfred Stieglitz, the son of German immigrants.

Motion picture history is unthinkable without such names as Marlene Dietrich, Erich von Stroheim, Peter Lorre, Ernst Lubitsch, Billy Wilder—all German immigrants.

429

In the world of sports, names like Johnny Weismuller, Babe Ruth, Lou Gehrig, Red Schoendienst, Heinie Zimmermann, Honus Wagner stand out.

The greatest cartoonist during and after the Civil War, Thomas Nast, arrived in New York from Germany at the age of six.

Ottmar Mergenthaler, a German immigrant, invented the Linotype machine, without which the modern newspaper would be unable to satisfy the demands of the reading public.

The famous Brooklyn Bridge was designed by the German immigrant, John A. Roebling, and completed by his son, Washington.

One can only mention in passing names like Cardinal Mundelein and Paul Tillich in religion, or Walter Reuther in labor. An immigrant scholar of the middle nineteenth century, Francis Lieber, founded the *Encyclopedia Americana*. The first American scientist to win a Nobel Prize (1907), Albert A. Michelson, was of German origin.

The much-neglected field of American forestry was enriched by immigrant-experts who brought with them the skills of a profession that was already highly cultivated in Germany.

Ironically, the two great leaders of World War I and World War II American forces respectively, were General John Pershing and General Dwight D. Eisenhower, both of German stock.

Politically the Germans are no match proportionately with the ubiquitous and energetic Irish. Nevertheless, names like Rockefeller, Hoover, Eisenhower, Herter stand out. Half of all elected governors and many U.S. senators and representatives are wholly or partially of German background.[1]

The Social Security Act and the famous National Labor Relations (Wagner) Act, which more than any single piece of legislation elevated the dignity and authority of labor to unprecedented heights, were introduced into Congress by the late Senator Robert F. Wagner, who was born in a mountain village in western Germany. His son, Robert, became mayor of New York City.

In business and industry, German names are an integral part of the American scene. In 1715 Johann Huber built a new kind of stove, and Baron von Stiegel with the help of German blacksmiths built up a steel industry in Pennsylvania. A family by the name of Studebaker changed from wagon construction to automobile manufacturing.

The northwestern railroad network owes its origins primarily to an immigrant by the name of Heinrich Gustav Hilgard, who changed his name to Henry Villard, who, as an avocation, wrote reports on the Lincoln-Douglas Debates, on the Civil War, and on the discovery of gold in California.

The great breweries in America are a litany of names like Pabst, Anheuser-Busch (Budweiser), Schlitz, and Schaefer, while other German names—Walter Chrysler, Heinz, Hershey, Kraft, Wurlitzer, Steinway, and Fleischmann—are household words. Henry Timken became famous for his "Timken Spring" and the Timken Roller Bearing Company in Canton, Ohio, is the world's largest manufacturer of tapered roller bearings.

"I have often thought," wrote the American author Karl Shapiro in his introduction to Henry Miller's *Tropic of Cancer,* "that the Germans make the best Americans, though they certainly make the worst Germans."

Some Famous Immigrants

From Colonial days to the present, German immigrants have made history. Among them: a printer by the name of John Peter Zenger, a military officer by the name of Friedrich Wilhelm von Steuben, a merchant by the name of John Jacob Astor, a statesman by the name of Carl Schurz, and a rocket scientist by the name of Wernher von Braun.

Zenger, who immigrated from Germany at the age of thirteen, published a little newspaper by the name of *New York Weekly Journal* and soon got into deep trouble for his forthright editorials criticizing the corrupt administration of the Colonial Governor William Cosby. Inevitably Zenger was arrested for his pains and brought to trial after spending nine months in prison. His wife, Anna, kept the paper going by receiving instructions and copy from a hole in the door in his cell.

The year was 1733. Zenger's friends succeeded in winning over Andrew Hamilton, a friend of Benjamin Franklin, to act as Zenger's defense attorney. Hamilton pleaded to the jury that what was at stake was not the freedom of one journalist but the right of free speech itself. In spite of advanced age and ill health (he was over eighty), Hamilton won the case and Zenger was acquitted. Shortly thereafter Cosby died and Zenger was appointed official printer for the governments of New Jersey and New York. The Zenger trial is regarded as a precedent for the free press in America.

The Prussian Officer at Valley Forge

A man of action who had taken part in seven campaigns with Frederick the Great, king of Prussia, and feeling uncomfortable in his new diplomatic role as Prussian ambassador-at-large, von Steuben was inspired by reports of the rebellion of the American colonies and was hankering to get back onto the battlefield again.

During a diplomatic trip to Paris he happened to meet the American Ambassador to France, Benjamin Franklin, who was so impressed by the burly Prussian that he recommended him to Congress as just the man to train Washington's troops at Valley Forge.

Undernourished, ragged, and badly housed, they were a motley crew with no inkling of formal military procedure. Used to the "guerrilla" tactics of the Indians, the civilian army of blacksmiths, farmers, wagonmakers, and carpenters could not hold their own with the spit-and-polish British Army trained in the ways of open attack.

Approved by Congress, von Steuben systematically began drilling the troops. He soon ran up against a major obstacle, the Americans' refusal to take orders blindly. "The spirit of this nation," von Steuben wrote to a friend in Germany, "is not comparable to that of the Prussians, Austrians, or French. Over there, if you say, 'do this' to a soldier, he does it. But here one is obliged to say, 'This is the reason why you ought to do this,' and then he will do it."

The German contribution to Washington's victory of the Revolutionary War is substantially weakened by the fact that Hessian mercenaries fought on the British side of the war. Nevertheless, the German involvement on the American side was considerable. General Johann Dekalb led a number of southern campaigns and died in action in the Battle of Camden, South Carolina, in 1780. His memory is preserved in the name of a city in Illinois and Dekalb counties in six states. A statue of him stands in front of the State House in Annapolis.

In addition, German troops were represented by the German Fusileers of Charleston, by the Mohawk Valley Germans, and by

George Washington's private German bodyguard under the command of Major Bartholomaeus. Through the desertion of more than 5,000 Hessians from the British forces, the Revolution was indirectly aided.

Von Steuben led one of the three divisions in the Battle of Yorktown, 1781, which brought final victory to the Revolutionary forces and brought about the surrender of the British Commander, Charles Cornwallis.

In gratitude for his services, Congress sent von Steuben a gold-hilted sword and granted him an annual pension. The poverty-stricken states of Pennsylvania, Virginia, New Jersey, and New York granted him land instead of cash, a total of over 30,000 acres.

Two states, New York and Indiana, have a Steuben county. Ohio commemorates the baron's memory with a city called Steubenville. And in Lafayette Square in Washington, D.C., just across the street from the White House stands a big bronze statue of General Friedrich Wilhelm von Steuben.

Every year on September 20, thousands of Americans of German extraction celebrate Von Steuben Day, which includes a parade down New York's Fifth Avenue. It doesn't quite match the flamboyance of St. Patrick's Day, but 20,000 marchers, 50 floats, and 40 bands, including representatives of German singing societies, and hundreds of costumes of the Rhineland, Black Forest, Bavaria, Palatinate, and other German provinces, in their own way give testimony to their German heritage.

John Jacob Astor

If Horatio Alger is the legendary fiction character of the American dream, the "rags to riches" success story has real life validity in the case of John Jacob Astor, who arrived in New York from a remote German village called Waldorf, a penniless youth who was to become America's first tycoon.

Working as a cake peddler, fur storage clerk, factory worker, and fur dealer, he rapidly rose to the pinnacles of business success. But his real millions were earned from shrewd real estate investments.

Inspiring as the Astor story may be, however, it is also tarnished by Astor's unscrupulous business dealings. The farm originally located on the present site of Times Square is said to have been obtained by him by mercilessly foreclosing the mortgage. When he died in 1848, his fortune was valued at $20 million, the largest sum ever accumulated at that time by any one man in America. Today Astor's name is kept alive by the world-famous Waldorf-Astoria on Park Avenue, and the public library on Fifth Avenue and Forty-second Street bears his name over its main entrance. But as a philanthropist Astor's name trails far behind that of Rockefeller or Carnegie. The sum total of all his charitable works did not even add up to one million dollars, and on his death the New York *Herald* angrily editorialized, "He doubled the value of his property through the industry, enterprise and commerce of the people in New York. It would not have been too much if he had left half of his fortune, ten million, for the city which made him rich."

Carl Schurz

However, Americans of German origin need make no apologies for Carl Schurz, one of the founders of the Republican Party, an ardent supporter of Abraham Lincoln, a Major General in the Union Army, a United States Senator, and a member of the cabinet under President Rutherford B. Hayes.

Born in the village of Liblar near Cologne in 1829, Schurz took part in the unsuccessful Revolution of 1848 at the age of nineteen, later fled to the United States where he learned English by translating Shakespeare into German and then back into English again.

During the Lincoln administration he served as ambassador to Spain and as Major General in the Union Army. In 1865 he was correspondent for Horace Greeley's *The New York Tribune* and subsequently became editor of the *Detroit Post* and the St. Louis German-language *Westliche Post*. Elected U.S. Senator from Missouri in 1868, he promoted the liberalization of immigration laws, opposed prohibition, and urged the adoption of the civil service system. As Secretary of the Interior, Schurz championed civil rights for American Indians and introduced the independent civil service merit system for government employees, replacing party allegiance with competence and experience as criteria for government work. He also created the national park system.

Wernher von Braun

Wernher von Braun, the German-born rocket and space expert, has become a legendary figure in his own lifetime, primarily as the scientist most associated with the free world's first satellite into space and man's first landing on the moon on July 21, 1969, by the United States. Ironically, it was Adolf Hitler who both promoted his rocket research and at the same time frustrated it and ultimately led von Braun and his coworkers to seek refuge and permanent hospitality in the United States.

Impressed by the success of von Braun's early rocket experiments, the Nazi regime established a rocket experimental station near Peenemünde on the Baltic Sea in 1937 and placed von Braun in charge. Although von Braun was primarily interested in space exploration, the regime was more interested in long-range artillery. When in October, 1942, von Braun and his team succeeded in launching a rocket that soared to a record-breaking height of sixty miles and a distance of 120 miles, the notorious V-2-*Vergeltungswaffe* (retaliation weapon) was born.

But von Braun was overwrought by impossible production schedules, which led to interrogations by the Gestapo for suspected sabotage. Toward the end of World War II, von Braun shrewdly decided to move his entire experimental rocketry station to southern Germany in order to be captured by American troops rather than by the Russians, in whose zone they were located. With counterfeit stickers, the team with the aid of two trains and over a hundred trucks, moved their entire equipment and supplies to Bavaria.

In 1950, by now in America, von Braun and his team of Germans joined American scientists in establishing the American rocket program in Huntsville, Alabama, which experimented in the production of long-range missiles with nuclear payload possibilities. However, the experimentation was continually bogged down by the lack of funds and internal bickering among the Navy, Army, and Air Force over jurisdictional rights regarding rockets. It took the launching of the Russian Sputnik, man's first space satellite, on October 4, 1957, to jolt the United States into action. Less than four months afterwards, on January 31, 1958, the Army rocket Jupiter C thrust Explorer I, the first U.S. satellite, into a perfect orbit around the earth.

"The moon," von Braun has said, "is a challenge very much as

Antarctica was. People went because they thought it would be fun and found uses they hadn't dreamed of. The value of discovery becomes clear only in the wake of the exploration itself. Columbus couldn't have predicted what the United States would be like today."

"Little Germanies"

Like other immigrant minorities—Italians, Czechs, Slovakians, Poles, Chinese—the Germans at first tended to settle among their own kind, established "Little Germanies" with their own schools, newspapers, fraternal and singing societies, national churches, shopping districts, and social activities. With the exception of a large contingent in San Francisco, the Germans settled mainly in the area between New York, Minneapolis, St. Louis, and Baltimore, which is popularly called "The German Quadrangle." Perhaps the most famous group is that known as the Pennsylvania Dutch ("Dutch" here being a distortion of the word "Deutsch" and having nothing to do with the Netherlands), a group which has preserved many elements of German culture.

The two most important cohesive forces of Americans of German descent and their immigrant parents and forefathers were the national churches and the German-language newspapers, both of which continued to exercise a great deal of influence well into the middle of the twentieth century. Today national churches, Protestant and Catholic, are gradually becoming a thing of the past.

The German-language newspaper not only provided a familiar atmosphere to the homesick immigrant, but was also one of the most important vehicles for introducing him to the New World. It was the German newspaper which helped newcomers find jobs, rent apartments, shop conveniently where German was spoken, make social and business contacts, and learn about their adopted country. As the newcomer, thanks to his paper, became more and more assimilated—and the Germans tended to assimilate faster and more completely than most other minorities—he became less and less dependent on his paper. Thus the more competently a German-language publication tried to serve its readers, the more rapidly it hastened its own demise.

As early as 1732 Benjamin Franklin actually launched the *Philadelphische Zeitung,* but his knowledge of German was poor, and the paper folded after the second issue.

The oldest seven-days-a-week periodical in New York is a German-language newspaper, *Die Staats Zeitung und Herold,* which first appeared only two years after Goethe's death in 1834.

The German-language press had its golden age around 1910, when there were 786 newspapers and periodicals. By 1941, when the U.S. entered World War II, their number had dropped to 220. Today, *Staats Zeitung und Herold,* whose motto is "An American newspaper in the German language," is making a last-ditch stand for survival, along with the only other German-language daily in Chicago, and about 25 weeklies in the U.S.

Successful Assimilation

The decline of German newspapers and national churches is evidence of the successful assimilation of German immigrants and their offspring, so that the hyphenated term, "German-American" was never less appropriate than now. Only a few "pockets" of German culture remain, such as the folkloristic Hermann, Missouri, with its annual *Maifest,* costume parades, maypole, knackwurst, and a wine cellar whose dozen 3,000-gallon casks are called the "Twelve Apostles."

New York City's Yorkville, roughly the area along Eighty-sixth Street between Second and Third avenues, is affectionately nicknamed "Sauerkraut Boulevard" or "German Broadway." But any comparison between this tourist center—overflowing with cuckoo clocks, beer steins, long-stem pipes, and *dirndl-* and *lederhosen*-clad waitresses and waiters—and modern Germany is strictly laughable.

Cities like New York, St. Louis (whose city hall resembles Hamburg's), Milwaukee, Cleveland, Cincinnati, Buffalo, Chicago, Detroit, Baltimore, Newark, Pittsburgh, and Jersey City still have their German movie houses, fraternal singing and gymnastic societies.

Meanwhile, interest in German life and culture is hardly on the wane; on the contrary, it has become intensified, but on a far more sophisticated level. If there are fewer German-language publications originating within the United States, the distribution of publications directly from Germany, thanks to light air-mail editions, is constantly increasing. Numerous American newsstands now provide dailies like *Die Welt,* weeklies like *Die Zeit, Der Spiegel,* and *Der Stern.*

437

More than ever before German language courses have been introduced into college and high school curricula, and Americans by the thousands are spending at least one semester in German universities.[2] The outstanding success of the Chicago-based Institute of European Studies, which sponsors European study programs in Vienna, Freiburg-im-Breisgau, Paris, and elsewhere is but one example.

Two distinguished private organizations which promote meetings with leaders in education, journalism, politics, and social sciences in the two countries are the American Council on Germany in New York City and its German affiliate, *Atlantik-Brücke* (Atlantic Bridge) in Hamburg.

The Carl Schurz Memorial Foundation located in Philadelphia is especially devoted to the preservation of the traditions of the Pennsylvania "Dutch," and maintains a folk art museum near Lancaster. A strictly private institution, it promotes German language instruction, grants scholarships to both German and American students, and publishes the *American-German Review.*

A committee of Germans and Americans have established cultural and educational centers called "Goethe House" in New York and Milwaukee. Developed along lines similar to the *Amerika Haus* in several German cities, it differs from the latter, which is U.S.I.A.-sponsored, in that it is run on a strictly private basis and operated entirely by American citizens.

The shortwave radio station, *Deutsche Welle* (Voice of Germany), is that country's counterpart to the Voice of America. But it too differs from the VOA. Although financed by the German government, it is operated by an independent board of directors composed of civic leaders, parliamentarians of the leading German parties. Housed in the building where the world-famous 4711 Eau de Cologne is manufactured, the *Deutsche Welle* broadcasts in twenty-seven languages including Amharic (Ethiopia) and Hausa (Nigeria).

Today Canada and Australia are preferred to the United States by German emigrants. However, more Germans than ever before are visiting the U.S.[3]

Immigrants today slip into the mainstream of American life almost as easily as they slip into an overcoat. Thanks to the comprehensive Americanization of Europe, the universal requirements of English in business and daily life, the overwhelming coverage of American life by communications media, adaptation is a relatively small problem. On the contrary, teams of West German servicemen, especially in the *Luftwaffe* (Air Force) adapt to such a degree that language experts are worried about the baffling new vocabulary that German servicemen bring with them when returning from the States. Dr. Hugo Moser, German language professor at the University of Bonn and director of the German language institute, published an article in a *Bundeswehr* publication, entitled *"Hoffentlich ist das bald over."* He points out that he is not against the use of the English language in communicating with other NATO units, but he is worried about the ruination of the German mother tongue through the complete mishmash with English terms.

Examples: *"Ich bin um 12 Uhr off-ge-taked* [I took off at 12 o'clock]"; *"Er ist noch nicht geklärt* [from "to clear," *i.e.,* He is not yet cleared]." One reason for this, Dr. Moser discovered, is that German servicemen are more familiar with English than with German technical terms because they learned the English terms first. Also, the English terms are simpler. A drastic example: *"Düsenflugzeugsgeschwindigkeitsverringerungskurve"* for as simple a term as "break."

The majority of current immigrants to the United States are more apt to be frustrated by the normal problems of daily life: finding a job, getting along with one's neighbors, sending the children to school, surviving the heat, and the continuous battle with bureaucracy.

Anti-German Sentiments

During and after World War I, a fierce anti-German wave swept across the United States. It shifted from the bizarre—anti-Sauerkraut and anti-Dachshund campaigns—to the irrational—physical violence and discrimination. "Hamburger" and "Sauerkraut" on restaurant menus were abruptly changed to "Salisbury Steak" and "Liberty Cabbage." Many Germans rapidly anglicized their names form Müller to Miller, Schmidt to Smith, Schwarz to Black.

Paradoxically, the greatest wave of Nazi films, magazine features, comic strips, TV movies inundated the Americans long after World War II, all the way into the seventies. The CBS series, *Hogan's Heroes,* seen by an estimated 30 million Americans, over a period of five years—longer than World War II itself—

439

relentlessly paraded stiff, monocled and stupid German Wehrmacht officers across the screen. Nazi-uniformed officers appear on the *Laugh-In* show, while in the *Evergreen Review* a leering Nazi officer takes whip in hand and "lashes Phoebe's defenseless breasts and loins, making the whip bite cruelly into the soft, supplicating skin . . . ."

"Through their Nazi films," commented *Der Spiegel*, "the U.S. film industry has produced an image of Germany that may well have penetrated far deeper into the American consciousness than World War II itself."

The CBS 1967 documentary, *The Germans* by Hughes Rudd, seen by millions of Americans and also shown in Scandinavia, South America, and Japan, created a furor in West Germany because in the Germans' view it presented a stereotyped, cliché German, complete with *Lederhosen,* Bavarian beer mug, and sauerkraut.

While most Germans do not experience much prejudice on account of the Nazi past, many of the more educated do encounter resentment, criticism, snide remarks. They are frequently asked to account for the Nazi atrocities and the alleged rise of neo-Nazism or anti-Semitism in today's Federal Republic. During an ABC-TV special a guest happened to remark that he had purchased a German clock, and the British singer Tom Jones brought down the house with the remark: "It shows the hour, the day, the year—and the particular war of the time."[4]

Hans Friedrichs, a reporter for West German television, was once asked by David Susskind during a press panel on American TV, "Do you as a German find it difficult to live in New York?" When he answered in the affirmative, he was asked, to the accompaniment of sneers from the studio audience, "As difficult as a Jew in Nazi Germany?"

German tourists, like many Europeans coming to the States for the first time, are often shocked and frustrated by the extremely small number of Americans who can speak any foreign language, while in Europe a second and third language is commonplace. The visitors are inevitably shocked by the prodigious waste on the streets and highways, the filth in the cities, the overheated apartments and sealed windows, the unhealthy coolness of air-conditioning, the absence of pedestrian and bicycle paths, and the few possibilities for taking a walk in America's cities "in communion with nature."

I have heard time and again of Germans being questioned or

even arrested by police because they were "suspiciously" *walking* late at night in residential districts and their explanation of "merely taking a walk" was found unbelievable.

But, in spite of all this, it appears as though the Germans today are loved by Americans far more than they realize. According to the Hooper Research Institute, Germans were the second most-liked people (29 percent), next to the English (34 percent), but way ahead of the Italians (19 percent), the French (10 percent), and the Mexicans (5 percent). The Russians were last. Only 6 percent of Americans have an outright dislike for the Germans, according to the recent survey.

"I find Americans," one German journalist returning from the States said to me, "more nervous, their tastes more luxurious, life more hectic. The American landscape is marred by endless rows of billboards. Television and radio programs are choked with commericals. I missed in the United States the sidewalk café, the leisurely pace, the larger number of holidays, the well-laid out parks, walks, and trees in the cities. I missed the sense of history and tradition that confronts you at every turn in Germany, the long hikes, the endless, penetrating debates on politics which bore people so easily there."

But far more often Germans returning from the States have raved to me about Americans' directness, generosity, and "completely uncomplicated way of getting to the point and helping you find your way." Americans, they say, are less envious. In Europe "one is always quick at suspecting there is something fishy about success, that 'connections' or little deals 'not quite above board' had played a role. . . . Over there, one rolls up one's sleeves and tries to make equally good. Perhaps this is the reason why Socialism never really caught on in the States and why social security falls far behind that of Europe."

Scholars and journalists find the American emphasis on the pragmatic approach refreshing—in Germany as elsewhere scientific, technical, and sociological literature is top-heavy with American references and allusions. Older Germans have repeatedly told me how friendly American students are, how willing and eager they are to learn from others. "I miss," said one, "the Americans' open door, their friendliness in everyday dealings, their fresh informality. It is true that in the States you can have many friends and yet none, but for everyday life the uncomplicated humanity of this people does one so much good."

◄26►

THE UGLY GERMANS

"THE GERMANS THEMSELVES, I am inclined to think, are natives of the soil and extremely little affected by immigration or friendly intercourse with other nations. . . . Who would leave Asia, Africa or Italy to visit Germany, with its unlovely scenery, its bitter climate, its general dreariness to sense and eye, unless it were his home. . . .

"The Germans have no taste for peace; renown is easier won among perils. . . . You will find it harder to persuade a German to plough the land and to await its annual produce with patience than to challenge a foe and earn the prize of wounds. He thinks it spiritless and slack to gain by sweat what he can buy with blood. . . . When not engaged in warfare, they spend some little time in hunting, but more in idling, abandoned in sleep and gluttony. . . . They are so strangely inconsistent. They love indolence, but they hate peace. . . . No business, public or private, is transacted except in arms. . . . The liberty of the Germans is a deadlier foe than the tyranny of the kings of Parthia. . . ."[1]

Thus as long ago as A.D. 98, the Roman historian Tacitus, in his famous book, *Germania,* already regarded the German people as a force to be reckoned with in Europe. His picture of the Germans is not all negative. Indeed, he praises their intense love of freedom, their extravagant hospitality, their keen sense of humor, the unique fidelity of their women, and the sanctity of their family life. Tacitus regarded them as overgrown children who needed the strong arm of Roman discipline to keep them in line. *Germania* has been assiduously taught in German schools and universities for generations, and it was Tacitus' exaggerated and naive impressions of the Germans' racial purity ("wild, blue eyes, reddish hair and huge frames") that made his book a kind of Bible to support the Nazi myth of *"Blut und Boden."*

Today nearly 2,000 years later and a quarter of a century after World War II, the Germans are still regarded with worldwide suspicion, sometimes with admiration and envy, but more often with condescension, reservation, and conditional acceptance. They are a people on parole.

Not long ago I sat in a restaurant in Amsterdam and happened to answer a German at the next table in his own language who had asked for the time. The waiter overheard me, and when I tried to order in English he snarled at me, "Why don't you Germans speak in your own language! Why do you try to hide your identity by speaking English?" It was only when I showed him my American passport that he was pacified. "My apologies," he said, "but these Germans make me retch with their obsequiousness. They think they can cover up all they have done by bowing and scraping with their phony humility."

Among a great many Dutch of the older generation the trauma of the Nazi invasion of May 10, 1940, is still not overcome and the nightmare of 104,000 murdered Jews and 23,000 other Dutch is still vivid in their memories, as is the German economic exploitation of their country. As Professor Patijn, a member of the Dutch parliament from the Workers' Party, once put it, "We have been afraid of the Germans since Kaiser Wilhelm II and have not stopped being afraid."

An opinion poll conducted among the Dutch people in 1963 revealed that they regarded the Germans as the least likable people on earth.

With the marriage of Crown Princess Beatrix to the German diplomat Claus von Amsberg in 1966, the Germans (and all but one of the Netherlands' kings and queens had a German spouse) appeared at last to be accepted by the Dutch people as a whole.

With the state visit of West German President Gustav Heinemann to the Netherlands in November, 1969, the first German head of state to visit the Netherlands since Kaiser Wilhelm II in 1907, a new era of friendly relations began for the two countries.

More than a century and a half ago, Madame Germaine de Staël, accompanied by her friend Benjamin Constant and much baggage, set forth from Paris to "discover" the Germans. Her book *De L'Allemagne,* published in 1813, is frequently quoted in Germany in the same breath as Tacitus. During her trip Madame de Staël met Wilhelm von Humboldt, Fichte, Schlegel. While her companion Constant translated Schiller's *Wallenstein,* Goethe flattered her with the express wish "soon to publish your observations about us honest Germans, so that we can look at ourselves in such a lovely mirror." The publication of her book proved to be a friendly but far from flattering "mirror."

She described the Germans as "generally sincere and upright; they never break their word. . ." but transformed the feint praise with inevitable damnation: "In Germany everyone stands behind his rank and position like a post. . . . Their respect for power proceeds more from fatalist belief than from self-interest. . . . They are so conscientious in carrying out every order that every order is a command. . . . The decided ability to work and to brood are also typical German characteristics. . . . They do not know how to get along with other people and the less one gives them the opportunity to make independent decisions, the happier they are. . . . Their thinkers move about on a heavenly plain, but once one sets one's feet on solid earth again, one finds only grenadiers. . . . The true Germany of Bach, Beethoven and Goethe is drowned out by the marching boots of German militarism."

Victor Hugo thought more kindly of the Germans. "Two nations have made Europe," he once wrote. "These two nations are Germany and France. Germany is to Western civilization what India is to the Orient, a kind of great ancestor. . . . Germany is one of the countries that I love and I admire the German people. I feel almost like a son of this noble and sacred Fatherland of all thinkers. If I were not a Frenchman I would wish to be a German."

An opinion poll conducted in France in the late sixties revealed that the French regarded the Germans as primarily "industrious, disciplined, intelligent, clean," but also "fanatic, brutal. '

"It is wrong," observed a German diplomat in Paris, "to depict France with the symbolic woman Marianne. For the French the Germans are the hussy that must be raped."

"When the Germans try to be gracious," once sighed former President Charles de Gaulle, "they jump out the window."

Yet de Gaulle signed the much disputed German-French Friendship Treaty with Konrad Adenauer on January 22, 1963, which provides for regular consultation between the two heads of state as well as economic, cultural, and recreational exchange. Many Germans have criticized the treaty for narrowing the scope of European integration and providing a dangerous vehicle for

French domination of all-European policy during the de Gaulle regime, which could just as easily lead to a German hegemony, with or without reunification.

Nevertheless writers like François Mauriac have since spoken of the "miracle" of German-French reconciliation. Unquestionably the bilateral friendship, and the burial of the *Erbfeindschaft* (hereditary enmity), was the cornerstone of the European movement, without which its two great architects, former French Premier Robert Schuman and the brilliant French economist and originator of the Common Market, Jean Monnet, might not have achieved even the limited results obtained so far.

However, French confidence in the Germans and vice versa is still a very fluctuating affair. In 1967 the majority of French youths questioned in a national survey responded in favor of improved relations with the Germans, while a third of Germans in a similar survey that same year said relations had worsened, and more than 40 percent were "uncertain."

"Britain's Best Friend"

When in 1961 the British were asked in the National Opinion Poll what they thought of the Germans, German men were regarded as "industrious, arrogant, ruthless and manly," and German women were considered "hard-working, good house-wives, fat and clever." Asked in 1963 which country is England's best friend on the continent, they opted for Denmark and Holland over Germany and Belgium. Queried again in 1964 which Europeans they liked most, the British placed the Germans last (5 percent), behind the Swiss (24 percent), Swedes, French, Norwegians, Italians, Danes, and Dutch.

"When the Germans are polite," observed British novelist Evelyn Waugh, "they are politer. When they are rough, they are rougher. When they are clever, they are cleverer. When they are drunk, they are drunker. And when they are nasty, they are nastier."[2]

Ethnically and culturally, the English and the Germans are closely related, taking into account the important Celtic element that is absent in Germany and the Slavic characteristics that have no equivalent in Britain. Charlemagne took English scholars along with him wherever he went, notably his greatest friend and

445

adviser, Alcuin of York. The "Apostle to the Germans," St. Boniface, was an English Benedictine monk. From 1714 a continuous flow of brides from Germany graced the British court, and during the entire eighteenth century British and German forces fought as allies in Europe, while the British army was noticeably influenced by Prussian methods of drill, dress, and tactics.

The British historian John K. Dunlop, who served on the Allied Control Commission in Germany at the end of World War II, compiled *A Short History of Germany* especially designed to help British troops stationed in Germany understand the historical background of the country. He also reminded them of their similarities. "Today," he writes in the 1964 edition of his study, "when school groups or students from the two countries meet it is difficult to identify from outward view, from color of hair or skin or from shape of head, which members of the cheerful company are from southern England and which from northern Germany."

But in that same book the author warns that while "the Germany that our fathers knew, the Germany of Edwardian days, has passed away, yet it still broods, an uneasy ghost, over central Europe."

By 1967, with the Federal Republic's support for the United Kingdom's entry in the Common Market, the image of the Germans began to change considerably. On December 22 that year, the London *Daily Telegraph* carried the headline: "Germany—Britain's Best Friend in Europe." After all, the Beatles first came to public attention in Hamburg's Reeperbahn, and the English pop singer, Engelbert Humperdinck, adopted the Germanic name, rightly believing it to be an asset.

Yet in 1969 polls showed that about a quarter of the British still said they dislike or strongly dislike the Germans, mostly the over-forty group, while only 6 percent say they would consider living in Germany if they had to emigrate. According to a survey jointly sponsored by *Der Stern* and London's *Daily Telegraph*, only 4 percent of the British speak German, compared to 15 percent of the Germans who speak some English. And only 10 percent of the British have been to Germany in the past twelve years. But German troops are now "old hat" in Wales and elsewhere for short training stints and have long been accepted, even marrying some British girls.

The "Revanchist" Federal Republic

In the Soviet Union and throughout the Eastern European countries the image of the Germans from World War II until the seventies was systematically kept alive as that of revanchists, new-Nazis, and *Störenfriede der Welt* (the world's mischiefmakers). Even the GDR relentlessly employed the most savage polemics imaginable in a continuous harrangue against the "revanchist" *Bundesrepublik.* The extremist National Democratic Party (NPD) is cited as an example of "rampant neo-Nazism raising its ugly head in militaristic *Bundesrepublik.*"

In Czechoslovakia, warned *Izvestia,* "one could feel the criminal hand of Bonn, where reactionary powers supported the Czechoslovakian counterrevolution with direct interference and aide."

Willy Brandt's foreign policy, according to *Pravda,* "is simply a carbon copy of Franz-Josef Strauss, leader of the revanchist, militaristic powers."

"In certain West German cities," according to the Soviet youth magazine *Smena,* "high school students can drop a coin in the slot of a vending machine, lift the receiver, and listen to the barbaric words of Hitler."

"West Germany is a neon-lighted jungle of decadence, lust, corruption, passion, desire, and nudity," a *Trud* reporter commented, describing the Federal Republic's night life.

The magazine *Sowjetskaja kultura* claims to have counted 230 witches in the Lüneburg heath, "while 95 percent of the inhabitants of the Lake of Constance region still believe in witches and ghosts."

At best, most of these wild charges are distorted, many of them, such as the claim that schoolboys can hear Hitler's speeches from a slot machine, are downright fabrications.

However that may be, it is actually beside the point whether or not the continuous Communist tirades against the Federal Republic are based on assumptions or demonstrable facts. Far more significant is the overriding factor behind this phenomenon: fear.

"The Soviet people," according to historian Jeschow, "have a right to be suspicious." Few Westerners are aware how deeply ingrained the *Koschmar* (nightmare) of the World War II holocaust is in a part of the world that has not enjoyed the distracting and compensating benefits of consumer prosperity and is virtually cut off from the West. Twenty million Soviet war dead (including seven million civilians) is the main fact that the average Soviet and East European citizen remembers about the Germans, and to make sure they do not forget, and that the younger generation is kept vividly aware of it, the Communist press of these countries has been pounding away relentlessly in an endless tirade against the Germans.

Soviet diplomats find it execrable taste to compare the Berlin blockade, with its handful of accidental deaths, to the nine-hundred-day Nazi siege of Leningrad in which nearly one million (estimated) lives were lost.

The average Soviet citizen learns precious little factual information about the Germans, officially very little about the division of the two Germanies. The Soviet press assiduously avoids publication of maps showing both Germanies and photos or films of the Berlin Wall have been almost totally absent from Soviet mass media.

In spite of all this, the average Russian appears to bear no animosity or ill will toward the Germans. Former German ambassador to Moscow, Hans Kroll, has said, "If one considers the extraordinary means of power and influence at the disposal of Soviet propaganda, and with what intensity and consistency it is carried out, one can only be amazed how relatively little effectiveness it has among the people. The results are disproportionate to the effort."

A survey conducted among German tourists to the Soviet Union (over 50,000 in 1968) revealed that they encountered virtually no ill will or animosity from Russians. Even in Leningrad, they were received with friendliness. Tourists to France and the Netherlands reported far more numerous incidents of insult and resentment.

At the time Otto von Bismarck served as ambassador at the czarist court at St. Petersburg, from 1859 to 1862, the Germans were held in high esteem in Russia. Even today every schoolboy is familiar with the legendary German opera, *Zar und Zimmermann,* which is about Peter the Great, who brought numerous German craftsmen and merchants to Russia on account of their skills. In a country without a middle class, the first image of the German burgher was formed, and stuck. German princesses married Russian czars. Catherine the Great, daughter of a Prussian prince, reigned over Russia for thirty-four years, rivaling the fame of Peter the Great himself. German scientists went to Russia and contributed to the image of German perfection. "The moon," quipped Gogol, "was built in Hamburg."

"In Germany," Dostoevsky once wrote in a letter to a friend, "I met a Russian who continually lives abroad. He travels every year to Russia for about three weeks and then returns to Germany, where he lives with his wife and children. All of them have become Germans through and through. Among other things I asked him, 'Why did you emigrate?' He replied testily, 'Here is civilization and there is barbarism.' "

"Learn from the Germans!"

In the twenties Illya Ehrenburg, Russian novelist, sat in a Berlin café and wrote, "In Europe there is only one modern city, Berlin. London, that is paradise and hell. But Berlin is simply a great city."

It was General Erich Ludendorff who arranged for the payment of fifty million gold marks from the Kaiser's treasury and the famous secret transport of Lenin in a sealed coach from Zurich, through Germany, to St. Petersburg, to lead the revolution of 1918. The Germans hoped thereby to divide Russia and weaken it for German conquest. And that same Lenin, whose maternal grandparents, Alexander Blank and Anna Groschopf, may have been Germans, is quoted in the Soviet edition of the complete writings of Lenin as saying "Learn from the Germans!" (Volume 27, page 137).[3]

Just as the Soviet writer Boris Pasternak studied at the University of Marburg an der Lahn in the twentieth century, so did the Russian universal genius Lomonossov before him in 1736. Marx and Engels, after all, were Germans, and German philosophers like Kant, Schelling, and Hegel have long exercised a strong influence. The Russians are avid readers of Schiller, Goethe, the Grimm brothers, Feuchtwanger, Heine, Hauff, Remarque, Rilke, and Thomas Mann. More than seventy million copies of books by German authors—contemporary Heinrich Böll alone, more than one million—have appeared in the Soviet Union in recent years. In the spring of 1970 some nine million Russian students were learning German, which is more than half of all students (94 percent) required to learn a foreign language, while only five million were studying English and one million French.

In their history books, Russian schoolchildren learn how Peter the Great successfully brought German experts to Russia, that in 1812 the Prussian General Yorck together with the Russian Diebitsch helped smash Napoleon. The same school books mention that at the end of the last century every second high officer of the Russian Army was of German descent and that German civil servants comprised the greater percentage of the staff of the foreign ministry.

Russian writers like Tolstoy, Dostoevsky, Gogol, Pasternak, and recent authors like the poet Yevgeny Yevtushenko, Mikhail Sholokhov, and controversial Aleksandr I. Solzhenitsyn are widely read in Germany.

In 1964 a group of Soviet journalists accompanying Alexej Adschubej, then editor-in-chief of *Izvestia* and son-in-law of former Soviet Premier Krushschev, made a visit to West Germany, but with many reservations. However, they avoided the usual polemics, complimented progressive methods of German agriculture and economics and industry. They even admitted that they thought more and more Germans in the Federal Republic are devoted to peace and that they are "using the Ruhr to produce steel for peace." They praised the beer, donned Bavarian hats, and Adschubej admitted that Germans and Russians have more in common than he had thought—"they are capable of crying." As for "revanchist odors, one can say that they are in evidence everywhere in the world."

"In reality," commented Heinz Schewe, the veteran German correspondent in Moscow, "Ivan Ivanovitch wants nothing so much as an alliance with the Germans. One hears frequently in confidential conversations, even among high diplomats, 'If the Germans and Russians would get together, then we have nothing more to fear. No power on earth could beat us.' "

The Poles Remember

Perhaps even more than in the Soviet Union, the trauma of Hitler's massacres is still painfully vivid in Poland. Next to the Jews, no other people have suffered so much in World War II as the Poles, whose country has been partitioned three times by her neighbors, Russia, Prussia, and Austria, and which lost its large eastern territories to the U.S.S.R., while being made custodian of the former German Oder-Neisse territories in the West.

The Poles remember the systematic destruction of Warsaw and the Nazi "Educational Program for Sub-humans" (a little bit of reading, ability to write their names and to count to five hundred). They remember the labor camps, the massacre of the Jews at Auschwitz, and the 4.5 million Poles who fell during the war.

During his regime, Wladyslaw Gomulka held stubbornly to an anti-German policy. The propaganda machinery in Warsaw continued up to the seventies to raise fears that West Germany would recover the territory now making up Poland's western frontier. By fanning the flames of hatred for the Germans the regime tried to keep alive one of the few issues that created a bond of unity between the predominantly Roman Catholic antiregime-minded pro-West people and the regime. Mindful of centuries of exploitation by Russia and eager to take up contacts with the West there was a gradual informal rapprochement among the ordinary people during the sixties. The famous exchange of letters between the German and Polish Roman Catholic bishops in 1965 and their proposals of "mutual forgiveness" is indicative of the growing climate of understanding between the two peoples, especially among the young.

With the increase in tourism and the rebellion of the youth, who favored fast motorcycles, beat, jazz, soul over ideology, and the increase in trade, notably with Krupp, economic and cultural bridges have been reected. By 1970, more than 100 guest performances of Polish plays, concerts, and films annually take place in West Germany.

In the Czech language the word for "German" is "Nemec," which means "the mute," *i.e.*, one who doesn't hear us, doesn't understand us, does not speak our language.

The Sudetenland question and World War II all but wiped out the strong affinities which bound Prague with Germany through its university and its numerous writers (notably Franz Kafka and Franz Werfel) who wrote in German. Until the Soviet invasion in August, 1968, relations with the Germans, in large part fostered by the large numbers of East German tourists, improved remarkably. Through the Soviet invasion West German sympathies for the Czechoslovakian people increased.

In 1967 Rumania became the first country of the Warsaw pact,

451

outside of the Soviet Union, to resume diplomatic relations with
Bonn. Economically the country has become an important
importer of German products. Culturally the Rumanians feel
themselves closer to the French than to the Germans. But they
never had border conflicts with Germany and were allied to the
Third Reich for a time. Nearly 400,000 ethnic Germans live in
Rumania, enjoy relative freedom, have their own customs,
newspaper, German language courses. The "revanchist, militarist"
image of the Germans is virtually unknown.

Yugoslavia has normalized relations with the Federal Republic
to a greater degree than perhaps any other communist country.
Diplomatic relations were broken off in 1957 when Yugoslavia
recognized East Germany, but were resumed again with the
revision of the Hallstein doctrine. A special factor fostering
improved relations is a trade agreement which enables thousands
of Yugoslavs to work in the Federal Republic (100,000 in 1970).
Better informed, their country inundated with German tourists,
Yugoslavians on the whole are very kindly disposed toward the
Germans today.

Relations between the Federal Republic and other neighbors—
Austria, Switzerland, Italy—have more or less normalized.

"We Austrians," says Chancellor Bruno Kreisky, "no longer see
Germany as the Reich to which we want to 'return home'."[4]

In Switzerland one senses a widespread uneasiness toward the
Germans. Many German-speaking Swiss feel uncomfortable
speaking High German which they regard as a foreign language;
they have the impression the Germans feel superior to them.
Psychologically the Swiss are said to be still waiting for the World
War II invasion that never came. "The Swiss," a Swiss psychologist once remarked to me, "have had two tragedies in their
recent history. Twice they were unable to take part in a world
war." His intentional irony was meant to underline the Swiss'
lack of opportunity to work off their agressions. "They don't
have to atone for anything."

The Italian, Altiero Spinelli, a high official of the EEC in
Brussels, who had been imprisoned by the Fascists for ten years,
wrote recently: "All in all, relations between the two countries
[West Germany and Italy] are excellent. . . . Nevertheless a quiet
fear continues to live in the breasts of all that Germany could
once again become too strong and once more be tempted by
ambitious thoughts of conquest."[5]

Israel—A New Relationship

In the spring of 1965 the West German Near-East policies were in a state of crisis. Israel was incensed over the lackluster West German performance in regard to the statute of limitations regarding murder, which included Nazi criminals, and over the presence of German rocket and aviation technicians in Egypt. East German boss Walter Ulbricht was invited to Egypt, and the secret German delivery of weapons to Israel was made public. The Arabs demanded the discontinuance of weapons delivery to Israel and declined to call off Ulbricht's visit. The Israelis on their part demanded the continued delivery of weapons and the dismissal of the German technicians from Egypt.

Among the Arabs ironically much admiration for the Germans abounds. Many a German technician even today, in Egypt, Algeria, Tunis, has to endure the frequent and uncomfortable outbursts of "Heil, Hitler!" which Arabs intend as a compliment. Even before Hitler, the Arabian world showed great sympathy for the Germans on account of their scientific and technical skills. In World War II, Field Marshal Erwin Rommel's tanks in North Africa awakened great sympathy among the Arabs, because they regarded the German conquests as a victory over French colonialism, and also because the Afrika Korps of Rommel was noted for its humanity toward captured enemies.

The Adenauer government had extended itself to individual restitution to the Jews and reparations toward Israel (Luxembourg Agreement of 1952), after a talk between Adenauer and Israel's President Ben-Gurion in 1960 in New York. They had also agreed to secret delivery of weapons, but not the formal establishment of diplomatic relations. Adenauer was for this in principle but when in August, 1963, Israel indicated its readiness to take up diplomatic relations, he demurred, fearing the reaction of the Arab nations.

But his successor, Chancellor Ludwig Erhard, in March, 1965, agreed to cancel the weapons delivery to Israel on the premise that the Federal Republic should refuse weapons delivery to any area of tension. He also offered to take up diplomatic relations with Israel, even at the risk that the Arab states would sever relations and recognize the GDR. When Egypt invited Ulbricht for a state visit, the Erhard regime reacted by canceling economic aid to the United Arab Republic. Ten of the thirteen Arab states

(Jordan, UAR, Yemen, Iraq, Saudi Arabia, Kuwait, Sudan, Algeria, Syria, and Lebanon) recalled their ambassadors from Bonn, but did not take up diplomatic relations with the GDR. A few weeks later, on May 12, the establishment of diplomatic relations between Bonn and Israel was announced. A new relationship with Israel had begun.

Although the GDR has done nothing toward restitution to the Jews and unequivocally sides with the Arabs, the Federal Republic is accused of a double standard of morality in the Jewish question.

The Israeli publicist Vera Elyashiv, in her book *Deutschland Kein Wintermärchen,* based on her trip through West Germany in 1964, accuses West Germans of abnormal attitudes toward the Jews and Israel. "Too many Germans," she writes, "give Israel preferred treatment. They admire her and her inhabitants to such an exaggerated degree that this admiration actually evokes disdain for the European and especially German Jews.

"The government does the exact opposite. It is ready to do everything for the tiny Jewish community in Germany. But Israel is treated as if it were any other nation and had nothing to do with the mass extermination of the Jews in Germany. Both obscure the truth, that the Israelis and the Jews are one and the same people, the Israelis are no less Jews than those that one knows in Germany, and that this state consists predominantly of the survivors of the Jewish catastrophe in Europe, and consequently after this experience will defend their existence to the very end, because this is the only guarantee that Jewish blood will never again be spilled in vain."

When in March, 1966, economic negotiations between Israel and the Federal Republic came to an impasse, Israel again referred to its special status. "The negotiations between West Germany and us," commented the Israeli publication *Jedioth Achronoth,* "cannot be compared with negotiations between Germany and other states in the world that have diplomatic relations with the Federal Republic."

Meanwhile, relations between the two have become "normal."

But, asks Rolf Breitenstein, diplomatic correspondent for the *Frankfurter Rundschau,* a Frankfurt daily, "Can there be 'normal relations' between 'abnormal' states, both with uncertain boundaries and traditions, both not universally recognized, both at once ancient and very young nations, in which the classic concepts of state, unity, executive power and jurisdiction are forged by means of painstaking juristic improvisation?"[6]

Breitenstein cites the odious comparison that the Germans in the past have made between themselves and the "chosen people" of the Bible. Long before Hitler the Germans regarded themselves as chosen and destined for a higher role than other folk. During the Third Reich even Roman Catholic leaders, such as Bishop Rudolf Graber of Regensburg, used the expression. And the poet Emmanuel Geibel exclaimed rapturously, "May the world one day enjoy the fruits of German substance." "We are the salt of the earth," once boasted Kaiser Wilhelm II.

Yet even Israeli critics like Elyashiv find a strange and ironic bond between Israelis and Germans. "We are two sides of a tragedy, and we are united by it. As long as this tragedy is alive in us, we won't be able to rid ourselves of the Germans and they from us. Even hate can be a binding force."[7]

No one knows how widespread or deep this hatred for the Germans is in Israel, but no one will deny it is very strongly present. Many Jews refuse on principle to visit Germany. I know a number of Israeli youths who would never knowingly buy a German product. An Israeli girl taking a shortcut through Germany from Holland to Switzerland said she "trembled the whole time." Many Israeli youth are openly hostile to their parents and older Israelis whom they regard as cowards for capitulating so easily to Hitler.

When in October, 1969, the Israel Philharmonic Orchestra attempted to play a work by the German composer Richard Strauss, who is branded in Israel for his known Hitler sympathies, it was compelled by an incensed public to postpone the performance.

"To hell with the musical shrine of one Richard Strauss," wrote Emanuel Bar-Kadman, one of Israel's most influential music critics.

The changed attitude toward the Germans was however also indicated in the dispute, when the respected daily *Ha 'aretz* denounced "this trend of public intolerance."

"We have long ago," it editorialized, "abandoned the idea of boycotting everything German. German cars are today the most popular in the country. TV sets, stereo equipment, records, heaters, and coffee percolators fill thousands of Israeli homes. Israelis go to Germany, and Germans come here. This normalization is admittedly painful, but it exists."

In the first three months of 1969, 31 percent more persons from the Federal Republic visited Israel than in the same period a year previously—according to the Israeli Travel Office in Frankfurt. And in March, 1969, West Berlin guests in Israel increased 56 percent over March, 1968. This rising tide of visitors, a German goal, put Israel in first place among Middle Eastern countries visited.

Tourism

The "ugly German" epithet is most often applied to the German tourist (over ten million in 1970) who annually inundates surrounding European countries. They spend over six billion DM's annually, three billion more than foreigners spend in West Germany. About 900,000 GDR citizens traveled to Eastern European countries in 1970.

Germans usually face a double-barreled dose of suspicion, first as tourists and second as Germans who still are expected to account for their ugly past wherever they go. But hard currency has replaced the hard invasion, and the annual soft invasion is often met, from Palermo to Tunis, with *"Deutsch gesprochen"* signs and German menus.[8]

The "Guest Workers"

During the 1960's and also in the 1970's West Germany has found it necessary to employ hundreds of thousands (over 1.3 million in 1968) of foreign workers, mostly from Italy, Greece, Turkey, and North Africa, to perform the menial work that the Germans decline to do in a country that has enjoyed over a decade of full employment. There was such a shortage of manpower that the Federal Republic reached all the way to North Africa to find workers. The *Bundesbahn* (Federal Railway) even went to the trouble of altering whole sections of railroad coaches and embellishing them with prayer rugs, so that Moslem workers could bow to Mecca at the appropriate times.

It is an open secret that Swiss cuckoo clocks are actually manufactured in the Black Forest because Swiss wage scales are even higher than in Germany, while certain German products are manufactured in Spain, Italy, Greece, and Turkey because wages there are much lower. It is not at all unusual for a German to be unable to make himself understood in countless German hotels, restaurants, or service shops because the waiters, maids, and attendants speak only their native Italian, Greek, Turkish, or Arabic.

While officially these workers are treated well—they are called *Gastarbeiter* (guest workers)—their actual working and living conditions often leave much to be desired. Although they can join trade unions, vote on general issues affecting workers in industry, they are all too often regarded as second-class human beings—relegated to sub-standard barracks to live, and socially ostracized by fellow-workers. Workers from Common Market countries are treated better than those from other nations. During the short recession of 1967 Germans became especially restive about the foreigners (who were under contract) holding jobs while their own countrymen were unemployed. One national survey conducted during a full-employment period revealed that over 50 percent of the German people would be willing to work an hour or two longer each week if thereby they could decrease the number of foreign workers.

Because the majority of these Mediterranean workers come from semi-literate, impoverished areas, and never had the opportunity or means to acquire the standards of cleanliness, order, and quiet that are so much a part of the German way of life, many Germans resent them. They are especially annoyed by the tendency of many of these workers, sometimes several thousand, to congregate in and around train terminals on weekends (the closest thing in Germany to a piazza). Germans object to their boisterousness, clannishness, and zest for life. They are irritated by their loud merrymaking, singing, guitar playing, gesticulating—and their sheer numbers. One *Hausfrau* said to me, "I wouldn't mind renting a room to one or two of them, but if you rent to one, you will inevitably have ten or more congregating there night after night."

There is widespread discrimination. Dance halls, restaurants, taverns frequently have signs, reading "No Greeks [Italians, Arabs, Spaniards] Wanted". In Konstanz, which lies directly on the Swiss border, signs reading "No Foreigners Admitted"

457

unleashed furious storms of protest from German-speaking Swiss, in spite of the fact that they were told, "We didn't mean you, but only the guest workers."

A headline, appearing on the front page of the Roman Catholic weekly *Publik* (November 6, 1970), speaks volumes: DEUTSCH-LAND'S NEUE JUDEN (Germany's New Jews).

Negroes in Germany

Blacks and other persons with dark complexions on the whole enjoy immense popularity in Germany. But this is rapidly becoming a dubious blessing, coupled as it is with frequent instances of unpredictable public and private discrimination. The situation of black American GI's has been described in Chapter 24. Sad to say, much of the discrimination in some German bars and restaurants is directly due to the contagious influence of bigoted white American GI's. Located in the vicinity of American bases, many of these establishments are dependent on GI trade. Another delicate situation in the vicinity of several American bases—notably the Kaiserslautern area—is the unhappy coincidence that some of those nightclubs most noted for rowdyism happen to be owned by Jews. Thus it is difficult if not impossible for German authorities to clamp down on these establishments for fear of being charged with anti-Semitism.

Racial discrimination is very common in university cities and towns, where black and Asian students are known to have great difficulty in renting suitable lodgings, at least at a price they can afford. Subsidized student apartment houses and dormitories are, of course, completely integrated, but cannot cope with the need.

In Hamburg I witnessed the following bizarre incident. An enterprising bar owner who had spent many years in the States decided to capitalize on the Germans' fascination for Negroes. So he sent for a Negro barman who had worked for him in the States, put a fancy red uniform on him, and put him to work behind the bar as his "star attraction." The idea is repugnant to anyone who opposes using humans as freaks, even if there wasn't a trace of discrimination but only good-natured fun intended. But it worked. In no time the proprietor had double the number of customers.

One evening I stopped for a beer, and noticed four overweight German businessmen plunk down at a corner table. When the

German waitress walked over to them, one of the men shouted, loud enough for all to hear, "We don't want you to wait on us! Go bring that 'nigger' over there. That's that we came in here for." To the credit of the proprietor, he immediately asked the men to leave and told them in no uncertain terms that he would not tolerate such insults to his coworker.

Black pop singers, actors, personalities, and good looking blacks of both sexes enjoy exuberant, sometimes sickening emotional acceptance from the German people, who at times applaud louder and longer for an inferior black rendition than for an artistically superior performance of a white singer. This partiality toward Negroes is exemplified by the fact that West German TV pays a "normal" top fee of 12,000 DM's (about $3,750) for star performances, and occasionally 25,000 DM's for single appearances by European stars, but didn't hesitate to pay Sammy Davis, Jr., 150,000 DM's (over $45,000) for a single show.

Negro men are much sought after by some German women, with disillusionment often following in the wake of a romance. The number of German women is legion who feel they must compensate for racial injustice with personal intimacy. According to West German government figures, 95 percent of marriages between German women and Asians or Africans break up.

"Don't you be fooled," a German friend told me, "as long as there are only a few Negroes in Germany, they will be received warmly. But if ever there were a couple of hundred thousand one day, you would soon see the same racial tension that you have in England or the States."

Development Aid

Germany's big opportunity to make herself loved among nations is development aid. She was never a great colonial power like Spain, Holland, France, or England. And she has been happily released of her African colonies since World War I.

According to figures released in Bonn in 1969, the Federal Republic is second to the United States among donors of foreign aid to developing countries. Public and private aid granted by the Federal Republic in 1968 totaled $1.6 million, a rise of 44 percent over 1967 and 1.24 percent of the Gross National Product (GNP). Over a thousand German youth were serving through the Development Aid Service (Peace Corps) in twenty countries in Asia, Africa, and Latin America in 1969.

As Germany entered the seventies, a new wave of confidence swept over the land. In view of the American blunders in the Sonmy and Mylai massacres of civilians, the loss of hydrogen bombs in the ocean, the fall of the French franc and the British pound, the loss of confidence in American leadership, the malaise in the Common Market, the invasion of Czechoslovakia in 1968, and, to some extent, the moral ambivalence of the 1967 Israeli blitzkrieg, the Germans feel relieved of a good share of the moral burden for the Third Reich.

But some observers are not so sure· Bonn, they say, has been riding a whole series of lucky waves. If it had rejected signing the nuclear nonproliferation pact, or if the extremist NPD party had entered parliament in 1969, or if they had not softened their stand toward the GDR, and had not relaxed their position on the Sudetenland and the Oder-Neisse territories—then the old bogeyman of the "German menace" might at any time arise. More than two decades after the defeat of Germany at least the western half of the former Reich can boast of being a stabilizing influence in the world. But one blunder, one false move, and the whole business of German rehabilitation will come crashing down and the "German-hating" syndrome will be in motion again.

Germany International

Without a doubt a new spirit has captured the Germans. The word in Germany these days is "Germany International." A leading cigarette firm has enjoyed a smashing success with a single advertising slogan that it has driven into the Germans' consciousness with relentless zeal, *"Mit der Duft der grossen weiten Welt* [With the Aroma of the Great, Wide World] ."

It was the exaggerated growth of nationalism at the close of the nineteenth century which led to the loss of European consciousness and the complete disappearance of the best European traditions. And it was this isolation of the European peoples from one another that created the atmosphere which enabled two world wars to take place.

It has been said that Hitler might never have so recklessly attempted his grandiose plan of conquering Europe, and probably the world, if he had done more homework in geography. It was his incredible ignorance of the outside world that enabled him to proceed with such asinine boldness.

Today the Federal Republic is fully involved in international affairs, from television to tourism, from the Common Market to exchange programs, from development aid to conferences—and more. It has realistically, but also eagerly, accepted the interdependence that has become a condition of modern life. It couldn't escape the internationalist fever even if it wanted to—and it doesn't want to.

The Federal Republic spends millions of Deutsche marks annually—improving its image, acting as hosts to hundreds of journalists, specialists, and scholars from all over the world, through its international center, Inter Nationes, and the foreign press office. In 1969, 118,000 students studied at its universities. Numerous German cities have joined the European game of "city twinning." A town in France, Belgium, or Holland will find its counterpart in Germany. The two mayors will meet and promise in a twinning ceremony called *jumelage* to be joined together in friendship. Outside of Hohenstein-an-der-Wald a sign will read "Twin City to Bonhomie-sur-le-Oeuf, France." The 114 foreign branches of the Goethe Institute have been teaching German to thousands of persons all over the world, as well as spreading knowledge of German culture.

Internationally Committed

The Federal Republic, of course, is not a member of the United Nations, since this ticklish matter is bound up with the question of reunification. It is believed that an application for membership by West Germany would automatically be followed by that of East Germany. As things stand, West Germany's membership would presumably be prevented by a Soviet veto and East Germany's application by vetoes of Western nations.

Some astute observers, however, assessing the situation realistically, forsee the eventual dual recognition of both Germanies as separate nations, both to be accepted as members of the United Nations.

Meanwhile, the Federal Republic is officially represented at the UN by a permanent observer group headed by an ambassa-

461

dor. In Switzerland the German ambassador is simultaneously observer at the European office of the UN in Geneva. In addition, several of the specialized UN agencies have national headquarters in the Federal Republic: the German UNESCO commission and the UNICEF committee, both in Cologne. The International Labor Organization (ILO) maintains a branch office in Bad Godesberg, and the High Commissioner for Refugees has an office in Bonn. The Bonn cabinet ministers maintain their respective contacts with the World Health Organization (WHO) in Geneva, and Food and Agriculture Organization (FAO), Rome, while the German Association for the United Nations is devoted to spreading information about the United Nations.

Like the other Western European countries, West Germany's role toward the creation of a United States of Europe is one of painstaking minutiae rather than dramatic visible victories. It is a member of Euratom, an organization established in 1957 devoted to coordinated action in developing and marketing nuclear resources for peaceful purposes, which also includes France, the Netherlands, Belgium, Luxembourg, and Italy.

The Federal Republic was one of the first states to sign the convention of human rights of the Council of Europe, founded in 1949, almost at the same time as the Federal Republic. In so doing it subjugated itself to the judgement of the European Commission for Human Rights. More than thirty conventions and agreements of the Council of Europe were ratified by the Federal Republic.

For Germans the Council of Europe offered the deputies of the German Bundestag the extremely valuable opportunity, only a few years after World War II, to assume contacts with parliamentarians of their former enemy countries. Through the Consultative Assembly in Strasbourg, the Europeans regained confidence in the Germans and the Germans won self-confidence and acceptance as equal partners on an international level.

Just a few years ago it was impossible to find a good Chinese restaurant in West Germany, except in a few large cities. Xenophobia, or at least fear of foreigners, contributed as much as anything else to the nationalist climate of old Germany. Today all this is changed. You can't walk down any West German street, even in remote villages and towns, without being confronted with the internationalist spirit. People of all complexions and nationalities, often with costumes, are everywhere. Indonesian, Italian,

Chinese, Baltic, Greek, Turkish restaurants can be found—even in small towns. Every second hick town has art exhibitions from all over the world. Guest artists and theatrical groups flow into the country continuously from near and far. If, as has been observed elsewhere in this book, the world is more German than it ever was before, the reverse is even truer: The Germans—at least in West Germany—have never been more international than they are now. The Germans have discovered the human race, and the revelation is mutual.

APPENDIX A

GERMAN HISTORY AT A GLANCE

B.C.

c. 500,000 | Heidelberg Man, believed to have lived between the second and third glacial periods of the Pleistocene Epoch, whose existence is inferred from certain fossil remains discovered in 1907 near Heidelberg. A cast of the jaw believed to be that of the prehistoric "Heidelberg Man" is on display at the Palatinate Museum in Heidelberg.

c. 58,000 | Neanderthal Man of Paleolithic Period. Famous skeleton found in a cave near Düsseldorf in 1856. Bones are on display in the Düsseldorf Prehistoric Museum, the skull in the Rhineland Museum, Bonn.

c. 1000-100 | Primitive tribes, which came to be known collectively as "Germani" lived along the Rhine and Danube rivers, later discovered by Romans. The words "Deutsch" and "Deutschland" are believed to have originated from an ancient High German word "diot" meaning "the people."

A.D.

9 | German victory at Teutoburg Forest suspends Roman efforts to colonize beyond the Rhine.

c. 370 | The mass migration of German tribes into the Roman Empire begins, called euphemistically *Völkerwanderung* (Migration of People) by Germans, barbarian invasion by others.

About the fourth century the Goths, cousins of the Germans, pour out of the plains of present-day Poland, move south and then west through Hungary and Italy and eventually to France and Spain. The Vandals, moving out of territory later to become Prussia, descend on Northern Italy, and the Burgundians into the territory that still bears their name. The Alemanni in Southern Germany cross the Rhine and establish themselves in Eastern France. The French word for Germany, *"Allemagne,"* derives from this tribe. From the Elbe estuary and the western shores of Denmark, the Angles, Saxons, and Jutes migrate to the British Isles.

378	Goths vanquish the Romans at Battle of Adrianople.
c. 450	Huns from Mongolia penetrate as far as France until checked at the Battle of Troyes.
	Slav tribes follow the German migration and settle lower Holstein, the middle Elbe, Thuringia, and Bohemia. Ironically, the western frontier of these Slav settlements is strikingly close to the line of demarcation today known as the Iron Curtain.
481-511	Clovis the Merovingian defeats and then unites various tribes, establishes the Frankish empire on what is today French and German territory.
c. 600	Most of the easterly thrust of the German and Slav peoples comes to an end. The Angles, Saxons, and Jutes settle in England; the Franks, Burgundians, and Alemanni occupy Gaul; the Lombards and Venetians stay in Italy, and the Goths live in Spain. East of the Rhine, between the Slavs and the old Roman frontiers, live the Saxons, Swabians, Frisians, and Bavarians. The Germanic tribes in what is now West and South Germany develop linguistic similarities. The "German people" begin to emerge.
	Christianization of the Germans east of the Rhine is initiated by Irish monks. The "German" people begin to assume a definite character.
732	Charles the Hammer (Charles Martel), a Merovingian Mayor of the Palace, defeats the Moors near Poitiers and preserves the Christian faith within Europe. During his reign, an English Benedictine monk, Boniface, establishes a monastery at Fulda, and from this center Christian teaching radiates out among the Germans. Slain while preaching to the Frisians in 755, Boniface was canonized and is known as the "Apostle to the Germans." His work paved the way for Charlemagne.
768-814	Reign of Charlemagne (Charles the Great), who consolidates and enlarges the Frankish kingdom, which now reaches from the Po River in Northern Italy to include most of Western Europe belonging to the Roman Empire except Britain.
	During a visit to Rome, Charlemagne is crowned emperor by Pope Leo III. Thus the "Holy Roman Empire of the German Nation" is born. The title implied that Charlemagne was the Christian successor to the Roman emperors.

843

Treaty of Verdun, signed by Charlemagne's three grandsons, which divides the great empire into three sections. The territory of the West Franks goes to Charles the Bald, and the territory of the East Franks is allotted to Louis the German, these regions being the nuclei of future France and Germany. The eldest grandson, Lothar, retained the imperial title and a narrow strip of country running from Belgium, through Lotharingia, Burgundy, and into Italy. This middle kingdom, today's Alsace-Lorraine, was to become a major bone of contention between France and Germany for generations and the scene of untold misery and bloodshed.

Unlike France, England, and Sweden, where life gradually coalesced around a central kingly house, a unified monarachy did not take hold in Medieval Germany. One reason was the lack of a fixed geographical boundary; indeed, for a long time the emperors had no fixed capital, but wandered from palace to palace. A second reason is attributed to the vastness of the areas covered by German tribes. A further reason was the continuous power struggle among the regional rulers.

Throughout the Middle Ages divisive forces were at work that profoundly influenced the course of German history and the structure of German society even to our day. The insecurity of the emperors in contraposition to the numerous tribal leaders who gradually emerged as leaders of states, induced the former to establish free cities, whose rulers were responsible to them alone. They threw up walls around the cities to protect them from feuding tribes and a great tradition of trade and craftsmanship developed. These conditions also fostered the rapid rise and dominance of monasticism.

A second significant development was the custom of dividing lands by inheritance, as if they were private property. As a result dependence on the emperor became less and less and jurisdiction passed to lesser princes and counts. The number of independent secular states steadily increased.

The concept of a nation as we know it today had little meaning for medieval man whose loyalty was attached to his tribe or his city and the Christian Church. Because that church was a political as well as a spiritual institution, it seemed only natural to him that there should be two leaders, the pope of the spiritual realm and the emperor of the secular world. But the areas of jurisdiction overlapped. Inevitably many bishops and abbots were endowed with secular powers, many of them became independent rulers and enormously wealthy prince bishops. Throughout the Middle Ages there was constant friction between people and bishops, between emperors and popes.

The unrealistic and, in retrospect, farfetched claim of the Holy Roman Empire not only proved itself to be the greatest obstacle to a centralized monarchy that would have given Medieval Germany stability and order, but it is the fundamental underlying factor shaping the whole course of German history and culture. More than a millennium ago the grand imperial illusion prepared the soil for the Reformation and the Second (Kaiser Wilhelm) and Third (Hitler) reichs.

900-1300	Great age of monasticism reaches its peak, radiating German culture, improving agriculture, imparting rudimentary knowledge of medicine, and inculcating the conception of a settled life. Flowering of Romanesque period of architecture. German expansionist movement. Crusading knights and traders push eastward along the Baltic as far as Reval (Tallinn). This was not a centrally organized invasion but sporadic infiltration of small independent groups. Many of these migrants were sought after and revered for their skills and scholarship.
919-1024	The Saxon Imperial House completes the union of the German tribes.
936-973	Reign of Otto I. Crowned emperor by Pope John XII, he establishes the imperial claim for future German kings.
1056-1105	Reign of Henry IV. Beginning of long power struggle between emperors and papacy.
1095	First Crusade proclaimed by Pope Urban II. Christians of Europe undertake military expeditions from 11th to 13th centuries for the recovery of the Holy Land from the Moslems. They brought in their wake as the price of dubious victory tremendous human misery, widened the gap with Eastern Christianity, and unleashed the world's first large-scale pogroms in Germany.
1122	Concordat of Worms: emperor-pope dispute temporarily settled by providing the pope with spiritual jurisdiction over church officials, and the emperor with the right to invest them with temporal powers.

1152-1190	Reign of Frederick Barbarossa of the Hohenstaufen dynasty—next to Charlemagne, the greatest figure of early and medieval German history. He conquers and Christianizes the Slavs of Eastern Germany, leads a crusading army through Asia Minor to the Holy Land.
	Age of chivalry.
c. 1200	Early Gothic period begins during which great cathedrals, such as Rheims and Cologne, are constructed.
1200-1400	Lands beyond the Elbe conquered for Germany.
1227	Emperor Frederick II colonizes "heathen" Prussians.
1254-1273	The Great Interregnum: infighting over imperial succession. Feuding princes terrorize the country.
1273	Election of Rudolf I, first emperor of Hapsburg dynasty which in 1438 saw Albert of Hapsburg elected Holy Roman Emperor. From his election to the abolition of the Holy Roman Empire by Napoleon in 1806, every emperor comes from House of Hapsburg. In 1500 Hapsburgs are dominant world power.
1348	First German university founded in Prague, followed by that of Heidelberg in 1386.
c. 1350	Origin of Hanseatic League, principally of North German towns for the promotion and protection of trading privileges.
1356	Golden Bull, proclaimed by Emperor Charles IV, regulates imperial succession.
1417	Friedrick of Nuremberg of the Hohenzollern family is appointed Elector of Brandenburg. (The Hohenzollerns later rule Prussia and Germany.)
	Thus at the close of the Middle Ages, two great houses, Hohenzollern in Berlin and Hapsburgs in Vienna, become opposite German centers of gravity. From these two cities the future destiny of Germany was shaped.
1450	Johann Gutenberg invents the art of printing.
1517	Martin Luther fastens his ninety-five theses attacking rampant ecclesiastical abuses to the door of the Wittenberg church. The Protestant Reformation begins.

1519-1558	Reign of Charles V.
1521	Charles V presides over Diet of Worms, which orders Luther's arrest. While in hiding, Martin Luther translates New Testament into German, invents new written form of High German.
1545-1563	Council of Trent codifies Catholic doctrine, reforms Church abuses, launches Counter Reformation.
1547	Catholic Charles V defeats free cities and Protestant princes in Schmalkaldic War.
1555	Peace of Augsburg introduces tenet of *cuius regio, eius religio,* whereby the people have to adopt the religion of their respective rulers or emigrate. Temporary cessation of religious wars.
1618-1648	Thirty Years' War: ostensibly a war between Catholics and Protestants. Involving every German state, it soon became a power struggle with political and dynastic overtones. At war's end nearly every German city and town had been sacked several times, agriculture was destroyed, and the population dropped from 20 million to 13.5 million.
1648	Peace of Westphalia, the last European treaty to be drafted in Latin, is signed at Osnabrück. Holy Roman Empire dissolved. Switzerland and the Netherlands receive independence, France is granted Alsace-Lorraine. By this time there were some three hundred and fifty different states in Germany. Period of princely absolutism begins.
1646-1716	Age of Pietism and Enlightenment, German baroque, Bach and Handel compose masterpieces of music.
1701	Frederick I of Prussia proclaims his duchy a kingdom.
1713-1740	Frederick William I of Prussia reigns, establishes a powerful army.
1724-1804	Immanuel Kant, great German philosopher.
1740-1786	Under reign of Frederick II (Frederick the Great), Prussia becomes a great power.
1740-1748	War of the Austrian Succession between Prussia and Austria brings new territories to victorious Prussia.
1749-1832	Johann Wolfgang von Goethe.

469

c. 1750	Rococo period. Beginning of golden age of German poetry (Herder, Lessing, Klopstock, Schiller).
1756-1763	Seven Years' War. Prussia again wins, remaining dominant over Austria, and gains more territories.
1770-1827	Ludwig van Beethoven.
1795	Franco-Prussian War. Prussia defeated.
1803-1815	Napoleonic Wars.
	Revolutionary armies at first arouse little hostility, are regarded as liberators. Germans welcome Napoleon's annexations. Beethoven dedicates, then later retracts, his third symphony, *Eroica*, to Napoleon. Napoleon annexes the Rhine, his Act of Mediation of 1803 abolishes 112 states and free cities, which are absorbed by larger kingdoms, and secularizes the monasteries, giving their lands as rewards to friends for loyalty.
1805-1807	Napoleon compels the emperor (Francis I of Austria) to renounce this title and position, bringing the Holy Roman Empire of the German Nation to an end.
1807	Prussia again defeated by Napoleon.
1813-1815	Prussia rallies the German states to rise and drive French from German soil. War of Liberation. Battle of Leipzig. Spirit of national unity sweeps through the German states.
1815	Napoleon's defeat at Waterloo. Congress of Vienna restores Prussian territories, reduces the number of independent states to thirty-nine by increasing new territories of Prussia and Austria. A loose Confederation of German States, including Prussia, is formed, with Austria presiding.
1830-1848	Local and regional patriotism begins to give way to a new spirit of national patriotism previously unknown. At a time of expanding industry and travel, thirty-nine German states, with their own currencies, tax laws, weights and measures regulations, and customs, were severe handicaps. The first railroad from Berlin to Hamburg needed the approval of five separate governments. It was Napoleon who more than any other influence spread pan-German thought.
1841	Heinrich Hoffmann von Fallersleben writes the text to the *"Deutschland Über Alles"* ("Song of the Germans") hymn

470

which at the time was not intended as an expression of German superiority over other nations but as the rallying cry of liberals urging national over Bavarian, Saxon, or Rhenish patriotism.

1848	Revolutions in various German states bring limited reforms. A self-appointed group of liberals meet in the Pauls Kirche in Frankfurt/Main to draft a constitution for a new German nation to include all German states except Austria. They offer the Imperial Crown for a greater Germany to the King of Prussia who, suspicious of liberalism, declines. One of the revolutionaries, Carl Schurz, emigrates to the United States to become a Civil War general and later, secretary of the interior. (Today the Pauls Church is used for solemn cultural or patriotic occasions.)
1862	Otto von Bismarck begins long career as a powerful leader in Prussia (later Germany).
1864	Prussia and Austria defeat Denmark.
1866	Prussia and Austria turn on each other, ending with Austria's defeat. Austria leaves the German Confederation.
1866-67	South German states join Prussia and North German states to form the North-German Confederation.
1870-71	South German states join Prussia in Franco-Prussian War.
1871	Prussia wins, acquires Alsace-Lorraine. German states unite to form an all-German nation. Wilhelm I of Prussia reluctantly accepts the title of Kaiser, is proclaimed German Emperor at Versailles. The second German Reich begins. Bismarck becomes first chancellor.
	Industrial age begins. Great scientific discoveries, including, among others, Robert Koch (cure of tuberculosis) and Wilhelm Conrad Roentgen (X rays).
1872-86	*Kulturkampf.* Conflict between imperial government and Roman Catholic Church chiefly over control of ecclesiastical and educational appointments.
1881	Bismarck begins his social policy.
1888-1918	Reign of Kaiser Wilhelm II, also affectionately called "Wilhelmine Age," German counterpart of Victorian age.

471

1914-1918	World War I.
1918	Kaiser abdicates. End of the second German Reich. Treaty of Versailles. Poland recreated, Germany forced to give up territories which Prussia had annexed in the eighteenth century. Part of Schleswig returned to Denmark. Alsace-Lorraine returned to France. These losses were later used by Hitler in his notorious "stab-in-the-back" speeches to whip up a spirit of revenge.
1919-1933	The Weimar Republic (named after the city where Goethe and Schiller once resided): noble but ill-fated German effort at parliamentary democracy.
1923	Adolf Hitler's beer-hall *Putsch* in Munich, arrest in Landsberg prison, where he uses time to write *Mein Kampf.*
1929-1934	Germany suffers mass unemployment and major depression during world wide financial crisis.
1933	Third Reich begins with Hitler's assumption of power as chancellor. National Socialist German Workers' Party (Nazis) begin rule of violence, terror: genocide, euthanasia, blitzkrieg, Gestapo, SS, and concentration camps characterize the regime.
1936	Rhineland remilitarized. Rome-Berlin Axis formed.
1938	Hitler annexes Austria, which jubilantly receives him. Munich Pact provides legal framework for Nazi occupation of Czechoslovakia.
1939	Nazi Germany invades Poland and starts World War II.
1945	Hitler commits suicide in his bunker in Berlin. End of World War II and the Third Reich. Allies assume "supreme authority." Germany is divided into four occupation zones and so is Berlin.
1948-1949	Berlin Blockade.
1949	Federal Republic of West Germany and German Democratic Republic (GDR) of East Germany created. Konrad Adenauer becomes first chancellor of West Germany.
1953	Unsuccessful uprising throughout East Germany on June 17 becomes symbol of German quest for unity in the Federal Republic, which annually observes this day as a national holiday.

1955	German Federal Government given sovereign power over the Federal area. West Germany admitted to NATO.
1957	West Germany joins European Common Market.
1961	Berlin Wall goes up.
1963	Ludwig Erhard, "Father of Economic Miracle" and former economics minister, succeeds Adenauer as chancellor.
1966	Kurt Georg Kiesinger becomes chancellor.
1969	Willy Brandt becomes chancellor, the Social Democrats assume power, in coalition with the Free Democrats, for the first time in the Federal Republic's twenty-year existence.
1970	March 19, Chancellor Willy Brandt meets with East German Premier Willi Stoph in Erfurt, GDR.
	August 12, Chancellor Brandt and Soviet Premier Alexei N. Kosygin sign non-aggression treaty in Moscow.
	December 7, Chancellor Brandt and Polish Premier Jozef Cyrankiewicz sign normalization pact in Warsaw. Oder-Neisse line acknowledged as Poland's western frontier.
1971	Walter Ulbricht resigns as first secretary of East Germany's communist party, SED, and is succeeded by Erich Honecker.

APPENDIX B

SOME DISTINGUISHED GERMANS

c. 1170-c. 1215	Hartmann von Aue, writer of epics and religious legends (*Gregorius, Der arme Heinrich*).
c. 1170-c. 1220	Wolfram von Eschenbach, writer of epics (*Parzival*).
1193-1280	St. Albert the Great (Albertus Magnus), teacher of St. Thomas Aquinas, scholastic philosophy.
c. 1400-1468	Johann Gensfleisch Gutenberg invented printing.
-1451	Stephan Lochner, painter of religious subjects: the *Dombild* in Cologne Cathedral, *Virgin with Violets*.
c. 1446-1488	Martin Schongauer, painter, engraver of religious and historical subjects.
c. 1465-1524	Hans Holbein the Elder, painter, draftsman, of historical and religious subjects.
c. 1470-1528	Mathias Grünewald, painter of religious subjects.
1471-1528	Albrecht Dürer, painter, draftsman, engraver of portraits, religious paintings, landscapes, drawings (*Adoration of the Magi*).
1472-1553	Lucas Cranach the Elder, painter, engraver (*Crucifixion*).
c. 1480-1545	Hans Baldung Grien, painter of religious and mythological subjects (*Coronation of the Virgin, Death*).
1483-1546	Martin Luther, Protestant reformer, German translation of the Bible; pamphlets; religious hymns.
1490-1553	Wolf Huber, painter of religious subjects (*Flight into Egypt*).
1493-1543	Hans Holbein the Younger, painter, portraitist, engraver of German Renaissance period. Religious subjects (*Dead Christ*).
1571-1630	Johannes Kepler, astronomer, mathematician. Propounded laws of plantary motion.

1585-1672	Heinrich Schütz, composer of church music. First German opera: *Dafne*.
1602-1686	Otto von Guericke, physicist, invented air pump, air balance.
1646-1716	Gottfried Wilhelm von Leibniz, philosopher, author, mathematician. Developed differential and integral calculus.
1681-1767	Georg Philipp Telemann, composer of church music, operas, overtures, sonatas, chamber music.
1685-1750	Johann Sebastian Bach, composer of church music (chorales, preludes, fugues, passion oratorios), organ compositions *(Passion According to St. John, Passion According to St. Matthew)*.
1685-1759	George Frederick Handel (emigrated to Britain), composer of oratorios, operas, cantatas, harpsichord and organ compositions *(Messiah)*.
1691-1766	Johann Michael Fischer, architect, sculptor, leading designer of late baroque and early rococo Bavarian churches.
1714-1787	C. W. von Gluck, composer of operas, reformer of operatic style *(Orpheus and Eurydice)*.
1724-1803	Friedrich Gottlieb Klopstock, epic poet *(Der Messias)*.
1724-1804	Immanuel Kant, philosopher *(Critique of Pure Reason, Critique of Practical Reason)*.
1729-1781	Gotthold Ephraim Lessing, critic and dramatist *(Nathan the Wise)*.
1729-1786	Moses Mendelssohn (grandfather of Felix Mendelssohn), philosopher.
1730-1794	Friedrich Wilhelm von Steuben, Prussian major general who served in American revolutionary army.
1744-1803	Johann Gottfried Herder, essayist, folk-song collector.
1749-1832	Johann Wolfgang von Goethe, writer, poet, essayist, playwright *(Faust)*.
1759-1805	Johann Friedrich von Schiller, poet, dramatist *(Mary Stuart, William Tell, The Maid of Orleans)*.

1767-1845	August Wilhelm von Schlegel, theorist of romanticism. Translated Shakespeare, Dante, Cervantes.
1768-1834	Friedrich Schleiermacher, philosopher *(The Christian Faith).*
1769-1859	Alexander von Humboldt, scientist, explorer, naturalist, statesman.
1770-1827	Ludwig van Beethoven, composer.
1770-1831	Georg Wilhelm Friedrich Hegel, philosopher *(Phenomenology of Mind, Philosophy of Right).*
1770-1843	Friedrich Hölderlin, novelist, poet *(Hyperion).*
1772-1829	Friedrich von Schlegel, theorist of romanticism, philosopher.
1772-1801	Novalis (pen name of Friedrich von Hardenberg), poet *(Hymnen an die Nacht).*
1775-1854	F. W. von Schelling, philosopher *(Ideen zu einer Philosophie der Natur).*
1776-1822	E. T. A. Hoffmann, author, composer, illustrator *(Weird Tales, The Nutcracker and the Mouse-King).*
1777-1811	Heinrich von Kleist, playwright, novelist *(Der Prinz von Homburg).*
1777-1855	Karl Friedrich Gauss, mathematician, astronomer. Wrote on theory of numbers, binomial equations.
1778-1842	Clemens Brentano, collector of folk songs.
1785-1863	Jakob Ludwig Grimm, philologist, mythologist, folklore collector *(Fairy Tales,* together with his brother, Wilhelm Karl Grimm).
1786-1826	Carl ·Maria von Weber, composer of masses, operas, concert works *(Der Freischütz).*
1788-1857	Josef von Eichendorff, writer of tales and romantic poems *(Happy Wanderer and Other Poems).*
1795-1886	Leopold von Ranke, historian.
1797-1856	Heinrich Heine, poet, satirist, travel writer, political commentator *(Last Poems, Wintermärchen).*

476

1800-1882	Friedrich Wohler, chemist, discovered aluminum, conducted experiments leading to first synthesis of an organic compound.
1803-1873	Justus von Liebig, chemist, improved organic analysis, made important contributions to agricultural chemistry.
1809-1847	Felix Mendelssohn-Bartholdy, composer of symphonies, oratorios, songs, piano pieces, overtures *(A Midsummer Night's Dream)*.
1810-1856	Robert Schumann, composer of symphonies, overtures, hymns, chamber music. Chief exponent of romantic period.
1811-1899	Robert Bunsen, chemist, discovered method of spectrum analysis (with Kirchhoff), rubidium, cesium, Bunsen burner.
1813-1837	Georg Büchner, dramatist *(Dante's Death, Wozzeck)*.
1813-1863	Christian Friedrich Hebbel, dramatist, poet, *(Maria Magdalena)*.
1813-1883	Richard Wagner, composer of operas, romanticist symphonic poems, choral works, chamber music *(Die Meistersinger, Tristan und Isolde, Parsifal)*.
1817-1903	Theodor Mommsen, historian.
1818-1883	Karl Marx (emigrated to England), socialist and political theorist, originator of Communist doctrines *(Das Kapital, Communist Manifesto* with Friedrich Engels).
1819-1898	Theodor Fontane, novelist.
1821-1894	H. L. von Helmholtz, physiologist, physicist. Noted for discoveries in optics and acoustics.
1821-1902	Rudolf Virchow, pathologist, founder of cellular pathology.
1822-1888	R. J. E. Clausius, physicist, pioneer in the field of thermodynamics.
1824-1887	Gustav Robert Kirchhoff, physicist, discovered (with Bunsen) method of spectrum analysis, founded astrophysics.
1829-1866	G. F. B. Riemann, mathematician, developed non-Euclidian geometry.

1829-1906	Carl Schurz, statesman, fighter in German 1848 Revolution, Northern general in U.S. Civil War, later American secretary of interior.
1833-1897	Johannes Brahms, romanticist composer. Symphonies, hymns.
1843-1910	Robert Koch, bacteriologist, discovered bacterial cause of tuberculosis and other infectious diseases. Nobel Prize, 1905.
1844-1900	Friedrich Wilhelm Nietzsche, philosopher.
1844-1929	Karl Benz, automobile inventor.
1845-1920	Wilhelm Pfeffer, plant physiologist, synthesized plant physiology.
1845-1923	Wilhelm Konrad Roentgen, physicist, discovered X rays. Nobel Prize, 1901.
1848-1896	Otto Lilienthal, aerial pioneer.
1850-1918	Karl Ferdinand Braun, physicist. Nobel Prize, 1909.
1852-1919	Emil Fischer, chemist, pioneered in organic chemistry, discovered structures of proteins, purines, sugars.
1853-1932	Wilhelm Ostwald, physical chemist, philosopher. Investigated reaction rates, principles governing equilibrium.
1854-1915	Paul Ehrlich, biochemist, discovered salvarsan arsenicals. Developed lateral chain theory of immunization. Nobel Prize for Medicine, 1908.
1854-1921	Engelbert Humperdinck, composer *(Hansel and Gretel)*.
1857-1894	Heinrich Rudolf Hertz, physicist, discovered telegraphic waves, studied relationship between light and electricity.
1858-1947	Max Planck, physicist, formulated quantum theory. Nobel Prize, 1918.
1862-1946	Gerhart Hauptmann, novelist, playwright *(Rose Bernd)*. Nobel Prize, 1912.
1864-1920	Max Weber, sociologist *(Protestant Ethic and the Spirit of Capitalism)*.
1864-1841	Walther Hermann Nernst, physicist, a founder of modern physical chemistry, pioneered in thermodynamics. Nobel Prize for Chemistry, 1920.

478

1864-1949	Richard Strauss, composer of symphonic poems, operas. Noted for complex modern style *(Death and Transfiguration, Der Rosenkavalier)*.
1867-1922	Walther Rathenau, industrialist, writer, and statesman.
1867-1945	Käthe Kollwitz, painter, lithographer, etcher. Her works are noted for their passionate social protest against war, poverty, exploitation.
1867-1956	Emil Nolde, artist, supernatural and religious subjects, noted for aquarelles and seascapes. A founder of Expressionism *(The Last Supper)*.
1868-1933	Stefan George, poet.
1870-1938	Ernst Barlach, sculptor, dramatist *(Man Drawing a Sword)*.
1873-1943	Max Reinhardt, theatrical director, producer, actor.
1875-1955	Thomas Mann, novelist *(The Magic Mountain, Buddenbrooks)*, lived in the United States after 1937. Nobel Prize, 1929.
1876-1967	Konrad Adenauer, statesman, chancellor of Federal Republic, 1949-1963.
1877-1947	Georg Kolbe, sculptor, public monuments in Berlin, Hamburg, Leipzig.
1877-1962	Hermann Hesse, novelist, poet. Nobel Prize, 1946.
1879-1955	Albert Einstein, theoretical physicist, formulated theory of relativity. U.S. citizen from 1940. Nobel Prize for physics, 1921.
1879-	Otto Hahn, physical chemist, split uranium atom (1939), showed possibility of chain reactions. Nobel Prize, 1944.
1879-1960	Max von Laue, physicist, discoverer of X-ray diffraction. Nobel Prize, 1914.
1880-1916	Franz Marc, artist, a leader of *Blaue Reiter* abstractionists, expressionist painter of animals and landscapes.
1880-1938	Ernst Ludwig Kirchner, artist, leader of expressionism *(Street)*.
1881-1919	Wilhelm Lehmbruck, expressionist sculptor *(Standing Youth)*.

479

1881-1965	Hermann Staudinger, chemist. His macro-molecule research helped pioneer plastics, synthetics.
1882-1970	Max Born, physicist, traced movements of nuclear particles, led to revision of classical physics. Nobel Prize, 1954.
1883-1969	Karl Jaspers, philosopher.
1883-1969	Walter Gropius, architect, pioneer of functional school, founder of *Bauhaus*. In the U.S. from 1937.
1883-1970	Erich Heckel, expressionist artist, co-founder of *Die Brücke* in Dresden, together with Emil Nolde and Max Pechstein.
1884-1950	Max Beckmann, expressionist artist *(The Dream)*.
1884-	Karl Schmidt-Rottluff, expressionist painter, sculptor, engraver. Noted for mosaics, tapestries, etchings.
1886-1965	Paul Tillich, philosopher, theologian in the United States for many years.
1885-1969	Romano Guardini, theologian, philosopher.
1886-1969	Ludwig Miës van der Rohe, architect, *Bauhaus* founder, in the U.S. from the thirties.
1887-1914	August Macke, expressionist artist.
1887-1953	Erich Mendelsohn, expressionist architect.
1889-	Martin Heidegger, philosopher.
1889-	Gerhard Marcks, sculptor, *Bauhaus* collaborator.
1890-1935	Kurt Tucholsky, humorist, satirist.
1891-	Max Ernst, artist, writer, proponent of surrealism and early dadaism.
1891-	Fritz Lang, movie director.
1893-1959	George Grosz, artist, in the U.S. from 1932 *(Germany, A Winter's Tale)*.
1895-1963	Paul Hindemith, composer of operas, concertos, chamber music, sonatas in modern style *(Mathis der Maler)*. Resided in U.S. from 1939.

1895-	Carl Orff, composer of operas, oratorios, theatrical music.
1898-1956	Bertolt Brecht, dramatist, poet *(Threepenny Opera, Mother Courage, Good Woman of Setzuan)*.
1898-1970	Erich Maria Remarque, novelist, many years in the U.S. *(All Quiet on the Western Front)*.
1900-1950	Kurt Weill, composer of operas, songs, musicals, choral and orchestral works *(The Threepenny Opera, Lady in the Dark)*. In the U.S. from 1935.
1901-	Werner Egk, composer of ballets, operas, orchestral pieces.
1901-	Werner Heisenberg, physicist, discovered allotropic forms of hydrogen, developed theory of quantum mechanics.
1904-1969	Theodor W. Adorno, philosopher, spiritual father of New Left.
1904-	Marlene Dietrich, singer and actress, in the U.S. for many years.
1904-	Karl Rahner, S.J., theologian.
1906-1945	Dietrich Bonhoeffer, theologian.
1912-	Wernher von Braun, rocket engineer, in the U.S. since 1945, played prominent role in the development of Saturn V, which thrust American astronauts to successful moon landing, July 21, 1969.
1927-	Günter Grass, novelist *(The Tin Drum)*.

A SELECTED BIBLIOGRAPHY

BOOKS

Adolph, Walter, *Verfälschte Geschichte-Antwort auf Rolf Hochhuth.* Zürich, Christiana-Verlag, 1963.

Adorno, Theodor W., *Was Bedeutet Aufarbeitung? In Gesellschaft, Staat, Erziehung.* Wiesbaden, 1960.

Allemann, Fritz René, *Bonn Ist Nicht Weimar.* Cologne, 1956.

Amery, Carl, *Die Kapitulation, Oder Deutscher Katholizismus Heute.* Hamburg, Rowohlt, 1963.

Andrae, Friedrich (with Sybil Gräfin Schönfeldt), *Deutsche Demokratie von Bebel bis Heuss.* Frankfurt/Main, Fischer Bücherei, 1968.

Arntz, Helmut, *Facts About Germany.* Bonn, Press and Information Office of the Federal Republic of Germany, 1964, revised, 1970.

Augstein, Rudolf, *Preussens Friedrich und die Deutschen.* Frankfurt/Main, S. Fischer-Verlag, 1969.

Barraclough, Geoffrey, *The Origins of Modern Germany.* London, Blackwell, 1947.

Baumgarten, Franziska, *Demokratie und Charactèr.* Zürich, 1944.

Bergsträsser, Ludwig, *Geschichte der Politischen Parteien in Deutschland.* Munich, 1960.

Breitenstein, Rolf, *Der Hässliche Deutsche?* Munich: Kurt Desche Verlag, 1968.

Bullock, Alan, *Hitler, a Study in Tyranny.* New York, Harper & Brothers, 1953, revised, 1969.

Chouraqui, Dr. A., *Die Geschichte des Judentums.* Hamburg, Verlag Johannes Marie Hoeppner, 1955.

Clay, Lucius D., *Decision in Germany.* New York, 1950.

Conant, James B., *Germany and Freedom.* Cambridge, Mass., 1958.

Dahms, Hellmuth Günther, *Kleine Geschichte Europas im 20. Jahrhundert.* Freiburg-im-Breisgau, Herder Bücherei, 1958.

Dönhoff, Marion Gräfin, *Die Bundesrepublik in der Ära Adenauer.* Hamburg, Rowohlt, 1963.

Dunlop, Sir John K., *A Short History of Germany.* London, Oswald Wolff, 1965.

Eich, Hermann, *Die Unheimlichen Deutschen.* Düsseldorf-Vienna, 1963.

Elon, Amos, *In Einem Heimgesuchten Land.* Munich, 1966.

Elyashiv, Vera, *Deutschland—Kein Wundermärchen.* Vienna-Düsseldorf, 1964.

Erfurt, Werner, *Moscow's Policy in Germany.* Esslingen, Bechtle Verlag, 1968.

Eyck, Erich, *Geschichte der Weimarer Republik,* 2 vols. Zürich and Stuttgart, E. Rentsch Verlag, 1954-56.

BIBLIOGRAPHY

Fehrle, Eugen, *Feste und Volksbräuche*. Kassel, Hinnenthal-Verlag, 1955.
Flenley, Ralph, *Modern German History*. New York, Dent, 1964.
Fodor, Eugene, ed., *Germany*. New York, MacGibbon & Kee, 1965.
Furtwängler, Franz Josef, *Die Gewerkschaften*. Hamburg, Rowohlt, 1956.
Gablentz, O. M. von der, *Documents on the Status of Berlin*. Munich, R. Oldenbourg-Verlag, 1959.
Gamm, Hans-Jochen, *Aggression und Friedens-fähigkeit in Deutschland*. Munich, Paul List-Verlag, 1968.
Greinacher, N. (with H. T. Risse), *Bilanz des Deutschen Katholizismus*. Mainz, Matthias-Grünewald-Verlag, 1966.
Gross, Johannes, *Die Deutschen*. Frankfurt/Main, Heinrich Scheffler Verlag, 1967.
Heigert, Hans, *Deutschlands falsche Träume*. Hamburg, Christian Wegner-Verlag, 1967.
Hellpach, Willy, *Der Deutsche Character*. Bonn, 1954.
_____ *Deutsche Physiognomik*. Berlin, 1949.
Hiscocks, Richard, *Democracy in Western Germany*. London: Oxford University Press, 1957.
Hitler, Adolf, *Mein Kampf*. New York: Reynal & Hitchcock, 1939.
Hochhuth, Rolf, *Der Stellvertreter*. Hamburg, Rowohlt, 1963.
Hofer, Walther, *Der Nationalsozialismus, Dokumente, 1933-45*. Frankfurt/Main, Fischer Bücherei, 1957.
Horne, Alistair, *Return to Power*. New York, Frederick A. Praeger, 1956.
Hornstein, Erika von, *Die Deutsche Not, Flüchtlinge Berichten*. Cologne, Rowohlt, 1960.
Jacobsen, Walter, *Der Neue Beamtentyp*. Detmold, Im Deutsches Verwaltungsblatt, 1951.
Jaeggi, Urs, *Macht und Herrschaft in der Bundesrepublik*. Frankfurt/Main, Fischer Bücherei, 1969.
Keynes, John M., *The Economic Consequences of the Peace*. New York, Harcourt, Brace and Howe, 1920.
Kogon, Egon, *The Theory and Practice of Hell*. New York, translated from the German by Heinz Norden, Farrar, Strauss, 1950.
Leber, Annedore, *Das Gewissen Steht Auf*. Berlin, Mosaik Verlag, 1959; English translation by Rosemary O'Neill, *Conscience in Revolt*, London, Vallentine, Mitchell & Co., 1957.
Leiser, Erwin, *Mein Kampf* (Documentation of Film). Frankfurt/Main, Fischer Bücherei, 1961.
Leonhardt, Rudolf Walter, *X-mal Deutschland*. Munich, 1961.
Lewy, Günter, *The Catholic Church and Nazi Germany*. New York, McGraw-Hill Paperback, 1964.
Liptzin, Solomon, *Germany's Stepchildren*. Cleveland, Meridian Books, 1961.
Matthias, Erich (with Morsey), *Das Ende der Parteien*. Düsseldorf, 1960.
Mehnert, Klaus, *Der Deutsche Standort*. Stuttgart, 1967.
Meinicke, Friedrich, *The German Catastrophe*. Cambridge, translated by Sidney B. Fay, Harvard University Press, 1950.
Mitscherlich, Alexander and Margarete, *Die Unfähigkeit zu Trauern*. Munich, Piper Verlag, 1967.
Mohler, Armin, *Was die Deutschen Fürchten*. Berlin, 1963.

Morsey, Rudolf (with Matthias), *Das Ende der Parteien, 1933.* Düsseldorf, 1960.

Muhlen, Norbert, *The Survivors, A Report on the Jews in Germany Today.* New York, Thomas Y. Crowell, 1962.

—— *The Incredible Krupps.* New York, Henry Holt & Co., 1959.

Neven-du-Mont, Jürgen, *Zum Beispiel 42 Deutsche.* Munich, Nymphenburger Verlagshandlung, 1968.

Odin, Karl-Alfred, *Die Denkschriften der EKD.* Neukirchen, Neukirchener Verlag, 1966.

Picard, Max, *Hitler in Uns Selbst.* Zürich, 1946.

Pinson, K. S., *Modern Germany: Its History and Civilization.* New York, Macmillan, 1954.

Plessner, Otto, *Die Verspätete Nation.* Stuttgart, 1959.

Pollock, James K., ed., *German Democracy at Work.* Ann Arbor: University of Michigan Press, 1955.

Prittie, Terence, *Germany.* New York, Time Inc., 1961.

Raab, Heribert, *Kirche und Staat.* Munich, Deutscher Taschenbuch Verlag, 1966.

Raddatz, Fritz J., *Summa Injuria oder Durfte der Papst Schweigen?* Hamburg, Rowohlt, 1963.

Reinhardt, Kurt F., *Germany: 2000 Years.* New York, Constable, 1961.

Risse, H. T. (with N. Greinacher), *Bilanz des Deutschen Katholizismus.* Matthias-Grünewald-Verlag, 1966.

Rosenberg, Arthur, *The Birth of the German Republic, 1871-1918.* London, New York, translated by I. F. D. Morrow, Oxford University Press, 1931.

Rothfels, Hans, *Die Deutsche Opposition Gegen Hitler.* Frankfurt/Main, Fischer Bücherei, 1958.

Schilling, Konrad, *Monumenta Judaica, 2000 Jahre Geschichte und Kultur der Juden am Rhein.* Special handbook published by the city of Cologne, 1963.

Schnabel, Franz, *Deutsche Geschichte im 19 Jahrhundert.* Freiburg-im-Breisgau, Herder-Bücherei, 1965.

Schönfeldt, Sybil Gräfin (with Friedrich Andrae), *Deutsche Demokratie von Bebel bis Heuss.* Frankfurt/Main, Fischer Bücherei, 1968.

Schudt, Johann Jakob, *Von der Frankfurter Juden Vergangenheit.* Berlin, Schocken Verlag, 1934.

Schultz, Hans Jürgen, *Juden, Christen, Deutsche.* Stuttgart, Kreuz Verlag, 1961.

Schulz, Eberhard, *Deutschland Heute.* Frankfurt/Main, Ullstein, 1958.

Shepherd, William R., *Historical Atlas.* London, George Philip & Son, 1956.

Shirer, William L., *The Rise and Fall of the Third Reich.* New York, Simon & Schuster, 1959.

Solberg, Richard W., *God and Caesar in East Germany.* New York, Macmillan, 1961.

Sontheimer, Kurt, *Der Uberdruss an der Demokratie, Neue Linke und Alte Rechte . . . Unterschiede und Gemeinsamkeiten.* Cologne, Markus Verlag, 1970.

Stäel, Madame Anne Louise Germaine de, *De L'Allemagne.* Paris, 1813.

Stahl, Walter; ed., *The Politics of Postwar Germany*. New York, Frederick A. Praeger, 1963.

Stehle, Hansjakob, *Nachbar Polen*. Frankfurt/Main, S. Fischer-Verlag, 1963.

Tacitus, P. Cornelius, *Germania* ("On the Origin and Geography of Germany"). Harmondsworth, Middlesex, England, English translation by H. Mattingly, Penguin Books, 1948. Written A.D. 97-98. See also Posidonius of Rhodes, Caesar's Gallic War, and Livy.

Thalheim, Karl C., "Eastern Germany" in *The Fate of East Central Europe* (Stephen D. Kertesz, ed.). South Bend, Ind., University of Notre Dame Press, 1956.

Thilenius, Richard, *Die Teilung Deutschlands*. Hamburg, Rowohlt Verlag, 1957.

Valentin, Veit, *The German People*. New York, Alfred A. Knopf, 1946.

Viereck, Peter, *Metapolitics, The Roots of the Nazi Mind*. New York, Capricorn Books, 1961.

Weymar, Paul, *Konrad Adenauer-Die Autorisierte Biographie*. Munich, Kindler-Verlag, 1955. English translation by Peter De Mendelssohn: *Adenauer—His Authorized Biography*. New York, E. P. Dutton & Co., 1957.

Wolff, Ilse R., ed., *German Jewry, Its History, Life and Culture*. Catalogue series No. 3. London, Wiener Library, 1958.

Zahn, Gordon C., *German Catholics and Hitler's Wars*. New York, Sheed & Ward, 1962.

———— *In Solitary Witness: The Life and Death of Franz Jaegerstätter*. New York, Holt, Rinehart & Winston, 1964.

BOOKLETS

Deutsche Rundschau (series), Stuttgart, Scherz Verlag, 1963ff.

East-West Tensions, vols. I-VI, documentation on American-German conferences, jointly sponsored by American Council on Germany, New York, together with Atlantik-Brücke, Hamburg.

The Evangelical Church in Berlin and the Soviet Zone, Berlin, Eckart Verlag, 1959.

German Social Science Digest, Hamburg, Classen Verlag.

Geschichte der Juden in Deutschland by Ernst Ludwig Ehrlich, Düsseldorf, Pädagogischer Verlag, Schwann.

Godesberger Programm, SPD.

Grundgesetz für die Bundesrepublik (Basic Law of the Federal Republic), West German Press and Information Office, Bonn.

Meet Germany, published annually by Atlantik-Brücke, Hamburg, 1957-70.

Das Oberammergauer Passionspiel 1970 (Text of the Oberammergau Passion Play 1970, available in several languages).

Report on Democratic Institutions in Germany by Hans Wallenberg, issued by the American Council on Germany, New York.

The Roman Catholic Church in Berlin and the Soviet Zone, Berlin, Morus Verlag, 1959.

485

PERIODICALS & NEWS SERVICES

Allgemeine Wochenzeitung der Juden in Deutschland, Düsseldorf.
Aussenpolitik.
Bulletin, West German Press and Information Office, Bonn.
Christ und Welt, Stuttgart, Evangelical weekly (since changed to *Deutsche Zeitung*).
Dokumente, Cologne.
Forum
Frankfurter Allgemeine.
Frankfurter Rundschau.
Freiburger Rundbrief.
The German Tribune, Hamburg.
The Guardian, London.
Handelsblatt.
Hannoversche Presse.
Herder Korrespondenz.
Industriekurier.
Institute für Demoskopie, *Informationsdienst,* Allensbach.
International Herald Tribune, Paris.
Jüdische Presse Dienst, Düsseldorf.
Kieler Nachrichten.
Kölner Stadt Anzeiger.
Konkret.
Los Angeles *Times.*
Monat, Hamburg.
National Zeitung, Basle.
Die Neue Gesellschaft.
Neue Zürcher Zeitung, Zürich.
Newsweek.
The New York Times.
Observer, London.
Politische Welt.
Die Presse, Vienna.
Publik, Frankfurt/Main, Roman Catholic weekly.
Rheinischer Merkur.
Sonntags Journal, Zürich.
Der Spiegel, Hamburg
Der Stern, Hamburg.
Stuttgarter Zeitung.
Süddeutsche Zeitung, Munich.
Die Tat, Zürich.
Tages Anzeiger, Zürich.
Time Magazine.
Times, London.
U.S. News & World Report.
Washington *Post.*
Die Welt, Hamburg.
Welt der Arbeit.

BIBLIOGRAPHY

Welt am Sonntag.
Die Weltwoche, Zürich.
Die Zeit, Hamburg.

ACKNOWLEDGEMENTS

It is a poor reporter indeed who would base his study solely on published material. So my thanks go out first to the several hundreds of men, women, and children of both Germanies with whom I have spent thousands of hours in conversation. I paid particular attention to the so-called "ordinary" people, because it has been my experience that they often have insights every bit as meaningful as those of erudite scholars. And sometimes the vision of the latter is rigidly circumscribed by tight compartments of their particular disciplines and frames of reference.

It was in East Germany that I once listened for two hours to a pompous professor exuding endlessly about the ideological situation of the German Democratic Republic, with all that special parlance that sounds so learned. Then I asked him to recommend a simple worker's family to interview, so that I could obtain a picture of everyday life.

"Well," he said condescendingly, "perhaps you can talk to my janitor there. But I doubt if you'll get much out of him. He hasn't very much education, you know." In the end I got infinitely more insights into the workings of the East German establishment from the observations of that janitor, who had to cope from morning to night with the ideological implications in the hard reality of shopping, sending the children to school, paying taxes, than the privileged professor with his ivory-tower view of the East German situation.

But ordinary people have their limitations too, and if a reporter bases his study solely on their impressions and his own very limited and subjective observations, it would rightly be challenged by responsible critics and scholars.

The biggest problem in this study was not one of finding material but rather sifting through the gigantic mass of information that bombarded me from all sides daily,[1] from the radio and TV that were churning out documentation night and day to the arm-breaking bundles of newspapers and magazines that I lugged home at regular intervals. But it was from these sources that I obtained authenticated, documented information. I tried to draw from such material even when it tended to contradict my personal impressions.

In evaluating this enormous source of information, of course, I had to consult with dozens of colleagues, educators, politicians, civic leaders. I am indebted to my colleagues in Switzerland and West and East Germany. I am grateful to the *Westdeutscher Rundfunk* and *Bayerische Rundfunk* for the generous use of their archives. Special thanks are due to Leo Waltermann and Hans Hübner of the *Westdeutscher Rundfunk*, as well as to Alfred Paffenholz, *Funkhaus Hannover*, Dr. Franz Hoyer, Munich, and to Reinhold Lehmann of the Pax Christi center in Frankfurt/Main, who all gave me valuable suggestions, references, and information.

I acknowledge with thanks the numerous services of the Press and Information Office of the Federal Republic, as well as the Cologne press office. I appreciate the help I have received by way of documentation, interviews, and information from the numerous ministries, agencies, embassies, consulates of many nations in Bonn, Munich, and Hamburg. I gratefully acknowledge the extremely useful documentation I received from Dr. Walter Stahl, Executive Vice-President of the Atlantik-Brücke, Hamburg. My thanks go out also to the fruitful cooperation I received some years ago from Dr. Gregor Siefer, University of Hamburg, in matters related to this book, as well as Professor H. C. Hans Fischer-Barnicol, University of Heidelberg.

I express my deep appreciation for the warm hospitality I enjoyed from author Carl Amery and his family and also from Professor Helmut Thielicke, former rector of Hamburg University. I am indebted to Professor Karl Rahner, S.J., Professor Hans Küng and Julius Cardinal Doepfner, Archbishop of Munich, as well as Dr. Martin Niemoeller and Rabbi Hans Isak Gruenewald for their valuable interviews.

I acknowledge with special appreciation the dedicated assistance of my former secretaries, Mrs. Anje Petrozzini, now an American citizen, and Fräulein Irmgard Burmeister, during my stint as editor of *The Bridge*, a monthly paper informing American servicemen about Germany. From them I obtained a wealth of knowledge about the German people and many observations that later proved useful in the compilation and writing of this book. Thanks also to Fräulein Marianne Meier for proofreading the manuscript and for her numerous suggestions.

I can only mention by name a few German families—the Broddas, the Burmeisters, the Meissners, the Oberles, the Jungs, the Westphals, the Wefers, the Lutzes, the Mayers, the Goldmanns, the Krälings, the Wiedorns, and their names stand for many—who have helped me so very much.

Surely some of the most valuable help for this volume came from several fellow Americans. There is Harry Golden, the well known humorist and civil rights champion, author, and columnist with whom I spent happy hours in Germany and who gave me the inspiration for the book in the first place. I am particularly indebted to U.S. Air Force Captain (Reserve) Thomas H. Nelson and family for their generous hospitality and extremely valuable information and documentation during their West German tour of duty, as well as to Major (Retired) Robert Fuerst who helped me so much to become acquainted with the American military scene in the Federal Republic.

489

Special mention must be made of my dear friend Jim Kulp, assistant city editor of the Alton *Evening Telegraph,* Illinois, whose generous stateside help was extremely valuable for the completion of this volume. I am also indebted to Professor Alan Scham of the Southern Connecticut State College, Department of History, for his valuable suggestions and documentary material.

I also thank my good friends, Dr. Sylvester P. Theisen, Institutional Coordinator, St. John's University, Collegeville, Minnesota, as well as Dr. Gordon C. Zahn, Professor of Sociology at the University of Massachusetts, in whose company I spent many productive hours in the Federal Republic. From their specialized knowledge of the country and their scholarly writings on German affairs I have derived much useful knowledge and valuable insights.

To my devoted friend, Bob Burns, executive editor of *U.S. Catholic,* I am especially grateful for the many German assignments that enabled me to research simultaneously for this book. I wish to thank him also for permission to use as Chapter 6 an article that originally appeared in that magazine, as well as additional material that has found its way in adapted form here and there in these pages. To James O'Gara and John G. Deedy, Jr., editors of *The Commonweal,* go my thanks for permission to use material originally appearing in that publication, as well as to Bob Hoyt, editor of *The National Catholic Reporter,* which likewise originally published some of the material in this book. Grateful acknowledgement goes to Penguin Books, for permission to quote at length from the English translation of Tacitus' *Germania* by H. Mattingly. I also express my appreciation to the editors of *Quinto Lingo* for their kind permission to include passages in this book that originally appeared as articles in that publication.

Special thanks should go also to Frau Ingeborg Godenschweger, of the German Information Center, New York, for her critique and invaluable insights.

Last but certainly not least, I am most indebted to the sustained encouragement and constructive directives from Bram Cavin, senior editor at Prentice-Hall, who helped me so much to bring this difficult project to a close. I regret that I cannot mention by name the countless other persons who have directly and indirectly helped me in the research, writing, and editing of this book.

Of course, the opinions and conclusions of this volume, except where they are otherwise identified in the text, cannot be attributed to anyone but myself.

A.S.

NOTES

Preface

[1] In an essay, "A Guide to German Politics," appearing in the booklet, *Meet Germany, 1969*, Atlantik-Brücke, Hamburg, p. 39.

[2] *Die Deutschen* by Johannes Gross, Heinrich Scheffler Verlag, Frankfurt/Main, 1967, p. 7.

Introduction: Some Observations About Germany

[1] A study, to be completed in 1973, is underway to examine the possibilities of reducing the present ten states of the Federal Republic to five. It is believed that the present arrangement irrationally permits inequality in size, wealth, and population. Under the present system there are "rich" and "poor" states, and administrative measures have to be taken to even out the differences.

The new states would be: 1) Bavaria, retaining its present size of 10.6 million inhabitants; 2) North Rhine-Westphalia retaining, with minor border adjustments, its present shape and 17 million inhabitants; 3) Baden-Württemberg, with minor changes and 9 million inhabitants; 4) a new "northwest state" to include the present states of Lower Saxony, Schleswig-Holstein, Bremen, and Hamburg and to have a population of 12.2 million; and 5) a new state, "Middle Rhine-Hesse," to be comprised of the present states of Hesse, Rhineland-Palatinate, and the Saar, which would then have 10.3 million residents.

There is strong opposition running through both major parties, CDU/CSU and SPD, who fear that the shifts in voting districts might change political party patterns. And, of course, many leading politicians in the two parties, faced with a loss of patronage and political power if the plan were to be enacted, have these added reasons for their opposition.

Backers of the project argue that the new plan would make each state economically viable and more rationally distribute federal tasks.

1. Main Street, Germany

[1] *Man and Superman* by George Bernard Shaw, Penguin Books, London, 1946, p. 181.

[2] In recent years many of these agencies, overtaxed by the demand, have begun to restrict their listings to upper- and middle-class hotels. However agencies in the smaller cities and towns still try to accommodate the low-budget-minded traveler.

[3] Due to full employment and manpower shortage, this custom is rapidly being replaced by impersonal shoe polishing machines in the corridors.

[4] In contrast to the average American hotel, which normally does not include breakfast with a night's lodging, the average German hotel has a special breakfast room and regards the serving of breakfast as an integral part of its normal service. The breakfast room frequently serves as a television room in the evening.

[5] Dear to their hearts as beer is to the Germans, they may eventually have to do without their purer version, which lacks such additives as sulphur dioxide, ascorbic acid, tannic acid or poteolytic enzymes, common in U.S. beers. The purity of German beer is protected by a Bavarian ordinance dating back to 1516, which stipulates that beer be made only of malt, hops, yeast, and water. However, this purer beer is far more expensive to make than those with additives, and doesn't keep long. But now the Common Market is developing a "Eurobeer," which would permit additives, standardizing it for the entire community. While the Germans would not be compelled to stop making their purer beer, the new drink could flood the German market and eventually replace the time-honored purer brew. An "action committee for pure beer" complete with pretty blonde lobbyists has been launched to save the reputation of West Germany's 1,800 breweries. Plastic vials containing unadulterated doses of the above-named additives have been sent to the country's 496 deputies, with the warning: "Don't let this happen to our beer!"

2. One Man's Family
[1] An Evangelical pastor in Nürnberg recently said to me, "This is the most often used word in Germany today."

3. What Is a German?
[1] For the purpose of this book we shall use the word German, as a noun, to mean any citizen of East or West Germany, or an emigrant therefrom, and as an adjective, to include the broad meaning of cultural, geographic, linguistic characteristics that have ethnically evolved as Germans.

[2] In the village of Unteruhldingen on the Lake of Constance, *Pfahlbauten* (houses on stilts), *i.e.*, prehistoric dwellings such as those presumably used by the ancient Germanic tribes, have been reconstructed. A small museum on the shore contains artifacts found during excavations.

4. "You Germans Are Too Stiff!"
[1] Just how great ethnic differences can be even within one generic people is illustrated by a classic comparison by the Austrian poet Hugo von Hofmannsthal. "The Prussian," he once wrote, "is self-righteous, arrogant and pedantic. The Austrian by contrast is bashful, vain and witty. The Prussians are self-reliant, the Austrians self-effacing. Prussians are incapable of understanding someone else's situation, the Austrian projects himself so much into the other person's plight that he loses his own character in the process. The Prussian tends to exaggeration, the Austrian to such a degree of irony that it evaporates." Quoted during a *"Telekolleg"* history lesson, West German TV, October 10, 1970.

[2] That there are exceptions to this tendency was recently illustrated during the November, 1970, state elections in Bavaria. In spite of

professional predictions that the Free Democrats (FDP) would not win enough votes to remain in the state parliament, it more than doubled the required 5 percent of the total and gained additional seats. This surprise comeback is attributed to the sympathy vote of many citizens who usually vote SPD but in this case wished to help the "underdog" and indirectly strengthen Willy Brandt's shaky SPD FDP coalition in Bonn.

[3] It should be pointed out that Germans don't have anything precisely like the American dictionary. Their lexicons have only selected listings and do not include every word.

[4] Holger Diezemann and Ulrich Weyland in *Der Stern*, September 6, 1970, pp. 68ff. Similar articles have appeared in *Düsseldorf Express, Rheinische Post, Frankfurter Allgemeine,* during August, 1970. A typical headline: "Are the Germans Really Pigs?"

[5] It has come to this: In Wesel, pedestrians are cajoled at street crossings with signs, reading: "Show character, wait until the light turns green."

[6] The passion for thoroughness sometimes drives Germans to incredible lengths. In Duisburg a civil court decided that twins born to a 32-year-old woman have different fathers. On the basis of blood tests and testimony by the woman that she had committed adultery while her husband was away on business, soon after having had intercourse with him, the court decided that the boy was illegitimate and the twin sister legitimate. AP report in *International Herald Tribune*, December 31, 1970, p. 3.

[7] In the Germans' view there is nothing stiff or formalistic about the *"Sie."* Sometimes they have a warm and cheerful relationship with someone on a *"Sie"* basis for many years. To them it is simply an arrangement, rather than a barrier. Although two forms of "you" are also used in French and in Spanish and other languages, it can be said that the *"Sie"* and *"Du"* are specifically German in character.

[8] *Der Grosse Duden*, Band 2., *Stilwörterbuch der deutschen Sprache,* Bibliographisches Institut, Dudenverlag, Mannheim/Zürich, quoted by Ludwig Reiners, p. 7.

[9] *German Catholics and Hitler's Wars* by Gordon Zahn, Sheed & Ward, New York, 1962, pp. 21, 22.

[10] *De L'Allemagne* by Madame Anne Louise Germaine de Staël, Paris, 1813.

5. Of Castles, Customs and Cults

[1] Heine's famous "Lorelei" still captures the imagination of Germans and tourists alike. The poem is based on a legend about a treacherous bend in the Rhine where fishermen would be enraptured by the melancholy singing of a blonde nymph high on a cliff, and so would perish in the rapids.

Every now and then enterprising Germans concoct new ideas about "promoting" the site of the famous Lorelei rock. The latest: a Lorelei statue, illuminated at night, and a nearby hotel and recreation center. At the foot of the cliff other hoteliers are planning a gambling casino, recreation and amusement center, to be called, "Las Vegas on the Rhine."

[2] Siegfried, the invincible warrior of the Bergstrasse gave Richard Wagner material for his *Ring of the Nibelungs* operas: *Das Rheingold, Die Walküre, Siegfried,* and *Götterdämmerung.*

493

[3] Nobility was officially abolished by the Weimar Constitution on August 11, 1919. Despite Hitler's dislike for nobility, 18.7 percent of the SS came from their ranks, but so did some of the men, notably Count Claus von Stauffenberg, associated with the famous July 20, 1944, attempt to assassinate him.

Prince Johannes Friedrich Bonifazius Lamoral von Thurn und Taxis is one of the five richest Germans, owns vast properties in Bavaria, is chairman of a number of concerns including a Munich bank and its far-flung affiliates, a brewery and large holdings in Brazil, where he "permits" employees, including men, to kiss his hand. Twenty percent of West German ambassadors are from noble families, but their number is gradually diminishing.

6. The Roots of German Anti-Semitism

[1] *Gesta Treverorum* (written before 1132), Patrol. lat. ed. Migne, 154, 1206-1209, as quoted in *Geschichte der Juden in Deutschland* by Ernst Ludwig Ehrlich, Pädagogischer Verlag Schwann, Düsseldorf, 1960, p. 16.

[2] *Geschichtsquellen der Stadt Cöln II*, Ennen-Eckertz, pp. 321ff.

[3] *Kirche Und Synagoge*, by W. Maurer, 1953, pp. 36ff, 88ff. Also *ibid.*

7. What Ever Happened to Prussia?

[1] Germany as a national entity only came into being in 1871, when King Wilhelm I of Prussia was proclaimed German Kaiser by Chancellor Bismarck, the creator of the "Second German Reich" (hence Hitler's use of the term "Third Reich").

The "First German Reich" came to an end in 1806, when Napoleon ruled Europe and the emperor laid down the crown of the Holy Roman Empire of the German Nation. That empire, however, had been in existence for more than a thousand years and included today's Austria, Switzerland, Italy, Belgium, the Netherlands, parts of France, and parts of eastern Europe. Central to the Holy Roman Empire was the unification of Christian Europe under the German emperors. But internal power struggles, religious strife, and petty regional animosities weakened the emperor's powers. By the eighteenth century, during the reign of Frederick the Great of Prussia, the Reich existed in name rather than in fact; the real power was tenaciously held by the Reich's individual states: Austria, Bavaria, Saxony, Hesse, numerous other kingdoms and duchies: and, notably, Prussia.

[2] Countess Marion Dönhoff, editor-in-chief, *Die Zeit*, in an article in that newspaper, February 17, 1967, p. 3.

[3] In a letter reacting to the above-named article, appearing in *Die Zeit* March 3, 1967, p. 44.

8. "Deutschland über Alles"

[1] According to Nordic mythology Wallhalla, or Valhalla, is the final resting-place for the souls of slain heroes.

[2] In 1970, the 200th anniversary year of Ludwig van Beethoven's birth in Bonn, the great musical genius was widely heralded around the world. A lesser-known aspect of the great *Meister's* personality is his sense of political

commitment. However, a close look at his life will again show how hard it is to find a political hero in the German past. For even Beethoven's political thought is at best ambivalent. He is admired as the composer of the famous "Freedom" chorus in his sole opera, *Fidelio*. It is known that he came into contact with the ideas of the "enlightenment" and the French Revolution early in life and admired Napoleon so much that he at first dedicated his symphony *Eroica* to him only to destroy the title page in angry disillusionment when the supposed champion of liberty had himself declared emperor.

Beethoven was known to be outspoken in his criticism of political figures. His secretary and biographer Anton Schindler destroyed more than 250 notebooks because they contained incriminating "attacks on persons in the highest places." Emperor Franz I even ordered secret reports to be made on *Der Meister*. But that same Beethoven was never reluctant to receive favors from the Vienna aristocracy, nor was he ever really deeply involved in political matters. His political consciousness was hardly sufficient to qualify him as a dedicated reformer or revolutionary.

[3] On the twentieth anniversary of the founding of the Federal Republic, 1969, scant notice was paid to the event inside the country or out. And on the centennial anniversary of modern Germany on January 18, 1971, solemn newspaper analyses appeared, but parades or festivals were not only totally absent, they were unthinkable.

[4] *Die Deutschen,* by Johannes Gross, Heinrich Scheffler Verlag, Frankfurt-am-Main, 1967, p. 7.

9. The Rocky Road of German Democratic Tradition

[1] *The German Phoenix* by William Henry Chamberlin, Duell, Sloan & Pearce, Inc., p. 187.

[2] *A Short History of Germany* by Sir John K. Dunlop, Oswald Wolff, London, 1965, pp. 4, 5.

[3] *Ibid.,* p. 53.

[4] The profusion of theaters and opera houses and subsidization of the arts in Germany today is in large part thanks to the tradition begun by these rulers.

[5] In an article, "German Character and History," *The Atlantic*, June, 1958.

[6] *Ibid.,* Theodor Heuss, first president of the Federal Republic, writes, "The Germans, too, 'fought for freedom'—in the peasant wars of the Reformation and in the civic uprisings of 1848, to name the most prominent examples. But theirs was a history of defeats which did not lend themselves to legends of glory. After the military collapse of 1918 and the abdication of all dynastic sovereigns, a democratic constitution was set up as the sole possible basis for a legitimate government. But this democracy was not a prize won in hard struggle; it was simply seized upon in desperation. There was no glamor in it, and a sentimental monarchism lingered on. Then came the 'licensed' democracy after 1945—differently interpreted by the four Occupation Powers and quickly perverted by the Russians into a red instead of a brown police state."

10. *Vergangenheitsbewältigung*
or
The National Guilt Complex

[1] Writing in *Commonweal* magazine, New York City, March 15, 1963.

[2] After months of investigation, the Munich prosecution closed its investigation of the auxiliary bishop. According to the Bavarian Justice Ministry the case was dropped because the prosecutor's office "came to the final conclusion that the innocence of the accused had been proven in accordance with the penal code."

The Defregger case has been portrayed as a play, *Eine Deutsche Szenerie (A German Scenario)* by the Austrian writer Hans-Georg Behr, which re-enacts the moral problems of a man ordered to kill. Other stage and film productions are reportedly under way.

In the wake of adverse publicity and public outcry both within and without the Roman Catholic Church, Bishop Defregger finally relinquished his post as regional bishop of the Munich archdiocese and quietly assumed duties, away from the public eye, as consultant for the training of religious. This position, however, is far less obscure than it sounds, as it involves some 100 religious communities with more than 8,000 members.

[3] The author is of Austrian descent, both parents having emmigrated to the United States in the 1920's from Austria.

[4] *Oekumenische Marienschwesternschaft*, Weg und Auftrag, by Mutter Basilea Schlink, published by Oekumenische Marienschwesternschaft, Darmstadt-Eberstadt, 1959, pp. 14, 15.

[5] Georg Ferdinand Duckwitz, State Secretary in the Foreign Office, was awarded the Heinrich Stahl Prize on April 19, 1970, by the Jewish Community in Berlin for rescuing more than 7,000 Jews in Denmark during the German occupation in World War II. Mr. Duckwitz was a naval attaché at the German legation in Denmark in 1943 and enabled Danish Jews to be rescued by boat with the help of the Danish resistance movement and Swedish support.

11. God and Man in East Germany

[1] According to statistics revealed by the West German border patrol headquarters in Munich on January 21, 1971, East Germany has planted 2.23 million mines along the strip dividing the two Germanies, and strung 50,000 miles of barbed wire along the border. In addition, obstacles along the 860 miles of frontier, running from the Baltic Sea to Czechoslovakia, include 1.9 million concrete pillars, 972 bunkers, 699 of which are of reinforced concrete, and 524 wooden watchtowers.

12. The German Question and Berlin

[1] October 31, 1969, p. 6.

[2] *International Herald Tribune,* August 5, 1969, p. 3.

PART TWO

13. That Little Town on the Rhine

[1] Front page editorial, *Die Zeit,* February 7, 1969.

14. How Stable a Democracy?
[1] *Frankfurter Rundschau*, August 5, 1969, p. 3.

15. The Jewish Community
[1] Historian Egmont Zechlin points out that the dedication and zeal with which Jews fought for the Kaiser in World War I has seldom been equaled by their Gentile compatriots. In his book, *Die Deutsche Politik und die Juden im Ersten Weltkrieg*, he writes that "the Jews were German to their very bones and offered their very souls and entire fortune in the service of the Fatherland. . . . Far beyond the call of duty they closed ranks behind the flag. Even the Zionist *Wanderbund* proclaimed: 'Joyfully we follow the call of the Fatherland.' " According to Zechlin, more than 100,000 of the 550,000 German Jews served in World War I, 80,000 of them on the front. At least 12,000 fell for the Kaiser. Some 35,000 were decorated. More than 2,000 were promoted to the rank of officer, and 23,000 received some kind of award for bravery or the like.

[2] From mimeographed documents accompanying correspondence with Rabbi Brickner and the author in 1967.

16. The Generation Gap—German Style
[1] *The Complete Travel Books of Mark Twain*, Vol. II, *A Tramp Abroad*, edited by Charles Neider, Doubleday & Co., New York, 1967, p. 26. Even today regular tuition fees do not exceed $75 a semester and many scholarships are available.

[2] November 7, 1969, p. 5.

[3] One is tempted to ask: Where are the student rebels of the sixties now? Today, just a few short years afterwards, Rudi Dutschke has assumed a respectable teaching post at Aarhus University, Denmark (his 1971 expulsion from Britain on the grounds of his former leftist activity is widely regarded as unjust); "Red Daniel" Cohn-Bendit has become the hero of Westerns and enjoys the royalties and profits from his films and books in plush hotels on the Côte d'Azur; the West Berlin rebels Fritz Teufel and Rainer Langhans have been employed as photographers' models, film producers, and organizers of pop festivals; the former Hamburg revolutionary Jens Litten has become a TV editor; and the erstwhile "angry young man" Bernd Rabehl has quietly assumed a teaching position at the Hamburg University. The Frankfurt APO leader, Günther Amendt, is now a radio scriptwriter of harmless family features, having come a long way from the writing of revolutionary pamphlets.

According to the government-sponsored weekly paper, *The Bulletin* (April 27, 1971), young Karl Marx during his student days in Bonn was very much of a grind. The report on his university conduct notes that he was a "very diligent and attentive visitor to the lecture hall." The spiritual father of world revolution also took up studies that rebels today hardly consider "relevant": aesthetics and Greek and Roman mythology. Once the student Marx was locked up for a day by university authorities for drunkenness and "disturbing the peace." But his conduct at the university's lock-up is laconically recorded at the University of Bonn as "very quiet."

[4] Editorial, *Schweizer Illustrierte*, March, 1970, p. 4.

497

[5] *Poems for People Who Don't Read Poems*, Hans Magnus Enzensberger, translated by Michael Hamburger, Jerome Rothenberg, and the author, with grateful acknowledgement to the publisher, Martin Secker & Warburg, Ltd., London, and Atheneum Publishers, New York, 1967.

17. "Citizens in Uniform"

[1] *Return to Power*, Alistair Horne, Frederick A. Praeger, New york, 1956, p. 28.

[2] *Ibid.*

18. The German Male—A Nonperson?

[1] In an effort to prove their masculinity in at least one area, German men are spending more and more money each year for fancy clothes, especially such as are inspired by the hippie culture. In 1969 German men spent 3 billion DM's (more than $900 million) for clothes, or 13.5 percent more than the year previously. In variety, color, and originality, men's clothes in West Germany know no bounds, with more than 100,000 designs and models per season.

21. "We Are Somebodies Again!"

[1] One should not rule out the possibility that all this could change in the event of a recession or some other national catastrophe. Moreover, it is no longer a foregone conclusion that West German workers, in spite of their good pay and social benefits, are content. One shocking example of abuse was reported on November 17, 1970, by the state employment ministry of Baden-Württemberg. It discovered 7,000 cases of abuse among 18,000 apprentices working at 3,300 firms. In one case, and not an isolated one, an apprentice cook, a boy of sixteen, was forced to work fifteen hours daily and up to ninety hours per week. One out of every three enterprises employing more than 1,000 persons was found to exploit apprentices, by making them work overtime or by assigning them exclusively to unpleasant tasks. All of the detected violaters were fined, but the unrest common among apprentices is believed to be widespread among skilled workers too.

22. A Matter of Life and Death

[1] In West Germany victims of accident or assault receive extremely small compensation monies. For example, a German may receive compensation of about 1,000 to 3,000 DM's ($290 to $900), in contrast to the United States, where such a victim might receive up to $150,000.

According to Hans-Eckhard Stegen, Hamburg traffic specialist, West German women are demonstrably worse—and more dangerous—motorists than men. They cause more accidents and are proportionately responsible for a greater number of injuries in accidents. In the five years between 1964 and 1968, according to a study supervised by Stegen, 25 percent more women were found to be responsible for serious accidents than men.

24. The Great American Inundation

[1] *The Complete Travel Books of Mark Twain*, Volume II, *A Tramp Abroad*, edited by Charles Neider, Doubleday & Co., New York, 1967, Appendix D. "The Awful German Language," pp. 326ff.

² Members of *Atlantik-Brücke* include: Countess Marion Dönhoff, editor-in-chief, *Die Zeit;* Dr. Fabian von Schlabrendorff, Judge at the Federal Constitutional Court, Karlsruhe; Dr. Kurt Birrenbach, member of the *Bundestag* and chairman of the board, Thyssen, GmbH, Düsseldorf; Walther A. Bösenberg, president, IBM Deutschland; Gerhard Geyer, chairman of the board, Esso AG; Dr. Joachim Zahn, member, managing board, Daimler-Benz AG, Stuttgart; Franz Heinrich Ulrich, member, managing board, Deutsche Bank AG, Düsseldorf; Helmut Schmidt, Minister of Defense; Prof. Dr. Karl Schiller, Minister of Economics.

³ An American executive intimately acquainted with internal IBM politics, who does not wish to be identified, to whom I showed this chapter before publication, regards my remarks about IBM as naive. He said, that if a German employed by IBM were to invent some new gadget, it is not at all unlikely that it would be marketed in the United States before it was ever used in Germany. As he put it, "All the IBM laboratories may claim to be equal, but one is more equal than all the others, the U.S."

⁴ In addition, American investors benefit on the German market from the decisions of the Bretton Woods, N.H., Conference, which in 1944 created the International Monetary Fund and the World Bank and is based on the American dollar. All western currencies are dependent on it and are convertible to gold through it. During the recent series of dollar crises, the Deutsche Bundesbank was forced to protect the dollar from the oath of manifestation with its own reserves.

25. Germans in the United States

¹ President Richard Nixon's mother-in-law, Käte Halberstadt—whom he never met—was born in the village of Ober-Rosbach, near Frankfurt-Main.

² While this statement is true, it needs to be qualified. For example, although the number of students studying the German language in the Denver public school system increased from 5,000 before the Soviet Sputnik satellite launching in 1957 to 15,000 (out of 100,000 students) in 1965, this number dropped back to 10,250 in 1969. In other words, the foreign language boom that followed the Sputnik shock is on the wane. One reason for this is that budgetary pressures are causing reassessments of academic priorities. In many colleges and high schools across the country foreign language studies are no longer required. Another reason is that far too few educational institutions have adapted language study to modern conversational needs. The stubborn emphasis on classics just doesn't attract students who can't get very excited about Goethe's *Faust*. The jet age to the contrary, the splendid geographical isolation of the United States continues to be a major psychological handicap. Americans by and large just don't see the need to undertake the tedious exercises required to master a modern foreign language. In 1966 German was the third most popular foreign language (214,000 students) studied in U.S. colleges, with French leading (570,000 students) and Spanish (310,000) taking second place. Among high school students, however, only 300,000 out of 12 million studied German, which was less than Latin (600,000), French (1.2 million) and Spanish (1.5 million).

³ With the abolishment of the national origins quota system in 1965, Germans, British, Irish, and Dutch, who once comprised the majority of

immigrants, have gone way down on the statistical ladder where emmigra-
tion to the United States is concerned. They are rapidly being replaced by
increasing numbers of Filipinos, Italians, Greeks, Portuguese, as well as
people from Africa and the West Indies. Between 1965 and 1970, Germany
went down from fourth place with 26,357 immigrants to fourteenth with
9,263. Britain dropped from third to eighth place, and Ireland, which
provided 5,563 immigrants in 1965, sent only 1,000 in 1970.

[4] *Der Spiegel*, Nov. 15, 1970, pp. 132ff.

26. The Ugly Germans

[1] *Tacitus on Britain and Germany*, a translation of *Agricola* and *Germania*
by H. Mattingly, Penguin Books, Harmondsworth, Middlesex, England,
1948, excerpted with permission, pp. 101ff.

[2] *Daily Mirror*, London, June 28, 1966, p.12.

[3] Germany played a central part in the thinking of Vladimir Ilyich
Ulyanov, alias Lenin, who lived in Western Europe from 1900 until 1917.
Moreover, he was deeply impressed by the size and organization of the
German labor movement. Prior to World War I, Germany boasted more than
one million Social Democrats and two million trade unionists, which
together formed the largest, most disciplined and modern movement of its
kind in Europe. The sporadic and divided left-wing in Czarist Russia was
pale by comparison. Lenin repeatedly cited the German example to his
followers and called for a Russian equivalent to the German Socialist August
Bebel.

[4])*So Sehen Sie Deutschland*, edited by Francois Bondy, Seewald Verlag,
1970, p. 35.

[5])*Ibid.*, p. 140.

[6])*Der Hässlich Deutsche?* by Rolf Breitenstein, Desch, 1968, Munich,
p. 104.

[7] To Franz Kafka is attributed the observation, "Jews and Germans have
much in common. They are industrious, efficient, diligent, and thoroughly
hated by others." *Typisch Deutsch*, Modern Verlag, 1965, p. 106.

[8] It should also be mentioned that more than 150,000 American students
annually spend a semester or more in Germany and thousands more
stampede the country every year as tourists. Numerous exchange programs
and study tours have reported extremely favorable results. Several American
colleges have branch campuses in the Federal Republic. Outstanding work
has also been done by the several *Amerika Häuser* (America houses) of the
U.S.I.A. in West Germany.

Acknowledgements

[1] Every day, on an average of at least three, books about Germany and
the Germans appear somewhere in the world, not to mention hundreds of
newspaper and magazine articles. *Der Spiegel*, Nov. 30, 1964, p. 26.

INDEX